sociology

9

sociology

exploring the architecture of everyday life

9

david m. newman

DePauw University

SAGE

Los Angeles | London | New Delhi
Singapore | Washington DC

Los Angeles | London | New Delhi
Singapore | Washington DC

FOR INFORMATION:

SAGE Publications, Inc.
2455 Teller Road
Thousand Oaks, California 91320
E-mail: order@sagepub.com

SAGE Publications Ltd.
1 Oliver's Yard
55 City Road
London EC1Y 1SP
United Kingdom

SAGE Publications India Pvt. Ltd.
B 1/I 1 Mohan Cooperative Industrial Area
Mathura Road, New Delhi 110 044
India

SAGE Publications Asia-Pacific Pte. Ltd.
33 Pekin Street #02-01
Far East Square
Singapore 048763

Acquisitions Editor: David Repetto
Assistant Editor: Terri Accomazzo
Editorial Assistant: Lydia Balian
Production Editor: Laureen Gleason
Copy Editor: Rachel Keith
Typesetter: C&M Digitals (P) Ltd.
Proofreader: Scott Oney
Indexer: Jeanne Busemeyer
Cover Designer: Candice Harman
Marketing Manager: Erica DeLuca
Permissions Editor: Karen Ehrmann

Copyright © 2012 by SAGE Publications, Inc.

Printed in the United States of America

Library of Congress Cataloging-in-Publication Data

Newman, David M., 1958-

Sociology : exploring the architecture of everyday life / David M. Newman. — 9th ed.

p. cm.
Includes bibliographical references and index.

ISBN 978-1-4129-8729-5 (pbk. : alk. paper)

1. Sociology. I. Title.

HM585.N48 2012
301—dc23—2011036350

This book is printed on acid-free paper.

11 12 13 14 15 10 9 8 7 6 5 4 3 2 1

Brief Contents

Detailed Contents

PART II
THE CONSTRUCTION OF SELF AND SOCIETY   53

3.   Building Reality: The Social Construction of Knowledge   55

PART III
SOCIAL STRUCTURE, INSTITUTIONS, AND EVERYDAY LIFE   275

9. The Structure of Society: Organizations, Social Institutions, and Globalization   277

10. The Architecture of Stratification: Social Class and Inequality 317

11. The Architecture of Inequality: Race and Ethnicity   358

About the Author

David M. Newman is Professor of Sociology at DePauw University. In addition to the introductory course, he teaches courses in research methods, family, social psychology, deviance, and mental illness. He has won teaching awards at both the University of Washington and DePauw University. His other written work includes *Identities and Inequalities: Exploring the Intersections of Race, Class, Gender, and Sexuality* (2012) and *Families: A Sociological Perspective* (2008). He received his Ph.D. from the University of Washington.

Preface

It was the first day of the fall semester in 1994. I had just finished making the final adjustments to the first edition of this book, which was due to be published the following January. I felt good, like I'd just accomplished something monumental. Even my two sons were impressed with me (although not as impressed as the time we went to a professional hockey game and I leaped out of my seat to catch an errant, speeding puck barehanded). I walked into the first meeting of my Contemporary Society class eager to start teaching wide-eyed, first-year students a thing or two about sociology.

In my introductory comments to the class that day, I mentioned that I had just written this book. The panicked look in their eyes—a curious combination of awe and fear—calmed when I told them I wouldn't be requiring them to read it that semester. I told them that the process of writing an introductory text helped me immensely in preparing for the course and that I looked forward to passing on to them the knowledge I had accumulated.

The next day after class, one of the students—a bright, freshly scrubbed 18-year-old—approached me. The ensuing conversation would leave a humbling impression even 18 years later:

Student: Hi. Umm. Professor Newman . . . I called my parents last night to, like, tell them how my first day in college went. I think they were, like, more nervous than I was. You know how parents can be.

Me: Yes, I sure do. I'm a parent myself, you know.

Student: Yeah, whatever. Anyway, I was telling them about my classes and my professors and stuff. I told them about this class and how I thought it would be pretty cool. I told them you were writing a book. I thought that would impress them, you know, make it seem like they were getting their money's worth and everything.

Me: Well, thanks.

Student: So, they go, "What's the book about?" [He laughs sheepishly.] I told them I didn't know, but I'd find out. So, like, that's what I'm doing . . . finding out.

Me: Well, I'm glad you asked. You see, it's an introductory sociology textbook that uses everyday experiences and phenomena as a way of understanding important sociological theories and ideas. In it I've attempted to . . .

Student: [His glazed eyes suddenly jump back to life.] Wait, did you say it was a textbook?

Me: Why, yes. You see, the purpose of the book is to provide the reader with a thorough and useful introduction to the sociological perspective. I want to convey . . .

Student: [Quite embarrassed now] Oh . . . Professor Newman, I'm really sorry. I misunderstood you. I thought you had written a real book.

Real book. *Real* book. *Real* book. Those words rang in my head like some relentless church bell. At first, I tried to dismiss the comment as the remark of a naive kid who didn't know any better. But the more I thought about it, the more I realized what his comment reflected. The perception that textbooks aren't *real* books is pervasive.

Not long ago, I heard a radio ad for a local Red Cross book drive asking listeners to donate any unused or unwanted books *as long as they weren't textbooks.* Torn copies of *The Cat in the Hat?* Fine, they'll take 'em. Grease-stained owner's manuals for 1976 Ford Pintos? Sure, glad to have 'em. Textbooks? No way!

Sadly, these sorts of perceptions are not altogether unwarranted. Textbooks hover on the margins of the literary world, somewhere between respectable, intellectual monographs on trailblazing research and Harlequin romance novels. Historically, they've been less than titillating: thick, heavy, expensive, and easily discarded for a measly five bucks at the end-of-semester "book buy-back."

My goal—from that very first edition to this one—has always been to write a textbook that reads like a *real* book. In the first eight editions I tried to capture simultaneously the essence and insight of my discipline and the reader's interest. From what reviewers, instructors, and students who've read and used the book over the years have said, I think I've been fairly successful. People seem to like the relaxed tone and appreciate the consistent theme that ties all the chapters together. Many instructors have commented on how the book enables students to truly understand the unique and useful elements of a sociological perspective.

Features of the Ninth Edition

To my younger son—who believes that I have nothing important to say about anything anyway—continually revising this book has always been clear evidence of my incompetence. Back when he was in middle school, he once asked me, "Why do you keep writing the same book over and over? My English teacher made me rewrite a book report on *To Kill a Mockingbird* because I answered a few questions wrong. Is that what's going on here? Is your publisher making you write the book again because you've put too much wrong stuff in it?" I told him no and that I'd make him read the book—cover to cover—if he continued to ask such questions. He stopped . . . although to this day, he's still not convinced I have anything useful to say.

Despite his concerns, sociology textbooks do need to be revised regularly and frequently. No book can be of lasting value if it remains static, locked into a particular style and content. I keep my ears and eyes open, always looking for some new example or current issue to include in the book. My office overflows with books, newspaper clippings, photocopied journal articles, Post-it notes, and shreds of paper napkins containing scribbled ideas that I write to myself at the breakfast table when I think of something interesting.

When revising a book, it's a lot easier to add new material than it is to cut out the old stuff. But simply inserting bits and pieces here and there tends to make books fat and unwieldy. So I've tried to streamline the book wherever possible. I've replaced outdated material with new material where appropriate, revised all the statistical information, condensed or deleted some sections, and changed the order of others.

Here are some of the specific changes I've made in this ninth edition to enhance the features that worked so well in the previous editions.

Updated Examples and Statistical Information

As in the first eight editions, each chapter is peppered with anecdotes, personal observations, and accounts of contemporary events. Many of the examples you will read come from incidents in my own life; others are taken from today's news headlines.

It would be impossible to write an introduction to the discipline of sociology without accounting for the life-altering occurrences—wars, natural disasters, political upheavals, legal developments, economic meltdowns, Snooki's latest escapades—that we hear about every day. So throughout this book, I've made a special effort to provide some sociological insight into contemporary events and trends, both large and small. In doing so, I intend to show you the pervasiveness and applicability of sociology in our ordinary everyday experiences in a way that, I hope, rings familiar with you.

Several specific recent developments have had—and will continue to have—a dramatic impact on sociological thought and on people's everyday lives: the persistent global economic recession, the presidency of Barack Obama, and the dramatic growth of communication technology, particularly social networking sites. As you will see throughout the book, it is impossible to understand what happens to us in our personal lives without taking into consideration broader social and historical phenomena. When the economy suffers, everyone—from tycoons to unemployed welfare recipients—experiences some kind of alteration in her or his day-to-day routine. As I was writing this edition, it was quite a challenge to keep up with the most current information on joblessness, hiring trends, home foreclosures, spending patterns, and so on. Likewise, major political events can change what we know and what we take for granted. Although it's still too early to know its full extent, the election of the country's first black president will no doubt influence perceptions of race and race relations—locally, nationally, and maybe even globally. And it's quite difficult to talk about the sociology of everyday life without acknowledging the powerful role online social networking has had in shaping the way we relate to others and define ourselves. Thus, I have made reference to these developments throughout the book to illustrate the interconnections between private life and massive historical occurrences.

I've also tried to provide the most current statistical information possible. I've updated all the graphic exhibits and, in the process, changed some of them from statistical tables to more readable charts and graphs, making trends and relationships more obvious. Much of the new statistical information is drawn from the most recent data from sources such as the U.S. Census Bureau, the Population Reference Bureau, the Centers for Disease Control and Prevention, the U.S. Bureau of Labor Statistics, and the U.S. Bureau of Justice Statistics.

Updated "Sociologists at Work" and "Micro-Macro Connections"

In the first eight editions, I provided many in-depth features that focused either on a specific piece of sociological research or on some issue that illustrates the connection between the everyday lives of individuals and the structure of their society. These extended discussions link social institutions to personal experiences and provide insight into the methods sociologists use to gather information and draw conclusions about how our world works.

Instructors and students alike have found these features very useful in generating classroom discussion. The features that I've updated from the previous edition focus on topics such as suicide, the language of war, cell phones, children's toys, cultural conceptions of obesity, dual-earner couples, clergy sexual abuse, the cultural impact of antidepressants, homelessness, the global health divide, multiracial identity, gender harassment in the military, residential segregation, and the shifting politics of immigration. In addition, I've added several new features on the use of American undergraduates as subjects in psychological research, consumption patterns of poor people worldwide, Facebook friendships, social structure and environmental catastrophe, and the technological erosion of privacy.

New Articles in the Companion Reader

Jodi O'Brien, a sociologist at Seattle University, and I have carefully edited a companion volume to this book, consisting of short articles, chapters, and excerpts written by other authors. These readings are provocative and eye-opening examples of the joys and insights of sociological thinking. Many of them vividly show how sociologists gather evidence through carefully designed research. Others are personal narratives that provide firsthand accounts of how social forces influence people's lives. The readings examine common, everyday experiences; important social issues; global concerns; and distinct historical events that illustrate the relationship between the individual and society. We've taken great pains to include readings that show how race, social class, gender, and sexual orientation intersect to influence everyday experiences.

Of the 41 selections in this edition of the reader, 15 are new. The new selections touch on important and relevant sociological issues such as the rules of gift giving, the questionable use of statistics, consumerism, race and class in everyday public encounters, gay parenting, covenant marriage, the power of fads, the everyday experience of race on college campuses, gender and technology, cyberbrides, and community organizing. In addition, we've brought back a few popular readings from past editions and have moved several others to different chapters to improve their usefulness and applicability.

Teaching Resources and Web Site to Accompany the Book and Companion Reader

For the Instructor

The password-protected Instructor Site at **www.sagepub.com/newman9e** gives instructors access to a full complement of resources to support and enhance their courses. The following assets are available on the instructor site:

- A **test bank** with multiple-choice, true/false, short-answer, and essay questions. The test bank is provided on the site in Word format as well as in our Diploma computerized testing software. Diploma is a question authoring and management tool that enables instructors to edit the existing test bank questions, add their own questions, and create customizable quizzes and exams. After tests have been created, they can be printed, exported into Word, or exported into popular course management systems such as Blackboard or WebCT.

- **PowerPoint** slides for each chapter, for use in lecture and review. Slides are integrated with the book's distinctive features and incorporate key tables, figures, and photos.
- **Video resources** that enhance the information in each chapter.
- **SAGE journal articles** for each chapter that provide extra content on important topics from SAGE's sociology journals.
- **Classroom exercises and discussion topics** that suggest group and individual activities to enhance student learning, as well as valuable tools to facilitate discussion.
- **Suggested readings and films** for each chapter that explore recommended literary resources, educational film resources, features films, and classic/exemplary sociological studies.
- **Web resources** that provide links to Web sites to encourage additional learning on specific topics.

For the Student

To maximize students' understanding of sociology and promote critical thinking and active learning, we have provided the following chapter-specific student resources on the open-access portion of **www.sagepub.com/newman9e**:

- **Flashcards** that reiterate key chapter terms and concepts.
- **Self-quizzes**, including multiple-choice and true/false questions.
- **Video resources** that enhance the information in each chapter.
- **SAGE journal articles** for each chapter that provide extra content on important topics from SAGE's sociology journals.
- **Web resources** that provide links to Web sites to encourage additional learning on specific topics.

A Word About the "Architecture of Society"

I have chosen the image of architecture in the subtitle to convey one of the driving themes of this book: Society is a human construction. Society is not "out there" somewhere, waiting to be visited and examined. It exists in the minute details of our day-to-day lives. Whenever we follow its rules or break them, enter its roles or shed them, work to change things or keep them as they are, we are adding another nail, plank, or frame to the structure of our society. In short, society—like the buildings around us—couldn't exist were it not for the actions of people.

At the same time, however, this structure that we have created appears to exist independently of us. We don't usually spend much time thinking about the buildings we live, work, and play in as human constructions. We see them as finished products, not as the processes that created them. Only when something goes wrong—the pipes leak or the walls crack—do we realize that people made these structures and people are the ones who must fix them. When buildings outlive their usefulness or become dangerous to their inhabitants, people must renovate them or, if necessary, tear them down.

Likewise, society is so massive and has been around for so long that it *appears* to stand on its own, at a level above and beyond the toiling hands of individual people. But here, too, when things begin to go wrong—widespread discrimination, environmental degradation, massive poverty, lack of affordable health care, escalating crime rates—people must do something about it.

So the fascinating paradox of human life is that we build society, collectively "forget" that we've built it, and live under its massive and influential structure. But we are not "stuck" with society as it is. Human beings are the architects of their own social reality. Throughout this book, I examine the active roles individuals play in planning, maintaining, or fixing society.

A Final Thought

One of the greatest challenges I face as a teacher of sociology is trying to get my students to see the personal relevance of the course material, to fully appreciate the connection between the individual and society. The true value of sociology lies in its unique ability to show the two-way connection between the most private elements of our lives—our characteristics, experiences, behaviors, and thoughts—and the cultures, groups, organizations, and social institutions to which we belong. The "everyday life" approach in this book uses real-world examples and personal observations as a vehicle for understanding the relationship between individuals and society.

My purpose is to make the familiar unfamiliar—to help you critically examine the commonplace and the ordinary in your own life. Only when you step back and examine the taken-for-granted aspects of your personal experiences can you see that there is an inherent, sometimes unrecognized organization and predictability to them. At the same time, you will see that the structure of society is greater than the sum of the experiences and psychologies of the individuals in it.

It is my conviction that this intellectual excursion should be a thought-provoking and enjoyable one. Reading a textbook doesn't have to be boring or, even worse, the academic equivalent of a trip to the dentist (although I personally have nothing against dentists). I believe that one of my responsibilities as an instructor is to provide my students with a challenging but comfortable classroom atmosphere in which to learn. I have tried to do the same in this book. Your instructor has chosen this book not because it makes his or her job teaching your course any easier but because he or she wants you, the student, to see how sociology helps us to understand how the small, private experiences of our everyday lives are connected to this thing we call society. I hope you learn to appreciate this important message, and I hope you enjoy reading this book as much as I enjoyed writing it.

Have fun,

David M. Newman
Department of Sociology and Anthropology
DePauw University
Greencastle, IN 46135
E-mail: dnewman@depauw.edu

Acknowledgments

A book project such as this one takes an enormous amount of time to develop. I've spent thousands of hours on this book—typing away at my computer, searching the Web, fretting over what I should and shouldn't include—all while holed up in my isolated and very cluttered third-floor office. Yet as solitary as this project was, I could not have done it alone. Over the years, many people have provided invaluable assistance to make this book a reality. Without their generous help and support, it wouldn't have been written, and you'd be reading some other sociologist's list of people to thank. Because I have revised rather than rewritten this book, I remain indebted to those who have helped me at some point during the writing of all eight editions.

First, I would like to thank the former publisher and president of Pine Forge Press, Steve Rutter. Nearly two decades ago, when I was a brand new author, he pushed, prodded, and cajoled me into exceeding my expectations and overachieving. The numerous suggestions he offered on the early editions of this book made it a better one. Likewise, my former editor, Becky Smith, must be thanked for helping me through the maze of details and difficulties that cropped up during the many previous versions of this book. Even though she no longer edits my books, hers is the grammar-correcting, thesaurus-wielding voice in my head whenever I write.

As for this edition, I would like to extend my sincere gratitude to Maggie Stanley, Lydia Balian, Dave Repetto, and Laureen Gleason at SAGE and copy editor Rachel Keith for their insight and guidance in putting together this newest edition. Having already written eight editions of this book, I was definitely an old dog with absolutely no desire to learn any new tricks when these individuals became involved. To their credit, they let me write as I have always written. For that, I am eternally grateful.

I would also like to express my thanks to Harvest Moon, The University of Texas at Arlington, for creating an excellent instructor's manual, to Julianne McNalley, Edmonds Community College, for creating the student study site materials, and to Pat Purdy for securing copyright permissions.

As always, I appreciate the many helpful comments offered by the reviewers of the nine editions of this book:

Sharon Abbott, Fairfield University

Deborah Abowitz, Bucknell University

Stephen Adair, Central Connecticut State University

Rebecca Adams, University of North Carolina, Greensboro

Ron Aminzade, University of Minnesota

Afroza Anwary, Carleton College

George Arquitt, Oklahoma State University

Carol Auster, Franklin and Marshall College

Ellen C. Baird, Arizona State University

Ellen Berg, California State University, Sacramento

Mildred Biaku, University of Alabama at Birmingham

Michael G. Bisciglia, Southeastern Louisiana University

David Bogen, Emerson College

Frances A. Boudreau, Connecticut College

David L. Briscoe, University of Arkansas at Little Rock

Todd Campbell, Loyola University, Chicago

Wanda Clark, South Plains College

Thomas Conroy, St. Peter's College

Norman Conti, Duquesne University

Maia Greenwell Cunningham, Citrus College

Doug Currivan, University of Massachusetts, Boston

Karen Dalke, University of Wisconsin, Green Bay

Jeff Davidson, University of Delaware

Kimberly Davies, Augusta State University

Tricia Davis, North Carolina State University

James J. Dowd, University of Georgia

Laura A. Dowd, University of Georgia, Athens

Charlotte A. Dunham, Texas Tech University

Donald Eckard, Temple University

Charles Edgley, Oklahoma State University

Rachel Einhower, Purdue University

June Ellestad, Washington State University

Shalom Endleman, Quinnipiac College

Rebecca Erickson, University of Akron

Kimberly Faust, Winthrop University

Patrick Fontane, St. Louis College of Pharmacy

Michael J. Fraleigh, Bryant University

Sarah N. Gaston, Texas A&M University

Farah Gilanshah, University of Minnesota–Morris

Barry Goetz, University of Dayton

Lorie Schabo Grabowski, University of Minnesota

Valerie Gunter, University of New Orleans

Roger Guy, Texas Lutheran University

John R. Hall, University of California, Davis

Charles Harper, Creighton University

Douglas Harper, Duquesne University

Tara Hardinge, California State University, Long Beach

Lori Heald, East Carolina University

Peter Hennen, University of Minnesota

Max Herman, Rutgers University

Cynthia Hewitt, Morehouse College

Christine L. Himes, Syracuse University

Susan Hoerbelt, Hillsborough Community College

Amy Holzgang, Cerritos College

Kate Hovey, Central New Mexico Community College

W. Jay Hughes, Georgia Southern University

Gary Hytreck, Georgia Southern University

Valerie Jenness, University of California, Irvine

Kathryn Johnson, Barat College

Richard Jones, Marquette University

Tom Kando, California State University, Sacramento

Steve Keto, Kent State University

Peter Kivisto, Augustana College

Lisa Konczal, Barry University

Marc LaFountain, State University of West Georgia

Sharon Melissa Latimer, West Virginia University

Joseph Lengermann, University of Maryland, College Park

Linda A. Litteral, Grossmont Community College

Julie L. Locher, University of Alabama at Birmingham

David G. LoConto, Jacksonville State University

David A. Lopez, California State University, Northridge

Fred Maher, Temple University

Kristen Marcussen, University of Iowa

Benjamin Mariante, Stonehill College

Joseph Marolla, Virginia Commonwealth University

Michallene McDaniel, University of Georgia

James R. McIntosh, Lehigh University

Jerome McKibben, Fitchburg State University

Ted P. McNeilsmith, Adams State College

Dan Miller, University of Dayton

Melinda Milligan, Sonoma State University

John R. Mitrano, Central Connecticut State University

Susannne Monahan, Montana State University

Harvest Moon, The University of Texas at Arlington

Kelly Murphy, University of Pittsburgh

Elizabeth Ehrhardt Mustaine, University of Central Florida

Daniel Myers, University of Notre Dame

Anne Nurse, College of Wooster

Marjukka Ollilainen, Weber State University

Toska Olson, Evergreen State College

Liza A. Pellerin, Ball State University

Larry Perkins, Oklahoma State University, Stillwater

Bernice Pescosolido, Indiana University, Bloomington

Mike Plummer, Boston College

Edward Ponczek, William Rainey Harper College

Tanya Poteet, Capital University

Sharon E. Preves, Grand Valley State University

Kennon J. Rice, North Carolina State University

Judith Richlin-Klonsky, University of California, Los Angeles

Robert Robinson, Indiana University, Bloomington

Mary Rogers, University of West Florida

Sally S. Rogers, Montgomery College

Wanda Rushing, University of Memphis

Michael Ryan, University of Louisiana, Lafayette

Scott Schaffer, Millersville University

Aileen Schulte, State University of New York, New Paltz

Dave Schweingruber, Iowa State University

Mark Shibley, Southern Oregon University

Thomas Shriver, Oklahoma State University

Toni Sims, University of Louisiana, Lafayette

Kathleen Slevin, College of William and Mary

Melissa Sloan, Drew University

Lisa White Smith, Christopher Newport University

Eldon E. Snyder, Bowling Green State University

Nicholas Sofios, Providence College

George Spilker, Clarkson College

Melanie Stander, University of Washington

Beverly Stiles, Midwestern State University

Kandi Stinson, Xavier University

Richard Tardanico, Florida International University

Robert Tellander, Sonoma State University

Kathleen Tiemann, University of North Dakota

Steven Vallas, George Mason University

Tom Vander Ven, Indiana University, South Bend

John Walsh, University of Illinois, Chicago

Gregory Weiss, Roanoke College

Marty Wenglinski, Quinnipiac College

Stephan Werba, Catonsville Community College

Cheryl E. Whitley, Marist College

Norma Williams, University of North Texas

Janelle Wilson, University of Minnesota, Duluth

Mark Winton, University of Central Florida

Judith Wittner, Loyola University, Chicago

Cynthia A. Woolever, Hartford Seminary

Don C. Yost, Mountain State University

Ashraf Zahedi, Stanford University

Stephen Zehr, University of Southern Indiana

I also want to express my appreciation to the many colleagues, students, and friends who have offered cherished assistance throughout the production of all nine editions of this book and have put up with my incessant whining about how hard it all was. Some offered bits of advice on specific topics; others provided general support and encouragement, which helped me retain my sanity. Christopher Bondy, Eiko Saeki, David Dietz, and Rhonesha Byng were especially helpful in providing specific illustrative examples for this edition. Jodi O'Brien, after close to 30 years of friendship and over a decade of coediting, continues to graciously remind me that there's more to life than writing a book. Thanks also to my administrative assistant, Krista Dahlstrom, who patiently explained to me—many, many times—how to fill out the Federal Express shipping vouchers.

I would also like to express gratitude to my sons, Zach and Seth, and to my students, who, throughout the years, have kept me curious and prevented me from taking myself too seriously. And finally, my deepest thanks must go to Rebecca Upton, whose eternal optimism, support, and confidence consistently inspire me to push beyond my intellectual limitations, and to Mokolodi Underfoot, whose wagging tail never fails to brighten my day.

PART I

The Individual and Society

What is the relationship between your private life and the social world around you? Part I introduces you to the guiding theme of this book: Our personal, everyday experiences affect and are affected by the larger society in which we live. Chapters 1 and 2 discuss the sociological perspective on human life and the ways in which it differs from the more individualistic approaches of psychology and biology. You will read about what society consists of and get a glimpse into sociologists' attempts to understand the two-way relationship between the individual and society.

As you read on, keep in mind a metaphor that will be used throughout the book to help explain the nature of society: architecture. Like buildings, societies have a design discernible to the alert eye. Both are constructed by bringing together a wide variety of materials in a complex process. Both, through their structure, shape the activities within. At the same time, both change. Sometimes they change subtly and gradually as the inhabitants go about their lives; other times they are deliberately redecorated or remodeled. As you make your way through this book, see if you can discover more ways in which buildings and societies are alike.

Taking a New Look
at a Familiar World

André graduated from college in 2011. He had been a model student. When not studying, he found time to help kids read at the local elementary school and actively participated in student government at his own school. He got along well with his professors, his grades were excellent, he made the dean's list all four years, and he graduated Phi Beta Kappa. As a computer science major with a minor in economics, André thought his future was clear: He would land a job at a top software company or perhaps a stock brokerage firm and work his way up the ladder so that he'd be earning a six-figure income by the time he was 30.

But when André entered the job market and began applying for jobs, things didn't go exactly according to plan. Despite his credentials, nobody seemed willing to hire him full time. He was able to survive only by taking temporary freelance programming jobs here and there and working nights at the Gap. Many of his friends from college had similar difficulties finding jobs. Nevertheless, André began to question his own abilities: "Do I lack the skills employers are looking for? Am I not trying hard enough? What the heck is wrong with me?" His friends and family were as encouraging as they could be, but some secretly wondered if André wasn't as smart as they'd thought he was.

Michael and Carole were both juniors at a large university. They had been dating each other exclusively for the past two years. By all accounts, the relationship seemed to be going quite well. In fact, Michael was beginning to imagine them getting married, having children, and living happily ever after. Then one day out of the blue, Carole dropped a bombshell. She told Michael she thought their relationship was going nowhere and perhaps they ought to start seeing other people.

Michael was stunned. "What did I do?" he asked her. "I thought things were going great. Is it something I said? Something I did? I can change."

She said no, he hadn't done anything wrong, they had simply grown apart. She told him she just didn't feel as strongly about him as she used to.

After the breakup, Michael was devastated. He turned to his friends for support. "She wasn't any good for you anyway," they said. "We always thought she was a little flighty. She probably couldn't be in a serious relationship with anybody. It wasn't your fault; it was hers."

In both of these stories, notice that people immediately try to explain an unhappy situation by focusing on the individual characteristics and attributes of the people involved. André blames himself for not being able to land a job; others question his intelligence and drive. Michael wonders what he did to sour his relationship with

Carole; his friends question Carole's psychological stability. Such reactions are not uncommon. We have a marked tendency to rely on *individualistic explanations*, attributing people's achievements and failures to their personal qualities.

Why can't André, our highly intelligent, well-trained, talented college graduate, land a permanent job? It's certainly possible that he has some personal defect that makes him unemployable: lack of motivation, laziness, negative attitude, bad hygiene, and so on. Or maybe he doesn't come across as particularly capable during job interviews.

But by focusing exclusively on such individual "deficiencies," we overlook the broader societal factors that may have affected André's job prospects. For instance, the employment situation for college graduates like André was part of a broader economic trend that began with the global financial crisis of 2008. By late 2010, 7.9 million jobs had disappeared, many permanently (Isidore, 2010). At the time I was writing this chapter, 9.5% of American adults (about 14 million people) were officially unemployed. Incidentally, the official unemployment rate only counts people who have been actively seeking employment for the past month. Thus it doesn't include the 8.5 million people who were employed part time even though they wanted to work full time and the 822,000 so-called "discouraged" workers who had lost hope and given up looking for employment (U.S. Bureau of Labor Statistics, 2011a).

Furthermore, college degrees are no longer the guarantee of fruitful employment they once were. Job opportunities for college graduates improved in the mid 2000s, only to take a steep dive in 2009. Each year between 2004 and 2008, employers increased their hiring of college graduates by an average of 13% over the previous year (cited in Hunsinger, 2009). In fact, the job market became so good in the mid 2000s that newspapers began providing advice to college graduates on how to be "picky" when choosing a place to work (Knight, 2006). As late as May 2008, economists were still predicting a favorable job market for new graduates (K. Murphy, 2008).

But all that quickly changed with the economic recession. Currently, the percentage of college-educated young Americans who are either unemployed or are no longer seeking work—roughly 17%—is the highest it's been since 1994, the first year such records were kept (Uchitelle, 2010). Indeed, about 20% of all unemployed people over the age of 25 are college graduates, up from 9.2% in 1979 (Mishel, Bernstein, & Allegretto, 2007; U.S. Bureau of Labor Statistics, 2011a). Only 56% of 2009 college graduates are currently working in jobs that actually require a college degree (cited in Rampell, 2011b).

According to the Collegiate Employment Research Institute (2011), about one third of employers reported definite plans to hire college graduates in the 2010–2011 academic year, a slight increase over 2010 and a sign of improvement. But that figure is well below the 47% of employers who had such intentions two years earlier. And the majority of employers who *did* intend to hire college graduates indicated they'd be hiring fewer people compared with the previous year.

For college graduates who do land jobs, starting salaries have stagnated. The average starting salary for those graduating in 2010 was $27,000, down from $30,000 for those who graduated between 2006 and 2008 (Godofsky, Zukin, & Van Horn, 2011). The "wage premium"—the taken-for-granted assumption that a college degree will bring higher wages—has lost steam in recent years. College graduates still earn nearly 46% more, on average, than people with high school diplomas (U.S. Bureau of the Census, 2011b). And having a degree brings higher pay even in fields that don't require a degree, such as dishwasher, hairdresser, and cashier (cited in Leonhardt, 2011). But the education-based wage gap has been shrinking for several years (Uchitelle, 2005).

So you see, André's employability and his chances of earning a good living were as much a result of the economic forces operating at the time he began looking for a job as of any of his personal qualifications. Had he graduated only a few years earlier (when the economy was doing better) or a few years later (when it is projected to improve), his prospects would have been much brighter.

And what about Michael and Carole? It seems perfectly reasonable to conclude that something about either of them or the combination of the two caused their breakup. We tend to view dating relationships—not to mention marriages—as situations that succeed or fail solely because of the traits or behaviors of the two people involved.

But how would your assessment of the situation change if you found out that Jason—to whom Carole had always been secretly attracted—had just broken up with his longtime girlfriend and was now available? Like it or not, relationships are not exclusively private entities; they're always being influenced by forces beyond our control. They take place within a larger network of friends, acquaintances, ex-partners, coworkers, fellow students, and people as yet unknown who may make desirable or, at the very least, acceptable dating partners. Social network Web sites such as Facebook and Twitter where people can post word of their relationship status are as popular as the more traditional places where people announce their weddings. As one columnist put it, "What good does it do to know that Joe and Jane are getting married? The news we really need is who's breaking up—so we can go and . . . hit on them" (quoted in Soukup, 2004, p. 15).

When people believe they have no better alternative, they tend to stay with their present partners, even if they are not particularly satisfied. When people think that better relationships are available to them, they may become less committed to staying in their present ones. Indeed, people's perceptions of what characterizes a good relationship (such as fairness, compatibility, affection) are less likely to determine when and if it ends than the presence or absence of favorable alternatives (Felmlee, Sprecher, & Bassin, 1990). Research shows that the risk of a relationship ending increases as the supply of potential alternative relationships increases (South & Lloyd, 1995).

In addition, Carole's decision to leave could have been indirectly affected by the sheer number of potentially available partners—a result of shifts in the birth rate 20 years or so earlier. Today, there are roughly 120 U.S. men in their 20s who are single, divorced, or widowed for every 100 women in the same categories (Roberts, 2006). For a single, heterosexual woman like Carole, such a surplus of college-age men increases the likelihood that she would eventually come across a better alternative to Michael. The number of available alternatives can even vary from state to state. For instance, Michael's attractiveness would have improved if he were living in New York (where there are more single women than men) but worsened if he were living in Alaska (where there are more single men than women; Kershaw, 2004). In sum, Michael's interpersonal value, and therefore the stability of his relationship with Carole, may have suffered not because of anything he did but because of population forces over which he had little, if any, control.

Let's take this notion beyond Carole and Michael's immediate dating network. For instance, the very characteristics and features that people consider desirable (or undesirable) in the first place reflect the values of the larger culture in which they live. Fashions and tastes are constantly changing, making particular characteristics (e.g., hairstyle, physique, clothing), behaviors (smoking, drinking, exercising), or life choices (occupation, political affiliation) more or less attractive. And broad economic forces can affect intimate choices even further. In China, where there is a large surplus of bachelors (see Chapter 13), young single women can be especially choosy when it comes to romantic partners, often requiring that suitors own their own homes before they'll even consider them for a date (Jacobs, 2011).

The moral of these two stories is simple: To understand experiences in our personal lives, we must move past individual traits and examine broader societal characteristics and trends. External features beyond our immediate awareness and control often exert more influence on the circumstances of our day-to-day lives than our "internal" qualities. We can't begin to explain an individual's employability without examining current and past economic trends that affect the number of jobs available and the number of people who are looking for work. We can't begin to explain why relationships work or don't work without addressing the broader interpersonal network and culture in which they are embedded. By the same token, we can't begin to explain people's ordinary, everyday thoughts and actions without examining the social forces that influence them.

Sociology and the Individual

Herein lies the fundamental theme of *sociology*—the systematic study of human societies—and the theme that will guide us throughout this book: Everyday social life—our thoughts, actions, feelings, decisions, interactions, and so on—is the product of a complex interplay between societal forces and personal characteristics. To explain why people are the way they are or do the things they do, we must understand the interpersonal, historical, cultural, organizational, and global environments they inhabit. To understand either individuals or society, we must understand both (C. W. Mills, 1959).

Of course, seeing the relationship between individuals and social forces is not always so easy. The United States is a society built on the image of the rugged, self-reliant individual. Not surprisingly, it is also a society dominated by individualistic understandings of human behavior that seek to explain problems and processes by focusing exclusively on the personality, the psychology, or even the biochemistry of each individual. Consequently, most of us simply take for granted that what we choose to do, say, feel, and think are private phenomena. Everyday life seems to be a series of free personal choices. After all, we choose what to major in. We choose what to wear when we go out. We choose what and when to eat. We choose our lifestyles, our mates, and so on.

But how free are these decisions? Think about all the times your actions have been dictated or at least influenced by social circumstances over which you had little control. Have you ever felt that because of your age or gender or race, certain opportunities were closed to you? Your ability to legally drive a car, drink alcohol, or vote, for instance, is determined by society's prevailing definition of age. When you're older, you may be forced into retirement despite your skills and desire to continue working. Some occupations, such as bank executive and engineer, are still overwhelmingly male, whereas others, such as registered nurse and preschool teacher, are almost exclusively female. Likewise, the doctrines of your religion may limit your behavioral choices. For a devout Catholic, premarital sex or even divorce is unlikely. Each day during the holy month of Ramadan, a strict Muslim must abstain from food and drink from sunrise to sunset. An Orthodox Jew would never drink milk and eat meat at the same meal.

Then there's the matter of personal style—your choices in hairstyle, dress, music, and the like. Large-scale marketing strategies can actually create a demand for particular products or images. Would the Jonas Brothers or Katy Perry or Justin Bieber have become so popular without a tightly managed and slickly packaged publicity program designed to appeal to adolescents and preadolescents? Your tastes, and therefore your choices as a consumer, are often influenced by decisions made in far-off corporate boardrooms.

National and international economic trends also affect your everyday life. You may lose your job or, like André, face a tight job market as a result of economic fluctuations brought about by increased global competition or a severe recession. Or, because of the rapid development of certain types of technology, the college degree that may be your ticket to a rewarding career today may not qualify you even for a low-paying, entry-level position 10 years from now. In one poll, 75% of young adults who dropped out of college cited the financial need to work full time as the principal reason why it would be hard for them to go back to school (Lewin, 2009b). And if you finish your degree but don't get a good job right out of college, you may have to move back home—like 40% of people in their 20s today (cited in Henig, 2010)—and live there for years after you graduate, not because you can't face the idea of living apart from your beloved parents but because you can't earn enough to support yourself.

Government and politics affect our personal lives too. A political decision made at the local, regional, national, or even international level may result in the closing of a government agency you depend on, make the goods and services to which you have grown accustomed either more expensive or less available, or reduce the size of your paycheck after taxes are taken out. Workplace family-leave policies or medical insurance regulations established by the government may affect your decision whether and when to have a baby. If you are homosexual, the government can determine whether or not you can be covered by your partner's health care policy and file a joint income tax return, whether or not you can inherit jointly acquired assets, or whether or not you can be involuntarily discharged from the military because of your sexual orientation. In the United States, decisions made by the U.S. Supreme Court can increase or limit your ability to control your fertility, sue an employer for discrimination, use your property however you please, buy certain products, or keep the details of your life a private matter.

People's personal lives can also be touched by events that occur in distant countries:

- In 2005, Hurricane Katrina killed thousands of people, rendered hundreds of thousands homeless and unemployed, contaminated local waterways, and decimated Gulf Coast industries such as tourism and steel, lumber, and oil production. Its economic effects were felt immediately in the rest of the country, where, for instance, gasoline prices skyrocketed. It also had a staggering impact on U.S. exports and on the travel industry—both nationally and internationally.
- In 2008, a stock market plunge in the United States instantly sent markets tumbling in Europe, South America, and Asia. The ensuing recession drove up unemployment rates in just about every industrialized nation around the world. Some countries, like Greece and Portugal, are on the verge of bankruptcy.
- In 2009, fear over the spread of swine flu dramatically reduced international travel—especially to Mexico, where the flu was purported to originate—thereby affecting global

airline companies and cruise operators in the United States and elsewhere. It even reduced exports of pork, despite assurance by health officials that there was no connection between the virus and food consumption.

- In 2011, a massive earthquake and deadly tsunami crippled many Japanese companies that manufacture car parts, resulting in a drop in automobile production in U.S. plants.
- Violent protests in Arab countries like Libya, Egypt, Syria, and Yemen sparked fears of reduced oil imports and drove U.S. gasoline prices up over $4.00 a gallon in the spring of 2011.
- The technologically interconnected nature of the world has made the effects of international events almost instantaneous. In 2011, a Florida pastor made headlines worldwide for his highly publicized burning of the Qur'an. This act incited waves of violent protest half a world away in Afghanistan that killed dozens of people, including seven United Nations employees.

These are only some of the ways in which events in the larger world can affect individual lives.

The Insights of Sociology

Sociologists do not deny that individuals make choices or that they must take personal responsibility for those choices. But they are quick to point out that we cannot fully understand the things happening in our lives, private and personal though they may be, without examining the influence of the people, events, and societal features that surround us. By showing how social processes can shape us, and how individual action can in turn affect those processes, sociology provides unique insight into the taken-for-granted personal events and the large-scale cultural and global processes that make up our everyday existence.

Other disciplines study human life, too. Biologists study how the body works. Neurologists examine what goes on inside the brain. Psychologists study what goes on inside the mind to create human behavior. These disciplines focus almost exclusively on structures and processes that reside *within* the individual. In contrast, sociologists study what goes on *among* people as individuals, groups, or societies. How do social forces affect the way people interact with one another? How do people make sense of their private lives and the social worlds they occupy? How does everyday social interaction create "society"?

Personal issues like love, sexuality, poverty, aging, and prejudice are better understood within the appropriate societal context. For instance, U.S. adults tend to believe that they marry purely for love, when in fact society pressures people to marry from the same social class, religion, and race (P. L. Berger, 1963). Sociology, unlike other disciplines, forces us to look outside the tight confines of individual anatomy and personality to understand the phenomena that shape us. Consider, for example, the following situations:

- A young middle school girl, fearing she is overweight, begins systematically starving herself in the hope of becoming more attractive.
- A 55-year-old stockbroker, unable to find work since his firm laid him off, sinks into a depression after losing his family and his home. He now lives on the streets.
- A 36-year-old professor kills herself after learning that her position at the university will be terminated the following year.
- The student body president and valedictorian of the local high school cannot begin or end her day without several shots of whiskey.

What do these people have in common? Your first response might be that they are all suffering or have suffered terrible personal problems. If you saw them only for what they've become—an "anorexic," a "homeless person," a "suicide victim," or an "alcoholic"—you might think they have some kind of personality defect, genetic flaw, or mental problem that renders them incapable of coping with the demands of contemporary life. Maybe they simply lack the willpower to pick themselves up and move on. In short, your immediate tendency may be to focus on the unique, perhaps "abnormal," characteristics of these people to explain their problems.

But we cannot downplay the importance of their *social* worlds. There is no denying that we live in a society that praises a lean body, encourages drinking to excess, and values individual achievement and economic success. Some people suffer under these conditions when they don't measure up. This is not to say that all people exposed to the same social messages inevitably fall victim to the same problems. Some people overcome wretched childhoods, others withstand the tragedy of economic failure and begin anew, and some people are immune to narrowly defined cultural images of beauty. But to understand fully the nature of human life or of particular social problems, we must acknowledge the broader social context in which these things occur.

The Sociological Imagination

Unfortunately, we often don't see the connections between the personal events in our everyday lives and the larger society in which we live. People in a country such as the United States, which places such a high premium on individual achievement, have difficulty looking beyond their immediate situation. Someone who loses a job, gets divorced, or flunks out of school in such a society has trouble imagining that these experiences are somehow related to massive cultural or historical processes.

The ability to see the impact of these forces on our private lives is what the famous sociologist C. Wright Mills (1959) called the *sociological imagination*. The sociological imagination enables us to understand the larger historical picture and its meaning in our own lives. Mills argued that no matter how personal we think our experiences are, many of them can be seen as products of society-wide forces. The task of sociology is to help us view our lives as the intersection between personal biography and societal history, and thereby to provide a means for us to interpret our lives and social circumstances.

Getting fired, for example, is a terrible, even traumatic private experience. Feelings of personal failure are inevitable when one loses a job. But if the unemployment rate in a community hovers at or above 20%—as it does in places hardest hit by the recent economic recession, like El Centro, California, and Yuma, Arizona—then we must see unemployment not as a personal malfunction but as a social problem that has its roots in the economic and political structures of society. Listen to how one columnist described his job loss:

> Five years ago, when the magazine dismissed me, fewer Americans were unemployed than are now, and I felt like a solitary reject in a nation of comfortable successes. . . . If I were to get the same news now, in an era of mass layoffs and major bankruptcies, I wonder if I would suffer as I did then. . . . Maybe I would just shrug instead and head outside for a relaxing bike ride. (Kirn, 2009, p. 13)

Such an easygoing response to being fired is probably uncommon. Nevertheless, his point is important sociologically: Being unemployed is not a character flaw or personal failure if a significant number of people in one's community are also unemployed. We can't explain a spike in the unemployment rate as a sudden increase in the number of incompetent or unprepared individual workers in the labor force. As long as the economy is arranged so that employees are easily replaced or slumps inevitably occur, the social problem of unemployment cannot be solved at the personal level.

The same can be said for divorce, which people usually experience as an intimate tragedy. But in the United States, 4 out of every 10 marriages that begin this year will eventually end in divorce, and divorce rates are increasing in many countries around the world. We must therefore view divorce in the context of broader historical changes occurring throughout societies: in family, law, religion, economics, and the culture as a whole. It is impossible to explain significant changes in divorce rates over time by focusing exclusively on the personal characteristics and behaviors of divorcing individuals. Divorce rates don't rise simply because individual spouses have more difficulty getting along with one another than they used to, and they don't fall because more husbands and wives are suddenly being nicer to each other.

Mills did not mean to imply that the sociological imagination should debilitate us—that is, force us to powerlessly perceive our lives as wholly beyond our control. In fact, the opposite is true. An awareness of the impact of social forces or world history on our personal lives is a prerequisite to any efforts we make to change our social circumstances.

Indeed, the sociological imagination allows us to recognize that the solutions to many of our most serious social problems lie not in changing the personal situations and characteristics of individual people but in changing the social institutions and roles available to them (C. W. Mills, 1959). Drug addiction, homelessness, sexual violence, hate crimes, eating disorders, suicide, and other unfortunate situations will not go away simply by treating or punishing a person who is suffering from or engaging in the behavior.

As I was working on the revision of this book, a tragic event occurred at the university where I teach. On a pleasant May night at the beginning of final exam week, a first-year student killed himself. The incident sent shock waves through this small, close-knit campus.

As you would expect in such a situation, the question on everyone's mind was, "Why did he do it?" Although no definitive answer could ever be obtained, most people simply concluded that it was a "typical" suicide. They assumed that he must have been despondent, hopeless, unhappy, and unable to cope with the demands of college life. Some students said they heard he was failing some of his courses. Others said that no one really knew much about him, that he was a bit of a loner. In other words, something was wrong with *him*.

As tragic as this incident was, it isn't unique. Between the 1950s and the 1990s, the U.S. suicide rate more than doubled for people between the ages of 15 and 24 (National Center for Health Statistics, 2005). Although the rate dropped during the early 2000s, it has recently increased again (cited in Tanner, 2007), especially among young girls (Centers for Disease Control and Prevention, 2007). Suicide remains the third leading cause of death among young Americans, following accidents and homicides (Kent, 2010). In 2009, 13.8% of U.S. high school students reported that they had seriously considered attempting suicide during the previous year, and about 6.3% had actually attempted suicide one or more times during the same period (Centers for Disease Control and Prevention, 2010).

Focusing on individual feelings such as depression, hopelessness, and frustration doesn't tell us why so many people in this age group commit suicide, nor does it tell us why rates of youth suicide increase—or for that matter decrease—from decade to decade. So, to understand why the student at my university made such a choice, we must look beyond his private mental state and examine the social and historical factors that may have affected him.

Clearly, life in contemporary developed societies is focused on individual achievement—being well dressed, popular, and successful—more strongly than ever before. Young people face almost constant pressure to "measure up" and define their identities, and therefore their self-worth, according to standards set by others (Mannon, 1997). Although most adjust pretty well, others can't. In addition, as competition for scarce financial resources becomes more acute, young people are likely to experience heightened levels of stress and confusion about their own futures. When the quest for success begins earlier and earlier, the costs of not succeeding increase. Such changes may explain why suicides among young African American men (ages 15–24), once quite rare and still relatively less frequent than suicides among other ethnic groups, increased from 4.1 deaths per 100,000 people in 1960 to 15.1 deaths in 1990 (see Exhibit 1.1). The rate has since fallen but is still double what it was five decades ago (National Center for Health Statistics, 2010). Some experts blamed the increase on a growing sense of hopelessness and a long-standing cultural taboo against discussing mental health matters. Others, however, cited broader social factors, brought about, ironically, by the growing economy of the late 20th century. As more and more black families moved into the middle class, they felt increasing pressure to compete in

Exhibit 1.1   Race, Gender, and Teen Suicide

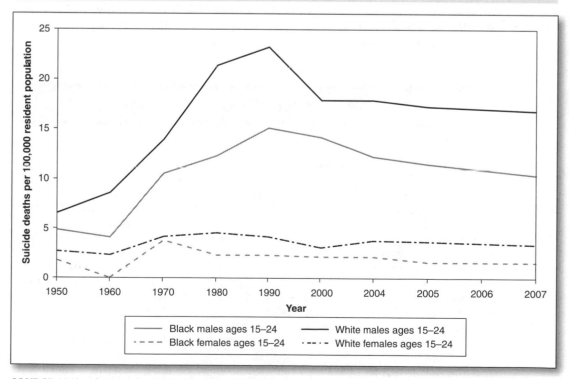

SOURCE: National Center for Health Statistics, 2010, Table 39

traditionally white-dominated professions and social environments. In fact, black teenagers who committed suicide were more likely to come from higher socioeconomic backgrounds than black teenagers in the general population (cited in Belluck, 1998).

You'll also notice in Exhibit 1.1 that the suicide rate of both black and white young men dropped in the early 2000s. Can you think of a sociological reason to account for this trend? Is it less stressful being a teenager today than it was 10 or 20 years ago?

In other societies, different types of social changes may account for fluctuations in suicide rates. In the late 1990s, Japan saw its unemployment and bankruptcy rates rise to record levels as companies grappled with a severe economic recession. Since then, suicide rates have risen steadily each year ("Japan Suicides Rise," 2010). According to Japan's National Police Agency, over 25% of suicides are caused by financial problems such as difficulty paying bills, finding a job, and keeping a business going (cited in Curtin, 2004). Although the elderly make up the largest segment of suicides in Japan, rates have increased dramatically among elementary school, middle school, and college students. In fact, suicide has become such a problem that the East Japan Railway Company recently installed blue lights above train platforms in its stations in hopes that they will have a soothing effect, thereby reducing the number of people who jump in front of trains to kill themselves ("Japanese Railways," 2009). Indeed, a veritable suicide subculture has arisen among Japanese youth, reflected in the dramatic growth of "suicide Web sites." One such site rates various methods of suicide in terms of "pain," "chance of success," and "annoyance to other people" (Brooke, 2004, p. 11).

The stress of change due to rapid development has been linked to increased suicide rates in China too, particularly among rural women, who are most likely to be displaced from their villages (E. Rosenthal, 2002). And in Ireland, which has the fastest-growing rate of suicide in the world, one in four suicides occurs among those ages 15 to 24 (Clarity, 1999). Experts there attribute much of this increase to the weakening of religious prohibition of suicide and the alteration of gender roles, which has left many young men unsure of their place in Irish society.

ÉMILE DURKHEIM

A Sociological View of Suicide

Sociologists' interest in linking suicide to certain processes going on in society is not new. In one of the classic pieces of social research, the famous sociologist Émile Durkheim (1897/1951) argued that suicide is more likely to occur under particular social circumstances and in particular communities. He was the first to see suicide as a manifestation of changes in society rather than of psychological shortcomings.

How does one go about determining whether rates of suicide are influenced by the structure of society? Durkheim decided to test his theory by comparing existing official statistics and historical records across groups, a research strategy sometimes referred to as the **comparative method**. Many sociologists continue to follow this methodology, analyzing statistics compiled by governmental agencies such as the U.S. Bureau of the Census, the Federal Bureau of Investigation, and the National Center for Health Statistics to draw comparisons of suicide rates among groups.

For about seven years, Durkheim carefully examined the available data on suicide rates among various social groups in Europe—from different regions of countries, certain religious or ethnic groups, and so on—looking for important social patterns. If suicides were purely acts of individual desperation, he reasoned, one would not expect to find any noticeable changes in the rates from year to year or from society to society. That is, the distribution of desperate, unstable, unhappy individuals should be roughly equal across time and culture. If, however, certain groups or societies had a consistently higher rate of suicide than others, something more than individual disposition would seem to be at work.

After compiling his figures, Durkheim concluded that there are actually several different types of suicide. Sometimes, he found, people take their own lives when they see no possible way to improve their oppressive circumstances. They come to the conclusion that suicide is preferable to a harsh life that will never improve. Think of prisoners serving life sentences or slaves who take their own lives to escape their miserable confinement and lack of freedom. Durkheim called this type of suicide *fatalistic suicide*.

Other suicides, what he called *anomic suicide*, occur when people's lives are suddenly disrupted by major social events, such as economic depressions, wars, and famines. At these times, he argued, the conditions around which people have organized their lives are dramatically altered, leaving them with a sense of hopelessness and despair. A study of suicide trends over the past 80 years found that overall rates tend to rise during economic recessions and fall during economic expansions (F. Luo, Florence, Quispe-Agnoli, Ouyang, & Crosby, 2011).

But he also discovered that suicide rates in all the countries he examined tended to be consistently higher among widowed, single, and divorced people than among married people; higher among people without children than among parents; and higher among Protestants than among Catholics. Did this mean that unmarried people, childless people, and Protestants were more unhappy, depressed, or psychologically dysfunctional than other people? Durkheim didn't think so. Instead, he felt that something about the nature of social life among people in these groups increased the likelihood of what he called *egoistic suicide*.

Durkheim reasoned that when group, family, or community ties are weak or deemphasized, people feel disconnected and alone. He pointed out, for instance, that the Catholic Church emphasizes salvation through community and binds its members to the church through elaborate doctrine and ritual; Protestantism, in contrast, emphasizes *individual* salvation and responsibility. This religious individualism, he believed, explained the differences he noticed in suicide rates between Catholics and Protestants. Self-reliance and independence may glorify one in God's eyes, but they become liabilities if one is in the throes of personal tragedy.

Durkheim feared that life in modern society tends to be individualistic and dangerously alienating. Over a century later, contemporary sociologists have found evidence supporting Durkheim's insight (e.g., Bellah, Madsen, Sullivan, Swidler, & Tipton, 1985; Riesman, 1950). Many people in the United States today don't know and have no desire to know their neighbors. Strangers are treated with suspicion.

In the pursuit of economic opportunities, we have become more willing to relocate, sometimes to regions far from family and existing friends and colleagues—the very people who could and would offer support in times of need. One study found that membership in volunteer organizations (Parent Teacher Association, Elks club, Red Cross, League of Women Voters, etc.) steadily declined in the United States in recent years (Putnam, 1995). Over the same period, the average number of hours a day that people watch television by themselves increased (cited in Roberts, 1995).

The structure of our communities discourages the formation of bonds with others, and, not surprisingly, the likelihood of suicide increases at the same time. In the United States today, the highest suicide rates can be found in Alaska and in the sparsely populated mountain states of Nevada, Montana, New Mexico, and Wyoming (U.S. Bureau of the Census, 2011b). Exhibits 1.2a and 1.2b show this pattern. These states tend to have a larger proportion of new residents who are not part of an established community. People tend to be more isolated, less likely to seek help or comfort from others in times of trouble, and therefore more susceptible to suicide than people who live in more populous states. It's worth noting that sparsely populated rural areas also have higher rates of gun ownership than other areas of the United States. Over 70% of suicides in rural counties in the United States are committed with firearms (Butterfield, 2005).

Durkheim also felt, however, that another type of suicide (what he called *altruistic suicide*) is more likely when the ties to one's community are too strong instead of too weak.

Exhibit 1.2a   Population Density and Suicide Rates in All 50 States (Suicides per 100,000 Residents)

State	Suicide Rate per 100,000 Resident Population	Persons per Square Mile	State	Suicide Rate per 100,000 Resident Population	Persons per Square Mile
United States	*11.3*	*86.8*	Missouri	13.5	86.9
Alabama	12.5	92.8	Montana	19.4	6.7
Alaska	22.1	1.2	Nebraska	10.2	23.4
Arizona	16.1	58.0	Nevada	18.3	24.1
Arkansas	14.3	55.5	New Hampshire	11.1	147.7
California	9.8	237.0	New Jersey	6.7	1,174.0
Colorado	16.4	48.4	New Mexico	20.4	16.6
Connecticut	7.4	726.2	New York	7.0	413.9
Delaware	10.7	453.1	North Carolina	11.7	192.6
District of Columbia	5.8	9,766.4	North Dakota	14.4	9.4
Florida	13.3	343.8	Ohio	11.0	281.9
Georgia	10.7	169.7	Oklahoma	14.7	53.7
Hawaii	9.7	201.7	Oregon	15.2	39.9
Idaho	15.1	18.7	Pennsylvania	11.2	281.3
Illinois	8.5	232.3	Rhode Island	8.7	1,007.9
Indiana	12.4	179.1	South Carolina	11.7	151.5
Iowa	10.6	53.8	South Dakota	12.5	10.7
Kansas	13.7	34.5	Tennessee	13.3	152.8
Kentucky	15.1	108.6	Texas	10.4	94.7
Louisiana	12.2	103.1	Utah	15.4	33.9
Maine	13.7	42.7	Vermont	13.8	67.2
Maryland	9.0	583.1	Virginia	11.2	199.1
Massachusetts	7.6	841.0	Washington	13.0	100.1
Michigan	11.0	175.5	West Virginia	15.9	75.6
Minnesota	10.8	66.2	Wisconsin	12.7	104.1
Mississippi	13.8	62.9	Wyoming	19.7	5.6

Exhibit 1.2b States With the Highest and Lowest Suicide Rates

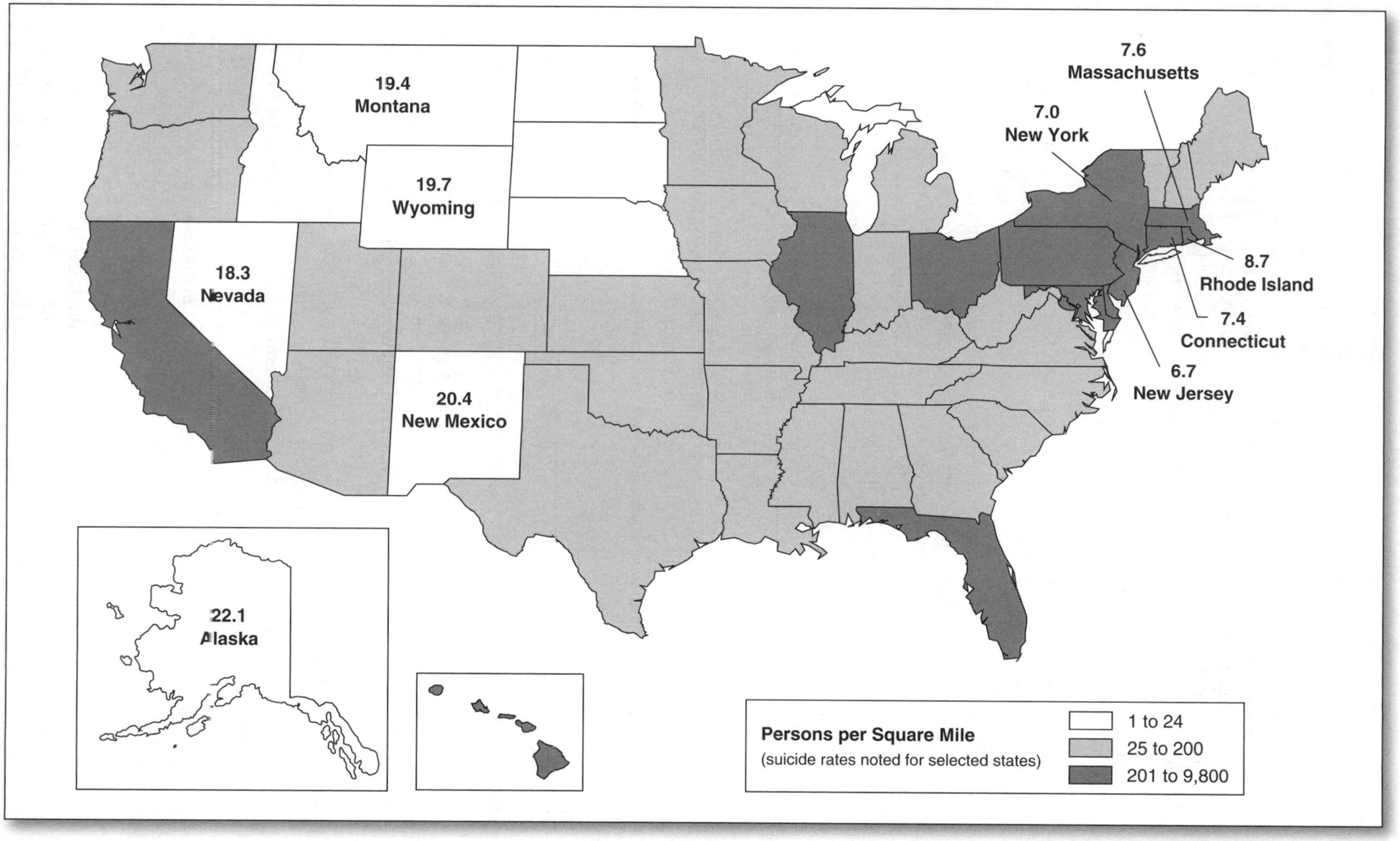

Massachusetts 7.6
New York 7.0
Rhode Island 8.7
Connecticut 7.4
New Jersey 6.7

Montana 19.4
Wyoming 19.7
Nevada 18.3
New Mexico 20.4
Alaska 22.1

Persons per Square Mile
(suicide rates noted for selected states)

1 to 24
25 to 200
201 to 9,800

SOURCE: U.S. Bureau of the Census, 2011b, Tables 13 and 121

15

He suggested that in certain societies individuality is completely overshadowed by one's group membership; the individual literally lives for the group, and personality is merely a reflection of the collective identity of the community. In some cases, commitment to a particular political cause can be powerful enough to lead some people to take their own lives. In India, the number of politically motivated suicides doubled between 2006 and 2008. For example, 200 people have taken their own lives in support of efforts to establish a separate state, Telangana, in southern India (Polgreen, 2010). Spiritual loyalty can also lead to altruistic suicide. Some religious sects require their members to reject their ties to outside people and groups and to live by the values and customs of their new community. When members feel that they can no longer contribute to the group and sustain their value within it, they may take their own lives out of loyalty to group norms.

A terrible example of the deadly effects of overly strong ties occurred in 1989, when four young Korean sisters, ranging in age from 6 to 13, attempted to kill themselves by ingesting rat poison. The three older sisters survived; the youngest died. The eldest provided startling sociological insight into this seemingly senseless act: Their family was poor; the father supported everyone on a salary of about $362 a month. The girl told the authorities that the sisters had made a suicide pact to ease their parents' financial burden and leave enough money for the education of their three-year-old brother. Within the traditional Korean culture, female children are much less important to the family than male children. These sisters attempted to take their lives not because they were depressed or unable to cope but because they felt obligated to sacrifice their personal well-being for the success of their family's male heir ("Korean Girls," 1989).

Just as the suicide pact of these young girls was tied to the social system of which they were a part, so, too, was the suicide of the young college student at my university. His choices and life circumstances were also a function of the values and conditions of his particular society. No doubt he had serious emotional problems, but these problems may have been part and parcel of his social circumstances. Had he lived in a society that didn't place as much pressure on young people or glorify individual achievement, he might not have chosen suicide. That's what the sociological imagination helps us understand.

Conclusion

In the 21st century, understanding our place within cultural, historical, and global contexts is more important than ever. The world is shrinking. Communication technology binds us to people on the other side of the planet. Increasing ecological awareness opens our eyes to the far-reaching effects of environmental degradations. The changes associated with colossal events in one country (political revolutions, terrorist attacks, natural disasters, economic crises, cultural upheavals) often quickly reverberate around the world. The local and global consequences of such events often continue to be felt for years.

When we look at how people's lives are altered by such phenomena—as they sink into poverty or ascend to prosperity; stand in bread lines or work at a job previously unavailable; or find their sense of ethnic identity, personal safety, or self-worth altered—we can begin to understand the everyday importance of large-scale social change.

However, we must remember that individuals are not just helpless pawns of societal forces. They simultaneously influence and are influenced by society. The next chapter provides a more detailed treatment of this theme. Then, in Part II, I examine how society and our social lives are constructed and ordered. I focus on the interplay between individuals and the people, groups, organizations, institutions, and culture that collectively make up our society. Part III focuses on the structure of society, with particular attention to the various forms of social inequality.

YOUR TURN

The sociological imagination serves as the driving theme throughout this book. It's not a particularly difficult concept to grasp in the abstract: Things that are largely outside our control affect our everyday lives in ways that are sometimes not immediately apparent; our personal biographies are a function of social history. Yet what does this actually mean? How can you see the impact of larger social and historical events on your own life? One way is to find out what events were going on at the time of your birth. Go to the library and find a newspaper and a popular magazine that were published on the day you were born. It would be especially useful to find a newspaper from the town or city in which you were born. What major news events took place that day? What were the dominant social and political concerns at the time? What was the state of the economy? What was considered fashionable in clothing, music, movies, and so forth? Ask your parents or other adults about their reactions to these events and conditions.

How do you think those reactions affected the way you were raised and the values of your family? What have been the lasting effects, if any, of these historical circumstances on the person you are today? In addition, you might want to check newspapers and magazines and the Internet to determine the political, economic, global, and cultural trends that were prominent when you entered high school. The emergence from adolescence into young adulthood is a significant developmental stage in the lives of most people. It often marks the first time that others—including parents and other adults—take us seriously. And it is arguably the most self-conscious time of our lives. Try to determine how these dominant social phenomena will continue to influence your life after college. Imagine how different your life might have been had these social conditions been different—for instance, a different political atmosphere, a stronger or weaker economy, a more tolerant or more restrictive way of life, and so on.

CHAPTER HIGHLIGHTS

- The primary theme of sociology is that our everyday thoughts and actions are the product of a complex interplay between massive social forces and personal characteristics. We can't understand the relationship between individuals and societies without understanding both.

- The sociological imagination is the ability to see the impact of social forces on our private lives—an awareness that our lives lie at the intersection of personal biography and societal history.

- Rather than studying what goes on within people, sociologists study what goes on between people, whether as individuals, groups, organizations, or entire societies. Sociology forces us to look outside the tight confines of our individual personalities to understand the phenomena that shape us.

KEY TERMS

altruistic suicide: Type of suicide that occurs where ties to the group or community are considered more important than individual identity

anomic suicide: Type of suicide that occurs when the structure of society is weakened or disrupted and people feel hopeless and disillusioned

comparative method: Research technique that compares existing official statistics and historical records across groups to test a theory about some social phenomenon

egoistic suicide: Type of suicide that occurs in settings where the individual is emphasized over group or community connections

fatalistic suicide: Type of suicide that occurs when people see no possible way to improve their oppressive circumstances

individualistic explanation: Tendency to attribute people's achievements and failures to their personal qualities

sociological imagination: Ability to see the impact of social forces on our private lives

sociology: Systematic study of human societies

STUDENT STUDY SITE

Visit the Student Study Site at **www.sagepub.com/newman9e** for these additional learning tools:

- Flashcards
- Web quizzes
- Sociologists at Work features
- Micro-Macro Connection features
- Video links
- Audio links
- Web resources
- SAGE journal articles

Seeing and Thinking Sociologically

2

How Individuals Structure Society

Social Influence: The Impact of Other People in Our Everyday Lives

Societal Influence: The Effect of Social Structure on Our Everyday Lives

Three Perspectives on Social Order

In 1994, ethnic violence erupted in the small African nation of Rwanda. The Hutu majority had begun a systematic program to exterminate the Tutsi minority. Soon, gruesome pictures of the tortured and dismembered bodies of Tutsi men, women, and children began to appear on television screens around the world. When it was over, close to a million Tutsis had been slaughtered—half of whom died within a three-month period. Surely, we thought, such horror must have been perpetrated by bands of vicious, crazed thugs who derived some sort of twisted pleasure from committing acts of unspeakable cruelty. Or maybe these were the extreme acts of angry soldiers, trained killers who were committed to destroying the enemy as completely as possible.

Actually, much of the responsibility for these atrocities lay elsewhere, in a most unlikely place: among the ordinary, previously law-abiding Rwandan citizens. Many of the participants in the genocide were the least likely brutes you could imagine. For instance, here's how one woman described her husband, a man responsible for many Tutsi deaths:

> He came home often. He never carried a weapon, not even his machete. I knew he was a leader. I knew the Hutus were out there cutting Tutsis. With me, he behaved nicely. He made sure we had everything we needed. . . . He was gentle with the children. . . . To me, he was the nice man I married. (quoted in Rwandan Stories, 2011, p. 1)

Pauline Nyiramasuhuko, a former social worker and the country's minister of family and women's affairs, promised the Tutsis in one village that they would be safe in a local stadium. When they arrived there, armed militia were waiting to kill them. She instructed one group of soldiers to burn alive a group of 70 women and girls, adding, "Before you kill the women, you need to rape them" (quoted in Zimbardo, 2007, p. 13). In 2011, a United Nations tribunal found that she had used her political position to help abduct and kill uncounted Tutsi men, women, and children and sentenced her to life in prison (Simons, 2011).

Some of the most gruesome attacks occurred in churches and missions (Lacey, 2006). Two Benedictine nuns and a National University of Rwanda physics professor stood trial for their role in the killings. The nuns were accused of informing the military that Tutsi refugees had sought sanctuary in the church and of standing by as the soldiers massacred them. One nun allegedly provided the death squads with cans of gasoline, which were used to set fire to a building where 500 Tutsis were hiding. The professor was accused of drawing up a list for the killers of Tutsi employees and students at the university and then killing at least seven Tutsis himself (Simons, 2001). A Catholic priest was sentenced to 15 years in prison for ordering his church to be demolished by bulldozers while 2,000 ethnic Tutsis sought refuge there.

A report by the civil rights organization African Rights provides evidence that members of the medical profession were deeply involved, too (M. C. Harris, 1996). The report details how doctors joined with militiamen to hunt down Tutsis, turning hospitals into slaughterhouses. Some helped soldiers drag sick and wounded refugees out of their beds to be killed. Others took advantage of their position of authority to organize roadblocks, distribute ammunition, and compile lists of Tutsi colleagues, patients, and neighbors to be sought out and slaughtered. Many doctors who didn't participate in the actual killing refused to treat wounded Tutsis and withheld food and water from refugees who sought sanctuary in hospitals. In fact, the president of Rwanda and the minister of health were both physicians who were eventually tried as war criminals.

Ordinary, well-balanced people—teachers, social workers, priests and nuns devoted to the ideals of charity and mercy, and physicians trained to heal and save lives—had changed, almost overnight, into cold-hearted killers. How could something like this have happened? The answer to this question lies in the sociological claim that individual behavior is largely shaped by social forces and situational contingencies. The circumstances of large-scale ethnic hatred and war have the power to transform well-educated, "nice" people with no previous history of violence into cruel butchers. Tragically, such forces were at work in many of the 20th and 21st centuries' most infamous examples of human brutality, such as the Nazi Holocaust during World War II and, more recently, large-scale ethnic massacres in Cambodia, Iraq, Bosnia, Kosovo, the Democratic Republic of the Congo, and the Darfur region of Sudan, as well as Rwanda.

But social circumstances don't just create opportunities for brutality; they can also motivate ordinary people to engage in astounding acts of heroism. The 2004 film *Hotel Rwanda* depicts the true story of Paul Rusesabagina, a hotel manager in the Rwandan capital, Kigali, who risked his own life to shelter over a thousand Tutsi refugees from certain death. Rusesabagina was a middle-class Hutu married to a Tutsi and the father of four children. He was a businessman with an eye toward turning a profit and a taste for the finer things in life. But when the genocide began, he used his guile, international contacts, and even water from the swimming pool to keep the refugees alive.

In this chapter, I examine the process by which individuals construct society and the way people's lives are linked to the social environment in which they live. The relationship between the individual and society is a powerful one—each continually affects the other.

How Individuals Structure Society

Up to this point, I have used the word *society* rather loosely. Formally, sociologists define **society** as a population living in the same geographic area who share a culture and a common identity and whose members are subject to the same political authority. Societies may consist of people with the same ethnic heritage or of hundreds of different groups who speak a multitude of languages. Some societies are highly industrialized and complex; others are primarily agricultural and relatively simple in structure. Some are very religious; others are distinctly secular.

According to the 19th-century French philosopher Auguste Comte, all societies, whatever their form, contain both forces for stability, which he called "social statics," and forces for change, which he called "social dynamics." Sometimes, however, people use the term *society* only to mean a "static" entity—a natural, permanent, and historical structure. They frequently talk about society "planning" or "shaping" our lives and describe it as a relatively unchanging set of organizations, institutions, systems, and cultural patterns into which successive generations of people are born and socialized.

As a result, sociology students often start out believing not only that society is powerfully influential (which, of course, it is) but also that it is something that exists "out there," completely separate and distinct from us (which it isn't). It is tempting to view society simply as a "top down" initiator of human activity, a massive entity that methodically shapes the lives of all individuals within it like some gigantic puppeteer manipulating a bunch of marionettes. This characterization is not completely inaccurate. Society does exert influence on its members through certain identifiable structural features and historical circumstances. The concept of the sociological imagination discussed in Chapter 1 implies that structural forces beyond our direct control do shape our personal lives.

But this view is only one side of the sociological coin. The sociological imagination also encourages us to see that each individual has a role in forming a society and influencing the course of its history. As we navigate our social environments, we respond in ways that may modify the effects and even the nature of that environment (House, 1981). As one sociologist has written,

> No [society], however massive it may appear in the present, existed in this massivity from the dawn of time. Somewhere along the line each one of its salient features was concocted by human beings. . . . Since all social systems were created by [people], it follows that [people] can also change them. (P. L. Berger, 1963, p. 128)

To fully understand society, then, we must see it as a human construction made up of people interacting with one another. Communication plays an important role in the construction of society. If we couldn't communicate with one another to reach an understanding about society's expectations, we couldn't live together. Through day-to-day communication, we construct, reaffirm, experience, and alter the reality of our society. By responding to other people's messages, comments, and gestures in the expected manner and by talking about social abstractions as real things, we help shape society (Shibutani, 1961).

Imagine two people sitting on a park bench discussing the United States' decade-long "war on terror." Person A is convinced that the actual threat to individual citizens, in the years since the attacks of September 11, 2001, does not warrant the erosion of civil rights and personal privacy through measures such as the USA PATRIOT Act, which allows the government to gain access to citizens' tax records, credit records, library records, bookstore records, and medical records without probable cause, consent, or knowledge. Person B counters that more recent terrorist attacks—such as those in Madrid, London, Bali, and Mumbai, as well as several highly publicized unsuccessful attempts to hijack airplanes—show that we're always potential targets and that any means of preventing U.S. deaths at the hands of foreign terrorists is worthwhile, even if it means sacrificing some freedoms. The debate becomes heated: One thinks that our nation's founding principles are the best protection for individual liberty; the other feels that individual liberty must be sacrificed if people's lives are in danger. These two people obviously don't agree on the need for or the effectiveness of sacrificing individual liberties as part of a war on terror. But merely by discussing it, they are acknowledging that such a war exists. In talking about such matters, people give shape and substance to society's ideals and values (Hewitt, 1988).

Even something as apparently unchangeable as our collective past can be shaped and modified by individuals. We usually think of history as a fixed, unalterable collection of social events that occurred long ago; only in science fiction novels or *Back to the Future* movies can one "go back" and change history. No one would question that the Declaration of Independence was signed in 1776; that John F. Kennedy was assassinated on November 22, 1963; that hijackers flew passenger jets into the Pentagon and the World Trade Center on September 11, 2001; or that the mastermind behind these attacks, Osama bin Laden, was killed on May 1, 2011.

Although such historical events themselves don't change, their meaning and relevance can. Consider the celebration in 1992 of the 500th anniversary of Columbus's voyage to the Americas. For generations, American schoolchildren have been taught that Columbus's 1492 "discovery" represented a triumphant step forward for Western civilization. We even have a holiday in his honor. However, increasing sensitivity to the past persecution of Native Americans has forced many people to reconsider the historical meaning of Columbus's journey. In fact, some historians now consider this journey and what followed it to be one of history's most dismal examples of reckless and deadly prejudice. So, you see, history might best be regarded as a work in progress.

When we view society this way, we can begin to understand the role each of us has in maintaining or altering it. Sometimes the actions of ordinary individuals mobilize larger groups of people to collectively alter some aspect of social life.

Consider the story of a young Canadian named Craig Kielburger. Over a decade ago, when he was 12, a front page article in the newspaper caught his eye. It described a Pakistani boy about his age who was sold into bondage as a carpet weaver, escaped, and was eventually murdered for speaking out publicly against child labor. Upset by the story, Craig gathered a few friends and formed an organization he called (Kids Can) Free the Children (KCFTC). Craig traveled throughout Canada and other countries addressing business groups, government bodies, educators, unions, and students on the plight of children around the world.

Since then, the organization, which now has over 350,000 young volunteers worldwide, has built more than 650 primary schools providing education to over 55,000 children a day (Free the Children, 2011). In addition, KCFTC supports clean water projects, health clinics, and alternative income cooperatives in 40 developing nations and has lobbied corporations to adopt standard labeling for child-labor-free products. Before Craig had even completed his college education, he had written a book, had met world leaders such as the Dalai Lama and the late Pope John Paul II, and had been nominated for the Nobel Peace Prize. He has won numerous awards and has been featured on *Oprah* and *60 Minutes.*

We live in a world in which our everyday lives are largely a product of structural, or **macrolevel**, societal and historical processes. Society is an objective fact that coerces, even creates us (P. L. Berger, 1963). At the same time, we are constantly creating, maintaining, reaffirming, and transforming society. Hence, society is part and parcel of individual-level human interaction (R. Collins, 1981). But although we create society, we then collectively "forget" we've done so, believe it is independent of us, and live our lives under its influence.

Throughout the remainder of this book, you'll see brief features called Micro-Macro Connections, which will help you see this interrelationship between macrolevel societal forces and many of the *microlevel* everyday phenomena we experience as individuals.

Social Influence: The Impact of Other People in Our Everyday Lives

We live in a world with other people. I know that's not the most profound statement you've ever read, so you can stop yawning. But it is key to understanding the sociology of human behavior. Our everyday lives are a collection of brief encounters, extended conversations, intimate interactions, and chance collisions with other people. In our early years, we may have our parents, siblings, uncles, aunts, and grandparents to contend with. Soon, we begin to form friendships with others outside our families. Over time, our lives also become filled with connections to other people—classmates, teachers, coworkers, bosses, spiritual leaders, therapists—who are neither family nor friends but who have an enormous impact on us. And, of course, we have frequent experiences with total strangers: the person at the local coffee shop who serves us our daily latte, the traveler who sits next to us on an airplane, the tech support specialist who helps us when our documents won't print or our iPods freeze.

If you think about it, understanding what it means to be alone requires that we know what it's like to be with other people. As I will discuss in Chapters 5 and 6, much of our private identity—what we think of ourselves, the type of people we become, and the images of ourselves we project in public—comes from our contact with others.

Sociologists tell us that these encounters have a great deal of *social influence* over our lives. Whether we're aware of their doing so or not, other people affect our thoughts, likes, and dislikes. Consider why certain songs, books, or films become blockbuster hits. We usually think their popularity is a consequence of a large number of people making their own independent decisions about what appeals to them. But research shows that popularity is a consequence of social influence (Salganik, Dodds, & Watts, 2006). If one object happens to be slightly more popular than others—such as a particular song that gets downloaded a lot from iTunes—it tends to become more popular as more people are drawn to it. As one sociologist put it, "People tend to like what other people like" (Watts, 2007, p. 22).

In a more direct sense, we often take people's feelings and concerns into account before we act. Perhaps you've decided to date someone, only to reconsider when you asked yourself, "What would my mother think of this person?" Those who influence us may be in our immediate presence or hover in our memories. They may be real or imagined, loved or despised. And their effects on us may be deliberate or accidental.

Imagine for a moment what your life would be like if you had never had contact with other people (assuming you could have survived this long!). You wouldn't know what love is, or hate or jealousy or compassion or gratitude. You wouldn't know if you were wealthy or poor, bright or dumb, witty or boring. You'd lack some basic information, too. You wouldn't know what day it was, how much a pound weighs, where Belgium is, or how to read. Furthermore, you'd have no language, and because we use language to think, imagine, predict, plan, wonder, and reminisce, you'd lack these abilities as well. In short, you'd lack the key experiences that make you a functioning human being.

Contact with people is essential to a person's social development. But there is much more to social life than simply bumping into others from time to time. We act and react to things and people in our environment as a result of the meaning we attach to them. At the sight of a dog barreling toward it, a squirrel instinctively runs away. A human, however, does not have such an automatic reaction. We've learned from past experiences that some animals are approachable and others aren't. So we can think, "Do I know this dog? Is it friendly or mean? Does it want to lick my face or tear me limb from limb?" and respond accordingly. In short, we usually interpret events in our environment before we react.

The presence of other people may motivate you to improve your performance—for example, when the high quality of your tennis opponent makes you play the best match of your life. But their presence may at other times inhibit you—as when you forget your lines in the school play because your ex-boyfriend's in the audience glowering at you. Other people's presence is also essential for the expression of certain feelings. Have you ever noticed that it's impossible to tickle yourself? Being tickled is the product of a *social* interaction. Indeed, according to one study of laughter, people are about 30 times more likely to laugh when they're around other people than when they're alone (Provine, 2000). And our personal contentment can be linked to others as well. One recent study found that just knowing someone who is happy—whether she or he is a relative, friend, or acquaintance—significantly increases your own chances of happiness (Fowler & Christakis, 2008).

The influence of others goes beyond performances and emotions. Even our physical well-being is affected by those around us. According to researchers in Japan, the risk of heart attack is three times higher among women who live with their husbands and their husbands' parents than among women who just live with their husbands (cited in Rabin, 2008).

Consider also the way people eat. Most of us assume that we eat when we're hungry and stop when we're full. But our eating tendencies reflect the social cues that surround us. For instance, when we eat with other people, we adjust our pace to their pace. We also tend to eat longer—and therefore more—when in groups than when we're by ourselves. One researcher found that people, on average, eat 35% more food when they're with one other person than when they're alone. That figure goes up to 75% more when eating with three other people (DeCastro, 1994, 2000). This may explain why a person's chances of becoming obese increase significantly when he or she has a close friend who is obese (Christakis & Fowler, 2007). As one researcher put it, "Weight can be inherited, but it can also be contagious" (Wansink, 2006, p. 99).

And, of course, other people can sometimes purposely influence our actions. I'm sure you've been in situations in which people have tried to persuade you to do things against your will or better judgment. Perhaps someone convinced you to steal a candy bar, skip your sociology class, or disregard the speed limit. On occasion, such social influence can be quite harmful.

STANLEY MILGRAM

Ordinary People and Cruel Acts

If a being from another planet were to learn the history of human civilization, it would probably conclude that we are tremendously cruel, vicious, and evil creatures. From ethnic genocides to backwater lynchings to war crimes to schoolyard bullying, humans have always shown a powerful tendency to viciously turn on their fellow humans.

The curious thing is that people involved in such acts often show a profound capacity to deny responsibility for their behavior by pointing to the influence of others: "My friend made me do it" or "I was only following orders." That leaves us with a very disturbing question: Can an ordinary, decent person be pressured by another to commit an act of extreme cruelty? Or, conversely, do cruel actions require inherently cruel people?

In a classic piece of social research, social psychologist Stanley Milgram (1974) set out to answer these questions. He wanted to know how far people would go in obeying the commands of an authority. He set up an experimental situation in which a subject, on orders from an authoritative figure, flips a switch, apparently sending a 450-volt shock to an innocent victim.

The subjects responded to an advertisement seeking participants in a study on memory and learning. On a specified day, each subject arrived at the laboratory and was introduced to a stern-looking experimenter (Milgram) wearing a white lab coat. The subject was also introduced to another person who, unknown to the subject, was actually an accomplice of the experimenter.

Each subject was told he or she would play the role of "teacher" in an experiment examining the effects of punishment on learning; the other person would play the role of the "learner." The teacher was taken to a separate room that held an ominous-looking machine the researcher called a "shock generator." The learner was seated in another room out of the sight of the teacher and was supposedly strapped to an electrode from the shock generator.

The teacher read a series of word pairs (e.g., blue–sky, nice–day, wild–duck) to the learner. After reading the entire list, the teacher read the first word of a pair (e.g., blue) and four alternatives for the second word (e.g., sky, ink, box, lamp). The learner had to select the correct alternative. Following directions from the experimenter, who was present in the room, the teacher flipped a switch and shocked the learner whenever he or she gave an incorrect answer. The shocks began at the lowest level, 15 volts, and increased with each subsequent incorrect answer all the way up to the 450-volt maximum.

As instructed, all the subjects shocked the learner for each incorrect response. (Remember, the learner was an accomplice of the experimenter and was not actually being shocked.) As the experiment proceeded and the shocks became stronger, the teacher could hear cries from the learner. Most of the teachers, believing they were inflicting serious injury, became visibly upset and wanted to stop. The experimenter, however, ordered them to continue—and many did. Despite the tortured reactions of the victim, 65% of the subjects complied with the experimenter's demands and proceeded to the maximum, 450 volts.

Milgram repeated the study with a variety of subjects and even conducted it in different countries, including Germany and Australia. In each case, about two thirds of the subjects were willing, under orders from the experimenter, to shock to the limit. Milgram didn't just show that people defer to authority from time to time. He showed just how powerful that tendency is (Blass, 2004). As we saw with the Rwandan genocide, given the "right" circumstance, ordinarily nice people can be compelled to do terrible things they wouldn't have done otherwise.

Milgram's research raises questions not only about why people would obey an unreasonable authority, but also about what the rest of us think of those who do. A study of destructive obedience in the workplace—investigating actions such as dumping toxic waste in a river and manufacturing a defective automobile—found that the public is more likely to forgive those who are responsible when they are believed to be conforming to company policy or obeying the orders of a supervisor than when they are thought to be acting on their own (V. L. Hamilton & Sanders, 1995).

Milgram's study has generated a tremendous amount of controversy. For over four decades, this pivotal piece of research has been replicated, discussed, and debated by social scientists (Burger, 2009). It has made its way into popular culture, turning up in novels, plays, films, and songs (Blass, 2004). Since the original study, other researchers have found that in small groups, people sometimes collectively rebel against what they perceive to be unjust authority (Gamson, Fireman, & Rytina, 1982). Nevertheless, Milgram's findings are discomforting. It would be much easier to conclude that the acts of inhumanity we read about in our daily newspapers (such as soldiers raping civilians or killing unarmed noncombatants) are the products of defective or inherently evil individuals—a few "bad apples." All society would have to do then is identify, capture, and separate these psychopaths from the rest of us. But if Milgram is right—if most of us could become evil given the "right" combination of situational circumstances—then the only thing that distinguishes us from evildoers is our good fortune and our social environment.

Societal Influence: The Effect of Social Structure on Our Everyday Lives

Social life is more than individual people affecting one another's lives. Society is not just a sum of its human parts; it's also the way those parts are put together, related to each other, and organized (Coulson & Riddell, 1980). Statuses, roles, groups, organizations, and institutions are the building blocks of society. Culture is the mortar that holds these blocks together. Although society is dynamic and constantly evolving, it has an underlying macrolevel structure that persists.

Statuses and Roles

One key element of any society is its collection of *statuses*—the positions that individuals within the society occupy. When most of us hear the word *status*, we tend to associate it with rank or prestige. But here we're talking about a status as any socially defined position a person can occupy: cook, daughter, anthropologist, husband, computer nerd, electrician, Facebook friend, shoplifter, and so on. Some statuses may, in fact, be quite prestigious, such as president. But others carry very little prestige, such as gas station attendant. Some statuses require a tremendous amount of training, such as physician; others, such as ice cream lover, require little effort or none at all.

We all occupy many statuses at the same time. I am a college professor, but I am also a son, uncle, father, brother, friend, sushi lover, dog owner, occasional poker player, aging athlete, homeowner, and author. My behavior at any given moment is dictated to a large degree by the status that's most important at that particular time. When I am training for a half marathon, my status as professor is not particularly relevant. But if I decide to run in a race instead of giving the final exam in my sociology course, I may be in big trouble!

Sociologists often distinguish between ascribed and achieved statuses. An *ascribed status* is a social position we acquire at birth or enter involuntarily later in life. Our race, sex, ethnicity, and identity as someone's child or grandchild are all ascribed statuses. As we get older, we enter the ascribed status of teenager and, eventually, old person. These aren't positions we choose to occupy. An *achieved status*, in contrast, is a social position we take on voluntarily or acquire through our own efforts or accomplishments, such as being a student or a spouse or an engineer.

Of course, the distinction between ascribed and achieved status is not always so clear. Some people become college students not because of their own efforts but because of their family's influence. Chances are the religion with which you identify is the one you inherit from your parents. However, many people decide to change their religious membership later in life. Moreover, as we'll see later in this book, certain ascribed statuses (sex, race, ethnicity, and age) influence our access to lucrative achieved statuses.

Whether ascribed or achieved, statuses are important sociologically because they all come with a set of rights, obligations, behaviors, and duties that people occupying a certain position are expected or encouraged to perform. These expectations are referred to as ***roles***. For instance, the role expectations associated with the status "professor" include teaching students, answering their questions, grading them impartially, and dressing appropriately. Any out-of-role behavior may be met with shock or suspicion. If I consistently showed up for class in a thong and tank top, that would certainly violate my "scholarly" image and call into question my ability to teach (not to mention my sanity).

Each person, as a result of her or his own skills, interests, and interactional experiences, defines roles differently. Students enter a class with the general expectation that their professor is knowledgeable about the subject and is going to teach them something. Each professor, however, may have a different method of meeting that expectation. Some professors are very animated; others remain stationary behind a podium. Some do not allow questions until after the lecture; others constantly encourage probing questions from students. Some are meticulous and organized, others spontaneous and absentminded.

People engage in typical patterns of interaction based on the relationship between their roles and the roles of others. Employers are expected to interact with employees in a certain way, as are doctors with patients and salespeople with customers. In each case, actions are constrained by the role responsibilities and obligations associated with those particular statuses. We know, for instance, that lovers and spouses are supposed to interact with each other differently from the way acquaintances or friends are supposed to interact. In a parent-child relationship, both members are linked by certain rights, privileges, and obligations. Parents are responsible for providing their children with the basic necessities of life—food, clothing, shelter, and so forth. These expectations are so powerful that not meeting them may constitute the crime of negligence or abuse. Children, in turn, are expected to abide by their parents' wishes. Thus, interactions within a relationship are functions not only of the individual personalities of the people involved but also of the role requirements associated with the statuses they occupy.

We feel the power of role expectations most clearly when we have difficulty meeting them or when we occupy two conflicting statuses simultaneously. Sociologists use the term ***role strain*** to refer to situations in which people lack the necessary resources to fulfill the demands of a particular role, such as when parents can't afford to provide their children with adequate food, clothing, or shelter. ***Role conflict*** describes situations in which people encounter tension in trying to cope with the demands of incompatible roles. People may feel frustrated in their efforts to do what they feel they're supposed to do when the role expectations of one status clash with the role expectations of another. For instance, a mother may have an important out-of-town conference to attend (status of sociologist) on the same day her 10-year-old son is appearing as a talking pig in the school play (status of parent). Or a teenager who works hard at his job at the local ice cream shop (status of employee) may be frustrated when his buddies arrive and expect him to sit and chat or to give them free ice cream (status of friend).

Role conflict can sometimes raise serious ethical or legal concerns. For instance, in states that use lethal injection as a means of execution, it is necessary to have a licensed anesthesiologist present to ensure that the prisoner is unconscious when paralyzing and heart-stopping drugs are administered. Ordinarily, the role expectations of doctors emphasize ensuring the health and well-being of the people they treat. But when doctors are part of an execution team, they are expected to use their medical skills and judgment to make killing more humane and less painful. Several medical organizations, including the American Medical Association, have condemned physicians' involvement in executions as unethical and unprofessional (P. Elias, 2006).

Groups

Societies are not simply composed of people occupying statuses and living in accordance with roles. Sometimes individuals form well-defined units called groups. A *group* is a set of people who interact more or less regularly with one another and who are conscious of their identity as a group. Your family, your colleagues at work, and any clubs or sports teams to which you belong are all social groups.

Groups are not just collections of people who randomly come together for some purpose. Their structure defines the relationships among members. When groups are large, enduring, and complex, each individual within the group is likely to occupy some named position or status—mother, president, supervisor, linebacker, and so forth.

Group membership can also be a powerful force behind one's future actions and thoughts. Sociologists distinguish between *in-groups*—the groups to which we belong and toward which we feel a sense of loyalty—and *out-groups*—the groups to which we don't belong and toward which we feel a certain amount of antagonism. For instance, a girl who is not a member of the popular clique at school, but wants to be, is likely to structure many of her daily activities around gaining entry into that group.

In addition, like statuses and roles, groups come with a set of general expectations. A person's actions within a group are judged according to a conventional set of ideas about how things ought to be. For example, a coworker who always arrives late for meetings or never takes his or her turn working an undesirable shift is violating the group's expectations and will be pressured to conform.

The smallest group, of course, is one that consists of two people, or a *dyad*. According to the renowned German sociologist Georg Simmel (1902/1950), dyads (marriages, close friendships, etc.) are among the most meaningful and intense connections we have. The problem, though, is that dyads are by nature unstable. If one person decides to leave, the group completely collapses. Hence, it's not surprising that for society's most important dyads (i.e., marriages), a variety of legal, religious, and cultural restrictions are in place that make it difficult for people to dissolve them.

The addition of one person to a dyad—forming what Simmel called a *triad*—fundamentally changes the nature of the group. Although triads might appear more stable than dyads because the withdrawal of one person needn't destroy the group, they develop other problems. If you're one of three children in your family, you already know that triads always contain the potential for *coalitions*—where two individuals pair up and perhaps conspire against the third.

Groups can also be classified by their influence on our everyday lives. A *primary group* consists of a small number of members who have direct contact with each other over a relatively long period of time. Emotional attachment is high in such groups, and members have intimate knowledge of each other's lives. Families and networks of close friends are primary groups. A *secondary group*, in contrast, is much more formal and impersonal. The group is established for a specific task, such as the production or sale of consumer goods, and members are less emotionally committed to one another. Their roles tend to be highly structured. Primary groups may form within secondary groups, as when close friendships form among coworkers, but in general, secondary groups require less emotional investment than primary groups.

Like societies, groups have a reality that is more than just the sum of their members; a change in a group's membership doesn't necessarily alter its basic structure. Secondary groups can endure changing membership relatively easily if some, or even all, individuals leave and new ones enter—as, for example, when the senior class in a high school graduates and is replaced the following year by a new group of students. However, change in primary groups—perhaps through divorce or death—produces dramatic effects on the structure and identity of the group, even though the group itself still exists.

Although people of the same race, gender, ethnicity, or religion are not social groups in the strictest sense of the term, they function like groups in that members share certain characteristics and interests. They become an important source of a person's identity. For instance, members of a particular racial or ethnic group may organize into a well-defined unit to fight for a political cause. The feelings of "we-ness" or "they-ness" generated by such group membership can be constructive or dangerous, encouraging pride and unity in some cases and anger, bitterness, and hatred toward outsiders in others.

Organizations

At an even higher level of complexity are social units called *organizations*, networks of statuses and groups created for a specific purpose. The International Brotherhood of Teamsters, Oxford University, Microsoft, the Federal Emergency Management Agency, the National Organization for Women, and the Methodist Church are all examples of organizations. Organizations contain groups as well as individuals occupying clearly defined statuses and taking on clearly defined roles.

Some of the groups within organizations are transitory; some are more permanent. For instance, a university consists of individual classes that form at the beginning of a semester and disband at its end, as well as more permanent groups such as the faculty, administration, secretarial staff, maintenance staff, and alumni.

Large, formal organizations are often characterized by a *hierarchical division of labor*. Each person in an organization occupies a position that has a specific set of duties and responsibilities, and those positions can be "ranked" according to their relative power and importance. At Honda, for instance, assembly line workers typically don't make hiring decisions or set budgetary policies, and the vice president in charge of marketing doesn't spray paint the underbodies of newly assembled Accords. In general, people occupy certain positions in an organization because they have the skills to do the job required of them. When a person can no longer meet the requirements of the job, she or he can be replaced without seriously affecting the functioning of the organization.

Organizations are a profoundly common and visible feature of everyday social life, as you'll see in Chapter 9. Most of us cannot acquire food, get an education, pray, undergo lifesaving surgery, or earn a salary without coming into contact with or becoming a member of some organization. To be a full-fledged member of modern society is to be deeply involved in some form of organizational life.

Social Institutions

When stable sets of statuses, roles, groups, and organizations form, they provide the foundation for addressing fundamental societal needs. These enduring patterns of social life are called *social institutions*. Sociologists usually think of institutions as the building blocks that organize society. They are the patterned ways of solving the problems and meeting the requirements of a particular society. Although there may be conflict over what society "needs" and how best to fulfill those needs, all societies must have some systematic way of organizing the various aspects of everyday life.

Key social institutions in modern society include the family, education, economics, politics and law, and religion. Some sociologists add health care, the military, and the mass media to the list.

Family. All societies must have a way of replacing their members, and reproduction is essential to the survival of human society as a whole. Within the institution of family, sexual relations among adults are regulated; people are cared for; children are born, protected, and socialized; and newcomers are provided an identity—a "lineage"—that gives them a sense of belonging. Just how these activities are carried out varies from society to society. Indeed, different societies have different ideas about which relationships qualify for designation as family. But the institution of family, whatever its form, remains the hub of social life in virtually all societies (J. H. Turner, 1972).

Education. Young people need to be taught what it means to be a member of the society in which they live and how to survive in it. In small, simple societies, the family is the primary institution responsible for socializing new members into the culture. However, as societies become more complex, it becomes exceedingly difficult for a family to teach its members all they need to know to function and survive. Hence, most modern, complex societies have an elaborate system of schools—preschool, primary, secondary, post-secondary, professional—that not only create and disseminate knowledge and information but also train individuals for future careers and teach them their "place" in society.

Economy. From the beginning, human societies have faced the problems of securing enough food and protecting people from the environment (J. H. Turner, 1972). Today, modern societies have systematic ways of gathering resources, converting them into goods and commodities, and distributing them to members. In addition, societies provide ways of coordinating and facilitating the operation of this massive process. For instance, banks, accounting firms, insurance companies, stock brokerages, transportation agencies, and computer networks don't produce goods themselves but provide services that make the gathering, producing, and distributing of goods possible. To facilitate the distribution of both goods and services, economic institutions adopt a system of common currency and an identifiable mode of exchange. In some societies, the economy is driven by the value of efficient production and the need to maximize profits; in others, the collective well-being of the population is the primary focus.

Politics and Law. All societies face the problem of how to preserve order, avoid chaos, and make important social decisions. The legal system provides explicit laws or rules of conduct and mechanisms for enforcing those laws, settling disputes, and changing outdated laws or creating new ones (J. H. Turner, 1972). These activities take place within a larger system of governance that allocates and acknowledges power, authority, and leadership. In a democracy, the governance process includes the citizens, who have a say in who leads them; in a monarchy, kings or queens can claim that their birthright entitles them to positions of leadership. In some societies, the transfer of power is efficient and mannerly; in others, it is violent.

Religion. In the process of meeting the familial, educational, economic, and political needs of society, some individuals thrive, whereas others suffer. Hence, all societies also face the problem of providing their less successful members with a sense of purpose and meaning in their lives. Religion gives individuals a belief system for understanding their existence as well as a network of personal support in times of need. Although many members of a given society may actively reject religion, it remains one of the most enduring and powerful social institutions. Although religion provides enormous comfort to some people, it can also be a source of hatred and irreparable divisions.

Health Care. One of the profoundly universal facts of human life is that people get sick and die. In some societies, healing the sick and managing the transition to death involves spiritual or supernatural intervention; other societies rely on science and modern technology. Most modern societies have established a complex system of health care to disseminate medical treatments. Doctors, nurses, hospitals, pharmacies, drug and medical equipment manufacturers, and patients all play an active role in the health care system.

Military. To deal with the possibility of attack from outside and the protection of national interests, many societies maintain an active military defense. However, militaries are used not only to defend societies but also, at times, to attack other countries in order to acquire land, resources, or power. In other cases, the military is used for political change, as when U.S. armed forces were mobilized to overthrow the government of Saddam Hussein in Iraq in 2003.

Mass Media. In very small, relatively close-knit societies, information can be shared through word of mouth. However, as societies become more complex, the dissemination of information requires a massive coordinated system. The modern mass media— radio, newspapers, television, and the Internet—provide coverage of important societal events so individuals can make informed decisions about their own lives. But the media do more than report events of local, national, and international significance. They also actively mold public opinion and project and reinforce a society's values.

From these very brief descriptions, you can see that the social institutions within a society are highly interrelated. Current debates over reforming the U.S. health care system make people aware of its links to the economy and politics. And religion and politics can play a major role in what gets taught in schools. For instance, in 2005, the Kansas State Board of Education, in response to pressure from anti-evolution religious organizations, held hearings to determine if it would require public school science classes to give equal time to religiously based ideas about the origins of life. The members voted to include criticisms of evolution in the curriculum, although that decision was reversed two years later, after the election of several new board members. Nevertheless, in 2007, the only candidate for president of the National Association of State Boards of Education—an organization that plays a major role in shaping national educational policy—was an anti-evolution member of the Kansas school board (Dean, 2007).

To individual members of society, social institutions appear natural, permanent, and inevitable. Most of us couldn't imagine life without a family. Nor could most of us fathom what society would be like without a stable system of government, a common currency, schools to educate our children, or an effective health care system. It is very easy, then, to think that institutions exist independently of people.

But one of the important themes that will be revisited throughout this book is that we each have a role to play in maintaining or changing social institutions, as when citizens alter the political shape of a country by voting out of office an administration with which they've grown displeased. Although the effects of changes can be felt at the organizational and institutional levels, they are ultimately initiated, implemented, or rejected, and, most important, experienced by individual people. The interrelationships between individuals and the various components of social structure can be seen in Exhibit 2.1.

Exhibit 2.1   Social Structure and the Individual

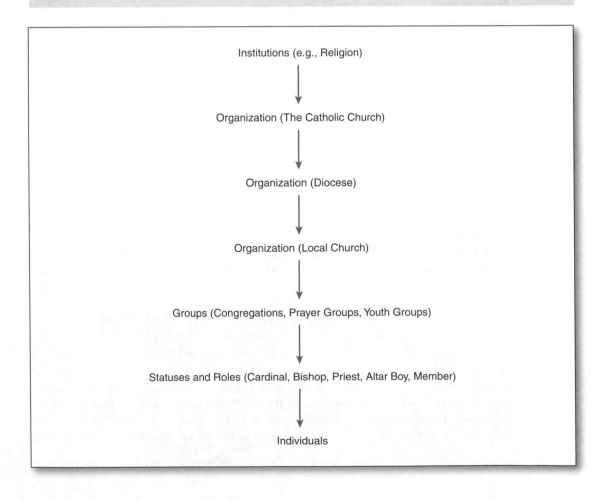

Institutions (e.g., Religion)

Organization (The Catholic Church)

Organization (Diocese)

Organization (Local Church)

Groups (Congregations, Prayer Groups, Youth Groups)

Statuses and Roles (Cardinal, Bishop, Priest, Altar Boy, Member)

Individuals

MARION NESTLE

The Economics and Politics of Food

Institutional influence is sometimes not so obvious. For instance, we usually think of nutrition as an inherent property of the foods we eat. Either something is good for us or it's not good for us, right? And we trust that the nutritional value of certain foods emerges from scientific discovery. We rarely consider the economic and political role that food companies play in shaping our tastes and our dietary standards (Pollan, 2007).

Marion Nestle (2002), a professor of nutrition and food studies, wanted to examine the institutional underpinnings of our ideas about health and nutrition. She faced an interesting data gathering dilemma, however. No one involved in the food industry was willing to talk to her "on the record." So she compiled information from government reports, newspapers, magazines, speeches, advocacy materials, conference exhibits, and supermarkets. She also used information that she'd previously received from lobbying groups and trade associations representing diverse interests such as the salt, sugar, vitamin, wheat, soybean, flaxseed, and blueberry industries.

Despite alarming levels of food hunger among the world's population (see Chapter 10), the United States has so much food that we could feed our citizens twice over. Many Americans regularly buy or prepare more food than they actually need (hence, the popularity of "doggie bags" and leftovers). The food industry is therefore highly competitive. But like all major industries, companies are beholden to their stockholders rather than to the consuming public. Marketing foods that are healthy and nutritious is a company's goal only if it can increase sales.

Food marketers have long identified children as their most attractive targets. According to Nestle, the attention paid to children has escalated in recent years because of their increasing responsibility for purchasing decisions. Children between 6 and 19 are estimated to influence upward of $500 billion in food purchases each year (cited in Nestle, 2002). By age seven, most children can shop independently, ask for information about what they want, and show off their purchases to other children.

Soft drink companies have become especially adept at targeting young people with diverse marketing strategies. Soft drinks have replaced milk as the primary beverage in the diets of American children as well as adults. Between 1985 and 1997, U.S. school districts decreased the amount of milk they bought by 30% and increased their purchases of carbonated sodas by 1,100% (cited in Nestle, 2002). Vending machines, which tend to be stocked with high-calorie soft drinks as well as other "junk" foods, exist in 17% of elementary schools, 82% of middle schools, and 97% of high schools (cited in Kalb, 2010a). The typical American teenage boy gets about 9% of his daily caloric intake from soft drinks, and about 20% of one- and two-year-olds regularly drink soda (Schlosser, 2001).

One of the most controversial marketing strategies in the soft drink industry is the "pouring rights" agreement, in which a company buys the exclusive right to sell its products in all schools in a particular district. For instance, several years ago one 53-school district in Colorado signed a 10-year, $8 million pouring rights agreement with Coca-Cola. In financially strapped districts, a pouring rights contract often supplies a significant part of the district's annual funding. It may be the only thing that allows a school system to buy much-needed resources like computers and textbooks.

Besides the lump sum agreed to in the contract, companies frequently offer school districts cash bonuses if they exceed certain sales targets. Hence, it is in the district's financial interest to encourage students to consume more soft drinks. In light of such incentives, ethical implications and health concerns become secondary. Indeed, many school districts justify these agreements by saying that soft drinks pervade the culture and students will drink them anyway, so why not get some benefit?

In addition to the long-term health effects of heavy soft drink consumption, however, Nestle points out that students learn a somewhat cynical lesson: that school officials are sometimes willing to compromise nutritional principles (and the students' physical well-being) for financial gain. Pouring rights contracts can also have a serious impact on long-term school funding. While they may solve short-term financial needs, they may also hamper efforts to secure adequate federal, state, and local funding for public education. Taxpayers may come to the conclusion that raising taxes to support public schools is unnecessary if the bulk of a district's operating budget comes from these commercial contracts.

In 2006, in response to criticism and the threat of lawsuits, beverage makers agreed to remove sweetened drinks from school cafeterias and vending machines (Burros & Warner, 2006). But the agreement is a voluntary one, so it remains to be seen what impact it will have on the overall health of young people. Some states have taken additional steps either to ban sugary soft drinks and junk food from school vending machines (Center for Science in the Public Interest, 2011; Morson, 2008) or to impose higher sales taxes on nondiet soft drinks (Kristof, 2008). No matter what the outcome of these actions, pouring rights agreements will continue to play a significant role in school district budgets. In these contracts, we can see how a child's food choices in school are linked deeply and profoundly to broader educational, political, and economic needs—often with little, if any, attention paid to nutritional considerations and individual health.

Culture

The most pervasive element of society is **culture**, which consists of the language, values, beliefs, rules, behaviors, and physical artifacts of a society. Think of it as a society's "personality." Culture gives us codes of conduct—proper, acceptable ways of doing things. We usually don't think twice about it, yet it colors everything we experience.

Human societies would be chaotic and unlivable if they didn't have cultures that allow people to live together under the same set of general rules. But culture can also sometimes lead to tragedy. In 2005, a high-speed Japanese commuter train crashed, killing close to 100 passengers. The driver was going too fast when the train jumped off the tracks on a curve and crashed into an apartment building. But on closer inspection, we can see that the root cause of the accident rested in the harmful effects of culture. The train was 90 seconds behind schedule, and in Japanese culture, where efficiency and punctuality take on vital importance, trains are considered late when they are a mere 60 seconds behind schedule. A 90-second delay was unacceptable, and the driver knew it. Everyday life in Japan is so tightly scheduled that it leaves little room for casual or slow-paced travel (Onishi, 2005)—or even, in some cases, for safety.

Culture is particularly apparent when someone questions or violates it. Those who do not believe what the majority believes, see what the majority sees, or obey the same rules the majority obeys are likely to experience punishment, psychiatric attention, or social ostracism. I will discuss the power of culture in more detail in Chapter 4, but here we should look at two key aspects of culture that are thoroughly implicated in the workings of social structure and social influence: values and norms.

Values

Perhaps no word in the English language carries more baggage than *values*. People throw around terms such as *moral values*, *traditional values*, *family values*, and *American values* with little thought as to what they actually mean. Sociologically speaking, a **value** is a standard of judgment by which people decide on desirable goals and outcomes (Hewitt & Hewitt, 1986). Values represent the general criteria on which our lives and the lives of others can be judged. They justify the social rules that determine how we ought to behave. For instance, laws against theft clearly reflect the value we place on personal property.

Different societies emphasize different values. Success, independence, and individual achievement are seen as important values in U.S. society. In other societies, such as Vietnam, people are more likely to value group obligation and loyalty to family.

Values within a society sometimes come into conflict. The value of privacy ("stay out of other people's business") and the value of generosity ("help others in need") may clash when we are trying to decide whether to help a stranger who seems to require assistance. Similarly, although the value of cooperation is held in high esteem in contemporary U.S. society, when someone is taking a final exam in a sociology class, cooperation is likely to be defined as cheating. When the key values that characterize a particular social institution come into conflict, the result may be widespread legal and moral uncertainty among individuals.

MICRO-MACRO CONNECTION

Family Privacy Versus Children's Welfare

One such conflict involves the cultural value of family privacy. Contemporary U.S. life is built on the assumption that what a family does in the privacy of its home is, or at least should be, its own business. Family life, many people believe, is best left to family members, not to neighbors, the government, the courts, or other public agencies. Consequently, American families are endowed with significant autonomy—the right to make decisions about their future or about treatment of their members (see Chapter 7).

Privacy has not always characterized American families. Before the 19th century, people felt free to enter others' homes and tell them what to wear and how to treat their children. The development of the value of family privacy and autonomy emerged with the separation of home and work and the growth of cities during the late 19th century (Parsons, 1971). Innovations in the amenities available within the home—indoor plumbing, refrigerators, telephones, radios, televisions, central air conditioning, and computers, for example—have all increased the privacy and isolation of American households. Our need to leave home for entertainment, goods, or services has been considerably reduced. Air conditioners, for instance, allow us to spend hot, stuffy summer evenings inside our own homes instead of on the front porch or at the local ice cream parlor. With the Internet, fax machines, text messaging, Facebook, and home shopping cable networks, family members can survive without ever leaving the privacy of their home. The institution of family has become increasingly self-contained and private.

But the ability to maintain family privacy has always varied along social class lines. In poor households, dwellings are smaller and more crowded than more affluent homes, making privacy more difficult to obtain. Thin walls separating cramped apartments hide few secrets. Mandatory inspections by welfare caseworkers and housing authorities further diminish privacy. And poor families must often use public facilities (health clinics, Laundromats, public transportation, etc.) to carry out day-to-day tasks that wealthier families can carry out privately.

Moreover, the value we place on the well-being of children can come into direct conflict at times with the value of family privacy. At what point should a state agency intervene and violate the privacy of the family to protect the welfare of a child? Does it better serve society's interests to protect family privacy or to protect children from harm?

Parents have never had complete freedom to do as they wish with their children. We're horrified at the thought of a parent beating his or her child to the point of injury or death. But we're equally horrified, it seems, at the thought of the state intruding on parents' right to raise their children as they see fit. In the United States, parents have the legal right to direct the upbringing of their children, to determine the care they receive, and to use physical means to control their children's behavior. From a sociological perspective, injuring children can sometimes be the extreme outcome of the widely practiced and accepted belief that parents have the right to use physical punishment to discipline their own kids.

Concern with parents' privacy rights is often framed as a freedom of religion issue. Forty-eight states allow parents to refuse certain medical procedures for their children on religious grounds, such as immunizations, screenings for lead poisoning, and physical examinations.

Six states even have statutes that excuse students with religious objections from simply *studying* about diseases in school (CHILD, 2011).

But it's unclear what ought to be done when parents' religious beliefs result in the injury or death of a child. Over the past 25 years, more than 300 children have died after their parents decided to withhold medical care because of their religious beliefs (cited in D. Johnson, 2009). Thirty-nine states allow religion as a defense in cases of child abuse or neglect. Eighteen states permit religious defenses for felony crimes against children. Oregon, West Virginia, and Arkansas allow religious defenses in cases of murder (CHILD, 2011).

Nevertheless, the government does sometimes violate the privacy of a family when that family's religious or cultural beliefs lead to the death or injury of a member. For instance, in 2010, a Philadelphia couple who prayed over their sick two-year-old son instead of taking him to a doctor was convicted of involuntary manslaughter when the boy died of bacterial pneumonia. They belonged to the First Century Gospel Church, a congregation that teaches faith healing. In 2008, the parents of a two-year-old girl who died of pneumonia were charged with manslaughter. In accordance with the teachings of their church, the Followers of Christ Church, they did not seek medical care for their daughter and instead anointed her with oil, laid on hands, and prayed. The girl's father was sentenced to 60 days in prison. Three months later, the girl's teenage uncle died of complications resulting from a blocked urinary tract. His parents were sentenced to 16 months in prison. It wasn't the first time members of this church had come to the attention of legal authorities. A 1998 investigation revealed that of the 78 children buried in its graveyard, 21 could have survived if they had received medical attention (Raftery, 2011).

Concern over increases in juvenile violence has led some cities and states to enact laws that punish parents for not properly supervising their children. Depending on the state, parental liability laws can hold parents responsible for their children's vandalism, theft, truancy, curfew violations, or illegal downloads (Sen, 2007). In 2005, a jury in Ohio determined that the parents of a 17-year-old boy who assaulted a young girl didn't do enough to stop him and were therefore responsible for paying the victim 70% of the damages she was awarded ($7 million; Coolidge, 2005). In 2007, a Virginia couple was sentenced to 27 months in jail for hosting an underage drinking party for their child, even though no one was hurt at the party and no one drove (Deane, 2007). Such cases illustrate the profound effects of cultural and political values on the everyday lives of individuals. Situations such as these pit the privacy and autonomy of families against society's institutional responsibility to protect children and create new citizens.

Norms

Norms are culturally defined rules of conduct. They specify what people should do and how they should pursue values. They tell us what is proper or necessary behavior within particular roles, groups, organizations, and institutions. Thousands of norms guide the minor and the grand details of our lives, from the bedroom to the classroom to the boardroom. You can see, then, that norms serve as the fundamental building blocks of social order.

Norms make our interactions with others reasonably predictable. Americans expect that when they extend a hand to another person, that person will grasp it and a brief handshake will follow. They would be shocked if they held out their hand and the other person spit on it or grabbed it and wouldn't let go. In contrast, people in some societies commonly embrace or kiss each other's cheek as a form of greeting, even when involved in a formal business relationship. A hearty handshake in those societies may be interpreted as an insult. In Thailand, people greet each other by placing the palms of their hands together in front of their bodies and slightly bowing their heads. This greeting is governed by strict norms. Slight differences in the placement of one's hands reflect the social position of the other person—the higher the hands, the higher the position of the person being greeted. Norms like these make it easier to "live with others" in a relatively harmonious way (see Chapter 4).

Social Structure in a Global Context

A discussion of social structure would not be complete without acknowledging the fact that statuses, roles, groups, organizations, social institutions, and culture are sometimes influenced by broad societal and historical forces at work in the world. One such force with deep implications for contemporary society is ***globalization,*** the process through which people's lives all around the world become increasingly interconnected—economically, politically, environmentally, and culturally (see Chapter 9 for more detail).

For instance, international financial institutions and foreign governments often provide money to support the building of hydroelectric dams in poor countries. According to the World Commission on Dams, 1,600 such dams in 40 countries were under construction in 2000 (Bald, 2000). These projects are meant to strengthen societies by providing additional energy sources in areas where power is dangerously deficient. However, they frequently transform individual lives, social institutions, and indigenous cultures in a negative way. A dam built along the Moon River in Thailand destroyed forests that for centuries were villagers' free source of food, firewood, and medicinal herbs. With the flooding created behind the dam, local farmers not only lost their farmland but also the value of their knowledge of farming methods developed over centuries to adapt to the ebb and flow of the river. A multidam project along the Narmada River in India displaced over 200,000 people and led to violent protests there. The Manantali Dam in Mali destroyed the livelihood of downstream farmers and has resulted in the spread of waterborne diseases (Fountain, 2005). None of these dams would have been built without the funding and political clout of global financial organizations and foreign corporations.

Cultures have rarely been completely isolated from outside influence, because throughout human history people have been moving from one place to another, spreading goods and ideas. What is different today, though, is the speed and scope of these interactions. Several decades ago, overnight mail service and direct long-distance telephone calls increased the velocity of cross-national communication. Advances in transportation technology have made international trade more cost effective and international travel more accessible to ordinary citizens. And today, the Internet has given people around the world instantaneous access to the cultural artifacts and ideals of other societies, no matter where they're located. Through search engines like Google, Yahoo, and Bing, children in Beirut, Baltimore, or Beijing can easily and immediately mine unlimited amounts of the same information on every conceivable topic.

Clearly, societies are more interdependent than ever, and that interdependence matters for individuals around the world. Sometimes the effects are positive. Pharmaceutical breakthroughs in the United States or Europe, for instance, can save lives around the world. Globalization gives us a chance to learn about other societies and learn from them. Other times, however, global influence can have disastrous consequences. Many of today's most pressing societal problems—widespread environmental devastation, large- and small-scale wars, economic crises, viral epidemics, and so on—are a function of globalization to some degree. Closer to home, the establishment of a toy factory in Southeast Asia or a clothing factory in Mexico may mean the loss of hundreds of manufacturing jobs in Kentucky or California.

In short, it is becoming increasingly difficult, if not impossible, to consider ourselves members of a single society unaffected by other societies. All of us are simultaneously members of our own society and citizens of a world community.

(Text continues on page 46)

The Old Ball Game

Douglas Harper

To watch a professional baseball game is to experience the world both as an individual and as a member of a larger social structure.

A baseball game offers a good example of how individuals participate in creating social life and, conversely, how social structure shapes our everyday experience. This essay features photographs from several ballparks. They take the perspective of a sociologist rather than a typical spectator or sports photographer.

When we watch a baseball game as fans, we're likely to focus on the interactions of the people on the field—what sociologists call a *micro* level of analysis. In this photo, several individuals carefully coordinate their actions, hoping to achieve different ends. The umpire, symbol of social control, defines actions as good or bad, successful or unsuccessful. The batter wants to drive the approaching ball into the outfield; the catcher wants the ball in his mitt after it crosses the strike zone. The game of baseball, seen from this perspective, consists of individuals acting on their interpretations of the actions of others. These interpretations require that people agree on the meaning of certain symbols, including words, gestures, and material objects such as uniforms.

This photograph was taken from roughly the same vantage point as the previous microlevel photo but with a different camera lens. The perspectives created by these lenses may be viewed as metaphors for different sociological perspectives. If the microlevel photo suggests an interactional level of analysis, this one suggests a middle-range level of analysis. Typical units of analysis at this level are statuses, roles, and norms.

Here we can see the coordination of several statuses within the realm of baseball, including first baseman, base runner from the opposing team, first-base coach, and two umpires. The roles that these people play in the game—their actions—are aligned with their statuses: The pitcher has the role of throwing the ball to the catcher, the first-base coach of guiding the base runner's actions, and so on. The positions of the players are determined by norms, or rules of behavior. Even an argument between an umpire and a player is socially choreographed: Only certain words, gestures, and forms of touch are allowed.

In what sociologists might call a macrolevel, structural view of baseball, we would look at the way that various social institutions—such as the economy, government, and the media—influence the way the sport is conducted. It's difficult to observe these large-scale influences, but we can observe the setting of the game and some of the elements that give the game meaning in a larger social context.

For instance, baseball, like other professional sports, is sustained and driven by corporate sponsorship. This influence shows up in the advertisements that plaster scoreboards and fences around the outfield but is especially obvious in the names of stadiums these days. Gone are the days when stadiums were simply named after the team that played there (Tiger Stadium, Astrodome), the location (County Stadium, Cleveland Stadium), features of the local physical landscape (Three Rivers Stadium, Candlestick Park), or influential individuals in the community (Comiskey Park, Forbes Field). Today, stadium names are sold to the highest corporate bidder and are more likely to reflect commercial investments than anything evoking the flavor of baseball (Comerica Park, Target Field, AT&T Park, Tropicana Field, U.S. Cellular Field, Safeco Field). To some sociologists, this trend indicates a shift from baseball as a microlevel, personal experience to a sport that seems overly impersonal and profit driven.

Such a conclusion is reinforced by the perception that today's baseball players, in the quest for ever-higher salaries, have lost any sense of team loyalty—a concept that seems quaint today. And it's certainly true that players have always given top priority to their personal financial interests over the organization's. But in general, in the past, a fan could count on a favorite player's remaining with the hometown team for years. Today, players come and go so frequently that a team's roster might be virtually unrecognizable from one year to the next. Cal Ripken, Jr., pictured here, was one of the very few exceptions in that he played with the same team, the Baltimore Orioles, for his entire 21-year career.

A macrolevel analysis of baseball can also be enhanced by a critical look at the history of professional baseball. Baseball was originally played in a narrow band of cities, such as New York, Pittsburgh, Chicago, and St. Louis. But it soon expanded to both the north and the south, to such cities as Minneapolis, Toronto, Houston, and Tampa, and the season lengthened well into autumn. Because of more extreme weather conditions in these areas, it became difficult to play the game outdoors all season long. The solution was to build many of the stadiums with permanent or retracting roofs and to replace the natural grass field with plastic carpet. The new parks, built from the mid 1960s through the 1980s, were dual-purpose facilities that often also accommodated football. However, these stadiums have been a failure. Most of them have been torn down and replaced or are in the process of being replaced by single-use facilities designed to evoke the more intimate ballparks of the past.

The extension of baseball into regions where it cannot easily be played, and the creation of stadiums to fit both baseball and football, can be seen as an example of something 19th-century sociologist Max Weber warned us about: focusing so much on rationality and efficiency that we lose sight of our real goals. It may seem quite practical to build a facility for both baseball and football and to cover a facility to keep out the weather. But the main point of baseball—a pleasurable fan experience—is diminished by these decisions. Similarly, plastic carpet may be more economically rational than grass, but it is ugly and changes the way the game is played.

Baseball began where the seasons invited outside activities from April to October. Because the pace of a baseball game is leisurely, it is a perfect summer event. The extension of major league baseball to more extreme climatological regions (whether it can be played and viewed in the way the game was intended or not) is a clear attempt to transform a leisure activity into an economic enterprise. Major league baseball (as well as other national-level sports) is a huge financial concern. It will likely continue to expand to new regions as long as it can be financially viable, whether or not this expansion makes sense for the game or for fans.

This is Olympic Stadium, home of the now defunct Montreal Expos. The stadium was originally built for the 1976 Summer Olympics. It had artificial turf and a retractable roof and accommodated well over 50,000 people. It was considered by many baseball aficionados to be one of the least appealing ballparks in the major leagues. This game, with only a few thousand spectators on hand, was played in early April. At that time of the year, watching a game in an uncovered stadium in Montreal—or Detroit or Chicago, for that matter—would be an unattractive experience for a fan.

The simple act of watching a baseball game might seem like a highly individual experience, far from the concerns of sociologists, but consider the differences between attending a game in a stadium and viewing the game on television. If we watch the game on television, TV personalities direct us to notice one set of events rather than another. The photographic style used to broadcast the game (especially the close-up) emphasizes the individual players and their accomplishments. We do not get as broad a view of the game experience or even see the way several players participate on a given play. Because the televised event emphasizes the individual player-as-hero, we often overlook the social context—namely the team—that gives his heroic actions meaning. The home run glorifies the batter and is exciting to witness, but the sacrifice fly may allow a run to score that is just as meaningful to the team.

If we attend a game in person, however, we become actively involved in constructing the "fan experience." We watch carefully to keep track of the players and the progress of the game; perhaps we keep inning-by-inning records, using the arcane symbols of scoring. We may even be able to affect the outcome of the game by vocally encouraging the home team and actively distracting the visiting team. Indeed, in some ballparks, the fans are given the honorary title of "10th man" to symbolize their contributions to the team. In short, the actions of all the players, all the other members of the crowd, and all the stadium personnel (hot dog vendors, security guards, announcers, and so on) become part of our experience of the game.

Being part of a collective event also has strong appeal. This photograph shows how thousands upon thousands of people can be drawn together to take part in an experience. Order is maintained through well-understood expectations and norms. Ironically, this was the last game played at Three Rivers Stadium in Pittsburgh, in October 2000. It drew a sold-out crowd of 54,000. Fans gathered to say good-bye to a stadium that was still functional but about to be torn down and replaced with a park resembling the one Three Rivers had itself replaced in 1970.

Although TV viewers get close-ups and biographical notes about players, they can't experience the thrill of interacting personally with the players. For an hour before the game, fans who can talk their way past the ushers who guard the passageway to the hitting area can watch the players practice and can call greetings and good wishes to their heroes. The players seldom look up as they trot back and forth to the dugout, but sometimes a player will toss a ball to a fan or meander to a designated area where the fan and player can intersect—the end of the dugout—to sign autographs. Note, though, that the early birds can occupy these most desirable seats only temporarily, because they are increasingly owned by corporations and given as favors to business partners.

General disillusionment with the sport, along with hard economic times and security concerns, have forced many teams to try to further enhance the fan experience. Baseball teams now regularly stage "fan friendly" events, such as live music, in an attempt to bolster sagging attendance. Here a fan dances with an even younger fan, on whom the typical barrage of beer advertising is wasted.

Luckily, the sport has a lot going for it. To be a baseball fan is to internalize heroic messages about the history of the game. Symbols communicate some of this history.

For Pittsburgh Pirate fans, few if any heroes can compare with Roberto Clemente, who is poised, larger than life, outside the Pirates' stadium.

Inside New York's Yankee Stadium the greatest player of all time, Babe Ruth, needs only a photograph and a neon sign to evoke a heroic tradition.

Fans also claim symbols as part of their own identity. Wearing a replica of the uniform of a hero is certainly a common form of fan behavior. But here we see an unusual degree of fan dedication: a tattoo indicating loyalty to the game of baseball itself.

Another important cultural element of the fan experience is the repeated events—called rituals—that define the audience experience in the park. They link the individual with the history of baseball and with all the fans who have attended ball games before. For example, at Yankee Stadium the groundskeepers groom the infield while marching in unison to the song "YMCA." At Fenway Park in Boston, Red Sox fans have been singing the Neil Diamond song "Sweet Caroline" in the eighth inning since the late 1990s, although the origin of this custom is a bit of a mystery. Rituals like these help define what it means to be an audience and contribute to the overall experience of the game.

Among the formal rituals in all ballparks are the singing of the National Anthem at the beginning of the game and the "seventh-inning stretch," where all fans stand and rock back and forth while singing "Take Me Out to the Ballgame." Like all rituals, these must be performed correctly. All men are instructed to remove their hats before singing the National Anthem, and everyone must stand. But there is some flexibility in the ritual as well. At Camden Yards, for example, home of the Baltimore Orioles, the crowd yells out a resounding "O" at the beginning of the phrase "O! say does that star-spangled banner yet wave . . . "

In the 1970s, fans began a strange ritual called "the wave." To start a wave, a group of fans stand simultaneously and throw their hands into the air. If they are successful, the wave moves around the stadium as adjoining sections take their turn. One watches the wave move around the stadium and then engulf one's own section. Here young girls are trying unsuccessfully to initiate a wave.

Since September 11, 2001, some ballpark rituals have been used to display patriotism. When "The Star-Spangled Banner" and "God Bless America" are played at Yankee Stadium, ushers ask fans to stop moving and even block the main aisles with chains.

A more compelling ritual is the singing of "Take Me Out to the Ballgame" during the seventh-inning stretch. Projecting the words of the song onto a screen, as at Camden Yards, home of the Baltimore Orioles, gives the ritual an "official" imprint that encourages participation.

Three Perspectives on Social Order

The question of what holds all these elements of society together and how they combine to create social order has concerned sociologists for decades. Sociologists identify three broad intellectual orientations they often use to address this question: the structural-functionalist perspective, the conflict perspective, and symbolic interactionism (see Exhibit 2.2). Each of these perspectives has its advantages and shortcomings. Each is helpful in answering particular types of questions. For instance, structural functionalism is useful in showing us how and why large, macrolevel structures, such as organizations and institutions, develop and persist. The conflict perspective sheds light on the various sources of social inequality that exist in our own and other societies. And symbolic interactionism is helpful in explaining how individuals construct meaning to make sense of their social surroundings. At times, the perspectives complement one another; at other times, they contradict one another.

Exhibit 2.2   Sociological Perspectives at a Glance

Sociological Perspective	*Key Concepts*	*Main Assumption*
Structural-functionalist perspective	Manifest and latent functions Dysfunctions Social stability	Social institutions are structured to maintain stability and order in society
Conflict perspective	Power Inequality Conflict Dominance	The various institutions in society promote inequality and conflict among groups of people
Symbolic interactionist perspective	Symbolic communication Social interaction Subjective meaning	Society is structured and maintained through everyday interactions and people's subjective definitions of their worlds

Throughout the remaining chapters of this book, I will periodically return to these three perspectives—as well as several other perspectives—to apply them to specific social phenomena, experiences, and events.

The Structural-Functionalist Perspective

According to sociologists Talcott Parsons and Neil Smelser (1956), two theorists typically associated with the ***structural-functionalist perspective***, a society is a complex system composed of various parts, much like a living organism. Just as the heart, lungs, and liver work together to keep an animal alive, so too do all the elements of a society's structure work together to keep society alive.

Social institutions play a key role in keeping a society stable. All societies require certain things to survive. They must ensure that the goods and services people need are produced and distributed; they must provide ways of dealing with conflicts between individuals, groups, and organizations; and they must provide ways to ensure that individuals are made a part of the existing culture.

As we saw earlier in this chapter, institutions allow societies to attain their goals, adapt to a changing environment, reduce tension, and recruit individuals into statuses and roles. Economic institutions, for instance, allow adaptation to dwindling supplies of natural resources or to competition from other societies. Educational institutions train people for the future statuses they will need to fill to keep society going. Religions help maintain the existence of society by reaffirming people's values and preserving social ties among individuals (Durkheim, 1915/1954).

Sociologist Robert Merton (1957) distinguishes between manifest and latent functions of social institutions. *Manifest functions* are the intended, obvious consequences of activities designed to help some part of the social system. For instance, the manifest function of going to college is to get an education and acquire the credentials necessary to establish a career. *Latent functions* are the *unintended*, sometimes unrecognized, consequences of actions that coincidentally help the system. The latent function of going to college is to meet people and establish close, enduring friendships. In addition, college informally teaches students how to live on their own, away from their parents. It also provides important lessons in negotiating the intricacies of large bureaucracies—registering for classes, filling out forms, learning important school policies—so that students figure out how to "get things done" in an organization. These latent lessons will certainly help students who enter the equally large and bureaucratic world of work after they graduate (Galles, 1989).

From the structural-functionalist perspective, if an aspect of social life does not contribute to society's survival—that is, if it is *dys*functional—it will eventually disappear. Things that persist, even if they seem to be disruptive, must persist because they contribute somehow to the survival of society (Durkheim, 1915/1954). Take prostitution, for example. A practice so widely condemned and punished would appear to be dysfunctional for society. But prostitution has existed since human civilization began. Some structural functionalists suggest that prostitution satisfies sexual needs that may not be met through more socially acceptable means, such as marriage. Customers can have their physical desires satisfied without having to establish the sort of emotional attachment to another person that would destroy a preexisting marriage, harm the institution of family, and ultimately threaten the entire society (K. Davis, 1937).

Structural functionalism was the dominant theoretical tradition in sociology for most of the 20th century, and it still shapes sociological thinking to a certain degree today. But it has been criticized for accepting existing social arrangements without examining how they might exploit or otherwise disadvantage certain groups or individuals within the society.

The Conflict Perspective

The *conflict perspective* addresses the deficiencies of structural functionalism by viewing the structure of society as a source of inequality that benefits some groups at the expense of other groups. Conflict sociologists are likely to see society not in terms of stability and acceptance but in terms of conflict and struggle. They focus not on how all the elements of society contribute to its smooth operation and continued existence but on how these elements promote divisions and inequalities. Social order arises not from the societal pursuit of harmony but from dominance and coercion. The family, government, religion, and other institutions foster and legitimate the power and privilege of some individuals or groups at the expense of others.

Karl Marx, perhaps the most famous scholar associated with the conflict perspective, focused exclusively on economic arrangements. He argued that all human societies are structured around the production of goods that people need to survive. The individuals or groups who control the means of production—land in an agricultural society, factories in an industrial society, computer networks and information in a postindustrial society—have the power to create and maintain social institutions that serve their interests. Hence, economic, political, and educational systems in a modern society support the interests of those who control the wealth (see Chapter 10).

Marx believed that when resources are limited or scarce, conflict between the "haves" and the "have-nots" is inevitable and creates a situation in which those in power must enforce social order. He said this conflict is not caused by greedy, exploitative individuals; rather, it is a by-product of a system in which those who benefit from inequality are motivated to act in ways that maintain it.

Contemporary conflict sociologists are interested in various sources of conflict and inequality. One version of the conflict perspective that has become particularly popular among sociologists in the past few decades is the *feminist perspective*. Feminist sociologists focus on gender as the most important source of conflict and inequality in social life. Compared with men, women in nearly every contemporary society have less power, influence, and opportunity. In families, especially in industrialized societies, women have traditionally been encouraged to perform unpaid household labor and childcare duties, whereas men have been free to devote their energy and attention to earning money and power in the economic marketplace. Women's lower wages when they do work outside the home are often justified by the assumption that their paid labor is secondary to that of their husbands. But as women in many societies seek equality in education, politics, career, marriage, and other areas of social life, their activities inevitably affect social institutions (see Chapter 12 for more details). The feminist perspective helps us understand the difficulties men and women face in their everyday lives as they experience the changes taking place in society.

Because this perspective focuses so much on struggle and competing interests, it tends to downplay or overlook the elements of society that different groups and individuals share. In addition, its emphasis on inequality has led some critics to argue that it is a perspective motivated by a particular political agenda and not the objective pursuit of knowledge.

Symbolic Interactionism

The structural-functionalist and the conflict perspectives differ in their assumptions about the nature of society, yet both analyze society mostly at the macro or structural level, focusing on societal patterns and the consequences they produce. In contrast, *symbolic interactionism* attempts to understand society and social structure through an examination of the microlevel interactions of people as individuals, pairs, or groups.

These forms of interaction take place within a world of symbolic communication. A *symbol* is something used to represent or stand for something else (Charon, 1998). It can be a physical object (like an engagement ring, standing for betrothal), a characteristic or property of objects (like the pink color of a triangle, standing for gay rights), a gesture (like a thumb pointed up, standing for "everything's OK"), or a word (like the letters d-o-g, standing for a particular type of household pet, or M-o-k-i, standing for *my* particular pet).

Symbols are created, modified, and used by people through their interactions with others. We concoct them and come to agree on what they should stand for. Our lives depend on such agreement. For instance, imagine how chaotic—not to mention dangerous—automobile travel would be if we didn't all agree that green stands for go and red stands for stop.

Symbols don't bear any necessary connection to nature. Rather, they're arbitrary human creations. There's nothing in the natural properties of "greenness" that automatically determines that green should stand for "go." We could have decided long ago that purple meant go. It wouldn't have mattered as long as we all learned and understood this symbol.

Most human behavior is determined not by the objective facts of a given situation but by the symbolic meanings people attach to the facts (Weber, 1947). When we interact with others, we constantly attempt to interpret what they mean and what they're up to. A gentle pat on the shoulder symbolizes one thing if it comes from someone with whom you are romantically involved but something quite different if it comes from your mother or your boss.

Society, therefore, is not a structure that exists independent of human action. It is "socially constructed," emerging from the countless symbolic interactions that occur each day between individuals. Each time I refer to "U.S. society," "the school system," "the global economy," "the threat of terrorism," or "the Newman family" in my casual conversations with others, I am doing my part to reinforce the notion that these are real things. By examining how and why we interact with others, symbolic interactionism reveals how the everyday experiences of people help to construct and maintain social institutions and, ultimately, society itself.

This perspective reminds us that for all its structural elements, society is, in the end, people interacting with one another. But by highlighting these microlevel experiences, symbolic interactionism runs the risk of ignoring the larger social patterns and structures that create the influential historical, institutional, and cultural settings for people's everyday interactions.

Conclusion

Living with others, within a social structure, influences many aspects of our everyday lives. But we must be cautious not to overstate the case. Although the fundamental elements of society are not merely the direct expressions of the personalities of individuals, we must also remember that people are more than "robots programmed by social structure" (G. Swanson, 1992, p. 94).

The lesson I hope you take from this chapter—and, in fact, from the entire book—is that the relationship between the individual and society is reciprocal. One cannot be understood without accounting for the other. Yes, this thing we call "society" touches our lives in intimate, important, and sometimes not altogether obvious ways. And yes, this influence is often beyond our immediate control. But society is not simply a "forbidding prison" that mechanically determines who we are and what we do (P. L. Berger, 1963). We as individuals can affect the very social structure that affects us. We can modify role expectations, change norms, create or destroy organizations, revolutionize institutions, and even alter the path of world history.

YOUR TURN

Alcohol occupies an important but problematic place in many societies. We decry its evils while simultaneously encouraging its use in times of leisure, celebration, despair, disappointment, anger, and worry.

The physical effects of being "under the influence"—vomiting, hangovers, liver damage—are a biological consequence of the presence of alcohol in the body. When a person's blood alcohol level reaches a certain point, that person will have trouble walking and talking; at a higher level, she or he will pass out.

But is the social behavior we see in drunken people reducible to a chemical reaction in the body? The traditional explanation for drunken behavior is that the chemical properties of alcohol do something to the brain that reduces inhibitions. If this were true, though, drunken behavior would look the same everywhere. The fact is, social behavior under the influence of alcohol can vary from culture to culture. The way people handle themselves when drunk "is determined not by alcohol's toxic assault on the seat of moral judgment, conscience, or the like but by what their society makes of and imparts to them concerning the state of drunkenness" (MacAndrew & Edgerton, 1969, p. 165).

Ask people who grew up in a culture different from yours (e.g., students who grew up in a different country or in a different socioeconomic class or geographic region) how people behave when drunk. Do these behaviors differ from those you've observed? Have them describe their first drunken experience. Are there similarities or differences in how people are introduced to alcohol?

Also ask the same questions of people from different sexes, races, ethnic groups, and age groups. Are there variations in the "drunken experience" within a society? What do these differences illustrate about the norms and values of these different groups? You might also ask some young children to describe how drunk people act. Are there any similarities in the images they have of drunkenness? Do you consider their ideas about drunkenness accurate? Where do you think their ideas about alcohol come from?

Use the results of these interviews to explain the role of social and societal influence on people's personal lives. Do you think your conclusions can be expanded to other private phenomena, such as sexual activity or religious experiences? Why or why not?

Note: Most colleges and universities require that any student research project involving human subjects—even if it just entails asking people questions—be approved by a campus or departmental review committee. For instance, you will probably be required to show that your interviewees have consented to participate and that you've guaranteed that their identities will not be divulged. Make sure you talk to your instructor before proceeding with this exercise to see what steps you have to take in order to have it approved by the appropriate campus committee.

CHAPTER HIGHLIGHTS

- Although society exists as an objective fact, it is also created, reaffirmed, and altered through the day-to-day interactions of the very people it influences and controls.

- Humans are social beings. We look to others to help define and interpret particular situations. Other people can influence what we see, feel, think, and do.

- Society consists of socially recognizable combinations of individuals—relationships, groups, and organizations—as well as the products of human action—statuses, roles, culture, institutions, and broad societal forces such as globalization.

- There are three major sociological perspectives. The structural-functionalist perspective focuses on the way various parts of society are structured and interrelated to maintain stability and order. The conflict perspective emphasizes how the various elements of society promote inequality and conflict among groups of people. Symbolic interactionism seeks to understand society and social structure through the interactions of people and the ways in which they subjectively define their worlds.

KEY TERMS

achieved status: Social position acquired through our own efforts or accomplishments or taken on voluntarily

ascribed status: Social position acquired at birth or taken on involuntarily later in life

coalition: Subgroup of a triad, formed when two members unite against the third member

conflict perspective: Theoretical perspective that views the structure of society as a source of inequality that always benefits some groups at the expense of other groups

culture: Language, values, beliefs, rules, behaviors, and artifacts that characterize a society

dyad: Group consisting of two people

feminist perspective: Theoretical perspective that focuses on gender as the most important source of conflict and inequality in social life

globalization: Process through which people's lives all around the world become economically, politically, environmentally, and culturally interconnected

group: Set of people who interact more or less regularly and who are conscious of their identity as a unit

in-groups: The groups to which we belong and toward which we feel a sense of loyalty

latent function: Unintended, unrecognized consequences of activities that help some part of the social system

macrolevel: Way of examining human life that focuses on the broad social forces and structural features of society that exist above the level of individual people

manifest function: Intended, obvious consequences of activities designed to help some part of the social system

microlevel: Way of examining human life that focuses on the immediate, everyday experiences of individuals

norm: Culturally defined standard or rule of conduct

organization: Large, complex network of positions created for a specific purpose and characterized by a hierarchical division of labor

out-groups: The groups to which we don't belong and toward which we feel a certain amount of antagonism

primary group: Collection of individuals who are together for a relatively long period, whose members have direct contact with and feel emotional attachment to one another

role: Set of expectations—rights, obligations, behaviors, duties—associated with a particular status

role conflict: Frustration people feel when the demands of one role they are expected to fulfill clash with the demands of another role

role strain: Situations in which people lack the necessary resources to fulfill the demands of a particular role

secondary group: Relatively impersonal collection of individuals that is established to perform a specific task

social institution: Stable set of roles, statuses, groups, and organizations—such as the institutions of education, family, politics, religion, health care, or the economy—that provides a foundation for behavior in some major area of social life

society: A population of people living in the same geographic area who share a culture and a common identity and whose members are subject to the same political authority

status: Any named social position that people can occupy

structural-functionalist perspective: Theoretical perspective that posits that social institutions are structured to maintain stability and order in society

symbol: Something used to represent or stand for something else

symbolic interactionism: Theoretical perspective that explains society and social structure through an examination of the microlevel, personal, day-to-day exchanges of people as individuals, pairs, or groups

triad: Group consisting of three people

value: Standard of judgment by which people decide on desirable goals and outcomes

STUDENT STUDY SITE

Visit the Student Study Site at **www.sagepub.com/newman9e** for these additional learning tools:

- Flashcards
- Web quizzes
- Sociologists at Work features
- Micro-Macro Connection features
- Video links
- Audio links
- Web resources
- SAGE journal articles

PART II

The Construction
of Self and Society

Part II examines the basic architecture of individual identities and of society: how reality and truth are constructed; how social order is created and maintained; how culture and history influence our personal experiences; how societal values, ideals, and norms are instilled; and how we acquire our sense of self. The tactical and strategic ways in which we present images of ourselves to others are also addressed. You will see how we form relationships and interact within small, intimate groups. The section closes with a look at how we define "acceptable" behavior and how we respond to those who "break the rules."

Building Reality

The Social Construction of Knowledge

3

Understanding the Social Construction of Reality

Laying the Foundation: The Bases of Reality

Building the Walls: Conflict, Power, and Social Institutions

Appreciating the Contributions of Sociological Research

The year was 1897. Eight-year-old Virginia O'Hanlon became upset when her friends told her there was no Santa Claus. Her father encouraged her to write a letter to the *New York Sun* to find out the truth. The editor's reply—which included the now famous phrase, "Yes, Virginia, there is a Santa Claus!"—has become a classic piece of American folklore. "Nobody sees Santa Claus," the editor wrote, "but that is no sign that there is no Santa Claus. The most real things in the world are those that neither children nor men [*sic*] can see" ("Is There a Santa Claus?" 1897).

In his book *Encounters With the Archdruid*, John McPhee (1971) examines the life and ideas of David Brower, who was one of the most successful and energetic environmentalists in the United States. McPhee recalls a lecture in which Brower claimed that the United States has 6% of the world's population and uses 60% of the world's resources and that only 1% of Americans use 60% of those resources. Afterward, McPhee asked Brower where he got these interesting statistics:

> Brower said the figures had been worked out in the head of a friend of his from data assembled "to the best of his recollection." . . . [He] assured me that figures in themselves are merely indices. *What matters is that they feel right* [italics added]. Brower feels things. (p. 86)

What do these two very different examples have in common? Both reflect the fickle nature of "truth" and "reality." Young Virginia was encouraged to believe in the reality of something she could and would never perceive with her senses. She no doubt learned a different sort of truth about Santa Claus when she got older, but the editor urged her to take on faith that Santa Claus, or at least the idea of Santa Claus, exists despite the lack of objective proof. That sort of advice persists. A survey of 200 child psychologists around the United States found that 91% of them advised parents not to tell the truth when their young children asked about the existence of Santa Claus (cited in Stryker, 1997).

Likewise, David Brower urges people to believe in something that doesn't need to be seen. What's important is that the information "feels right," that it helps one's cause even if it is not based on hard evidence. More recently, former MTV star Jenny McCarthy published several best-selling books in which she claims that the measles, mumps, and rubella vaccine—something most infants in this country routinely receive—had probably given

55

her son autism. Rather than provide research evidence (principally because there really is none), McCarthy based her conclusion on her own intuition, or what she called "mommy instinct." In fact, the Centers for Disease Control and Prevention, the Institute of Medicine, and the National Academy of Sciences have all concluded there is no link between vaccines and autism. Nevertheless, the contention that vaccines could harm children struck an emotional chord with many fretful parents. Consequently the percentage of children who get this vaccine as well as others has consistently dropped over the past several years. Perhaps not coincidentally, measles outbreaks have recently occurred in several states including New York, California, and Illinois (Mnookin, 2011).

Such precarious uses of truth may appear foolish or even deceitful. Yet much of our everyday knowledge is based on accepting as real the existence of things that can't be seen, touched, or proved—"the world taken-for-granted" (P. L. Berger, 1963, p. 147). Like Virginia, we learn to accept the existence of things such as electrons, the ozone layer, black holes in the universe, love, and God, even though we cannot see them. And like David Brower and Jenny McCarthy, we learn to believe and use facts and figures as long as they sound right or support our interests.

How do we come to know what we know? How do we learn what is real and what isn't? In this chapter, I examine how sociologists discover truths about human life. But to provide the appropriate context, I must first present a sociological perspective on the nature of reality. How do individuals construct their realities? How do societal forces influence the process?

Understanding the Social Construction of Reality

In Chapter 2, I noted that the elements of society are human creations that provide structure to our everyday lives. They also give us a distinctive lens through which we perceive the world. For example, because of their different statuses and their respective occupational training, an architect, a real estate agent, a police officer, and a firefighter can each look at the same building and see very different things: "a beautiful example of early Victorian architecture," "a moderately priced fixer-upper," "an easy target for a thief," or "a dangerous fire hazard." Mark Twain often wrote about how the Mississippi River—a waterway he saw every day as a child—looked different after he became a riverboat pilot. What he once saw as a place for recreation and relaxation, he later saw for its treacherous currents, eddies, and other potential perils.

What we know to be true or real is always a product of the culture and historical period in which we exist. It takes an exercise of the sociological imagination, however, to see that what we ourselves "know" to be true today—the laws of nature, the causes and treatments of certain diseases, and so forth—may not be true for everyone everywhere or may be replaced by different truths tomorrow (Babbie, 1986). For example, in some cultures, the existence of spirits, witches, and demons is a taken-for-granted part of everyday reality that others might easily dismiss as fanciful. On the other side of the coin, the Western faith in the curative powers of little pills—without the intervention of spiritual forces—might seem far-fetched and naive to people living in cultures where illness and health are assumed to have supernatural causes.

Ideas about reality also change over time. In 1900, a doctor might have told a patient with asthma to go to the local tobacconist for a cigarette; people with colds may have been told to inhale formaldehyde (Zuger, 1999). Early-20th-century child development experts offered parents advice such as "Kissing a baby after it's eaten will likely cause vomiting" and "Never let a baby sit on your lap" (P. Cohen, 2003). Doctors encouraged parents to paint "Thum," a fiery concoction of cayenne pepper, acetone nail polish, and isopropyl alcohol, on their baby's fingernails to discourage thumb-sucking (Critchell, 2005). Fifty years ago, obstetricians encouraged pregnant women to have a martini or a glass of wine each night to calm their nerves. Doctors also believed that alcohol prevented premature labor. Hence, women arriving at the hospital in early labor were often handed vodka or even given alcohol intravenously (Hoffman, 2005).

In 2004, federal health officials in the United States lowered the threshold level for harmful cholesterol (Kolata, 2004). Millions of people went to bed one night with cholesterol levels in the "healthy" range and woke up the next day with levels suddenly considered "unhealthy" and "risky." For decades, medical studies have shown that raising levels of high-density lipoproteins (HDL, or so-called good cholesterol) could help reduce people's risk of heart attack. But in 2011, a large government study concluded that increasing levels of HDL does not lower the risk of heart attacks, perhaps influencing the way doctors treat the millions of patients with heart disease each year (cited in G. Harris, 2011a). Around the same time, the Institute of Medicine concluded that there is no medically justifiable need for people to take Vitamin D supplements or calcium pills because just about everyone has enough Vitamin D for bone health (Begley, 2011).

According to one researcher, about a third of major medical studies are eventually contradicted by further research (Ioannidis, 2005). The frequency with which medical "truths" emerge only to be reversed or debunked later on led one columnist to write, with a fair amount of exasperation, "Sometimes you really do want to tell the medical profession to just make up its mind" (G. Collins, 2011, p. A23). Quite possibly, people 100 years from now will look back at the early 21st century and regard some of our taken-for-granted truths as mistaken, misguided, or downright laughable.

On some occasions, taken-for-granted realities change almost instantaneously. In 2006, this curious newspaper headline caught my eye: "Pluto Is No Longer a Planet, Astronomers Say" (Kole, 2006). Did that little celestial body orbiting in the far reaches of the solar system unexpectedly implode or turn into an asteroid? No. A panel of leading astronomers simply reclassified it based on new criteria for determining what is and isn't a planet (it is now officially a "dwarf planet"). So literally overnight, a reality that we all take for granted suddenly changed. Think of all the schoolbooks that will have to be rewritten to account for this new "truth."

The process through which facts, knowledge, truth, and so on are discovered, made known, reaffirmed, and altered by the members of a society is called the ***social construction of reality*** (P. L. Berger & Luckmann, 1966). This concept is based on the simple assumption that knowledge is a human creation. Ironically, most of us live our lives assuming that an objective reality exists, independent of us, and accessible through our senses. We are quite sure trees and tables and trucks don't exist simply in our imaginations. We assume this reality is shared by others and can be taken for granted as reality (Lindesmith, Strauss, & Denzin, 1991).

At times, however, what we define as real seems to have nothing to do with what our senses tell us is real. Picture a five-year-old child who wakes up in the middle of the night screaming that monsters are under her bed. Her parents comfort her by saying, "There aren't any monsters. You had a nightmare. It's just your imagination." The next day, the child comes down with the flu and wants to know why she is sick. The parents respond by saying,

> You've caught a virus, a bug.
>
> A bug? You mean like an ant or a beetle?
>
> No. It's the sort of bug you can't see, but it's there.

Granted, viruses can be seen and verified with the proper magnification equipment, but without access to such devices the child has to take her parents' word for it that viruses are real. In fact, most of us accept the scientific reality of viruses without ever having seen them for ourselves. The child learns to accept the authoritative claims of her parents that something that was "seen" (the nightmare monster) is not real, although something that was not seen (the virus) is real.

Hence, reality often turns out to be more a matter of agreement than something inherent in the natural world. In the early 1990s, Brazil's economy was on the edge of ruin. Inflation had reached 80% *a month*. That means that if you bought something for $10 one day, it would cost $18 a month later, $340 six months later, and a whopping $10,000 a year later. When inflation is that high, the value of the currency drops accordingly. So the *cruzeiro* (Brazil's unit of currency at the time) was worth only a fraction of what it went for a year earlier. Not surprisingly, Brazilians completely lost faith in the value of their currency and stopped buying consumer goods. Several government economists got together and decided that the solution to this decades-old problem was to trick people into thinking that Brazil's money had real, stable value. They invented a new form of currency and named it the "unit of real value" (URV). People's wages were paid in URVs, taxes were deducted in URVs, price tags were marked in URVs. People paid for things in URVs. URVs were kept stable—what changed was how many *cruzeiro*s each URV was worth at a given point in time. Every night, the National Bank of Brazil published a table in newspapers showing the conversion rate of URVs to *cruzeiros*. Let's say a gallon of milk costs 1 URV. At one point in time, that URV might be worth 10 *cruzeiros*. A month later, the gallon of milk will still cost 1 URV, but that 1 URV might now be worth 20 *cruzeiros*. People started to trust the URV because they knew its value and that the prices of things would remain constant. They began to purchase more. Inflation went down. In 1994, the government officially got rid of the *cruzeiro* and turned the virtual currency, the URV, into real currency, aptly called the *real brasileiro*. Because 150 million people tricked themselves into believing the fake money was real, it became real. Brazil now has the eighth-largest economy in the world (This American Life, 2011a).

Sociologists, particularly those working from the conflict perspective and symbolic interactionism, strive to explain the social construction of reality in terms of both its causes and its consequences. Their insights help explain many of the phenomena that influence our daily lives.

Laying the Foundation: The Bases of Reality

Think of society as a building constructed by the people who live and work in it. The building's foundation, its underlying reality, determines its basic shape and dimensions.

And the foundation is what makes that building solid and helps it stand up through time and the elements. For students of architecture as well as sociology, the first thing to understand is the way the foundation is prepared.

Symbolic interactionism encourages us to see that people's actions toward one another and interpretations of situations are based on their definitions of reality, which are in turn learned from interactions with those around them. What we know to be real, we share with other members of our culture. Imagine how difficult it would be to believe in something no one else around you thought existed. Psychiatrists use terms such as *hallucination* and *delusion* to describe things experienced by people who see, hear, or believe things that others don't.

The social construction of reality is a process by which human-created ideas become so firmly accepted that to deny them is to deny common sense. Of course, some features of reality are grounded in physical evidence—fire is hot, sharp things hurt. But other features of reality are often based not on sensory experiences but on forces such as culture and language, self-fulfilling prophecies, and faith.

Culture and Language

As I mentioned in Chapter 2, we live in a symbolic world and interact chiefly through symbolic communication—that is, through language. Language gives meaning to the people, objects, events, and ideas of our lives. In fact, language reflects and often determines our reality (Sapir, 1949; Whorf, 1956). Thus, language is a key tool in the construction of society.

Within a culture, words evolve to reflect the phenomena that have practical significance. Solomon Islanders have nine distinct words for *coconut*, each specifying an important stage of its growth, but they have only one word for all the meals of the day (M. M. Lewis, 1948). The Hanunóo people of the Philippines have different names for 92 varieties of rice, allowing them to make distinctions all but invisible to English-speaking people, who lump all such grains under a single word: *rice* (Thomson, 2000). Yet a traditional Hanunóo coming to this country would be hard pressed to see the distinction between the vehicles we call *sedans*, *SUVs*, *hatchbacks*, and *station wagons*.

Language also reflects prevailing cultural values. Consider, for instance, the words we use to describe spatial positioning. In most Western languages, English included, if you wanted to give someone directions to your house, you'd say something like, "After the stop sign, take the first left, then the second right. You'll see a brown duplex in front of you. Ours is the door on the right." You wouldn't say, "After the stop sign, drive north, then on the second street drive east and you'll see a brown duplex directly to the east. Ours is the southern door." The two sets of directions may identify the same route, but the first uses *egocentric* coordinates, which rely on the location of our own bodies relative to the destination in question. The second set of directions—which would be common in some areas of the world like Polynesia, northern Australia, Namibia, and Bali—uses fixed *geographic coordinates*, which stay the same no matter which way we're facing (Deutscher, 2010). Speakers of Guugu Yimithirr, an Australian Aboriginal language, orient their lives exclusively around geographic coordinates. If they wanted to warn a walking companion of impending danger on the path, they'd say, "There's a hole in the ground north of your western foot" rather than, "There's a hole in front of your left foot." Indeed, the Guugu Yimithirr have no idea what *left*, *right*, *in front of you*, or *behind you* mean. Notice how these two linguistic approaches reflect very different cultural beliefs about the importance of the individual:

If you saw a Guugu Yimithirr speaker pointing at himself, you would naturally assume he meant to draw attention to himself. In fact, he is pointing at a [geographic] direction that happens to be behind his back. While we [English speakers] are always at the center of the world, and it would never occur to us that pointing in the direction of our chest could mean anything other than to draw attention to ourselves, a Guugu Yimithirr speaker points through himself, as if he were thin air and his own existence were irrelevant. (Deutscher, 2010, p. 47)

In addition to affecting perceptions of reality, language reinforces prevailing ideas and suppresses conflicting ideas about the world (Sapir, 1929). In a highly specialized market economy such as the United States, for example, the ability to distinguish linguistically between "real" work and "volunteer" work allows us to telegraph our attitudes about a person's worth to society. In small agricultural societies, where all people typically perform tasks to provide the basic necessities and to ensure the survival of their tight-knit community, work is work whether you're paid to do it or not.

The way words are defined, especially by governments, can have serious implications. In 2008, the U.S. Congress began debating how to define "homeless." For two decades, only those living on the streets or in shelters were counted. But many legislators wanted to expand the definition to include people forced to live with friends or relatives or those living in day-to-day motels. Such a redefinition would increase the number of people eligible for federally funded housing and other services provided by the Department of Housing and Urban Development (Swarns, 2008c).

Language can also pack an enormous emotional wallop. Words can make us happy, sad, disgusted, or angry, or even incite us to violence. Racial, ethnic, sexual, or religious slurs can be particularly volatile. Among heterosexual adolescents, for example, homophobic name-calling (*queer, fag, dyke*) is one of the most common modes of bullying and coercion in school (Pascoe, 2010). In 2007, comedian Michael Richards—famous for playing the goofy character Kramer on the popular TV show *Seinfeld*—was caught on video calling a black heckler a "nigger" during his stand-up comedy show. In 2011, MSNBC radio host Ed Schultz was suspended for calling rival radio personality Laura Ingraham a "right-wing slut." That same year, star bastketball player Kobe Bryant was fined $100,000 after television cameras caught him calling referee Bennie Adams a "faggot" during a game. Bryant wasn't disparaging Adams's sexual orientation. I doubt if he even knew whether Adams was gay or straight. Instead, he was enraged by a call Adams had just made and found this word to be the most effective means of communicating his utter contempt for what he perceived to be terrible officiating.

The emotional effect of words can have economic implications, too. In January 2008, Orange County, California, opened a $480 billion "groundwater replenishment system." The massive plant purifies wastewater so that it is safe to drink. Repeated chemical analyses show that the water from this filtration system is actually purer (and therefore healthier) than bottled water. It even tastes better. Yet many residents were opposed, even sickened, by the thought of drinking this water. Their aversion had nothing to do with the quality of the water; it had to do with words: Few people could get past the fact that the water the system purifies—no matter how clean and safe it is—is *wastewater from flushed toilets* (Royte, 2008). So the county decided to combine the purified wastewater with the "dirtier" water supply from local reservoirs to avoid its association with raw sewage.

The broader demands of everyday life influence the way language is used. For instance, as societies become more developed, the pace of life quickens, and we become impatient. This phenomenon is reflected in the compression (and subsequent speedup) of language over the years. Contractions (like *we're* and *isn't*) shorten words. Portmanteaus combine two existing words into one, like *brunch* for "breakfast and lunch," *docudrama* for "documentary and drama," and *webinar* for "web seminar" (Garner, 2010). Technology contracts language even further. If you do a lot of instant messaging, tweeting, or texting, you have no doubt made use of "shortspeak"—the reduction of words and sentences through the use of abbreviations, acronyms, and emoticons. We don't even have to finish typing our words anymore. The search engine Google now offers an enhancement called Google Instant, which begins to reveal search results even before you're done entering the key words. The company claims this feature saves two to five seconds per search.

Within a culture, certain professions or groups sometimes develop a distinctive language, known as *jargon*, which allows members of the group to communicate with one another clearly and quickly. Surfers, snowboarders, and techies each have a specialized vocabulary (not understandable to most outsiders) through which they can efficiently convey to others information about wave quality, snow conditions, or the latest innovations in microprocessors. Teenagers must keep up with a constantly evolving vocabulary to avoid falling out of favor with their peers. At the same time, jargon can sometimes create boundaries and therefore mystify and conceal meaning from outsiders (Farb, 1983). For instance, by using esoteric medical terminology when discussing a case in front of a patient, health care professionals define who is and who isn't a member of their group, reinforce their image as highly trained experts, and keep the patient from interfering too much in their decision making. Often medical information has to be conveyed quickly, making it even more incomprehensible to outsiders. See if you can figure out the patient's condition from how this intensive care nurse described it to an attending physician:

> IL-2 patient, hypotensive, B.P. hovering between 70 over 40 to 60 over 30, occasionally tachy, bolused once this morning for a pressure of 80 over 50, getting another bolus right now, already fluid overloaded, crackles at the bases. (Brown, 2010, p. 5)

This sort of communication roadblock has become a cause for concern in the field of medicine. Many books and Web sites now help patients overcome their position of powerlessness by instructing them on how and when to ask physicians the right questions so they can make informed decisions about a course of treatment. For their part, many medical schools now require their students to be trained in how to avoid jargon and how to listen to their patients (D. Franklin, 2006).

Language is sometimes used to purposely conceal as well. A *euphemism* is an innocuous expression substituted for one that might be offensive. On the surface, people use such terms in the interests of politeness and good taste, such as saying "perspiration" instead of "sweat," "bathroom tissue" instead of "toilet paper," or "no longer with us" instead of "dead." However, euphemisms also shape perceptions and emotions. Does it matter, for instance, whether an economic crisis is called a *downturn, slump, recession, crash, depression,* or *meltdown*? Political regimes routinely use euphemisms to cover up, distort, or frame their actions in a more positive light. Here are a few examples of euphemisms, followed by their real meanings. Can you think of others?

- Pre-owned—used
- Seasoned—old
- Misinformation—lies
- Economically nonaffluent—poor
- Big boned—overweight

- Lady of the night—prostitute
- Revenue enhancement—taxes
- Postconsumer waste material—garbage
- Deselected, involuntarily separated, downsized, nonretained, given a career change opportunity, vocationally relocated, streamlined, or dehired—fired

In sum, words help frame or structure social reality and give it meaning. Language also provides people with a cultural and group identity. If you've ever spent a significant amount of time in a foreign country or even moved to a new school, you know you cannot be a fully participating member of a group or a culture until you share its language.

MICRO-MACRO CONNECTION

The Language of War

The governmental or political use of language illustrates how words can determine the course of people's everyday lives both at home and abroad. We all know what the word *war* means: It's when two opposing forces wage battle against one another, either until one side surrenders or until both agree to a truce. The vocabulary of war is vast, containing words such as *troops*, *battle*, *regiments*, *ammunition*, *artillery*, *allies*, *enemies*, *heroes*, *casualties*, and so forth.

In wartime, there is good and evil, us and them, victory and defeat. The language of war contains euphemisms, too, designed to minimize the public's discomfort and increase its support: *collateral damage* (civilian deaths during military combat), *friendly fire* (accidental shooting at fellow soldiers), *pullback* (retreat), *sectarian violence* (civil war), and *insurgency* (deadly attacks by people who resent being occupied by a foreign country).

Once a conflict is defined as a "war," people's lives are subjected to a different set of rules and expectations. "War" rallies people around their collective national identity and a common objective, creating obligatory expressions of patriotism and a willingness to fight and make sacrifices (Redstone, 2003). The interpretation of people's behavior dramatically changes as well. For example, some characterized the atrocities that occurred during the conflict in Bosnia-Herzegovina in the 1990s as the normal consequences of war. However,

> Is wide-scale sexual violence, including the rape of women and the forced oral castration of men, neighbors burning down their neighbors' homes, the murder and targeting for murder of civilians—men and women, children, the elderly, and infirm—"normal" simply because it takes place within the context of something we call "war"? (Wilmer, 2002, p. 60)

Immediately after the attacks of September 11, 2001, then-President Bush unofficially declared a "war" on terrorism, which continues to this day. But the administration later opted for the term "War on Terror" and then "Global War on Terror" rather than "War on Terrorism," evoking both the violent actions of terrorists and the fear they're trying to create:

> "The war on terror" . . . suggests a campaign aimed not at human adversaries but at a pervasive social plague. At its most abstract, terror comes to seem as persistent and inexplicable as evil itself, without raising any inconvenient theological qualms. And in fact, the White House's use of "evil" has declined by 80 percent over the same period that its use of "terror" has been increasing. (Nunberg, 2004, p. 7)

Whether this decade-long conflict is a war on terror or on terrorism, it is—in the traditional sense of the word *war*—linguistically impossible. This war has no geographically or nationally identifiable enemy and no achievable end. Technically, a nation can no more declare war on "terror" or "terrorism" than it can declare a war on guns or bombs or drunk driving. In 2005, the administration shifted its language and began testing a new slogan, "A Global Struggle Against Violent Extremism," in an attempt to convey the impression that the war is as much an ideological battle as it is a military mission (Schmitt & Shanker, 2005). In 2009, the Obama administration tried the equally ambiguous term "overseas contingency operation," thereby avoiding reference to "war" and "violence" altogether.

As one columnist put it, "In wartime, words are weapons" (Safire, 2006, p. 16). Whether the enemy is "terror," "terrorism," "Islamofascism," or "violent extremism," invoking the vocabulary of war has some strategic advantages—among them, justifying actions that would not be acceptable in any other context. By continually using wartime terms and expressions, an administration can frame the expansion of government powers and the limitation of civil liberties as steps we need to take to protect freedom, bring "enemies" and "evildoers" to justice, and avoid another catastrophe.

Governments must also try to control language during wartime. In the spring of 2004, we all saw the horrible pictures of Iraqi prisoners being mistreated by U.S. soldiers at the Abu Ghraib prison. Some were shown being attacked by dogs; others were stripped naked and forced to simulate sexual acts to the laughter of their captors; still others were hooded and attached to electrical wires. The ensuing battle over words was as heated as the battle to determine criminal responsibility for these acts.

The International Committee of the Red Cross (2007) issued a report in 2007 that the treatment to which high-value detainees were subjected at the U.S. Marine base in Guantánamo Bay, Cuba (waterboarding, forced nudity, sleep deprivation, food deprivation, prolonged standing, beatings, kickings, and confinement in boxes), "constituted torture." Liberal journalists and critics of the Bush administration used the term *torture* freely and frequently. A popular conservative radio talk show host, however, encouraged his listeners to see the incidents as no worse than "fraternity pranks." The administration itself went to great pains to avoid using the word *torture*, opting instead for euphemisms like "enhanced interrogation techniques" and "alternative procedures." The secretary of defense said that they weren't prisoners of war at all but were "unlawful combatants" and, therefore, didn't have any rights to be treated humanely (Sontag, 2004). The issue arose again in 2009, when the U.S. Justice Department released secret Bush administration memos that detailed the harsh tactics used by the Central Intelligence Agency against suspected terrorists. For years, the Justice Department maintained that these "interrogation techniques" were essential and effective in protecting the United States from further terrorist attacks.

In 2008, a government agency called the Counterterrorism Communications Center (CTCC) distributed a memo to the Departments of State, Homeland Security, and Defense advising representatives of those departments on how to discuss this war with "target audiences." Among other things, the CTCC suggested that spokespersons "change the discussion from 'the West vs. Islam' . . . to the fight between civilization as a whole and terrorists," thereby emphasizing that "terrorists misuse religion as a political tool to harm innocent civilians" (CTCC, 2008, p. 2).

In a wartime mode, even though concerns about national security are warranted and fears of attack are very real, the system, according to one prominent law professor, "by definition sweeps very broadly and ends up harming hundreds if not thousands of people" (quoted in Liptak, 2003, p. A1). Otherwise unacceptable actions occur largely without debate or opposition, reflecting the power of language in shaping the social reality of everyday life.

Self-Fulfilling Prophecies

As you will recall from Chapter 2, we do not respond directly and automatically to objects and situations; instead, as the symbolic interactionist perspective points out, we use language to define and interpret them, and then we act according to those interpretations. By acting on the basis of our definitions of reality, we often create the very conditions we believe exist. A *self-fulfilling prophecy* is an assumption or prediction that, purely as a result of having been made, causes the expected event to occur and thus confirms the prophecy's own "accuracy" (Merton, 1948; Watzlawick, 1984). Every holiday season, we witness the stunning effects of self-fulfilling prophecies on a national scale. Each September the toy industry releases the results of its annual survey of retailers, predicting which toys will be the top sellers at Christmas. Usually, one toy in particular emerges as the most popular, hard-to-get gift of the year. In the 1980s, it was Cabbage Patch Kids. In the early 1990s, it was Mighty Morphin Power Rangers and Ninja Turtles. More recently, items such as Beanie Babies, SpongeBob SquarePants toys, Razor scooters, Bratz dolls, toy digital cameras, Harry Potter paraphernalia, and Xbox Kinect and Wii video games have taken their turn as the "must have" toy of the year. By around November, we begin to hear the hype about unprecedented demand for the toy and the likelihood of a shortage. Powerful retail store chains, such as Toys"R"Us and Wal-Mart, may announce the possibility of rationing: one toy per family. Fueled by the dreaded image of a disappointed child's face at Christmas, thousands of panicked parents and grandparents rush to stores to make sure they're not left without. Some hoard extras for other parents they know. As a result, supplies of the toy—which may not have been perilously low in the first place—become severely depleted, thereby bringing about the predicted shortage. The mere belief in some version of the reality creates expectations that can actually make it happen.

Self-fulfilling prophecies are particularly powerful when they become an element of social institutions. In schools, teachers can subtly and unconsciously encourage the performance they expect to see in their students. For instance, if they believe their students are especially intelligent, they may spend more time with them or unintentionally show more enthusiasm when working with them. As a result, these students may come to feel more capable and intelligent and actually perform better (R. Rosenthal & Jacobson, 1968).

Self-fulfilling prophecies can often affect people physically. For years, doctors have recognized the power of the "placebo" effect—the tendency for patients to improve because they have been led to believe they are receiving some sort of treatment even though they're not. For instance, in one study, 42% of balding men taking a placebo drug either maintained or increased the amount of hair on their heads (cited in Blakeslee, 1998). Researchers estimate that in studies of new drugs, between 35% and 75% of patients benefit from taking dummy pills. In 1999, a major pharmaceutical company halted development of a new antidepressant drug it had been promoting because studies showed that placebo pills were just as effective in treating depression (Talbot, 2000b). Even when patients know they're taking placebos, the effects can be significantly better than if they underwent no treatment at all (Kaptchuk et al., 2010).

The inverse of the placebo effect is the creation of expectations that make people worse, sometimes referred to as the "nocebo" effect. Anthropologists have documented numerous mysterious and scientifically difficult-to-explain deaths that follow the pronouncement of curses or evil spells (Watzlawick, 1984). In Japan, researchers carried out an experiment on 13 people who were extremely allergic to poison ivy. The experimenters rubbed one of their arms with a harmless leaf and told them it was poison ivy and rubbed the other arm with poison ivy and told the subjects it was a harmless leaf. All 13 broke out in a rash where the harmless leaf had touched their skin; only two reacted to the real poison ivy leaves (cited in Blakeslee, 1998). In another study, patients with asthma were given a bronchodilator (a drug that widens air passages, making breathing easier) but were told it was a broncho-constrictor (a drug that narrows air passages, making breathing more difficult). Half of them experienced difficulty breathing after the treatment (cited in "The Nocebo Response," 2005). In other words, in many cases where people expected to get worse, they did. Once again, we see how reality is shaped by human beings as much as reality shapes them.

Faith and Incorrigible Propositions

David Blaine is a famous street performer and illusionist who combines sophisticated magic tricks with a hint of comedy. In one of his more astounding stunts, he appears to rise up and float several inches off the ground for a few seconds. Suppose you saw him perform such a feat in person. He looks as if he is levitating, but you "know better." Even though your eyes tell you he is floating in midair, you have learned that it's just not possible. Rather than use this experience to entirely abandon your belief that people can't float in midair, you'll probably come up with a series of "reasonable" explanations: "Maybe it's an optical illusion, and it just appears like he's floating." "Perhaps there are wires holding him up." To acknowledge the possibility that he is literally floating is to challenge the fundamental reality on which your everyday life is based. It is an article of faith that people aren't capable of levitating.

Such an unquestionable assumption, called an ***incorrigible proposition***, is a belief that cannot be proved wrong and has become so much a part of common sense that one continues to believe it even in the face of vast contrary evidence. By explaining away contradictions with "reasonable" explanations, we strengthen the correctness of the initial premise (Watzlawick, 1976). In the process, we participate in constructing a particular version of reality. For instance, if an incorrigible proposition for you is that women are inherently less aggressive than men, seeing an especially violent woman might lead you toward explanations that focus on the peculiar characteristics of *this particular* woman. Maybe *she's* responding to terrible circumstances in her life; maybe *she* has some kind of chemical imbalance or neurological disorder. By concluding that she is an exception to the rule, the rule is maintained.

In 2011, some evangelical Christians claimed that on May 21 of that year, God would send devastating earthquakes and begin a process that in five months would destroy the world. Believers would be spared and raised to heaven in "the rapture." When doomsday didn't materialize and the world still existed on May 22, those who believed in the prophecy provided a variety of rationalizations that allowed them to maintain the original belief. For instance, some argued that May 21 only marked the beginning of a five-month countdown to the end of the world and that the *real* day to worry about was *October* 21. Others claimed that the prayers of the believers actually worked and that God delayed judgment so that more people could be saved. Still others pointed to human fallibility: "I don't know where we went wrong other than that we obviously don't understand Scriptures in the way that we should" (quoted in Hagerty, 2011, p. 1).

HUGH MEHAN AND HOUSTON WOOD

The Infallible Oracle

Sociologists Hugh Mehan and Houston Wood (1975) furthered our understanding of incorrigible propositions by examining the research of the anthropologist E. E. Evans-Pritchard (1937). Evans-Pritchard described an elaborate ritual practiced by the Azande, a small African society located in southwestern Sudan. When faced with important decisions—where to build a house, whom to marry, and so on—the Azande consulted an oracle, or a powerful spirit. They prepared for the consultation by following a strictly prescribed ceremony. A substance was extracted from the bark of a certain type of tree and prepared in a special way during a séance-like ritual. The Azande believed that a powerful spirit would enter the potion during this ceremony. They then posed a question to the spirit in such a way that it could be answered either yes or no and fed the substance to a chicken. If the chicken lived, they would interpret the answer from the spirit as yes; if the chicken died, the answer was no.

Our Western belief system tells us the tree bark obviously contains some poisonous chemical. Certain chickens are physically able to survive it, others aren't. But the Azande had no knowledge of the bark's poisonous qualities or of chicken physiology. In fact, they didn't believe the tree or the chicken played a part in the ceremony at all. The ritual of gathering bark and feeding it to a chicken transformed the tree into the spirit power (not unlike how consecrated bread and wine *become* the body and blood of Christ in the Roman Catholic Eucharist). The chicken lived or died not because of a physical reaction to a chemical but because the oracle "hears like a person and settles cases like a king" (Evans-Pritchard, 1937, p. 321).

But what if the oracle was wrong? What if an Azande was told by the oracle to build a house by the river and the river overflowed its banks, washing away the house? How could they reconcile these sorts of inconsistencies with a belief in the reality of the oracle?

To us, the answer is obvious: There was no spirit, no magic, just the strength of the poison and the fitness of the chickens it was fed to. We see these bad decisions as contradictions, because we view them from the reality of Western science. We observe this ritual to determine if in fact there is an oracle, and of course we're predisposed to believe there isn't. We are looking for proof of the existence of something of which we are highly skeptical.

For the Azande, though, the contradictions were not contradictions at all. They *knew* the oracle existed. This was their fundamental premise, their incorrigible proposition. It was an article of faith that could not be questioned. All that followed for the Azande was experienced from this initial assumption, and they had ways of explaining contradictions to their truths, just as we do. When the oracle failed to give them proper advice, they would say things like, "A taboo must have been breached" or "Sorcerers must have intervened" or "The ceremony wasn't carried out correctly."

Protecting incorrigible propositions is essential for the maintenance of reality systems. By explaining away contradictions, we are able to support our basic assumptions and live in a coherent and orderly world.

Building the Walls: Conflict, Power, and Social Institutions

We, as individuals, play an important role in coordinating, reproducing, and giving meaning to society in our daily interactions. But we are certainly not completely free to create whatever version of social reality we want to create. We are, after all, born into a preexisting society with its norms, values, roles, relationships, groups, organizations, and institutions. Just as the walls of a building constrain the ability of the inhabitants to move about, directing them through certain predetermined doorways and corridors, these features of society influence our thoughts and deeds and consequently constrain our ability to freely construct our social world (Giddens, 1984). As Karl Marx (1869/1963) wrote, "[People] make their own history, but they do not make it just as they please; they do not make it under circumstances chosen by themselves, but under circumstances directly encountered, given and transmitted from the past" (p. 15).

As the conflict perspective points out, certain people or groups of people are more influential in defining reality than others. In any modern society, where socioeconomic classes, ethnic and religious groups, age groups, and political interests struggle for control over resources, there is also a struggle for the power to determine or influence that society's conception of reality (Gans, 1971). Those who emerge successful gain control over information, define values, create myths, manipulate events, and influence what the rest of us take for granted. Conflict theorists therefore argue that people with more power, prestige, status, wealth, and access to high-level policymakers can turn their perceptions of the world into the entire culture's perception. In other words, "He who has the bigger stick has the better chance of imposing his definitions of reality" (P. L. Berger & Luckmann, 1966, p. 109). That "bigger stick" can be wielded in several ways. Powerful social institutions and the people who control them play a significant role in shaping and sustaining perceptions of reality for everybody else. But if you wish to develop the sociological imagination, you need to understand the role of not only these larger forces in shaping private lives but also private individuals who struggle to shape public reality.

The Economics of Reality

Definitions of reality frequently reflect underlying economic interests. Consider, for instance, the story of a very successful painter named Marla Olmstead. Marla's paintings have been compared in style and spirit with the work of Jackson Pollock, Pablo Picasso, and Claude Monet and sell for thousands of dollars apiece. One gallery owner thought they could easily sell for $50,000 (Marla Olmstead, 2004). Her work has appeared at some of New York's finest art galleries. Many art critics note that her pieces are rhythmic, beautiful, and magical. She has been featured on *Today* and *60 Minutes* as well as in the *New York Times* and *Time* magazine. Marla has garnered all this attention not because of the quality of her work alone but because of who she is. When she first burst onto the artistic scene, Marla was four years old—and she'd already been "painting" for two years.

At that young age, Marla used bright acrylic paints, which she splattered and scraped on large 36-square-foot canvases. She sometimes worked on one piece for days at a time, and her parents never knew exactly when she was done. When she decided she'd finished, she gave her paintings titles, printed her name at the bottom, and went on to a more typical interest for a young girl: a TV show, a doll, a swim in the pool.

While some critics doubted whether she was solely responsible for her work (in 2007, she was the subject of a skeptical documentary called *My Kid Could Paint That*), there's no doubt that she was a force in the art world. But was Marla's early work the expression of creative, artistic vision, or was it the result of a child playing around with paint? More important, who gets to decide if her work is defined as "art" or as "childish doodles"? The investors and collectors who pay thousands of dollars for each of her paintings clearly have a stake in its being defined as art. But what if she had never come to their attention and never sold a single piece? For something to be considered art, does it have to have some economic exchange value? And how do you think all the thousands of struggling artists who never sell anything their entire lives feel about Marla's instant and apparently effortless success? Would they be less inclined to define her as an "artist" than the investors who buy her work? These questions are not trivial. They reflect a deeper issue regarding the role of economics in shaping the way social reality is defined.

The key concerns from the conflict perspective are who benefits economically and who loses from dominant versions of reality. Take mental illness, for example. The number of problems officially defined by the American Psychiatric Association (APA) as mental disorders and defects has now reached nearly 400 (Horwitz, 2002). In defining what constitutes a mental disorder, the APA unwittingly reflects the economic organization of U.S. society. In the United States, individuals seldom pay the total costs of health care services out of their own pockets. Most of the money for medical treatment comes from the federal and state governments or from private insurance companies. Only if problems such as gambling, depression, anorexia, and cocaine addiction are formally defined as illnesses is their treatment eligible for medical insurance coverage. In 2010, the U.S. Department of Veterans Affairs changed its definition of posttraumatic stress disorder, making it substantially easier for hundreds of thousands of veterans to receive compensatory benefits. Posttraumatic stress disorder is a condition characterized by emotional numbness, irritability, and flashbacks following the experience or observation of some traumatic event. In the past, only soldiers who had been in combat and who could document specific firefights, bomb blasts, or mortar attacks qualified for benefits. Under the new rule, veterans only have to prove they served in a war zone and in a job consistent with the events they say caused their condition. The rule also allows compensation for service members who have a good reason to fear traumatic events even if they didn't experience them firsthand. It's estimated that this new rule will cost the government $5 billion in treatment costs over the next several years (Dao, 2010b).

Another example of how economics affects the social construction of reality is our society's history of attempts to protect people with disabilities. Approximately 25 million adult Americans and 6 million children have some type of disability (U.S. Bureau of the Census, 2011b). The 1990 Americans with Disabilities Act (ADA) defines disability as "a physical or mental impairment that substantially limits one or more of the major life activities of such individuals" (U.S. Department of Labor, 2004, p. 1). Under this law, employers are required to accommodate employees who have a documented disability and are forbidden to fire them simply because of their disability. For instance, a company that has wheelchair-bound employees must have ramps or elevators that give these workers access to all areas of the building. Ironically, the added cost of employing disabled workers may actually work to their disadvantage by making them less attractive to potential hirers in the first place. One study found an 11% drop in the employment rate of people with disabilities after the ADA was enacted (DeLeire, 2000). Moreover, highly publicized stories of employees with questionable disabilities seeking accommodations—for example, an office worker allergic to perfume demanding that his employer install an expensive new air filtration system—give the impression that the ADA is placing an excessive economic burden on companies. Although powerful businesses and industries were not able to prevent this act from being passed in the first place, they have been able to create a reality that still works in their interest.

The Politics of Reality

The institution of politics is also linked to societal definitions of reality. To a great extent, politics is about controlling public perceptions so people will do things or think about issues in ways that political leaders want them to. During important political campaigns, we can see such attempts to influence public perception. Mudslinging, euphemistically called "negative campaigning," has become as common an element of the U.S. electoral process as speeches, debates, baby kissing, and patriotic songs.

Most politicians know that if you say something untrue or unproven about an opponent often enough, people will believe it. In fact, while companies that sell consumer products must meet some standard of accuracy in their advertising, we have no federal truth-in-advertising for political campaign ads. Candidates have the legal right to lie ("Bunk Busters," 2007). Ironically, constant public denials of bogus charges often reinforce their reality and keep them in the news. In 2011, President Obama was forced to hold a news conference and present his birth certificate because the false claims that he isn't a U.S. citizen—which first arose during the 2008 election campaign—wouldn't go away. In some states, over half of Republican registered voters believed he was born outside the United States (D. Jackson, 2011). The validity of claims becomes irrelevant as accusations are transformed into "fact" and become solidified in the minds of the voting public. The problem has become so acute that a Web site, FactCheck.org, exists solely to monitor the factual accuracy of what major U.S. politicians say in TV ads, debates, speeches, interviews, and news releases.

When the lives of thousands of citizens are at stake and public opinion is crucial, information control becomes particularly tight. Between September 2001 and the invasion of Iraq in March 2003, the Bush administration worked diligently to foster a belief that Iraq and its then dictator, Saddam Hussein, played a direct role in the September 11 attacks and had stockpiles of weapons of mass destruction. They were quite successful. Immediately after the attacks, national opinion polls showed that only 3% of Americans mentioned Iraq or Saddam Hussein when asked who was responsible. But by January 2003, 44% of Americans reported that either "most" or "some" of the hijackers were Iraqi citizens. In fact, none were (Feldmann, Marlantes, & Bowers, 2003). Two years after the attacks, 69% of Americans said in a *Washington Post* poll that they thought it at least likely that Hussein was involved in the attacks, even though the link between Iraq and al-Qaeda was never established (Milbank & Deane, 2003). Nevertheless, these beliefs provided the kind of public support necessary to justify the military invasion and occupation of Iraq. In 2008, the Center for Public Integrity (2008) concluded that the administration had made close to 1,000 false public statements on either the existence of weapons of mass destruction or the link between al-Qaeda and Iraq. Such a molding of public perception is accomplished most notably through the media.

The Medium Is the Message

Communication media are the primary means by which we are entertained and informed about the world around us (see Chapter 5). But the messages we receive from the media also reflect dominant cultural values (Gitlin, 1979). In television shows and other works of fiction, the way characters are portrayed, the topics addressed, and the solutions imposed on problems all link entertainment to the economic system and prevailing societal tastes in consumption.

The media are also our primary source of information about local, national, and international events and people. News broadcasts and newspapers tell us about things we cannot experience directly, making the most remote events meaningful (Molotch & Lester, 1974). The way we look at the world and define our lives within it is therefore shaped and influenced by what we see on Internet news sites, watch on TV news shows, hear on the radio, or read in our daily papers.

Because the news is the means by which political realities are disseminated to the public, it is an essential tool in maintaining social order (Hallin, 1986; Parenti, 1986). In many societies, news sources don't even try to hide the fact that they are mouthpieces of one faction or another. In repressive societies, the only news sources allowed to operate are those representing the government. In North Korea, for instance, the flow of news information is clearly controlled by the government. People who live in societies with a cultural tradition of press independence, in contrast, assume that news stories are purely factual—an accurate, objective reflection of the "world out there" (Molotch & Lester, 1975). Like everything else, however, news is a constructed reality.

Hundreds, perhaps thousands, of potentially newsworthy events occur every day. Yet we'll see maybe 10 of them on our favorite evening broadcast or the homepage of our favorite online news service. These events exist as news not because of their inherent importance but because of the practical, political, or economic purposes they serve. The old newsroom adage "If it bleeds, it leads" attests to the fact that events with shocking details—which appeal to the public's fondness for the sensational—are those most likely to be chosen. At its most independent, the news is still the product of decisions made by reporters, editors, network executives, and corporation owners, all of whom have their own interests, biases, and values (Molotch & Lester, 1974).

The manipulation of events for political gain is such an ordinary part of the cultural landscape that it's become institutionalized with its own term: *spin*. To put a spin on an event is to give it a particular interpretation, often one that is to the speaker's advantage. Spin is a valuable political resource. Every U.S. president, whether Republican or Democrat, has staff members who spin the facts to put his policies in the best possible light, often by withholding information from the public, fudging statistics, issuing nondenial denials, or exaggerating the progress or benefits of particular actions and policies (Stolberg, 2004). And it's not just politicians who spin reality. Blogs are a continuing source of spin as they mix fact with the blogger's opinion, much of it selected and phrased to present a clearly one-sided version of reality. During the contentious debate over health care reform in 2009, interest groups on both sides attempted to sway public opinion by spending nearly $60 million on television advertisements in a span of six months (Seelye, 2009). Spin has become a profession in its own right. Immediately following a televised presidential debate, for instance, a gaggle of trained supporters (the "spin doctors") for both candidates situate themselves in a specified area—called "spin alley"—where they creatively provide television viewers with a version of the outcome that benefits their candidate. Top aides and party officials are dispatched to cable news programs and local news studios. Teams of researchers send dozens of messages to reporters covering the debate, accusing the other candidate of misstatements or lies.

Although "freedom of expression" and "freedom of the press" are core American values, media manipulation of information has been not only tolerated but encouraged in some situations. Take the coverage of the current military actions in Iraq and Afghanistan. During the initial stages of the war, press coverage seemed to be relatively open. The Pentagon allowed hundreds of "embedded" reporters to accompany fighting forces and transmit their stories from the front lines throughout the war. According to one study, 61% of their reports during the first three days of the war were live and unedited (Project for Excellence in Journalism, 2005). By granting such unprecedented access, Pentagon officials hoped that these reporters would convey the "heroism and hard work" of American soldiers to a worldwide audience and in the process discredit Iraqi propaganda (Getlin & Wilkinson, 2003).

But even then, some media critics were concerned that the reporters were tools of the military, especially given their often close attachment to the soldiers with whom they were traveling. The Pentagon required embedded journalists to sign a contract giving the military control over the content of their stories (Jamail, 2007). According to one study, 80% of early embedded reports included no commentary at all from soldiers (Project for Excellence in Journalism, 2005). In addition, there is evidence that military personnel and news organizations fabricated stories to present the war in a favorable light. For instance, after the former NFL (National Football League) player Pat Tillman was killed in Afghanistan, the Army told his family (and the country via the media) that he had died in a heroic struggle with the enemy, when in fact he'd been killed by "friendly fire." Yet the Army used his death as an opportunity to create a feel-good media story, going so far as to keep eyewitnesses from talking to the press, cutting off Internet service to the base, and even burning Tillman's uniform (Alter, 2007).

For everyday news stories, even in societies that restrict the press, official censorship is usually unnecessary. Because of the economic pressures to attract audiences and keep their attention, TV networks and newspapers usually censor themselves (Bagdikian, 1991). Reporters pursue stories that are relatively easy to research and that have immediate interest for audiences. Less exciting, more complicated stories don't get enough journalistic resources or are cut in the editing process. We usually have no way of knowing which events have *not* been selected for inclusion in the day's news or which plausible alternatives are kept out of the public eye.

The economic and political motivation for such selectivity becomes apparent when we consider who owns the media. For instance, one company, Clear Channel, owns about 850 radio stations in all 50 states, reaching more than 154 million listeners—or 75% of the 18 and older U.S. population—every week (Clear Channel Communications, 2011). By comparison, the next top company, Cumulus Media, owns only 303 stations (Project for Excellence in Journalism, 2006). Another, the Sinclair Broadcast Group (2011), owns and operates 58 television stations in 35 markets and reaches an estimated 22% of U.S. television-watching households. In 1983, 50 companies controlled over half of all U.S. media outlets; by 2009, six companies—General Electric, Viacom, Disney, Time Warner, CBS, and News Corp—owned over half of all media outlets, concentrating control over what we see, hear, and read (Free Press, 2010).

Many media observers fear that the consolidation of corporate-owned news outlets twists certain stories to promote particular economic or political interests. In recent years, media owners have refused to run advertisements, stories, or commentaries that supported single-payer health insurance, criticized U.S. military intervention, or opposed certain international trade agreements. Television and print journalists have been fired, forced to resign, or reassigned for presenting stories critical of subsidiaries owned by the parent company (Parenti, 2006).

As the viewing and listening public, our recourse is difficult. To criticize faulty government policies and consider solutions to difficult social problems, we need solid information, which is frequently unavailable or difficult to obtain. The recent growth in popularity of podcasting, blogs, Internet Protocol television, micro radio stations, and subscription satellite networks may be a sign that some citizens are growing weary of the filtered and sometimes partisan information they receive from traditional news sources. Indeed, distrust of the news media has become so acute that some people turn to deliberately fake news/comedy shows like *The Daily Show* and *The Colbert Report* to keep abreast of national and world events.

So the challenge we face in our own private lives is to recognize the processes at work in the social construction of reality and to take them into account as we "consume" the news. A critical dimension of the sociological imagination is the ability to "read silences"—to be attentive to what the mass media *don't* say. Fortunately, one of the purposes of sociology is to scientifically amass a body of knowledge that we can use to assess how our society really works.

Moral Entrepreneurs

Individual efforts to control the construction of reality are difficult. But we are not consigned to meekly accept the reality presented to us by powerful organizations and institutions. Individuals banding together in interest groups have managed time and again to contribute to the construction of social reality. For instance, they have created new understandings of the rights of ethnoracial minorities, brought environmental degradation to the public's attention, and changed our attitudes toward particular crimes.

Although economic and political power have been the motivating concerns of many of these groups, certain people have had moral concerns they passionately want translated into law. Groups that seek to outlaw or increase the punishment for such things as pornography, drunk driving, sexually explicit song lyrics, abortion, gambling, and homosexuality, as well as groups that promote gun control, literacy, awareness of domestic violence, and support for AIDS research, are crusading for the creation of a new public conception of morality. These *moral entrepreneurs* (Becker, 1963) need not be wealthy or influential individuals. Instead, by virtue of their initiative, access to decision makers, skillful use of publicity and public relations, and success in neutralizing any opposing viewpoints, they are able to turn their interests into public policy (Hills, 1980). Sometimes groups seek to convince the public that a phenomenon that is currently a crime ought not be. For instance, people trying to convince legislators to legalize the use of marijuana for medicinal purposes have shown moderate success by emphasizing the medical properties of marijuana (pain or nausea relief) and disregarding the psychoactive effects associated with its recreational use (getting "high"). Indeed, many avoid the term *marijuana* entirely, opting instead for the more scientific-sounding *cannabis* (Chapkis, 2010).

(Text continues on page 81)

Personal Billboards

Liz Grauerholz and Rebecca Smith

Virtually everything we experience in our lives is mediated through language and symbols. At times, we sit back and passively accept the linguistic reality that others create. At other times, through our selective use of language and imagery, we actively attempt to construct, or at least influence, others' perceptions of reality. Bumper stickers and T-shirts are powerful forms of this sort of communication, pithy and to the point.

These "personal billboards" communicate messages cheaply and are available to any group or individual with a vehicle or a wardrobe. They are not reserved solely for powerful people or those whom the media deem worthy of coverage. In fact, personal billboards are some of the most powerful "voices" for underprivileged groups. No matter who uses them or what their messages are, they advertise a reality to others about who we are, what we stand for, and what we consider important.

The messages on T-shirts cover the cultural spectrum . . .

...as do the messages on bumper stickers.

Personal billboards are often used as a means of communicating group pride and identity. They reinforce the reality and vitality of the groups they represent.

Such communicative displays are especially prominent during crises, although different cultures might present very different realities. In the days immediately following the terrorist attacks of September 11, 2001, Americans and people living in southern Asia felt a similar need to express solidarity but with very different messages.

This Pakistani Muslim cleric displays a T-shirt lauding Osama bin Laden as Hero of Islam.

T-shirts and bumper stickers can also provide greater awareness of oppressed groups and their causes. Certain classes, ethnic and religious groups, age groups, sexual minority groups, and political interest groups struggle for control over resources and for the power to determine or influence society's conception of reality.

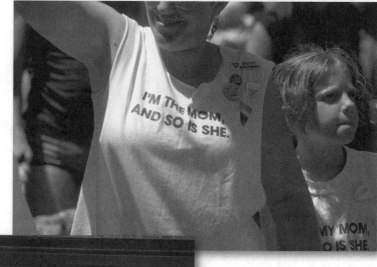

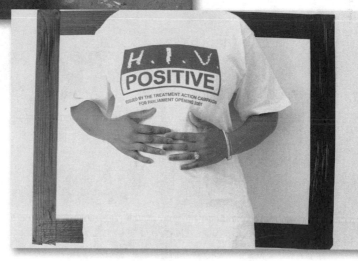

Oppressed Americans are not unique in displaying messages on their cars or clothing.

In Australia…

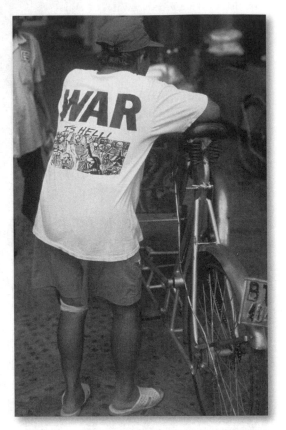

In Vietnam…

In England…

Moral entrepreneurs have social concerns they passionately want translated into law. Often, their personal billboards are designed to dramatize the emotional impact of the underlying message.

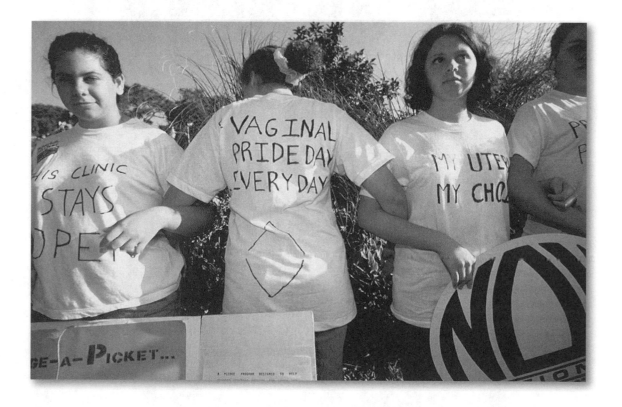

Moral entrepreneurs need not be wealthy or influential individuals. If they succeed in turning their interests into public policy, it is by virtue of their access to decision makers, skillful use of publicity, success in neutralizing any opposing viewpoints—and most of all, their initiative in making their desires known. For instance, the citizens of Northern Ireland were a key element in forcing the political compromise designed to stop decades of sectarian violence between Catholics and Protestants. Ordinary people like the men pictured here, whose voices had long been drowned out by strident and violent radicals on both sides of the conflict, helped to give political leaders the moral authority to move toward peace.

Appreciating the Contributions of Sociological Research

Up to this point, I've been describing how individuals, groups, organizations, and various social institutions go about constructing reality. We've seen that these realities sometimes shift with time, place, and individual perception. Faced with this type of fluctuation, sociologists, as well as scholars in other disciplines, seek to identify a more "real" reality through systematic, controlled research. The rules sociologists abide by when conducting research give them confidence that they are identifying more than just a personal version of reality. They hope to determine a reality as it exists for a community of people at a particular point in time.

Moving beyond the level of individual conclusions about the nature of social reality is crucial if we are to escape the distortions of personal interests and biases. A danger of relying solely on individual perceptions is that we are likely to conclude that what we experience is what everyone experiences. For example, the famous psychiatrist Sigmund Freud used his own childhood as the ultimate "proof" of the controversial concept called the Oedipus complex (the belief that sons are secretly in love with their mothers and jealous of their fathers). He wrote to a friend in 1897, "I have found, in my own case too, being in love with the mother and jealous of the father, and I now consider it a universal event of early childhood" (quoted in Astbury, 1996, p. 73).

To avoid the risk of such overgeneralizations, sociologists try to determine what most people believe or how most people behave. But in doing so, they sometimes run the risk of simply restating what people already know. Indeed, a criticism of sociology you hear from time to time is that it is just a fancy version of common sense. A lot of the things that we think are obvious based on our personal observations, however, turn out not to be so straightforward under the closer scrutiny of social research. Consider the following "commonsense facts":

- Rape, assault, and murder occur most often between total strangers.
- Because of the high divorce rate in the United States, people are reluctant to get married.
- American children today are more likely to live in a single-parent household than they were 100 years ago.

Most of us probably assume these statements are true. Given what you've read or seen on television, they probably make a lot of sense. But how accurate are they?

According to the U.S. Bureau of Justice Statistics (2011), over the past three decades, only 14% of all homicides in the U.S. were perpetrated by strangers. In addition, only 44% of assaults, 28% of rapes, and 46% of attempted rapes involve strangers. The rest occur between acquaintances, friends, colleagues, romantic partners, and family members. In 61% of rapes and sexual assaults, the victim knew the attacker (U.S. Department of Justice, 2008). Among female college students, that figure increases to 74% (Hart, 2003).

According to the U.S. Bureau of the Census (2011b), less than 8% of people between the ages of 55 and 64 have never been married. In fact, about two thirds of divorced women and three fourths of divorced men eventually remarry (Cherlin, 1992). Although we have become increasingly willing to end a bad marriage, we still tend to place a high value on the institution of marriage itself.

The percentage of children who don't live with both their parents—about 33% of all children (U.S. Bureau of the Census, 2010)—is roughly the same as it was a century ago.

At that time, life expectancy was much lower than it is today, so it was highly likely that before reaching adulthood a child would lose at least one parent to death (Kain, 1990).

As you can see, sometimes commonsense "facts" don't hold up under the weight of evidence provided by social research.

The Empirical Nature of Sociological Research

Research is all around us. Throughout our lives, we are flooded with statistics that are supposedly the result of scientific studies—which detergents make clothes brighter, which conditioners repair hair better, which dog food tastes best, which wireless providers have the widest 4G coverage, which chewing gum dentists recommend for their gum-chewing patients. Many of the important decisions we make, from purchasing a car to opting for a particular surgical procedure, are supported by some sort of research.

In addition, a significant proportion of our own lives is spent *doing* research. Every time we seek out the opinions of others, gauge the attitude of a group, or draw conclusions about an event, we engage in a form of research. Say, for example, you thought your exam scores would improve if you studied with others, so you formed a study group. After the exam, you compared your grade with the grade you received on the previous exam (when you just studied on your own) to see if there was any significant improvement. If there was, you would likely attribute your better performance to the study group. This is the essence of research: You had an idea about some social process, and you went out and tested it to see if you were correct.

Although useful and common, such casual research is fraught with problems. We may make inaccurate or selective observations, overgeneralize on the basis of a limited number of observations, or draw conclusions that protect our own interests (Babbie, 1992). Maybe your exam score would have improved even without the study group because you had a better understanding of the material this time and had a better sense of what the instructor expected.

Sociological research, which is a much more sophisticated and structured form of the sort of individual inquiry we use every day, can avoid some of these pitfalls. Of course, sociological researchers are human beings, and they too make errors in observation, generalization, and analysis. But they have a greater chance of avoiding these errors because, first and foremost, sociological research is an empirical endeavor. *Empirical research* operates on the assumption that answers to questions about human behavior can be ascertained through controlled, systematic observations in the real world. Individuals can reach naive conclusions based on their personal impressions of what happens in society. Great scholars can spend years thinking about human life and developing logical explanations about particular social phenomena. But for most sociologists, the strength of an explanation depends on how much empirical support it has.

Another characteristic of sociological research that makes it a better reflection of social reality than individual inquiry is that it is *probabilistic.* Instead of making absolute predictions, most sociologists prefer to state that under certain conditions particular phenomena are likely to occur. In other words, human behavior operates within the laws of probability. Whenever sociologists set out to find the reasons, say, for why people hold prejudiced beliefs or why some countries have a higher birth rate than others, they are searching for the factors that would explain these phenomena most but not all of the time. For instance, adults with less than a high school education are more likely than adults with college degrees to be prejudiced against members of other ethnoracial groups. But that doesn't mean that every single high school dropout is a bigot or that every person with a Ph.D. embraces those who are ethnically or racially different. By focusing on the probability of some phenomenon occurring while at the same time allowing for exceptions and variations, sociologists provide a view of reality that simultaneously reflects the way things are and the way they can be.

Qualitative and Quantitative Research

In contrast to the casual way we carry out our personal research, sociologists seek to define reality through a careful process of collecting information and answering questions. Some sociologists collect nonnumeric information (text, written words, phrases, symbols, observations) that describes people, actions, or events in social life (called *qualitative research*; Neuman, 1994). Others collect numeric data and rely on precise statistical analysis (called *quantitative research*). And some use a combination of both.

Qualitative researchers often go out and observe people and events as they happen in society. For instance, qualitative researchers interested in how additional children affect parents' ability to balance the demands of work and home may spend an entire day with a family, listening, observing, and asking questions (Upton, in press). Once they've collected enough information, they go about interpreting their observations, looking for identifiable patterns in people's everyday lives.

Quantitative sociological researchers methodically record observations across a variety of situations; they design and choose questions in advance and ask them in a consistent way of a large number of people; they use sophisticated techniques to ensure that the characteristics of the people in a study are similar to those of the population at large; and they use computers to generate statistics from which confident conclusions can be drawn.

Both kinds of sociological research are subjected to the scrutiny of peers, who will point out any mistakes and shortcomings. Researchers are obligated to report not only their results but also the methods they used to record observations or collect data and the conditions surrounding the study. Such detailed explanations allow other researchers to replicate a study—that is, to perform it themselves to see if the same results are obtained. The more a particular research result is replicated, the greater its acceptance as fact in the sociological community.

Theories, Variables, and Hypotheses

Whether qualitative or quantitative, social research is purposeful. Unlike personal research, which may be motivated by a hunch, whim, or immediate need, most social research is guided by a particular theory. A *theory* is a set of statements or propositions that seeks to explain or predict a particular aspect of social life (Chafetz, 1978). Theory does not, as is popularly thought, mean conjecture or speculation. Ideally, theories explain the way things are, not the way they ought to be.

Research and theory closely depend on each other. Research without any underlying theoretical reasoning is simply a string of meaningless bits of information (C. W. Mills, 1959); theory without research is abstract and speculative.

Some theories—such as structural functionalism, the conflict perspective, and symbolic interactionism—are quite broad, seeking to explain why social order exists or how societies work overall. Other theories are more modest, seeking to explain more narrowly certain behaviors among specific groups of people. For example, Travis Hirschi (1969) developed a theory of juvenile delinquency called "social control theory," in which he argued that delinquent acts occur when an individual's bond to society is weak or broken. These bonds are derived from a person's attachments to others who obey the law, the rewards a person gains by acting nondelinquently (commitments), the amount of time a person engages in nondelinquent activity (involvements), and the degree to which a person is tied to society's conventional belief system.

To test theories, sociologists must translate abstract propositions into testable hypotheses. A ***hypothesis*** is a researchable prediction that specifies the relationship between two or more ***variables.*** A variable is any characteristic, attitude, behavior, or event that can take on two or more values or attributes. For example, the variable "marital status" has several categories: never married, cohabiting, married, separated, divorced, widowed. The variable "attitudes toward capital punishment" has categories ranging from "strongly in favor" to "strongly oppose."

Hirschi was interested in why juveniles engage in delinquent behavior. Such a question is far too general to study empirically, so he developed a clear, specific, empirically testable prediction, or hypothesis, specifying a relationship between two variables: Strong "social bonds" will be associated with low levels of "delinquency."

In developing their hypotheses, sociologists distinguish between independent and dependent variables. The ***independent variable*** is the factor presumed to influence or create changes in another variable. The ***dependent variable*** is the one assumed to depend on, be influenced by, or change as a result of the independent variable. If we believe that gender affects people's attitudes toward capital punishment, then "gender" would be the independent variable influencing "attitudes toward capital punishment," the dependent variable. For Hirschi's theory of juvenile delinquency, the strength of the social bond was the independent variable, and level of delinquency was the dependent variable.

The assumption behind most research that tests a hypothesis is that the independent variable *causes* changes to occur in the dependent variable—for instance, that a weak social bond *causes* a young person to become delinquent. But just because two variables seem to be related doesn't necessarily mean a causal relationship exists.

In fact, the two variables may not be related at all but merely seem to be associated with each other due to the effect of some third variable. Sociologists call such false relationships spurious. A classic example of a ***spurious relationship*** is the apparent association between children's shoe size and reading ability. It seems that as shoe size increases, reading ability improves (Babbie, 2007). Does this mean that the size of one's feet (independent variable) *causes* an improvement in reading skills (dependent variable)? Certainly not. This illusory relationship is caused by a third factor, age, that is related to shoe size (older kids have bigger feet) as well as reading ability (older kids can read better than younger kids). Hence, when researchers attempt to make causal claims about the relationship between an independent and a dependent variable, they must control for—or rule out—other variables that may be creating a spurious relationship. Can you think of a third variable that might strengthen or weaken a person's social bond *and* influence his or her tendency toward delinquent behavior?

Aside from concern with spuriousness, quantitative social researchers, like Hirschi, face the problem that many of the concepts that form the basis of theories are abstract and not easy to observe or measure empirically. We can't directly see concepts such as "attachments" or "commitments." So they must be translated into *indicators*: events, characteristics, or behaviors that can be observed or quantified.

In his survey of 1,200 boys in Grades 6 through 12, Hirschi derived a set of indicators for his independent variable, the strength of the social bond. To determine young people's attachments to law-abiding others, Hirschi measured their attraction to parents, peers, and school officials. To determine the degree to which they derived rewards from acting nondelinquently (commitment), he asked them to assess the importance of things such as getting good grades. To determine the proportion of their lives spent in conventional activities (involvement), he asked them how much time they spent in school-oriented activities. Finally, to determine their ties to a conventional belief system, he asked them questions about their respect for the law and the police.

Hirschi measured the dependent variable, delinquent activity, by asking the boys if they'd ever stolen things, taken cars for rides without the owner's permission, banged up something on purpose that belonged to somebody else, or beaten up or hurt someone on purpose. In addition, he used school records and police records to measure delinquent acts that had come to the attention of authorities.

The empirical data he collected supported his hypothesis. The boys who indicated close attachments to their parents and peers, who got good grades, who were involved in lots of school-related activities, and who had high levels of respect for the law were the boys who didn't get into trouble. Hirschi was therefore able to use these results to strengthen the power of his original theory.

Modes of Research

Although the answers to important sociological questions are not always simple or clear, the techniques sociologists use to collect and examine data allow them to draw informed and reliable conclusions about human behavior and social life. The most common techniques are experiments, field research, surveys, and unobtrusive research.

Experiments

An *experiment* is typically a research technique designed to elicit some sort of behavior under closely controlled laboratory circumstances. In its ideal form, the experimenter randomly places participants into two groups, then deliberately manipulates or introduces changes into the environment of one group of participants (called the experimental group) and not the other (called the control group). Care is taken to ensure that the groups are relatively alike except for the variable that the experimenter manipulates. Any observed or measured differences between the groups can then be attributed to the effects of the experimental manipulation.

Experiments have a significant advantage over other types of research because the researcher can directly control all the relevant variables. Thus, conclusions about the independent variable causing changes in the dependent variable can be made more convincingly. The artificial nature of most laboratory experiments, however, may make subjects behave differently than the way they would in their natural settings, leading some people to argue that laboratory experimentation in sociology is practically impossible (Silverman, 1982).

To overcome this difficulty, some sociologists have created experimental situations outside the laboratory. Arthur Beaman and his colleagues (Beaman, Klentz, Diener, &

Svanum, 1979) conducted an experiment to see whether self-awareness decreases the likelihood of engaging in socially undesirable behavior—in this case, stealing. The researchers set up situations in which children arriving at several homes on Halloween night were sent into the living room alone to take candy from a bowl. The children were first asked their names and ages and then told, "You may take only one of the candies." For the experimental group, a large mirror was placed right next to the candy bowl so that the children couldn't help but see themselves. For the control group, there was no mirror. In the control group, 37% of the children took more than one candy, but only 4% of the children in the experimental group took more than one candy. The researchers concluded from this experiment that self-awareness—brought about by seeing one's reflection in a mirror—can significantly reduce dishonesty.

Experimental research outside the laboratory can also be used to inform public policy. In 2010, the City of New York embarked on a two-year experimental test of the effectiveness of its six-year-old homelessness prevention program, a $23 million endeavor called Homebase. Half of the test subjects—people who are unable to pay their rent and therefore risk eviction—are being denied assistance from the program as researchers observe them to see if they become homeless. The other half receive the program's regular assistance services, including tenant-landlord mediation, emergency rental assistance, and job training (Buckley, 2010). The city hopes to determine if the program's intervention actually makes a difference in reducing the number of homeless. Some public officials have denounced the experiment as unethical and cruel.

Field Research

In *field research*, qualitative sociologists observe events as they actually occur, without selecting experimental and control groups or purposely introducing any changes into the subjects' environment. Field research can take several forms. In *nonparticipant observation*, the researcher observes people without directly interacting with them and without their knowing that they are being observed. Sociologist Lyn Lofland (1973), for example, studied how strangers relate to one another in public places by going to bus depots, airports, stores, restaurants, and parks and secretly recording everything she saw.

Participant observation requires that the researcher interact with subjects. In some cases, the researcher openly identifies herself or himself. For instance, to gain insight into how people balance work and family, sociologist Arlie Russell Hochschild (1997) observed employees over a period of three years at a large public relations company she called Amerco. She was particularly interested in why employees tend not to take advantage of available family leave policies. At Amerco, only 53 of 21,000 employees—all of them women—chose to switch to part-time work in response to the arrival of a new baby. Less than 1% of the employees shared a job or worked at home, even though the company permits it. Most of the workers worked a lot of overtime, coming in early and staying late. So why were these workers so unwilling to change their work lives to spend more time with their families even when the company would have supported them in doing so? Through her long-term observations of Amerco, Hochschild came to the conclusion that work has become a form of "home" and home has become "work." For many people at Amerco, home had become a place of frenzied activity and busy schedules, whereas work had become a sort of nurturing refuge where they could relax and share stories with friends. So they actually preferred spending more time at work.

This type of qualitative field research can be quite time-consuming. Researchers can conduct only a limited number of interviews and can observe only a limited number of people and events. Hochschild collected rich information about people's work-family trade-offs, but she could study only one corporation. It's risky to generalize from the experiences of a small group of workers in one company in one society to all workers in all sorts of work environments.

In more delicate situations where the people being studied don't want their actions made public, the researcher may have to conceal his or her identity in order to gather accurate information. For instance, researchers have gone "undercover" to study everything from doomsday cults (Festinger, Riecken, & Schacter, 1956) to college sororities (Robbins, 2004). Sociologist Julia O'Connell Davidson (2002) wanted to examine the issue of power and control in the relationships between prostitutes and their clients. To study this topic, she posed as a "receptionist" for a prostitute she called "Desiree," fielding phone calls and supervising the "waiting room" for the clients who had arrived to see Desiree. While Desiree knew O'Connell Davidson was a sociologist, the clients did not. If these men knew they were being studied, they might have altered their conversations and behaviors to cover up potentially damaging information.

Surveys

When it is impossible or impractical to carry out field observations or to set up a controlled experimental situation, social researchers use the survey method. *Surveys* require that the researcher pose a series of questions to respondents either orally, electronically, or on paper. The questions should be sufficiently clear so they are understood by the respondent the way the researcher wants them to be understood and measure what the researcher wants them to measure. In addition, the respondent is expected to answer the questions honestly and thoughtfully. The answers are often recorded in numerical form so they can be statistically analyzed.

All of us have experienced surveys of one form or another. Every 10 years, people who live in the United States are required to fill out questionnaires for the U.S. Census Bureau. You've probably filled out an evaluation form at the end of a college course. Or perhaps you've been interviewed in a shopping mall or have received an e-mail asking you to respond to a "brief survey" about a particular product or service.

Surveys typically use standardized formats. All subjects are asked the same questions in the same way, and large samples of people are used as subjects. One survey that has provided the basis for much sociological research on families is the National Survey of Families and Households. First conducted in the late 1980s, it includes information derived from interviews with over 13,000 respondents. A second wave of the survey, conducted between 1992 and 1994, and a third wave between 2001 and 2003 included interviews with surviving members of the original sample. The sample covers a diverse array of households, including single-parent families, families with stepchildren, cohabiting couples, and recently married persons. A great deal of family information was collected from each respondent, including family arrangements in childhood, dating experiences, experiences of leaving home, marital and cohabitation experiences, details of contact with kin, and data on economic well-being, as well as education, childbearing, and employment histories. Some of the research discussed in this book is based on analyses of data collected from this survey.

When sociologists Philip Blumstein and Pepper Schwartz (1983) undertook a massive study of intimate couples in the United States, they sent questionnaires to people from every income level, age group, religion, political ideology, and educational background. Some of their respondents were cohabiting; others were married. Some had children; others were childless. Some were heterosexual, others homosexual. All couples filled out a 38-page questionnaire that asked questions about their leisure activities, emotional support, housework, finances, sexual relations, satisfaction, relations with children, and so forth. More than 6,000 couples participated. From these surveys, Blumstein and Schwartz were able to draw conclusions about the importance of money, work, sexuality, power, and gender in couples' lives.

Unobtrusive Research

All the methods I've discussed so far—whether quantitative or qualitative—require the researcher to have some contact with the people being studied: giving them tasks to do in an experiment, watching them (with or without their knowing that they are participating in social research), or asking them questions. But the very act of intruding into people's lives may influence the phenomena being studied. This problem, known as *reactivity*, calls into question the accuracy of the data that are collected, thereby threatening the credibility of the research.

In the late 1920s, an engineer and a time study analyst (Roethlisberger & Dickson, 1939) were hired to study working conditions and worker productivity at an electric company in Hawthorne, Illinois. They were interested in finding out whether changing certain physical conditions in the plant could improve workers' productivity and satisfaction. They quickly discovered that increasing the lighting in the workroom was linked with workers' producing more. Increasing the brightness of the lights again the next day increased productivity even further. To bolster their conclusion, they decided to dim the lights to see if productivity dropped. Much to their dismay, productivity increased again when they darkened the room. They soon realized that the workers were responding more to the attention they were receiving from the researchers than to changes in their working conditions. This phenomenon is known as the "Hawthorne effect."

To avoid such influence, sociologists sometimes use another research technique, unobtrusive research, which requires no contact with people at all. *Unobtrusive research* is an examination of the evidence of social behavior that people create or leave behind. There are several types of unobtrusive research.

Analysis of existing data (also known as secondary data) relies on data gathered earlier by someone else for some other purpose. Émile Durkheim used this technique when he examined different suicide rates for different groups to gain insight into the underlying causes of suicide (see Chapter 1). Analysis of existing data is still used extensively by sociologists today. One of the most popular and convenient sources of data is the U.S. Census. Studies that examine broad, nationwide trends (e.g., marriage, divorce, or premarital childbearing rates) typically use existing census data.

Content analysis is the study of documented communications—books, speeches, poems, song lyrics, television commercials, Web sites, and so forth. For example, sociologists Bernice Pescosolido, Elizabeth Grauerholz, and Melissa Milkie (1997) analyzed close to 2,000 children's picture books published from 1937 to 1993 to see if there were any changes in the way African Americans were portrayed. They believed that these depictions could tell a lot about the shifting nature of race relations in the larger society. The researchers looked not only at the number of black characters in these books but also at whether they were portrayed positively or negatively. They found, among other things, that in times of high uncertainty in race relations and substantial protest and conflict over existing societal norms, Blacks virtually disappeared from picture books. Furthermore, depictions of intimate, equal interracial interactions and portrayals of Blacks as primary characters remained rare.

Similarly, sociologists Sarah Brabant and Linda Mooney (1999) were interested in how families and race were portrayed in Sunday newspaper comics and, therefore, what messages readers receive about families through the media. They studied three cartoon families (in *Dennis the Menace, Calvin and Hobbes,* and *Curtis*) by analyzing all the strips from these cartoons appearing in one year. They found that the comic strip *Curtis,* which depicts an African American family, showed more family unity and social engagement than the ones that depicted white families. White families were portrayed as more isolated from other families and the community at large, and from one another.

Historical analysis relies on existing historical documents as a source of research information. Sociologist Kai Erikson (1966) was interested in how communities construct definitions of acceptable and unacceptable behavior. For his book *Wayward Puritans,* he studied several "crime waves" among the Puritans of the Massachusetts Bay Colony in the late 17th century. Erikson examined court cases, diaries, birth and death records, letters, and other written documents of the period. Piecing together fragments of information 300 years old was not easy, but Erikson was able to draw some conclusions. He found that each time the colony was threatened in some way—by opposing religious groups, betrayals by community leaders, or the king of England's revocation of its charter—the number of convicted criminals and the severity of punishments significantly increased. Erikson believed that these fluctuations occurred because the community needed to restate its moral boundaries and reaffirm its authority.

Visual sociology is a method of studying society through photographs, video recordings, and film. Some visual sociologists use these media to gather sociological data—much as documentary photographers and filmmakers do. The visual images they create are meant to tell a sociological story. Other visual sociologists analyze the meaning and purpose of existing visual texts, such as sports photographs, TV advertisements, and the photographic archives of corporations. The visual essays that appear throughout this book use this methodology to examine important issues of sociological interest.

All these methods allow sociological researchers to collect information without intruding on and possibly changing the behavior of the people and groups they're studying.

The Trustworthiness of Social Research

Most sociologists see research as not only personally valuable but central to improving human knowledge and understanding. However, as consumers of this research, we must always ask, "How accurate is this information?" Sometimes it's difficult to interpret the evidence we come across in scholarly research articles (see Exhibit 3.1). Moreover, because we have a tendency to believe what we read in print or see reported on television or posted on Web sites, much of what we see may be either inaccurate or misleading. To evaluate the results of social research, we must examine the researcher's samples, the indicators used to measure important variables, and the researcher's personal qualities—namely, values, interests, and ethics.

Exhibit 3.1   Questions to Ask When You Read a Research Article

As you read a piece of published sociological research, you may be more able to assess the value of the research and the results if you ask yourself some questions about the article:

- What is the basic research problem the researcher is investigating?
- Is the research question derived from a particular sociological theory?
- Were any hypotheses stated? How were these hypotheses different from those tested in previous research?
- What type of research was used? Experiment? Survey? Use of existing statistics? Field research? Unobtrusive research?
- What were the independent and dependent variables? Did the author explain how the variables were measured?
- Who were the subjects in the study? How were they selected? Did the author think the sample was representative of the general population?
- What did the research find? How clearly were the statistical results discussed?
- Is there anything else you'd want to know about how the research was carried out that wasn't discussed by the author?

SOURCE: Adapted from Schutt, 2006

Samples

Frequently, sociological researchers are interested in the attitudes, behaviors, or characteristics of large groups—college students, women, sports enthusiasts, single parents, and so on. It would be impossible to interview, survey, observe, or experiment on all these people directly. Hence, researchers must select a smaller **sample** of respondents from the larger population. The characteristics of this subgroup are supposed to approximate the characteristics of the entire population of interest. A sample is said to be **representative** if the small group being studied is in fact typical of the population as a whole. For instance, a sample of 100 students from your university should include roughly the same proportion of first-year students, sophomores, juniors, and seniors that characterizes the entire school population. Sampling techniques have become highly sophisticated, as illustrated by the relative accuracy of polls conducted to predict election results.

In the physical sciences, sampling is not such an issue. Certain physical or chemical elements are assumed to be identical. One need only study a small number of vials of liquid nitrogen, because one vial of nitrogen should be the same as any other. Human beings, however, vary widely on every imaginable characteristic. You couldn't make a general statement about all Americans on the basis of an interview with one person. For that matter, you couldn't draw conclusions about all people from observing a sample consisting only of Americans, men, or teenagers. Samples that are not representative can lead to inaccurate and misleading conclusions.

Note the sampling problems revealed in the following letter to the editor of a small-town newspaper in the rural Midwest:

> I went to a restaurant yesterday for lunch. I began to feel guilty, when I reached into my pocket for a cigarette. . . . I was thinking of the government figures which estimated cigarette smokers at 26% of the population of the United States. But everywhere I looked inside that room, people were smoking. I decided to count them. There were 22 people in the room. . . . I was surprised to discover that the government's figures were an outright fabrication. . . . Seventeen people out of the 22 were cigarette smokers . . . that accounts for over 77% of the people in that restaurant. . . . The government's figures are understated by 51% and just plain wrong! (*Greencastle Banner Graphic*, 1992)

This letter writer assumed that the 22 people who frequented a small restaurant in a small, relatively poor rural town on a single day were an accurate representation of the entire U.S. population. Such a conclusion overlooks some important factors. Government studies show that the lower a person's income, the greater the likelihood that person will be a smoker. Furthermore, people in blue collar or service jobs are more likely to smoke than people in white collar jobs. Finally, the prevalence of smoking tends to be higher in rural areas of the Midwest and South than in other parts of the country (U.S. Department of Health and Human Services, 2006).

MICRO-MACRO CONNECTION

The WEIRDest People in the World

Biased samples can be especially misleading when researchers attempt to make broad statements about human nature. For instance, American undergraduate students make up about two thirds of subjects in all U.S. psychological studies, the topics of which range from visual perceptions to beliefs about fairness and cooperation. However, according to one recent review of such experiments, these subjects are totally unrepresentative of people worldwide. They may be similar to other subjects from societies that are Western, educated, industrialized, rich, and democratic (WEIRD), but not representative of humans at large:

> Sampling from a thin slice of humanity would be less problematic if researchers confined their interpretations to the populations from which they sampled. However, despite their narrow samples, behavioral scientists often are interested in drawing inferences about the *human* mind and *human* behaviour. . . . Leading scientific journals and university textbooks routinely publish research findings claiming to generalize to "humans" or "people" based on research done entirely with WEIRD undergraduates. (Henrich, Heine, & Norenzayan, 2010, p. 63)

In one common experiment on fairness and cooperation in decision making, one subject (the "proposer") in a pair is given a sum of money and told that she or he can offer any portion of it to a second subject (the "responder"), who then decides whether to accept or reject the offer. If the responder accepts the offer, both subjects receive the proposed amount; if the responder rejects the offer, both subjects get nothing. Among WEIRD undergraduate subjects, proposers typically offer about 50% of the original amount and responders tend to reject offers below 30%. From these findings researchers have concluded that humans have a highly evolved sense of justice, leading us to make fair offers and to punish unfair ones, even if it comes at our own expense.

But when this experiment was conducted with subjects drawn from 23 small-scale societies in Africa, the Amazon rain forest, Oceania, Siberia, and Papua New Guinea, proposers made much smaller offers—in some cases, around 25%—and responders usually didn't reject them. In fact, in half of these societies, responders tended to reject offers only when they were *too high* (Henrich et al., 2010). Hence, experiments that utilize samples of WEIRD subjects may be measuring a specific set of social norms that emerge in societies where people regularly deal with money, markets, and strangers and not some universal component of human nature.

Indicators

As you recall, one problem sociologists face when doing research is that the variables they are interested in studying are often difficult to see. What does powerlessness look like? How can you identify marital satisfaction? How would you recognize alienation or social class? Sociologists thus resign themselves to measuring indicators of things that cannot be measured directly. Researchers measure events and behaviors commonly thought to accompany a particular variable, hoping that what they are measuring is a valid indicator of the concept they are interested in.

Suppose you believe that people's attitudes toward abortion are influenced by the strength of their religious beliefs, or "religiosity." You might hypothesize that the stronger a person's religious beliefs, the less accepting he or she will be of abortion rights. To test this hypothesis, you must first figure out what you mean by "religious." What might be an indicator of the strength of someone's religious beliefs? You could determine whether the subjects of your study identify themselves as members of some organized religion. But this indicator might not tell you how religious your subjects are because many people identify themselves as, say, Catholic or Jewish but are not religious at all. Likewise, some people who consider themselves quite religious don't identify with any organized religion. So this measure would focus on group differences but would fail to capture the intensity of a person's beliefs or the degree of religious interest.

Perhaps a better indicator would be some quantifiable behavior, such as the frequency of attendance at formal religious services (Babbie, 1986). Arguably, the more someone attends church, synagogue, or mosque, the more religious that person is. But here, too, we run into problems. Church attendance, for instance, may reflect family pressure, habit, or the desire to visit with others rather than religious commitment. Furthermore, many very religious people are unable to attend services because they are sick or disabled. As you can see, indicators seldom perfectly reflect the concepts they are intended to measure.

Surveys are particularly susceptible to inaccurate indicators. A loaded phrase or an unfamiliar word in a survey question can dramatically affect people's responses in ways unintended by the researcher. For instance, opinion polls show a majority of people oppose programs that give "preferences to minorities." However, polls also show a majority of people *in favor of* programs that "make special efforts to help minorities get ahead in order to make up for past discrimination" (Sussman, 2010, p. 5). In 2009, during the heated debate over health care reform, several news agencies conducted polls to determine people's feelings about altering the health care system. A New York Times/CBS News poll found overwhelming support (66%) for the so-called public option. Fox News, however, reported the support at a much lower 44%. Such an inconsistency had more to do with the way each agency worded its survey question than with the fluid, fluctuating nature of people attitudes. The New York Times/CBS poll asked people how they felt about "a government administered health insurance plan—something like the Medicare coverage that people 65 and older get." Fox News asked about "a government-run health insurance plan" (Sussman, 2010, p. 5).

Values, Interests, and Ethics in Sociological Research

Along with samples and indicators, the researcher's own qualities can influence social research. Ideally, research is objective and nonbiased and measures what is and not what should be. However, the questions researchers ask and the way they interpret observations always take place in a particular cultural, political, and ideological context (Ballard, 1987; Denzin, 1989).

Consider the impact of values and interests. If prevailing social values identify an intact nuclear family as the best environment for children, then most researchers will be prone to notice the disadvantages and perhaps ignore the advantages of other family arrangements. Furthermore, research is sometimes carried out to support a narrowly defined political interest (as when environmental groups fund research showing the damaging effects of global warming) or economic interest (as when tobacco companies fund research that downplays the relationship between cigarette smoking and cancer). Following the 2011 killing of six people and the wounding of Arizona representative Gabrielle Giffords outside a Tucson supermarket, the National Rifle Association used its political sway to choke off government funding for scientific research on the impact of firearms in society (M. Luo, 2011). In 2009, a legal investigation found that between 1998 and 2005, 26 scientific journal articles on the use of the hormone replacement drugs Premarin and Prempro for menopausal women were written by ghostwriters who were on the payroll of Wyeth, the pharmaceutical company that manufactured Premarin (Singer, 2009). That same year, an investigation by the Department of Health and Human Services found that the Food and Drug Administration does almost nothing to monitor financial conflicts of interest of doctors who conduct clinical trials of drugs and medical devices (cited in G. Harris, 2009).

But it's not just a problem of unscrupulous researchers or financial benefactors. Academic journals are notoriously reluctant to publish studies that show no relationship between one variable and another. A reexamination of clinical trial studies of antidepressants conducted between 1987 and 2004 found that medical journals had a significant bias toward publishing studies with positive results (E. H. Turner, Matthews, Linardatos, Tell, & Rosenthal, 2008). This problem has become so bad that an organization of 12 major medical journals proposed that pharmaceutical companies be required to register clinical trials at *the beginning* of drug studies so that negative and not just positive results would be publicly available (Meier, 2004).

We must remember that sociologists are people just like the rest of us, with their own biases, preconceptions, and expectations. Sociologists' values determine the kinds of information they gather about a particular social phenomenon. If you were conducting research on whether the criminal justice system is fair, would you study criminals, politicians, law enforcement personnel, judges, or victims? Each group would likely provide a different perception of the system. The most accurate picture of reality is likely to be based on the views of all subgroups involved.

In fact, values can influence the questions that researchers find important enough to address in the first place (Reinharz, 1992). For instance, research on families has historically reflected the interests of men. The term *labor force* has traditionally referred to those working for pay and has excluded those doing unpaid work, such as housework and volunteer jobs—areas that have always been predominantly female. Thus, findings on labor force participation are more likely to reflect the significant elements of men's lives than of women's lives. You can see that a lack of data does not necessarily indicate that a phenomenon or a problem doesn't exist. Perhaps all it indicates is that no researcher has yet undertaken a systematic study of it.

Ethics is another personal quality that affects the trustworthiness of social research. Research, as I mentioned earlier, often represents an intrusion into people's lives; it may disrupt their ordinary activities, and it often requires them to reveal personal information about themselves. Ethical researchers agree, therefore, that they should protect the rights of subjects and minimize the amount of harm or disruption subjects might experience as a result of being part of a study. Ethical researchers agree that no one should be forced to participate in research, that those who do participate ought to be fully informed of the possible risks involved, and that every precaution ought to be taken to protect the confidentiality and anonymity of participants. Sociologists almost always conduct their research under the scrutiny of university review committees for the protection of human participants.

At the same time, however, researchers must attempt to secure the most accurate—and perhaps most useful—information possible. Sometimes, this requirement conflicts with ethical considerations. In 2007, the federal government began a five-year, $50 million project designed to improve the way hospital patients are treated after car accidents, shootings, heart attacks, and other emergencies. Because such patients are often unconscious when they arrive at the hospital, researchers were allowed to conduct medical experiments on them without their consent, something that goes against usual ethical research protocol (R. Stein, 2007).

And what about research that requires information about people who may be involved in dangerous or criminal behavior or who do not want or cannot have their identities revealed? Sociologist Patricia Adler (1985) was interested in studying the worlds of drug dealers and smugglers. The illegal nature of their work makes them, by necessity, secretive, deceitful, and mistrustful—not the sort of individuals who make ideal surveyor interview respondents. So Adler had to establish a significant level of rapport and trust. Although she never became actively involved in drug trafficking, she did become a part of the dealers' and smugglers' social world and participated in their daily activities. Only by studying these criminals in their natural setting was she able to see the full complexity of the world of drug smuggling. Her research, however, raises important questions related to trustworthiness and ethics: Did her closeness to her subjects make it impossible to study them objectively? Did she have an obligation to report illegal activity to law enforcement officials?

LAUD HUMPHREYS

The Tearoom Trade

Most sociologists agree that the need to understand the depth and complexity of the drug world outweighed the ethical issues raised by Adler's research strategy. There is less agreement and more controversy, however, over situations in which researchers misrepresent their identities in order to gather information. Consider the 1970 study called *The Tearoom Trade* by Laud Humphreys, a study many sociologists find ethically indefensible. Humphreys was interested in studying anonymous and casual homosexual encounters among strangers. He decided to focus on interactions in "tearooms," which are places, such as public restrooms, where male homosexuals go for anonymous sex. (This study was done well before the HIV/AIDS epidemic significantly curtailed such activity.)

Because of the potentially stigmatizing nature of this phenomenon, Humphreys couldn't just come right out and ask people about their actions. So he decided to engage in a secretive form of participant observation. He posed as a lookout, called a "watchqueen," whose job was to warn of intruders as the people he was studying engaged in sexual acts with one another in public restrooms. In this way, he was able to conduct very detailed observations of these encounters.

Humphreys also wanted to know about the regular lives of these men. Whenever possible, he wrote down the license numbers of the participants' cars and tracked down their names and addresses with the help of a friend in the local police department.

About a year later, he arranged for these individuals to be part of a simple medical survey being conducted by some of his colleagues. He then disguised himself and visited their homes, supposedly to conduct interviews for the medical survey. He found that most of the men were heterosexual, had families, and were respected members of their communities. In short, they led altogether conventional lives.

Although this information shed a great deal of light on the nature of anonymous homosexual acts, some critics argued that Humphreys had violated the ethics of research by deceiving his unsuspecting subjects and violating their privacy rights. Some critics also noted that Humphreys might have been sued for invasion of privacy if he had not been studying a group of people rendered powerless by their potential embarrassment. Others, however, supported Humphreys, arguing that he couldn't have studied this topic any other way. In fact, his book won a prestigious award. But 40 years later, the ethical controversy surrounding this study remains.

Conclusion

In this chapter, I have described some of the processes by which reality is constructed, communicated, manipulated, and accepted. Reality, whether in the form of casual observations or formal research, is ultimately a human creation. Different people can create different conceptions of reality.

This issue can be raised from a personal level to a global one. People in every culture believe that their reality is the paramount one. Who is right? Can we truly believe that a reality in direct conflict with ours is equally valid? If we profess that everyone should have the right to believe what she or he wants, are we acknowledging the socially constructed nature of reality or merely being tolerant of those who are not "smart enough" to think as we do? Do we have the right to tell other people or other cultures that what they do or believe is wrong only because it conflicts with our definition of reality? Exasperating and complex, these questions lie at the core of international relations, global commerce, and everyday life.

YOUR TURN

The reality we take for granted is a social construction. This is particularly apparent when we look at the information presented to us as fact through published academic research, word of mouth, or the media. Reality is influenced by the individuals and organizations responsible for creating, assembling, and disseminating this information.

Choose an event that is currently making national headlines. It could be a story about the president or Congress, a major tragedy or natural disaster, a celebrity scandal, or a highly publicized criminal trial. Over the course of a week, analyze how this story is being covered by the following:

- Your local newspaper
- The major national newspapers (*USA Today, The New York Times, The Washington Post, The Wall Street Journal*)
- Mainstream news magazines (*Time, Newsweek, U.S. News & World Report*)
- Alternative magazines (*Utne Reader, Mother Jones, In These Times,* etc.)
- A local radio station
- National Public Radio (NPR)
- A local TV station
- A major TV network (NBC, CBS, ABC, Fox, CNN)
- A blog
- Late-night talk shows featuring topical comedy (such as *The Daily Show, The Colbert Report, The Late Show With David Letterman, Late Night,* or *The Tonight Show*)

Pay particular attention to the following:

- The amount of time or space devoted to the story
- The "tone" of the coverage (Supportive or critical? Purely factual or reflective of certain political opinions? Specific, objective language or biased, inflammatory language?)

Summarize your findings. What were the differences in how the story was covered by the different media outlets? What were the similarities?

Interpret your findings. What do these differences and similarities suggest about the people who run these organizations? Whose political or economic interests are being served or undermined by the manner in which the story is being presented to the public? Which medium do you think is providing the most accurate, objective coverage? Why?

CHAPTER HIGHLIGHTS

- The social construction of reality (truth, knowledge, etc.) is the process by which reality is discovered, made known, reinforced, and changed by members of society.

- Language is the medium through which reality construction takes place. It enables us to think, interpret, and define. Linguistic categories reflect aspects of a culture that are relevant and meaningful to people's lives.

- Not all of us possess the same ability to define reality. Individuals and groups in positions of power have the ability to control information, define values, create myths, manipulate events, and ultimately influence what others take for granted.

- The purpose of a discipline such as sociology is to amass a body of knowledge that provides the public with useful information about how society works. This is done, quantitatively and qualitatively, through systematic social research—field research, surveys, and unobtrusive research. It is important to keep in mind, however, that this form of reality is also a social construction, shaped by the people who fund, conduct, and report on social research.

KEY TERMS

analysis of existing data: Type of unobtrusive research that relies on data gathered earlier by someone else for some other purpose

content analysis: Form of unobtrusive research that studies the content of recorded messages, such as books, speeches, poems, songs, television shows, Web sites, and advertisements

dependent variable: Variable that is assumed to be caused by, or to change as a result of, the independent variable

empirical research: Research that operates from the ideological position that questions about human behavior can be answered only through controlled, systematic observations in the real world

experiment: Research method designed to elicit some sort of behavior, typically conducted under closely controlled laboratory circumstances

field research: Type of social research in which the researcher observes events as they actually occur

historical analysis: Form of social research that relies on existing historical documents as a source of data

hypothesis: Researchable prediction that specifies the relationship between two or more variables

incorrigible proposition: Unquestioned cultural belief that cannot be proved wrong no matter what happens to dispute it

independent variable: Variable presumed to cause or influence the dependent variable

indicator: Measurable event, characteristic, or behavior commonly thought to reflect a particular concept

moral entrepreneurs: Groups that work to have their moral concerns translated into law

nonparticipant observation: Form of field research in which the researcher observes people without directly interacting with them and without letting them know that they are being observed

participant observation: Form of field research in which the researcher interacts with subjects, sometimes hiding his or her identity

probabilistic: Capable only of identifying those forces that have a high likelihood, but not a certainty, of influencing human action

qualitative research: Sociological research based on nonnumeric information (text, written words, phrases, symbols, observations) that describes people, actions, or events in social life

quantitative research: Sociological research based on the collection of numeric data that uses precise statistical analysis

reactivity: A problem associated with certain forms of research in which the very act of intruding into people's lives may influence the phenomenon being studied

representative: Typical of the whole population being studied

sample: Subgroup chosen for a study because its characteristics approximate those of the entire population

self-fulfilling prophecy: Assumption or prediction that in itself causes the expected event to occur, thus seeming to confirm the prophecy's accuracy

social construction of reality: Process through which the members of a society discover, make known, reaffirm, and alter a collective version of facts, knowledge, and "truth"

spurious relationship: A false association between two variables that is actually due to the effect of some third variable

survey: Form of social research in which the researcher asks subjects a series of questions verbally, online, or on paper

theory: Set of statements or propositions that seeks to explain or predict a particular aspect of social life

unobtrusive research: Research technique in which the researcher, without direct contact with the subjects, examines the evidence of social behavior that people create or leave behind

variable: Any characteristic, attitude, behavior, or event that can take on two or more values or attributes

visual sociology: Method of studying society that uses photographs, video recordings, and film either as means of gathering data or as sources of data about social life

STUDENT STUDY SITE

Visit the Student Study Site at **www.sagepub.com/newman9e** for these additional learning tools:

- Flashcards
- Web quizzes
- Sociologists at Work features
- Micro-Macro Connection features
- Video links
- Audio links
- Web resources
- SAGE journal articles

Building Order

Culture and History

4

Dimensions of Culture

Cultural Expectations and Social Order

Cultural Variation and Everyday Experience

In Madagascar, the harvest months of August and September mark the *famadihana*—the "turning of the bones." Families receive messages from *razana*—their dead loved ones—who may say they are uncomfortable or need new clothes. In an elaborate ceremony that can last for days, families feast, sing, and dig up the graves of the deceased. The bodies are wrapped in shrouds and seated at the dinner table. Loved ones run their fingers over the skeletons through the shroud. Family news is whispered to them, and toasts are drunk. Widows and widowers can often be seen dancing with the bones of their dead spouses. The exhumed bones are then oiled and perfumed and laid back onto their "beds" inside the family tomb (Bearak, 2010; Perlez, 1991).

In the late 19th and early 20th centuries, dating and courtship in North America were based on a ritualized system known as "calling." Although the process varied by region and social class, the following general guidelines were involved:

> When a girl reached the proper age or had her first "season" (depending on her family's social level), she became eligible to receive male callers. At first her mother or guardian invited young men to call; in subsequent seasons the young lady . . . could bestow an invitation to call upon any unmarried man to whom she had been properly introduced at a private dance, dinner, or other "entertainment" . . . young men . . . could be brought to call by friends or relatives of the girl's family, subject to her prior permission. . . . The call itself was a complicated event. A myriad of rules governed everything: the proper amount of time between invitation and visit (two weeks or less); whether or not refreshments should be served . . . ; chaperonage (the first call must be made on mother and daughter . . .); appropriate topics of conversation (the man's interests, but never too personal); how leave should be taken (on no account should the woman accompany [her caller] to the door nor stand talking while he struggles with his coat). (B. L. Bailey, 1988, pp. 15–16)

How could anybody dig up a relative's corpse? Why would young men and young women follow such elaborate rules just so they could go on a date? Such practices seem peculiar, silly, or backward to most of us, but to the people involved, they are or were simply the taken-for-granted, "right" ways of doing things.

Some of the things you do may seem equally incomprehensible to an outside observer. For instance, you may not think twice about eating a bloody T-bone steak, but someone from a culture that views cows as sacred would be disgusted at the thought. You may think a Spaniard's fondness for bullfighting is "absurd," yet millions of people in the United States shell out a lot of money each year to watch large men in brightly colored shirts and helmets knock each other down while they chase, throw, carry, and kick an inflated object made out of the hide of a dead animal. You may pity the turn-of-the-century woman who squeezed her body into an ultratight corset to achieve the wasp-waisted figure men considered attractive. Yet many women today (and some men) routinely use harsh chemicals to change the color of their hair, pay to have someone cut into their faces to decrease the size of their noses or tighten the skin around their chins, or reduce their food intake to the point of starvation in order to become slender.

The legitimacy of certain practices and ideas can be understood only within the unique context of the group or society in which they occur. What is considered abnormal in one case may be perfectly normal, even necessary, in another. It takes a sociological imagination to see that time and place have a great influence on what people consider normal.

Ancestor worship in Madagascar is a custom that has been around for centuries, impervious to the arrival of Christian churches and Western ideals. To the people who practice it, the ritual of burial, disinterment, and reburial is more important than marriage. The physical body may die, but the *fanahy*, or soul, lives on. The Malagasy believe that spirits stay with the bones and have needs for earthly goods like food and clothing. It's up to the living to provide these things. In exchange, the dead take care of living relatives by determining their health, wealth, and fertility and by helping them communicate with God. As one man said after tending to the remains of his dead grandfather, "It is good to thank the ancestors in person because we owe them everything. . . . I am asking them for good health, and of course if they would help me to accumulate wealth, this is also a good idea" (quoted in Bearak, 2010, p. A7). In short, the custom is quite rational and beneficial: The individual's own earthly well-being and spiritual salvation depend on it.

Likewise, the practice of calling was an integral part of late-19th-century U.S. culture. It maintained the social class structure by serving as a test of suitability, breeding, and background (B. L. Bailey, 1988). Calling enabled the middle and upper classes to protect themselves from what many at the time considered the "intrusions" of urban life and to screen out the disruptive effects of social and geographic mobility, which reached unprecedented levels at the turn of the century. It also allowed parents to control the relationships of their children, thereby increasing the likelihood that their pedigree would remain intact.

These phenomena illustrate the important role played by culture and history in creating social order. Whether we're talking about our own ordinary rituals or those practiced by some distant society, the normative patterns that mark the millions of seemingly trivial actions and social encounters of our everyday lives are what make society possible. They tell us what to expect from others and what others should expect from us. In this chapter, by looking at the various taken-for-granted aspects of culture that lend structure to our daily lives, I examine how order is created and maintained in society. In the process, I compare specific aspects of our culture with others, past and present.

Dimensions of Culture

In Chapter 2, you saw that culture is one of the key elements that shape the structure of a society. It consists of the shared, taken-for-granted values, beliefs, objects, and rules that guide people's lives. In everyday conversation, however, the term *culture* is often used only when discussing something "foreign." We rarely feel the need to question why we do certain things in the course of our daily lives—we just do them.

It's other people in other lands whose rituals and beliefs need explaining. What we often fail to realize is that culture is "doing its job" most effectively when it is unnoticed. Only in times of dramatic social change and moral uncertainty or when circumstances force us to compare our society with another—like when you travel abroad—do we become aware that a distinct set of cultural rules and values influences us too.

To a large degree, we are products of the culture and historical epoch in which we live. From a very young age we learn, with a startling amount of accuracy, that certain types of shelter, food, tools, clothing, modes of transportation, music, sports, and art characterize our culture and make it different from others. Without much conscious effort, we also learn what to believe, what to value, and which actions are proper or improper both in public and in private.

Material and Nonmaterial Culture

Culture consists of all the products of a society that are created over time and shared by members of that society. These products may be tangible or intangible. The term *nonmaterial culture* refers to all the nonphysical products of society that are created over time and shared: knowledge, beliefs, customs, values, morals, symbols, and so on. Nonmaterial culture also includes common patterns of behavior and the forms of interaction appropriate in a particular society. It is a "design for living" that distinguishes one society from another. Like an owner's manual for social life, nonmaterial culture tells us how our society works, what is possible, what to value, how to conduct our everyday lives, and what to do if something breaks down. Without an understanding of a society's nonmaterial culture, people's behaviors—not to mention the symbolic significance of their material world—would be thoroughly incomprehensible.

The values that reside in nonmaterial culture often support a given society's economic and political systems. For example, in most Western industrialized countries, individual success is typically measured in financial terms, like a high-paying job and substantial accumulated wealth. In fact, in the United States, the entire country's well-being is gauged by the gross national product—the total dollar value of all goods and services produced for consumption during a particular time period. However, in Bhutan—a tiny Buddhist kingdom in the Himalaya Mountains—the country's well-being is judged not by its economic output but by how happy its people are. Bhutanese officials have even developed an index of gross national happiness, which determines the country's level of happiness by measuring things such as psychological and physical fitness, environmental health, educational attainment, living standards, time use, and community vitality (Mydans, 2009).

Material culture includes the physical artifacts and objects that shape or reflect the lives of members of a particular society: distinctive clothing and architecture, inventions, food, artwork, music, and so on. Elements of material culture occasionally take on powerful emotional value. If you followed the 2010 World Cup soccer tournament on television you no doubt noticed the loud buzzing drone that accompanied every game. The *vuvuzela*, that ubiquitous plastic horn responsible for all the racket, became a major cultural subplot during the tournament. In the 1990s, *vuvuzelas* became a common fixture at South African soccer matches (Walker, 2010). To opposing players, they were a nuisance; many complained that the swarming-insect noise was an unfair distraction. But to local fans, the horns became a tangible symbol of South African cultural pride.

Some of the most important elements of material culture are technological achievements, which are the ways in which members of a society apply knowledge to adapt to changing social, economic, or environmental conditions. For instance, plastic products have provided people with cheaper and more convenient packaging of needed goods—and in the process have forever altered shopping and consumption patterns.

Similarly, the advent of the automobile in the early 20th century gave people greater mobility to take advantage of economic or residential opportunities elsewhere and thereby dramatically changed how and where they lived. It's impossible to imagine society without cars. Today, the average number of cars per household (2.2) almost matches the average number of people per household (2.6; Bureau of Transportation Statistics, 2011; U.S. Bureau of the Census, 2011b). Since the interstate highway system was developed in 1956, the distance Americans drive annually has increased from 628 million miles to close to 3 billion (cited in R. Sullivan, 2006). This system made suburban living and cross-country travel possible. Moreover, our national economy would crumble without the ubiquitous long-haul trucks transporting needed goods to every corner of the country. The influence of the automobile is especially noticeable today in places such as Nepal and rural China, where it is just beginning to have a similar dramatic impact on people's lives.

Changes in material culture often transform the physical environment, creating the need for additional alterations in material and nonmaterial culture. The enormous amount of nonbiodegradable plastic piling up in overflowing landfills, for example, has spawned a vast array of advances in recycling and other ecofriendly technologies. Likewise, a heavy reliance on automobiles has created several serious problems throughout the world: air pollution, depletion of fossil fuel reserves, suburban sprawl, and constant traffic. These problems in turn have created the need for changes in travel patterns and arrangements as well as further material developments, such as an entire "green" industry that includes pollution-reducing devices, hybrid automobiles, and alternative-fuel sources (for more, see Chapter 14).

MICRO-MACRO CONNECTION

The Chair

Even the simplest and most taken-for-granted material objects of our everyday lives carry enormous cultural weight. Take, for example, the common chair. We spend a huge chunk of our lives sitting in chairs—in dining rooms, living rooms, classrooms, offices, cars, movie theaters, restaurants, and so on. You're probably sitting in one at this very moment.

Chairs supposedly make our lives comfortable. To be able to relax, kick off your shoes, and plop down on the old La-Z-Boy after a hard day's work is one of life's great pleasures. But such comfort has a steep cost. Ironically, lower back pain, often caused by bad sitting posture or poorly designed chairs, is second only to the common cold as the leading cause of absenteeism from work (Cranz, 1998). Our sedentary lifestyle has created a nation of people who are woefully out of shape.

Like all pieces of material culture, chairs are human creations. But once they're built, they start to shape us. The type of chair you use in your sociology class immediately places you in the role of student. And whether these chairs are arranged in rows or in a circle determines the degree of interaction expected of you in class. Children's first institutional lessons in controlling their bodies typically involve the chairs they are told to "sit still" in. Sitting quietly in rows of hard, straight chairs is not a natural state of being for young children. But it certainly helps teachers maintain authority and contain disruptive behaviors.

Chairs often take on important cultural significance beyond their functionality. For instance, the chair a person sits in may define that person's social status. In antiquity, only the most powerful and prestigious members of a society had access to chairs; the throne is one of the most enduring symbols of royalty worldwide. When the Pope issues an authoritative decree to Catholics around the world, he is said to be speaking *ex cathedra*, which literally means "from the chair." In some families, children know the consequences of sitting in or otherwise sullying "Dad's chair." The "chair" of an academic department can wield a great deal of power. On the other end of the spectrum, the "electric chair" is reserved for the lowest and most despicable of citizens, whose heinous crimes have led society to pronounce them unfit to live.

The right-angled posture required to sit in a chair, which we assume to be the universally proper way to sit, is used by only a third to half of people worldwide (Cranz, 1998). In many parts of the world people sit on floors, mats, carpets, or platforms. A Chinese man will likely squat when waiting for a bus, a Japanese woman kneels when eating, and an Arab might sit cross-legged on the floor when reading.

Regardless of whether we use a chair or what sort of chair we use, one thing is clear: This habit was created, modified, nurtured, and reformed in response to cultural—and not anatomical—forces. Our subjective experiences of comfort are socially constructed, and our bodies respond accordingly. For the American it *really is* more comfortable to sit in a chair, and for the rural Arab it *really is* more comfortable to sit on the floor. That these choices are experienced subjectively as personally pleasant shows that culture is at work here.

Global Culture

Although culture gives each society its distinctive character, cultural "purity" is all but obsolete (Griswold, 1994). Transnational media, global communication and transportation systems, and centuries of international migration have contributed to a worldwide swapping of cultural elements. For instance, despite the recent economic downturn, U.S. retailers remain a common fixture around the globe. More than 200 million people worldwide shop at one of Wal-Mart's nearly 9,000 stores in Asia, Latin America, and North America each year (Wal-Mart, 2011). Starbucks has over 17,000 coffeehouses in 50 countries (Starbucks, 2011). American pizza, too, which originally came to us from Naples, Italy, has migrated to every corner of the globe. Domino's Pizza now has over 9,000 stores worldwide (Domino's, 2011). And Yum! Brands—which owns fast food chains such as Taco Bell, Kentucky Fried Chicken, Pizza Hut, and Long John Silver's—has over 38,000 restaurants in 110 countries and territories (Yum! Brands, 2011). According to the Canadian Broadcasting Corporation (2003), only 30% of television shows, 18% of English language magazines, 28% of books, 13% of music recordings, and 2% of feature films that Canadians consume are actually produced in Canada. What were once unique features of U.S. material culture—such as blue jeans and fast food—can now be found on nearly every continent.

In some societies, people see the imported elements of culture as dangerous encroachments on long-held traditions and national unity. Of special concern is the increasing influence of U.S. culture on other countries. A decade ago, culture ministers from 20 different countries on four continents met to discuss how best to maintain their own cultures in a global environment dominated by U.S. media (Croteau & Hoynes, 2000). They were responding to examples like these:

- Approximately two thirds of French respondents to a survey felt that the United States exerted too much cultural influence on Europe (Daley, 2000). A French sheep farmer named José Bové became something of a national hero for vandalizing McDonald's restaurants, a symbol of what many French consider to be the unwanted intrusion of U.S. food culture.

- In Austria, an organization called the Pro-Christkind Association launched a campaign against Santa Claus, claiming that he is nothing more than an advertising symbol of American culture and consumption habits (Landler, 2002).
- Okinawa, Japan, has historically had the highest proportion of people over the age of 100 in the world and the greatest life expectancy of any region in Japan. But, increasingly, Okinawans are living and eating like Americans. They walk less, eat fewer vegetables, and eat more hamburgers than they used to. Okinawa now has the most American-style fast food restaurants of any city in Japan. As a result, average weight and rates of heart disease, cerebral hemorrhage, and lung cancer have all increased. Okinawans now rank 26th in life expectancy among the Japanese administrative regions (Onishi, 2004a; Takayama, 2003).

Emotions can run especially high when the integrity of a culture's language is at stake. About 60% of all existing languages have fewer than 10,000 speakers (R. G. Gordon, 2005). These languages are highly vulnerable to disappearance in a global culture. Indeed, linguists predict that of the 7,000 or so languages spoken worldwide today, nearly half are likely to disappear this century (cited in Wilford, 2007). Taking their place will be a handful of dominant languages that, in a technologically connected world, are seen as "linguistic passports" to education and a successful economic future (P. H. Lewis, 1998).

Foremost among these major languages is English, which today shapes communication all over the world. Japanese will order bottles of *bi-ru* (pronounced bee-roo) in pubs and spread *bata* on their bread. In many Spanish-speaking countries, people type e-mails on their *computadoras*. The French commonly use words like *le weekend* and *le shopping*. People are recognizing that in a world of collapsing borders, a common language is useful. And because of pervasive U.S. cultural influences and technologies, English is an understandable choice. For instance, even though the number of non-English Internet users grows each year, about 80% of the world's electronically stored information is in English (Crystal, 2003). It is estimated that 500 million to 1 billion people now speak English as either a first or a second language (N. Cohen, 2006). In fact, there are more people who speak English as their second language than there are people who speak it as their first (Mydans, 2007).

The growth of English as a sort of world language—what one author refers to as "Globish" (Chotiner, 2010)—has had a profound effect on the way people in other countries go about their business. For example, a while back the Swiss government decreed that all Swiss children above the age of six must learn English. In Chile, the government wants to make all its 15 million citizens fluent in English within a generation (Rohter, 2004).

But not everyone is happy about such developments. In 1994, France enacted the Toubon Law, which makes French the mandatory language in a variety of situations, ranging from advertising to the workplace documents employees need to do their jobs. In 2004, workers at a French branch of General Electric that manufactures health equipment sued the company for violating this law because all its internal e-mails, instruction manuals, and software applications were printed only in English. In 2006, the president of Iran proposed to ban English words like *helicopter*, *chat*, and *pizza* (N. Cohen, 2006).

In the United States, many people are concerned with the encroaching influence not of English but of Spanish. Over 34 million U.S. residents speak Spanish as their first language; in Los Angeles 44% of residents over the age of five speak Spanish at home (U.S. Bureau of the Census, 2011b). Immigrants are actually making the transition to speaking English more quickly than in the past, and over 90% of residents with a foreign-born parent prefer to speak only English at home (Kent & Lalasz, 2006). Indeed, about three quarters of the children who speak Spanish as their first language speak English "very well" (U.S. Bureau of the Census, 2011b). Nevertheless, many U.S. citizens fret about the primacy of English when they see street signs, billboards, election ballots, and automated teller machines in Spanish. In 2009, a city councilman in Nashville, Tennessee, introduced a bill that would have prevented government workers from communicating in *any* language other than English. Even though the bill failed, it illustrated a deep-seated fear among many Americans that the United States is moving toward becoming a bilingual or multilingual nation. Indeed, 31 states (including Tennessee) and at least 19 cities have declared English as their official language (Robbie Brown, 2009; U.S. English, 2011).

Subcultures and Countercultures

Sociologists and anthropologists usually speak of culture as a characteristic of an entire society. But culture can also exist in smaller, more narrowly defined units. A *subculture* consists of the values, behaviors , and physical artifacts of a group that distinguish it from the larger culture. Think of it as a culture within a culture. Certain racial and ethnic groups, religions, age groups, and even geographic areas can all constitute subcultures.

We don't usually think of people with sensory deficits as constituting a subculture, but many people who are deaf identify themselves as members of a subculture and take pride in its unique values and norms. This issue received national attention in 2006, when the board of trustees at Gallaudet University, a liberal arts university for the deaf, proposed hiring a new president. But students immediately protested because they felt the candidate—who was deaf herself—wasn't committed enough to deaf identity and culture. They mocked her for not learning sign language until she was 23 and criticized her for focusing too much attention on technologies to "fix" deafness, like cochlear implants and more powerful hearing aids, and not enough on advocating for deaf rights (Schemo, 2006b). The university eventually relented and abandoned their candidate.

To see a more common subculture, you don't have to look any further than your own school. You're probably well aware of the material and nonmaterial subculture that is unique to your campus. Perhaps some landmark—a bell tower or ornate archway—is the defining symbol of the university, or maybe a boulder or tree or fountain occupies a hallowed place in campus lore. I'm sure you know your school mascot and the school colors. In addition, when you first arrived at school, you probably had to learn a tremendous amount of new information about the nonmaterial subculture just to survive—how to register for courses, how to address a professor, where to eat and study, what administrators, faculty, and fellow students expect of you, and so on. At my university, the student newspaper publishes a glossary of common words, phrases, acronyms, and nicknames at the beginning of each academic year to aid first-year students in their adjustment to life on campus. Just as you have to learn how to be a member of your society, you have to learn how to be a member of your university subculture.

Some subcultures—called *countercultures*—go beyond just being different from the dominant culture to actively opposing its values and behavior patterns. Countercultures range from those that simply reject the way of life of the dominant culture (like the "hippie" movement of the 1960s) to those that use violence to try to destroy that way of life (like violent religious extremist groups). But even though certain countercultures may appear to dramatically conflict with the beliefs and values of the dominant culture, they never exist completely independent of that culture. For instance, alienated youth may adorn themselves in the angry and rebellious fashion trappings of gangsta rappers or antiglobal anarchists, but they still must conform to many of the dictates of the larger culture—for example, by exchanging money for necessary goods and services, going to school, and eventually getting a job so they can support themselves.

History: The "Archives" for Everyday Living

Like culture, history is simultaneously everywhere and invisible. We rarely see the connection between our personal lives and the larger historical context in which we live. Just as culture tends to be equated with the foreign, history tends to be equated with the past. Yet it too has a pervasive influence on today's society.

It is all too easy to use contemporary criteria to try to understand the thoughts and actions of people who lived long ago. Abraham Lincoln, known as one of history's most influential proponents of liberty and equality, once said, "There is a physical difference between the white and black races which I believe will forever forbid the two races living together on terms of social and political equality" (quoted in Gould, 1981, p. 35). Similar views of racial separation were voiced by important historical figures such as Benjamin Franklin, Thomas Jefferson, and Charles Darwin. Such comments, if uttered today, would be taken as indications of a deeply held prejudice.

However, we must understand such beliefs and behaviors not merely as signs of personal bigotry but as reflections of the dominant cultural belief system of the times. In other words, they are social constructions. As repugnant as we might find these attitudes, they were taken as undeniable truths by the scientific communities of their era. Innate "racial inferiority" was as much an established "scientific fact" as the germ theory of disease is today. (See Chapter 11 for more detail on the belief in innate racial inferiority.) The norms and values that govern everyday life in a given society are also likely to change over time. Some cultural practices that were wholly unacceptable in the past have now become commonplace. Premarital sex and househusbands no longer incite the sort of moral outrage or suspicion that they once did.

Other acts have become less acceptable, even criminal. In the United States, there was a time when people could smoke cigarettes anywhere and anytime they pleased—in supermarkets, airplanes, movie theaters, even hospitals. Now, with the increase in health awareness, smoking in public buildings (and even outdoor public facilities) has been severely restricted or outlawed in many locales. Hospitals in some states have begun enacting hiring policies that make smoking a reason to turn down job applicants. They argue that they want to increase worker productivity, cut health care costs, and encourage healthier living. Application forms warn of "tobacco-free hiring" and job seekers must submit to urine tests for nicotine as part of the application process (Sulzberger, 2011).

Historical shifts in the cultural acceptance of certain behaviors involve more than just a societal realization of the danger of such behaviors. Actually, as the conflict perspective would point out, such designations are greatly influenced by social and economic concerns. Take, for instance, the criminalization of opium—the substance from which heroin is derived. During the 19th century, the use of opium was legal in many parts of the world; it was commonly used for therapeutic purposes as a pain reliever, a cold medicine, and a cough suppressant (Inciardi, 1992). The typical "heroin addict" at that time in the United States was a white middle-class housewife.

By the early 20th century, however, things had changed considerably. In the United States, there was a growing fear, particularly on the West Coast, of economic competition from Chinese laborers who had been "imported" to work on the railroads. Workers began to see Chinese immigrants as a direct threat to their material interests. At the same time, these immigrants became equated with opium use (Hagan, 1985). A moral consensus soon emerged that focused on the presumed link between the Chinese and narcotics (Bonnie & Whitebread, 1974). It wasn't long before opium use became the dreaded "Oriental dope problem." By 1914, tight legislative controls restricted U.S. distribution of opium to authorized medical prescriptions only. By 1925, opium was completely outlawed (Becker, 1963).

Cultural Expectations and Social Order

Despite periodic shifts in the acceptability of certain acts, culture and history provide people with a common bond—a sense of shared personal experiences. That we can live together at all depends on the fact that we share a tremendous amount of cultural and historical knowledge. This knowledge allows us to predict, with a fair amount of certainty, what most people will do in a given situation. For instance, I can assume that when I say, "Hi, how are you?" you will reply "Fine." You probably won't launch into some long-winded explanation of your mental, physical, and emotional condition at that precise moment, because doing so would violate the cultural rules governing such casual greetings.

The actions of individuals are not simply functions of personality types or psychological predispositions; rather, they are also a reflection of shared cultural expectations. Culture provides us with information about which of these actions are preferred, accepted, or disapproved of at a given time (McCall & Simmons, 1978). Take, for example, sexuality. American culture is often characterized as a ***heteronormative culture***—that is, a culture where heterosexuality is accepted as the normal, taken-for-granted mode of sexual expression. Social institutions and social policies reinforce the belief that sexual relationships ought to exist between males and females. Cultural representations of just about every aspect of intimate and family life—dating, sex, marriage, childbearing, retirement, and so on—presume a world in which men are sexually and affectionately attracted to women and women to men (Macgillivray, 2000). Think of the flurry of magazine and TV advertisements we're subjected to in the weeks prior to Valentine's Day that depict men and women embracing, gazing longingly into each other's eyes, and buying each other expensive jewelry. Adolescent women seeing a gynecologist for the first time can expect to be given information on birth control, highlighting the assumption that they will have sex with men—it's just a matter of when. In 2008, the online dating service eHarmony was sued for discrimination because the site offered only two options to its customers: "man seeking woman" or "woman seeking man" (L. Miller, 2008). Even some sports reflect a heteronormative culture. In competitive figure skating, the "pairs" competition always consists of women partnered with men (Wildman & Davis, 2002). The 2007 film *Blades of*

Glory humorously satirized this basic assumption by depicting two men skating with one another in the pairs event.

In heteronormative cultures, heterosexuals are socially privileged because their relationships and lifestyles are affirmed in every facet of society. Such privilege includes having positive media images of people with the same sexual orientation; not having to lie about who you are, what you do, and where you seek entertainment; not having to worry about losing a job because of your sexual orientation; receiving validation from your religious community; being able to legally marry and adopt children; and being able to join the Boy Scouts or serve openly in the military (Macgillivray, 2000, p. 304).

Recall from Chapter 2 that norms are the rules that govern the routine social encounters in which we all participate. Although many everyday norms are sometimes difficult to identify and describe, they reflect commonly held assumptions about conventional behavior. Consider the unspoken norms in a situation we've all experienced: shopping at a supermarket:

> There is a customer role to be played in grocery stores. There generally is a standard of orderliness. Shoppers are not seen pushing each other out of the way, picking things out of each other's shopping carts, or sitting on the floor eating from a recently opened can. How does one "know" how the role of customer is to be played? Aside from the "No Shirt. No Bare Feet" sign on the door . . . there is no clear listing of shopping rules.
>
> Evidence of the implied existence of such rules can be found in the way people react to a fellow shopper dressed in a gorilla suit or to someone who violates the norms for waiting in line at the checkout counter. One may feel that rules are being broken when one finds oneself standing in line with melting ice cream behind a grandmother who takes out her grandchildren's photographs to show the clerk. Such behavior violates the norms of universalism (all customers are to be treated equally) and efficiency; the grocery store is not a context in which one shares one's private self with others, particularly anonymous others. (Kearl & Gordon, 1992, p. 274)

The power of such norms was illustrated recently in Clayton, Missouri, where a café run by Panera Bread began refusing payment from customers. Instead, "suggested" prices of meals were posted and patrons were politely asked to "take what you need, leave your fair share" in wooden lockboxes. The company argued that it was a way of providing free or low-cost food to those in need while sustaining the business off the money honest paying customers decided to put in the box (Strom & Gay, 2010). The responses of patrons—who were used to the scripted norms that govern the restaurant experience—ranged from curious to bewildered. How do you think you'd respond to such an arrangement?

Norms can be generalized to similar situations within a culture. That is, we can be reasonably certain that grocery store or restaurant behavior that is appropriate in Baton Rouge will be appropriate in Bakersfield or Butte as well. Our experiences in these places would be chaotic if there weren't a certain degree of agreement over how we should act. Without such unspoken rules and expectations, every situation would have to be interpreted, analyzed, and responded to as if it were an entirely new occasion. Social life would be utterly unmanageable.

Cultural norms are not static rules, however. They often change as the culture itself changes. A compelling reason for norms to change is to accommodate new technologies.

MICRO-MACRO CONNECTION

Can You Hear Me Now?

One of the most popular technological devices in contemporary society today is the cell phone. Cell phones were first mass-marketed to the public in 1984. Ten years later there were 24 million U.S. cell phone subscribers. Today, that figure exceeds 302 million—over 97% of the U.S. population (see Exhibit 4.1). About one quarter of American adults now live in households that have no traditional landlines, only cell phones (Tavernise, 2011d). In 2010, people talked for 2.2 *trillion* minutes and sent 2 *trillion* text messages on their cell phones (Cellular Telecommunications and Internet Association [CTIA], 2011). What was once the sole province of the well-to-do is now a mass-market item that virtually everyone can obtain. The federal government even provides financial assistance to low-income individuals so they can afford cell phones (Richtel, 2009). And

Exhibit 4.1   Trends in Cell Phone Usage

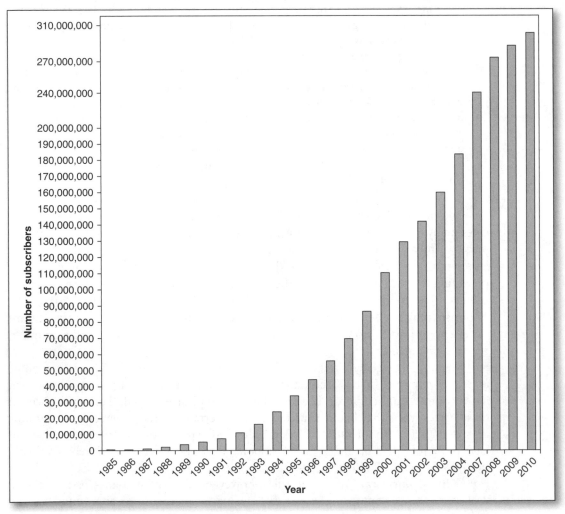

SOURCE: CTIA, 2011. Figure for the year-end 2010 semi-annual survey results, from CTIA–The Wireless Association®'s Semi-annual Wireless Industry Survey. Used with the permission of CTIA–The Wireless Association®.

the U.S. isn't even near the top worldwide when it comes to cell phone usage. According to the World Economic Forum, Americans rank below 71 other countries in the degree to which cell phones have come to dominate contemporary communication (cited in Giridharadas, 2010b). Many developing countries in Africa and Asia have gone from very low percentages of traditional telephone ownership a decade ago to very high percentages of cell phone ownership today, completely leapfrogging past the landline technology stage of growth.

Moreover, phones aren't simply phones anymore. In fact, the amount of time people actually spend talking on their phones hasn't increased at all over the past several years, even though cell phone ownership has grown (see Exhibit 4.1). Instead, people spend the bulk of their time using all the extras on today's "smart" phones: global navigation systems, Web browsers, MP3 players, video cameras, e-mail, Facebook, Instagram, Twitter, and text messaging. As one iPhone user put it, "I probably only talk to someone verbally on it once a week" (quoted in Wortham, 2010, p. A1). Clearly cell phones have completely revolutionized the way we communicate, work, find information, entertain ourselves, and form relationships.

Telephone conversations used to be activities people took great pains to keep private. And they were by necessity stationary: Phones were either in people's own homes or their workplaces. When people had to use a phone away from home or work, they turned to public telephone booths—relics of material culture that have gone the way of the dinosaur. In these enclosed boxes, people could deposit a dime or a quarter and shut out the rest of the world while talking privately on the phone.

Cell phones have changed all that. For one thing, these devices have completely altered our sense of place. When phones were anchored in a particular location, you knew when you called someone where that person was. Now the first question people typically ask when calling someone's cell phone is, "Where are you?" The other day I called a friend's cell phone. There was no answer, and the voicemail greeting started out with the common "I'm not here right now." I had to laugh. What does "here" actually mean when someone's phone is, by design, not here (or anywhere in particular, for that matter)?

More important, people speaking on cell phones today often seem more engaged in a public broadcast than in an intimate conversation. Perhaps you've experienced a variation of this common scene:

> With just five minutes to takeoff, the young man across the aisle . . . whipped out his cell phone and began a hurried and boisterous conversation, explaining the fine points of marketing his new Christmas-gift web site to an unseen underling. With glazed eyes staring at the seat in front of him, the executive unconsciously pounded his foot in rhythm to his conversation, oblivious to the 15 surrounding passengers glaring at this human loudspeaker in seat 23B. (Taub, 2001, p. D1)

Cellular technology did not develop in response to millions of people clamoring for constant access. It was the other way around. People's "need" to constantly talk to (or text) others as they go about their daily lives grew *as a result of* access to wireless technology that makes communication possible anywhere and anytime. My students know to turn off their ringers before coming to class. But it's rare these days to get through a class period without hearing the telltale buzzing sound of a cell phone on "vibrate." And it's common on campuses all across the country to see scores of students spilling from rooms into the hallway at the end of class already engaged in conversations on their cell phones (and I doubt it's to share the scintillating sociological insight they've just attained!). People talking or texting on their phones while riding stationary bikes in fitness centers, using toilets in public restrooms, or, of course, driving has become ubiquitous.

This last tendency has become, in many states, a major focus of legislative action designed to outlaw drivers' use of cell phones. Currently, eight states ban the use of handheld cell phones by all drivers, 30 states ban all cell phone use (including hands-free phones) among drivers under 18, and 32 states ban texting while driving (Governors Highway Safety Association, 2011). The New York State legislature is even considering a bill that would ban *pedestrians'* use of cell phones (and other electronic devices) while crossing streets (Saulny & Richtel, 2011).

Some airlines now allow passengers to use their phones until the plane pushes back from the gate and again the instant the plane touches down. But that's not good enough for some, and so the Federal Communications Commission is considering a change in federal aviation policy that would allow cell phone use on planes in flight. The European Union has already approved such a policy in flights over European airspace. Such conversational urgency was unknown a mere five years ago. Indeed, some experts liken this sort of cell phone use to an addiction (Hubert, 2005). As one author put it, cell phones are the "cigarettes of this decade" (quoted in Leland, 2005, p. 2).

The rapid diffusion of such a visible technology caught us unawares. As one author put it, "We should recognize that we're on a technological roller coaster and things are changing fast and there are levels of rudeness that we are just discovering" (quoted in Belson, 2004, p. 14). But a cultural backlash has imposed limits on people's behavior. At company business meetings all across the country, the tapping sound of people using smartphones to text and check e-mail has become routine. But such usage is so annoying and distracting to some that a few companies have already imposed bans on BlackBerrys in meeting rooms (A. Williams, 2009).

In public places, huffs of disgust and resentful rolled eyes await the person whose Black Eyed Peas ringtone goes off while in line at the supermarket. And people are beginning to lose patience with those who decide to take a call in the middle of a face-to-face conversation:

> I'm fine with people stepping aside to check something, but when I'm standing in front of someone and in the middle of my conversation they whip out their phone, I'll just stop talking to them and walk away. If they're going to be rude, I'll be rude right back. (quoted in Carr, 2011, p. 12)

Movie theaters, concert halls, libraries, and business conferences routinely post reminders to people to turn off their cell phones. In 2011, a passenger was removed from an Amtrak train and charged with disorderly conduct for talking loudly on her cell phone in one of the train's designated quiet cars. A few enterprising companies have begun marketing retro-style "cell phone booths" to nightclubs and restaurants in response to complaints about loud and annoying cell phone users (Mummolo, 2006). Some go even further. A small but growing group of annoyed business owners and commuters on public transportation use cell phone jammers, devices that create a temporary "dead zone" in their immediate vicinity, rendering nearby mobile phones useless (Richtel, 2007).

As with other forms of technology, people will eventually come to some normative agreement about proper cell phone etiquette in different social situations, and order will be restored.

Social Institutions and Cultural Norms

Large social institutions are closely tied to culture. For one thing, some institutions reflect deeply held cultural values. A free-market economy, for instance, reflects the cultural values of achievement, competition, material acquisition, and so on. A democratic government reflects the values of individual freedom and citizen participation. As we'll see in the following chapter, other institutions—such as education, religion, and family—provide the mechanisms through which culture and subculture are transmitted across generations.

Institutions are also strongly supported by cultural norms. When a pattern of behavior becomes widely accepted within a particular social institution and is taken for granted in society, sociologists say it has become an ***institutionalized norm*** (DiMaggio & Powell, 1991). For instance, the institutionalized (i.e., culturally acceptable) way of becoming financially successful in many developed societies is to earn a college degree, get a job in an entry-level position somewhere, and eventually work your way to the top. Even things that most of us would condemn have, at times, been institutionalized and encouraged by society. Slavery, for example, was for several hundred years a culturally, politically, and economically acceptable practice in the United States. The buying and selling of slaves was strongly approved by the nation's most powerful forces as well as by many ordinary people (Birenbaum & Sagarin, 1976).

Institutionalized norms constrain people's behavior by making some lines of action unthinkable. But they don't just limit options; they also establish the setting in which people discover their preferences and begin to see the world in a particular way (DiMaggio & Powell, 1991). The military ritualizes the process of becoming a full-fledged member through training, oaths of allegiance, and public recognition of the passage from one rank to another. In doing so, it ensures conformity to military norms and an understanding of the "rules of engagement," the specific norms that govern fighting on the battlefield. Religious congregations reinforce "appropriate" lifestyles and downplay inappropriate ones through collective worship services.

Shifts in one institution are often linked to shifts in another. The abolition of slavery in the United States, for instance, meant that the entire economic system of the South had to be restructured, from a plantation economy to one characterized by smaller landholdings and increased industrial production. In Russia, the collapse of communism two decades ago strengthened the role of religious organizations in providing people with normative guidelines. In the United States today, the fact that women are no longer expected to be the sole caretakers of children has meant an increase in the number of mothers who enter the paid labor force, which in turn has created a higher demand for organized day care as well as increased pressure on legislatures to enact laws protecting the interests of working parents.

MICRO-MACRO CONNECTION

I've Got a Feeling

We all experience emotions as physical, sometimes instantaneous responses to life events. Thus, we're inclined to see emotions as natural and universal. Yet emotional display comes under the strict control of cultural norms. In rural areas of Greece, widows traditionally are expected to mourn over the loss of their husbands—most notably by wearing black—for the rest of their lives. That would be seen as excessive in the United States, where more than two months of grieving might be considered an indicator of major depression (Horwitz, 2002).

Every society has unwritten rules about which emotions are appropriate to feel, which are appropriate to display, and how intense the emotional display should be under specific circumstances. For instance, in our culture, we're supposed to be sad at funerals, happy at weddings, and angry when we are insulted. We're supposed to feel joy when we receive good news but not show too much of it if our good fortune is at someone else's expense. In extreme cases, the violation of emotional display norms can lead to grave sanctions, such as a diagnosis of mental illness (Pugliesi, 1987; Thoits, 1985).

When people hide or alter their emotions to fit the situation, they are playing a significant role in maintaining social order within broader social institutions. Take the popular TV show *American Idol*, for example. In the season finale, when the field is finally reduced to the last two contestants, the camera zooms in on both of them. They stand on stage holding hands in shaky anticipation of the final verdict. The lights are dimmed. When the winner is announced, the runner-up is the picture of grace and charm, all smiles and congratulations. But we know better. This person has just lost the contest of her or his life on national television and has got to be sad, angry, or at the very least disappointed. To add insult to injury, she or he is then gently escorted offstage so the winner can have the spotlight. Why does the runner-up suppress the urge to show true emotions? Part of the reason is that he or she understands that there's more at stake than personal feelings. Imagine what would happen to the *American Idol* phenomenon if the runners-up started displaying their bitterness onstage—screaming at the host, threatening the judges, shunning the winners, or demanding a recount.

Norms about expressing emotions are often linked to institutional concerns and needs. In her book *The Managed Heart*, Arlie Russell Hochschild (1983) describes the feeling rules required by occupations in which employees have a great deal of contact with the public. Flight attendants, for example, must constantly be good natured and calm under dangerous conditions. They must make their work appear effortless and handle other people's feelings as deftly as their own. This ability is not just a matter of living up to social expectations—it is part of their job description. A "smile" becomes an economic asset and a public relations tool.

Likewise, doctors and nurses are trained to show compassionate concern for their patients, not disgust or alarm. Furthermore, they cannot become too emotionally involved with patients, because they see pain, suffering, and death every day. It is difficult not to become attached to patients, but such emotional outlay would inevitably lead to burnout, making effective job performance impossible. We want our health care providers to show that they like us, but doctors and nurses are most successful in their jobs when they can keep their emotions under control.

Some companies include explicit instructions on emotional control and display as part of their training programs for new employees. This is especially true in service sector jobs where contact with customers occurs over the phone. The telephone performance guidelines for one insurance company included the following directives:

> Remember, smiling can be heard as well as seen. . . . Have a smile in your voice and avoid sounding abrupt. . . . Try to make the caller feel you are there for them . . . [avoid] a disinterested, monotonous tone to voice. . . . Use language which conveys understanding of and empathy for the caller's individual situation, e.g., "are you OK?" "was anyone hurt?" "that must have been very distressing for you." (D. Cameron, 2000, pp. 334–335)

The ability to enact convincing performances has become even more important given the rise of management techniques that use customer or client input as a means of assessing employees. Many service sector companies survey customers, monitor phone calls, and use undercover "secret shoppers" or other forms of surveillance to gather information on workers, making appropriate emotional display even more important. Hochschild (1983) warns that this kind of "emotional labor" eventually takes a heavy psychological toll on the workers, who are required to adopt a display of emotions that reflects corporate needs and not their own. These people become increasingly estranged from their true feelings.

Although it is not surprising that organizations would have an interest in emotional displays by members, it is perhaps less obvious that particular emotions are linked to larger societal concerns such as politics and economics, often as a method of social control (Kearl & Gordon, 1992). For instance, the conflict perspective points out that some regimes may use fear to quell dissent and enforce obedience. In the early 20th century, in response to the increasing political and economic strength of African Americans, many white Southerners used fear to control Blacks through the threat of lynching and other forms of violence. Similarly, religious leaders often use the fear of eternal damnation to make sure their followers cooperate.

The effectiveness of invoking emotions such as guilt, anxiety, and shame waxes and wanes as social climates change. In the past, when communities were smaller and more interdependent, social behavior could be easily regulated by the threat of shame. If people broke a law or violated some norm of morality, they would bring humiliation on themselves, their families, and the community at large. But as societies became more complex, such close ties began to disappear. Today, the political control of behavior through emotion is more likely to be directed inward, in the form of guilt and anxiety. For instance, if working mothers are implicated by politicians as contributing to the "breakdown" of the traditional family by leaving the raising of their children to others, more and more mothers will experience guilt when they seek employment outside the home (Berg, 1992).

Norms governing the expression of emotions give us a way to communicate and maintain social order. They perpetuate institutions by creating powerful cultural expectations that are difficult to violate.

Norms and Sanctions

Most norms provide only a general framework of expectations; rarely do they tell us exactly how to act, and rarely are they obeyed by all people at all times. Furthermore, norms may be ambiguous or contradictory. It is no surprise, then, that actual behavior sometimes departs markedly from normative expectations. When it does, negative *sanctions* may be applied. A sanction is a direct social response to some behavior; a negative sanction is one that punishes or otherwise discourages violations of social norms and symbolically reinforces the culture's values and morals.

Different norms evoke different sanctions when violated. *Mores* (pronounced MORE-ayz) are norms, sometimes codified into laws, that are taken very seriously by society. Violation of some mores can elicit severe, state-sponsored sanctions, such as serving time in prison for armed robbery. Other mores may be equally serious but much less formally stated. Sanctions for violating these norms may take the form of public ostracism or exclusion from the group, as when one is excommunicated for going against the moral doctrine of one's church.

The vast majority of everyday norms are relatively minor, however; violations of these norms, called *folkways*, carry much less serious punishment. For instance, if I chew with my mouth open and food dribbles down my chin, others may show outward signs of disapproval and consider me a "disgusting pig." I may receive fewer dinner invitations as a result, but I won't be arrested or banished from my community.

According to the structural-functionalist perspective, each time a community moves to sanction an act, it strengthens the boundaries between normative and nonnormative behavior (Erikson, 1966). In the process, the rest of us are warned of what is in store if we, too, violate the norms. In the 17th century, for example, criminals and religious heretics were executed at high noon in the public square for all to see. The spectacle was meant to be a vivid and symbolic reaffirmation of the community's norms. Today, such harsh sanctions are likely to be hidden from the public eye. However, the publicity surrounding executions, as well as the visibility of less severe sanctions, serves the same purpose—to declare to the community where the line between acceptable and unacceptable behavior lies. By sanctioning the person who violates a norm, society informs its members what type of person cannot live "normally" within its boundaries (Pfohl, 1994).

Cultural Relativism and Ethnocentrism

When it comes to examining the cultures of different societies, sociologists are inclined to adopt a position of *cultural relativism*, the principle that people's beliefs and activities should be interpreted in terms of their own culture. In other words, practices that might conflict with our cultural values are still considered valid because they reflect the values of that culture. Maintaining a culturally relativist position becomes especially difficult when the practice in question is considered brutal or oppressive. Take, for instance, the practice of female genital mutilation/cutting (FGM/C), a procedure that entails the removal of a young girl's clitoris and/or the destruction of the labia and vulva. In the countries where FGM/C is practiced, women are expected to be virgins when they marry. The ritual therefore serves to control young women's sexuality and ensure their "marriageability." But to people in societies that acknowledge or even celebrate female sexuality, such a practice is abhorrent and a violation of human rights. A decades-long worldwide campaign to end FGM/C has led many countries to ban the practice. However, it persists as a local custom in 28 African countries and a few others in Asia and the Middle East. An estimated 100 million to 140 million girls and women worldwide have undergone the procedure and over 3 million girls are at risk for cutting each year on the African continent alone (Population Reference Bureau, 2010b).

Cultural relativism is not part of the way most of us are raised. People tend to evaluate other cultures in comparison to their own. This tendency is called *ethnocentrism*. As children, most people are taught that they live in the greatest country on earth. Many also learn to take pride in their religious, racial, or ethnic group. But the belief that one group or country is the "best" means that others are "not the best." Sixty percent of Americans believe that their culture is superior to others. The figure rises to 90% in South Korea and Indonesia (cited in Rieff, 2006).

ABHIJIT BANERJEE AND ESTHER DUFLO

The Economic Lives of Poor People

Ethnocentrism often reveals itself in harsh judgments of lifestyles that seem to challenge one's own cultural values. People often look incredulously at others who make decisions that contradict what they would do under similar circumstances. When such decisions lead to additional—or from the observer's perspective, avoidable—suffering, sympathy wanes.

Take, for instance, the way poor families with very little money prioritize their purchases. Two MIT economists, Abhijit Banerjee and Esther Duflo (2006), studied spending patterns among poor households in 13 countries in Africa, Asia, and Latin America. They examined both "poor" households—where people live on less than $2 a day per capita—and "extremely poor" households—where they live on less than $1 a day.

The researchers started with a basic—and perhaps ethnocentric—assumption: that when people have very little money, they should spend what they do have on basic necessities such as food, clothing, and education for their children. Instead, much to their chagrin, they found that families in some of the poorest areas in the world spend a relatively high proportion of their meager money on "frivolous" things like alcohol and cigarettes. In rural Mexico, for example, families spend less than half their budget on food, even though hunger and malnutrition are common. Especially surprising to the researchers was the tendency for spending on celebratory festivals to be an important part of the budget of many extremely poor households. In South Africa, 90% of households living on less than $1 a day spent some of their money on festivals. In one Indian state, Udaipur, more than 99% of extremely poor households had spent money the previous year on weddings, funerals, or religious celebrations. As the authors put it:

> It is hard to escape the conclusion that the poor do see themselves as having a significant amount of choice, and choose not to exercise it in the direction of spending more on food—the typical poor household in Udaipur could spend up to 30 percent more on food than it actually does, just based on what it spends on alcohol, tobacco, and festivals. (A. V. Banerjee & Duflo, 2006, p. 6)

An American newspaper columnist responding to this study was even less forgiving:

> If the poorest families spent as much money educating their children as they do on wine, cigarettes, and prostitutes, their children's prospects would be transformed. Much suffering is caused not only by low incomes, but also by shortsighted private spending decisions by heads of households. . . . I've seen too many children dying of malaria for want of a bed net that the father tells me is unaffordable, even as he spends larger sums on liquor. If we want . . . children to get an education and sleep under a bed net . . . the simplest option is for their dad to spend fewer evenings in the bar. (Kristof, 2010, p. 9)

These researchers based their assessment on existing surveys of people's consumption patterns. They had no information on the reasons people bought what they did or the cultural belief systems under which they live their lives. In some cultures, for instance, festivals celebrating gods or goddesses are the expressions of devotion that can lead to a better eternal life. In other cultures, buying something beyond one's means or something that appears frivolous, like a bottle of wine, might be the only way a family can establish its social status in the community; and these social needs may outweigh the more immediate needs of individual family members. Some indigenous peoples of the Pacific Northwest practice a ritual called *potlatch*, where people with very few economic resources give away or destroy much of what they have. In these cultures, the status of any given family is determined not by who has the most, but by who gives away the most. In short, all cultures may not abide by the same definition of "basic needs." Hence, to an outsider focused on survival issues who doesn't understand the broader cultural context in which people make their choices, the kinds of consumption patterns these researchers identified do indeed look ill considered and irrational.

Ethnocentrism results from the nature of human interaction itself. Much of our everyday lives are spent in groups and organizations. By their very character, these collectivities consist of individuals with some, though not necessarily all, shared interests. The same is true for larger cultures. To the extent that we spend a majority of our time with others "like us," our interactions with others "not like us" will be limited, and they will remain "foreign" or "mysterious." Similarity breeds comfort; difference breeds discomfort. For example, despite laws against the practice, many Japanese shopkeepers are so uncomfortable dealing with foreigners that they refuse to serve them (French, 1999a). In fact, when Japanese citizens who have lived abroad for a long time return to Japan, they find that they are no longer regarded as fully Japanese and are treated with the sort of cold disdain foreigners there often experience (French, 2000).

Another reason for the existence of ethnocentrism is the loyalty we develop to our particular culture or subculture (Charon, 1992). Different values, beliefs, and behaviors come to be seen not merely as different ways of thinking and acting but as threats to our own beliefs and values. Such perceptions, for instance, underlie much of the resentment of and hostility toward recently arrived immigrants. Even groups whose position in society is strong and secure can find the encroachment of other ways of life threatening:

- A Honolulu restaurant made headlines recently for its policy of adding a 15% gratuity to the checks of all non-English-speaking patrons. The owner claimed he put the policy into place because Asian guests routinely fail to tip. "It's not a part of their culture," he said. "They spend a lot of money, but they don't tip" (quoted in McKinley, 2011, p. A16).
- A school superintendent in Mustang, Oklahoma, got into trouble a few years ago for including references to Kwanzaa and Chanukah as well as Christmas in an annual school play and for removing a live nativity scene from the conclusion of the play so as not to highlight one faith too much over others. Christian parents became outraged, suing the school for discrimination and voting down an $11 million school bond (Zernike, 2004).
- In 2011, a bill introduced in the California legislature sought to ban the sale and possession of shark fins because of the brutal way the fins are hacked off live sharks. Similar bills have been presented in Oregon and Washington. But shark fins are a centuries-old delicacy among Chinese residents, who perceive the proposed law as an assault on their cultural traditions (P. L. Brown, 2011).

Cultural loyalty is also encouraged by institutional ritual and symbolism. In this country, saying the Pledge of Allegiance at the beginning of the school day, playing the "Star-Spangled Banner" and "God Bless America" at sports events, and observing holidays such as Memorial Day, the Fourth of July, Veterans Day, and Flag Day all reinforce loyalty to U.S. culture. The American flag is considered such an important national symbol that an entire code of etiquette with specific instructions on how to display it exists to ensure that it is treated with reverence. These are the "sacred objects" of U.S. culture (Durkheim, 1915/1954). The importance of these objects is especially pronounced when people in society feel threatened. You will recall the enormous number of American flags, patriotic songs, pins, T-shirts, and magnetic ribbons on cars that exploded onto the cultural landscape after the September 11, 2001, attacks and during the wars in Iraq and Afghanistan. Religious artifacts and symbols, uniforms and team colors, and distinctive ethnic clothing all foster a sense of pride and identity and hold a community of similar people together, often to the exclusion of others.

Sometimes respect for these cultural objects must be enforced under threat of punishment. In 2008, a fan at a New York Yankees' baseball game was forcibly removed by police for not standing by his seat as "God Bless America" was being played during the seventh-inning stretch. For years, some members of the U.S. Congress have been trying to ensure loyalty to the American flag by proposing a constitutional amendment banning its desecration. In Japan, 243 teachers were punished in 2004 for not standing and singing the national anthem at the beginning of the school day (Onishi, 2004b).

Cultural Variation and Everyday Experience

As populations grow more ethnically and racially diverse and as the people of the world become linked more closely by commerce, transportation, and communication, the likelihood of individuals from different cultures and subcultures living together increases. An awareness of cultural differences helps ease everyday interactions in a multicultural society and can be crucial in international relations:

- In Iran, people are expected to give false praise and make insincere promises. They are expected to tell others what they want to hear in order to avoid conflict or offer hope when, clearly, there is none. This practice, known as *taarof*, is considered polite, not offensive. Children learn from an early age to pick up on nuances in others' comments. The practice has its historical roots in centuries of occupation by foreign powers, which taught Iranians the value of hiding their true feelings. As one Iranian psychologist put it, "When you tell lies, it can save your life" (quoted in Slackman, 2006, p. 5).
- In Afghanistan and Iraq, the thumbs-up gesture—a sign of approval in the United States—is the equivalent of giving someone "the finger." To reduce potentially dangerous cultural clashes, the U.S. Marine Corps distributes "Culture Smart Cards" to U.S. military personnel on their arrival in these countries. The cards contain instructions on matters such as how to shake hands, what gestures are appropriate, and how to act when in Iraqi or Afghan homes (Edidin, 2005).
- In India, waiting lines do not carry the same set of cultural expectations they do in the U.S. When a line appears to be too long to some, they will create their own lines by standing next to someone toward the front of the original line and hoping that others will line up behind them. Pretty soon the original line has sprouted multiple branches. People will push their entire bodies against the person in front of them in hopes of deterring cutters. But that rarely works:

    [Cutters] hover near the line's middle, holding papers looking lost in a practiced way, then slip in somewhere close to the front. When confronted, their refrain is predictable: "Oh, I didn't see the line." (Giridharadas, 2010a, p. 5)

In all these cases, you can see how important it is for soldiers, diplomats, negotiators, and tourists to know of such tendencies. Without such knowledge, the risk of misunderstandings and perhaps even conflict increases.

Cultural variation reflects more than just differences in people's habits and customs. It indicates that even the most taken-for-granted truths in our lives, the things we assume are universal and unambiguous, are subject to different interpretations and definitions worldwide. Two important examples of such variation are beliefs about health and illness and definitions of sex.

Health and Illness

A prominent doctor once said, "A disease does not exist until we name it" (quoted in Kolata, 2011, p. 3). In other words, we can't claim to have a disease that is not recognized as real in our culture. In Malaysia, a man may be diagnosed with *koro*, a sudden, intense anxiety that his sexual organs will recede into his body, causing death. In some Latin American countries, a person can suffer from *susto*, an illness tied to a frightening event that makes the soul leave the body, causing unhappiness and sickness (American Psychiatric Association, 2000). One psychiatrist estimates that as many as one million Japanese youth (or about 1% of the population) suffer from *hikikomori*, a phenomenon whereby alienated adolescents withdraw from social life and sequester themselves in their rooms for six months or longer (some have lived in isolation for over a decade; M. Jones, 2006). None of these conditions exists as a medical diagnosis in other parts of the world. But they are not simply anthropological curiosities. They show that culture shapes everyday notions of health and illness.

Even more compelling, though, are the dramatic cultural differences in medical treatment among societies that share many other values, beliefs, norms, and structural elements. In the United States, medical treatment tends to originate from an aggressive "can do" cultural spirit. Doctors in the United States are much more likely than European doctors to prescribe drugs and resort to surgery (Payer, 1988). Women in the United States are more likely than their European counterparts to undergo radical mastectomies, deliver their babies by cesarean section, and undergo routine hysterectomies while still in their 40s. People in the United States tend to see their bodies as machines that require annual checkups for routine maintenance. Diseases are enemies that need to be conquered. Words like "fight" and "battle" are frequently invoked to describe the struggles of people receiving cancer treatment. Their stoicism in facing the disease, undergoing surgery, or enduring the powerful side effects of chemotherapy are often considered signs of "bravery." If they recover, they've "beaten" or "defeated" the cancer; if they succumb, they've "lost the good fight" (Jennings, 2010).

In contrast, British medicine is much more subdued. British physicians don't recommend routine examinations, seldom prescribe drugs, and order about half as many X-ray studies as U.S. doctors do. British patients are also much less likely to have surgery. These attitudes also influence perceptions of patients. People who are quiet and withdrawn—something U.S. doctors might consider symptoms of clinical depression—tend to be seen by British psychiatrists as perfectly normal.

Ironically, despite their more aggressive approach, Americans are actually much sicker than their British counterparts. They suffer higher rates of conditions like diabetes, heart disease, and obesity and have a lower life expectancy. These differences exist even when controlling for social class. According to one study, the richest one third of U.S. citizens are in worse health than the poorest one third of Britons (Banks, Marmot, Oldfield, & Smith, 2006).

In addition to determining the nature of illness, cultural attitudes determine what it means to be sick and how individuals experience sickness. Each society has a **sick role**, a widely understood set of rules about how people are supposed to behave when sick (Parsons, 1951). The sick role entails certain obligations (things sick people are expected to do) as well as certain privileges (things sick people are entitled to). Here are some common elements of the sick role in U.S. society:

- Because we tend to think of most illnesses as things that happen to people, individuals may be exempted from responsibility for the condition itself. At the same time, though, they're expected to recognize the condition as undesirable and something that should be overcome as soon as possible.

- Individuals who are allowed to occupy the sick role are excused from ordinary daily duties and expectations. This privilege varies with the severity of the illness. Compare someone with cancer to someone with a cold, for instance. National legislation—in the form of the Family and Medical Leave Act—and private workplace sick leave policies are the institutional manifestations of these expectations.
- Depending on the magnitude of the malady, sick people may be given relief from the ordinary norms of etiquette and propriety. Think of the nasty moods, actions, or insults you're able to "get away with" when you're sick that people wouldn't tolerate from you if you were well.
- Sick people are entitled to ask for and receive care and sympathy from others. But sympathy requests operate under their own set of cultural regulations. For instance, one should not claim too much sympathy, for too long, or for too many problems. In other words, sick people are expected to downplay their problems to avoid the appearance of self-pity. At the same time, though, they are expected to graciously accept some expressions of sympathy so as not to appear ungrateful (C. Clark, 1997).
- People occupying the sick role are required to take the culturally prescribed actions that will aid in their recovery, including, if the condition is serious enough, seeking help from a culturally appropriate health care professional (Parsons, 1951). Sometimes, to obtain the privilege of exemption from normal social obligations, people must be documented as officially ill from a culturally acceptable source. In the United States, that means a "doctor's note" (Lorber, 2000). Without such validation, your boss might not give you the day off, or your instructor might not allow you to miss an exam and reschedule it for a later date.
- Sick people are obligated to think of others as well as themselves. Hence, they are required to take precautions to avoid infecting those around them. In some cultures, sick people are expected to wear surgical masks in public to prevent contamination.

Failure on the part of sick people either to exercise their rights or to fulfill the obligations of the sick role—as when a person shows up at work with a persistent cough and a 102-degree fever—may elicit sanctions from the group (Crary, 2007). Moreover, those who do not appear to want to recover or who seem to enjoy being sick quickly lose sympathy. A person may also give up legal rights by not seeking or following expert advice. Parents who, because of their religious beliefs, prevent culturally approved medical intervention for their sick children have been arrested and charged with child endangerment or worse. If you are hospitalized and your attending physician doesn't think you ought to be discharged, but you leave anyway, your records will indicate that you have left "AMA"—against medical advice. This designation protects the doctor and the hospital from any liability should your condition worsen.

Like illness itself, sick role expectations are culturally influenced. For instance, when recent Latin American immigrants to the United States fall ill, they are likely to make a visit to the local *botanica* rather than a doctor. *Botanicas* are stores that sell all manner of folk remedies, religious objects, amulets, oils, perfumes, and other products purported to have curative powers. These practices, which combine alternative medicine with Roman Catholicism and other spiritual practices, are used to treat everything from arthritis to financial problems (Trotter & Chavira, 1997).

While different cultures define the sick role differently, it can also vary considerably along social class lines within the same culture (Freund & McGuire, 1991). Someone might have a debilitating disease, but without health insurance she or he may not have the wherewithal to seek the care of health professionals (and receive an official diagnosis) or may not be able to take time off from work for fear of losing her or his job. In short, socioeconomic factors may preclude such people from claiming sick role status.

(Text continues on page 129)

Funeral Rituals in the Netherlands

Marrie Bot

Rituals for the dead are typically dominated by religious beliefs and norms. In the Netherlands, however, rapid secularization and massive immigration have had a great impact on death ceremonies.

The sudden death of my father in 1984 made me reflect on death, funerals, and mourning rituals. I realized then how little is known about the manner in which the dead are cared for among either the native Dutch population or the ethnic minorities who have settled in the Netherlands over the past decades. I began my project in 1990 by setting up a network of informants and mediators of 10 population groups. From 1990 to 1998 I attended more than 100 funerals of Roman Catholic, Protestant, Jewish, and secular Dutch groups. I also photographed the death rituals of many ethnic groups living in the Netherlands, including Creoles and Hindus from Surinam; Pakistani, Iranian, and Surinam-Javanese Muslims; Cape Verdeans; and Chinese.

These photos are from my book *A Last Farewell: Funeral and Mourning Rituals in the Multi-cultural Society of the Netherlands*. It shows the rituals and death customs from the moment the dead person is washed to the last mourning rituals, which are sometimes repeated many years after the death of a person. I also conducted a comprehensive study into the origin and the meaning of the different rituals. This book was the first overview of death in a multicultural society.

The deceased person, a young woman, is taken to the cemetery by a traditional Dutch funeral coach drawn by Friesian horses. In the past the entire cortege was made up of coaches, which have now been replaced by black funeral cars. For nostalgic reasons the horse-drawn funeral coach is now only used at the request of the relatives.

At the end of the cremation ceremony of a 13-year-old Dutch boy, white balloons were sent up in the presence of his parents, brother, fellow pupils, and scouting friends.

A man and a woman looked after a friend who suffered from Hodgkin's disease. After he died, they washed their friend themselves and dressed him in his favorite party suit. Because they did not want him to be laid out in an impersonal funeral parlor, they laid him in his own bed at home. From time to time during the days preceding the funeral ceremony, they sat with him and with other friends.

Although I was interested in the ethnic experience, I noticed that secularization has also changed funeral rituals in the Netherlands. Under the influence of the predominantly Protestant culture, Dutch death ceremonies were always very formal and sober. But by 1997, 60% of the Dutch population had become secular, 19% Roman Catholic, and only 21% Protestant. Traditionally the dead were buried, but nowadays more than half of the population prefer cremation. And by the end of the 1980s, AIDS and cancer patients were asking for personalized farewell rituals. The media reported on these new types of rituals, and planning one's own cremation or funeral became a generally accepted option.

The arrival of immigrants with their own diverse funeral and mourning rituals also caused many changes. The Dutch law regulating the disposal of the dead has been adjusted to meet the needs of these groups. Every population group in the Netherlands may now bury or cremate its dead as they see fit.

Jewish Funeral Rituals

Since the 16th century, Jews from southern and eastern Europe have emigrated to the Netherlands. More than 140,000 mainly poor Jews lived in the Netherlands around 1940, but most of them died in the German concentration camps during World War II. Currently around 30,000 Jews live in the Netherlands. Only 25% of them belong to an orthodox or liberal religious community. The other Jews have assimilated and consider their Jewishness a cultural identity based on ancestry.

For those who do observe the religious rules, the dead are buried at a Jewish cemetery, where graves are left eternally. At most Dutch cemeteries, graves are sometimes removed after 30 years.

The traditional Jewish mourning period lasts seven days to a year, depending on the relationship of the next of kin. The relatives have to adhere to strict rules.

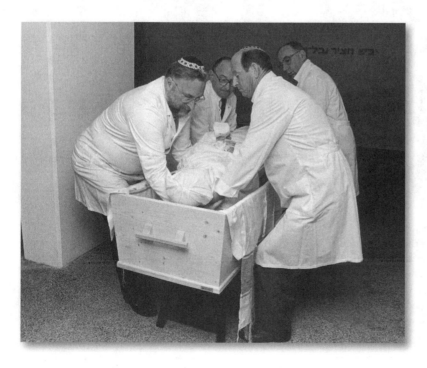

Under traditional Jewish law, the dead are buried. The deceased person is immediately covered with a sheet. Nobody, not even a close relative, is allowed to see the dead person. Viewing the dead is common among other groups in the Netherlands. With the Jews, neither relatives nor the undertaker lay out the deceased; rather, a Jewish funeral association handles this task. Its members dress the deceased in white clothes, because after death everybody is the same to God, regardless of position in life.

Surinam-Creole Death Rituals

Creoles are the descendants of the African slaves in the former Dutch colony of Surinam. Many Surinam people emigrated to the Netherlands when Surinam became independent in 1975. Some 100,000 Creoles now live in the Netherlands, mainly in the large cities. They have assimilated into Dutch society but have kept many of their own cultural and religious traditions. Protestant-Christian and Winti beliefs play an important role in their funeral rituals.

When a Creole dies, the relatives hire a Creole brotherhood that specializes in laying out the dead. Their members, the *Dinari*, perform the washing and dressing rituals with great care in a funeral parlor. The deceased is asked for permission before each ritual is performed, while Creole and Christian songs are sung. The songs are alternated with the drinking of rum and brandy. The next of kin may not be present during these "secret" rituals.

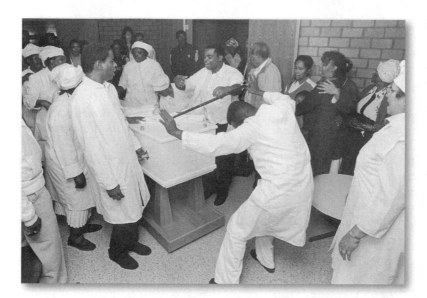

At the wake, the deceased is carried into the room while the *Dinari* sing and dance. To the accompaniment of loud crying and lamenting, the relatives carry out the farewell rituals. However, no tears may fall on the dead person, because then his or her soul could not leave in peace, which would bring bad luck for the relatives.

After the burial, the relatives and friends gather on the eighth day (*aiti dey*) and during the sixth week (*siksi wiki*) at home. A meal for the deceased is put outside, and in the living room a candle and a glass of water are put on a table laid with a white tablecloth. According to Winti belief, this arrangement will maintain the contact between the living and the soul of the dead and the spirits of the ancestors. All those present read from the Bible and sing Christian and Creole songs from 8 o'clock in the evening until 5 o'clock in the morning. After midnight the atmosphere can become more cheerful, and people drink, dance, and reminisce about the deceased.

Islamic Funeral Rituals

There are some 600,000 Muslims in the Netherlands. They come from a great many different countries, such as Turkey, Morocco, Pakistan (migrant workers), Surinam, Indonesia (a former Dutch colony), Iran, and many African countries (asylum seekers). They are a heterogeneous population who combine the general rules of the Koran with their own cultural and religious traditions, which are expressed during the burial ceremonies.

Muslims are allowed to bury their dead at cemeteries in the Netherlands according to their rules: They can bury their dead within 24 hours, without a coffin, and at graveyards that are only for Muslims. The largest group of Muslims, the Turks and Moroccans, still prefer taking their dead to their native country and burying them there.

Death is the will of Allah, and therefore deep mourning may last only three days. The condolence reception is at the home of the deceased person's family. Most Muslims continue the death rituals for 40 days, however. On certain days the men read the Koran for the salvation of the soul of the deceased. After they have finished reading, relatives show their gratitude by offering them a large meal on behalf of the deceased. Women keep themselves apart in the kitchen or bedroom.

Relatives or volunteers of the same gender as the dead person wash him or her following standard Islamic rules. The Surinam-Javanese in the photo are liberal and sometimes allow the washing rituals to be performed by someone of the opposite sex. The dead person must be wrapped in a white shroud, because after death everyone is the same to Allah.

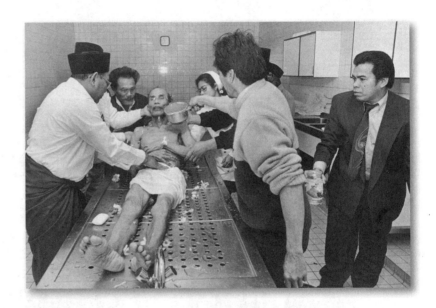

After the ritual washing, Pakistani men recite the death prayers, led by an imam. Women are not allowed to be present because the sexes are routinely segregated and also because it is believed that their loud wailing and sobbing would disturb the peace of the dead. At the end of the ceremony, the men bid farewell by walking past the coffin.

Chinese Ancestor Worship

At the beginning of the 20th century, the Chinese came to the Netherlands from China, Hong Kong, Surinam, Indonesia, and Vietnam. It is a diverse group consisting of some 60,000 people. Most Chinese keep themselves apart from mainstream Dutch society. They work mostly in restaurants owned by other Chinese and have relationships among themselves based on their country of origin and language.

The death cult plays an important role for all traditional Chinese. It is a combination of elements of the three Chinese religions: Taoism, Confucianism, and Buddhism. Faith teaches that the dead continue to live in the dangerous underworld while they are on their way to the Western Paradise. The dead continue to influence the lives of the relatives. The living have a lifelong obligation to help their ancestors on their journey to paradise by making sacrifices. They hope that their ancestors will show their gratitude by keeping them healthy, making them rich, and granting them sons.

At the burial the relatives place a meal and incense at the grave, and they also burn paper clothes and large stacks of fake money called "hell bank notes." The son must conduct these rituals. Three times a year relatives visit the graves to honor all ancestors. The Surinam-Chinese family in the photo is making a threefold sacrifice at the Rotterdam cemetery—for the father in the grave, for their grandparents buried in Surinam, and for their great-grandfather in China.

Surinam-Hindu Death Rituals

The Surinam-Hindustani are descendants of the contract workers who were taken from north India (Hindustan) to Surinam around 1900. Since the independence of Surinam, some 100,000 Surinam Hindustani have emigrated to the Netherlands. About 80% of them are Hindus, 16% Muslims, and 4% Christians.

The Surinam Hindus live predominantly in the larger cities and have adopted the lifestyle and work pattern of the Western world. At home they adhere to the Hindu faith and rules, which are mainly practiced during the obligatory ceremonies, the *sanskaars*, connected to rites of passage. The rituals for the dead are most important. The deceased is carefully washed and smartly dressed in the funeral parlor by the relatives.

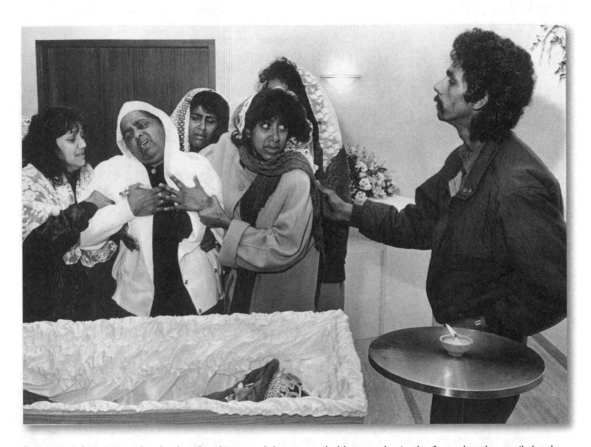

Receptions for viewing the dead and making condolences are held every day in the funeral parlor until the day of the cremation. Just as at Creole funerals, the closest relatives participate in the ritual crying and wailing, and sometimes people faint. With orthodox Hindus, the son or husband carries out all the rituals for the deceased. On the day of the cremation his head is shaved, except for a small tuft of hair on the top, which is regarded as the seat of his wisdom. He is now clean and ready to perform his task.

On the same day that the cremation takes place, the son, supervised by the Hindu priest, called *Pundit*, carries out a sacrifice ritual that lasts hours. Its purpose is to protect the deceased father until the moment of the cremation. One of the funeral parlors in Rotterdam has special facilities for Hindus and Chinese so that they can perform their fire offerings.

The relatives, and often hundreds of friends of the deceased, bid a ritual farewell in the funeral parlor. These gatherings are often very emotional.

During the year of mourning, the four offering rituals for the soul of the dead person are very important. On the 10th day and the 13th day, and in the 6th and 12th month, the entire extended family gathers at the home of the deceased. This photo shows the offering ritual on the 13th day. The ceremony begins at 10 o'clock in the morning and continues until 3 o'clock in the afternoon. The home bar has been covered, as alcohol is banned during the mourning rituals. In this special case the brother of the deceased woman, who is divorced, conducts the offering rituals because the woman's son is still too young. Nevertheless, the boy's head was also shaven, and he had to participate in the ritual with his uncle on the 10th and 13th day.

The person making the offerings has to carry out a number of complicated proceedings under the supervision of the *Pundit*. He takes care that the deceased will have a new cosmic body and hence will be able to complete the difficult journey to Yama, the realm of the dead. There the deceased will be united with his or her ancestors and await reincarnation. During every ceremony, a meal for the deceased is put outside, and gifts are offered to the *Pundit* to help the deceased during his or her journey.

After the rituals the guests will eat a special vegetarian meal and usually stay chatting for a long time.

The Sexes

The culture we grow up in shapes our most fundamental beliefs, even about what most people would consider the basic, universal facts of life. For instance, we take for granted that humans can be divided into two clearly identifiable sexes that are genetically determined at the moment of conception. If you asked someone how to distinguish between males and females, the response would probably focus on observable physical characteristics—body shape, hair, voice, facial features, and so on. When biologists distinguish between the sexes, they too refer to biological traits—for example, chromosomes (XX for female, XY for male), sex glands (ovaries or testes), hormones (estrogen or testosterone), genitalia (vagina or penis), reproductive capacities (pregnancy or impregnation), germ cells produced (ova or sperm), and secondary sex characteristics (hips and breasts or facial hair and deep voice).

These characteristics, and hence the two sex categories, male and female, are usually assumed to be biologically determined, permanent, universal (males are males and females are females no matter what country or what era you live in), exhaustive (everyone can be placed into one or the other category), and mutually exclusive (you can only be one or the other sex; you can't be both). This set of beliefs is called the *sexual dichotomy.*

If you think about it, our entire culture is built around the sexual dichotomy. We have separate clothing sections for men and women, separate hygienic products, separate sections in shoe stores, separate public restrooms, and so on. The sexual dichotomy is so obvious that we simply assume it to be in the nature of things. Our casual references to the "opposite" sex reinforce how much we take the sexual dichotomy for granted; when two things are opposite, it implies there's nothing in between.

But on closer inspection, the natural reality of the sexual dichotomy begins to break down. Throughout human history and across all societies, certain people have transcended the categories of male and female. They may be born with anatomical and/or genital configurations that are ambiguous. Or they may simply choose to live their lives in ways that don't conform to existing gender expectations associated with their sex (see Chapter 5 for more information about the distinction between sex and gender). *Transsexuals*—people who identify with a different sex and sometimes undergo hormone treatment and surgery to change their sex—challenge the idea that male and female are permanent biological characteristics. It's estimated that 1 in 30,000 men and 1 in 100,000 women in the United States undergo sex reassignment surgery each year, although many advocates consider this figure an underestimate (cited in Jost, 2006a). In 2008, a female-to-male transsexual named Thomas Beatie made international headlines when he gave birth to a baby girl. Although Thomas had his breasts removed, was taking testosterone (which deepened his voice and gave him facial hair), and was legally a man, he had kept his female reproductive organs.

The growing number of young transsexuals who transition in their late teens and early 20s has placed new pressures on colleges to accommodate them or risk charges of discrimination. The problem is especially acute for women's colleges that must find ways to house and meet the needs of their female students who become men while on campus. At Smith College, many restrooms have been redesigned as "gender neutral," and some professors have their students fill out forms indicating their preferred pronouns (Quart, 2008).

The impermanence of sex received official recognition of sorts when the International Olympic Committee's executive board approved a proposal to allow transsexuals to compete in the 2004 Athens Olympic Games. Athletes who had undergone sex reassignment surgery were eligible to compete as long as they had been legally recognized as a member of the "new" sex and it had been at least two years since their surgery. Shortly afterward, the Ladies European Golf Tour enacted a similar policy, allowing a 37-year-old Danish male-to-female transsexual to play in one of their professional tournaments. In 2006, the City of New York began allowing people to change the sex listed on their birth certificates.

Although transsexuals challenge the assumption of sexual permanence, they don't challenge the belief that there are only two sex categories. But that assumption is contested in some cultures. In Navajo culture, for instance, one could be identified as male, female, or *nadle*—a third sex assigned to those whose sex-typed anatomical characteristics were ambiguous at birth (Lang, 1998). Physically normal individuals also had the opportunity to choose to become *nadle* if they so desired. The gender status of *nadle* is simultaneously masculine and feminine. They are allowed to perform the tasks and take up the occupations of both men and women. For the Chuckchi of eastern Siberia, a biological male child with feminine physical traits gradually transforms into a "soft man." Although he keeps his masculine name, he is expected to live as a woman (W. L. Williams, 1992). The *hijras* of India are born as men, but by choice they have their genitals surgically removed (Reddy, 2005). This operation transforms them not into women but into *hijras*, who appear feminine—dressing, standing, walking, and sitting as women. Many figures in Hindu mythology are neither male nor female. Hence, Indian culture not only accommodates the *hijras* but views them as meaningful, even powerful beings.

Such cross-cultural examples illustrate that our taken-for-granted beliefs about sex and gender are not held worldwide. In other cultures, sex is not dichotomous, exhaustive, or permanent.

The sexual dichotomy is not challenge-free in the United States either. Consider the standard of mutual exclusivity, for example. **Intersexuals** are individuals in whom sexual differentiation is either incomplete or indistinct. They may have the chromosomal pattern of a female but the external genitals of a male, or they may have both ovaries and testicles. Experts estimate that about 1% of all babies born have some form of intersexuality, meaning that they are born with sexual organs that don't completely fit into the standard sex categories (Fausto-Sterling, 2000; Jost, 2006a).

It is interesting to note that the medical response to intersexuals supports the cultural and historical belief that there are two and only two sexes. Intersexuality is usually defined by doctors and medical researchers as a defective combination of the two existing categories and not as a third, fourth, or fifth category unto itself. Furthermore, on diagnosis of intersexuality, a decision is always made to define the individual as either male or female. In societies with advanced medical technology, surgical and chemical means may be used to establish consistency between visible anatomy and the social label. Every month, dozens of sexually ambiguous newborns are "assigned" a sex and undergo surgery to confirm the designation (Cowley, 1997). About 90% are designated female because creating a vagina is considered surgically easier than creating a penis (Angier, 1997b).

However, an increasingly vocal group of intersexuals protest that many of the surgical techniques used to "correct" the problem of visually ambiguous genitals are mutilating and potentially harmful. They cite cases of intersexuals being robbed of any sexual sensation in the attempt to surgically "normalize" them—that is, give them the physical appearance of either a male or a female. The founder of the Intersex Society of North America eloquently summed up her organization's frustration: "They can't conceive of leaving someone alone" (quoted in Angier, 1997a, p. A10).

The medical profession can't leave these individuals alone because to do so would undermine our cultural understanding of sex. Drastic surgical intervention is undertaken in these cases not because the infant's life is threatened but because our entire social structure is organized around having two and only two sexes (Lorber, 1989). The male-female dichotomy in our culture is so essential to our way of life that those who challenge it are often considered disloyal to the most fundamental of biological "facts." To suggest that the labels "male" and "female" are not sufficient to categorize everyone is to threaten a basic organizing principle of social life. So pervasive is the sexual dichotomy that one doctor estimated her chances of persuading the parents of an intersexual child *not* to choose surgery at zero (Weil, 2006).

Conclusion

Over the span of a year or two, most cultures seem to have a stable set of norms about the acceptability of certain behaviors. This stability is illusory, however. From the perspective of a generation or even a decade later, that sense of order would give way to a sense of change (McCall & Simmons, 1978). Behaviors, values, beliefs, and morals fluctuate with startling frequency. Thus, comparisons across eras, in addition to comparisons across cultures, can provide rich insight into shifting definitions of acceptability, the nature of everyday life, and ultimately large-scale social change and stability.

The cultural and historical underpinnings of our private lives help us see the relationship among the individual, society, and social order. Cultural practices add continuity and order to social life.

To an individual, culture appears massive and unrelenting; but at the same time, it cannot exist without people. Norms govern our lives, whether we live by them or rebel against them. But to fully understand the relationship between the individual and society, we must look beyond the fact that culture and history shape our lives; we must see them as human constructions as well.

YOUR TURN

Although everyday cultural norms underlie all we do, they remain largely unnoticed and unquestioned. The best proof of the existence of these norms lies in our reactions when they are violated. This exercise entails a small breach of a common cultural norm. The following suggestions are based on an exercise used by sociologist Jodi O'Brien at Seattle University:

- Make a purchase in a department store and offer to pay more than the listed price. Try to convince the clerk that you think the merchandise is worth the price you are offering.
- Send a close family member a birthday card months away from his or her actual birthday.
- Quietly talk to yourself in a public place.
- Stand or sit close to a stranger or, conversely, stand far away from a good friend or lover during the course of an ordinary conversation.
- Select an occasion—going to class, going on a date, going to the library—and dress differently from the expected "uniform." Treat your attire as absolutely appropriate to the circumstances.

- Whenever someone says to you, "See you later," ask her or him probing questions: "When?" "Do you have some plans to get together later?" "What do you mean by 'see'?" and so on. Or when someone says, "How's it going?" ask, "What do you mean by 'it'?" or "What do you mean by 'going'?"
- In a restaurant, offer to pay for your meal before you order it, or order dessert first, then the main course, then appetizers, and then drinks.

If you like, you can choose a different unspoken norm as long as it is one that lends order and predictability to daily social interactions. Be creative!

It is particularly important that this behavior be neither flagrantly bizarre—such as going to class dressed as a chicken—nor a violation of the law. Such acts do not address the power of the subtle, unspoken norms that, symbolic interactionism argues, make social life orderly. Also, do not do anything that might seriously inconvenience or humiliate someone else or put you in danger. Finally, make sure the norm has something to do with keeping order in face-to-face interactions. For instance, coming to class 10 minutes late violates a cultural norm, but it doesn't disrupt interactional order. Above all, remember to treat your violation as perfectly normal. You must give the impression that what you are doing is perfectly acceptable and ordinary.

As you conduct your exercises, record your own feelings and reactions as well as those of the people around you. What were people's initial responses to you? What did they do to try to "normalize" your behavior? How did you feel breaching this norm? Were you nervous? Was it uncomfortable? If so, why?

If possible, try also to debrief your subjects afterward: Tell them what you were really doing, and then interview them regarding their interpretations of the experience. You are likely to collect additional information on how people attempt to "explain away" unusual and strange circumstances and how they attempt to restore order to the situation. What are the implications of these sorts of "experiments" for understanding human behavior and the nature of social order in this society?

CHAPTER HIGHLIGHTS

- Culture provides members of a society with a common bond, a sense that we see certain facets of society in similar ways. That we can live together at all depends on the fact that members of a society share a certain amount of cultural knowledge.

- Norms—the rules and standards that govern all social encounters—provide order in our lives. They reflect commonly held assumptions about conventional behavior. Norm violations mark the boundaries of acceptable behavior and symbolically reaffirm what society defines as right and wrong.

- The more ethnically and culturally diverse a society, the greater the likelihood of normative clashes between groups.

- Over the span of a few years, most cultures present an image of stability and agreement regarding normative boundaries. This agreement is illusory, however. Over a generation or even a decade, that sense of order is replaced by a sense of change.

KEY TERMS

counterculture: Group that actively opposes the values and behavior patterns of the dominant culture

cultural relativism: Principle that people's beliefs and activities should be interpreted in terms of their own culture

ethnocentrism: Tendency to judge other cultures using one's own as a standard

folkway: Informal norm that is mildly punished when violated

heteronormative culture: Culture in which heterosexuality is accepted as the normal, taken-for-granted mode of sexual expression

institutionalized norm: Pattern of behavior within existing social institutions that is widely accepted in a society

intersexuals: Individuals in whom sexual differentiation is either incomplete or ambiguous

material culture: Artifacts of a society that represent adaptations to the social and physical environment

mores: Highly codified, formal, systematized norms that bring severe punishment when violated

nonmaterial culture: Knowledge, beliefs, customs, values, morals, and symbols that are shared by members of a society and that distinguish the society from others

sanction: Social response that punishes or otherwise discourages violations of a social norm

sexual dichotomy: Belief that two biological sex categories, male and female, are permanent, universal, exhaustive, and mutually exclusive

sick role: Set of norms governing how one is supposed to behave and what one is entitled to when sick

subculture: Values, behaviors, and artifacts of a group that distinguish its members from the larger culture

transsexuals: People who identify with a different sex and sometimes undergo hormone treatment and surgery to change their sex

STUDENT STUDY SITE

Visit the Student Study Site at **www.sagepub.com/newman9e** for these additional learning tools:

- Flashcards
- Web quizzes
- Sociologists at Work features
- Micro-Macro Connection features
- Video links
- Audio links
- Web resources
- SAGE journal articles

Building Identity

Socialization

5

When I was little, my family lived in a suburb just outside New York City. One day, shortly after my ninth birthday, my parents sat me down and told me that we were going to be moving. They had narrowed down our ultimate destination to two possibilities: Laredo, Texas, or a suburb of Los Angeles called Burbank. After some rather intense debate, they chose Burbank. And so we headed "out West," where from age 9 to age 18, I lived in the shadow of the entertainment industry and all its glamour, glitz, and movie stars.

It wasn't long before I became a typical sun-worshipping Southern California kid. I often wonder how differently I would have turned out if my parents had chosen Laredo and I had spent my formative years along the Texas-Mexico border instead of in the middle of Tinseltown. Would I have a fondness for cowboy hats and snakeskin boots instead of flip-flops and shorts? Would I have grown up loving country music instead of the Beach Boys? Would my goals, beliefs, or sense of morality be different? In short, would I be a different person?

Try to imagine what your life would be like if you had grown up under different circumstances. What if your father had been a harpsichord enthusiast instead of a diehard Cubs fan? What if your family had been Muslim instead of Episcopalian? What if you had an older brother instead of a younger sister? What if you had lived on a farm instead of in a big city? What if you had been born in the 1960s instead of the 1990s? Your tastes, preferences, and hobbies, as well as your values, ambitions, and aspirations, would no doubt be different. But more profoundly, your self-concept, self-esteem, personality—the very essence of who you are—would be altered too.

Consider the broader social and historical circumstances of your life. What kind of impact might they have had on the type of person you are? Talk to elderly people who were children back in the 1930s, and they will speak of the permanent impact that the Great Depression had on them (Elder & Liker, 1982). Imagine spending your childhood as a Jew in Nazi Germany. That couldn't help but shape your outlook on life. The same can be said for growing up poor and black in the American South in the segregated 1950s or wealthy and white in Salt Lake City during the George W. Bush presidency.

Becoming the person you are cannot be separated from the people, historical events, and social circumstances that surround you. In this chapter, I examine the process of socialization—how we learn what's expected of us in our families, our communities, and our culture and how we learn to behave according to those expectations.

The primary focus will be on the development of identity. ***Identity*** is our most essential and personal characteristic. It consists of our membership in various social groups (race, ethnicity, religion, gender, etc.), the traits we show to others, and the traits they ascribe to us. Our identity locates us in the social world, thoroughly affecting everything we do, feel, say, and think in our lives. Most people tend to believe that our self-concept, our sense of "maleness" or "femaleness," and our racial and ethnic identities are biologically or psychologically determined and therefore permanent and unchangeable. But as you will discover, these characteristics are social constructions: as much a product of our social setting and the significant people in our lives as a product of our physical traits and innate predispositions.

Genes, Social Structure, and the Construction of Human Beings

The question of how we become who we are has for centuries occupied the attention of biologists, psychologists, anthropologists, sociologists, philosophers, poets, and novelists. The issue is typically framed as a debate between *nature* (we are who we are because we were born that way) and *nurture* (we are who we are because of the way we were treated while growing up). Are we simply the predetermined product of our genes and biochemistry, or are we "created" from scratch by the people and the social institutions that surround us?

The answer to this question swings back and forth depending on the dominant cultural mood. In the late 19th and early 20th centuries, genetic inheritance became a popular explanation for human behavior, including a host of social problems ranging from poverty and crime to alcoholism and mental deficiency. Scientists, borrowing from the selective breeding practices used with racehorses and livestock, advocated programs of ***eugenics***, or controlled mating, to ensure that the "defective" genes of troublesome individuals would not be passed on to future generations. Theories of genetic inferiority became the cornerstone of Adolf Hitler's horrors in Nazi Germany during World War II. After the war, most people wanted to get as far away from such "nature" arguments as possible. So in the 1950s and 1960s, people heavily emphasized environmental influences on behavior, especially the role of early family experiences in shaping children's future personalities (Gould, 1997).

Today, because of the growing cultural emphasis on scientific technology, genetic explanations of human behavior have again become fashionable. In recent years, researchers have claimed that such diverse social phenomena as shyness, impulsiveness, intelligence, aggression, obesity, alcoholism, and addiction to gambling are at least partly due to heredity. An economist raised eyebrows recently when he argued in his book that because of the power of genetic inheritance, parenting hardly matters. Children's destiny is pretty much genetically predetermined. Healthy, smart, happy, virtuous parents tend to have matching offspring no matter what they do to and for their children. So, he wrote, they should just relax and let their children do, essentially, what they want (B. Caplan, 2011). Similarly, the authors of the best-selling book *Freakonomics* wrote, "It isn't so much a matter of what you *do* as a parent; it's who you are (Levitt & Dubner, 2009, p. 175). The success of the Human Genome Project—an undertaking, completed in 2003, that mapped all the 20,000 to 25,000 genes in human DNA—will no doubt add fuel to "nature" arguments in the years to come.

Yet we are apparently not ready to say that nurture plays no role. In 2011, a prominent Yale law professor struck a blow for the environmental influence on kids when she argued in her popular book that the educational success of Asian children is due largely to the heavy-handed role of mothers, whom she refers to as "Tiger Mothers." She recommends—to all parents, no matter what their ethnic backgrounds—that the prescription for a successful child consists of stressing academic performance, never accepting a mediocre grade, insisting on drilling and practice, and instilling unwavering respect for authority (Chua, 2011). Some affluent parents have even gone so far as to move to another country for a year so their children can be immersed in another culture and become cultivated, global citizens (L. Miller, 2011).

Indeed, when it comes to certain traits, heredity is meaningful only in the context of social experiences. Take intelligence. Many geneticists argue that heredity determines the limits of intelligence (Kirp, 2006). They base this claim on studies that have found that differences in IQ scores between identical twins (who share all their genes) are smaller than differences between fraternal twins (who share only half their genes). But it's impossible to understand intelligence without examining how our genetic makeup interacts with our social experiences. As one author put it,

> You've got genes that are going to give you a certain range of height, or a certain range in the color of your eyes, and a certain range of your intelligence. But we can't say that there's this separate nature that just does its thing separately from nurture. The genes literally do come first, but the way the genes act, their influence, actually doesn't take place before they interact with their environment. Everything is dependent on this interaction. (Shenk, 2010, p. 44)

Other researchers have found that children's socioeconomic environment can make an enormous difference in their intelligence. One study of seven-year-old children found that while genetics accounts for most of the variation in IQ scores among twins with wealthy parents, the opposite is the case for twins from impoverished families. In these families, the IQs of identical twins vary just as much as the IQs of fraternal twins (Turkheimer, Haley, Waldron, D'Onofrio, & Gottesman, 2003). The researchers conclude that home life is critical for children at the lower end of the economic spectrum. In a chaotic and unstable environment, children's genetic potential cannot be reached. Conversely, affluent families are better equipped to provide the cognitive stimulation needed for neurological development.

As you might suspect, most sociologists would argue that human beings are much more than a collection of genetic predispositions and biological characteristics; they reflect society's influence as well. But that doesn't mean that genes are irrelevant. Certainly, our outward appearance, our physical strength, and our inherited predisposition to sickness have some effect on our personal development. Furthermore, our every thought and action is the result of a complex series of neurological and electrochemical events in our brains and bodies. When we feel the need to eat we are reacting to a physiological sensation—stomach contractions—brought about by a lowering of blood sugar. Satisfying hunger is clearly a biological process. But the way we react to this sensation cannot be predicted by physiology alone. What, when, how, and how often we eat are all matters of cultural forces that we learn over time. When you say something like, "I'm starving, but it's too early to eat dinner," you're signaling the power of cultural training in overriding physiological demands.

Likewise, society can magnify genetic and physical differences or cover them up. We've collectively decided that some differences are socially irrelevant (e.g., eye color) and that some are important enough to be embedded in our most important social institutions (e.g., sex and skin color), giving rise to different rights, duties, expectations, and access to educational, economic, and political opportunities.

So while our genes and brains may have a role to play in who we become, the behaviors and attitudes of significant people in our lives and the cultural and institutional forces that structure our lives are just as, if not more, influential (Eliot, 2010). As these things change, so do we. This proposition is not altogether comforting. It implies that who we are may in some ways be "accidental," the result of a series of social coincidences, chance encounters, decisions made by others, and political, economic, and historical events that are in large measure beyond our control—such as growing up in California rather than Texas.

Socialization: Becoming Who We Are

The structural-functionalist perspective reminds us that the fundamental task of any society is to reproduce itself—to create members whose behaviors, desires, and goals correspond to those that particular society deems appropriate and desirable. Through the powerful and ubiquitous process of *socialization*, the needs of the society become the needs of the individual.

Socialization is a process of learning. To socialize someone is to train that person to behave appropriately. It is the means by which people acquire a vast array of important social skills, such as driving a car, converting fractions into decimals, speaking the language correctly, or using a fork instead of a knife to eat peas. But socialization is also the way we learn how to perceive our world; how to interact with others; what it means to be male or female; how, when, why, and with whom to be sexual; what we should and shouldn't do to and for others under certain circumstances; what our society defines as moral and immoral; and so on. In short, it is the process by which we internalize all the cultural information I discussed in Chapter 4.

This learning process is carried out by the various individuals, groups, organizations, and institutions a person comes into contact with during the course of his or her life. These entities—whom sociologists refer to as *agents of socialization*—can be family, friends, peers, teammates, teachers, schools, religious institutions, and the media. They can influence our self-concepts, attitudes, tastes, values, emotions, and behavior.

Although socialization occurs throughout our lives, the basic, formative instruction of life begins early on. Young children must be taught the fundamental values, knowledge, and beliefs of their culture. Some of the socialization that occurs during childhood—often called *anticipatory socialization*—is the primary means by which young individuals acquire the values and orientations found in the statuses they will likely enter in the future (Merton, 1957). Household chores, a childhood job, organized sports, dance lessons, dating, and many other types of experiences give youngsters an opportunity to rehearse for the kinds of roles that await them in adulthood.

The Acquisition of Self

The most important outcome of the socialization process is the development of a sense of self. The term *self* refers to the unique set of traits, behaviors, and attitudes that distinguishes one person from the next. The self is both the active source of behavior and its passive object (Mead, 1934).

As an active source, the self can initiate action, which is frequently directed toward others. Imagine, for example, that Donna and Robert are having dinner in a restaurant. Donna has a self that can perceive Robert, talk to him, evaluate him, tell him what to order, and maybe even try to persuade him to act in a way that is consistent with her interests. Donna also has a self that is a potential object of others' behavior: She can be perceived, talked to, evaluated, directed, or persuaded by Robert.

Donna can also direct these activities toward herself. She can perceive, evaluate, motivate, and even talk to herself. This is called *reflexive behavior*. To have a self is to have the ability to plan, observe, guide, and respond to one's own behavior (Mead, 1934). Think of all the times you have tried to motivate yourself to act by saying something such as, "All right, if I read 20 more pages of my boring sociology book, I'll make myself a hot fudge sundae" or, "I won't go on Facebook until I write five more pages of this chemistry paper." To engage in such activities, you must simultaneously be the motivator and the one being motivated—the seer and the seen.

At this very moment, you are initiating an action: reading this non-boring sociology book. But you also have the ability (now that I've mentioned it!) to be aware of your reading behavior, to reflexively observe yourself reading, and even to evaluate how well you are doing. This may sound like some sort of mystical out-of-body experience, but it isn't. Nothing is more fundamental to human thought and action than this capacity for reflexive self-awareness. It allows us to control our own behavior and interact smoothly with other self-aware individuals.

At birth, human babies have no sense of self. This is not to say that infants don't act on their own. Anyone who has been around babies knows that they have a tremendous ability to initiate action, ranging all the way from snapshot-worthy cute to downright disgusting. They cry, eat, sleep, play with squeaky rubber toys, and eliminate waste, all with exquisite flair and regularity. From the very first days of life, they respond to the sounds, sights, smells, and touches of others.

But this behavior is not characterized by the sort of reflexive self-awareness that characterizes later behavior. Babies don't say to themselves, "I wonder if Mom will feed me if I scream" or "I can't *believe* how funny my babbling sounds right now." As children grow older, though, they begin to exert greater control over their actions. Part of this transformation is biological. As they mature, they become more adept at muscle control. But physical development is only part of the picture. Humans must acquire certain cognitive capacities through interactions with others, including the abilities to differentiate between self and others, to understand and use symbolic language, and to take the roles of others.

The Differentiation of Self

To distinguish between yourself and others, you must at minimum be able to recognize yourself as a distinct being (Mead, 1934). The first step in the acquisition of self, then, is learning to distinguish our own faces and bodies from the rest of the physical environment. Surprisingly, we are not born with this ability. Not only are newborns incapable of recognizing themselves, but they also cannot discriminate the boundaries between their bodies and the bodies of others. Infants will pull their own hair to the point of excruciating pain but aren't yet able to realize that the hair they're pulling with their hands and the hair that they feel being pulled out of their heads is the same hair.

With cognitive growth and social experience, infants gradually recognize themselves as unique physical objects. Most studies in this area indicate that children usually develop this ability at about 18 months (Bertenthal & Fischer, 1978). There's a quick way to tell if a child has reached this stage: Make a large mark on a baby's forehead with a washable marker and hold the youngster up to a mirror. If the child reaches up to wipe away the smudge, you can be reasonably sure she or he recognizes that the image in the mirror is her or his own.

Language Acquisition and the Looking-Glass Self

The next important step in the acquisition of self is the development of speech (Hewitt, 1988). Symbolic interactionism points out that mastery of language is crucial in children's efforts to differentiate themselves as distinct social as well as physical objects (Denzin, 1977). Certainly, language acquisition relies on neurological development. But the ability to grasp the nuances of one's own language requires input from others. Most parents talk to their children from the start. Gradually, children learn to make sounds, imitate sounds, and use sounds as symbols for particular physical sensations or objects. Children learn that the sounds "Mama" and "Dada" are associated with two important objects in their life. Soon children learn that other objects—toys, animals, foods, Aunt Anita, Uncle Marc—have unique sounds associated with them as well.

This learning process gives the child access to the preexisting linguistic world in which his or her parents and others live (Hewitt, 1988). The objects named are not only those recognized within the larger culture but also those recognized within the child's family and social groups. The child learns the names of concrete objects (balls, buildings, furniture) as well as abstractions that cannot be directly perceived (God, happiness, peace, idea).

By learning that people and other objects have names, the child also begins to learn that these objects can be related to one another in a variety of ways. Depending on who is talking to whom, the same person can be called several different names. The object "Dad" is called "David," "Dave," "Dov," "Dr. Newman," "Professor Newman," "Mr. Newman," and "New Man" by various other people. Furthermore, the child learns that different people can be referred to by the same name. All those other toddlers playing in the park have someone they also call "Mama."

Amid these monumental discoveries, young children learn that they too are objects that have names. A child who learns that others are referring to him when they make the sound "Ethan," and that he too can use "Ethan" to refer to himself, has taken a significant leap forward in the acquisition of self. The child now can visualize himself as a part of the named world and the named relationships to which he belongs.

The self that initially emerges from this process is a rather simple one. "Ethan" is just a name associated with a body. A more sophisticated sense of self is derived from the child's ability to learn the meaning of this named object.

Children learn the meaning of named objects in their environment by observing the way other people act toward those objects. By witnessing people sitting on a chair, they learn what *chair* means. Parental warnings allow them to learn that a "hot stove" is something to be avoided. Similarly, by observing how people act toward them, they learn the meaning of themselves. People treat children in a variety of ways: care for them, punish them, love them, neglect them, teach them. If parents, relatives, and other agents of socialization perceive a child as smart, they will act toward her or him that way. Thus, the child eventually comes to define herself or himself as a smart person. One of the earliest symbolic interactionists, Charles Horton Cooley (1902), referred to this process as the acquisition of the ***looking-glass self****.* He argued that we use the reaction of others toward us as looking glasses (that is, mirrors) in which we see ourselves and determine our self-worth. Through this process, we imagine how we might look to other people, we interpret their responses to us, and we form a self-concept. If we think people perceive us favorably, we're likely to develop a positive self-concept. Conversely, if we detect unfavorable reactions, our self-concept will likely be negative. Hence, self-evaluative feelings like pride or shame are always the product of the reflected appraisals of others.

But the development of a self-concept is not just a function of an individual's traits and experiences. How the child-as-named-object is defined by others is also linked to larger societal considerations. Every culture has its own way of defining and valuing individuals at various stages of the life cycle. Children are not always defined, and have not always been defined, as a special subpopulation whose innocence requires nurturing and protection (Ariès, 1962). In some societies, they are expected to behave like adults and are held accountable for their actions just as adults would be. Under such cultural circumstances, a five-year-old's self-concept may be derived from how well he or she contributes economically to the family, not from how cute or playful he or she is. Moreover, every society has its own standards of beauty and success. If thinness is a culturally desirable characteristic, a thin child is more likely to garner positive responses and develop a positive self-image than a child who violates this norm (i.e., an obese child).

The Development of Role Taking

The socialization process would be pretty simple if everyone in our lives saw us in exactly the same way. But different people expect or desire different things from us. Children eventually learn to modify their behavior to suit different people. Four-year-old Ahmed learns, for instance, that his three-year-old sister loves it when he sticks his thumb up his nose, but he also knows that his father doesn't find this behavior at all amusing. So Ahmed will avoid such conduct when his father is around but proceed to amuse his sister with this trick when Papa is gone. The ability to use other people's perspectives and expectations in formulating one's own behavior is called ***role taking*** (Mead, 1934).

Role taking ability develops gradually, paralleling the increasing maturation of linguistic abilities. Operating from the symbolic interactionist perspective, George Herbert Mead (1934) identified two major stages in the development of role taking ability and, ultimately, in the socialization of the self: the play stage and the game stage. The ***play stage*** occurs when children are just beginning to hone their language skills. Role taking at the play stage is quite simple in form, limited to taking the perspective of one other person at a time. Very young children cannot yet see themselves from different perspectives simultaneously. They have no idea that certain behaviors may be unacceptable to a variety of people across a range of situations. They know only that this particular person who is in their immediate presence will approve or disapprove of this particular act. Children cannot see that their father's displeasure with public nose picking reflects the attitudes of a larger group and is always unacceptable no matter where or when it takes place. This more sophisticated form of self-control develops at the next stage of the socialization process: the game stage.

The ***game stage*** occurs about the time when children first begin to participate in organized activities such as school events and team sports. The difference between role taking at the play and game stages parallels the difference between childhood play and game behavior. "Play" is not guided by a specific set of rules. It has no ultimate object, no clearly organized competition, and no winners and losers. Children playing baseball at the play stage have no sense of strategy and may not even be aware of the rules and object of the game. They may be able to hit, catch, and throw the ball but have no idea how their behavior is linked to that of their teammates. If a little girl is playing shortstop and a ground ball is hit to her, she may turn around and throw the ball to the left fielder, not because it will help her team win the game but because that's where her best friend happens to be.

Game behavior, in contrast, requires that children understand the object of the game. They realize that each player on the team is part of an organized network of roles determined by the rules of the game. Children know they must continually adapt their behavior to the team's needs in order to achieve a goal. To do so, they must imagine the group's perspective and anticipate how both their teammates and their opponents will act under certain circumstances. Now our little shortstop will throw the ball to first base to get the batter out, but only after assessing how many outs there are and checking to make sure the opposing runner on second base is not trying to advance to third. It doesn't matter whether she likes or hates the first baseman; her team's success depends on her making this play.

With regard to role taking at the game stage, not only does the child learn to respond to the demands of several people, but she or he can also respond to the demands of the community or even society as a whole. Sociologists call the perspective of society and its constituent values and attitudes the *generalized other*. The generalized other becomes larger as a child matures, growing to include family, peer group, school, and finally the larger social community. "Mama doesn't like it when I take off my pants in a restaurant" (play stage) eventually becomes "It's never acceptable to take off one's pants in public" (game stage). Notice how such an understanding requires an ability to generalize behavior across a variety of situations and audiences. The child realizes that "public" consists of restaurants, shopping malls, school classrooms, parks, neighbors' living rooms, and so forth.

This ability is crucial because it enables the individual to resist the influence of specific people who happen to be in his or her immediate presence. The boy who defies his peers by not joining them in an act of petty shoplifting is showing the power of the generalized other ("Stealing, no matter where or with whom, is bad"). During the game stage, the attitudes and expectations of the generalized other are incorporated into one's values and self-concept.

Real life is not always that simple, though. Sometimes people succumb to the pressures of particular others and engage in behaviors they know are socially unacceptable. Furthermore, individuals from markedly different backgrounds are likely to internalize different sets of group attitudes and values. A devout Catholic contemplating divorce, for instance, is taking the role of a different generalized other than an atheist contemplating divorce. Likewise, the social worlds and social standards of men and women are different, as are those of children and adults, parents and nonparents, middle-class and working-class people, and people who grew up in different cultures.

Nor is role taking ability static. It changes in response to interactions with others. When people feel that they can understand another person's perspective—say, that of an intimate partner—they are likely to become concerned about or at least aware of how their behavior will affect that other person (Cast, 2004). Furthermore, as we move from one institutional setting to another, we adopt the perspective of the appropriate group and can become, for all intents and purposes, a different person. At school we behave one way, at church another, and at Grandma's house still another. We are as many different people as there are groups and organizations to which we belong.

Common sense suggests that people who have a great deal of knowledge and experience should be the best role takers. For example, parents should be more sensitive to their children's views than vice versa, because they are older and wiser and were children once themselves. However, given the dynamics of power and dependence, people in superior positions actually tend to be less sensitive and, as a result, may not be required to conform their behavior to—or even be aware of—the wishes and desires of their subordinates (Tsushima & Gecas, 2001). You can see this phenomenon in many areas of social life. Younger siblings, for instance, are typically more aware of the actions and interests of their older siblings than vice versa. Low-level employees must be sensitive to the behaviors and preferences of those above them if they want to achieve occupational success and mobility. On a broader scale, less powerful nations must have heightened sensitivity to the activities of their more powerful neighbors. I have heard some Canadians complain that they are expected to know virtually everything about the United States—its culture as well as its economic and political systems—whereas most people in the United States tend to be rather oblivious to even the most accessible elements of Canadian politics and culture, like the name of the prime minister or the provincial capital of Nova Scotia.

In sum, the ability to imagine another person's attitudes and intentions and thereby to anticipate that person's behavior is essential for everyday social interaction. Through role taking, we can envision how others perceive us and imagine what their response may be some action we're contemplating. Hence, we can select behaviors that are likely to meet with the approval of the person or persons with whom we are interacting and can avoid behaviors that might meet with their disapproval. Role taking is thus a crucial component of self-control and social order. It transforms a biological being into a social being who is capable of conforming her or his behavior to societal expectations. It is the means by which culture is incorporated into the self and makes group life possible (Cast, 2004).

Resocialization

Socialization does not end when childhood ends; it continues throughout our lives. Adults must be *resocialized* into a new set of norms, values, and expectations each time they leave behind old social contexts or roles and enter new ones (Ebaugh, 1988; Pescosolido, 1986; Simpson, 1979). For instance, we have to learn how to think and act like a spouse when we marry (P. L. Berger & Kellner, 1964), like a parent when we have kids (A. Rossi, 1968), and like a divorced person when a marriage ends (Vaughan, 1986). Every new group or organization we enter, every new friendship we form, every new life-changing experience we have, requires the formation of new identities and socialization into new sets of norms and beliefs.

Certain occupations require the formal resocialization of new entrants. Often, the purpose is simply to make sure people who work in the organization share the same professional values, methods, and vocabulary. Many large companies, for example, have orientation programs for new employees to teach them what will be expected of them as they begin their new jobs. Sometimes the purpose is to make new entrants abandon their original expectations and adopt a more realistic view of the occupation. Police recruits who believe their job is to protect people must learn that deadly force is appropriate and sometimes necessary in the line of duty (Hunt, 1985). Many medical students become less idealistic and more realistic as they learn about the exhausting demands of their profession (Becker & Geer, 1958; Hafferty, 1991). Such resocialization is especially important in occupations that deal with highly emotional matters, like death.

SPENCER CAHILL

The Professional Resocialization of Funeral Directors

Funeral directors routinely deal with death and corpses. They are exposed to sights, smells, and sounds that most people have learned to find frightening or repulsive. And they must discuss cold, practical matters, such as prices and methods of payment, with grief-stricken clients, without appearing callous. Thus, the occupational resocialization of funeral directors is as important as that in any other profession that deals with human tragedy (clergy, doctors, nurses, police detectives, etc.). But unlike these other professionals, for whom death is merely one aspect of the job, funeral directors exist solely for the purpose of dealing with death.

To study the process of becoming a funeral director, sociologist Spencer Cahill (1999) spent five months as a participant observer in a mortuary science program at a community college. In most states, funeral directors must complete an accredited program in mortuary science before getting their license to practice. Cahill regularly attended classes on topics such as health and sanitation science, psychology of grief, and embalming. He also talked informally with the other students and interviewed eight of them formally. What was especially unique about his research approach was that instead of taking the stance of the detached, objective researcher, Cahill incorporated his own feelings and emotional reactions into his analysis.

He found that the entire mortuary science education program serves to normalize the work, so that students become comfortable with death. Reminders of death are a constant presence. Nothing is hidden. For instance, all the classrooms contain some artifacts of death, such as refrigerated compartments that hold corpses, stainless steel embalming tables, and caskets. All the instructors Cahill observed spread their lecture notes on a body gurney, forgoing the traditional lectern and table. It was also common practice for instructors to leave the door open between the classroom and the embalming laboratory, allowing the lingering smell of decomposing bodies to drift into the classroom.

Because other students on campus tend to shun them, the mortuary science students often stick together, providing an almost constant network of support. From these casual interactions (as well as conversations with their instructors), these students learn an occupational language that communicates professional authority and calm composure toward things most of the public would find upsetting. For example, the students learn to see the corpse not as an individual person with a history and a family but as a series of technical puzzles and problems posed by the cause of death (e.g., ingested substances, chemical changes, injuries sustained before death).

However, Cahill points out that professional socialization is not enough to create funeral directors. He notes that students for whom death has always been a mystery or students who are predisposed to becoming queasy don't last very long in the program. In contrast, those who are familiar with death or who have somehow worked with the dead before (such as the sons or daughters of funeral directors) are the most likely to succeed.

Eventually, the mortuary science students who complete the program adopt the identity of funeral director. They learn to normalize death and acquire the perceptions, judgments, and emotional management skills required of this occupation.

As one well-socialized student put it, "What we do is far less depressing than what nurses and doctors do. We only get the body after the death and do not have to watch all the suffering" (quoted in Cahill, 1999, p. 109).

Sometimes resocialization is forceful and intense. According to sociologist Erving Goffman, this type of resocialization often occurs in ***total institutions*** (E. Goffman, 1961). Total institutions are physical settings in which groups of individuals are separated from the broader society and forced to lead an enclosed, formally administered life. Prisons, mental hospitals, monasteries, and military training camps are examples of total institutions. In these locations, previous socialization experiences are systematically destroyed and new ones developed to serve the interests of the larger group. Take military boot camp, for example. The Army alone spends several billion dollars a year and employs thousands of people to turn civilians into battle-ready warriors who look, act, and think like soldiers and learn to see the world from the soldier's perspective (Tietz, 2006). The process is called "total control." To aid in this transformation, recruits are stripped of old civilian identity markers (clothes, personal possessions, hairstyle) and forced to take on new ones that nullify individuality and also identify the newcomers' subordinate status (uniforms, identification numbers, similar haircuts). The newcomer is also subjected to constant scrutiny. Conformity is mandatory. Any misstep is met with punishment or humiliation. Eventually, the individual learns to identify with the ideology of the total institution.

In the boot camp, the uniformity of values and appearance is intended to create a sense of solidarity among the soldiers and thereby make the military more effective in carrying out its tasks. Part of the reason for all the controversy over diversity in the military—first with the inclusion of African Americans, then with women, and now with gay men and lesbians—is that it introduces diverse beliefs, values, appearances, and lifestyles into a context where, from an institutional perspective, similarity is essential.

The Self in a Cultural Context

When we imagine how others will respond to our actions, we choose from a limited set of lines of conduct that are part of the wider culture. In the United States, the self is likely to incorporate key cultural virtues such as self-reliance and individualism. Hence, personal goals tend to be favored over group goals (Bellah, Madsen, Sullivan, Swidler, & Tipton, 1985). In the United States, people will readily change their group membership as it suits them—leaving one career for another, moving from neighborhood to neighborhood, switching political allegiances or even religions.

The United States is said to be an *individualist culture*, where personal accomplishments are a key part of one's self-concept. We've always admired independent people whose success—usually measured in financial terms—is based on their own achievements and self-reliance (Bellah et al., 1985). Hence, the amount of respect people deserve is determined in large part by their level of expertise. For example, before a public speech, a guest lecturer in the United States will likely be introduced to her audience as "a distinguished scholar, a leader in her field" along with a list of academic credentials and scholarly achievements.

In many non-Western cultures, however, people are more likely to subordinate their individual goals to the goals of the larger group and to value obligations to others over personal achievements. In such a setting, known as a *collectivist culture*, personal identity is less important than group identity (Gergen, 1991). In India, for instance, feelings of self-esteem and prestige originate more from the reputation and honor of one's family than from any individual attainments (Roland, 1988). In a collectivist setting, high value is placed on preserving one's public image so as not to bring shame on one's family, tribe, or community (Triandis, McCusker, & Hui, 1990). Overcoming personal interests and temptations to show loyalty to one's group and other authorities is celebrated. Guest lecturers in a collectivist culture would be considered self-centered and egotistical if they mentioned their personal accomplishments and credentials. Asian public speakers, for instance, commonly begin their talk by telling the audience how *little* they know about the topic at hand (Goleman, 1990).

But even in an individualist society such as the United States, our personal identities are inseparable from the various groups and organizations to which we belong. Thus, to fully understand how we become who we are, we must know the norms and values of our culture, family, peers, coworkers, and all the other agents of socialization who are a part of our lives.

Socialization and Stratification: Growing Up With Inequality

Socialization does not take place in a vacuum. Your social class, your race and ethnicity, and your sex and gender all become significant features of your social identity. Were you born into a poor or a well-to-do family? Are you a member of a racial minority or a member of the dominant group? Are you male or female? These elements of identity shape your experiences with other people and the larger society and will direct you along a certain life path. In most societies, social class, race and ethnicity, and gender are the key determinants of people's opportunities throughout their lives.

Social Class

Social classes consist of people who occupy similar positions of power, privilege, and prestige. People's positions in the class system affect virtually every aspect of their lives, including political preferences, sexual behavior, religious affiliation, diet, and life expectancy. The conflict perspective points out that even in a relatively open society such as the United States, parents' social class determines children's access to certain educational, occupational, and residential opportunities. Affluent children grow up in more abundant surroundings than less affluent children and therefore have access to more material comforts and enriching opportunities such as good schools, opportunities to travel to far-off places, private music lessons, and so on. Furthermore, the lower the income of a child's family, the greater that child's risk of living in a single-parent household, having unemployed parents, having more than one disability, and dropping out of school (Mather & Adams, 2006).

But the relationship between class and socialization is not simply about parents' providing (or not providing) their children with the trappings of a comfortable childhood. Parents' class standing also influences the values and orientations children learn and the identities they develop.

In Chapter 10, you will learn much more about how social class affects attitudes, behaviors, and opportunities. The important point here is that social class and socialization are linked. Sociologist Melvin L. Kohn (1979) interviewed 200 working-class and 200 middle-class American couples who had at least one child of fifth grade age. He found that the middle-class parents were more likely to promote values such as self-direction, independence, and curiosity than were the working-class parents. A more recent study found that middle-class parents are more likely than working-class parents to foster their children's talents through organized leisure activities and experiences that require logical reasoning (Lareau, 2003). Other researchers have found this tendency especially strong among middle-class mothers (Xiao, 2000).

Conversely, working-class parents are more likely than middle-class parents to emphasize conformity to external authority, a common characteristic of the blue collar jobs they're likely to have later on (M. L. Kohn, 1979). Principally, they want their children to be neat and clean and to follow the rules.

Of course, not all middle-class parents, or working-class parents, raise their children in these ways, and many factors other than social class influence parental values (J. D. Wright & Wright, 1976). Nevertheless, Kohn found that these general tendencies were consistent regardless of the sex of the child or the size and composition of the family. In a study of African American women, those from middle-class backgrounds reported that their parents had higher expectations of them and were more involved in their education than African American women from working-class backgrounds reported (N. E. Hill, 1997). Moreover, others have found that despite cultural differences, social class standing influences child socialization in societies in Europe (Poland, Germany) and Asia (Japan, Taiwan; Schooler, 1996; Williamson, 1984; Yi, Chang, & Chang, 2004).

Sudden shifts in social class standing—due, for instance, to an unexpected job loss—can also affect the way parents socialize their children. Parents who lose their jobs can become irritable, tense, and moody and their disciplinary style more arbitrary. They may come to rely less on reasoning and more on hostile comments and physical punishment. As a result, children's sense of self, their aspirations, and their school performance suffer (cited in Rothstein, 2001).

Class differences in socialization are also directly related to future goals. Working-class parents tend to believe that eventual occupational success and survival depend on their children's ability to conform to and obey authority (M. L. Kohn, 1979). Middle-class parents are likely to believe that their children's future success will result from assertiveness and initiative. Hence, middle-class children's feelings of control over their own destiny are likely to be much stronger than those of working-class children.

Race and Ethnicity

Several years ago, shortly after an unarmed West African immigrant was shot and killed by four white police officers in Bronx, New York, some of my students became embroiled in a heated discussion of the incident. One student, who was white, expressed concern that because of the terrible actions of these individual officers, young children of all races would now grow up mistrusting or even hating the police. As a child, she said, she had been taught that the role of the police is to help people and that if she were ever in trouble or lost she could approach an officer for assistance. She never questioned whether or not the police could be trusted.

Some of the African American students in class quickly pointed out that their socialization experiences had been quite different. Parents and others in their neighborhoods had taught them not to trust the police, because officers were just as likely to harass them as to help them: They were taught to seek out neighbors and relatives, not the police, if they ever needed help. To them, the police were not knights in shining armor but bullies with badges. Now, in the wake of several other incidents around the country where police have injured or killed innocent people of color, some parents and civic leaders feel it is essential to teach black and Latino/a children how to respond safely when approached by the police. The NAACP (National Association for the Advancement of Colored People), the Allstate insurance company, and the National Organization of Black Law Enforcement Executives have published brochures and held community forums on "guidelines for interacting with law enforcement officials." Among other things, children are taught to speak when asked to speak, to stop when ordered to stop, to never make any sudden movements, and to always display their open hands to show they aren't armed (D. Barry, 2000).

Although the two perspectives of my students are not representative of every white or every black person in the United States, the interchange illustrates the impact race and ethnicity can have on socialization. For white children, learning about their racial identity is less about defining their race than it is about learning how to handle the privileges and behaviors associated with being white in a predominantly white society (Van Ausdale & Feagin, 2001). Chances are good that schools and religious organizations will reinforce the socialization messages expressed to white children in their families—for example, that "you can be anything you want as long as you work hard."

For children who are members of ethnoracial minorities, however, learning about their race occurs within a different and much more complex social environment (Hughes & Chen, 1997). These children must live simultaneously in two different worlds: their ethnoracial community and the "mainstream" (i.e., white) society. Hence, they're likely to be exposed to several different types of socialization experiences while growing up: those that include information about the mainstream culture, those that focus on their minority status in society, and those that focus on the history and cultural heritage of their ethnoracial group (L. D. Scott, 2003; Thornton, 1997). Parents often emphasize one type of orientation over others. In ethnoracial groups that have been able to overcome discrimination and achieve at high levels—such as some Asian American groups—ethnic socialization can focus simply on the values of their culture of origin. But among groups that by and large remain disadvantaged, such as African Americans, Native Americans, and Latino/as, parents' discussion of race is more likely to focus on preparing their children for prejudice, ethnic hatred, and mistreatment in a society set up to ignore or actively exclude them (McLoyd, Cauce, Takeuchi, & Wilson, 2000; Staples, 1992). For instance, these children may be taught that "hard work" alone may not be enough to get ahead in this society. Even African American children from affluent homes in racially integrated neighborhoods need reassurances about the racial conflicts they will inevitably encounter (Comer & Poussaint, 1992). These are lessons that children in the dominant racial group seldom require, for reasons explored in greater depth in Chapter 11.

Gender

As you recall from Chapter 4, the sexual dichotomy—the belief that there are two and only two sexes—is not universal. Cultures are even more likely to differ in what is expected of people based on their sex and in how male and female children are to be socialized.

Before discussing this aspect of socialization, it's necessary to distinguish between two concepts: sex and gender. *Sex* is typically used to refer to a person's biological maleness or femaleness. *Gender* designates masculinity and femininity: the psychological, social, and cultural aspects of maleness and femaleness (Kessler & McKenna, 1978). This distinction is important because it reminds us that male-female differences in behaviors or experiences do not spring naturally from biological differences between the sexes (Lips, 1993).

The gender socialization process begins the moment a child is born. A physician, nurse, or midwife immediately starts that infant on a career as a male or female by authoritatively declaring whether it is a boy or a girl. In most U.S. hospitals, the infant boy is wrapped in a blue blanket, the infant girl in a pink one. From that point on, the developmental paths of U.S. males and females diverge. The subsequent messages that individuals receive from families, books, television, and schools not only teach and reinforce gender-typed expectations but also influence the formation of their self-concepts.

If you were to ask parents whether they treated sons any differently from daughters, most would probably say no. Yet there is considerable evidence that what parents do and what they say they do are two different things (H. Lytton & Romney, 1991; McHale, Crouter, & Whiteman, 2003). In one study, 30 first-time parents were asked to describe their infants at less than 24 hours old. They frequently resorted to common gender stereotypes. Those with daughters described them as "tiny," "soft," "fine featured," and "delicate." Sons were seen as "strong," "alert," "hardy," and "coordinated" (J. Z. Rubin, Provenzano, & Luria, 1974). A replication of this study two decades later found that U.S. parents continue to perceive their infants in gender-stereotyped ways, although less so than in the 1970s (Karraker, Vogel, & Lake, 1995). Parents also tend to engage in rougher physical play with infant sons than with infant daughters and use subtle differences in tone of voice and different pet names, such as "Sweetie" versus "Tiger" (MacDonald & Parke, 1986; Tauber, 1979).

New parents can be very sensitive about the correct identification of their child's sex. Even parents who claim to consider sex and gender irrelevant may spend a great deal of time ensuring that their child has the culturally appropriate gender appearance. Parents of a girl baby who has yet to grow hair (a visible sign of gender in many cultures) will sometimes tape pink ribbons to their bald daughter's head to avoid potential misidentification. In many Latin American countries, families have infant girls' ears pierced and earrings placed in them to provide an unmistakable indicator of the child's sex and gender.

In a culture where sex and gender are centrally important and any ambiguity is distasteful, the correct gender identification of babies maintains social order. When my elder son was an infant, I dressed him on several occasions in a pink, frilly snowsuit in order to observe the reactions of others. (Having a sociologist for a father can be rather difficult from time to time!) Inevitably, someone would approach us and start playing with the baby and some variation of the following interchange would ensue:

Oh, she's so cute! What's your little girl's name?

Zachary.

Isn't Zachary a boy's name?

He's a boy.

At this point, the responses would range from stunned confusion and awkward laughter to nasty looks and outright anger. Clearly, people felt that I had emotionally abused my son somehow. I had purposely breached a fundamental gender norm and thereby created, in their minds, unnecessary trauma (for him) and interactional confusion (for them).

Both boys and girls learn at a very young age to adopt gender as an organizing principle (Hollander, Renfrow, & Howard, 2011). By the age of three or so, most children can accurately answer the question, "Are you a boy or a girl?" (e.g., Kohlberg, 1966). To a young child, being a boy or a girl is simply another characteristic, like having brown hair or 10 fingers. The child at this age has no conception that gender is a category into which every human can be placed (Kessler & McKenna, 1978). But by the age of five or so, most children have developed a fair number of gender stereotypes (often incorrect) that they then use to guide their own perceptions and activities (C. L. Martin & Ruble, 2004). They also use these stereotypes to form impressions of others. A boy, for instance, may avoid approaching a new girl who's moved into the neighborhood because he assumes that she will only be interested in "girl" things. Acting on this assumption reinforces the original belief that boys and girls are different. Indeed, to children at this age, gender is typically seen as a characteristic that is fixed and permanent. Statements such as "Doctors are men" and "Nurses are women" are uttered as inflexible, objective "truths." A few years later, though, their attitudes toward gender become considerably more flexible, although such flexibility isn't always reflected in their actual behaviors (C. L. Martin & Ruble, 2004).

It's important to note that gender socialization is not a passive process in which children simply absorb the information that bombards them. As part of the process of finding meaning in their social worlds, children actively construct gender as a social category (Liben & Bigler, 2002). From an early age, they are like "gender detectives," searching for cues about gender, such as who should and shouldn't engage in certain activities, who can play with whom, and why girls and boys differ (C. L. Martin & Ruble, 2004, p. 67).

Parents and other family members sometimes provide children with explicit instructions on proper gender behavior, such as "Big boys don't cry" or "Act like a young lady." Decades' worth of research shows that parents speak differently to and play differently with their sons and daughters. For instance, one study of mothers' reactions to their children's misbehaviors found that they tend to be more concerned about injuries and safety issues with their daughters and tend to focus more on disciplinary issues with their sons (Morrongiello & Hogg, 2004). In another study, parents were instructed to tell their children stories about their own childhoods. In doing so, they were more likely to highlight themes of autonomy and independence when they had sons than when they had daughters (Fiese & Skillman, 2000). Fathers spend more time with their sons and engage in more physical play with them than with their daughters, whereas mothers are more emotionally responsive to girls and encourage more independence with boys (Lanvers, 2004; Raley & Bianchi, 2006).

As children grow older, parents tend to encourage increasingly gender-typed activities (Liben & Bigler, 2002). Research consistently shows that children's household tasks differ along gender lines (Antill, Goodnow, Russell, & Cotton, 1996). For instance, boys are more likely to mow the lawn, shovel snow, take out the garbage, and do the yard work, whereas girls tend to clean the house, wash dishes, cook, and babysit their younger siblings (L. White & Brinkerhoff, 1981). These discrepancies are clearly linked to the different social roles ascribed to men and women, which are discussed in more detail in Chapter 12.

Gender instructions seem to be particularly rigid and restrictive for U.S. boys. Indeed, the social costs for "gender-inappropriate" behavior are disproportionately severe for boys. One study found that girls' play patterns become less stereotypical as they age; boys, however, must remain ardently masculine (Cherney & London, 2006). As one author put it, girls can still be girls, but boys *must* be boys (Orenstein, 2008).

Consider the different implications of the words *sissy* and *tomboy*. The girl who is a tomboy may fight, use profanity, compete in sports, and climb trees, but her entire gender identity is not called in question by the label. Girls, in general, are given license to do "boy things" (Kimmel, 2004). Indeed, "tomboyness," if considered negative at all, is typically defined as temporary—a stage that a girl will eventually grow out of. But the chances for boys to play "girl games" without ridicule are rare, and the risks for doing so are steep. The sissy is not simply a boy who enjoys female pursuits. He is suspiciously soft and effeminate. His "sissyness" is likely to be seen as reflective of his sexual essence, a sign to some of his imminent homosexuality.

Parents participate in gender socialization through the things they routinely provide for their children: clothes, adornments, books, videos, and so forth. Recently, a friend of mine who was visiting from Japan—and who is an expectant father—commented while shopping in a department store that even baby clothes in gender-neutral colors convey gendered images, such as yellow or beige pajamas sporting pictures of baseballs or footballs. Moreover, clothes not only provide visible markers of gender; they also send messages about how that person ought to be treated and direct behavior along traditional gender lines (Shakin, Shakin, & Sternglanz, 1985). Frilly outfits do not lend themselves easily to rough-and-tumble play. Likewise, it is difficult to walk quickly or assertively in high heels and tight miniskirts. Clothes for boys and men rarely restrict physical movement in this way. Toys and games are an especially influential source of gender information parents provide their children.

MICRO-MACRO CONNECTION

Girls' Toys and Boys' Toys

Like most people over the age of 50, I can remember a time when toys played a very different role in children's lives than they do now. When I was a child, my friends and I didn't have many toys, and we usually ended up improvising playthings out of available materials like tree branches, empty boxes, and old stringless tennis rackets. When we did receive a new toy, it was usually a special occasion, like a birthday, a holiday, or a cavity-free dental checkup. Every once in a while we'd save up enough money, walk down to the local toy shop, and buy some toy for ourselves that we'd been coveting for months. The toys were simple and straightforward—wagons, fire engines, dolls, balls, trains, board games—and we'd use them until they broke or wore out. When our parents detected a significant spurt in our maturity, they might get us a toy that required special caution: a chemistry set, an Easy-Bake Oven, an electric racing car set.

Today, toys have changed. Toys are now a multibillion-dollar business, part of a giant transnational, interconnected industry. It's virtually impossible to buy a toy these days that's not linked to some new film, television show, fast food restaurant, or other high-powered marketing campaign. Toy companies now regularly produce TV cartoons based on their own toy lines (C. L. Williams, 2006). Parents find it difficult to resist their children's wishes, which are likely to be formed by television advertisements. Try taking a small child to McDonald's without feeling the pressure to buy a Happy Meal with a toy. The quaint, independent toyshop of the past has been replaced by the massive toy mega-warehouse filled with endless aisles stocked from floor to ceiling with boxes sporting eye-popping colors and screaming images. Even serious world events are now linked to toys. In 2003, the video game industry kept a close eye on the war in Iraq for battle weapons and tools that could be turned into toys ("Toymakers Study Troops," 2003). Shortly after Navy SEALs killed Osama bin Laden in 2011, toy companies began to manufacture and market "SEAL Team 6" toys, ranging from posable action figures to plastic weapons.

But the current state of the toy industry is not simply a result of profit-hungry corporations trying to find new ways to exploit the child market (G. Cross, 1997). Toys have always played a significant socializing role in teaching children about the prevailing cultural conceptions of gender. In the 1950s—a time in U.S. history when most adults had endless faith in the goodness of technological progress—Erector Sets and chemistry sets were supposed to encourage boys to be engineers and scientists. Dollhouses and baby dolls taught girls to be modern homemakers and mothers during a time when girls typically assumed they'd occupy those roles in adulthood.

Today, a quick glance at Saturday morning television commercials, toy store shelves, or manufacturers' Web sites reveals that toys and games remain solidly segregated along gender lines. For instance, the Web site of the retail giant Toys"R"Us gives shoppers the option of selecting "girls' toys" or "boys' toys" when searching their collection. The featured categories for boys include "Horror," "Battle Action & Role Play," "Sports," and "Robots & Robotics." The featured categories for girls include "Dolls," "Doll Accessories," "Dollhouses," "Princess & Fairy Dolls," and "Horse & Pony Dolls."

"Girls' toys" still revolve around themes of domesticity, fashion, and motherhood. They encourage creativity, nurturing, and physical attractiveness. "Boys' toys" emphasize action and adventure and encourage exploration, competition, and aggression (C. L. Miller, 1987; Renzetti & Curran, 2003). Gender-specific toys foster different traits and skills in children and thereby further separate boys and girls into different patterns of social development.

The iconic and highly stereotypical "Barbie" doll has been one of the best-selling girls' toys for 50 years. Barbie takes in around $1 billion in annual sales (Bhatnagar, 2005). Ninety-five percent of girls ages 3 to 11 own at least one Barbie; the average number of Barbie dolls a U.S. girl owns is eight (G. Cross, 1997). In recent years, competitors such as American Girl dolls have gained in popularity, challenging Barbie's market primacy. These dolls are advertised as celebrating "all that girls can be" and come in a variety of historical characters, each with her own backstory. "Addy Walker" lived in the 19th century and was an escaped slave. "Molly McIntire" grew up during World War II. "Julie Albright" was a fun-loving girl in the 1970s who struggled to adjust to a new school.

Toy manufacturers also continue to make fortunes promoting war toys, competitive games of strategy, and sports paraphernalia for boys. In 1983, the popular action figure G.I. Joe got his own TV show; by 1988, two thirds of American boys between the ages of 5 and 11 owned Joes (G. Cross, 1997). Today, the boys' toy market is saturated with the plastic descendants of Joe: high-tech soldiers, muscle-bound action figures from popular comic books and movies, and intergalactic warriors. A live-action G.I. Joe film hit the theaters in 2009.

Video games have become a particularly lucrative product in recent years. Most video games are designed by males for other males. Female characters in these games are often provocatively sexual, scantily clad, and voluptuous. The developers of one game, *BMX XXX*, were forced to add clothing to their topless female riders after major retailers refused to carry the game. Many games portray female characters as prostitutes and strippers, who are frequent targets of violence at the hands of psychopathic male characters. In *Grand Theft Auto 3*, players can beat prostitutes to death with baseball bats after having sex with them (Media Awareness Network, 2005). In the online game *Boneless Girl*, players poke, pull, and throw a bikini-wearing girl across the screen to get her through a maze of bubbles. *Duke Nukem Forever* allows players to slap semi-naked women if they don't cooperate. To promote this game, 2K Games launched an accompanying Web site that contained a flash game in which female targets take off a piece of clothing for every successful shot until they are topless. The gender messages in such games may have a detrimental effect on both boys' attitudes toward girls and women and their conceptions of appropriate male behavior.

From time to time, toy manufacturers have attempted—usually only halfheartedly—to blur the lines between boys' and girls' toys. Several years ago, the Hasbro toy company tried to interest boys in troll dolls, which are traditionally popular among girls. What it came up with were old-fashioned action figures in the shape of a troll, with names like "Troll Warrior" and "Battle Troll" (Lawson, 1993). Other companies have tried to sell girls action figures and building blocks, which are typically the province of boys, but have drifted into traditional gender stereotypes. A few years ago, "Get Real Girl" dolls appeared on the scene. They were advertised as action figures for girls, emphasizing toughness rather than sexiness, and came dressed for activities such as snowboarding and camping. But they still resembled Barbie—albeit slightly bigger—and came with the accoutrements of feminine appearance, such as jewelry and hairbrushes. The popular Lego building blocks that boys have used for decades to make towers and monsters still come in vivid primary colors. But they are also available in more feminine, pastel colors and come in kits that can be used to make jewelry and dollhouses. In addition, Lego now markets a play system for girls, called "Lego Belville," that offers games with fairy tale and princess themes.

For the most part, toy manufacturers are still quick to exploit the gender-distinct roles children are encouraged to pursue when they become adults. They know full well that the few adults who do object to gender-specific toys will face disappointed children scowling at the sight of some gender-neutral alternative (C. L. Williams, 2006). Fisher-Price offers the "Little Mommy" doll, a soft, cuddly baby that drinks from a bottle and comes with a potty seat for toilet training. Playmates Toys' "Amazing Amanda" laughs, talks, cries, asks for hugs, and changes facial expressions. Mattel makes a pregnant version of Barbie's friend Midge (called "Happy Family Midge"). She comes with a distended tummy that, when removed, reveals a 1¾-inch baby nestled in the doll's plastic uterus. The doll comes with everything a girl needs to play out the birth and care of the new baby, including diapers (pink if it's a girl, blue if it's a boy), birth certificate, bottles, rattles, changing table, tub, and crib. All these dolls clearly teach young girls the cultural value of motherhood, a role most girls are encouraged and expected to enter later in life. You'd be hard pressed to find a comparable toy, popular among boys, that prepares them for future roles as fathers.

Institutions and Socialization

It should be clear by now that becoming who we are is a complex process embedded in the larger social structure. We are much more than the sum of our anatomical and neurological parts. Not only can cultural attitudes toward class, race, and gender dramatically affect our personal identities, but various social institutions—in particular, the educational system, religious organizations, and the mass media—exert considerable influence on our self-concept, our values, and our perspectives as well.

Education

In contemporary industrial societies, the most powerful institutional agent of socialization, after the family, is education. In fact, according to the structural-functionalist perspective, the primary reason why schools exist is to socialize young people. Children formally enter the school system around age five, when they begin kindergarten, although many enter earlier in preschool or nursery school. At this point, the "personalized" instruction of the family is replaced by the "impersonalized" instruction of the school, where children in most developed countries will remain for the next 13 years or longer. No other nonfamily institution has such extended and consistent control over a person's social growth.

Although schools are officially charged with equipping students with the knowledge and skills they need to fulfill various roles in society (e.g., reading, writing, mathematics, science), they also teach students important social, political, and economic values. When students set up simulated grocery stores or banks, they are learning about the importance of free enterprise and finance in a capitalist society; when they hold mock elections, they are being introduced to a democratic political system; when they spend time tending a school garden or setting up recycling bins, they are learning to nurture the earth.

More subtly, schools teach students what they can expect for themselves in the world. In many school districts, children are grouped into different programs, or tracks, based on an assessment of their academic abilities. In a typical high school, for example, some students will take courses designed to prepare them for college, whereas others will take more general or vocational courses designed to prepare them for work after they graduate. *Tracking* clearly determines future outcomes: Students in the higher tracks often go on to prestigious universities; those in the lower tracks may not go to college at all. Tracking can, therefore, ultimately affect employment opportunities, income levels, and overall quality of life.

Not surprisingly, some parents will go to great lengths to increase the likelihood of their children's success in school. For instance, some parents nowadays choose to delay enrolling their children in kindergarten for a year—a practice known as "academic redshirting"—to allow extra time for social, emotional, and intellectual growth as well as to ensure that the child is not the smallest in the class (Gootman, 2006). Between 1968 and 2005, the proportion of American six-year-olds enrolled in first grade or above dropped from 96% to 84%. It's not that the school enrollment rate for six-year-olds has decreased. It's that they're increasingly likely to be in kindergarten at this age rather than first grade (Deming & Dynarski, 2008).

Some research has shown that children who are older than their classmates perform better academically and athletically (cited in Weil, 2007). However, others point out that the consequences of redshirting reverberate beyond the kindergarten classroom. For instance, disadvantaged students are more likely than others to drop out of school. If they also started school late, they lose time at the beginning and at the end of their education. Moreover, children who start school late will experience delayed entry into the paid labor force, which means there will be fewer workers paying into the social security system that will support a growing number of retirees (Deming & Dynarski, 2008).

Ironically, although individual accomplishment is stressed in U.S. schools, through grades and report cards, students learn that their future success in society may be determined as much by who they are as by what they achieve. Ample evidence shows that teachers react to students on the basis of race, religion, social class, and gender (Wilkinson & Marrett, 1985). It is in school that many children are first exposed to the fact that people and groups are ranked in society, and soon they get a sense of their own standing in the social hierarchy.

Some sociologists argue that schooling in most cultures is designed not so much to provide children with factual information and encourage creativity as to produce passive, nonproblematic conformists who will fit into the existing social order (Gracey, 1991). This training in conformity involves several different dimensions (Brint, 1998). First, there is *behavioral* conformity. Teachers in the early grades typically keep children in line by controlling their bodily movements, such as making them sit still or forcing them to raise their hands before speaking. Some schools still work to ensure such conformity through strict punishment of misbehavior. According to the U.S. Department of Education, about 223,000 students are subjected to corporal punishment annually (cited in Frosch, 2011). Second, schools teach *moral* conformity. Teachers often instruct children about virtues such as honesty, courage, kindness, fairness, and respect. Finally, schools teach children to conform to *culturally* approved styles and outlooks. In some societies, teachers reward their students for showing a quick wit; in other societies, children are rewarded for demonstrating thoughtfulness and asking deep, probing questions. Such training socializes students to adopt traits that people consider culturally desirable within that society.

Sometimes these different dimensions overlap. Rules against arguing with the teacher, for instance, teach children the moral "goodness" of respecting authority. But they can also foster passivity and give students their first taste of control by authoritative adults other than their parents. Such classroom regulations, then, help impose discipline; at the same time, they prepare children for what they will face in the larger culture. Obeying the kindergarten teacher today prepares the individual for obeying the high school teacher, the college professor, and the boss tomorrow.

Unfortunately, children who seek ways to express their creativity often become underachievers who resent the constraining structure of the classroom, excessive rules and regulations, and the emphasis on conformity at the expense of independence (Kim & Van Tassel-Baska, 2010). Not surprisingly, numerous studies have found that American children's creativity—sometimes referred to as "CQ," or "creativity quotient"—has declined significantly over the past two decades, especially among younger children (cited in Bronson & Merryman, 2010).

Other countries have made childhood creativity a national priority. In 2008, Great Britain revamped its secondary school curricula to emphasize "idea generation" and not just traditional academic subjects. The European Union designated 2009 as "the European Year of Creativity and Innovation." Chinese schools have begun to adopt a problem-solving approach to education rather than drilling and rote memorization (Bronson & Merryman, 2010).

Although American schools still, for the most part, emphasize order and discipline, educators are beginning to pay more attention to the importance of creativity, developing curricula that incorporate innovation and problem-solving into all subject areas, not just the arts. Some schools even work to instill values that seem at odds with existing social arrangements. One school system in Minnesota, for example, is experimenting with a novel approach to teaching and learning in its elementary schools. Instead of forcing students to sit still during class time, teachers allow them to stand up and move around as much as they want. Even the desks are adjustable so students can stand at them to work if they like. Teachers claim that students sustain their attention longer and learn better than those in more traditional classrooms (Saulny, 2009b).

Because formal education is so important in the everyday lives of most children, the agenda of a particular school system, regardless of its philosophy or method, cannot help but influence the types of people they will eventually become.

(Text continues on page 161)

Becoming a Mariner

Liz Grauerholz and Rebecca Smith

The U.S. Merchant Marine is the country's fleet of commercial ships, which becomes an auxiliary to the Navy during wartime. In peacetime, merchant mariners are responsible for safely and efficiently transporting cargoes and passengers on the oceans and through inland waterways. Even in peacetime, it is a job fraught with physical and mental challenges.

The importance of the merchant seamen to the war effort was reflected in the establishment of the U.S. Merchant Marine Academy at King's Point on Long Island in New York in 1943. It is a four-year institution of higher learning that prepares young men and women to become naval reserve officers or merchant mariners. It is one of the five official U.S. service academies, in the same category as West Point and the U.S. Air Force Academy. Approximately 960 men and women are enrolled at any given time. Six state marine academies sanctioned by the U.S. Department of Transportation offer training for mariners as well.

Transporting a full load of iron ore through the ice-choked waters of the Great Lakes in winter requires a high level of training and commitment.

All the merchant marine academies put students through an extensive resocialization process. Students not only take academic courses leading to a college degree but also acquire the professional skills of mariners and the norms and values of people who are required to work in harmony in close quarters in difficult circumstances.

The Merchant Marine has existed in this country since 1775. As a new country with no navy, the United States relied heavily on its merchant seamen for defense against the British during the War of 1812. After the outbreak of World War II, many ordinary seamen were recruited to staff supply ships running a gauntlet of German submarines.

First-year students at the Maine Maritime Academy begin their orientation with a challenge course that requires teams to cooperate to solve problems and watch out for each other's safety.

As midshipmen at the Academy, students are required to take courses in the humanities, social sciences, math, and science. The curriculum is similar to that found in many engineering and business programs. However, Academy students spend almost a year on board a ship. They also learn a wide variety of practical skills, such as reading maps and radar screens, administering to sick shipmates, maintaining and repairing ship engines and other equipment, and deploying lifeboats.

Learning to tie ship cables

Reading maps on the bridge of a ship

Some aspects of indoctrination at the U.S. Merchant Marine Academy are more militaristic, as at the other service academies or in Reserve Officers' Training Corps (ROTC) programs at non-military universities. Students at the academy are required to march in formation as they move from one activity to another, learning discipline and the subordination of personal preferences to the unit's needs and rhythms. Unique outward expressions of individuality conflict with the Academy's goal of transforming a motley group of cadets into like-minded mariners.

Much of the responsibility for indoctrination falls on fellow students. Below, an upper-class student sanctions an infraction of the academy's norms. None of the other students in the mess hall question this form of discipline; in fact, they studiously concentrate on finishing their meal.

Everyday life is also tightly controlled. Meticulous attention to outward appearance is considered a crucial element of personal discipline.

At the Academy, as at other total institutions, the authorities frequently check the success of the resocialization process. Formal inspections are commonplace.

Life outside the Academy is also strictly regulated. Within strict rules and guidelines, students may be granted occasional "liberty"—they may have a dinner outside school grounds or attend a local sports event. Whether or not students can enjoy these privileges depends on how closely they follow the behaviors that are expected of them inside the Academy.

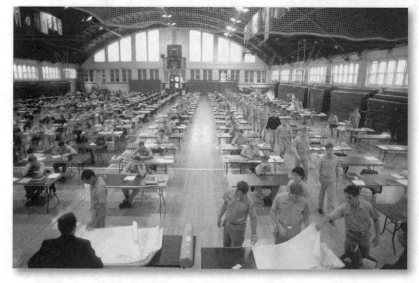

In order to graduate, students at the Academy have to take one or more licensing exams administered by the U.S. Coast Guard.

Unlike their nonmilitary counterparts, the graduating midshipmen must take an oath, pledging their unwavering commitment to the service of their country.

The solemnity of graduation is broken by a variety of celebratory rituals, including the tossing of caps into the air—much like the ritual at many college graduation ceremonies. Unique to the U.S. Merchant Marine Academy, though, is a fully dressed leap into the pool. It symbolizes release but is far from spontaneous. Note that the female graduates are wearing bathing suits under their uniforms, indicating that this ritual too is an artifact of the resocialization process.

Religion

As the structural-functionalist perspective tells us, religion is the social institution that tends to the spiritual needs of individuals and serves as a major source of cultural knowledge. It plays a key role in developing people's ideas about right and wrong. It also helps form people's identities by providing coherence and continuity to the episodes that make up each individual's life (Kearl, 1980). Religious rites of passage, such as baptisms, bar and bat mitzvahs, confirmations, and weddings, reaffirm an individual's religious identity while impressing on him or her the rights and obligations attached to each new status (J. H. Turner, 1972).

Religion occupies a complex and curious place in U.S. life. Structural changes in society have made religious affiliation somewhat unstable in recent years. For instance, as people move from one location to another, many of the ties that bind them to the same religion—most notably, networks of family and friends—are broken. Less than 40% of U.S. residents attend religious services once a week or more (Pew Forum on Religion and Public Life, 2008). Most U.S. residents are actually quite ignorant about basic religious history and texts (Prothero, 2007). When 3,400 Americans were asked 32 questions about the Bible, world religions, and religious figures, they only got about half of the questions right on average, even when the questions concerned their own religion. In fact, self-described atheists and agnostics scored significantly higher on this test of religious knowledge than Protestants and Catholics (Pew Forum on Religion and Public Life, 2010b).

The number of Americans who identify with *no* religion grew from 13 million in 1990 to more than 30 million in 2008 (U.S. Bureau of the Census, 2011b). Over that time, many of the most powerful religious groups experienced a decline in membership. For instance, the Lutheran Church and the Presbyterian Church each suffered a 5% drop in membership; the United Methodist Church saw its membership decline by 20% and the Episcopal Church by 21% (U.S. Bureau of the Census, 2011b). Over one quarter of American adults have left the religion of their childhood and joined another religion (Pew Forum on Religion and Public Life, 2008). But decline in membership does not necessarily mean that all religions are losing their socializing influence in U.S. society. Indeed, at the same time that membership in some religions has shrunk, that of so-called conservative churches (Roman Catholic Church, Church of Jesus Christ of Latter-Day Saints, Assemblies of God, United Church of Christ, and Southern Baptists) has increased (Kosmin & Keysar, 2009). And new religions are constantly emerging. Of the 1,600 or so recognized religions and denominations in the United States today, half were founded after 1965.

Membership in a variety of non-Christian religious groups grew significantly as well, including Muslim, Buddhist, Hindu, Unitarian Universalist, Scientologist, Baha'i, Taoist, New Age, Eckankar, Sikh, Wiccan, Druid, and Santerian (American Religion Data Archive, 2002). For instance, between 1990 and 2008, the number of Muslims and Buddhists in the United States increased from a little under 1 million to over 2.5 million (U.S. Bureau of the Census, 2011b). In fact, population experts project that over the next 20 years, the number of Muslims will grow at twice the rate of non-Muslims (Pew Forum on Religion and Public Life, 2011). Immigration has helped fuel this growth. More than four times as many immigrants as native-born Americans report non-Christian religious affiliations (Pew Forum on Religion and Public Life, 2008).

Religion may not look the same as it did 50 years ago, but it still remains a fundamental socializing agent in most Americans' lives (see Exhibit 5.1). Indeed, compared with most other Western democracies—such as Canada, Germany, France, Great Britain, and Australia—people in the United States stand out for the depth of their religious beliefs (Zoll, 2005). Consider these facts:

- Eighty-four percent of U.S. adults say that religion plays a big role in their lives (cited in Zoll, 2005). In contrast, 52% of Norwegians and 55% of Swedes say that God doesn't matter to them at all (cited in Ferguson, 2004).
- Sixty-nine percent of Americans definitely believe there is a personal God, and another 12% believe in a "higher power," though not in a personal God (Kosmin & Keysar, 2009).
- Two thirds of Americans believe that God is best described as the all-powerful, all-knowing perfect creator of the universe who rules the world today (The Barna Group, 2007).
- Eighty-three percent of Americans pray in a given week (The Barna Group, 2007).
- Two thirds of Americans feel that it is important that an American president have strong religious beliefs (Pew Forum on Religion and Public Life, 2004) and that they'd be less likely to vote for a political candidate who didn't believe in God (cited in M. Luo, 2007).
- Two thirds of married Americans had religious weddings and two thirds of Americans, in general, expect to have a religious funeral (Kosmin & Keysar, 2009).
- Among 18- to 29-year-olds who are *not* affiliated with any existing religion, 46% believe in heaven, 54% believe in life after death, and 58% believe in miracles (Pew Forum on Religion and Public Life, 2010a).

Exhibit 5.1 How U.S. Adults Rate Their Religiosity

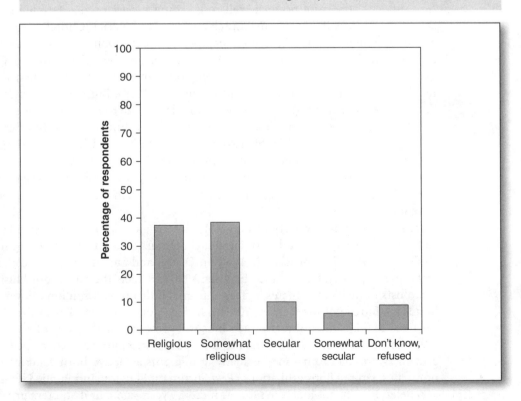

SOURCE: Kosmin and Mayer, 2001

Furthermore, we still consider ourselves "one nation under God," and our money still proclaims our trust in God. It's virtually impossible these days to watch a music awards show without seeing a winner acknowledging God's role in her or his success or a sporting event without seeing a baseball player cross himself before batting, a football player point skyward after scoring a touchdown, or a basketball player in a postgame interview thank God for guiding the shot that led to his team's victory. Sports stadiums around the country—including some major league ballparks—now offer "Faith Nights," religiously themed promotions that feature such things as Bible giveaways and revival-style testimonials from players (St. John, 2006). Sales of Christian books, computer games, videos, and toys are going up each year. Enrollment in evangelical colleges has grown steadily in recent years, as has the number of families choosing to homeschool their children for religious reasons (Talbot, 2000a).

Religion is also a key component of the American political system. Americans are far more likely than people in other industrialized countries to be willing to mix politics and religion. No sitting president would ever dare end a State of the Union speech without asking God to bless the United States of America. As one author put it, "America is the last country left whose citizens don't laugh out loud when their leader asks God to bless the country" (Ignatieff, 2005, p. 47). In one study, close to 40% of U.S. adults said religious leaders should try to influence policymakers (cited in Zoll, 2005). In 2011, Republican presidential candidate Rick Perry organized a Christian revival event that drew more than 20,000 people.

Mass Media

Another powerful institutional agent of socialization is the media. Newspapers, magazines, television, radio, film, and the Internet transmit persuasive messages on the nature of reality. They are the gatekeepers of political, economic, and social information, defining what is and isn't important (Marger, 2005). They also tell us the type of person we "should" be, from how we should perform our jobs to how different social classes live to what our sexual relationships and families are supposed to look like. The media teach us about prevailing values, beliefs, myths, stereotypes, and trends (Gitlin, 1979) and provide an avenue through which we learn new attitudes and behavior (Bandura & Walters, 1963).

Media exposure is pervasive in the United States. Young people between the ages of 8 and 18 spend an average of six and a half hours a day—or about 45 hours a week—with some type of media, such as television, radio, magazines, and computers (Rideout, Roberts, & Foehr, 2005). Researchers estimate that U.S. children spend more time with their televisions or computers than they do interacting directly with parents or teachers (Hofferth & Sandberg, 2001). So it's not surprising that sociologists, psychologists, and, of course, politicians continue to debate the degree to which sex and violence in film, television, and video games influence behavior, particularly among young people.

While U.S. television and other media entertain and expose us to diverse ways of life, they also send powerful messages about important cultural values like individual success. Consider the role of televised sports. Television has reduced the sports experience to a sequence of personal achievements—a cultural value on which the entire U.S. social structure is based. We have grown used to hearing descriptions such as "world record holder," "superstar," and "greatest player of all time." Praise is heaped not only on individuals and the occasional "dynasty" team but also on more specific actions: "best 3-point shooter," "best backhand," "best at hitting with two outs and runners in scoring position," "best open field tackler," "best chip out of a sand trap." Such characterizations not only perpetuate the importance of individual achievement but also give the impression that it is always possible to find something, however narrowly defined, at which one can be "best" (Gitlin, 1979).

Nowhere is the media emphasis on individual athletic achievement more obvious than in the most emblematic play in professional basketball today: the slam dunk. It's impossible to watch television highlights of a basketball game without seeing a thunderous, explosive, gravity-defying dunk:

> The dunk is a declaration of power and dominance, of machismo. In a team game, an ensemble of five players a side, it is an expression of self. In a sport devoted to selling sneakers, the dunk is a marketing tour de force, the money shot at the end of every worthy basketball sequence. (Sokolove, 2005, p. 42)

To some observers, though, fans' obsession with acrobatic dunks has made the fundamentals of success—namely, teamwork and sacrifice—seem irrelevant (Sokolove, 2005). In a world where muscled-up athletes, whose only reliable offensive skill is the ability to dunk the ball, can earn millions and where ESPN nationally televises the games of high school phenoms, it's not surprising that individual athleticism has overshadowed the collaborative aspect of the game. Consequently, many young players today are more concerned with perfecting their individual moves than with developing other skills—passing, rebounding, shooting from various spots on the floor, playing defense, and other less glamorous but no less essential elements of a team effort.

The socializing role of the media is especially apparent when it comes to gender. Children's books, for instance, teach youngsters what other little boys or girls in their culture do and what is expected of them. In the early 1970s, Lenore Weitzman and her colleagues studied the portrayal of gender in popular U.S. preschool books (Weitzman, Eifler, Hodada, & Ross, 1972). They found that boys played a more significant role in the stories than girls by a ratio of 11 to 1. Boys were more likely to be portrayed in adventurous pursuits or activities that required independence and strength; girls were likely to be confined to indoor activities and portrayed as passive and dependent. These gender stereotypes in children's books decreased only slightly over the next several decades (S. B. Peterson & Lach, 1990). Recent attempts to publish more nonsexist children's books have had little impact on the overall market. For instance, elementary school reading textbooks still primarily portray males as aggressive, argumentative, and competitive (L. Evans & Davies, 2000). "Gender equality" in children's books usually involves female characters taking on characteristics and roles typically associated with males. These books rarely, if ever, portray male characters exhibiting feminine traits (Diekman & Murnen, 2004).

Similarly, film and television continue to portray males and females in stereotypical ways. A study of the top-grossing fictional films of 2008 found that only 32% of characters with speaking roles were female, even though women compose over half the population. Forty percent of female characters were depicted in sexy, alluring attire, compared with less than 7% of male characters (S. L. Smith & Choueiti, 2010). Although it's changed somewhat in recent years, men on television are typically shown as rational, competitive, and violent, while women are sensitive, romantic, peaceful, and submissive. Programming often emphasizes male characters' strength and skill and female characters' attractiveness and desirability (cited in Witt, 2005). A study of 41 Saturday morning cartoons found that male characters are more likely than female characters to occupy leadership roles, act aggressively, give guidance to or come to the rescue of others, express opinions, ask questions, and achieve their goals. In addition, males are more likely to be portrayed in some kind of recognizable occupation, whereas females are more likely to be cast in the role of caregiver (T. L. Thompson & Zerbinos, 1995). Even the media coverage of female sports events tends to focus on the physical appearance and sexual attractiveness of the athletes and not just their competitive accomplishments (Billings, Angelini, & Eastman, 2005; Shugart, 2003).

Media advertising also perpetuates gender stereotypes. Three quarters of the central characters in radio advertisements are men. And men are significantly more likely than women to be portrayed as authorities on products rather than users (Monk-Turner, Kouts, Parris, & Webb, 2007). A study of 467 TV commercials shown between children's cartoons found that, as in the shows themselves, male characters are more likely than female characters to be in a major role, to be active rather than passive, and to be depicted in an occupational setting (S. Davis, 2003). Similarly, an analysis of more than 500 U.S. and Australian commercials targeting children found that girls were much more likely than boys to be portrayed as shy, giggly, and passive (Browne, 1998). The differences were less pronounced in Australia, however, where activists have had more success in countering gender stereotypes in the media than in the United States. Such images are not trivial, given that U.S. children watch more than 20,000 TV commercials a year.

All these gender images have a strong influence on children's perceptions and behaviors (Witt, 2005). Children who watch a lot of television are more likely to hold stereotypical attitudes toward gender, exhibit gender-related characteristics, and engage in gender-related activities than children who watch little television (M. Morgan, 1987; Signorielli, 1990). In one study, girls who did not have stereotypical conceptions of gender to begin with showed a significant increase in such attitudes after two years of heavy television watching (M. Morgan, 1982). The more high school students watch talk shows and prime time programs that depict a lot of sexual activity, the more likely they are to hold traditional sexual stereotypes (Ward & Friedman, 2006).

Conclusion

Becoming the people we are is a complex social process. Those intimate characteristics we hold so dear—our self-concept, our gender, and our racial and ethnic identity—reflect larger cultural attitudes, values, and expectations. Yet we are not perfect reflections of society's values. Despite all the powerful socializing institutions that pull our developmental strings, we continue to be and will always be individuals.

Sometimes we ignore our generalized others and strike out on our own with complete disregard for community standards and attitudes. Sometimes we form self-concepts that contradict the information we receive from others about ourselves. Sometimes we willingly violate the expectations associated with our social class, gender, or race. Societal influence can go only so far in explaining how we become who we are. The rest—that which makes us truly unique—remains a fascinating mystery.

YOUR TURN

Being a child or an adolescent is not simply a biological stage of development. It is a social identity. People's experiences with this identity emerge from a particular cultural and historical context as well as the process of socialization that takes place within their families.

But many other social institutions assist in the process of raising children, often in ways that aren't immediately apparent.

To see firsthand how such socialization works, visit a large shopping mall. Most malls today have children's clothing stores (e.g., Baby Gap). If yours doesn't, go to one of the large department stores and find the children's clothing section. Start with the infants' clothes. Is there a difference between "girls' clothes" and "boys' clothes"? Note the differences in the style, color, and texture of boys' versus girls' clothes. Collect the same information for clothes designed for toddlers, preschoolers, and elementary school age children.

Now find a store that specializes in clothes for preteens and teenagers. How do clothing styles and materials differ along gender lines at this age level?

After collecting your data, try to interpret the differences you noticed. Why do they exist? What do these differences say about the kinds of social activities in which boys and girls are expected or encouraged to engage? For instance, which clothes are "rugged" and which are "dainty"? How do such differences reinforce our cultural conceptions of masculinity and femininity? Turning your attention to teenagers, how do popular clothing styles encourage sexuality?

The next stop on your sociological shopping trip is a toy store. Can you detect a boys' section and a girls' section? How can you tell? How do the toys differ? What sorts of interactions with other children do the toys encourage? Competition? Cooperation? Which toys are designed for active play? Which seem to encourage passive play? For what sorts of adult roles do the toys prepare children? Provide specific examples.

Finally, find a bookstore that has a children's book section. Which books are more likely to interest boys? Which will interest girls? Are there different sections for "boy" and "girl" books? What are the differences in the sorts of characters and plots that are portrayed? Does the bookstore have a section that contains books designed to help adolescents through puberty? If so, do these books offer different advice to adolescent boys and girls?

Use your findings in all these areas—clothing, toys, and books—or any others you come across to analyze the role that consumer products play in socializing children into "appropriate" gender roles. Is there more or less gender segregation as children get older? Do you think manufacturers, publishers, retail outlets, and so on are simply responding to market demands (i.e., do they make gender-specific products because that's what people want), or do they play a role in creating those demands?

CHAPTER HIGHLIGHTS

- Socialization is the process by which individuals learn their culture and learn to live according to the norms of a particular society. It is how we learn to perceive our world, gain a sense of our own identity, and interact appropriately with others. It also tells us what we should and should not do across a range of situations.

- One of the most important outcomes of socialization for an individual is the development of a sense of self. To acquire a self, children must learn to recognize themselves as unique physical objects, master language, learn to take the roles of others, and, in effect, see themselves from another's perspective.

- Socialization is not just a process that occurs during childhood. Adults must be resocialized into a new galaxy of norms, values, and expectations each time they leave or abandon old roles and enter new ones.

- Through socialization, we learn the social expectations that go with our social class, racial or ethnic group, and gender.

- Socialization occurs within the context of several social institutions—family first, and then schools, religious institutions, and the mass media.

KEY TERMS

agents of socialization: Various individuals, groups, and organizations who influence the socialization process

anticipatory socialization: Process through which people acquire the values and orientations found in statuses they will likely enter in the future

collectivist culture: Culture in which personal accomplishments are less important in the formation of identity than group membership

eugenics: Control of mating to ensure that "defective" genes of troublesome individuals will not be passed on to future generations

game stage: Stage in the development of self during which a child acquires the ability to take the role of a group or community (the generalized other) and conform his or her behavior to broad societal expectations

gender: Psychological, social, and cultural aspects of maleness and femaleness

generalized other: Perspective of the larger society and its constituent values and attitudes

identity: Essential aspect of who we are, consisting of our sense of self, gender, race, ethnicity, and religion

individualist culture: Culture in which personal accomplishments are a more important component of one's self-concept than group membership

looking-glass self: Sense of who we are that is defined by incorporating the reflected appraisals of others

play stage: Stage in the development of self during which a child develops the ability to take a role, but only from the perspective of one person at a time

reflexive behavior: Behavior in which the person initiating an action is the same as the person toward whom the action is directed

resocialization: Process of learning new values, norms, and expectations when an adult leaves an old role and enters a new one

role taking: Ability to see oneself from the perspective of others and to use that perspective in formulating one's own behavior

self: Unique set of traits, behaviors, and attitudes that distinguishes one person from the next; the active source and passive object of behavior

sex: Biological maleness or femaleness

socialization: Process through which one learns how to act according to the rules and expectations of a particular culture

total institution: Place where individuals are cut off from the wider society for an appreciable period and where together they lead an enclosed, formally administered life

tracking: Grouping of students into different curricular programs, or tracks, based on an assessment of their academic abilities

STUDENT STUDY SITE

Visit the Student Study Site at **www.sagepub.com/newman9e** for these additional learning tools:

- Flashcards
- Web quizzes
- Sociologists at Work features
- Micro-Macro Connection features
- Video links
- Audio links
- Web resources
- SAGE journal articles

Supporting Identity

The Presentation of Self

6

Forming Impressions of Others

Managing Impressions

Mismanaging Impressions: Spoiled Identities

On Christmas Day, 1981, I met my soon-to-be wife's family for the first time. For this group of important strangers, I knew I had to be on my best behavior and say and do all the right things. I wanted to make sure the impression they formed of me was that of a likable fellow whom they'd be proud to call a member of the family someday.

As people busily opened their presents, I noticed the wide and gleeful eyes of my wife's 14-year-old sister as she unwrapped what was to her a special gift—her very own basketball. Being the youngest in a family of eight kids, she didn't have much she could call her own, so this was a significant moment for her. She had finally broken away from a life filled with hand-me-downs and communal equipment. She hugged that ball as if it were a puppy.

I saw my chance to make the perfect first impression. "I'm not a bad basketball player," I thought to myself. "I'll take her outside to the basketball hoop in the driveway, dazzle her with my shooting skills, become her idol, and win family approval."

"Hey, Mary," I said, "let's go out and shoot some hoops." After we stepped outside, I grabbed the new ball from her. "Watch this," I said as I flung it toward the basket from about 40 feet away. We both watched as the ball arced gracefully toward its destination, and for a brief moment, I actually thought it was going to go in. But that was not to be.

As if guided by the taunting hand of fate, the ball struck an exposed bolt that protruded from the supporting pole of the hoop. There was a sickeningly loud pop, followed by a hissing sound as the ball fluttered to the ground like a deflated balloon. It sat there lifeless, never having experienced the joy of "swishing" through a net. For that matter, it had never even been bounced on the ground in its short-lived inflated state.

For a few seconds, we both stood numb and motionless. Then I turned to apologize to the 14-year-old girl, whose once cheerful eyes now harbored the kind of hate and resentment usually reserved for ax murderers and IRS auditors. In a flash, she burst into tears and ran into the house shrieking, "*That guy* popped my ball!" It was hardly the heroic identity I was striving for. As the angry mob poured into the backyard to stare at the villainous and still somewhat unknown perpetrator, I became painfully aware of the fragile nature of the self-images we try to project to others.

We all have been in situations—a first date, a job interview, a first meeting with a girl-friend or boyfriend's family—in which we feel compelled to "make a good impression." We try to present a favorable image of ourselves so that others will form positive judgments of us. This phenomenon is not only an important and universal aspect of our personal lives but a key element of social structure as well.

In this chapter, I examine the social creation of images. How do we form impressions of others? What do we do to control the impressions others form of us? I also discuss the broader sociological applications of these actions. What are the institutional motivations behind individuals' attempts to control others' impressions of them? How do groups and organizations present and manage collective impressions? Finally, what happens when these attempts fail and images are spoiled, as mine was when my errant jump shot killed a girl's brand-new basketball?

Forming Impressions of Others

When we first meet someone, we form an immediate impression based on observable cues such as age, ascribed status characteristics such as race and gender, individual attributes such as physical appearance, and verbal and nonverbal expressions. This process of **impression formation** helps us form a quick picture of the other person's identity.

Keep in mind that the importance of this information—the value attached to a certain age, race, or gender; the particular physical or personality traits a society defines as desirable; the meaning of certain words and gestures—varies across time and place. Hence, the impressions that people form of others must always be understood within the appropriate cultural and historical contexts. For instance, an emotionally expressive person in the United States may give the impression of being energetic and outgoing; in the United Kingdom such a person may seem boorish and rude; and in Thailand or Japan that person may be considered dangerous or crazy.

Social Group Membership

Age, sex, race, and to a certain degree ethnicity can often be determined merely by looking at someone; social class is less obvious but sometimes becomes known early in an encounter with another person through her or his language, mannerisms, or dress. Our socialization experiences have taught us to expect that people displaying these signs of social group membership have certain characteristics. For instance, if all you know about a person you've not yet met is that she's 85 years old, you might predict that she has low energy, a poor memory, and a conservative approach to life. Think about your expectations when you learn that a new roommate is from a different region of this country—or, for that matter, from a different country. Of course, such expectations are rarely completely accurate. Nevertheless, we begin social interactions with these culturally defined conceptions of how people from certain social groups are likely to act, what their tastes and preferences might be, and what values and attitudes they are likely to hold.

This information is so pervasive and so quickly processed that we usually notice it only when it isn't there. If you spend a lot of time texting or tweeting with strangers, you may have noticed how difficult it can be to form a friendship or carry on a discussion when you don't know whether you are interacting with someone of the same sex or with someone of a different sex or whether the person is much older or much younger than you are. Social group membership provides the necessary backdrop to all encounters between people who have little if any prior knowledge of one another.

Physical Appearance

We confirm or modify early impressions based on social group membership by assessing other characteristics that are easily perceivable, such as a person's physical appearance (Berndt & Heller, 1986). The way people dress and decorate their bodies communicates their feelings, beliefs, and group identity to others. People's clothes, jewelry, hairstyles, and so on can also indicate their ethnicity, social class, age, cultural tastes, morality, and political attitudes.

But again, these impressions can be influenced by our cultural background. Physical appearance is enormously important in U.S. culture. Everywhere we turn, it seems, we are encouraged to believe that if our skin isn't free of blemishes, if we are too short or too tall, if we are over- or underweight, if our hair isn't stylish, if our clothes don't reflect the latest fashion trend, we have fallen short of some attractiveness threshold. Although we readily acknowledge that using a person's physical appearance to form an impression is shallow and unfair, most of us do it anyway.

Research confirms that physical appearance affects our perceptions of others. Attractive men are perceived as more masculine and attractive women more feminine than their less attractive counterparts (Gillen, 1981). We often assume that physically attractive people possess other desirable traits, such as sensitivity, kindness, strength, and sexual responsiveness (Dion, Berscheid, & Walster, 1972). Such judgments can sometimes be converted to financial gain. Economists have coined the term "beauty premium" to refer to the advantages attractive people enjoy:

> Handsome men earn, on average, 5% more than their less-attractive counterparts (good-looking women earn 4% more); pretty people get more attention from teachers, bosses, and mentors. . . . Fifty seven percent of hiring managers [in a recent survey indicated that] qualified but unattractive candidates are likely to have a harder time landing a job, while more than half advised spending as much time and money on "making sure they look attractive" as on perfecting a résumé. (J. Bennett, 2010, p. 47)

Impressions based on appearance can also work their way into the legal system. In 2010, a Florida judge ruled that a defendant in a murder trial was entitled to a $125 cosmetic makeover each day he was in court to hide his offensive tattoos, which included a large swastika on his neck. The defense attorney had successfully argued that his client's fearsome appearance could prejudice the jury:

> There's no doubt in my mind—without the makeup being used, there's no way a jury could look at [my client] and judge him fairly. It's too frightening when you see him with the tattoos. It's a scary picture. (quoted in J. Schwartz, 2010, p. A18)

In a recent study, undergraduate subjects at Cornell University were provided with profiles of defendants in criminal trials and asked to assess their guilt and suggest a punishment. The profiles included information about the defendant's race, gender, height, weight, and eye color, and a high-resolution color photograph, which previous subjects had coded as either attractive or unattractive. In addition, they were given a trial summary (these were all aggravated assault cases), transcripts of the attorneys' closing arguments, and the judge's instructions to the jury. The researchers found that unattractive defendants were 22% more likely to be convicted and, if convicted, spend an average of 22 months *longer* in prison than their better-looking counterparts (Gunnell & Ceci, 2010). The findings of this study did not come as a surprise to the spokesperson for the National Association of Criminal Defense Lawyers, who stated, "We usually want our clients in a suit, with their hair combed and trying to appear as clean-cut as possible. [This study] bears out what many of us knew in our gut" (quoted in Baldas, 2010, p. 1).

On the flip side, ugliness has always occupied a lowly place on the social landscape. In literature and film, ugliness is usually associated with evil and fear, characterizing all manner of monsters, witches, and villains (Kershaw, 2008). Beyond fictional portrayals, unattractiveness can have serious everyday consequences. For instance, one study found that even in occupations where looks have no bearing on a person's ability to do his or her job—like computer programming—unattractive workers suffer discrimination (Mobius & Rosenblat, 2006). Many parents these days are becoming less tolerant of any flaw in their children's appearance. Numerous Web sites now offer retouching services so that parents can airbrush photos of their children to remove blemishes, crooked teeth, and other facial imperfections (J. Bennett, 2008).

Physical attractiveness is still a more salient interpersonal and economic issue for women than for men, even though women have more money, political clout, and legal recognition today than ever. For instance, 61% of hiring managers indicate that it's advantageous for a woman to "show off her figure" in the workplace (cited in J. Bennett, 2010). An article about a talented, all-female chamber music trio called Eroica stated, "The Eroica Trio not only plays beautiful music, it has also created a marketing sensation for being 'easy on the eye'" (W. Smith, 2002, p. 4). Hillary Clinton's unsuccessful 2008 presidential campaign was marked by almost constant media focus on her clothing and hairstyle. Here's how one columnist described the breathless attention being paid to the attractiveness of some female Republican politicians:

> Something pretty creepy has been happening to conservative women lately. There seems to be an insistent, increasingly excitable focus on the supposed hotness of Republican women in the public eye, like Sarah Palin, Michele Bachmann, Michelle Malkin, and Nikki Haley. . . . The sexual references are pervasive: they come from left, right, and center, and range from gushing to highly offensive. (Baird, 2010, p. 37)

It's hard to imagine physical attractiveness being the hub of this kind of attention for male political leaders, not to mention male salespeople or classical musicians.

Women around the world routinely cause themselves serious pain and injury as they alter their bodies to conform to cultural definitions of beauty. In China, for example, hundreds of women each year, convinced that being taller would improve their job and marriage prospects, subject themselves to a procedure in which their leg bones are broken, separated, and stretched. Metal pins and screws pull the bones apart a fraction of a millimeter a day, sometimes for close to two years. Many Chinese women have lost the ability to walk from this treatment; others have suffered permanent, disfiguring bone damage (C. S. Smith, 2002). In the United States, a growing number of affluent women undergo potentially dangerous cosmetic foot surgery each year to reduce the size of their toes so that they can fit into today's fashionable, narrow high-heeled shoes (G. Harris, 2003). In 2010, girls and women began wearing decorative "circle lenses," brightly colored contact lenses that make eyes appear larger because they cover not just the iris, as ordinary lenses do, but part of the whites as well (Saint Louis, 2010). These lenses, which give wearers a childlike, doe-eyed appearance, are available online without a prescription, much to the chagrin of eye doctors who fear the damage they may cause. A spokesperson for the Food and Drug Administration wrote that consumers risk significant eye injury, even blindness, when they buy contact lenses without a valid prescription.

At the individual level, the emphasis on physical appearance devalues a person's other attributes and accomplishments; at the institutional level, it plays an important role in the nation's economy by sustaining several multibillion-dollar enterprises, including the advertising, fashion, cosmetics, and weight loss industries (Schur, 1984).

MICRO-MACRO CONNECTION

Sizing People Up

In U.S. society and in most industrialized societies, the negative effects of being considered unattractive are perhaps felt most strongly by those whose body size does not meet cultural standards (Carr & Friedman, 2006; English, 1991). Sometimes the disapproval of people's weight is motivated by health concerns. For instance, some elementary, middle, and high schools around the country monitor students' weight gain (and loss) and regularly report their body mass index scores—a measure of the ratio of height to weight that is used to determine "fatness" and "thinness"—to parents via obesity report cards (Kantor, 2007). This strategy is meant to guard against dangerous weight fluctuations and eating disorders. And because of its financial effects—childhood obesity alone costs more than $14 billion annually in direct health expenses, and it's estimated that almost 17% of U.S. medical costs are obesity related (Stobbe, 2010)—some health insurance companies are now debating whether to charge higher premiums to anyone over a certain body mass index (Singer, 2010).

But against a cultural backdrop that glorifies thinness, fat is seen not only as unhealthy and costly but as repulsive, ugly, and unclean (LeBesco, 2004). People are likely to judge an overweight person as lacking in willpower and as being self-indulgent, personally offensive, and even morally and socially unfit (Millman, 1980). One study found that mental health caseworkers were more likely to assign negative psychological symptoms (e.g., being too emotional, being unhygienic, engaging in inappropriate behavior) to obese patients than to thin patients (Young & Powell, 1985). In another study, one out of four nurses reported being "repulsed" by obese patients (cited in Puhl & Brownell, 2001).

It is often said that obese people are the last acceptable targets of unequal treatment (Carr & Friedman, 2006). Some commercial airlines have obesity seating policies that require a passenger to purchase a second seat if she or he is unable to fit comfortably into a single seat in the ticketed cabin, is unable to properly buckle the seatbelt using a single seatbelt extender, and/or is unable to put the seat's armrests down when seated. In the workplace, researchers have found significant discrimination against obese and overweight people at every stage of the employment cycle, including hiring, placement, compensation, promotion, discipline, and discharge (Roehling, 1999). Like unattractiveness in general, research has consistently shown a wage penalty for obese employees, especially women. One study that followed young adults over eight years found that overweight women earned an average of $6,000 less than nonobese women (Pagan & Davila, 1997).

In high-visibility occupations such as public relations and sales, overweight people are often regarded as unemployable because they might project a negative image of the company they are working for. Flight attendants have been fired for exceeding airline weight requirements, even though their job-related abilities met company standards (Puhl & Brownell, 2001). A casino in Atlantic City once warned its cocktail waitresses that if they gained more than 10% of their current weight, they'd be suspended without pay for 90 days while they tried to lose the extra pounds. If their weight loss efforts were unsuccessful, they'd be fired (I. Peterson, 2005).

Negative perceptions of obese people are not universal. In Niger, for example, being overweight—ideally with rolls of fat, stretch marks, and a large behind—is considered an essential part of female beauty. Women who aren't sufficiently round are considered unfit for marriage (R. Popenoe, 2005). In Mauritania, girls as young as 5 and as old as 19 years are sometimes forced by their parents to drink five gallons of fat-rich camel's milk each day so they become fat (LaFraniere, 2007). In Botswana, fatness is equated with fertility, especially among women, and is therefore a positive sign of one's marriageability. Large women are said to have "fat eggs" and are therefore fit to bear children (Upton, 2010). In many developing countries, where food supplies are scarce, being overweight is associated with being middle class or wealthy.

Indeed, some anthropologists argue that cultural tastes in female body shape are always influenced by women's role in society. For instance, men tend to prefer larger female bodies in industrial societies where women are economically independent (e.g., Britain and Denmark) and in nonindustrial societies where they bear responsibility for finding food. Only in societies where women are economically dependent on men (such as Japan and Greece) do men have a strong preference for thin, hourglass figures in women. As one anthropologist put it, men's preferences in female body type depend "on the degree to which they want their mates to be strong, tough, economically successful, and politically competitive" (Cashdan, 2008, p. 1104).

Rates of obesity have been rising worldwide, due principally to the increased production of more processed and affordable food than ever before (Swinburn et al., 2011). At the same time, though, Western images of thinness—and perhaps the stigmatization of obesity as well—have begun to infiltrate places that once had positive attitudes toward large bodies, such as Mexico, Tanzania, and Puerto Rico (Brewis, Wutich, Falletta-Cowden, & Rodriguez-Soto, 2011). For instance, the 2001 Miss World was a Nigerian woman named Agbani Darego, an extremely tall and thin woman who conformed to Western rather than Nigerian weight ideals. Older Nigerians considered her sickly thin. But younger Nigerians, more likely to be exposed to negative Western attitudes toward fatness, felt otherwise (Onishi, 2002). An Indian businesswoman recently stated, "I think all around the ideal of beauty is skinny thin. I had a highly educated friend confess that she would prefer for her children to be anorexic rather than overweight" (quoted in Parker-Pope, 2011, p. A3).

In the United States, the value attached to body size is linked to race, education level, and social class. By official measures, about 65% of Whites are either overweight or obese. Among African Americans and Mexican Americans, the figures are about 72% and 76%, respectively. Sixty-seven percent of U.S. adults who have taken at least some college courses are either overweight or obese as compared with 71% of people who have only a high school diploma (U.S. Bureau of the Census, 2011b).

As in contemporary developing countries, obesity was once considered a sign of wealth in the U.S., but today, being overweight is likely to be equated with poverty, where sedentary lifestyles and high-fat diets can be commonplace (Gilman, 2004). About 20% of poor children are obese, as compared with 15% of nonpoor children (M. Lee, 2006). Weight problems are compounded in poor communities because the key determinants of physical activity—safe playgrounds, access to high-quality, low-cost food, and transportation to play areas—are either inadequate or nonexistent. And because of poor grocery distribution in low-income neighborhoods, fresh fruits and vegetables are actually more expensive than in suburban stores. Poor black and racially mixed neighborhoods have significantly fewer large-chain supermarkets, natural food stores, fruit and vegetable markets, and bakeries than wealthier white neighborhoods. What they have more of are local grocery stores, convenience stores, and fast food restaurants—all of which provide fewer healthy choices and tend to charge higher prices for the healthier food they do offer (M. Lee, 2006). These areas are sometimes referred to as "food deserts" because of their nutritional isolation and the lack of mainstream, high-quality grocery stores.

In addition, fast food companies have grown more aggressive in targeting poor, inner city neighborhoods. One out of every four McDonald's hamburgers is purchased by a consumer in the inner city (Critser, 2000). Such facts are not inconsequential. Researchers have found that obesity rates among ninth graders increase by an average of 5% when their school is located within one tenth of a mile of a fast food restaurant (Currie, DellaVigna, Moretti, & Pathania, 2009). The problem became so acute that in 2008 the Los Angeles City Council adopted legislation mandating a one-year moratorium on the building of new fast food restaurants in an inner city area with a 30% obesity rate (Kurutz, 2008).

The association of obesity, class, and race is often tinged with prejudice. The cultural devaluation of fat tends to combine with the devaluation of poverty and of "nonwhiteness":

> The fact that African, Native American, and Latin cultural traditions [define] large bodies as beautiful—and that, in general, poor people of all colors are heavier and eat fattier diets than the well-to-do—allows an ugly stew of hatreds to come together in the abhorrence with which we regard fleshy bodies, especially if they are dark-skinned, ineptly groomed, or cheaply dressed. (Weismantel, 2005, p. 51)

Many cases have been reported of fat children being removed from their homes because their obesity is taken as a sign that they are victims of abuse and neglect. These incidents almost always involve people of color and the poor or working class. Caseworkers tend to blame the parents for unacceptable cultural traditions and, allegedly, their ignorance of healthy lifestyles (LeBesco, 2004).

As with physical appearance in general, women feel the contemporary distaste for obesity particularly strongly. Clothing companies contribute to women's heightened weight concern through the way they size women's clothes. Several companies now manufacture size zero outfits. In 2007, the fashion designer Nicole Miller became the first to introduce a "subzero" size for women with 23-inch waists—roughly the circumference of a junior soccer ball—and 35-inch hips (the average U.S. woman has a 34-inch waist and 43-inch hips; Schrobsdorff, 2006). It is feared that less-than-zero sizes will become a status symbol among young girls who glorify razor-thin bodies. For older women, clothing companies also engage in a common practice known as "vanity sizing," whereby garments with the same size number become larger over time. A size 12 in the 1950s is now a size 6 (B. Swanson, 2006). Such a practice allegedly makes older women feel better about themselves because it gives the illusion that they are thinner than they really are.

Female weight concern has large-scale economic implications because of the role it plays in the growth and success of the diet "industry": low-calorie foods and beverages, diet books, prescription medicines, weight loss organizations, and so forth. Pharmaceutical companies spend billions of dollars each year on research designed to develop new obesity drugs with names like "Slim Seduction," "PowerThin," and "the size zero pill." It's estimated that global sales of diet foods and beverages will exceed $200 billion by 2014 (Markets and Markets, 2011).

But weight concerns may not be shared equally by all U.S. women. About 76% of African American women and 74% of Latina women are overweight or obese, compared with 60% of white women (U.S. Bureau of the Census, 2011b). Yet white women are significantly more likely than women of ethnoracial minorities to be concerned about their weight and to exhibit disordered eating behaviors (Abrams, Allen, & Gray, 1993). In one study, 90% of white junior high and high school girls voiced dissatisfaction with their bodies, compared with 30% of black teens (S. Parker et al., 1995). Indeed, black adolescents tend to perceive themselves as thinner than they actually are, whereas white adolescents tend to perceive themselves as heavier than they actually are.

African American women, especially poor and working-class African American women, worry less than women of other races about dieting or about being thin (Molloy & Herzberger, 1998). One study found that although African American women are more likely than white women to weigh more than 120% of their recommended body weight, they are much less likely to perceive themselves as overweight or to suffer blows to their self-esteem as a result (Averett & Korenman, 1999). When black women do diet, their efforts to lose weight are more realistic and less extreme than white women's attempts.

However, researchers have recently begun to challenge the suggestion that women of color are somehow immune to body weight concerns (e.g., Beauboeuf-Lafontant, 2009). Some have suggested that women of color have always suffered from body dissatisfaction and disordered eating but have largely been overlooked by researchers because they are less likely than white women to seek treatment (Brodey, 2005). Others speculate that body dissatisfaction among women of color has actually increased recently because they are more likely than their predecessors to be exposed to and adopt for themselves dominant white preferences, attitudes, and ideals about beauty and weight. One study found that the risk of disordered eating increases for African American women who have a strong desire to assimilate into the dominant white culture (Abrams et al., 1993). Concern over weight shows how powerful cultural beliefs are in the formation of self-concepts. At best, the failure to meet broad cultural standards of thinness can lower self-esteem and generate antagonism toward one's own body. At worst, it can lead to life-threatening eating disorders. Such drastic responses indicate the importance of body size—and physical appearance in general—in forming impressions of other people.

Verbal and Nonverbal Expression

Another important piece of information we use in forming impressions of others is what people express to us verbally or nonverbally. Obviously, we form impressions of others based on what they tell us about themselves. But beyond speech, people's movements, postures, and gestures provide cues about their values, attitudes, sentiments, personality, and history (Stone, 1981). Sometimes people use these forms of communication purposely to convey meaning, as when they put on a smile so that others will find them approachable. However, some physical expressions, such as a shaky voice, a flushed face, and trembling hands, are difficult to control. They transmit an impression whether we want to or not.

Most of us are quite proficient at "reading" even the subtlest nonverbal messages. We learn early on that a raised eyebrow, a nod of the head, or a slight hand gesture can mean something important in a social encounter. So crucial is this ability in maintaining orderly interactions that some psychologists consider a deficiency in it to be a learning disability akin to severe reading problems (Goleman, 1989).

Managing Impressions

People form impressions of others and present impressions of themselves at the same time. This ability to influence the impressions others make of us is the defining feature of human interaction. Naturally, we try to create impressions of ourselves that give us advantages—by making us seem attractive or powerful or otherwise worthy of people's attention and esteem. Of course, that's what I was trying to do when I attempted the ill-fated jump shot with my future sister-in-law's new basketball.

The process by which people attempt to present a favorable public image of themselves is called *impression management*. Erving Goffman (1959), the sociologist most responsible for the scholarly examination of impression management, portrays everyday life as a series of social interactions in which a person is motivated to "sell" a particular image to others. The primary goal of impression management is to project a particular identity that will increase the likelihood of obtaining favorable outcomes from others in particular social situations (E. E. Jones & Pittman, 1982; Stryker, 1980). To do so, we can strategically furnish or conceal information. At times, we may need to advertise, exaggerate, or even fabricate our positive qualities; at other times, we conceal or camouflage behaviors or attributes that we believe others will find unappealing.

The prominent role that social network sites now play in our lives has created new challenges for impression management. Recall our discussion of role taking in Chapter 5. In our "offline" lives, we interact with various people each day: family, acquaintances, coworkers, friends from different corners of our lives. Consequently, we have the opportunity to express multiple selves and manage different impressions that suit our different immediate needs. You may not be the same person with your friends as you are with your grandparents. But online—when, say, we're creating a Facebook profile of ourselves—we have one shot at managing the impression we want others to form of us. And it's an impression all our different "friends," who have come to know us under very different circumstances, will have access to. That's a lot of pressure.

Whether it occurs online or in offline, face-to-face interaction, obtaining favorable outcomes through impression management is usually associated with social approval— that is, with being respected and liked by others. However, different circumstances may require projecting different identities (E. E. Jones & Pittman, 1982). Perhaps you've been in situations where you've tried to appear helpless in order to get someone else to do a task you really didn't want to do, or maybe you've tried to appear mean and fearsome to intimidate someone. Perhaps you've "played dumb" to avoid challenging a superior (Gove, Hughes, & Geerkin, 1980). As social beings, we have the ability to tailor our images to fit the requirements of a particular situation.

Various psychologists argue that managing artificial impressions can sometimes have therapeutic value. For instance, during the economic recession, some therapists are encouraging their laid-off clients to project the illusion of employment by maintaining their job routine—waking up early, dressing in their usual work clothes, and commuting—even though they don't have a job to go to. They claim that "keeping up appearances" may seem deceitful but can be useful in sustaining good habits and personal pride (Carey, 2009).

Goffman argues that impression management is not just used to present false or inflated images of ourselves. Many authentic attributes we possess are not immediately apparent to others; sometimes our actions may be misinterpreted. Imagine yourself taking the final exam in your sociology course. You look up from your paper and make brief eye contact with the instructor. You're not cheating, but you think the instructor may interpret your wandering eyes as an indication of cheating. What do you do? Chances are you will consciously overemphasize your noncheating behavior by acting as though you're deep in thought or by glancing up at the clock to highlight your "law-abiding" image.

Frequently people try to present a favorable image of themselves by altering their physical appearance. Clothing and body adornment can be used to manipulate and manage the impressions others form of us. People can dress to convey the impression that they are worthy of respect or, at the very least, attention (Lauer & Handel, 1977). Businesspeople are acutely aware of and usually conform to a corporate dress code, even if the code is "business casual"; those who dress too casually are not taken seriously. Children often signal their entry into the world of adolescence by wearing the clothing of their peers and refusing to wear the clothing chosen by their parents (Stone, 1981). The purveyors of pop, hip-hop, crunk, heavy metal, lounge, rave, dance/house/techno, goth, and other musical subcultures use clothing and hairstyle as an expression of identity and social rebellion. And as you are well aware, fashion is a significant element of the student subculture on most college campuses (Moffatt, 1989). In short, by what they wear, people tell one another who they are, where they come from, and what they stand for.

Dramaturgy: Actors on a Social Stage

"All the world's a stage, / And all the men and women merely players: / They have their exits and their entrances; / And one man in his time plays many parts," wrote William Shakespeare in *As You Like It*. Analyzing social interaction as a series of theatrical performances—what sociologists call *dramaturgy*—has been a staple of symbolic interactionism for decades. Like Shakespeare, sociologist Erving Goffman (1959) argues that people in everyday life are similar to actors on a stage. The "audience" consists of people who observe the behavior of others, "roles" are the images people are trying to project, and the "script" is the content of their communication with others. The goal is to enact a performance that is believable to a particular audience and that allows us to achieve the goals we desire. Just about every aspect of social life can be examined dramaturgically, from the ritualized greetings of strangers to the everyday dynamics of our family, school, and work lives.

Front Stage and Back Stage

A key structural element of dramaturgy is the distinction between front stage and back stage. In the theater, front stage is where the performance takes place for the audience. In contrast, back stage is where makeup is removed, lines are rehearsed, and performances are rehashed, and where people can fall "out of character."

In social interaction, *front stage* is where people maintain the appropriate appearance as they interact with others. For workers in a restaurant, front stage is the dining room where the customers (the audience) are present. Here, the servers (the actors) are expected to present themselves as upbeat, happy, competent, and courteous. *Back stage*, however, is the region where people can knowingly violate their impression management performances. In the restaurant, back stage is the kitchen area where the once courteous servers now shout, shove dishes, and even complain about or mock the customers.

As in the theater, the barrier between front and back stage is crucial to successful impression management because it blocks the audience from seeing behavior that would ruin the performance. During a therapy session (front stage), psychiatrists usually appear extremely interested in everything their patients say and show considerable sympathy for their problems. At a dinner party with colleagues or at home with family (back stage), however, they may express total boredom with and disdain for their patients' disclosures. If patients were to see such back stage behavior, not only would it disrupt the performance, but it would damage the psychiatrist's professional credibility and reputation as well. One study found that beneath their mask of neutrality, many psychiatrists harbor strong and professionally inappropriate feelings—including hatred, fear, anger, and sexual arousal—toward their patients (cited in Goleman, 1993).

PETER UBEL

Elevator Talk Among Doctors and Nurses

We all take for granted, when visiting a doctor's office or a hospital, that the doctors and nurses will protect the confidentiality of their patients. Yet even for these professionals, the temptation to talk about patients behind their backs ("back stage") is often hard to resist. Dr. Peter Ubel and his colleagues (1995) sent observers to five Pennsylvania hospitals to determine the frequency and nature of inappropriate talk about patients among hospital personnel. The researchers were particularly interested in conversations that could easily be overheard by people who shouldn't be privy to such information. They decided to focus on elevator talk.

Of the 259 elevator rides they observed during which passengers had a chance to converse, inappropriate comments were made 14% of the time. The observers found that the remarks fell into four distinct categories:

1. *Comments violating patient confidentiality:* The majority of back stage comments inappropriately disclosed factual information about a patient's condition. These remarks were usually simple declarations, such as "Mr. X was readmitted last night for more chemo." In other situations, the comments exposed professional disagreement over a particular course of action. For instance, in one case two physicians had a heated debate over the merits of removing parts of either one or two lungs from a patient.

2. *Unprofessional remarks and motivation:* Another category of comments consisted of remarks that raised questions about medical personnel's ability or desire to provide quality care. For instance, doctors or nurses sometimes complained that they were too tired or too sick to do their jobs well. On some occasions, physicians were heard talking about how they were just biding their time in the hospital until they could go elsewhere and make large amounts of money. Such comments clearly call into question their professionalism.

3. *Comments raising questions about the quality of patient care:* Some conversations consisted of personnel complaining about hospital resources and facilities, thereby raising doubts about whether the institution offered good patient care. Other times, nurses or doctors would question the qualifications of a colleague. Although the motivation behind such remarks is not always clear, people who come to visit their loved ones in a hospital and overhear these casual conversations are not always capable of weighing unsubstantiated information.

4. *Derogatory comments about patients or their families:* The last category of inappropriate back stage comments were direct insults about patients, focusing on traits such as weight or body odor. Such comments reflect poorly on the compassion of health care workers. In addition, visitors' anxiety about the quality of care may increase if they are led to believe that the staff don't like them or their loved ones.

This research points to the institutional importance of maintaining boundaries between front stage and back stage. Health care workers will always talk about patients behind their backs. But in a field such as medicine, which deals with extremely delicate personal information and life-and-death decisions, the credibility of the profession depends on workers' ability to correctly determine when a location is, in fact, private back stage. Public awareness of these sorts of remarks can have serious economic, political, and perhaps even legal consequences. The problem has become so bad that elevators in some hospitals carry posted warnings reminding medical personnel to refrain from talking about patients.

Props

Successful impression management also depends on the control of objects, called props, that convey identity. In the theater, props must be handled deftly for an effective performance. A gun that doesn't go off when it's supposed to or a chair that unexpectedly collapses can destroy an entire play. The same is true in social interaction. For instance, college students may make sure their schoolbooks are in clear view and beer bottles disposed of as they prepare for an upcoming visit from their parents. Similarly, someone may spend a great deal of time setting a romantic mood for a dinner date at home—the right music, the right lighting, pictures of former lovers hidden from view, and so on.

Sometimes people use props to create an environment that reinforces some individuals' authority over others. Note the way props were used to intimidate this professor as he testified before Congress:

> And then I was called to the witness stand. Now, the chair is something nobody talks about. It is low and extremely puffy. When you sit in it your butt just keeps sinking, and suddenly

the tabletop is up to your chest. The senators peer down at you from above, and the power dynamic is terrifying. (H. Jenkins, 1999, p. 21)

Props needn't be inanimate objects. To convey to potential clients and investors what they believe will be an air of prestige, money, and crucial global connections, some Chinese companies now "rent" white foreigners to pose as fake employees. The companies hope that the presence of these individuals will help to secure a contract or simply support the company's claim of being internationally successful. An ad in a Chinese newspaper for a company called Rent-a-Laowai (Chinese for "foreigner") read: "Occasionally companies want a foreign face to go to meetings and conferences or to go to dinners and lunches and smile at the clients and shake people's hands" (quoted in Farrar, 2010, p. 1).

Viewing impression management from a dramaturgical perspective reminds us that our everyday actions rarely occur in a social vacuum. Indeed, our behaviors are often structured with an eye toward how they might be perceived by particular "audiences."

Image Making

In our individualistic, competitive society, appearances can sometimes provide a critically important edge. A person's desire to maximize prestige, wealth, and power can be the driving force behind a thorough makeover. Two prominent examples are Americans' pursuit of improved looks through the invasive alteration of their bodies and politicians' pursuit of a popular identity through a carefully controlled public image. As you will see, these efforts are not things a person undertakes on his or her own. Whole industries have evolved that are devoted to making and remaking images for the public eye.

The Alteration of Appearance

The desire to manage impressions by changing physical appearance motivates some people to do far more than try a new hairstyle, get a tattoo, or buy a new outfit or two. Even in economic hard times, people in the United States are willing to spend huge sums of money to medically alter their looks. According to the American Society of Plastic Surgeons (2011), there were 1.6 million cosmetic surgery procedures and close to 12 million minimally invasive, nonsurgical procedures (such as Botox injections, cellulite treatments, and chemical peels) in the United States in 2010. Ninety-one percent of the patients were women. These figures represent a 77% increase over 2000. The overall cost for these procedures was about $10.2 billion. Exhibit 6.1 shows recent trends in the popularity of cosmetic procedures.

The desire to surgically alter one's appearance is not unique to the United States. Doctors perform more plastic surgeries per capita in Brazil than anywhere else in the world. In fact, according to some reports, there's even been an increase in such procedures among women over the age of 80 (Rohter, 2007). In 2001, the Brazilian contestant in the Miss Universe contest scandalized many non-Brazilians by speaking freely and publicly about her breast implants, cheekbone reconstruction, silicone remolding of her chin, pinned-back ears, and liposuction. She told reporters, "I have to work on my figure to get it where I want it. It's something I need for my

Exhibit 6.1   The Popularity of Cosmetic Surgery in the United States

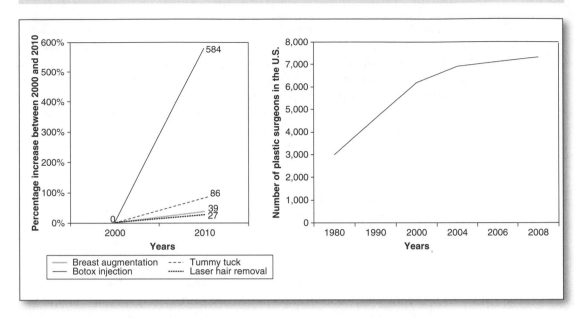

SOURCES: American Society of Plastic Surgeons, 2011; U.S. Bureau of the Census, 2011b, Table 160

profession. . . . I have a doctorate in body measurement" (Kulick & Machado-Borges, 2005, p. 128).

In China, the growing cosmetic surgery industry takes in over $2.4 billion a year as people with newfound affluence rush to go under the knife to become *renzao meinu*, or "man-made beauties." The number of Chinese receiving cosmetic plastic surgery doubles each year. The most commonly requested procedure is one designed to make the eyes appear larger and more "Western" (LaFraniere, 2011). In fact, China now hosts an "Artificial Beauty" contest, where people from all over the globe compete to become the world's most beautiful product of plastic surgery (Ang, 2004).

The growing popularity of cosmetic surgery reflects an alarming level of discontent among people about the way they look. Researchers estimate that 30% to 40% of U.S. adults have concerns about some aspect of their physical appearance (Gorbis & Kholodenko, 2005). And about 2% of the population is so self-conscious about their looks that their lives are constricted in some significant way, from feeling inhibited during lovemaking to becoming homebound or even suicidal. This condition, called "body dysmorphic disorder," has become more common over the past decade or so (Wartik, 2003). About half of these individuals seek some sort of professional medical intervention, like surgery or dermatological treatment (Gorbis & Kholodenko, 2005).

The television industry has taken advantage of this overall sense of bodily dissatisfaction. The popular reality show *The Biggest Loser* portrays the week-to-week thinning of dangerously obese people. With the help of professional personal trainers (as well as occasional input from nutritionists, fashion consultants, hair stylists, and makeup artists), contestants literally shrink and transform right before viewers' eyes. *Extreme Makeover: Weight Loss Edition* has a similar premise, although here the trainer works with "superobese" people one at a time to lose half their body weight in one year. Now-defunct shows like *The Swan* took people who were unhappy with the way they looked and, with the help of extensive plastic surgery, changed them into what they hoped were reborn beauties.

Political Portraits

If you have ever seen a U.S. political party's national convention the summer before a presidential election, you have witnessed a highly professional, meticulously planned effort at impression management. Music, balloons, lighting, logos, colors, even individual delegates in the audience are all transformed into props that are manipulated to project images of patriotism, unity, organization, strength, and, above all, electability. At the center is the candidate, who must personally present an image (also professionally crafted) that will appeal to the voting public. Campaign staffs are concerned as much with ensuring that their candidate "appears presidential" as they are with his or her positions on key political issues.

Consider the images crafted for the 2008 presidential candidates. The Republican candidate, John McCain, was a war hero who spent more than five years in a North Vietnamese prison camp in the 1960s. Nonetheless, he had to work hard to overcome negative impressions of him based on his age (he was 72 at the time of the election). Critics subtly tried to frame each verbal gaffe or memory lapse as a sign of senility. At one point, his campaign balked at disclosing all 1,200 pages of his medical record for fear it would fuel speculation that his health was feeble. Not surprisingly, his public appearances were choreographed to highlight his youthful energy; he often wore casual clothes and a baseball cap on the campaign trail. His running mate, Sarah Palin, had her own impression management challenges. She was so tightly handled in the early stages of the campaign that she remained hidden from the media for the first three weeks after the Republican nominating convention. And when she did emerge to speak in public, she performed so poorly that she quickly became a common late-night-television parody. As Election Day approached, she had to withstand a flurry of criticism over the fact that the campaign paid more than $150,000 for her new wardrobe.

Barack Obama was not spared the task of managing his public persona. Indeed, he had to deal with his own problems in casting a presidential image, such as not wearing an American flag lapel pin (which he started doing), "fist bumping" his wife on the campaign trail (which he stopped doing), and having the middle name "Hussein" (which he could do nothing about). He successfully managed his most obvious image problem—his race and ethnicity—by repeatedly telling audiences on the campaign trail that he didn't look like the presidents on our currency and acknowledging that he had a funny name. In doing so, he neutralized opposition attempts to paint him as un-American. Well into his presidency, Obama's political enemies still paint him as an alien threat, calling attention to his "exotic" upbringing and questioning his religious affiliation or whether he is even a U.S. citizen (Alter, 2010).

Once elected, a president, with the help or hindrance of the media, must play simultaneously to international and domestic audiences (P. Hall, 1990). The international audience consists of foreign allies and adversaries, whom he must convince of his authority and his ability to fulfill commitments. The domestic audience is the voting public, whom he must impress through the portrayal of "presidential character": good health, decisiveness, control, a stable home and family life, and so forth. Like all politicians, a president must be prepared to use impression management throughout his tenure to get a favorable result in an opinion poll or a desired vote in Congress or some international body, like the United Nations.

Moreover, the president is but one member of an entire administration made up of various departments, commissions, and agencies, each of which must engage in its own impression management so as not to reflect poorly on the government. For instance, as we saw in Chapter 3, the Counterterrorism Communications Center provides detailed directives for how government officials ought to talk about the War on Terror. Here we see the importance of projecting a trustworthy, knowledgeable image:

> Try to limit the number of non-English terms you use. . . . Mispronunciation could make your statement incomprehensible and/or sound ill-informed. If you must use such a word, make sure your pronunciation is validated by an expert. Don't use words that require use of consonants that do not exist in English and whose nearest English approximation has a totally different meaning. (Counterterrorism Communications Center, 2008, p. 2)

The White House, no matter who is in office, has an entire staff of media and public relations consultants to ensure that images and messages are tightly controlled so as to depict the president in the most favorable light possible. When the president travels—whether it be an excursion to a small town in the heartland or a major state trip to Asia—a small advance team arrives at the location days or perhaps weeks beforehand to coordinate every logistical component of the trip. But it's not just about making sure limousines arrive on time or security personnel know their duties. The advance team functions as an impression management extension of the president by making sure every factory he visits, every walk he takes, and every meal he eats at a local diner runs as smoothly as possible (The White House Blog, 2010). Advance teams must even develop plans for dealing with demonstrators and protestors, should they be present (Office of Presidential Advance, 2002).

Often a president's goals are accomplished through "gesture politics"—actions or initiatives that are largely symbolic and convey, whether purposefully or not, particular characteristics. National leaders frequently find themselves judged not so much by the effectiveness of their policies as by how the public responds to their gestures:

> At least one European newspaper described [former] President Bush's effort to aid tsunami victims [in 2004] as a bid to show U.S. compassion. What was important was not the particulars of Bush's own aid plan, but whether the public would find it convincingly noble. . . . In the public mind [programs] are secondary to (and their success is dependent on) the personal gestures that accompany them. (Caldwell, 2005, p. 11)

Like all of his predecessors, Barack Obama has had his share of "gesture politics" appearances following such tragedies as the mass shootings in Tucson, Arizona; floods in the Mississippi Delta; tornadoes in Tuscaloosa, Alabama, and Joplin, Missouri; and

Hurricane Irene in New Jersey. At each of these events, Obama was judged more by the comfort and sympathy his gestures symbolized than by the specific details of his plans. But "gesture politics" always carry the risk of criticism if actions fail to convey the precise level of empathy, sympathy, or strength the general public thinks is appropriate. Obama was highly criticized in 2011 for appearing on ESPN to discuss his predictions for the NCAA basketball championship tournament at a time when violent political uprisings in many Arab countries, a possible nuclear disaster in the aftermath of the Japanese earthquake and tsunami, and persistent economic woes at home were dominating the news. To some, this appearance made him look as if he didn't care about the human suffering associated with these crises.

Social Influences on Impression Management

Up to this point, I've described impression management and dramaturgy from the viewpoint of individual actors driven by a personal desire to present themselves in the most advantageous light possible. But social group membership may also influence the sorts of images a person tries to present in social interaction. The elements of one's identity—age, gender, race and ethnicity, religion, social class, occupational status—influence others' immediate expectations, which can be self-fulfilling. In other words, members of certain social groups may manage impressions somewhat differently than nonmembers because of society's preconceived notions about them. Race or ethnicity and social status are among the most notable influences on impression management.

Race and Ethnicity

In a society where race is a primary source of inequality, people of color often learn that they will be rewarded if they assimilate to "white norms" and hide the elements of their ethnoracial culture. According to Kenji Yoshino (2006), a law professor, the pressure to "act white" means that people of color must suppress the nonwhite aspects of their hairstyle, clothing, and speech. They must also monitor their social activities, participation in ethnic or race-based organizations or political causes, and friendship networks. The comedian Dave Chappelle once said that African Americans must be "bilingual" if they want to make it in this society. In other words, they become adept at identifying situations, like job interviews, where they must eliminate "black" patterns of speech and "speak white" (Chaudhry, 2006).

Such impression management strategies may increase the likelihood of economic benefit, but they are not without social costs. As then-Senator Barack Obama said in a 2004 speech at the Democratic National Convention, "Children [of color] can't achieve unless we raise their expectations and . . . eradicate the slander that says a black youth with a book is acting white" (quoted in Fryer, 2006, p. 53). People of color who "act white" in some situations but perform a different version of their identity when with others like themselves run the risk of being considered sellouts or tagged as "Oreo cookies," "bananas," or "coconuts"—that is, black or yellow or brown on the outside and white on the inside—by members of their ethnoracial community (Chaudhry, 2006).

Moreover, it's only the relatively affluent who have the opportunity to learn how to act white. Others—Pakistani cab drivers, Latina housekeepers, Korean grocery store clerks, to name a few—have no such option. Indeed, living up (or down) to certain ethnoracial stereotypes may be one of the few ways people can participate actively in public life while retaining their own cultural identity. In the past, for example, Native Americans often complained that in interactions with members of other ethnoracial groups, they were expected to "act Indian" by wearing traditional garb or speaking in the stilted manner of media stereotypes. Contemporary rap and hip-hop stars are often criticized for conforming to unflattering black stereotypes in order to appeal to white, middle-class audiences. But while individuals from disadvantaged groups may appear to fit common racial or ethnic stereotypes in public (front stage), an analysis of private (back stage) behavior often indicates that they are keenly aware of the identities they've been forced to present. Impression management is obviously an important survival tactic.

ELIJAH ANDERSON

Streetwise

Sociologist Elijah Anderson carried out observational research in a racially, ethnically, and economically diverse area of Philadelphia he called Village Northton. The area is home to two communities: one black and poor, the other middle to upper income and predominantly white. Anderson was particularly interested in how young black men—the overwhelming majority of whom were civil and law abiding—managed public impressions to deal with the assumption of Village Northton residents that all young black men are dangerous.

Anderson discovered that a central theme for most area residents was maintaining safety on the streets and avoiding violent and drug-related crime. Incapable of making distinctions between law-abiding black males and others, people relied for protection on broad stereotypes: Whites are law abiding and trustworthy; young black men are crime prone and dangerous.

Residents of the area, including black men themselves, were likely to be suspicious of unknown black males on the street. Women—particularly white women—clutched their purses and edged up closer to their companions as they walked down the street. Many pedestrians crossed the street or averted their eyes from young black men, who were seen as unpredictable and menacing.

Some of the young black men in the area developed certain dramaturgical strategies to overcome the assumption that they were dangerous. For instance, many came to believe that if they presented a certain appearance or carried certain props with them in public that represented law-abiding behavior (e.g., a briefcase, a shirt and tie, a college identification card), they would be treated better in contacts with the police or others in the neighborhood. In addition, they often used friendly or deferential greetings as a kind of preemptive peace offering, designed to advise others of their civil intentions. Or they went to great lengths to behave in ways contrary to the presumed expectations of Whites:

> I find myself being extra nice to whites. A lot of times I be walking down the streets . . . and I see somebody white. . . . I know they are afraid of me. They don't know me, but they intimidated. . . . So I might smile, just to reassure them. . . . At other times I find myself opening doors, you know. Holding the elevator. Putting myself in a certain light, you know, to change whatever doubts they may have. (E. Anderson, 1990, pp. 185–186)

Such impression management requires an enormous amount of effort and places responsibility for ensuring social order on this man. He feels compelled to put strangers at ease so he can go about his own business. He understands that his mere presence makes others nervous and uncomfortable. He recognizes that trustworthiness—an ascribed characteristic of Whites—is something Blacks must work hard to achieve.

Other young black men, less willing to bear the burden of social order, capitalized on the fear they knew they could evoke. Some purposely "put on a swagger" or adopted a menacing stance to intimidate other pedestrians. Some purposely created discomfort in those they considered "ignorant" enough to be unnecessarily afraid of them. According to Anderson, law-abiding youth have an interest in giving the impression that they are dangerous: It is a way to keep others at bay. The right looks and moves ensure safe passage on the street.

The irony of such survival tactics is that they make it even more difficult for others to distinguish between those who are law abiding and those who are crime prone. By exhibiting an air of danger and toughness, a young black man may avoid being ridiculed or even victimized by his own peers, but he risks further alienating law-abiding Whites and Blacks. Members of racial and ethnic minorities face many such special dilemmas in impression management, whether they attempt to contradict stereotypes or embrace them.

Social Status

A person's relative position in society can also influence impression management. Like the young black men in Anderson's study, some working-class youths, frustrated by their lack of access to the middle-class world and their inability to meet the requirements of "respectability" as defined by the dominant culture, may present themselves as malicious or dangerous. A tough image helps them gain attention or achieve status and respect within their group (A. Campbell, 1987; A. K. Cohen, 1955).

Conversely, those who occupy the dominant classes of society can get the attention and respect we all want with very little effort (Derber, 1979). They get special consideration in restaurants, shops, and other public settings. They monopolize the starring roles in politics and economics and also claim more than their share of attention in ordinary interactions. By displaying the symbolic props of material success—large homes, tasteful furnishings, luxury cars, expensive clothes and jewelry—people know that they can impress others and thereby reinforce their own sense of worth and status.

Prior to the recent economic recession, the visual trappings of social class had become harder to spot. When credit was easily available, more U.S. adults had access to the traditional high-end props of the well-to-do. A middle-class family could own a flat screen television or a fancy sports car. Just a few years ago, 81% of respondents in one study indicated that they had felt some pressure to buy high-priced goods (cited in Steinhauer, 2005). So the extremely wealthy ratcheted up the visual display of social status, buying even more expensive products, such as $130,000 cars and $400 bottles of wine, and using posh services like personal chefs and private jets. Tough times, however, have led even the super rich to become a bit more discreet in their public displays of wealth: "Out are private jets, glitzy high-profile parties and see-and-be-seen vacations to hot spots such as St. Barts. In are flying first-class, tasteful low-profile affairs and getaways to more remote resorts in the likes of Laos and Panama" (Gomstyn, 2009, p. 1).

Indeed, ostentatious displays of wealth have become the object of public anger and ridicule. You may recall the firestorm that erupted in the media in 2009, when the chief executives of the major U.S. automakers flew to Washington, D.C., in their private jets to appeal for federal bailout money. In fact, some public figures take great pains to distance themselves from their upper class or "elite" backgrounds. The 2010 Republican gubernatorial candidate in the state of Connecticut went to Andover prep school and Harvard. He owned a private plane, a yacht, six cars, and three motorcycles. His

Democratic opponent went to Exeter prep school and Harvard, owned six cars and a 16-room mansion, and was worth more than $90 million. Yet their television ads highlighted their working-class roots and depicted them as blue-jeans-wearing, homespun everyday folk (D. W. Chen, 2010). Today, the Tea Party movement, a political faction that espouses the values of individual liberty and limited government, is composed mostly of white working-class Americans who view upper-class, college-educated politicians with angry disdain and suspicion. Their message resonated with enough voters in 2010 that several Tea Party candidates won election to Congress.

Status differences in impression management permeate the world of work as well. Those at the very top of an organization need not advertise their high status because it is already known to the people with whom they interact regularly. Their occupational status is a permanently recognized "badge of ability" (Derber, 1979, p. 83). Others, however, must consciously solicit the attention to which they feel they are entitled. For example, physicians in hospitals may wear stethoscopes and white lab coats to communicate their high-status identity to patients; female doctors are especially inclined to wear the white coats so they will not be mistaken for nurses. These status markers become especially powerful when compared with patients, who are often required to shed their own clothes and don revealing hospital-issue garments. It's hard to appear powerful and be taken seriously in a conversation with a doctor when you're barefoot and naked under a paper gown (D. Franklin, 2006).

Impression management plays a prominent role in the socialization process within many professions (Hochschild, 1983). Managers and CEOs in large companies, for instance, become acutely aware through their rise up the corporate ladder of the image they must exude through their dress and demeanor. Salespeople are trained to present themselves as knowledgeable, trustworthy, and, above all, honest. Medical students learn how to manage their emotions in front of patients and to present the image of "competent physicians." New teachers learn what images are most effective in getting students to comply. This teacher's assessment of the importance of impression management more than 50 years ago still rings true today:

> You can't ever let them get the upper hand on you or you're through. So I start out tough. The first day I get a new class in, I let them know who's boss. . . . You've got to start off tough, then you can ease up as you go along. If you start out easygoing, when you try to be tough, they'll just look at you and laugh. (E. Goffman, 1959, p. 12)

In any given interaction, one person is likely to have more power than others (Wrong, 1988). When we first hear the word *power*, we think of it in terms of orders, threats, and coercion. But noncoercive forms of power—the signs and symbols of dominance, the subtle messages of threat, the gestures of submission—are much more common to impression management in social encounters (Henley, 1977). The humiliation of being powerless is felt by people who are ignored or interrupted, are intimidated by another's presence, are afraid to approach or touch a superior, or have their privacy freely invaded by another.

The norms that govern the way people address each other also reflect underlying power differences. For instance, the conversations that take place between friends or siblings are commonly marked by the mutual use of informal terms such as first names or nicknames. When status is unequal, though, the lower-status person is often required to use terms of respect such as *Sir* or *Ma'am* or *Doctor.* In the South in years past, every white person had the privilege of addressing any black person by first name and receiving the respectful form of address in return. A president's fondness for making up funny nicknames for people on his staff or members of Congress may appear amiable and friendly, but it also reinforces power differences. These people are still required to address him as "Mr. President."

Status differences are even more clearly institutionalized in some languages. In Spanish, *tu* is the familiar word for "you," which is used when one is talking to a subordinate or to a person of equal status. *Usted* also means "you," but it is the formal version, used when one is addressing a person of superior status. The terms we use to address others may on the surface appear simply to be forms of etiquette. However, forms of address convey a great deal of information about who we think we are in relation to the others we encounter.

Collective Impression Management

We often find ourselves in situations that require a "couple," "group," or "organizational" image of some sort. These impressions are more complex than individual ones, and their management often requires the help and cooperation of others. For example, business partners often present a united front and a joint image of trustworthiness to their clients. Goffman (1959) uses the term ***performance team*** to describe individuals who intimately cooperate in staging a performance that leads an audience to form an impression of one or all of the team members.

Team members are highly dependent on one another and must show a fair amount of trust and loyalty, because each member has the power to disrupt or "give away" the performance at any moment. Individuals who can't be trusted—such as political advisers who have worked for another party or people who are emotionally unstable—thus make poor teammates.

One of the most obvious performance teams is the married couple. Couples are socially obligated to present a believable and cooperative image, particularly if the audience does not know them very well. Few things are as uncomfortable as being in the presence of a couple who are openly fighting, bickering, or putting each other down. The cultural value of marriage—and, by extension, the institution of family—is publicly reinforced by the ability of couples to collectively project contented images of a loving relationship.

Like individual impression management, successful teamwork depends on maintaining the boundary between front stage and back stage. If a couple's teamwork is cohesive and the performance believable, the partners can give the impression that they are happy and content even if they have had a bitter fight moments before going out in public. But the boundary between front stage and back stage is fragile, and third parties may undermine the best efforts at impression management. Imagine a dinner guest being informed by a precocious four-year-old that "Mommy and Daddy stopped yelling those bad words at each other when you showed up." Young children who can speak but are not yet schooled in the social conventions of everyday interaction are not, from a dramaturgical perspective, trustworthy performance teammates. They are often too honest to maintain a front. They are naturally inclined to let audiences back stage, thereby disrupting both the order of the situation and the identities the actors have attempted to claim. The ability to go back stage periodically is crucial to maintaining a sound team relationship. Not only does it give the team a place to rehearse public performances, but it also provides a refuge from outside scrutiny. For married couples, tensions can rise if they must constantly be "on" for an audience. This is precisely why out-of-town house guests become a burden after a long visit or why living with one or the other partner's parents becomes so difficult. The couple has no back stage, no chance for privacy, no place to go to escape the demands of audience expectations.

Organizations must carefully manage their impressions, too, as a way of establishing their legitimacy (Ginzel, Kramer, & Sutton, 2004). Those that depend on public approval for their survival have to develop effective team performances to manage public perceptions (Taylor & Bogdan, 1980). Take, for instance, the way U.S. law enforcement organizations present high-profile crime suspects to the public. The suspect being transported from one place to another is usually in shackles, with armed officers on either side. Occasionally the officers halfheartedly try to hide the alleged perpetrator's face with a coat or a hat, even though we are likely to know who she or he is. If the suspect is well known, a raincoat will often be draped over her or his handcuffs. The "perp walk," as it is known, is a decades-long American tradition designed not only to satisfy the press but to give the police an opportunity to gloat over their latest capture and, in the process, humiliate the suspect (Roberts, 2011). Moreover, if staged well, the perp walk makes the suspect look dangerous—the kind of person who would mail letter bombs, blow up federal office buildings, or commit sexual assault. If prisoners are left unshaven and unkempt, and presented in orange prison jumpsuits at a court hearing, the public gets the impression that they've already been convicted.

Individual impression management and organizational impression management are governed by the same principles (Hochschild, 1983). Take, for instance, the management of props and physical space. Hospitals usually line their walls with soothing paintings designed to calm, not agitate; children's wards are often filled with colorful images of familiar cartoon characters. Other types of physical structures may be managed to convey images of power and dominance. For instance, the White House is symbolically the center of world politics. Some of the most important international decisions are made within its walls. But at the same time,

> the building itself—with its white walls, serene proportions, classical Greek tympanum and colonnade—has become the symbol of a power that radiates not only strength but also peace, freedom, and harmony. The rich and positive symbolism has been daily reinforced by the media broadcasting throughout the world pictures of this resplendent mansion, the opulent elegance of the Oval Room, the . . . professionalism and impeccable white shirts of the president's men, the beautiful green lawns with a cheerful and self-confident president and his playful dog nimbly stepping out of the helicopter as if he were a Greek God alighting from Olympus. (Hankiss, 2001, p. 1)

In any society, people often find themselves in situations where they must depend on others for the successful performance of the roles they play as individuals. Without teamwork, many individual and organizational performances would fail, interactions would fall apart, and ultimately social order would be threatened (Henslin, 1991).

Mismanaging Impressions: Spoiled Identities

While impression management is universal, it's not always successful. We may mishandle props, blow our lines, mistakenly allow the audience back stage, or otherwise destroy the credibility of our performances. Some of us manage to recover from ineffective impression management quite quickly; others suffer an extended devaluation of their identities. What happens when impression management is unsuccessful? What do we do to regain identities and restore social order?

Embarrassment

A common emotional reaction to impression mismanagement is ***embarrassment***, the spontaneous feeling we experience when the identity we are presenting is suddenly and unexpectedly discredited in front of others (E. Gross & Stone, 1964). An adolescent boy trying to look "cool" in front of his friends may have his tough image shattered by the unexpected arrival of his mother in the family minivan. We can see his embarrassment in the fixed smile, the nervous hollow laugh, the busy hands, and the downward glance that hides his eyes from the gaze of others (E. Goffman, 1967). Embarrassment can come from a multitude of sources: lack of poise (e.g., stumbling, saying something stupid, spilling a drink, inappropriately exposing body parts), intrusion into the private settings of others (a man walking into a women's restroom), improper dress for a particular social occasion, and so on.

Embarrassment is sociologically important because it has the potential to destroy the orderliness of a social situation. Imagine being at your high school graduation. As the class valedictorian is giving the commencement address, a gust of wind blows her note cards off the podium. As she reaches down to collect them, she hits her head on the microphone and tears her gown. In front of hundreds of people she stands there, flustered, not knowing what to say or do. The situation would be uncomfortable and embarrassing not only for her but for you and the rest of the audience as well.

Because embarrassment is disruptive for all concerned, it is in everyone's best interest to cooperate in reducing or eliminating it. To call attention to such an act may be as embarrassing as the original episode itself, so we may pretend not to notice the faux pas (Lindesmith, Strauss, & Denzin, 1991). By suppressing signs of recognition, we make it easier for the person to regain composure (E. Goffman, 1967). A mutual commitment to supporting others' social identities, even when those identities are in danger, is a fundamental norm of social interaction.

At times, however, embarrassment is used strategically to disrupt another person's impression management. Practical jokes, for instance, are intentional attempts to rein in conceit or overconfidence and cause someone to lose identity. More seriously, groups and organizations may use embarrassment or the threat of embarrassment (e.g., hazing) to encourage a preferred activity or discourage behavior that may be damaging to the group. In that sense, embarrassment reasserts the power structure of the group, because only certain people can legitimately embarrass others. A low-status employee, for instance, has much less freedom to embarrass a superior or make him or her the target of a joke than vice versa (Coser, 1960).

Groups and organizations themselves may also experience embarrassment from time to time. In 2009, the Colorado Veterans Alliance, an advocacy group that led a drive to help homeless veterans, announced that its founder—former Marine Captain Rick Duncan, a recipient of the Purple Heart and a Silver Star—was, in fact, never in the military. It turned out he was a 32-year-old drifter with a criminal record. The organization immediately disbanded. In 2010, British Petroleum (BP) faced a massive public image crisis when a deepwater oil rig in the Gulf of Mexico exploded, creating a catastrophic oil spill that devastated the local economy. As if the accident weren't bad enough, Tony Hayward, chief executive officer of BP, and Carl-Henric Svanberg, its chairman, embarrassed the company further when they made insensitive public comments belittling the disaster, shirking responsibility for it, and trivializing the suffering of the Gulf Coast residents affected by it.

In a collectivist culture like Japan, organizational misdeeds or mistakes can create considerable public humiliation, shame, and embarrassment for top officials. In 2010, Toyota faced worldwide condemnation and was forced to recall some 8 million vehicles when it could no longer deny published reports of fatal accidents in which accelerator pedals had gotten stuck at high speeds. A year later, some officials in Japanese government agencies were forced to resign for trying to downplay the public health crisis that occurred after a nuclear reactor sustained major damage from the earthquake and tsunami.

When events challenge an organization's public image, leaders are often compelled to engage in activities that protect, repair, and enhance that image (Ginzel et al., 2004). For example, every year, *U.S. News & World Report* publishes its rankings of the top American universities. Schools that receive high rankings boast of that fact in their recruitment materials and on their Web sites. When a university falls in its ranking from one year to the next, though, officials face the unenviable task of scrambling to mend the school's reputation so that alumni continue to donate money and prospective students still consider applying. Typically, schools that have dropped in the rankings opt to downplay the survey's relevance and criticize the magazine's methodology and ranking criteria, which only a year earlier (when they were ranked higher) were considered sound and trustworthy.

Most government agencies and large corporations like BP and Toyota have massive public relations departments or crisis management teams that carefully oversee the organization's image by controlling negative publicity. One insurance company offers a corporate liability policy that pays policyholders up to $50,000 for the emergency hiring of an image consultant to help manage embarrassing public relations disasters (Landler, 1996). Southwest Airlines has a full-time employee, called "Senior Manager of Proactive Customer Communications," whose only job is to write apology letters to customers who are annoyed about flight delays, cancellations, or shoddy plane conditions. He writes about 20,000 such letters a year (J. Bailey, 2007).

Remedies for Spoiled Identities

Organizations and governments can enlist the aid of experts to overcome the debilitating effects of negative images, but individuals are usually left to their own devices. Fixing a spoiled identity is not easy. The mere knowledge that we are being evaluated negatively can impede our thoughts, speech, and action. Nevertheless, the major responsibility for restoring order lies with the person whose actions disrupted things in the first place.

To restore social order and overcome a spoiled identity, the transgressor will use an ***aligning action*** (Stokes & Hewitt, 1976). Sometimes aligning can be done easily and quickly. If you step on a person's foot while standing in line at a cafeteria, a simple apology may be all that's needed to avoid the impression that you're a clumsy oaf.

By apologizing, you acknowledge that such an act is wrong and send the message that you are not ordinarily a breaker of such social norms. Other situations, however, call for more detailed repair:

- An *account* is a verbal statement designed to explain unanticipated, embarrassing, or unacceptable behavior (C. W. Mills, 1940; M. Scott & Lyman, 1968). For example, an individual may cite events beyond her or his control ("I was late for the wedding because there was a lot of traffic on the highway") or blame others ("I spilled my milk because somebody pushed me"). An alternative is to define the offending behavior as appropriate under the circumstances, perhaps by denying that anyone was hurt by the act ("Yeah, I stole the car, but no one got hurt"), by claiming that the victim deserved to be victimized ("I beat him up, but he had it coming"), or by claiming higher, unselfish motives ("I stole food, but I did it to feed my family").
- A *disclaimer* is a verbal assertion given before the fact to forestall any complaints or negative implications (Hewitt & Stokes, 1975). If we think something we're about to do or say will threaten our identity or be used by others to judge us negatively, we may use a disclaimer. Phrases such as "I probably don't know what I'm talking about, but . . ." or "I'm not a racist, but . . ." introduce acts or expressions that ordinarily might be considered undesirable. As long as a disclaimer is provided, a self-proclaimed nonexpert can pretend to be an expert and a person claiming to be nonracist feels he or she can go ahead and make a racist statement.

Accounts and disclaimers are important links between the individual and society. We use them to explicitly define the relationship between our questionable conduct and prevailing cultural norms. That is, by using aligning actions, we publicly reaffirm our commitment to the social order that our conduct has violated and thereby defend the sanctity of our social identities and the "goodness" of society.

Other people may also try to deal with a transgressor's spoiled identity through a process called *cooling out* (E. Goffman, 1952): gently persuading someone who has lost face to accept a less desirable but still reasonable alternative identity. People engaged in cooling out seek to persuade rather than force offenders to change. It's an attempt to minimize distress. The challenge is to keep the offender from realizing that he or she is being persuaded.

Cooling out is a common element of social life; it is one of the major functions of consumer complaint departments, coaches, doctors, and priests. Cooling out also plays a major part in informal relationships. A partner who terminates a dating or courting relationship might persuade the other person to remain a "good friend," gently pushing the person into a lesser role without completely destroying her or his self-worth.

Cooling out is often motivated by institutional pressures. Consider the environment of higher education. The aspirations of many people in U.S. society are encouraged by open door admission policies in some universities and most community colleges (Karabel, 1972). There is a widely held cultural belief that higher education is linked to better employment opportunities and that anyone can go to college. Discrepancies, however, inevitably arise between people's aspirations and their ability to succeed. If educational institutions simply kicked unqualified students out of school, the result would likely be widespread public pressure and anxiety over the system itself. Hence, most community colleges opt for a "soft response" of cooling out the unqualified student (B. Clark, 1960). A counselor may direct a poor student toward an alternative major that would be easier but "not that different" from the student's original goal—for example, nurse's aide instead of registered nurse. Or the counselor might encourage the student to seek employment after graduation from a two-year program rather than transfer to a four-year university. That is, the student is gently persuaded to redefine himself or herself.

Institutional cooling-out processes such as these are inherent in an educational system that doesn't have clear selection criteria. In the United States, admission into college is based on some combination of achievement (course grades), aptitude (standardized test scores), and personality traits (interviews, letters of recommendation). In contrast, educational selection in China is based on the *gao kao*, or "high test"—a nine-hour, SAT-like aptitude test offered just once a year. This test is the sole determinant of admission to all Chinese colleges and universities (LaFraniere, 2009). Because one's eligibility for college study is so clearly and quickly defined, Chinese higher education has no need for an institutionalized cooling-out process.

Stigma

The permanent spoiling of someone's identity is called **stigma**. A stigma is a deeply discrediting characteristic, widely viewed as an insurmountable obstacle preventing competent or morally trustworthy behavior (E. Goffman, 1963). Stigmas spoil the identities of individuals regardless of other attributes those individuals might have. According to Goffman, the three types of stigma are (1) defects of the body (e.g., severe scars, blindness, paralyzed or missing limbs), (2) defects of character (e.g., dishonesty, a weak will, a history of imprisonment or substance abuse), and (3) membership in devalued social groups, such as certain races, religions, or ethnicities. The impression management task when faced with stigma is not so much to recapture a tarnished identity as to minimize the social damage.

Some stigmas are worse than others. For instance, the use of eyeglasses to compensate for one sensory deficiency (poor vision) is usually considered far less stigmatizing than the use of hearing aids to compensate for a different sensory deficiency (poor hearing). Contemporary hearing aids are designed to be as small and unnoticeable as possible. Eyeglasses, on the other hand, have become a common fashion accessory, often sold in their own trendy boutiques.

Stigma varies across time and culture as well. Being a Christian in the 21st century is very different from being one in AD 100, and being a Christian in the United States is different from being one in the Arab Middle East (Ainlay, Becker, & Coleman, 1986). Ancient Mayans considered being cross-eyed desirable, so parents encouraged babies to focus on objects that forced their eyes to cross (Link & Phelan, 2001). As you saw earlier in this chapter, obesity is stigmatized in contemporary Western societies but was seen as desirable, attractive, and symbolic of status and wealth in the past (Clinard & Meier, 1979) and is still seen that way in some other cultures today.

Interactions between the stigmatized and the nonstigmatized—called "mixed contacts"—can sometimes be uneasy. We have all felt uncomfortable with people who are "different" in appearance or behavior. Stigma initiates a judgment process that colors impressions and sets up barriers to interaction (E. E. Jones et al., 1984).

Whether intentionally or not, nonstigmatized individuals often pressure stigmatized people to conform to "inferior" identities. A person in a wheelchair who is discouraged from going camping or a blind person who is discouraged from living on her or his own is not given the chance to develop important skills and is thus kept dependent.

Nonstigmatized people often avoid mixed contacts because they anticipate discomfort and are unsure how to act (E. Goffman, 1963). Research shows that when interacting with a person who is physically disabled, an able-bodied person is likely to be more inhibited and more rigid and to end the interaction sooner than if the other person were also able bodied (Kleck, 1968; Kleck, Ono, & Hastorf, 1966). On the one hand, the able-bodied person may fear that showing direct sympathy or interest in a disabled person's condition could be regarded as rude or intrusive. On the other hand, ignoring it may make the interaction artificial and awkward or create impossible demands (Michener, DeLamater, & Schwartz, 1986).

As for people with stigmatizing conditions, they often sense that others are evaluating them negatively. One study of people diagnosed with a mental disorder found that they had all at one time or another been shunned, avoided, patronized, or discriminated against when others found out about their condition (Wahl, 1999). Consider also the case of Mark Breimhorst, a Stanford University graduate. Mr. Breimhorst has no hands. When he was applying to business schools in 1998, he was given 25% more time to complete the Graduate Management Admission Test. His results were mailed to prospective graduate schools with the notation "Scores obtained under special circumstances." Mr. Breimhorst was not admitted to any of the business schools to which he applied. He filed a federal lawsuit against the testing service, challenging the way they flagged the scores of students who needed accommodations. Such notations, he argued, were stigmatizing because they created suspicion that the scores were less valid than others (Lewin, 2000). In 2003, the testing service stopped flagging the results of students who receive special accommodations.

Faced with the strong possibility of discrimination, people with stigmatizing conditions often use coping strategies to establish the most favorable identity possible. One strategy is to try to hide the stigma. People who are hard of hearing, for instance, may learn to read lips or otherwise interact with people as if they could hear perfectly; those with bodily stigmas may opt for surgery to permanently conceal their condition.

Some stigmatized individuals, particularly those whose conditions are not immediately observable, use a strategy of selective disclosure. Sociologist Charlene E. Miall (1989) interviewed and surveyed 70 infertile women, nearly all of whom characterized infertility as something negative, an indication of failure, or an inability to function "normally." Most of the women were concerned that others' knowledge of their infertility would be stigmatizing. So they engaged in some form of information control. Many simply concealed the information from everyone except medical personnel and infertility counselors. Others used medical accounts, saying, "It's beyond my control." Some disclosed the information only to people they felt would not think ill of them. Some even used the disclosure of their infertility to gain control of a situation by deliberately shocking their "normal" audience (Miall, 1989).

Of course, not all stigmas can be hidden. Some individuals can only minimize the degree to which their stigmas intrude on and disrupt the interaction. One tactic is to use self-deprecating humor—telling little jokes about their shortcomings—to relieve the tension felt by the nonstigmatized. Others may try to focus on attributes unrelated to the stigma. For instance, a person in a wheelchair may carry around esoteric books in a conspicuous manner to show others that he or she still has a brain that works well. Still others with stigmas boldly call attention to their condition by mastering areas thought to be closed to them (such as mountain climbing for an amputee).

And some organize a movement to counter social oppression. For instance, organizations like the National Association to Advance Fat Acceptance and the Council on Size and Weight Discrimination help fat people (*fat* is their preferred adjective, by the way) cope with a society that hates their size by lobbying Congress and state legislatures to combat "size discrimination" and promote "weight diversity" (Saulny, 2009a).

They have organized civil rights protests in Washington, D.C., lobbied health care professionals for tolerance and acceptance, and organized campaigns against insurance discrimination and the dubious "science" of weight loss programs (LeBesco, 2004).

But overcoming the problems created by stigma cannot be accomplished solely through individual impression management or collective demonstrations. Long-lasting improvements can be accomplished only by changing cultural beliefs about the nature of stigma (Link, Mirotznik, & Cullen, 1991). As long as we hold stigmatized individuals solely responsible for dealing with the stigma, only some of them will be able to overcome the social limitations of their condition.

Conclusion

After reading this chapter, you may have an image of human beings as cunning, manipulative, and cynical play actors whose lives are merely a string of phony performances carefully designed to fit the selfish needs of the moment. The impression manager comes across as someone who consciously and fraudulently presents an inaccurate image in order to take advantage of a particular situation. Even the person who seems not to care about her or his appearance may be consciously cultivating the image of "not caring."

There's no denying that people consciously manufacture images of themselves that allow them to achieve some desired goal. Most of us go through life trying to create the impression that we're attractive, honest, competent, and sincere. To that end we carefully manage our appearance, present qualities we think others will admire, and hide qualities we think they won't. When caught in an act that may threaten the impression we're trying to foster, we strategically use statements that disclaim, excuse, or justify it.

So who is the real you? If people freely change their images to suit the expectations of a given audience, is there something more stable that characterizes them across all situations?

If you are aware that the impression you are managing is not the real you, then you must have some knowledge of what *is* the real you. And what you are may, in fact, transcend the demands of particular situations. Some basic, pervasive part of your being may allow you to choose from a repertoire of identities the one that best suits the immediate needs of the situation. As you ponder this possibility, realize that your feelings about impression management reflect your beliefs about the nature of individuals and the role society and others play in our everyday lives.

YOUR TURN

Impression management is a tool most of us use to present ourselves as likable people. Occasionally, however, our attempts fail. Survey several friends or classmates and have them describe their most embarrassing moment. Prompt them for specific details: What were the circumstances surrounding the incident? What identities were they trying to present? How did the attempt to claim these identities fail? How did these people immediately react, physically and behaviorally, to the embarrassment? How did they try to overcome the embarrassment and return order? Did they offer some sort of account? Were the consequences of the failed impression management temporary or permanent? What did the witnesses to the embarrassing incident do? Did their reactions alleviate or intensify the embarrassment?

Once you've gathered a substantial number of stories (about 12 or 15), see if you can find some common themes. What are the most frequent types of embarrassing situations? What are the most frequent reactions? If your class is large, your instructor can have you report your results to a small group of fellow students or to the entire class. What kinds of patterns can you identify in the embarrassing stories people tell? Are there gender, ethnic, or age differences in what people find embarrassing?

Sociologists Edward Gross and Gregory Stone have written, "In the wreckage left by embarrassment lie the broken foundations of social transactions" (1964, p. 2). What do you suppose they meant by that? Discuss the sociological importance of embarrassment (and, more important, reactions to embarrassment) in terms of the maintenance of interactional and social order.

CHAPTER HIGHLIGHTS

- A significant portion of social life is influenced by the images we form of others and the images others form of us.

- Impression formation is based initially on our assessment of ascribed social group membership (race, age, gender, etc.), individual physical appearance, and verbal and nonverbal messages.

- While we are gathering information about others to form impressions of them, we are fully aware that they are doing the same thing. Impression management is the process by which we attempt to control and manipulate information about ourselves to influence the impressions others form of us. Impression management can be both individual and collective.

- Impression mismanagement can lead to the creation of damaged identities, which must be repaired in order to sustain social interaction.

KEY TERMS

account: Statement designed to explain unanticipated, embarrassing, or unacceptable behavior after the behavior has occurred

aligning action: Action taken to restore an identity that has been damaged

back stage: Area of social interaction away from the view of an audience, where people can rehearse and rehash their behavior

cooling out: Gently persuading someone who has lost face to accept a less desirable but still reasonable alternative identity

disclaimer: Assertion designed to forestall any complaints or negative reactions to a behavior or statement that is about to occur

dramaturgy: Study of social interaction as theater, in which people ("actors") project images ("play roles") in front of others ("the audience")

embarrassment: Spontaneous feeling experienced when the identity someone is presenting is suddenly and unexpectedly discredited in front of others

front stage: Area of social interaction where people perform and work to maintain appropriate impressions

impression formation: The process by which we define others based on observable cues such as age, ascribed status characteristics such as race and gender, individual attributes such as physical appearance, and verbal and nonverbal expressions

impression management: Act of presenting a favorable public image of oneself so that others will form positive judgments

performance team: Set of individuals who cooperate in staging a performance that leads an audience to form an impression of one or all team members

stigma: Deeply discrediting characteristic that is viewed as an obstacle to competent or morally trustworthy behavior

STUDENT STUDY SITE

Visit the Student Study Site at **www.sagepub.com/newman9e** for these additional learning tools:

- Flashcards
- Web quizzes
- Sociologists at Work features
- Micro-Macro Connection features
- Video links
- Audio links
- Web resources
- SAGE journal articles

Building Social Relationships

Intimacy and Families

7

Life With Others

Social Diversity and Intimate Choices

Family Life

Family and Social Structure

Family Challenges

So far, the 21st century has been a strange and challenging time for the types of close relationships we commonly think of as the foundation of social life:

- Among college students, traditional dating has seemingly been replaced by *hooking up*—in which two people hang out in a dorm room or meet at a party, go somewhere private, and engage in some form of sexual behavior, which can range from kissing to intercourse (England & Thomas, 2007). Alcohol is usually involved, but intimacy and romance rarely are.
- In 2011, Facebook introduced an app called the "Breakup Notifier" that alerts users via e-mail when a friend's relationship status changes. That same year, the Boston Public Health Commission held a one-day conference on "healthy breakups" to provide teens with guidance on online break-up etiquette (Denizet-Lewis, 2011).
- For the first time in more than a century, the number of adults between the ages of 25 and 34 who have never been married has surpassed the number who are married (Eckholm, 2010).
- Thirty-one percent of men and 23% of women between the ages of 18 and 34 live with their parents (Fields, 2004). These figures include people who have never left home and those who have left and returned, perhaps more than once. According to one survey, 13% of parents with grown children said that one of their sons or daughters had moved back home within the past year (Wang & Morin, 2009).
- Nearly four in 10 respondents to a national survey said they felt marriage is becoming obsolete (Pew Research Center, 2010a).
- The number of Americans with children who live together but are not married has increased 12-fold since 1970; children are now more likely to have unmarried parents than divorced parents (cited in Tavernise, 2011c).
- Of all births in the United States, close to 40% are to unmarried mothers (U.S. Bureau of the Census, 2011b); and 61% of women and 55% of men in a national survey said they'd be willing to raise a child on their own without a spouse or partner (cited in T. M. Edwards, 2000).
- At the time of this writing, two people of the same sex can legally marry in six states— Massachusetts, New Hampshire, Vermont, Iowa, Connecticut, and New York.

Some people might see these events as "proof" that society is going downhill fast; others may see them as signs that relationships are keeping up with a changing culture.

Like every other aspect of our individual lives, intimacy and family must be understood within the broader contours of our society. This chapter takes a sociological peek into their private and public aspects and explores the role that close relationships, especially family bonds, play in our everyday experience. Why are these relationships so important to us? How do societal factors such as social institutions, gender, race, and social class affect our perceptions of intimacy and belonging? How do they affect family life? And why are the desirable aspects of these relationships so often outweighed by the negative aspects, such as family violence?

Life With Others

The quality and quantity of our close relationships are the standards against which many of us judge the well-being of our lives (A. Campbell, Converse, & Rodgers, 1976). We spend a tremendous amount of time worrying about these relationships, contemplating new ones, obsessing over past ones, trying to make current ones more satisfying, or fretting over how to get into or out of one.

Although we hunger for closeness in our lives, it can often be a challenge to maintain. For more than a century, sociologists have been writing that people who live in complex, urban, industrial, or postindustrial societies gradually become less integrated and connected to others (Durkheim, 1893/1947; Riesman, 1950; Tönnies, 1887/1957). Membership in church-related groups, civic organizations (e.g., Red Cross, Boy Scouts, PTA), and fraternal organizations (e.g., Lions, Elks, Shriners) has decreased (Putnam, 1995). According to one study, only 43% of Americans know all or most of their neighbors by name (cited in Blow, 2010). Today, more than 31 million U.S. adults live by themselves, and single people who have never married make up 26% of the adult population in this country—up from 22% in 1990 (U.S. Bureau of the Census, 2011b).

Because we're more mobile in our careers and more willing to relocate, we are more likely to break social ties than people were, say, a century ago. In the United States, the number of people who have friends and family they can talk to about important matters has declined dramatically over the past two decades. In fact, a U.S. adult today is much more likely than an adult two decades ago to be completely isolated from others (McPherson, Smith-Lovin, & Brashears, 2006).

Some sociologists attribute these trends to U.S. culture's emphasis on individualism, which takes away a sense of community, diminishes our ability to establish ties with others, and makes it easier for people to walk away from groups they see as unfulfilling (Bellah, Madsen, Sullivan, Swidler, & Tipton, 1985; Sidel, 1986). The high value that contemporary society places on self-reliance and individual achievement can sometimes make social relationships, even family relationships, seem expendable.

In contrast, in collectivist societies such as India and Japan, group ties play a more substantial role in people's everyday lives. There, people consider duty, sacrifice, and compromise more desirable traits than personal success and individual achievement. They assume that group connections are the best guarantee for an individual's well-being. Hence, feelings of group loyalty and responsibility for other members tend to be strong.

In several cross-cultural studies, people have been asked to complete the sentence "I love my mother, but . . ." In the United States and other Western societies, the typical response is critical and somewhat hostile, like "I love my mother, but she's just so difficult." Such a response reflects a powerful cultural expectation that we step away from our closest bonds and rely instead on ourselves. In contrast, in collectivist societies such as those in Southeast Asia, the typical response is something like, "I love my mother, but I can never repay all that she has done for me" (Olds & Schwartz, 2009).

Despite the inevitable conflicts in close relationships and the difficulties of maintaining these ties in an individualistic, mobile, high-tech society, people still place a high value on belonging and intimacy and take great pains to achieve them. For instance, a growing number of older women who are single, widowed, or divorced look for support not through marriage but through long-term friendships with other women who are at a similar stage in their lives (J. Gross, 2004a). Similarly, we spend more time than ever at work (Galinsky et al., 2006), perhaps to the detriment of relationships with our families. But for many people, forming ties with coworkers can be just as emotionally fulfilling (Wuthnow, 1994). And many of us spend a great deal of time in local hangouts (such as bars and coffee shops), where we can find comfort and good company (Oldenburg & Brissett, 1982). Many people find the sense of belonging they crave in these small groups of friends and like-minded neighbors and coworkers.

MICRO-MACRO CONNECTION

That's What (Facebook) Friends Are For

And how have new communication and information technologies—mobile phones, social networking sites, video phone services, and so on—influenced people's relationships and connections to others? At this time, the question is open. Some evidence points to a serious isolating effect of these technologies. One study found that users of social networking services are 28% less likely to seek out their neighbors as sources of companionship than nonusers (cited in Blow, 2010). Others argue that the more digitally connected we are, the less emotionally connected we become. The more we expect from technology, the less we expect from each other:

> We are offered . . . a whole world of machine-mediated relationships on networked devices. As we instant-message, e-mail, text, and Twitter, technology redraws the boundaries between intimacy and solitude. . . . Teenagers avoid making telephone calls, fearful that they will "reveal too much." They would rather text than talk. Adults, too, choose keyboards over the human voice. . . . After an evening of avatar-to-avatar talk in a networked game, we feel, at one moment, in possession of a full social life and, in the next, curiously isolated, in tenuous complicity with strangers. We build a following on Facebook . . . and wonder to what degree our followers are friends. . . . Sometimes people feel no sense of having communicated after hours of connection. (Turkle, 2011, pp. 11–12)

However, other evidence suggests that these technologies merely give people an additional means of establishing important interpersonal ties both within and outside their immediate neighborhoods. They can often provide a meaningful substitute for or enhancement of traditional types of interpersonal involvement, thereby expanding the scope of peoples' social support networks. The Internet, for instance, allows people to obtain support from a social circle that extends far beyond their geographic community. In addition, it gives people an opportunity to establish more diverse personal networks:

> Social media activities are associated with several beneficial social activities, including having discussion networks that are more likely to contain people from different backgrounds. For instance, frequent Internet users, and those who maintain a blog are much more likely to confide in someone who is of another race. Those who share photos online are more likely to report that they discuss important matters with someone who is a member of another political party. (Hampton, Sessions, Her, & Rainie, 2009, p. 3)

To illustrate the dramatically different ends of this debate, consider the following two letters that appeared in the same edition of the *New York Times* in response to an earlier column on the perils of new communication technologies. The first is from an eighth grader, the second from a high school junior:

I feel it detracts from my "real" relationships. I have never had an interesting conversation over social networking. . . . Often when I try to have an in-person conversation with someone about a real-world event, they are looking at a screen, their mind somewhere else, and even as they are eternally "connected," I can feel them drifting away from me. (Grossbard, 2011, p. 8)

Never before could a high-school student so brazenly reach out to a Harvard graduate student and ask for mentorship on his research paper. Never again will we think it odd for someone from the farthest corner of the globe to be exchanging witticisms on Twitter with a well-known celebrity. (Kaufman, 2011, p. 8)

So, has technology enhanced or destroyed our ties to others? Is a weekly Skype chat with your best friend from high school any more or less gratifying than going out to lunch with him or her every Friday? Certainly all would agree that the way we establish and maintain close relationships is different than it was, say, 50 or even 10 years ago. But does that mean that the importance of others in our everyday lives—be they neighbors, coworkers, family members, personal friends, or Facebook "friends"—has diminished?

Social Diversity and Intimate Choices

Our bonds with coworkers, neighbors, relatives, and friends (real or virtual) are certainly an important part of our social lives, but the sense of belonging and closeness that comes from intimate, romantic relationships has become one of the prime obsessions of the 21st century. Magazines, self-help books, supermarket tabloids, Web sites, blogs, and talk shows overflow with advice, warnings, and pseudoscientific analyses of every conceivable aspect of these relationships.

Most people in the United States assume that love is all they need to establish a fulfilling, long-lasting relationship. But their intimate choices are far from free and private. The choices they make regarding whom to date, live with, or marry are governed by two important social rules that limit the field of eligible partners: exogamy and endogamy.

Exogamy

At any given time, each of us is a member of many groups simultaneously. We belong to a particular family, a friendship group, a set of coworkers, a religion, a race, an ethnicity, an age group, a social class, and so on. Entering into intimate relationships with fellow members of some of these groups is considered inappropriate. So society follows a set of customs referred to as *exogamy* rules, which require that an individual form a long-term romantic or sexual relationship with someone *outside* certain social groups to which she or he belongs. For instance, in almost all societies, exogamy rules define marrying or having sex with people in one's own immediate family—siblings, parents, and children—as incest. Presumably, these rules exist in order to prohibit procreation between people who are genetically related, thereby reducing the chance that offspring will inherit two copies of a defective gene.

Exogamy prohibitions typically extend to certain relatives outside the immediate family too, such as cousins, grandparents, aunts, uncles, and, in some societies, stepsiblings. In the United States, 25 states completely prohibit marriage between first cousins; 6 others allow it under certain circumstances, such as when both partners are over 65 or when one is unable to reproduce (National Conference of State Legislatures, 2009). Informally, opposition to romantic relationships between coworkers or, on college campuses, between people who live on the same dorm floor (called "dormcest") illustrates a common belief that relationships work best when they occur between people who aren't in constant close proximity. One college advice blog identifies some the pitfalls of dormcest—mismatched expectations, seeing sex partners at their worst, nonexclusivity in a shared living space, keeping things fresh—and provides some strategies to overcome them (A. Jones, 2010).

Different cultures apply the rules of exogamy differently. For example, in South Korea, it was once illegal to marry someone with the same surname—not a trivial law, considering that 55% of the population is named Kim, Park, Lee, Choi, or Chong (WuDunn, 1996b). This rule originated centuries ago as a way of preventing marriages between members of the same clan and was written into Korean law in 1957. The ban was deemed unconstitutional in 1997. However, most single people still try to avoid lovers with the same name. As one college student put it, "When I'm introduced to someone, I very casually ask what her name is, and if I find out that it's the same as mine, it puts a mark against her right there" (WuDunn, 1996b, p. A4).

In other places, the violation of exogamy rules can lead to severe sanctions. In 2003, a young Indian couple was beaten to death by members of their own families for being lovers. In their community, it was considered incest for two people from the same village to fall in love. A resident of the village said, "In our society all the families living in a village are all sons and daughters of the whole village. We are like brothers and sisters. The marriage of brothers and sisters is not accepted" (quoted in Waldman, 2003, p. A4).

Endogamy

Simultaneously, less formal, but just as powerful, are the rules of **endogamy**, which limit people's intimate choices to those *within* certain groups to which they belong. The vast majority of marriages in the United States, for example, occur between people from the same religion, ethnoracial group, and social class. These rules of endogamy increase the likelihood that the couple will have similar backgrounds and therefore share common beliefs, values, and experiences. But more important, from a sociological point of view, rules of endogamy reflect our society's traditional distaste for relationships that cross social-group boundaries.

Religious Endogamy

Throughout history, many societies have had endogamy rules relating to religion: Only people with the same religious background were allowed to marry. Marrying outside one's religion is more common than it once was in industrialized countries, however, because greater mobility and freer communication bring people from diverse religious backgrounds into contact. In the United States, it's estimated that between one quarter and one half of all marriages occur between people of different religions ("Breaking the Rules," 2002; B. A. Robinson, 1999).

Nevertheless, most religious leaders still actively discourage interfaith marriages. They worry about maintaining their religion's influence over how people identify themselves within a diverse and complex society (M. M. Gordon, 1964). In 2004, the Vatican issued an official church document discouraging marriage between Catholics and non-Christians, especially Muslims (Feuer, 2004). The concern is that such marriages may further weaken people's religious beliefs and values, lead to the raising of children in a different faith, or encourage family members to abandon religion entirely.

The situation facing U.S. Jews provides a good example of the consequences of marriages that break rules of religious endogamy. Although only one Jew in 10 married a non-Jew in 1945, close to one in two does so today (InterfaithFamily.com, 2011). A lower birth rate among Jews compared with other groups, coupled with the likelihood that interfaith couples will not raise children as Jews, explains, in part, why the Jewish population has been dropping steadily (Goodstein, 2003). Between 1990 and 2008, the number of Jews in the U.S. population declined from 3.1 million to 2.7 million (U.S. Bureau of the Census, 2011b). Many Jewish leaders fear that the outcome of this trend will be not only the shrinking of the Jewish population but also the erosion and perhaps extinction of an entire way of life.

Racial and Ethnic Endogamy

Racial and ethnic endogamy is a global phenomenon, forming the basis of social structure in most societies worldwide (Murdock, 1949). The issue is an especially volatile one in U.S. society, however, given how racially and ethnically diverse we are. The first law against interracial marriage was enacted in Maryland in 1661, prohibiting Whites from marrying Native Americans or African slaves. Over the next 300 years or so, 38 more states put such laws on the books, expanding their coverage to include Chinese, Japanese, and Filipino Americans. It was believed that a mixing of the races (then referred to as "mongrelization") would destroy the racial purity (and superiority) of Whites. The irony, of course, is that racial mixing had been taking place since the 17th century, much of it through white slave owners raping and impregnating their black slaves.

Legal sanctions against interracial marriage persisted well into the 20th century. In 1958, for example, when Richard Loving (who was white) and his new wife, Mildred Jeter Loving (who was black), moved to their new home in Virginia, a sheriff arrived to arrest them for violating a state law that prohibited interracial marriages. The Lovings were sentenced to one year in jail but then learned that the judge would suspend the sentence if they left the state and promised not to return for 25 years. At the time, the majority of states, including California, Oregon, Indiana, all the mountain states, and every state in the South, legally prohibited interracial marriage (Liptak, 2004). The Lovings found a home in Washington, D.C., where interracial marriage was not prohibited, and had three children. While there, they embarked on an appeal of their conviction. In 1967, the U.S. Supreme Court ruled in favor of the Lovings, concluding that using racial classifications to restrict freedom to marry was unconstitutional.

A half-century later, attitudes are becoming more tolerant, and people are no longer banished for violating racial endogamy rules. Although the vast majority of U.S. marriages remain racially endogamous, relationships that cross racial or ethnic lines are becoming more common. The number of interracial marriages in the U.S. has grown exponentially, from 651,000 in 1980 to more than 2.4 million today (U.S. Bureau of the Census, 2011b). About 4% of existing American marriages involve people of different races. In addition, marriages between Latino/as and non-Latino/as (regardless of race) increased from 1.8% of all marriages in 1980 to 4.0% today (U.S. Bureau of the Census, 2011b). These figures grow each year. Approximately 14.6% of couples who married in 2008 consisted of two people of different racial or ethnic groups, up from 6.7% in 1980 (cited in Thomas, 2010).

To put it another way, 4% of currently married women over the age of 55 are in interracial or Latino/non-Latino marriages. But that figure rises to 13% among currently married women between the ages of 15 and 24 (Kreider & Ellis, 2011).

Attitudes toward interracial marriage have steadily improved over the past 50 years (see Exhibit 7.1). Nevertheless, people involved in interracial relationships report that they still face problems (Rosenblatt, Karis, & Powell, 1995). About half of the black-white couples in one study felt that biracial marriage makes things harder for them, and about two thirds reported that their parents had a problem with the relationship, at least initially (Fears & Deane, 2001). Many interracial couples—especially black-white couples—still experience a lack of family support when choosing to marry each other (R. Lewis & Yancey, 1997). Everyday activities may require more time and effort for interracial couples than for couples of the same race. For instance, when planning vacations, interracial couples often have to do extensive advance research of potential leisure destinations to see how accepting they are of relationships like theirs (Hibbler & Shinew, 2005). Even today, judges can sometimes make it difficult for interracial couples to marry. In 2009, newspapers reported that a Louisiana justice of the peace regularly refused to issue marriage licenses to interracial couples, claiming that he was doing it to protect children because of the instability of such marriages. As one woman in an interracial marriage put it, "In a perfect world, race wouldn't matter, but that day's a while off" (quoted in Saulny, 2011a, p. 4).

Exhibit 7.1   Changing Attitudes Toward Interracial Marriage

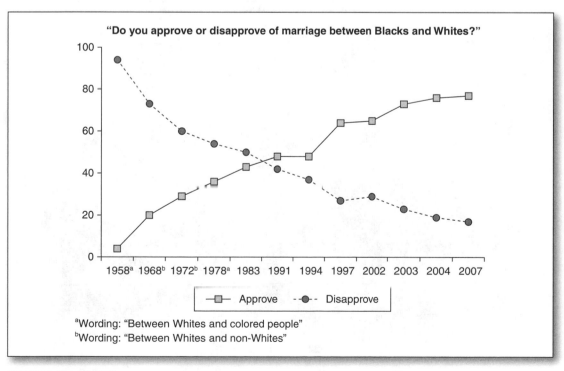

SOURCE: Carroll, 2007

(Text continues on page 207)

The Blending of America: Mixed Race

Jerome Krase

It has been projected that over the next several decades, as American society becomes more culturally and linguistically diverse, the population of the United States will also look like the rest of the globe, that is, less white. As the population becomes more ethnically diverse it also seems to be becoming more racially "mixed." In my own lifetime, the marriage of Italians and Slavs, even when both bride and groom were Roman Catholic, was looked upon somewhat as a "mixed marriage," and marriages between Jews and Gentiles were extremely unusual. Historically the most problematic forms of social integration or blending have been racial. For example, socially created racial categories like black and white (as well as even more arbitrary human colors of "yellow" for Asian and "red" for indigenous Americans), despite the lack of a scientifically biological basis, were seen as fixed. The hierarchy of racism argued that just one drop of black blood would essentially contaminate an otherwise apparently "white" and allegedly also superior person. In fact, marriages between arbitrarily defined white and nonwhite races were illegal in many states. Following are a number of 19th-century illustrations that cast racial mixing, or miscegenation, as sinister and threatening to society.

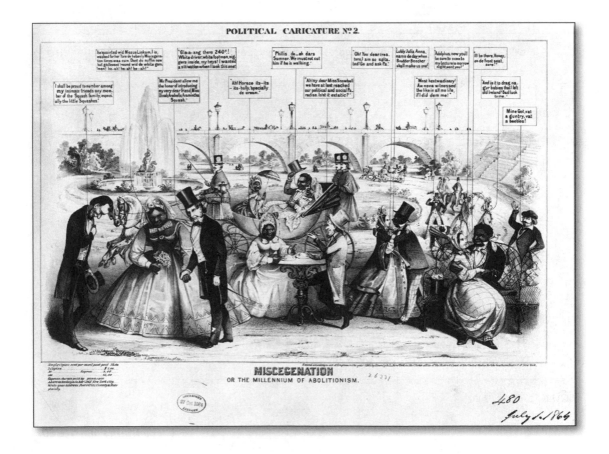

Jack Johnson (pictured at right) was the first African American heavyweight champion. There was a campaign of hatred and bigotry waged against him by Whites who wished to regain the heavyweight title and who also resented his intimate relationships with white women.

After his first interracial marriage and his defeat of several white hopefuls, Johnson was convicted in 1913 under contrived circumstances for violating the Mann Act, which made it a crime to transport women across state lines for "immoral" purposes.

Popular media reflected and in some cases helped the movement in the United States for racial equality. Films such as *Guess Who's Coming to Dinner?* (1967; see below), which starred Sidney Poitier, presented the issue of interracial marriage, once a virtually taboo subject in the media, in a humorous way. The opening of Hollywood for black movie stars

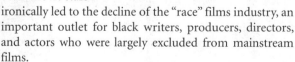

ironically led to the decline of the "race" films industry, an important outlet for black writers, producers, directors, and actors who were largely excluded from mainstream films.

Having stars like Sidney Poitier in leading roles side by side with white men and (once even more unthinkable) white women has greatly enhanced the American movie industry.

Racially mixed gatherings and residential neighborhood integration continued to be unusual in the 1970s even after the many successes of the civil rights movement.

Although it might seem that we have come a long way since the days when miscegenation was illegal, both interracial dating and interracial marriage continue to evoke hostility and, in too many cases, violence as well.

But things are changing. Perhaps the strongest indication of the belated acceptance of interracial mixing in the United States today is the fact that some of the most celebrated idols of beauty and athletics could be called "blended Americans." Moreover, many of our newest immigrants are in one way or another "mixed," such as European- and African-blended Latinos. Other groups, such as those from Asia and the Middle East, also challenge the old racial categories.

Social Class Endogamy

If we based our ideas about the formation of romantic relationships on what we see in movies, we might be tempted to conclude that divisions based on social class don't matter in U.S. society or perhaps don't exist at all. Popular films such as *Titanic*, *The Wedding Planner*, *Maid in Manhattan*, *Good Will Hunting*, *Sweet Home Alabama*, *The Prince and Me*, and *Pretty Woman* send the message that the power of love is strong enough to blow away differences in education, pedigree, resources, and taste. When it comes to love, Hollywood's United States is a classless society.

In reality, however, social class is a powerful determinant of whom we choose to marry. Around the world, people face strong pressures to choose marital partners of similar social standing (H. Carter & Glick, 1976; Kalmijn, 1994). Even if two individuals from different races, ethnic groups, or religions marry, chances are they will have similar socioeconomic backgrounds (Rosenfeld, 2005). Certainly some people do marry a person from a different social class, but the class tends to be an adjacent one—for instance, an upper-middle-class woman may marry a middle-class man. Cinderella-like marriages, between extremely wealthy and extremely poor people, are quite rare.

One reason this occurs is because individuals of similar social classes are more likely to participate in activities together, where they come into contact with people who share their values, tastes, goals, expectations, and backgrounds (Kalmijn & Flap, 2001). Our education system plays a particularly important role in bringing people from similar class backgrounds together. The proportion of married couples who share the same level of schooling is the highest it's been in 40 years. The odds of someone with only a high school education marrying a college graduate have been decreasing since the 1970s (C. R. Schwartz & Mare, 2005).

Moreover, neighborhoods—and thus neighborhood schools—tend to be made up of people from similar social classes. College often continues this class segregation. People from upper-class backgrounds are considerably more likely to attend costly private schools, whereas those from the middle class are most likely to enroll in state universities and those from the working class are most likely to enroll in community colleges. These structural conditions increase the odds that the people with whom college students form intimate relationships will come from the same class background.

Family Life

To most people's way of thinking, committed intimate romantic relationships form the cornerstone of families. Of all the groups we belong to, family is usually the most significant. Our ancestors provide us with a personal history, and they, along with the families we build later in life, provide much of our identity. Because of its importance in everyday life, sociologists consider family one of the main social institutions, a social structure that addresses not only our personal needs but also the fundamental needs of society (see Chapter 2).

Defining Family

Ironically, as important as family is, it is an elusive term to define. When most people hear the word *family*, they usually think of the ***nuclear family***: a unit consisting of parents and siblings. Others may think of the ***extended family***: other kin, such as grandparents, aunts, uncles, and cousins. In everyday usage, people may use the word *family* more loosely to describe those with whom they've achieved a significant degree of emotional closeness and sharing, even if they're not related. If I choose to think of my father's best friend, my barber, and even my dog as members of my family, I can.

But we don't live our lives completely by ourselves, and so we don't have complete freedom to define our own families. Not only do we come into fairly regular contact with people who want to know what our family looks like, but we also must navigate a vast array of organizations and agencies that have their own definitions of family and may, at times, impose them on us. Local, state, and federal governments manage many programs that provide certain benefits only to groups they officially define as "families."

The federal government regularly compiles up-to-date statistics on the number of individuals, married couples, and families that live in this country. Obviously it must have some idea of what a family (or what a marriage) is before it can start counting. In its official statistics, the U.S. Bureau of the Census distinguishes between households and families. A **household** is composed of one or more people who occupy the same housing unit. A **family** consists of "two or more persons, including the householder, who are related by birth, marriage, or adoption, and who live together as one household" (U.S. Bureau of the Census, 2005). Not all households contain families. If we accept this narrow definition of family, then other arrangements—people living alone, roommates, same-sex and opposite-sex cohabitors, and various forms of group living—cannot be considered families in the strict sense of the word. Such a definition is reflected in many people's beliefs. In a recent national study, respondents were twice as likely to identify unmarried couples (both heterosexual and homosexual) *with* children as families as they were to identify unmarried couples *without* children as families (B. Powell, Bolzendahl, Geist, & Steelman, 2010). According to the government's definition, over 40% of U.S. households are not families (see Exhibit 7.2).

Exhibit 7.2   The Diversity of U.S. Households

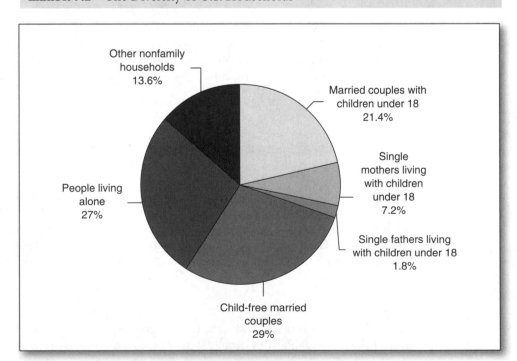

SOURCE: U.S Bureau of the Census, 2011b, Table 59

Having one's living arrangement legally recognized as a family has many practical implications. Benefits such as inheritance rights, insurance coverage, spousal immigration benefits, savings from joint tax returns, the ability to make medical decisions for another person, and visitation rights in prisons and hospital intensive care units are determined by marital or family status. Members of relationships not defined as family relationships, no matter how committed, economically interdependent, or emotionally fulfilling, are not eligible. For instance, homosexual partners of victims of the September 11 attack on the Pentagon were not eligible for the same survivor benefits in the state of Virginia that surviving heterosexual spouses were entitled to (Farmer, 2002).

Historical Trends in Family Life

Many functionalist sociologists have voiced concern over the current state of family as a social institution. Over time, they argue, the family has lost many, if not all, of its traditional purposes (Lasch, 1977). Historically, the family was where children received most of their education and religious training. It was where both children and adults could expect to receive emotional nurturing and support. It was the institution that regulated sexual activity and reproduction. And it was also the economic center of society, where family members worked together to earn a living and support one another financially.

But as the economy shifted from a system based on small, privately owned agricultural enterprises to one based on massive industrial manufacturing, the role of family changed. Economic production moved from the home to the factory, and families became more dependent on the money that members earned outside the home. Schools began to take over the teaching of skills and values that were once a part of everyday home life. Even the family's role as a source of emotional security and nurturing began to diminish as it became less able to shield its members from the harsh realities of modern life (Lasch, 1977).

For all these reasons many people are concerned about the survival of the contemporary family. Anxiety over the future of families has generated some strident calls for a return to the "good ol' days" of family life. The belief in a lost "golden age" of family has led some to depict the present as a period of rapid decline and inevitable family breakdown (Coontz, 2005; Hareven, 1992; Skolnick, 1991). Critics often pessimistically cite high divorce rates, large numbers of out-of-wedlock births, changing gender roles (most notably, the increase in working mothers), and a de-emphasis on heterosexual marriage as troublesome characteristics of contemporary families (The National Marriage Project, 2010). However, families have always been diverse in structure and have always faced difficulties in protecting members from economic hardship, internal violence, political upheaval, and social change. Calls for a return to the "good ol' days" are calls for a return to something that has never truly existed. By glorifying a mythical and idealized past, we artificially limit ourselves to an inaccurate image of what we think a "normal" family ought to look like.

Trends in Family Structure

The reality of U.S. family life has never quite fit its nostalgic image. According to sociologist William J. Goode (1971), the traditional family of the past that people in the United States speak so fondly of and want to re-create is somewhat of a myth. He calls the idealized image of the past "the classical family of Western nostalgia":

It is a pretty picture of life down on grandma's farm. There are lots of happy children, and many kinfolk live together in a large rambling house. Everyone works hard. Most of the food to be eaten during the winter is grown, preserved, and stored on the farm. . . . Father is stern and reserved and has the final decision in all important matters. . . . All boys and girls marry, and marry young. . . . After marriage, the couple lives harmoniously, either near the boy's parents or with them. . . . No one divorces. (p. 624)

Like most stereotypes, this one is not altogether accurate. In the 19th century, U.S. adults had a shorter life expectancy than adults today, so due to the death of a parent, children were actually more likely then than they are now to live in a single-parent home (Kain, 1990). Even children fortunate enough to come from intact families usually left home to work as servants or apprentices in other people's homes. Furthermore, although nearly 22% of U.S. children live in poverty today (DeNavas-Walt, Proctor, & Smith, 2011), a comparable proportion lived in orphanages at the beginning of the 20th century—but not just because their parents had died. Many were there because their parents simply couldn't afford to raise them. Rates of alcohol and drug abuse, domestic violence, and school dropouts were also higher a century ago than they are today (Coontz, 1992).

Also contrary to popular belief, father-breadwinner/mother-homemaker households were not the universal family form in the 19th and early 20th centuries. For instance, by 1900 one fifth of U.S. women worked outside the home (Staggenborg, 1998). But the experiences of employed women varied along class and race lines. For middle- and upper-class white women, few professions other than teaching and nursing were available. Because their income was probably not essential for the survival of the household, most could enter and exit the labor force in response to family demands. In contrast, poor women were likely to work long hours, mostly in unskilled jobs in clothing factories, canning plants, or other industries.

Family life for women of color was even more affected by economic necessity. Black domestic servants, for instance, were often forced to leave their own families and live in their employer's home, where they were expected to work around the clock. And most of them had little choice. Throughout U.S. history, black women have rarely had the luxury of being stay-at-home spouses and parents. In 1880, 73% of black single women and 35% of black married women reported holding paid jobs. Only 23% of white single women and 7% of white married women reported being in the paid labor force at that time (cited in Kessler-Harris, 1982).

Trends in Household Size

Perhaps the most pervasive myth regarding U.S. families of the past is that of the primacy of the extended family with several generations living under the same roof. Today's more isolated nuclear family is often compared unfavorably with the image of these large, close-knit support networks. But research shows that U.S. families have always been fairly small and primarily nuclear (Blumstein & Schwartz, 1983; W. J. Goode, 1971; Hareven, 1992). The United States has no strong tradition of large, extended multigenerational families living together. In fact, the highest proportion of extended family households ever recorded existed between 1850 and 1885 and was only around 20% of all households (Hareven, 1978). Because people didn't live as long then as they do today, most died before ever seeing their grandchildren. Even in the 1700s, the typical family consisted of a husband, a wife, and approximately three children.

When households of the past were large, it was probably due to the presence of nonfamily members: servants, apprentices, boarders, and visitors. The reduction in average household size we've seen over the past several centuries was caused not by a decline in the number of extended relatives but by a decrease in the number of nonfamily members living in a household, a reduction in the number of children in a family, and an increase in the number of young adults living alone (Kobrin, 1976).

As people migrated to the United States from countries that did have a tradition of extended families, such as China, Greece, and Italy, often their first order of business was to leave their extended family members so they could create their own households. Reducing the size of their families was seen as a clear sign that they had become American. Large, multigenerational families simply didn't make economic sense. Being able to move to a different state to pursue a job would be next to impossible with a bunch of grandparents, aunts, uncles, and cousins in tow.

In addition, it's not at all clear that families today are as isolated as some people make them out to be. More U.S. residents than ever have grandparents alive, and most adults see or talk to a parent on the phone at least once a week (Coontz, 1992). Extended family members may not live under the same roof, but they do stay in contact and provide advice, emotional support, and financial help when needed (K. Newman, 2005).

Trends in Divorce

Another oft-cited indicator of the demise of the U.S. family based on faulty conceptions of the past is the current high divorce rate. Many observers fear that the intact middle-class family depicted in 1950s television shows such as *Ozzie and Harriet*, *Father Knows Best*, and *Leave It to Beaver* has crumbled away forever. The rise in the divorce rate in the late 20th century has been attributed to the cultural movement toward "swinging singles, open marriages, alternative lifestyles, and women's liberation" in the 1960s and 1970s (Skolnick, 1991). True, this was a revolutionary period in U.S. history, and norms governing all aspects of social life were certainly changing.

What these conclusions overlook, however, is the longer historical trend in divorce in this country. Until World War II, it had been increasing steadily for more than 100 years. It rose sharply right after the war, most likely because of short courtships before the young men shipped out and the subsequent stress of separation. In the 1950s, the rate dropped just as sharply. The high divorce rates of the 1960s and 1970s, then, represented a return to a national trend that had been developing since the beginning of the 20th century. Indeed, since the mid 1980s, the rate has actually been declining (see Exhibit 7.3).

Furthermore, the rate of "hidden" marital separation 100 years ago was probably not that much less than the rate of "visible" separation today (Sennett, 1984). For financial or religious reasons, divorce was not an option for many people in the past. For instance, divorce rates actually fell during the Great Depression of the 1930s. With jobs and housing scarce, many couples simply couldn't afford to divorce. Rates of marital unhappiness and domestic violence increased. A significant number of people turned to the functional equivalents of divorce—desertion and abandonment—which have been going on for centuries. So you can see that the divorce rate may have been lower in the past, but families found other ways to break up. The image of a warm, secure, stable family life in past times is at odds with the actual history of U.S. families (Skolnick, 1991).

Exhibit 7.3 Historical Trends in U.S. Divorce, 1950–2008

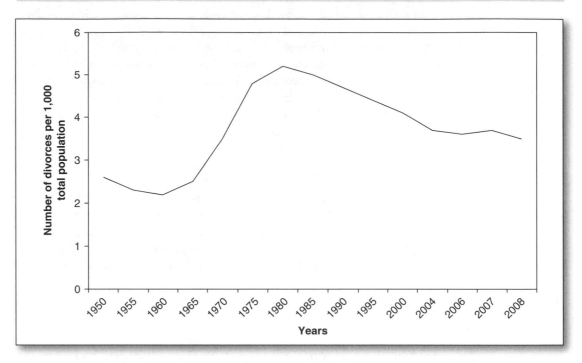

SOURCES: Eldridge & Sutton, 2007, Table A; Tejada-Vera & Sutton, 2009, Table A; U.S. Bureau of the Census, 2011b, Table 78

Cultural Variation in Intimacy and Family

Families can be found in every human society, and from a structural-functionalist perspective, they all address similar societal needs. However, the way families go about meeting these needs—their structure, customs, patterns of authority, and so on—differ widely across cultures. Thus, ideas about what a family is and how people should behave within it are culturally determined.

Most of us take for granted that *monogamy*, the practice of being married to only one person at a time, is the fundamental building block of the family. Some families do exist without a married couple, and some people may have several spouses over their lifetimes. But monogamous marriage is the core component of our image of family (Sudarkasa, 2001).

In the United States, monogamous marriage between one man and one woman continues to be the only adult intimate relationship that is legally recognized, culturally approved, and endorsed by the Internal Revenue Service. It's still the only relationship in which sexual activity between the partners is not only acceptable but expected. No other relationship has achieved such a status. Despite the growing number of couples choosing cohabitation over marriage and overall public concern regarding the disintegration of marriage, monogamous heterosexual marriage remains the cultural standard against which all other types of intimate relationships are judged.

In religious circles, the primacy of marriage can create biases against those who are single, especially when it comes to leadership roles. In 2011, for instance, a conservative

Christian organization called The Family Leader encouraged all candidates for president to sign a pledge document in which they vow, among other things, personal fidelity to their spouses and vigorous opposition to any attempt to expand the definition of family beyond heterosexual monogamy. Pastors in some Christian denominations often find it difficult to land a permanent position if they are not married. In conservative, evangelical churches, 1 pastor in 20 is single; among mainline Protestant denominations, the figure is 1 in 6. In fact, there are more female pastors in mainline churches—about 28%—than there are single pastors. One minister, who had more than 50 (unsuccessful) job interviews, said, "They often acted like I'm not quite whole because I'm single" (quoted in E. Eckholm, 2011, p. A3).

It may be hard to imagine a society that is not structured around the practice and primacy of monogamy, but many societies allow an individual to have several husbands or wives at the same time. This type of marriage is called **polygamy**. Some anthropologists estimate that about 75% of the world's societies prefer some type of polygamy, although few members within those societies actually have the resources to afford more than one spouse (Murdock, 1957; Nanda, 1994). Often polygamy is an adaptation to population or economic conditions. In Russia, for instance, some people, mostly women, have lobbied the government to legalize polygamy because of population pressures: The Russian population is falling by 3% each year and there are 9 million fewer men than women. Polygamy would give more women, particularly in rural areas, an opportunity to have a husband and therefore legal rights to his financial and physical support as well as legitimacy for their children. According to one anthropologist, the scarcity of potential husbands has led many Russian women to conclude that "half a good man is better than none at all" (quoted in Katbamna, 2009, p. 3).

Even in the United States, certain groups practice polygamy. Thousands of members of a dissident Mormon sect in Utah live in households that contain one husband and two or more wives (T. McCarthy, 2001). Although these marriages are technically illegal, few polygamists are ever prosecuted. For most of the past century, practitioners were tolerated as long as they kept to themselves. However, every once in a while a case garners widespread publicity. For instance, in 2006, Warren Jeffs, leader of the Fundamentalist Church of Jesus Christ of Latter Day Saints, drew national attention when he was placed on the FBI's Ten Most Wanted list for unlawful flight to avoid prosecution on charges that he arranged illegal marriages between his adult male followers and underage girls. In 2007, he was convicted of this crime as well as rape and incest and sentenced to 10 years to life in a Utah prison. In 2008, law enforcement officials removed 400 children from his polygamous compound in Eldorado, Texas, and placed them in state custody. The popularity of recent television shows such as *Big Love* and *Sister Wives* has sparked even more public interest in the private everyday lives of American polygamists.

Societies differ in other taken-for-granted facets of family life as well. Take living arrangements, for example. In U.S. society, families tend to follow the rules of **neolocal residence**; that is, young married couples are expected to establish their own households and separate from their respective families when financially possible. However, only about 5% of the world's societies are neolocal (Murdock, 1957; Nanda, 1994). In most places, married couples are expected to live with or near either the husband's relatives (called "patrilocal" residence) or the wife's relatives (called "matrilocal" residence).

Even the belief that members of the same nuclear family ought to live together is not found everywhere. Among the Kipsigis of Kenya, for instance, the mother and children live in one house and the father lives in another. The Kipsigis are polygamous, so a man might have several homes for his several wives at one time (Stephens, 1963). Among the Tsonga of southern Africa, children live with their grandmothers once they stop breast-feeding. They remain there for several years and are then returned to their parents. On the traditional Israeli kibbutz, or commune, children are raised not by their parents but in an "infants' house," where they are cared for by a trained nurse (Nanda, 1994).

Child-rearing philosophies vary cross-culturally, too. Most people in the United States believe that young children are inherently helpless and dependent: They feel that if parents attend to the child's drives and desires with consistency, warmth, and affection, that child will learn to trust the parents, adopt their values, develop a sturdy self-concept, and turn out to be a well-rounded, normal individual. In contrast, in the highlands of Guatemala, parents believe that their child's personality is determined by the date of birth. The parents are almost entirely uninvolved in the child's life, standing aside so he or she can grow as nature intended. In many societies—Nigeria, Russia, Haiti, the Dominican Republic, and Mexico, to name a few—most parents think that the best way to teach children to be respectful and studious is to beat them when they misbehave. In contrast, most U.S. child development experts believe that physical punishment can deaden the child's spirit and lead to violence later in life (Dugger, 1996). Despite these dramatic differences in child rearing practices, most children in all these cultures grow up equally well adapted to their societies.

Family and Social Structure

All of us have experience with families of one form or another, so it's very tempting to look at this topic in individualistic, personal terms. However, the sociological imagination encourages us to think about how social forces affect this aspect of our private lives. As you will see, a focus on the influence of social structure—social institutions as well as sources of social inequality, such as gender, race, and class—can help us understand some of the dilemmas facing contemporary families.

How Other Institutions Influence Family

As a social institution, family is connected to other institutions in important ways. Consider, for instance, the effect that the wars in Iraq and Afghanistan have had on family life. For as long as there have been wars, military families have been disrupted when one parent—almost always the father—either shipped out to sea or was deployed in another part of the world. But the structure of U.S. families had changed in many ways by the time the current wars began. According to the Pentagon, the number of single mothers and fathers in the military increased from under 50,000 in the Persian Gulf War of 1991 to about 140,000 in 2007 (cited in Associated Press, 2007; Piore, 2003). However, the military as an institution has no special programs in place to assist single parents when they are deployed. Raising a child in the military has always been hard, but being a single parent raises special challenges and difficult choices, not the least of which is what to do with the children while the parent is gone. According to the Servicemembers' Civil Relief Act, military personnel cannot be evicted or have their property seized during deployment. But this law does not protect them from losing custody of their children, if that's what a judge decides. In 2010, a single mother was days away from her yearlong deployment in Afghanistan when her mother backed out of an agreement to take care of her 10-month-old son while she was away. With no other choice, she stayed home and missed her flight to Afghanistan. She was immediately arrested by military police and faced court martial charges and jail time until she agreed to a "less-than-honorable discharge" (Dao, 2010a).

The legal, political, religious, and economic forces that shape society are perhaps the institutions that most influence the identities and actions of individuals within family relationships. Keep in mind that individuals within families can act to influence society as well.

The Influence of Law and Politics

The relationship between the family and the law is obvious. Marriage, for instance, is a legal contract that determines lawful rights and responsibilities. In the United States, each state legislature determines the age at which two people can marry, the health requirements, the length of the waiting period required before marriage, rules determining inheritance, and the division of property in case of divorce (Baca Zinn & Eitzen, 1996). Sometimes the legislature sets limits on specific types of marriage. For instance, to protect noncitizens from potential abuse, the U.S. Congress enacted the International Marriage Broker Regulation Act, which requires that men who seek foreign brides over the Internet disclose information about their criminal record and marital history before any contracts are signed (Porter, 2006).

In the case of same-sex unions, the law's power to either forbid or grant family rights and privileges is especially obvious . . . and controversial. In some countries, gay men and lesbians can have their relationships legally ratified. Belgium, Spain, Canada, Iceland, South Africa, Argentina, the Netherlands, Norway, and Sweden allow gay couples to legally marry. France, Denmark, Portugal, Germany, and several other European countries allow same-sex couples to enter "civil unions" (sometimes called "domestic partnerships" or "registered partnerships"), which grant them many of the legal and economic benefits and responsibilities of heterosexual marriage.

The matter is far from resolved in the United States, however. In 2004, Massachusetts became the first state to allow same-sex couples who are state residents to legally marry. Since then, Connecticut, Iowa, New Hampshire, Vermont, New York, and the District of Columbia have followed suit. California, Maine, Wisconsin, Nevada, New Jersey, Oregon, Illinois, Hawaii, and Washington provide at least some spousal rights to same-sex couples (Davey, 2010; Human Rights Campaign, 2009). In addition, 285 of the Fortune 500 companies provide domestic partner health benefits for their gay and lesbian workers (Human Rights Campaign, 2011b). Almost a third of all private sector gay and lesbian workers now have access to employer-provided health care benefits for their partners (Human Rights Campaign, 2011a).

But most states have moved in the opposite direction. Twenty-nine states have constitutional amendments restricting marriage to one man and one woman. (This number includes California, where a 2008 vote to amend the state constitution to prohibit same-sex marriage has been challenged and at the time of this writing remains unsettled.) Another 13 states have laws restricting marriage to one man and one woman (Human Rights Campaign, 2009). In 2005, the Michigan state legislature ruled that its law defining marriage as a relationship between one man and one woman meant that gay and lesbian state workers were not entitled to health benefits for their partners (Lyman, 2005).

At the federal level, the status of same-sex marriage is just as murky. The 1996 Defense of Marriage Act—written at a time when there was no legal same-sex marriage in any state—formally reaffirms the definition of marriage as the union of one man and one woman; authorizes all states to refuse to accept same-sex marriages from other states where it is legal; and denies federal benefits such as Social Security survival payments and spousal burials in national military cemeteries to same-sex couples. However, in 2010, a federal judge in Massachusetts ruled that this restrictive definition of marriage is discriminatory in that it violates the equal-protection provisions of the Constitution. In 2010, President Obama approved policies allowing gay workers to take family and medical leave to care for sick or newborn children of a same-sex partner and authorizing them to make medical decisions on behalf of their partners (Pear, 2010; Stolberg, 2010). That same year he mandated that hospitals extend visitation rights to the partners of gay and lesbian patients and respect patients' choices about who may make critical health care decisions on their behalf (Shear, 2010). In 2011, he called the Defense of Marriage Act unconstitutional and directed the Department of Justice to stop defending the law in court.

State and federal laws usually reflect public opinion, which, as you might suspect, is mixed on the matter of legalizing same-sex marriage. While acceptance of gays and lesbians in the workplace, in elementary schools, in the military, and in elected office has grown over the past several decades, support of laws allowing gay couples to marry has been slower to materialize. In 2008, a poll found that while an overwhelming majority of respondents approved of inheritance rights, health insurance coverage, Social Security benefits, and hospital visitation rights for same-sex partners, only 39% approved of legal marital rights (Campo-Flores, 2008). Opposition to same-sex marriage can be strong even in areas where residents tend to be prosperous and well educated. And when communities face trouble—increasing crime rates, decreasing rates of home ownership, high unemployment, and so on—opposition to same-sex marriage tends to increase (McVeigh & Diaz, 2009).

Yet support—or at least tolerance—does seem to be growing. In 2011, for the first time in its history of tracking this issue, a nationwide Gallup poll found that a majority of Americans (53%) believe same-sex marriage should be recognized by the law as valid, with the same rights as traditional marriages; in 1996, only 27% supported such rights (Newport, 2011). And younger people seem especially inclined to support it. Sixty percent of 18- to 34-year-olds in a recent survey believed that not allowing same-sex couples to marry amounts to discrimination, compared with 38% of people over 55 (cited in Bai, 2009).

Incidentally, heterosexual cohabitors have also faced difficulty achieving legal recognition. Between 1990 and 2008, the number of heterosexual cohabiting couples increased from 3.2 million to 5.6 million, constituting almost 5% of all U.S. households (Fields, 2004; U.S. Bureau of the Census, 2011b). But although public attitudes have grown more tolerant of unmarried heterosexual adults living together, the law has been slower to adjust. Massachusetts did repeal a 1784 law banning "lewdly and lasciviously associating and cohabitating without the benefit of marriage"—but not until 1987 (J. Yardley, 2000). New Mexico and Arizona didn't repeal their "unlawful cohabitation" laws until 2001. In 2008, voters in Arkansas approved a proposition that bans people who are "cohabiting outside a valid marriage" from serving as foster parents or adopting children (Savage, 2008, p. A31).

Politics and family are interconnected in other ways, too. Many of today's most pressing political issues, such as affordable health insurance, quality education, guaranteed parental leave in the workplace, Social Security, and poverty are fundamentally family problems. For example, abortion didn't become a significant political issue until the late 1960s, when it became part of the larger movement for women's rights and reproductive freedom. Later, the right-to-life movement framed the abortion debate not only as a moral and political issue but also as a symbolic crusade to define (or redefine) the role of motherhood and family within the larger society (Luker, 1984).

The Influence of Religion

You saw in Chapter 5 that religion is an important feature of everyday life and a powerful agent of socialization. Religion can also play a role in virtually every stage of family life. One of the key aspects of religion is that it constrains people's behavior, or at the very least encourages them to act in certain ways. This normative aspect of religion has important consequences for people's family experiences. For instance, all the major religions in the United States are strong supporters of marriage and childbearing.

In recent years, more churches have begun requiring engaged couples to participate in premarital counseling and education programs before the wedding. In addition, religions almost universally prohibit sexual relations outside marriage. Some religions prohibit divorce or don't permit remarriage after divorce. In 2003, the Roman Catholic Pope publicly urged women worldwide to pay heed to what he called their "lofty vocation" as wives and mothers ("Pope Exalts Women," 2003). In highly religious families, a sacred text such as the Bible, the Qur'an, or the Talmud may serve not only as a source of faith but as a literal guidebook for every aspect of family life, from dating, marriage, and sexuality to child discipline, responses to illness and death, and household division of labor.

Religion's influence on family life needn't be so direct, however. For example, among Muslims and members of certain Christian denominations, families are expected to tithe, or donate, a certain amount of their income (10% in most cases) to support their religious establishment. Although it is a charitable thing to do, tithing obligations can create problems for families that are already financially strapped.

Most evidence suggests that religious involvement has positive effects, especially for families raising children, such as higher levels of marital commitment (Larson & Goltz, 1989) and more positive parent-child relationships (L. D. Pearce & Axinn, 1998; Wilcox, 2000). "Spiritual wellness" is often cited as one of the most important qualities of family well-being (Stinnett & DeFrain, 1985).

However, in some situations the link between religious beliefs and actual family behavior may not be as strong as we might think. Even in highly religious families, the practical demands of modern life can make it difficult for people to always subscribe to religious teachings. For instance, although fundamentalist Christians believe wives should stay at home and submit to the authority of their husbands, many fundamentalist women do work outside the home and exert powerful influence over family decisions (Ammerman, 1987). Moreover, although many religions stress the value of keeping families intact, increased religious involvement does not do much to strengthen troubled marriages (Booth, Johnson, Branaman, & Sica, 1995). It may slightly decrease thoughts about divorce, but it doesn't necessarily enhance marital happiness or keep spouses from fighting.

The Influence of Economics

The economy affects virtually every aspect of family life, from the amount of money coming into the household to the day-to-day management of finances and major purchasing decisions. Money matters are closely tied to feelings of satisfaction within family relationships. When couples are disappointed with how much money they have or how it is spent, they find all aspects of their relationships less satisfying (Blumstein & Schwartz, 1983). Sustaining a supportive, nurturing family environment is nearly impossible without adequate income or health care. When economic foundations are weak, the emotional bonds that tie a family together can be stretched to the breaking point.

Financial problems are not just private troubles. Rather, they are directly linked to larger economic patterns. A deep recession and an unemployment rate that hovers around 9% nationally have obvious effects on family life. At the global level, the competitive pressures of the international marketplace have forced many businesses and industries to make greater use of so-called disposable workers—those who work part time or on a temporary contract. These jobs offer no benefits and no security and therefore make family life less stable. Other companies have reduced their costs by cutting salaries, laying off workers, or encouraging early retirement. Some businesses end up relocating either to other countries or to other parts of the United States where they can pay lower wages (see Chapter 10 for a more detailed discussion). Relaxed rules on foreign investment and export duties have made it easy for U.S. companies to open low-wage assembly plants abroad. The companies obviously benefit from higher profits, and the impoverished workers in these countries benefit from the added income. But displaced U.S. workers and their families may suffer.

MICRO-MACRO CONNECTION

Dual-Earner Parents

The financial strains of living in the 21st century have made it difficult for most young couples to survive on only one income. For instance, it's estimated that it will cost two-parent, middle-income families more than $222,360 to raise a child from birth to the age of 17, up from $25,230 in 1970 (Lino, 2010; U.S. Department of Agriculture, 2001). Since the mid 1970s, the amount of an average family budget earmarked for mortgage payments increased 69%. And the cost of sending a child to college, when adjusted for inflation, is double what it was a generation ago (cited in Tyagi, 2004).

But incomes have not risen proportionately. In fact, in constant dollars, median household incomes have remained stagnant since 1999 (U.S. Bureau of the Census, 2011b). Consequently, about 66% of married-couple households with at least one child under the age of 18 consist of two working parents. That figure is up from 39% in 1970 (Coontz, 2005; U.S. Bureau of the Census, 2011b).

Some sociologists feel that the single most important step society could take to help these dual-earner families would be to assist them with childcare demands. The Family and Medical Leave Act (FMLA), signed into law by President Clinton in 1993, was a step in that direction: It guarantees some workers up to 12 weeks of unpaid sick leave per year for the birth or adoption of a child or to care for a sick child, parent, or spouse. However, it has some important qualifications that seriously limit its usefulness to the working population:

- The law covers only workers who have been employed continuously for at least one year and who have worked a total of at least 1,250 hours (or about 25 hours a week). So temporary and part-time workers are not eligible.
- The law exempts companies with fewer than 50 workers.
- The law allows an employer to deny leave to a "key" employee—that is, one who is in the highest-paid 10% of its workforce—if allowing that person to take the leave would create "substantial and grievous injury" to the business's operations.

In 2008, an amendment was added to FMLA that permits a spouse, child, parent, or next of kin to take up to 26 weeks of unpaid leave to care for a member of the Armed Forces who is undergoing medical treatment for a serious injury or illness. Other than that, FMLA provisions have not changed in nearly 20 years.

Currently, only about 60% of the civilian U.S. workforce is eligible for FMLA benefits. In 2005, 17% of eligible employees actually took leave (U.S. Department of Labor, 2007). Many of those who don't take leave are parents who need the time off but can't afford to go without a paycheck. According to one survey, of those eligible workers who needed leave but didn't take it, 78% cited the inability to afford unpaid leave as the principal reason. In fact, 1 out of 10 workers who take unpaid leave under FMLA ends up going on public assistance to make up for the lost wages (National Partnership for Women and Families, 2005). Moreover, relatively few private employers go beyond the minimum unpaid leave policies mandated by FMLA. For instance, only about one quarter of U.S. employers offer fully paid "maternity-related leave" of any length, and one fifth of U.S. employers offer no maternity-related leave of any kind, paid or unpaid (Ray, Gornick, & Schmitt, 2009).

Although FMLA represents an improvement over past conditions, the United States still lags behind other countries in its support of dual-earner families. A 2007 report found that of the 173 countries studied, 168 offer guaranteed paid leave to women in connection with childbirth; 98 of these countries offer at least 14 weeks of paid leave. In addition, 66 countries ensure paid paternity leave for fathers. Only Liberia, Papua New Guinea, Swaziland, Australia, and the United States offer no paid leave to new parents in any segment of the workforce (Heymann, Earle, & Hayes, 2007). France and Spain, for example, provide 5½ and 4½ months of paid leave, respectively, and allow both parents to stay at home until their child's third birthday, at which point they can return to their prior jobs. Germany and Sweden provide almost a full year of paid leave to both parents (Ray et al., 2009). Exhibit 7.4 shows how much paid and unpaid leave two parents are allowed for a new child in wealthy, industrialized nations.

Exhibit 7.4   Leave Policies for Two Parents With a New Child in 21 Countries

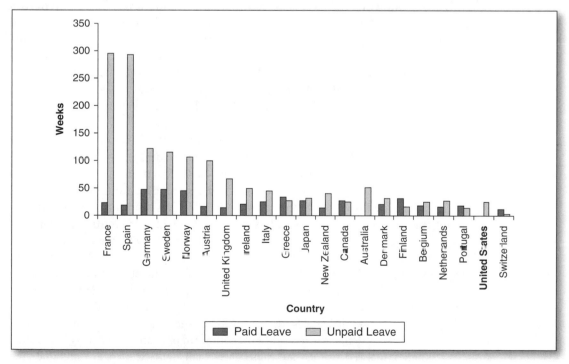

SOURCE: Ray, Gornick, & Schmitt, 2009, Figure 1, p. 6

If we are truly concerned about preserving and helping families, then perhaps we need to find more effective ways to reduce the conflict between work life and family life. In 2009, a bill called the Healthy Families Act was introduced in Congress. This bill would guarantee employees one paid hour off for every 30 hours they work, enabling them to get up to seven paid sick days a year. They could use their days to care for a sick child, parent, or spouse, or anyone else close to them. The law would apply only to workplaces that employ 15 or more workers. However, business groups have fought the legislation, arguing that in tight economic times it would impose added financial hardships on employers (S. Greenhouse, 2009). The bill remains in committee and has never come to a vote. Another piece of legislation, the Federal Employees Paid Parental Leave Act, was also introduced in 2009. This bill would have given all federal employees four weeks of *paid* leave each year for the birth or adoption of a child. It was approved by the House of Representatives but never came to a vote in the Senate and, hence, never became law. In 2011, lawmakers reintroduced this legislation. As of this writing, that bill is still pending.

How Social Diversity Influences Family

We cannot talk about structural influences on family life without discussing the role of gender, class, and race. Gender is especially influential, explaining a variety of phenomena in family relationships, such as the way people communicate, how they express themselves sexually, how they deal with conflict, and what they feel their responsibilities are. Culturally defined gender expectations in families are certainly changing. But men and women are still likely to enter relationships with vastly different prospects, desires, and goals.

As you learned in Chapter 5, traditional gender role socialization encourages women to be sensitive, express affection, and reveal weakness, whereas men are taught to be competitive, strong, and emotionally inexpressive. These stereotypes have some basis in fact. Research has consistently shown that women have more close friends than men and are more romantic in their intimate relationships (Perlman & Fehr, 1987). Furthermore, women have been shown to be more concerned about, attentive to, and aware of the dynamics of their relationships than men are (see, e.g., Fincham & Bradbury, 1987; Rusbult, Zembrodt, & Iwaniszek, 1986). Women even think more and talk more about their relationships than men do (Acitelli, 1988; Holtzworth-Munroe & Jacobson, 1985).

Ironically, such attentiveness and concern do not necessarily mean that women get more satisfaction out of family relationships than men do. In fact, the opposite may be true. According to one sociologist, every marriage actually contains two marriages—"his" and "hers"—and "his" seems to be the better deal (J. Bernard, 1972). Both married men and married women live longer and healthier lives than their single counterparts, but husbands typically are sick less often and have fewer emotional problems (Gove, Style, & Hughes, 1990; Ross, Mirowsky, & Goldstein, 1990; Waite & Gallagher, 2000). They are more likely to receive regular checkups, maintain healthy diets, and exercise regularly than unmarried men (Fustos, 2010b). One study found that compared with married women, married men have lower rates of back pain, headaches, serious psychological distress, and physical inactivity (Schoenborn, 2004).

The reason for these differences may lie in the relationship between cultural gender expectations and family demands. Because of the continued pressures of gender-specific family responsibilities, married women are more likely than married men to experience the stresses associated with parenthood and homemaking. Men have historically been able to feel they are fulfilling their family obligations by simply being financial providers. While some evidence suggests that fathers are struggling just as much as mothers in balancing work and family obligations (Harrington, Van Deusen, & Ladge, 2010), most people still interpret a father's long hours on the job as an understandable sacrifice for his family's sake. Fathers rarely spend as much time worrying about the effect their work will have on their children as mothers do.

In contrast, even in the relatively "liberated" United States, women's employment outside the home is often perceived as optional or, more seriously, as potentially damaging to the family. Even though women work for the same reasons men work—because they need the money—and bring home paychecks that cover a major chunk of the family's bills (Warren & Tyagi, 2007), women have traditionally had to justify why working outside the home is not an abandonment of their family duties. You'd be hard pressed to find many journalists and scholars fearfully describing the perilous effects of men's outside employment on the family. But a mountain of articles, editorials, and research reports over the years—not to mention a steady stream of Hollywood films—have focused on the difficulties women have in juggling the demands of work and family and on the negative effects of mothers' employment on their children's well-being. Newspaper accounts of studies showing that children who spend time in day care have more behavioral problems than children who don't—even if the effect is slight—perpetuate the idea that mothers' labor force choices can have dire consequences (Carey, 2007).

Social class has a substantial effect on family life, too. You saw in Chapter 5 that social class can determine the lessons that parents instill in their children. Social class affects families in other ways, too. All families, no matter what their class standing, face the same issues: work, leisure, child rearing, and interpersonal relations (L. Rubin, 1994). But beneath the similarities, we see dramatic differences in how these issues are handled. For example, because of heightened concern over class boundaries, ancestry, and maintenance of prestige, upper-class parents exert much more control over the dating behaviors of their children than lower-class parents do (Domhoff, 1983; M. K. Whyte, 1990). Upper-class families are also better able to use their wealth and resources in coping with some of the demands of family life. Finding adequate childcare arrangements will probably not pose much of a dilemma to parents who can afford a full-time, live-in nanny. The picture for middle-class families, though, can be different, especially when it intersects with race.

MARY PATTILLO-MCCOY

Privilege and Peril in Middle-Class Black Families

Concerned about how the combination of race and social class affects family life, sociologist Mary Pattillo-McCoy (1999) spent three and a half years in a middle-class black Chicago neighborhood she called "Groveland." She interviewed residents of all ages, including children. The only people she wasn't able to interview were the young adults who had gone off to college. As a black middle-class woman herself, Pattillo-McCoy quickly developed an affinity with the people she studied. She even had friends in common with some of her interviewees.

In many respects, the Groveland families were just like families in any other middle-class neighborhood. Parents saw their children's development into self-sufficient adults as their primary family goal. And they had the financial and social resources to help achieve this goal. Most of them had the wherewithal to pay for private schools, sports equipment, dance lessons, and other enriching activities for their children. Groveland children had access to technology and other resources that their counterparts in poor black neighborhoods did not.

Pattillo-McCoy also found that the Groveland middle-class families had to deal with problems markedly different from those of their white counterparts. For one thing, she found that the neighborhoods where many urban, middle-class African Americans live are likely to be adjacent to poor neighborhoods. In contrast, white middle-class neighborhoods are typically geographically separated from poor areas. In Chicago, for example, 79% of middle-class Blacks were likely to be living within a few blocks of a neighborhood where at least one third of the residents are poor; only 36% of white middle-class Chicago dwellers lived so close to a poor neighborhood (Pattillo-McCoy, 1999).

Thus, Groveland parents had to spend a lot of time trying to protect their children from the negative influences found in the nearby poor, inner city areas. In doing so, they faced some challenges other middle-class parents were unlikely to face:

> Groveland parents . . . set limits on where their children can travel. They choose activities—church youth groups, magnet schools or accelerated programs in the local school, and the Boy Scouts and Girl Scouts—to increase the likelihood that their children will learn positive values and associate with youth from similar families. Still, many parents are working long hours to maintain their middle-class incomes. They cannot be with their children at all times. On their way to the grocery store or to school or to music lessons, Groveland's youth pass other young people whose parents are not as strict, who stay outside later, who have joined the local gang, or who earn enough money being a lookout at a drug house to buy new gym shoes. They also meet these peers in school and at the park. . . . For some teenagers, the fast life looks much more exciting than what their parents have to offer them, and they are drawn to it. The simple fact of living in a neighborhood where not all families have sufficient resources to direct their children away from deviance makes it difficult for parents to ensure positive outcomes for their children and their neighborhood. (Pattillo-McCoy, 1999, pp. 211–212)

Pattillo-McCoy found that, in many other respects as well, black middle-class families face social realities that are quite different from those faced by white middle-class families. Still, her research also shows that most families within a particular social class face many of the same opportunities and barriers.

Family Challenges

Given all the pressures on families from the society around them, it should be no surprise that some families experience serious problems. Those problems include divorce and its aftereffects and family violence.

Divorce

Although divorce is more common and more acceptable in some places than in others, virtually all societies have provisions—legal, communal, or religious—for dissolving marriages (McKenry & Price, 1995). As a general rule, divorce rates worldwide tend to be associated with socioeconomic development. The developing countries of Latin America (e.g., Ecuador, Nicaragua, and Panama) and Asia (e.g., Malaysia, Mongolia, and Sri Lanka) have substantially lower divorce rates than the developed countries of Western Europe and North America (Nugman, 2002).

Iran provides a vivid example of how development and modernization can influence divorce rates, even in a restrictive environment. Recent economic development there has created more job opportunities for women than ever before. And female college undergraduates now outnumber males two to one. Hence, more women now see divorce as an available way out of an unsatisfying marriage. As one Iranian sociologist put it,

> This economic freedom has had an effect on the behavior of women in the home. In the past, if a housewife left her home, she would go hungry; now there is a degree of possibility of finding a job and earning an income. (quoted in Yong, 2010, p. A4)

Consequently, between 2000 and 2010, the number of Iranian divorces per year tripled.

Even in societies that we would consider modern and developed, powerful religious forces can sometimes suppress divorce. For instance, in 1995 the Irish government began a campaign against the Catholic Church over the country's constitutional ban on divorce. The government estimated at that time that at least 80,000 people were trapped in broken marriages and that they deserved the right to end them and remarry. The Catholic bishops launched a massive advertising counterattack, arguing that even unhappily married people have an obligation to keep their marriages intact to provide a good example for society. The referendum passed by a minuscule margin, and in 1997, for the first time, people in Ireland had the right to legally divorce.

Although the dissolution of marriage is virtually universal, no society values divorce highly. In fact, in most societies, people who divorce are somehow penalized, either through formal controls such as fines, prohibitions against remarriage, excommunication, and forced alimony and child support or through informal means such as censure, gossip, and stigmatization.

The Normalization of Divorce

Fifty years ago, divorce was a topic people talked about in whispers if they talked about it at all. Today, of course, things are quite different. You'd be hard pressed to find an eight-year-old who doesn't know what the word *divorce* means or who hasn't witnessed the end of a marriage, either that of her or his parents or of someone close. Divorce has become a part of everyday life. It's in our movies, television shows, and novels. The children's sections of bookstores stock picture books showing little dinosaurs or bears worrying about the possibility of their parents divorcing. Hallmark has an entire line of greeting cards for parents whose children live elsewhere.

Although the U.S. divorce rate has declined a bit since reaching a peak in 1981 (Stevenson & Wolfers, 2007), it still remains high, especially compared with other industrialized countries (see Exhibit 7.5). Consider these statistics:

- Roughly 2 million U.S. adults divorce each year (Kreider, 2005). That works out to a little less than 20 divorces per 1,000 existing marriages.
- About 40% of men and women in their 50s have been divorced at least once (U.S. Bureau of the Census, 2007).
- About 23% of marriages—not to mention 55% of cohabitations—end in divorce or separation within the first five years (Fustos, 2010a). The figure jumps to 33% after 10 years and 43% after 15 years (Bramlett & Mosher, 2002).
- Eighty-three percent of women who married between 1960 and 1964 reached their fifth anniversary, but only 74% of women who married between 1990 and 1994 did so (Kreider & Ellis, 2011)

Exhibit 7.5 Divorce Rates in Selected Developed Countries

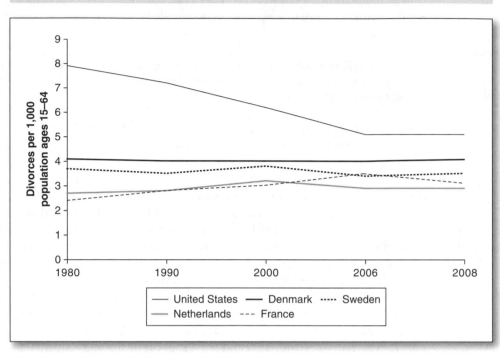

SOURCE: U.S. Bureau of the Census, 2011b, Table 1335

Such figures frighten people who are about to enter a "lifetime" relationship and distress those already married who want some sense of permanence.

Despite the traditional "family values" rhetoric we hear so much about these days, divorce in the United States tends to be unaffected by religious restrictions or political conservatism. For instance, several studies have found that born-again Christians are just as likely as anyone else to divorce (cited in Belluck, 2004). In addition, divorce rates are lowest in the so-called liberal states of the Northeast and upper Midwest and are highest in the conservative, heavily religious states of the South, such as Alabama, Arkansas, Oklahoma, and Kentucky (D. Elliott & Simmons, 2011). Some sociologists argue that other factors more commonly found in these states—namely younger age at marriage, less education, and lower socioeconomic status—render religiosity irrelevant. No matter how religious they are, young people who drop out of school and marry quickly not only lack emotional maturity but are highly susceptible to the economic strains that can create insurmountable problems in a marriage.

At a cultural level, the causes of the high divorce rates in Western societies include things such as the weakening of the family's traditional economic bonds and the stress of shifting gender roles (D. Popenoe, 1993). One particularly important factor has been a cultural change in the perception of marriage. Marriage has become a voluntary contract system that can be ended at the discretion of either spouse. In the past, when economic needs—not to mention constraints such as parental expectations or religious norms—held couples together, people "made do" with loveless, unsatisfying marriages because they had to. But when these constraints do not exist, people are less willing to make do (Coontz, 2005). Women's increasing earning power and decreasing economic dependence on men have made it easier to end an unsatisfying marriage.

In addition, people's overall attitudes toward divorce have become more accepting. In the 1960s, a divorced politician didn't stand a chance of being elected in the United States. Today, many of our most influential lawmakers are divorced. In the 1980s, Ronald Reagan's divorce and remarriage didn't prevent him from being elected—twice. In the 2008 presidential election, people barely mentioned candidate John McCain's divorce and remarriage. Most people now recognize that a divorce may be preferable to an unhappy marriage. In short, divorce is as much a part of U.S. family life as, well, marriage.

Changing perceptions of marriage and changing cultural attitudes toward divorce are typically accompanied by other institutional changes. In the United States, modifications of existing divorce laws in the past four decades have made it easier for people to end an unsatisfying marriage. Historically, evidence of wrongdoing—adultery, desertion, abuse, and so forth—was required for courts to grant a divorce. But since the early 1970s, every state has adopted a form of no-fault divorce. No-fault laws have eliminated the requirement that one partner be found guilty of some transgression. Instead, marriages are simply declared unworkable and terminated. Today, for fees ranging from $50 to $300—a small fraction of what most lawyers would charge— couples can download the appropriate forms and get online help filling them out. As one divorcing man put it, "I filled out the forms in the course of a night—it took three hours—and saved $2,000" (quoted in Crary, 2003, p. A6).

Many critics argue that these laws and innovations have made divorce *too* easy and *too* quick. Indeed, there seems to be a desire in some areas of the country to return to more restrictive divorce laws. Some states—Indiana, New Hampshire, Colorado, and Georgia, to name a few—have laws that impose mandatory waiting periods on couples contemplating divorce. Other states have toyed with the idea of providing discounted marriage licenses to couples who participate in premarital counseling. In 1997, the Louisiana State Legislature passed a measure forcing engaged couples to choose between a standard marriage contract that permits no-fault divorce and a "covenant marriage," which can be dissolved only by a mutually agreed-on two-year separation or proof of fault—chiefly adultery, abandonment, or abuse (Loe, 1997). Arizona followed suit in 1998, as did Arkansas in 2001. Critics of such measures note that instead of having a positive impact on family life, the result might be an increase in contentious, expensive, potentially child-harming divorces and unhappy, perhaps even dangerous marriages.

Children, Divorce, and Single Parenting

More than 1 million U.S. children see their parents divorce each year (D. Elliott & Simmons, 2011). When we combine divorce, separation, widowhood, and out-of-wedlock births, a significant number of children grow up living with one parent. In 1960, 9% of children under 18 lived with a single parent; by 2009, the figure had increased to over 30% (U.S. Bureau of the Census, 2011b). In fact, 8% of children who live with their mothers will witness three or more maternal partnerships (either marriage or cohabitation) by the time they reach 15 (Fustos, 2010a). The odds of growing up in a single-parent family are higher for some racial groups than for others (see Exhibit 7.6).

Exhibit 7.6   Family Composition and Race

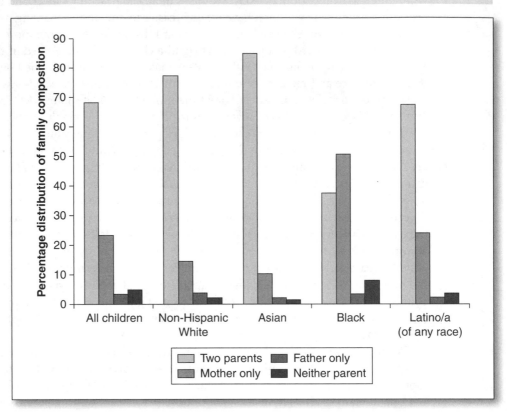

SOURCE: U.S. Bureau of the Census, 2011b, Table 69

Although divorce can be traumatic for adults, most recover after a period of years. Children, however, have a more difficult time adjusting. For them, divorce may set a series of potentially disruptive changes in motion. They may have to move to a new home in a new neighborhood, make new friends, and go to a new school. Because the overwhelming majority of children of divorced parents live with their mothers (D. Newman, 2009), they often experience a decline in their standard of living. The earning capacity of women is generally lower than that of men to begin with. Furthermore, noncustodial fathers do not always pay child support. In 57% of divorces in which mothers have sole physical custody, fathers are required to pay child support (U.S. Bureau of the Census, 2011b). Of these, only 46.8% of noncustodial fathers pay the full amount, 29.5% pay a partial amount, and 23.7% pay nothing. Hence, more than half of divorced mothers with custody of children don't receive the total financial assistance they have been awarded. Award rates are especially low for African American and Latina women, who are likely to suffer from higher poverty rates already (Grall, 2007).

The relationship that children have with their noncustodial parent also tends to deteriorate over time. Some research indicates that noncustodial fathers rarely see their children regularly or maintain close relationships with them (Furstenberg & Harris, 1992). What contact they do have with their children often diminishes over time (W. D. Manning & Smock, 1999). One study found that 75% of noncustodial fathers never attend their child's school events, 85% never help them with their homework, and 65% never take them on vacations (Teachman, 1991). Another found that fewer than one in five noncustodial fathers have a significant influence over their children's health care, education, religion, or other matters important to their welfare (Arendell, 1995).

What are the long-term effects of divorce on children? A substantial body of research shows that regardless of race or education of parents, children raised in single-parent homes have more problems at every stage of life than children from two-parent families. An extensive review of studies published during the 1990s found that children from divorced families fare worse in terms of academic success, psychological adjustment, self-concept, social competence, and long-term health than children from intact, two-parent families (Amato, 2000). When they reach adulthood, they are at greater risk of low socioeconomic attainment, increased marital difficulties, and divorce (Diekmann & Engelhardt, 1999).

These differences are typically attributed to factors such as the absence of a father, increased strain on the custodial parent to keep the household running, and emotional stress and anger associated with the separation. However, the causes of these problems are more likely to be factors that can also be found in two-parent families: low income, poor living conditions, lack of parental supervision, and marital discord (Amato & Sobolewski, 2001; Cherlin, 1992).

Some critics argue that the standard research design in studies on the impact of divorce on children—comparing children whose parents have divorced with children in happy, intact families—is flawed. Indeed, if we compare kids from divorced families with kids from intact families whose parents are unhappily married or whose families experience a great deal of conflict, we find that the type and frequency of emotional and interpersonal problems are similar for both sets of children (Cherlin et al., 1991). In fact, children who grow up in intact families marked by frequent conflict may actually suffer more. This research suggests that behavioral problems are caused not by the divorce itself but by exposure to conflict between the parents both before and after the divorce (Stewart, Copeland, Chester, Malley, & Barenbaum, 1997). In short, the simple fact of growing up in a single-parent family may not be as important in the development of a child as the way parents relate to each other and to the child.

Remarriage and Stepfamilies

About 29% of existing marriages in the United States today involve at least one partner who was previously married (Kreider & Ellis, 2011). This statistic suggests that although people are quite willing to escape a bad marriage, they have not necessarily given up on the concept of marriage entirely.

Although they are fairly common, remarriages are not without their difficulties. The divorce rate for remarriages is actually slightly higher than the rate for first marriages. In the United States, about 25% of remarriages end in divorce within five years, compared with 23% of first marriages (Bramlett & Mosher, 2002; Fustos, 2010a).

Remarriages may be less stable than first marriages because the traditional roles, relationships, and norms of family don't apply. We have no institutionalized expectations for relationships between former and current spouses, between stepparents and stepchildren, between step- and half-siblings, and with extended kin (Ahrons & Rodgers, 1987). Laws and customs have been slow to catch up. For instance, do stepchildren have legal claims to their stepparents' property? Do incest rules apply to stepsiblings?

Remarriage is particularly difficult when children are involved. Although many stepparents build strong, durable, loving relationships with their partner's children, others face difficulties. When a new stepparent enters the formerly single-parent family, the entire system may be thrown out of balance. He or she may be seen as an outsider or, worse, an intruder. Stepsiblings may be asked to share bedrooms or other possessions. They may see their connection to their biological parent as giving them greater claim on that parent's affection and resources. Rules and habits change and, for a time, confusion, resentment, and hostility may be the norm. Conflict is common in all types of families, but conflict over issues such as favoritism, divided loyalties, the right to discipline, and financial responsibility is particularly likely in stepfamilies.

The high divorce rate of remarriages and the high levels of conflict within some stepfamilies are not simply an outgrowth of people's psychological inability to sustain intimate relationships, as some analysts have claimed. The fact that remarriages are not fully institutionalized makes them susceptible to failure. The lack of clear role definitions, the absence of established societal norms, and the increased complexity of the family structure itself increase the likelihood of tension and turmoil. Perhaps as we develop standard ways of defining and coping with reconstructed families, remarriage will become more institutionalized and less problematic. Until then, remarriage will continue to create a great deal of tension and confusion.

Family Violence

Ironically, relationships in families—with the people who are supposed to nourish us when the outside world has sucked away our life energy—can also be some of the most violent relationships in a society.

Intimate-Partner Violence

Wife beating occurs in about 85% of the world's societies. According to the World Health Organization, women everywhere face the greatest threat of violence in their own homes (Garcia-Moreno, Jansen, Ellsberg, Heise, & Watts, 2006). A study of intimate violence in developing countries found that about one third of women in Egypt and Nicaragua and close to one half of women in Peru, Colombia, and Zambia have been beaten by their spouses or partners (Kishor & Johnson, 2004). In some countries—Indonesia, Ghana, India, and Uganda, for instance—it's not unusual for women to condone intimate violence against them. They are actually more likely than men to believe that it's acceptable for a husband to beat his wife if she argues with him or refuses to have sex with him (Population Reference Bureau, 2011b).

Husband beating occurs less frequently—in about 27% of societies—and occurs less often than wife beating in societies where both are present (Levinson, 1989). In the United States, for instance, women are eight times more likely than men to be beaten by an intimate partner (Rand, 2008).

Exact statistics about the prevalence of violence among intimates are notoriously difficult to collect. In the United States, domestic violence typically occurs in private, beyond the watchful eyes of relatives, neighbors, and strangers. Even with the more stringent rules for police reporting that have been instituted in the past decade or two, most incidents of domestic violence are never reported; others are dismissed as accidents. It's been estimated that only about half of the cases of nonlethal violence against women are reported to the police (Rennison & Welchans, 2000).

The statistics on intimate-partner abuse that do exist indicate that it is a widespread problem, although it has declined somewhat in recent years. In 2007 (the last year for which figures were available at the time of this writing), there were about 650,000 reported nonlethal assaults committed by current spouses, former spouses, boyfriends, or girlfriends (U.S. Bureau of the Census, 2011b). Women accounted for about 87% of the victims of these incidents.

Other studies place the prevalence rate for intimate-partner violence significantly higher. For instance, the National Violence Against Women Survey of 16,000 women and men across the country found that nearly 25% of surveyed women and 7.6% of men said they'd been raped or physically assaulted by a spouse, partner, or date at some point in their lifetimes. Within the previous 12 months, 1.5% of women and 0.9% of men reported being raped or physically assaulted. According to these estimates, about 1.5 million women and more than 800,000 men are assaulted by an intimate partner annually in the United States, well above the official Bureau of Justice Statistics figures. And if we add relatively minor acts of violence—pushing, grabbing, shoving, and slapping—the figures would rise to more than 3 million incidents for men and more than 5 million for women (Tjaden & Thoennes, 2000).

About 1,200 women were killed by an intimate partner in 2007 (U.S. Bureau of the Census, 2011b). Overall, about 30% of all female murder victims were killed by an intimate partner (Fox & Zawitz, 2007). One study found that almost half the women murdered by their intimate partners had visited the emergency room within the two years before they were killed (Crandall, Nathens, Kernic, Holt, & Rivara, 2004).

But women don't just suffer disproportionate physical consequences. Female victims of intimate violence are also more likely than male victims to suffer psychologically (e.g., from depression, anxiety, or low self-esteem) and socially (e.g., isolation from friends). The economic costs can be steep, too. It's estimated that intimate violence costs about $8.3 billion a year in direct costs (medical and mental health care) and indirect costs (lost productivity due to time away from work; Centers for Disease Control and Prevention, 2009). Women who experience severe forms of abuse are also more likely than women who experience less serious forms of abuse to lose their jobs or to go on public assistance.

Although domestic violence between heterosexual partners gets most of the attention, same-sex couples are not immune to the problem. Indeed, same-sex intimate violence is widespread. It's estimated that between 42% and 79% of gay men and 25% and 50% of lesbians have experienced some type of intimate violence (cited in Burke & Owen, 2006). In fact, some researchers claim that more violence occurs in long-term homosexual relationships than in heterosexual relationships (P. Cameron, 2003).

Child Abuse

Children are even more likely to be victims of intimate violence than adult family members. In some poverty-stricken countries, children may be consigned to unpleasant and dangerous labor, sold to buy food for the rest of the family, or even murdered in infancy if their parents don't want them or can't afford them. In the United States, there were about 774,000 substantiated cases of child abuse and/or neglect in 2008 (U.S. Bureau of the Census, 2011b). Because the vast majority of child abuse incidents involve victims who can't protect themselves or report the abuse and remain hidden from the police and social service agencies, many researchers think the actual figure is much higher. And if we take violence against children to mean any act of physical aggression directed by an adult toward a child—including spanking and slapping— perhaps as many as 9 of every 10 U.S. children under the age of three have been the object of violence at the hands of their parents or caretakers (Straus & Gelles, 1990).

Because of the relative size of victims and abusers, child abuse can sometimes be fatal. It's estimated that 1,740 children nationally died from abuse or neglect in 2008, and 71% were killed by one or both parents. About 80% of these victims were younger than four at the time of their death (Child Welfare Information Gateway, 2010).

Intimate Violence in a Cultural Context

Individual-level factors such as frustration over money, stress, and alcohol and drug use are frequently cited as major causes of domestic violence. To some analysts, batterers are either psychopaths or people who are just plain prone to violence. Although it would be comforting to believe that domestic violence is rare and occurs only in families that harbor a "sick" partner, parent, or spouse, it actually happens with alarming frequency and is likely to be committed by people we would otherwise consider "normal." Intimate-partner abuse and child abuse—not to mention elder abuse and violence between siblings—occur in every culture, class, race, and religion. It is not an aberration; it is a fundamental characteristic of the way we relate to one another in private, intimate settings. So to fully understand domestic violence, we must take a look at some important characteristics of the society in which it occurs.

The United States is fundamentally committed to the use of violence to achieve desirable ends (Straus, 1977). For many people, violence is considered the appropriate means by which to resolve certain problems. Furthermore, violence pervades the culture. It is in our schools, our movies, our toy stores, our video games, our spectator sports, and our government. It's even in our everyday language. How many times have you heard a parent "playfully" warn a misbehaving child that she or he is "cruisin' for a bruisin'"?

In addition to the pervasiveness of violence in the culture, families have several characteristics that increase the probability of conflict. For instance, we spend a lot of time with family members and interact with them across a wide range of situations. The intimacy of these interactions is intense. Emotions run deep. The anger we may feel toward a stranger or an acquaintance never approaches the intensity of the anger we feel toward a spouse—or for that matter, toward a sibling or a child.

Moreover, we also know more about family members than we know about other people in our lives. We know their likes and dislikes, their fears, and their desires. And they know these things about us, too. If someone in your family insults you, you know immediately what you can say to get even. Spouses usually know the "buttons" they can push to hurt or infuriate each other. Arguments can escalate into violence when one partner focuses on the other's vulnerabilities and insecurities.

Finally, family life contains endless sources of stress and tension. For one thing, we expect a lot from our families: emotional and financial support, warmth, comfort, and intimacy. When these expectations aren't fulfilled, stress levels escalate. Life circumstances also contribute to family tension (Gelles & Straus, 1988). The birth and raising of a child, financial problems, employment transitions, illness, old age, death, and so on are all events that potentially increase stress. Indeed, a pregnant or recently pregnant woman is more likely to be the victim of a homicide than to die of any other cause (Horon & Cheng, 2001).

We must also look at the broader conceptions of gender that exist within a society. Male dominance in human societies has a long and rather infamous history. Roman law, for instance, justified a husband's killing his wife for reasons such as adultery, wine drinking, and other so-called inappropriate behaviors (Steinmetz, Clavan, & Stein, 1990). Most societies in the world remain dominated by and built around the interests of men. Men typically occupy the high-status positions, make important decisions and exercise political power, tend to dominate interpersonal relationships, and occupy the roles society defines as most valuable (see Chapter 12).

Men who beat their partners are not necessarily psychotic, deranged, "sick" individuals. Rather, they are often men who believe that male dominance is their birthright. Such men are actually living up to cultural prescriptions that are cherished in many societies—aggressiveness, male dominance, and female subordination (Dobash & Dobash, 1979). We have a deeply entrenched tendency to perceive domestic violence as "normal"—as something that, although not necessarily desirable, is not surprising or unexpected either. Consequently, much of the research in this area has focused on the victims rather than on the perpetrators.

Personal and Institutional Responses to Intimate Violence

One question that has captured the attention of many marriage and family researchers is why people, especially women, stay in abusive relationships in societies where divorce is readily available. During the 1960s, *the masochism thesis*—that is, that women like being humiliated and hurt—was the predominant reason offered by psychiatrists (see, e.g., Saul, 1972). Even today, many psychiatrists believe that masochism—or *self-defeating personality disorder*, as it is now called—is a "legitimate" medical explanation for women who stay in abusive relationships. Other contemporary explanations focus on the woman's character flaws, such as a weak will or a pathological emotional attachment.

All these explanations focus on the victim while paying little attention to her social situation. From a conflict perspective, we can see that in a society reluctant to punish male abusers, many women may perceive that they have no alternatives and may feel physically, economically, and emotionally trapped in their relationships. Many of them leave, sometimes on several occasions, but find that the opportunities outside the relationship are not sufficient and end up returning (D. J. Anderson, 2003). Indeed, the broader economic structure conspires to keep vulnerable women in abusive relationships. Women who are unemployed and cannot support themselves financially are significantly less likely to leave an abusive marriage than women who are employed and who therefore have their own source of income (Strube & Barbour, 1983).

The perception that battered women simply sit back and take the abuse, thinking they somehow deserve it, is inaccurate. One study of 1,000 battered and formerly battered women nationwide found that they had tried a number of active strategies to end the violence directed against them (Bowker, 1993). They tried to talk men out of beating them, extracted promises that the men wouldn't batter them anymore, avoided their abuser or avoided certain volatile topics, hid or ran away, and even fought back. Many of these individual strategies had limited effectiveness, however, and so most of these battered women eventually turned to people outside the relationship for informal support, advice, and sheltering. From these informal sources, the women generally progressed to organizations in the community, such as the police, social service and counseling agencies, women's groups, and battered women's shelters. Some of these women were able, eventually, to end the violence; others weren't. In any case, as the study points out, most women actively try to end their victimization.

It's also important to keep in mind that leaving the relationship doesn't always end the violence. In fact, it may escalate it. One study found that victims who temporarily leave an abusive relationship suffer increased violence compared with those who never leave. Moreover, almost three quarters of visits battered women make to hospital emergency rooms occur after a separation (D. J. Anderson, 2003). About 90% of U.S.

women who are killed by ex-husbands or ex-boyfriends were stalked prior to their murders (S. A. D. Moore, 2003).

In some cases, the social organizations and institutions that are designed to help battered women contribute to their inability to escape abuse. As recently as 20 years ago, for instance, emergency room workers routinely interviewed battered women about their injuries with their husbands present. The courts, too, historically treated spousal violence less seriously than other crimes, making it even more difficult for women to seek help. Even today, about 80% of domestic violence victims don't have lawyers to guide them through the legal process (Prah, 2006). Most states require that volunteers who work on domestic violence hotlines complete 40 to 50 hours of training, but no such training is required for police personnel, lawyers, and judges (Prah, 2006).

Sometimes the resources in place to assist battered women are simply inadequate. Several states have waiting lists of intimate violence victims in need of counseling. If shelters are filled—as is often the case—victims may have to be bused hundreds of miles away to a place where shelter is available. This remedy may get them out of harm's way, but it may also wreck their work lives, endanger welfare checks, take them away from the support of extended family and friends, and disrupt their children's schooling.

In rural areas, there may be no services available at all. And if there's no public transportation, the shelters that do exist may be inaccessible to women who live miles away and don't own a car. In small towns, confidentiality is virtually impossible. The fact that people tend to know one another can dissuade a woman from calling a local sheriff's office for help, because the person answering might be a friend or relative of her abusive partner.

In sum, the decision to stay in an abusive relationship is the result not of irrationality or mental dysfunction but of rational choices women make in response to an array of conditions, including fear of and harassment by the abuser, the everyday realities of dependence, and the lack of institutional support (P. L. Baker, 1997). Broader societal circumstances may also play a role. In the months following the September 11, 2001, attacks, for instance, many battered women made the decision not to leave their relationships, clinging to familiar surroundings and coming to believe that a bad home was better than none in such unstable times. As a consequence, shelters reported dwindling demand for beds in their facilities in the immediate aftermath of the attacks (Lewin, 2001). In their need to acknowledge such realities, battered women are no different from any other individuals seeking to negotiate the complexities of social life.

Conclusion

Close relationships form the center of our personal universes. Life with intimates provides us with the sense of belonging that most of us need. However, although these relationships are the principal source of identity, community, happiness, and satisfaction for many, they can be the source of tremendous anguish and suffering for others.

Family, the most structured and culturally valued intimate relationship, is simultaneously a public and a private institution. True, most intimate and family behavior occurs away from the watchful eyes of others; we alone have access to our thoughts, desires, and feelings regarding those with whom we are intimately involved. But people around us, the government, and even society as a whole have a vested interest in what happens in our intimate lives.

The social institutions and culture that make up our society also shape the very nature and definition of "family." Today, the boundaries of that definition are being pushed by rapidly increasing numbers of "nontraditional" families—dual-earner couples, single-parent households, cohabitors, same-sex married couples, and so on.

Every family relationship, whether it violates or conforms to current social norms, reflects the dominant ideals and beliefs regarding what a marriage or a family ought to look like. Although each relationship is unique, this uniqueness will always be bounded by the broader constraints of our cultural, group, and institutional values.

YOUR TURN

There is no universal definition of "family." Our ideas about what a family is depend on the culture we grew up in. Within a particular culture, people may also debate what a family is and which groups get to be defined as a family.

With so much disagreement, it would be interesting to find out how people actually define a family. Go to a spot on campus with a lot of foot traffic and ask passersby for their definition of the word *family*. See if you can find any patterns in people's responses. Do you see a tendency to focus on blood or legal relations, or is the emotional component of family more important? Do definitions of family require children?

To delve deeper into the diversity of family definitions and experiences, pose the following questions to several friends or classmates. Try to acquire as diverse a sample of respondents as possible by talking to people from different cultural, racial, ethnic, religious, gender, and age groups:

- How many brothers and sisters do you have?
- If they are younger, did your parents expect you to help take care of them?
- Did you share a room with any of them while you were growing up?
- How many different houses and/or apartments did you live in while growing up?
- Did you live with both of your parents as you were growing up? If not, who did you live with?
- How often do you see your grandparents?
- Did you ever have grandparents or other relatives living in your house?
- How did your parents or guardians discipline you when you misbehaved?
- How would you characterize the marital status of your parents while growing up? Single? Married? Divorced? Separated?
- Do you address your relatives by family terms ("Uncle Bob," "Aunt Judy," "Grandpa," "Grandma") or by first name?
- Do you expect to help support your parents when you are older?

Did you notice any interesting trends in people's responses? What do their answers say about the structure of their families? Did you find any consistent differences across cultural, gender, class, race, or age lines? For instance, does the likelihood of sharing a room with a sibling differ for people who grew up in different eras? Do members of different ethnic groups maintain different degrees of contact with grandparents or other relatives? Do age and class affect the likelihood of growing up with one or both parents? Do people have different expectations about supporting their parents in the future? What do these different responses tell us about the broader structural context within which we live our family lives?

A variation on this exercise would be to examine the content of the personal Web pages that more and more families are now posting on the Internet. (If you are using a search engine like Yahoo, narrow your search by going to the following subcategories: Society and Culture → People → Personal Homepages → Families.) Randomly select 50 or so (or more if you have time or are able to work in groups), and try to document the different categories of information families include about themselves—factual information (e.g., size and location of family), likes and dislikes, opinions on political or social issues, links to other Web sites, and so on. Do these pages tend to focus on nuclear families or do they include information about extended family members? Are certain racial, ethnic, or religious groups over- or underrepresented? Did you notice any differences in the Web pages of U.S. families versus families from other societies? What do the content and design of these home pages tell us about the nature and importance of family in people's lives? How can you explain the willingness of these families to expose such private aspects of their lives to the vast, public domain of the Internet?

CHAPTER HIGHLIGHTS

- In this culture, close relationships are the standard against which we judge the quality and happiness of our everyday lives. Yet in complex, individualistic societies they are becoming more difficult to establish and sustain.

- Many people in the United States long for a return to the "golden age" of the family. But the image of the U.S. family of the past is largely a myth.

- Although monogamous marriage is the only sexual relationship that has achieved widespread cultural legitimacy in the United States, other forms of intimacy (e.g., extra- and premarital sex, polygamy) are considered legitimate in other societies.

- Although we like to think that the things we do in our family relationships are completely private experiences, they are continually influenced by large-scale political interests and economic pressures. Furthermore, our choices of romantic partners are governed to some degree by cultural rules that encourage us to form relationships within certain social groups and outside others.

- Divorce is not a solely private experience either. It occurs within a cultural, historical, and community context. The high rate of remarriage after divorce indicates that people still view the institution of marriage as desirable.

- Instead of viewing domestic violence (spouse abuse and child abuse) as a product of "sick" individuals, sociologists are likely to view it as the product of a culture that tolerates violence in a variety of situations, traditionally grants men authority over women in family roles, and values family privacy and autonomy over the well-being of individual members.

KEY TERMS

endogamy: Marriage within one's social group

exogamy: Marriage outside one's social group

extended family: Family unit consisting of the parent-child nuclear family and other relatives, such as grandparents, aunts, uncles, and cousins

family: Two or more persons, including the householder, who are related by birth, marriage, or adoption and who live together as one household

household: Living arrangement composed of one or more people who occupy a housing unit

monogamy: The practice of being married to only one person at a time

neolocal residence: Living arrangement in which a married couple sets up residence separate from either spouse's family

nuclear family: Family unit consisting of at least one parent and one child

polygamy: Marriage of one person to more than one spouse at the same time

STUDENT STUDY SITE

Visit the Student Study Site at **www.sagepub.com/newman9e** for these additional learning tools:
- Flashcards Web quizzes
- Sociologists at Work features
- Micro-Macro Connection features
- Video links
- Audio links
- Web resources
- SAGE journal articles

Constructing Difference

Social Deviance

8

Defining Deviance

Explaining Deviant Behavior

Linking Power, Deviance, and Social Control

In 1984, 22-year-old Kelly Michaels moved to New York to pursue her dream of becoming an actress. She was a mild-mannered, devout Catholic who loved children. To support herself, she began working at the Wee Care Preschool in a New Jersey suburb. By all accounts, the kids there loved her (Hass, 1995).

Two weeks after Michaels left Wee Care for a better-paying job at another preschool, a four-year-old boy who was enrolled at Wee Care was taken to a doctor. A nurse rubbed his back and explained that she was going to take his temperature rectally. He said something like, "That's what teacher [Michaels] does to me at nap time." Although it was unclear exactly what he meant by this—Michaels sometimes rubbed children's backs to get them to sleep and did take their temperature with a plastic forehead strip—the boy's alarmed mother, who happened to be the daughter of a local judge, called the school and the police (Michaels, 1993). The police questioned the child, as well as other children at Wee Care, searching for evidence that Michaels had sexually abused them. As word spread of the investigation, worried parents phoned other parents to share stories about the latest allegations. The police encouraged parents to seek state-funded psychological help for themselves as well as their children. In turn, the therapists encouraged the parents to cooperate with authorities in investigating Michaels.

That casual comment made by one little boy in a doctor's office touched off a 16-month investigation by the Division of Youth and Family Services, which eventually ended in a 235-count indictment against Michaels. During the investigation, scores of parents became convinced that Michaels had raped their children with silverware, wooden spoons, Legos, and lightbulbs; that she had played "Jingle Bells" on the piano while naked; and that she had licked peanut butter off children's genitals, made them drink her urine, and forced them to eat excrement off the floor (Hass, 1995).

By the time the trial began, Kelly was already being called the "most hated woman in all of New Jersey." The 10-month trial was filled with a host of inconsistencies and questionable legal tactics. Prosecutors never provided any substantiated evidence of abuse, yet they portrayed Michaels as "actressy" and "deviously charming." Everything she did was interpreted from the assumption that she was a "monster." For instance, if she was kind and patient with the children, that meant she was trying to seduce them.

None of the other teachers at the day care center had heard or seen anything, even though most of the alleged abuse took place during the children's nap time in a room set off only by a plastic curtain. The judge in the trial allowed the children to testify on closed-circuit TV while seated on his lap and denied the defense attorneys the opportunity to cross-examine them. One of the prosecution's witnesses—a child therapist—testified that the children who denied being molested by Ms. Michaels suffered from something called "child sexual abuse accommodation syndrome," a psychological condition that made them deny the abuse. In fact, the more the children denied it, the more certain the child therapist was that the abuse had actually happened.

Michaels was found guilty on 115 counts of assault, sexual abuse, and terrorist threats and sentenced to 47 years in prison. As if to add insult to injury, while in prison she received a bill from the Essex County public defenders office charging her $800,000 in legal fees (L. Manning, 2007). In 1993, after she had spent five years in prison—including an 18-month stint in solitary confinement—a state appellate court overturned the conviction. Later, the New Jersey Supreme Court upheld the appellate court's decision, decrying the original conviction with outrage. The court wrote that all 20 children who testified against Michaels had been led, bribed, or threatened (Hass, 1995).

You might think that a formal declaration of innocence from such a powerful body as a state supreme court would change people's feelings about Kelly Michaels. Yet she remained a target of hate. Several civil suits were filed against Michaels by parents who still believed their children had been sexually abused. One mother said she would try to kill Michaels with her bare hands if she had the chance. To date, no Wee Care parents have ever publicly retracted their accusations against their child's former teacher (L. Manning, 2007).

Why was it so hard for people to admit that Michaels was innocent? For one thing, at a time when child molestation was becoming a national obsession, the case reflected our darkest collective fears. The terrifying message was that our children could be hurt not only by creepy, middle-aged men but also by seemingly safe, 22-year-old college women. In the frenzy over children's safety, no one seemed willing to protect the principle that a defendant is innocent until proven guilty.

Even more striking about this case is what it says about the way people think. Once members of the community concluded that Kelly Michaels had committed these horrible acts, no amount of conflicting evidence was going to sway them to believe otherwise. Deviant labels and what they imply in people's minds can overshadow everything else about that person. When Michaels was convicted and formally tagged a criminal, the public degradation acquired legal legitimacy. From that point on, she would never again be able to reclaim a normal life and in many people's minds would forever be a "child molester." Long after Michaels's conviction on sexual abuse charges had been overturned, the media continued to identify her as a criminal. An Associated Press news release about her thwarted attempt to sue the county and the state was titled "Sex Offender's Case Denied in Court" (2001).

Few of us have spent five years in prison as a wrongly convicted child molester. But people are unjustifiably tagged as deviant all the time. Perhaps there have been times in your life when you acquired some sort of unflattering but inaccurate reputation that you couldn't shed. In this chapter, I examine several questions related to this phenomenon: What is deviance? How does society attempt to control deviant behavior? Who gets to define what is and is not deviant? And what are the consequences of being identified by others as deviant?

Defining Deviance

In its broadest sense, *deviance* refers to socially disapproved behavior—the violation of some agreed-on norm that prevails in a community or in society at large. Staring at a stranger in an elevator, talking to oneself in public, wearing outlandish clothes, robbing a bank, and methodically shooting dozens of students on a college campus can all be considered deviant acts. If we define deviance simply as any norm violation, then most deviance is rather trivial—even "normal"—like driving over the speed limit or walking across an intersection when the light is red. Most of us, at some point in our lives, occupy statuses or engage in behaviors that others could regard as deviant. But most sociologists focus on deviant acts that are assaults on mores, the most serious of a society's norms. It's this type of deviance to which I will devote most of my attention in this chapter.

The determination of which behaviors or characteristics are deviant and which are normal is complex. We usually assume there's a fair amount of agreement in a society about what and who is deviant. For instance, no one would challenge the notion that child abuse is bad and that child abusers ought to be punished. But the level of agreement within a given society over what specific acts constitute child abuse can vary tremendously. Spanking may be a perfectly acceptable method of discipline to one person but be considered a cruel form of abuse by another.

To further complicate the issue, some sociologists who are identified with structural functionalism (e.g., Durkheim, 1895/1958; Erikson, 1966) argue that deviance, as a class of behaviors, is not always bad for society and may actually serve a useful purpose. As you recall from Chapter 4, norm violations help define the cultural and moral boundaries that distinguish right from wrong and increase feelings of in-group togetherness among those who unite in opposition to deviance from group norms. At the surface level, individual acts of deviance are disruptive and generate varying degrees of social condemnation, but at a deeper level, they can contribute to the maintenance and continuity of every society. Deviance can also create needed change in a society (Durkheim, 1895/1958). During the 1950s and 1960s, civil rights protestors purposely broke laws they considered discriminatory, such as those that prevented Blacks from entering certain establishments or attending certain schools. These acts of deviance eventually helped convince many voters and politicians to support legislation ending legal segregation.

As you may have guessed, sociologists usually don't judge whether a given behavior should or shouldn't be considered deviant. Instead, they examine how deviance comes about and what it means to society. One of their primary concerns is whether people respond to deviance from the perspective that all human behavior can be classified as essentially good or bad (absolutism) or from the perspective that definitions of deviance are socially constructed (relativism).

Absolutist Definitions of Deviance

According to **absolutism**, there are two fundamental types of human behavior: (1) that which is inherently proper and good and (2) that which is obviously improper, immoral, evil, and bad. To those who subscribe to such a position, the distinction is clear and identifiable. The rightness or wrongness of an act exists prior to socially created rules, norms, and customs and independently of people's subjective judgments (Erich Goode, 1994).

Absolutist definitions of deviance are often accompanied by strong emotional reactions toward those considered deviant. For instance, speaking about the issue of same-sex marriage, the televangelist Jimmy Swaggart once expressed these sentiments:

> I'm trying to find the correct name for it . . . this utter absolute, asinine, idiotic stupidity of men marrying men. . . . I've never seen a man in my life I wanted to marry. And I'm gonna be blunt and plain; if one ever looks at me like that, I'm gonna kill him and tell God he died. (Brutally Honest, 2004, p. 1)

Such extreme reactions might seem at odds with what appears to be a growing cultural acknowledgment and tolerance of homosexuality. You will recall from Chapter 7 that public support for same-sex marriage has grown recently. In addition, the percentage of people who believe homosexuals should be allowed to teach in college increased from below 50% in the early 1970s to close to 80% in the mid 2000s (Schott, 2007). A majority of Americans now favor allowing gays and lesbians to serve openly in the military, and opposition to gay adoption has decreased significantly in the past decade (Pew Research Center, 2006b; Talbot, 2010). In fact, in 2011, the U.S. Department of State began using gender-neutral language on U.S. passports—using "Parent One" and "Parent Two" instead of "mother" and "father"—to make it easier for same-sex couples to get passports for their children (L. Weeks, 2011). That same year, the Presbyterian Church (USA) voted to allow openly gay people in same-sex relationships to be ordained as ministers, elders, and deacons (Goodstein, 2011). Even in Indianapolis, Indiana—a state not considered to be especially gay friendly—the 2011 gay pride parade included representatives from the city police and fire departments, the county sheriff's department, and the mayor, and attracted between 60,000 and 70,000 onlookers.

As a consequence of greater acceptance and visibility, gays and lesbians are more likely than ever to "stand up and be counted." According to U.S. Census Bureau estimates, the number of documented gay and lesbian couples increased by 50% between 2000 and 2010. The growth has been most rapid not in large cities or traditional safe havens like San Francisco and West Hollywood, but in smaller towns and suburbs in states like Delaware, Michigan, Florida, Massachusetts, and Pennsylvania (cited in Tavernise, 2011a).

But many people still see homosexuality as absolutely deviant. In 2011, a bill was introduced in the Tennessee General Assembly that would prohibit elementary and middle school teachers from discussing any sexual orientation other than heterosexuality in the classroom. The Pentagon classifies homosexuality as a "defect," along with conditions like bed-wetting, dyslexia, obesity, and stuttering (Rosenberg, 2006). When such absolutist attitudes make their way into institutions and organizations, they become the justification for various types of prohibitions against gays and lesbians:

- In 1993, the U.S. Department of Defense enacted the "Don't ask, don't tell" policy. According to this rule, military personnel could not be asked about their sexual orientation. However, openly professing one's homosexuality or engaging in sexual conduct with a member of the same sex could still constitute grounds for discharge. Between 1993 and 2010, more than 13,000 soldiers were discharged under this policy (C. McLean & Singer, 2010). Nearly 1,000 specialists with important skills—fluency in Arabic, for instance—were forced out. One organization estimates that it cost the U.S. Armed Forces between $22,000 and $43,000 to replace each individual discharged under this policy (cited in Conant, 2010). In 2010, the Pentagon issued a report in which it concluded that allowing gay men and lesbians to serve openly in the armed forces presents little risk to the military's effectiveness. Later that year, President Obama signed a law repealing the "Don't ask, don't tell" policy. It remains to be seen how ending this policy will affect the everyday lives of gay, lesbian, and bisexual military personnel.
- Boy Scouts of America prohibits openly gay men from becoming troop leaders, claiming that they do not provide the sort of role model it wants young scouts exposed to, and in 2000 the U.S. Supreme Court upheld this policy.
- The Vatican excludes men from the Catholic priesthood who "are actively homosexual, have deep-seated homosexual tendencies, or support the so-called 'gay culture'" (quoted in Fisher & Goodstein, 2005, p. A1).

Absolutist definitions of deviance imply something about society's relationship with the person who is considered deviant. Many people consider "deviants" to be psychologically, and perhaps even anatomically, different from ordinary, rule-abiding people. The attribute or behavior that serves as the basic reason for defining a person as deviant in the first place is considered pervasive and essential to his or her entire character (Hills, 1980). Respectable, conventional qualities become insignificant. It doesn't matter, for instance, that the "sexual deviant" has an otherwise ordinary life, that the "drug addict" no longer uses drugs, or that the violent act of the "wife batterer" was completely atypical of the rest of his life. In short, the deviant act or trait determines the overall worth of the individual (J. Katz, 1975). Being defined as deviant means being identified as someone who cannot and should not be treated as an ordinary member of society.

There's another element of unfairness involved in the absolutist approach to deviance. People routinely make judgments about deviants based on strongly held stereotypes. If you ask someone to imagine what a typical drug addict looks like, for instance, chances are she or he will describe a dirty, poor, strung-out young man living on the streets and resorting to theft to support his illegal habit. The image probably wouldn't be one of a middle-class alcoholic, stay-at-home mother, or clean-shaven, hardworking physician hooked on prescription drugs, even though these groups constitute a higher percentage of drug addicts than any other in U.S. society (Pfohl, 1994). In Ohio, fatal overdoses of prescription pain-killers among young people have more than quadrupled over the past decade, surpassing car crashes as the leading cause of accidental death (cited in Tavernise, 2011b).

In U.S. society, the consequences of absolute deviant stereotypes fall heavily on members of ethnoracial minorities. Latino/as and African Americans make up over 60% of the U.S. inmate population even though they compose only about 27% of the general population. In fact, Blacks and Latino/as make up over two thirds of drug offenders behind bars (U.S. Sentencing Commission, 2009). Black males are incarcerated at a rate 2.6 times higher than Latino males and almost 7 times higher than white males (West, 2010). According to the Justice Policy Institute (2002), the number of black men in jail or prison has grown so much in the past two decades that there are now more black men behind bars than there are enrolled in colleges and universities.

Although some people may see such figures as clear evidence of higher rates of minority involvement in crime, other statistics seem to suggest something different. For instance, African Americans make up about 13% of the population, but they account for 39% of all arrests for violent crime, 30% of arrests for property crimes, and 34% of arrests for drug violations. In addition, African Americans account for 39% of convictions for violent crimes, 34% of convictions for property crimes, and 46% of convictions for drug crimes (U.S. Bureau of Justice Statistics, 2009). Since the death penalty was reinstated in 1977, 42% of defendants who have been executed have been Latino/a or African American, and 54% of the current death row population is Latino/a or African American (Snell, 2010).

Absolutist images of deviants are often oversimplified and fall short of accounting for every individual. The vast majority of African Americans do not commit crimes, just as the vast majority of gay men are not sexual predators, the vast majority of Italians are not involved in the Mafia, and the vast majority of Muslims are not terrorists. Nevertheless, the degree to which an entire group is characterized by an absolutist stereotype is important, because it determines individual and societal responses. If affluent housewives and businesspeople who abuse drugs are not considered typical drug addicts, they will never be the focus of law enforcement attention, collective moral outrage, political rhetoric, or public policy.

Relativist Definitions of Deviance

Reliance on a strict absolutist definition of deviance can lead to narrow and often inaccurate perceptions of many important social problems. This shortcoming can be avoided by employing a second approach to defining deviance, *relativism*, which draws from symbolic interactionism and the conflict perspective. This approach—which parallels the more general "cultural relativism" discussed in Chapter 4—states that deviance is not inherent in any particular act, belief, or condition; instead, it is socially constructed, a creation of collective human judgments and ideas. Like beauty, it is in the eye of the beholder. Consequently, no act is universally or "naturally" deviant. The relativist approach is useful when the focus of study is the process by which some group of people or some type of behavior is defined as deviant.

For the relativist, complex societies consist of different groups with different values and interests. Sometimes these groups agree and cooperate to achieve a common goal, as when different segments of society join together to fight a foreign enemy. But more often than not there is conflict and struggle among groups to realize their own interests and goals.

Different people or groups can thus have dramatically different interpretations of the same event. In 1995, a 35-year-old white ex-Marine named William Masters was taking his usual armed, late-night walk through a barren neighborhood in Los Angeles. He came upon two young Latino men spray painting graffiti beneath a freeway overpass. Masters wrote down the license number of their car on a small piece of paper. When the men saw him and demanded the paper, Masters pulled out his 9-millimeter pistol and shot them, wounding one and killing the other. He told the police that the men had threatened him with a screwdriver and he had acted in self-defense, even though both were shot in the back. He was not charged with murder. Eventually, he was found guilty on one count of carrying a concealed gun in public and one count of carrying a loaded gun in public—charges that carried a maximum of 18 months in jail and a $2,000 fine.

Shortly after his arrest, Masters made a case for why his actions shouldn't be defined as deviant. He told one interviewer he was sure people were glad that he, the intended victim, had gotten away and that no jury would ever convict him (Mydans, 1995). Many people agreed. Callers to radio talk shows and letters to newspapers applauded him for his vigilant anti-graffiti efforts and for his foresight in carrying a weapon for self-protection. A few suggested that society would be better off with more people like William around (Mydans, 1995). But others expressed dismay at the verdict and argued that Masters was simply a racist out looking for trouble. They felt he was a deviant who literally got away with murder.

All those who expressed opinions on this case would likely agree on one thing: "Murder" is a deviant act at the far end of the spectrum of social acceptability. However, their perceptions of whether William Masters was a "murderer" were quite different. Was he a "hero" or a "killer"? The answer lies not in the objective act of taking another's life but in the way others define and respond to such an act.

To fully understand the societal and personal implications of deviance designations, we must look at how these definitions are created and perpetuated. One key factor is who is doing the defining. One person's crime is another person's act of moral conscience; one group's evil is another group's virtue; one culture's terrorist is another culture's freedom fighter.

Definitions of deviance are also relative to particular cultural standards:

- In Singapore, a young vandal is a serious deviant (punishable by caning), as is a person who leaves chewed gum where it can be stepped on. The fine for bringing one stick of gum into Singapore is $10,000.
- In Thailand, it is illegal to step on a *baht*, the nation's currency.

- In Malaysia, a Muslim woman can be whipped for drinking alcohol in public or arrested for snacking during the daylight fasting hours of Ramadan.
- In Japan, a drunk driving conviction carries the possibility of a three- to five-year prison sentence, depending on the level of intoxication, and passengers who either provide the alcohol or provide the vehicle face criminal charges as well.

Deviance definitions undergo changes over time as well. For instance, several states at one time had laws designed specifically to protect women's virtue. Florida had a law that prohibited women from parachuting on Sundays. Michigan law made it a crime for men to use profanity in front of women. In Texas, it was a crime for women to adjust their stockings in public. The state of Washington still has a law on the books that makes it illegal to call a woman a "hussy" or "strumpet" in public (Kershaw, 2005). Sometimes new laws outlawing previously acceptable behavior seem just as ludicrous.

Conflict over deviance definitions often reflects differing cultural expectations. In 2005, for instance, an appeals court in Florida upheld a judge's earlier ruling that a Muslim woman could not wear a burka—a traditional veil that covers all but a woman's eyes—in her driver's license photo. In 2005, the U.S. Supreme Court ruled that the federal government could prohibit the medicinal use of marijuana even in the 11 states that explicitly permit it (L. Greenhouse, 2005). Even though people in the United States who wear burkas or smoke marijuana for medical purposes don't consider themselves deviant, these court rulings meant they could be defined and treated as such by the dominant culture.

The absolutist approach assumes that certain individual characteristics are typical of all deviants, but the relativist approach acknowledges that there is no typical deviant. In fact, the same act committed by two different people may yield very different community responses. In 1980, a Bayonne, New Jersey, teacher named Diane Cherchio was caught kissing and groping a 13-year-old male student at an eighth-grade dance. A few years later, after being promoted to guidance counselor, she had sex with an 11th grader, became pregnant, and eventually married him upon his graduation in 1985. Yet instead of being fired or even reprimanded, she was allowed to continue working in the public school district for two decades. When the son she gave birth to grew to be a teenager, Ms. Cherchio began having sex with one of his friends. She used her school authority to rearrange the boy's schedule so they had time for their sexual trysts. When that boy's parents found out and complained to the police, she was arrested. Again, she was not fired. School officials instead allowed her to take an early retirement package that increased her pension. They even gave her a gala farewell party. When she finally pled guilty to sexual assault charges in 2005, glowing references from coworkers convinced the judge to sentence her to probation and to spare her from registering as a sex offender (Kocieniewski, 2006).

Cherchio was eventually punished, as have been other older women who've had sexual relationships with teenage boys. Nevertheless, it's hard to imagine a school accommodating or defending a male teacher who seduced teenage girls in such a way. Because she was a young, attractive, intelligent woman whose victims were willing teenage boys, people in her community looked the other way. When *she* did it, somehow it wasn't so bad. One author summed up the public response to such incidents: "A teenage boy who gets to live his fantasy? What can be the harm?" (Levy, 2006, p. 2).

From a relativist approach, immediate situational circumstances, such as the time and location of an act, can also influence definitions of deviance. For example, drinking alcohol on the weekend is more acceptable than drinking during the week, and drinking in the evening is more acceptable than drinking in the morning. In 2005, the state of Florida expanded its self-defense law so that people could use concealed guns or other deadly force to defend themselves in public places without first trying to escape the attacker (Goodnough, 2005). In fact, 15 states have adopted "stand-your-ground" laws that allow victims to use deadly force in situations that aren't life threatening (Liptak, 2006). Had William Masters lived in any of these places instead of Los Angeles, he wouldn't have even faced minor criminal charges; he would have simply been a citizen exercising his legal right.

If deviance is relative, then even acts of extreme violence may be defined as acceptable under certain circumstances. Killings committed under the auspices of the government—shooting looters during a riot, killing enemy soldiers during wartime, or executing convicted murderers—fall outside the category of behaviors deemed deviant and problematic in society. However, a relativist approach to defining deviance doesn't mean that we can't be upset by activities that some people consider acceptable:

> Relativity does not require moral indifference, and it does not mean that one can never be . . . horrified by what one experiences in another group or culture. . . . [It] just reminds us that our personal beliefs or our cultural understandings are not necessarily found everywhere. (Curra, 2000, p. 13)

Relativists, like absolutists, acknowledge that every society identifies certain individuals and certain behaviors as bothersome and disruptive and therefore as justifiable targets of social control, whether through treatment, punishment, spiritual healing, or correction. However, to a relativist the main concerns in defining deviance are not so much what is committed but rather who commits the act, who labels it, and where and when it occurs. Some people have the wherewithal to avoid having their acts defined as deviant; others may fit a certain profile and be defined as deviant even if they've done nothing wrong. Definitions of deviant behavior change over time, and certain acts are acceptable to some groups and not others. The definitions most likely to persevere and become part of the dominant culture are those that have the support of influential segments of the population or have widespread agreement among the members of that society.

The Elements of Deviance

The two perspectives on defining deviance raise some complex and controversial issues. The definition of *deviance* most applicable to both perspectives is this: behavior (how people act), ideas (how people think), or attributes (how people appear) that some people in society—though not necessarily all people—find offensive, wrong, immoral, sinful, evil, strange, or disgusting.

This definition has three important elements (Aday, 1990):

- *An expectation:* Some sort of behavioral expectation must exist, a norm that defines appropriate, acceptable behavior, ideas, or characteristics. The expectations may be implicit or explicit, formal or informal, and more or less widely shared.
- *A violation:* Deviance implies some violation of normative expectations. The violation may be real or alleged; that is, an accusation of wrongdoing may be enough to give someone the reputation of being a deviant.
- *A reaction:* An individual, group, or society must react to the deviance. The reaction can take several forms: avoidance, criticism, warnings, punishment, or treatment. It may accurately reflect the facts, or it may bear little relation to what really happened, as when people are punished or ostracized for acts they did not commit.

Deviance, then, cannot exist if people don't have some idea of what's appropriate, if someone hasn't been perceived as or accused of violating some social norm, and if others haven't reacted to the alleged transgression.

(Text continues on page 248)

A Culture of Tramps

Douglas Harper

People typically see their own culture as normal and may be surprised to learn that other people around them have a different culture. That may especially be the case for subcultures defined by mainstream society as "deviant," such as the "tramp" culture pictured here.

Like any other culture, however, even the tramp culture has a clear set of norms. For example, after a tramp has worked for weeks or months, within the tramp culture it is appropriate to drink up one's wages in a drunken binge that may last for days or even weeks. Excessive drinking causes problems for tramps, but they define it as a normal part of their culture, like a football player who regards his injuries as inevitable.

I met this tramp, Carl, in Minneapolis. Suffering through a hangover after a three-week drunk, he was heading 2,000 miles to the apple harvest in Washington State. He accepted my company because I had a sack of food. We "buddied up," which is a tramp expression noting a relationship of limited but specific commitment.

Carl's gear for a 2,000-mile migration to the apple harvest included a razor and a mirror. He was finished with his drunk, and he knew he needed to shave and clean up to get a job. After he shaved, he handed me the razor and told me that either I shaved or I'd be heading the rest of the way by myself. The tramp understood that his life consisted of several identities and that the shift from a skid row drunk to a worker required specific attention to his appearance.

Freight trains are a particularly important and challenging part of tramp culture. They are complicated and dangerous. Tramps watch others ride trains and are quick to point out amateurs who don't know the cultural ropes or failures in the culture who may be smart but remain incompetent in the ways of tramps.

Tramps know where and how to ride freights. Here we rode on an exposed auto carrier, which is one of the least desirable places on a freight train. Riders are exposed to the elements, but worse than that, they are visible to yard police. Tramps prefer to ride inside empty boxcars or under the truck trailers bolted onto flatcars, called "piggybacks." There are at least 20 different places a tramp may ride a freight, and tramps spend a great deal of time arguing their comparative advantages.

There were eventually 38 men in this boxcar as it approached the towns where the apple orchards were situated. During the hot afternoon a tramp entered the car with a bottle of wine, but most tramps shied away. It is a strong tramp norm not to get drunk on a freight train, because to do so places the rider in great danger. Most tramps remembered the norms and passed on a tempting cold drink.

The culture of tramps is connected to the "macro" or structural aspect of society. We look at homeless people and see only a social problem or evidence of individual failure. But the tramps I met on trains and during apple harvests are homeless only some of the year, and then they ride a freight perhaps thousands of miles to become workers somewhere else. In the Pacific Northwest tramps pick fruit. They usually leave their wages in the harvest towns, where they either spend it getting drunk or have it stolen by "jackrollers" or the police.

Tramps define this way of spending money as normal, and their behavior serves an agricultural economy that needs intensive but intermittent labor. We take for granted that our fruits and vegetables await us in clean and orderly stores, but these products have come to us because a culture of probably homeless workers have labored for paltry wages in circumstances where they have little if any social power. In the case of tramps, their own cultural definition of their lives and fate justifies what is, in fact, an exploitative labor situation.

While waiting to be hired for the apple harvest, tramps assembled at one of many "jungles" in the area. In the jungles, tramps lived by norms: Food was shared, the camp was kept clean, and firewood was replaced. But when we were hired to work in an orchard, we were given a one-room cabin in which to live. Suddenly we had transformed from tramps to workers. We got an advance on our wages, bought cans of beans and SpaghettiOs, and began living under a roof. The change in Carl was remarkable. Suddenly he was master of a different world.

Note that I refer to these men as "tramps" because that is how they define themselves. The existence of a distinctive culture is often signaled by words that have meaning only within the framework of that culture. When tramps see another man in a freight car, they see a bindlestiff, an Airedale, a mission stiff, a rubber tramp, a jackroller, or one of many other categories of tramps. Each of these labels defines a certain set of actions, possessions, behaviors, and beliefs. In other words, they are not casual definitions but definitions that indicate an individual's identity. They are no less important or socially powerful than our own cultural definitions.

Tramps define themselves by how they travel and what they do. This man is a "bindlestiff" because he carries his gear in an old-fashioned manner, tied into what are called bindles. A bindlestiff usually spends his time in the less threatening environments of smaller cities or freight yards in the American West. His identity is made complete by his dog on a handmade leash. Here he enters the relatively hostile environment of Seattle, where many will prey on an elderly tramp. He may be visiting family, for many tramps keep family connections. Or he may be on his way to the freight yard to catch a train to a jungle, an orchard, or another city.

When a tramp can no longer take care of himself on the open road, he retires to a mission. He then becomes a "mission stiff," like the tramp in this photograph. Since tramps value independence, the admission that one must leave the road to retire to a mission is a radical redefinition of one's self. Tramps talk of retiring to a small cabin in the woods but seldom accumulate enough money to do it. Rather, they end their days in a homemade shack by a freight yard or in a mission when the weather turns too cold to live outside. It is at the ends of their lives that the inconsistencies in their self-definitions and their actual situations become most apparent.

The tramps pictured here live in Boston. On the surface they appear to be the same as the tramps pictured earlier. Yet their culture is profoundly different. In the East, single homeless men are not an agricultural labor force, and it is more difficult for them to ride freights. Without work and mobility, the tramp becomes a stationary homeless man, reduced to begging and scavenging. Still, the homeless man lives in a culture. These two men are in a "bottle gang," furtively sharing a pint of cheap wine they have purchased from a day's work panhandling and scavenging for spare change.

To study a culture one must participate as well as observe. To study tramps I rode freight trains, lived in hobo jungles and skid row missions, and picked apples in orchards where all the workers were tramps. I became something of an expert in tramp culture, which eventually made these arcane cultural situations part of my own understanding of the world and the nature of deviance.

MICRO-MACRO CONNECTION

Sexual Abuse and the Clergy

Some waves of deviance are considered so horrible that they fundamentally change previously positive perceptions of the individuals and institutions involved. In 2002, the *Boston Globe* published a story about a Catholic priest who had sexually molested children in six Boston parishes between 1962 and 1993 (cited in Jost, 2002). It wasn't the first time such behavior had received media or Church attention. For decades, stories about priests sexually abusing children had periodically popped up in the press.

What gave the 2002 *Boston Globe* story unusual impact was that it focused on the Church's handling of sexual abuse allegations over the years. In the past, priests had routinely been allowed to remain in their posts despite repeated accusations and even admissions of sexual misconduct. In other cases, the Church quietly reassigned abusive priests to different parishes. The 2002 story pointed out that Church officials had known of this particular priest's behavior since 1984, nine years before he was finally removed from his last parish. Further investigation revealed that the Archdiocese of Boston had quietly settled suits against 70 priests over the preceding decade, often stipulating that in exchange for financial settlement, the victims were not to discuss the cases publicly (Jost, 2002). Under mounting public pressure, the Boston archdiocese agreed to give prosecutors the names of 100 other priests who had been accused of sexual molestation.

Eventually, similar stories began appearing all over the country. Since that first newspaper story appeared, some 4,400 priests have faced allegations of sexual abuse (U.S. Conference of Catholic Bishops, 2011). The majority of victims were between the ages of 11 and 14 at the time of the abuse, and 81% were male (Terry, 2004). Often the most vulnerable children made the easiest victims. One Wisconsin priest molested as many as 200 deaf boys from the 1950s to the 1970s.

Reports of clergy sexual abuse began to surface in other countries as well, like Australia, Canada, New Zealand, Germany, and Great Britain. A government commission in Ireland found that between 1930 and 1990, thousands of children were sexually abused by Catholic priests in orphanages and reform schools (Jordan, 2009). Even a decade after this scandal came to the public's attention, allegations continue to emerge on a weekly basis worldwide.

And it soon became clear that although the problem was most severe in the Catholic Church, it wasn't unique to Catholics. Charges involving Orthodox Jewish rabbis, Protestant ministers, and Hare Krishna gurus were disclosed. The three companies that insure the majority of Protestant churches in the United States receive about 260 reports each year of children being sexually abused by ministers, church staff, or volunteers ("Protestant Church Insurers," 2007). Even nuns have been found guilty of sexual abuse (Einhorn, 2007). What many had hoped was an isolated problem of a few individual bad priests has now become a full-scale, national scandal that crosses geographic and denominational boundaries.

One sociologically interesting element of this scandal is that it clearly shows the limitations of relying on absolute stereotypes about what "deviants" look like. If there is any profession that fails to fit the image of "deviance," it's the clergy. Priests, ministers, nuns, rabbis, and imams are often the most respected individuals in their communities. Most of them are able to confidently preach against sin and extol a virtuous life. Like Kelly Michaels or even Diane Cherchio, they don't fit the stereotype of the sleazy, drooling "child molester."

So it's no surprise that there wasn't much of an institutional response or even considerable public outrage when allegations of clergy abuse were reported decades ago. Even when such charges are substantiated, the collective response tends to be that these were "sick" priests, glaring exceptions to the stereotype of the clergy as benevolent shepherds. In 2010, the Vatican secretary of state, Cardinal Tarcisio Bertone, linked the sexual abuse to the "pathological" homosexuality of a few wayward priests (Donadio, 2010a). They were troubled individuals who, with enough compassion and psychiatric treatment, could change their ways. One church official in the 1960s even put a down payment on a Caribbean island that he planned to use as a retreat to sequester sexually predatory priests (Goodstein, 2009). Interestingly, however, according to a massive five-year study of the scandal commissioned by the United States Conference of Catholic Bishops (2011), less than 5% of abusive priests exhibited behavior consistent with a psychiatric diagnosis of pedophilia. In other words, this phenomenon is not simply a matter of a few "bad apples."

Consequently, these kinds of "sympathetic" responses to abusive priests have drawn widespread public outrage as more and more charges of institutional deception and cover-ups continue to surface. The scandal has created an ongoing crisis within the Church that pits those who support the traditional approach of protecting bishops and priests above all else against those calling for more openness and accountability (Donadio, 2010b). While these internal battles rage, devout Catholics have found their everyday lives shattered and their faith in their Church crushed. As one theologian put it,

> This is the greatest crisis in the modern history of the Catholic Church. It raises serious questions about the integrity of its priesthood, and the Catholic Church just can't function without a priesthood that has the support and trust of its people. (quoted in Jost, 2002, p. 395)

The financial fallout from this scandal has been steep. In 2003, the Boston archdiocese agreed to pay $85 million to settle more than 500 lawsuits brought by people who claimed they were sexually abused as children. In 2007, the San Diego diocese settled a lawsuit for $200 million (Archibold, 2007). That same year, the Los Angeles archdiocese agreed to pay $660 million to the more than 500 people who had made allegations of sexual abuse (Flaccus, 2007). In Delaware, one man—who was sexually abused more than 100 times by a Catholic priest—was awarded $30 million in 2011, the largest single victim award to date (Goodstein, 2010b). That same year, the Northwest Jesuits, a Roman Catholic religious order covering Oregon, Washington, Idaho, Montana, and Alaska, agreed to pay $166 million to 500 victims, many of whom were American Indians and Alaska natives abused in Indian boarding schools decades ago (W. Yardley, 2011). In addition to monetary settlements, nearly one third of U.S. Catholics in a nationwide survey said they had withheld weekly monetary offerings to the Church in the wake of the scandal (cited in Mulrine, 2003). With shrinking financial support, several dioceses around the country have been forced to close down churches. The Boston archdiocese, for instance, closed down 65 of its 357 parishes in 2004 ("Boston Archdiocese," 2004). The Milwaukee diocese filed for bankruptcy in 2011.

Victims' advocacy groups continue to put pressure on the Church to adopt a "zero tolerance" policy. As a result, changes have occurred in the way the Church deals with the problem. Proven perpetrators are now removed from ministry, and church personnel are trained to detect and investigate abuse allegations (T. D. Lytton, 2007). In 2002, the U.S. Conference of Catholic Bishops drafted the *Charter for the Protection of Children and Young People*, which requires churches to implement "safe environment" programs designed to ensure the security of all children as they participate in church and religious activities.

When there are only a few cases of deviance, they're easy to dismiss as individual anomalies. However, when they occur by the thousands, all across the world and in a variety of settings, they come to represent a glaring problem at the institutional level and thus become more likely to provoke serious societal reaction.

Explaining Deviant Behavior

The question of how certain acts and certain people come to be defined as deviant is different from the question of why people do or don't commit acts that are considered deviant. Psychological or biological theories addressing this question might focus on the personality or physical characteristics that give rise to deviant behavior, such as psychological proneness to violence or addiction, genetic predispositions, chemical imbalances, or neurological defects. Most sociological theories, however, focus on the environmental forces that act upon people and the effectiveness of various methods to control them.

The structural-functionalist perspective, for instance, tells us that it is in society's interest to socialize everyone to strive for success so that the most able and talented people will come to occupy the most important positions. Sociologist Robert Merton's "strain theory" (1957) argues that the probability of committing deviant acts increases when people experience a strain or contradiction between these culturally defined success goals and access to legitimate means by which to achieve them. The despair and hopelessness that accompany sudden economic hardship can sometimes evoke anger and blame, leading to violence. For instance, some criminologists noted an unprecedented spike in mass murders in 2009 during the height of the economic recession. In the span of one month, there were eight mass murders that took the lives of 57 people (cited in Rucker, 2009).

More commonly, though, those who believe that being wealthy and achieving the "American dream" are important goals but have no money, employment opportunities, or access to higher education will be inclined to achieve the goal of financial success through illegitimate means (Merton, 1957). One of the most consistent findings in criminal research is the correlation between unemployment (a factor closely associated with economic disadvantage) and property crime (Hagan, 2000). In this sense, people who sell, say, illegal drugs or stolen cell phones to get rich are motivated by the same desire as people who sell real estate or flat screen TVs to get rich. But people who lack access to legitimate means to achieve success may also reject the culturally defined goal of success and retreat from society altogether. According to Merton, deviants such as vagrants, chronic drunks, drug addicts, and the mentally ill fall into this category.

Another sociologist, Edwin Sutherland, bases his theory of deviance (Sutherland & Cressey, 1955) on the symbolic interactionist principle that we all interpret life through the symbols and meanings we learn in our interactions with others. Sutherland argues that individuals learn deviant patterns of behavior from the people with whom they associate on a regular basis: friends, family members, peers. Through our associations with these influential individuals, we learn not only the techniques for committing deviant acts (e.g., how to pick a lock or how to snort cocaine) but also a set of beliefs and attitudes that justify or rationalize such behavior (Sykes & Matza, 1957). To commit deviant acts on a regular basis, we must learn how to perceive those acts as normal.

Deterring Deviance

Some sociologists have turned away from the issue of why some people violate norms to the issue of why most people don't (see, e.g., Hirschi, 1969). Their concern is with the mechanisms society has in place to control or constrain people's behavior. **Deterrence theory** assumes that people are rational decision makers who calculate the potential costs and benefits of a behavior before they act. If the benefits of a deviant act (e.g., money or psychological satisfaction) outweigh the costs (e.g., getting caught and punished), we will be inclined to do it. Conversely, if the costs exceed the benefits, the theory predicts that we'll decide it's not worth the risk (van den Haag, 1975).

The controversy surrounding capital punishment is, essentially, a debate over its true capacity to deter potentially violent criminals. According to deterrence theory, a punishment, to be effective, must be swift as well as certain and severe. However, capital punishment is anything but swift. Currently, about 3,200 inmates are on death row in the United States, but only 1,188 prisoners have been executed since 1977, when the death penalty was reinstated. On average, death row inmates spend 14 years awaiting execution, a figure that has been growing steadily for three decades (Snell, 2010; see Exhibit 8.1).

Exhibit 8.1   Time Spent on Death Row

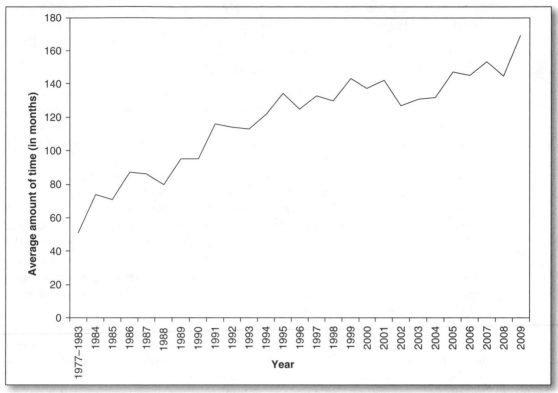

SOURCE: Snell, 2010, Table 12

In addition, opponents of the death penalty argue that violent offenders are often under the influence of drugs or alcohol or are consumed by passion when they commit an act of violence; their violence is more or less spontaneous. Hence, they may not be thinking rationally (weighing the potential benefits of the act against the costs of punishment) at the time of the crime. The threat of being condemned to death may not deter such people when they are committing the act. Researchers have, indeed, found little empirical support for the argument that the threat of capital punishment reduces murders (W. C. Bailey, 1990; Galliher & Galliher, 2002). Nor have they found that well-publicized executions deter homicides (R. D. Peterson & Bailey, 1991). In fact, over the past two decades, the homicide rate in the 38 states with the death penalty has been 48% to 100% higher than in the 12 states without the death penalty (Bonner & Fessenden, 2000).

Most societies around the world have abandoned the use of capital punishment for both moral and practical reasons: It's inhumane, and it doesn't deter crime. Even in China, a country responsible for most of the world's court-ordered executions, legislators voted in 2006 to bar all but the nation's highest court from approving death sentences ("China Changes," 2006). Nevertheless, the majority of U.S. citizens—about 64% according to one study—continue to favor the death penalty (Pew Research Center, 2007b). Legislative efforts to increase the number of offenses punishable by death and to reduce the number of "death row" appeals an offender can file reflect this popular attitude. However, such a position can sometimes conflict with economic realities. During the current recession, lawmakers in several states have pushed bills to abolish the death penalty, not on moral grounds but to cut costs. Some have argued that capital punishment cases cost states nearly three times as much as homicide cases where the death penalty is not sought (Urbina, 2009).

Labeling Deviants

These theories help us explain why some people engage in deviant acts and others don't, but they bypass the question of why certain acts committed by certain people are considered deviant in the first place. ***Labeling theory*** attempts to answer this question by characterizing a deviant person as someone—such as the preschool teacher Kelly Michaels—to whom the label "deviant" has been successfully applied (Becker, 1963; Lemert, 1972). According to this theory, the process of being singled out, defined, and reacted to as deviant changes a person in the eyes of others and has important life consequences for the individual. Once the label sticks, others may react to the labeled deviant with rejection, suspicion, withdrawal, fear, mistrust, and hatred (A. K. Cohen, 1966). A deviant label suggests that the person holding it is habitually given to the types of undesirable motives and behavior thought to be typical of others so labeled. The "ex-convict" is seen as a cold-blooded and ruthless character incapable of reforming, the "mental patient" as dangerous and unpredictable, the "alcoholic" as weak willed, the "prostitute" as dirty and immoral.

The problem, of course, is that such labels overgeneralize and can be misleading. For instance, a study by two marketing professors found that convicted felons showed just as much integrity as MBA (Master of Business Administration) students on a test of ethics related to difficult business situations. In fact, the convicts were less likely than the students to indicate that they'd steal employees from competitors or scrimp on customer service to increase profits ("MBA vs. Prison," 1999).

The type of deviant who receives the harshest expressions of public outrage changes with some regularity. At various times, child molesters, crack addicts, and drug dealers have claimed the title of society's most despised deviant. Currently, foreign terrorists, greedy Wall Street executives, and cyberstalkers fit the bill. Often, collective hostility is directed toward people who don't seem to pose a grave societal threat, like those who talk loudly on cell phones. Cigarette smoking used to be seen as a sign of sophistication; nowadays many people consider smoking filthy and disgusting, and smokers are often banished from buildings and forced to keep their distance from entryways. Across the country, landlords of privately owned multiple housing units have begun to forbid smoking *inside* people's apartments.

Cities around the country sometimes use humiliating labels as an alternative to incarceration. For example, an Illinois man convicted of assault was once required to place a large sign at the end of his driveway that read WARNING: A VIOLENT FELON LIVES HERE. TRAVEL AT YOUR OWN RISK. In some states, convicted drunk drivers have to put special license plates on their cars, and convicted shoplifters must take out ads in local newspapers that use their photograph and announce their crimes. The Chicago police department posts on its Web site photographs and partial addresses of men arrested for soliciting prostitution, even though they've not yet been convicted. Other cities, like Denver, Akron, and Durham, post this information on local television stations. Oakland and Omaha display photographs of such offenders on prominent billboards (Ruethling, 2005).

Sometimes the humiliation doesn't even involve law enforcement. When security guards at a Chinese grocery store in Queens, New York, catch suspected shoplifters, the store manager photographs them holding the items they're suspected of stealing. In lieu of contacting the police, the store imposes a fine. If the suspects don't or can't pay, the store prominently displays their photos at the entrance (Kilgannon & Singer, 2010). Such penalties are designed to shame the labeled individuals into behaving properly and to deter others from committing such crimes. In the process, they satisfy the public's need for dramatic moral condemnation of deviants (Hoffman, 1997).

Deviant labels can impair an individual's eligibility to enter a broad range of socially acceptable roles. Many state penal systems use an instrument called the "Psychopathy Checklist–Revised" to decide if an inmate should be awarded parole. The battery of questions yields a score that allegedly determines if the individual is a "psychopath" or not. If an inmate is found to be a "psychopath" and therefore not eligible for parole, the label stays on his or her permanent record, rendering future positive parole decisions unlikely or even impossible ("This American Life," 2011b).

Consider also the impact of the 1994 Federal Crime Bill on convicted sex offenders. This law requires states to register and track convicted sex offenders for 10 years after their release from prison and to privately notify police departments when the sex offenders move into their community. A Web site, NeighborhoodScan.com, provides information on released sexual offenders in all 50 states, including their names, addresses, and photographs. Many states have "sexually violent predator" statutes that give officials the power to commit violent sex offenders to mental hospitals involuntarily or to retain them in prison indefinitely *after* their prison terms are up (C. Goldberg, 2001). These convicts have "paid their debt" to society by serving their mandated punishment. But under these laws, convicted sex offenders can never fully shed their deviant identity. Finding a decent place to live or a decent job may be a problem for the rest of their lives.

And it's not just sex offenders who must navigate the stigmatizing effects of their deviant labels. Several states are seeking to establish online registries for offenders who engage in a wide range of crimes including arson, drunk driving, methamphetamine production, and animal cruelty (Erica Goode, 2011b). The appeal of these laws is hard to understate. According to one law professor, "You'd be hard pressed to find a more politically popular movement in recent years. Whether it's actually good public policy is a distinct and independent question from whether it's politically popular and makes us feel good" (quoted in Erica Goode, 2011b, p. A12).

All ex-offenders experience the "stickiness" of labels to some degree, despite legislative efforts to help them. In 2007, Congress passed the Second Chance Act, which funds a variety of services and resources for ex-offenders in hopes of aiding their reentry into society. Nevertheless, potential employers still commonly refuse to hire ex-convicts, even when the crime has nothing to do with the job requirements. Like the public at large, many employers believe that prisons do not rehabilitate but actually make convicts more deviant by teaching them better ways to commit crimes and by providing social networks for criminal activity outside the prison (R. Johnson, 1987). In recent years—particularly in the wake of the attacks of September 11, 2001—the criminal background check industry has grown dramatically. The public now has greater access to criminal history records of ex-offenders than ever before through such Web sites as CriminalSearches.com and ScreenStaff.com. Nine out of 10 companies—both large and small—now use criminal background checks as part of their hiring process.

An examination of jobs posted on Craigslist found several hundred ads that contained statements that the company wouldn't consider applicants with criminal records: for example, "Do not apply with any misdemeanors/felonies," "You must not have any felony or misdemeanor convictions on your record. Period," and "We are looking for people with . . . spotless background/criminal history" (M. N. Rodriguez & Emsellem, 2011).

In addition, being labeled as deviant may actually increase the probability that the behavior itself will stay the same or become worse (Archer, 1985). A great many ex-convicts in the United States do return to prison. According to the U.S. Department of Justice, a little over two thirds of all ex-convicts released in 1994 were arrested for a new offense within three years, and 47% were convicted again (see Exhibit 8.2).

Exhibit 8.2   Recidivism Rate of Prisoners Released in 1994

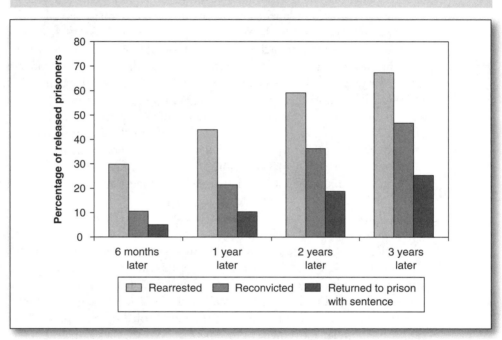

SOURCE: Langan & Levin, 2002, Table 2

Deviant labels are so powerful that a mere accusation of dangerous activity can taint a person's character. In 2009, two Muslim immigrants from Morocco enlisted in the Army National Guard. They both successfully completed basic training, but just prior to leaving the base in South Carolina they were questioned by military investigators who suspected them and three other Moroccan immigrants of plotting to poison fellow soldiers. They were placed under military arrest. For the next month and a half, the Army prevented them from calling their families without military personnel present, barred them from speaking to each other in Arabic, and required them to go to the mess hall and bathroom with an escort. It wasn't until 2010 that the Army concluded that the allegations against them were completely unfounded. However, despite their innocence, the FBI has kept its investigation open. As a result the two men have been unable to receive security clearances, become citizens, obtain concealed weapons permits, or get government jobs (Dao, 2011).

NANCY HERMAN

Becoming an Ex-Crazy

Sociologist Nancy Herman (1993) was interested in how labeling can weaken a person's self-image, create "deviant" patterns of behavior, and lead to social rejection. She was especially concerned about how former mental patients are reintegrated into society after their release from a psychiatric hospital. She decided to study ex–mental patients because her father had been an occupational therapist at a large psychiatric institute in Ontario, Canada. She spent most of her childhood and adolescence roaming the halls talking to patients. From time to time, the patients would spend Thanksgiving and Christmas with her family.

For this study, she conducted in-depth interviews with 146 former nonchronic mental patients (hospitalized in short intervals for less than two years) and 139 former chronic mental patients (hospitalized continuously for two or more years). She interviewed them in a variety of settings, such as coffee shops, malls, and their own homes. Many subjects invited her to their self-help group meetings and therapy sessions.

Herman found that these ex-patients, on release, noticed right away that friends, neighbors, coworkers, and family members were responding to them on the basis of their "mental illness" label and not on the basis of their identity prior to hospitalization. Although their treatment was complete (i.e., they were "cured" of their "illness"), others still saw them as defective. They were often made to feel like failures for not measuring up to the rest of "normal" society. As one woman put it,

> When I was released, I presumed that I could resume with the "good times" once again. I was treated—I paid my dues. But I was wrong. From the first moment I set foot back onto the streets of "Wilsonville" and I tried to return to my kids . . . I learned the hard way that my kids didn't want nothing to do with me. They were scared to let me near the grandkids—that I might do something to them. They told me this right to my face. . . . Having mental illness is like having any other illness like heart troubles, but people sure do treat you different. If you have heart troubles, you get treated, and then you come out good as new and your family still loves you. But that's not so with mental illness . . . you come out and people treat you worse than a dog! (quoted in Herman, 1993, p. 303)

On release, some of the former patients Herman interviewed were quite open about their illness and attempted to present themselves in as "normal" a way as they could. Others became political activists who used their "ex–mental patient" label to try to dispel common myths about mental illness or to advocate for patients' rights. But most of the former patients spent a great deal of time selectively concealing and disclosing information regarding their illness and treatment. Strategies of concealment included avoiding certain individuals, redirecting conversations so that the topic was less likely to come up, lying about their absence, and withdrawing from social interaction. Constant concern that people might "find out" created a great deal of anxiety, fear, and frustration, as described by this 56-year-old woman:

> It's a very difficult thing. It's not easy to distinguish the good ones from the bad ones. . . . You've gotta figure out who you can tell about your illness and who you better not tell. It is a tremendous stress and strain that you have to live with 24 hours a day! (quoted in Herman, 1993, p. 306)

The stickiness of the "crazy" label is difficult for former mental patients. However, Herman's research also shows that ex-patients are not powerless victims of negative societal reactions, passively accepting the deviant identity others attribute to them. Rather, they are strategists and impression managers who play active roles in transforming themselves from "abnormal" to "normal."

Linking Power, Deviance, and Social Control

Because deviance is socially defined, the behaviors and conditions that come to be called "deviant" can at times appear somewhat arbitrary. Sociologists working from the conflict perspective would say that definitions of and responses to deviance are often a form of social control exerted by more powerful people and groups over less powerful people and groups. In U.S. society, the predominant means of controlling those whose behavior does not conform to the norms established by the powerful are criminalization and medicalization. Labeling people either as criminals or as sick people gives socially powerful individuals, groups, and organizations a way to marginalize and discount certain people who challenge the status quo. Criminalization and medicalization also have economic and other benefits for certain powerful groups.

The Criminalization of Deviance

Presumably, certain acts are defined as crimes because they offend the majority of people in a given society. Most of us trust our legal institutions—legislators, courts, the police, and prisons—to regulate social behavior in the interest of the common good. But according to the conflict perspective, most societies ensure that offenders who are processed through the criminal justice system are members of the lowest socioeconomic class (Reiman, 2007). Poor people are more likely to get arrested, be formally charged with a crime, have their cases go to trial, get convicted, and receive harsher sentences than more affluent citizens (Parenti, 1995; Reiman, 2007). In 2002, 69 poor people in Atlanta who had been arrested on petty charges—shoplifting, trespassing, public drunkenness—and who couldn't afford bail remained in jail for weeks, and in some cases months, awaiting a lawyer and a court date, despite a law that requires anyone arrested for a misdemeanor to go before a judge or lawyer within 48 hours. All of them had spent more time behind bars than they would have had they been convicted (Rimer, 2002).

The quality of legal representation for defendants in criminal cases is also skewed along socioeconomic lines. When wealthy or powerful individuals are tried for capital crimes (an occurrence that, in and of itself, is rare), they are usually able to afford effective legal representation. In contrast, poor defendants in such cases are often represented by public defenders, who have fewer resources available for investigative work and who may have little, if any, experience in such matters. For instance, in one Alabama case, the public defender for a poor man facing the death penalty had never tried a capital case and had no money to hire an investigator before the case went to trial. The defendant was sentenced to death. In 2008, three North Carolina death row inmates were released in a span of six months because appeals courts found that evidence that would have favored the defendants was withheld during their trials. As one critic of capital punishment put it, "The problem with the death penalty [is] not the method of execution . . . [it's] poor people getting lousy lawyers" (quoted in Dewan, 2008, p. A1).

Cases like these have intensified the national debate over class—not to mention racial—disparities in the quality of legal representation. Ninety-eight percent of chief district attorneys in death penalty states are white; 1% are black. Since 1977, 15 white defendants have been executed for murdering black victims; during the same period, 246 black defendants have been executed for killing white victims (Death Penalty Information Center, 2010). In response, some states have taken steps to address biases, especially in the way capital cases are handled:

- In 2001, the governor of Illinois called for a moratorium on executions in his state after 13 men on death row—most of whom were either Latino or African American and all of whom were poor and had been represented in their trials by public defenders—were proven innocent. Two years later, he commuted all death sentences in the state to prison terms of life or less after declaring the system fundamentally flawed and unfair (Wilgoren, 2003).
- Concerned about the inadequate legal representation poor defendants were receiving, the American Bar Association in 2001 passed a resolution calling for a nationwide moratorium on executions (Fleischaker, 2004).
- In 2002, the governor of Maryland imposed a moratorium on executions in his state because of concerns over racial bias. In Maryland, 81% of homicide victims are African American, yet 84% of death sentences were cases involving white victims. Two thirds of the people on death row there are African American (Amnesty International, 2004a).
- In 2006, the state of New Jersey enacted a one-year moratorium on executions by the state. In 2007, New Jersey joined 13 other states in abolishing the death penalty altogether. As a result, all eight inmates on death row had their sentences commuted to life in prison.

Persistent imbalances in the justice system go beyond the way disadvantaged people are treated by the police, judges, attorneys, and juries. If they were simply a matter of discrimination, the situation would be relatively easy to address. Instead, they occur because the actions of poor individuals are more likely to be ***criminalized***—that is, officially defined as crimes in the first place. When poor people do commit certain crimes—car theft, burglary, assault, illegal drug use, and so on—they become "typical criminals" in the public eye (Reiman, 2007).

The Social Reality of Crime

Followers of the conflict perspective point out that powerful groups often try to foster a belief that society's rules are under attack by deviants and that official action against them is needed. The strategy has worked well. In polls taken in the United States in the 1980s and 1990s, an average of 83% of respondents felt that the justice system was not harsh enough in dealing with criminals (Gaubatz, 1995). Ever since, governments at the state and federal level have responded to popular sentiment by "getting tough on crime"—cracking down on drug users and dealers, reviving the death penalty, scaling back parole eligibility, lengthening prison sentences, and building more prisons. By 1999, 15 states had abolished parole boards and early-release programs, resulting in more prisoners serving their full sentences (Butterfield, 1999).

Not surprisingly, the inmate population in this country has swelled. In 1970, there were fewer than 200,000 people in state and federal prisons; by 2009, that figure had grown to 2.3 million (West, 2010). Another 5.1 million are under community supervision—that is, on probation, or on parole. That adds up to a little over 3% of the entire adult population who've been convicted of a crime and whose lives are under the jurisdiction of the state, at a cost of close to $50 billion a year (S. Moore, 2009). Add in the 1.5 million or so ex-offenders who exit supervision each year because they've completed their probation (Glaze & Bonczar, 2010) and you get what one author called "a nation of ex-cons" (Gonnerman, 2004). This situation is less a function of some staggeringly high number of serious criminals in this country than it is of the "tough on crime" policies that have taken hold in the last few decades. In 2009, the U.S. incarceration rate was 748 prisoners per 100,000 people (West, 2010). No other industrialized country comes close to this figure (see Exhibit 8.3).

Exhibit 8.3   Incarceration Rates Worldwide

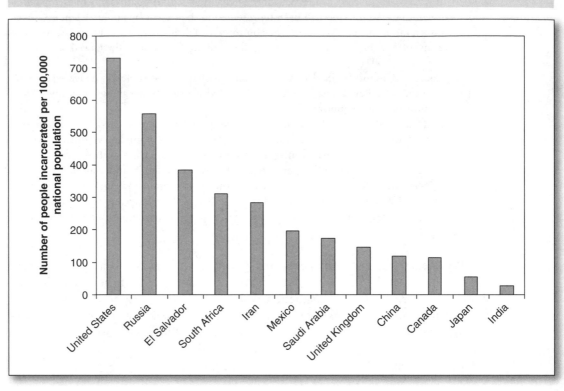

SOURCE: International Centre for Prison Studies, 2011

But other problems have popped up. For instance, increasing rates of incarceration have been accompanied by heightened police surveillance and supervision in poor communities. The number of police per capita has increased dramatically in the past several decades (A. Goffman, 2009). Hovering police helicopters and video cameras mounted on streetlights have become the ubiquitous markers of poor urban neighborhoods. As a consequence, a climate of fear and suspicion has gripped these communities. In such an environment, life for everyone is anxious and unsettled: "Family members and friends are pressured to inform on one another and young men live as suspects and fugitives, with the daily fear of confinement" (A. Goffman, 2009, p. 353).

Newly released inmates—who are likely to be poor and members of ethnoracial minorities—are also significantly less likely than their counterparts of two decades ago to find jobs and stay out of the kind of trouble that leads to further imprisonment (Butterfield, 2000). Many states have sharply curtailed education, job training, and other rehabilitation programs inside prison. In addition, parole officers are quicker to rescind a newly released inmate's parole for relatively minor infractions, such as failing a drug test. In California, for instance, four out of five former inmates who return to prison do so *not* for committing new crimes but for violating the conditions of their parole.

The question you might ask is, "Who benefits when it becomes so hard for ex-convicts to stay out of prison?" According to advocates of the conflict perspective, the law is not merely a mechanism that protects good people from bad people; it is a political instrument used by specific groups to further their own interests, often at the expense of others' (W. Chambliss, 1964; Quinney, 1970). Law is, of course, determined by legislative action. But legislatures are greatly influenced by powerful segments of society, such as lobbying groups, political action committees, individual campaign contributors, and so on.

Tellingly, the acts that threaten the economic or political interests of the groups that have the power to influence public policy are more likely to be criminalized (and more likely to be punished) than are the deviant acts these groups commit. For instance, it's against the law to fail to report income on one's annual tax return. But poor working people are far more likely to be audited by the Internal Revenue Service (IRS) than wealthy people (Johnston, 2002). That's not surprising, given that the IRS looks for tax cheating by wage earners much more closely than it does for cheating by corporations or by people whose money comes from their own businesses, investments, partnerships, and trusts.

Through the mass media, dominant groups influence the public to look at crime in ways that are favorable to them. The selective portrayal of crime plays an important role in shaping public perceptions of the "crime problem" and therefore its "official" definition. For instance, decades of research show that the crimes depicted on television are significantly more likely to be violent than actual crimes committed in the real world (cited in Reiman, 2007). When politicians talk about fighting the U.S. crime problem or when news shows report fluctuations in crime rates, they are almost always referring to street crimes (illegal drug use, robbery, burglary, murder, assault, etc.) rather than corporate crimes, governmental crimes, or crimes committed by people in influential positions.

Such coverage creates a way of perceiving crime that becomes social reality. We accept the "fact" that certain people or actions are a threat to the well-being of the entire society and therefore a threat to our own personal interests.

Corporate and White Collar Crime

Consequently, people in the United States take for granted that street crime is our worst social problem and that corporate crime is not as dangerous or as costly (Reiman, 2007). U.S. citizens simply shake their heads over the exploitative practices of corporations or wealthy despots in places such as the rain forests of Brazil and Indonesia and the sweatshops of Southeast Asia. However, unsafe work conditions; dangerous chemicals in the air, water, and food; faulty consumer products; and unnecessary surgery actually put people who live in the United States in more constant and imminent physical danger than do ordinary street crimes (Mokhiber, 1999). Approximately 16,000 Americans were murdered in 2008 (U.S. Bureau of the Census, 2011b). At the same time, about 5,000 Americans died while on the job (U.S. Bureau of Labor Statistics, 2011c). According to the Centers for Disease Control and Prevention, approximately 20,000 U.S. cancer deaths each year are attributable to occupational exposure (Centers for Disease Control and Prevention, 2011b), and almost 100,000 people die annually from infections they contract in hospitals or clinics (Klevens et al., 2007). Add in the 3.3 million Americans who suffer from nonfatal workplace injuries and illnesses each year (U.S. Bureau of Labor Statistics, 2010f) and you can see that street crime is not our biggest threat.

Corporate and white collar crimes also pose greater economic threats to U.S. citizens than does street crime. The FBI estimates that burglary and robbery cost the United States $3.8 billion a year. The total cost of white collar crimes like corporate fraud, bribery, embezzlement, insurance fraud, and securities fraud amounts to perhaps as much as $500 billion a year (Reiman, 2007).

To be fair, some people actually do view certain types of corporate misbehavior as more serious than street crimes (Mokhiber, 2000). Indeed, the financial crisis that first gripped the nation in 2008 created a firestorm of public anger that cast unprecedented scrutiny on white collar misconduct. President Obama vowed to crack down on Wall Street bankers for their "reckless practices" (P. Baker & Herszenhorn, 2010). Across the country, attorneys began to indict loan processors, mortgage brokers, and bank officials on various types of financial fraud. Congress and the Department of Justice plotted strategies for an all-out federal attack. As one lawyer who represents white collar clients put it, "It's going to be open season" on corporate officials (Segal, 2009, p. A19).

In a few high-profile cases, executives convicted of corporate malfeasance have, indeed, received harsh prison sentences:

- In 2006, Jeffrey Skilling, former CEO of Enron, received a 24-year sentence for securities fraud and other crimes.
- In 2009, a wealthy stockbroker and financial adviser named Bernard Madoff pled guilty to charges of securities fraud, investment fraud, mail fraud, wire fraud, money laundering, and theft from an employee benefit plan, to name a few. Prosecutors estimated that these schemes cost his clients about $65 billion. The judge called Madoff's actions "extraordinarily evil" and sentenced him to 150 years in prison, an act that was largely symbolic considering that Madoff was 71 years old at the time (Henriques, 2009).
- In 2011, billionaire hedge fund manager Raj Rajaratnam was found guilty of securities fraud and conspiracy. He's looking at 25 years in prison.

But responses like these have been directed largely at individual white collar criminals. Corporations themselves rarely receive heavy criminal punishment when their dangerous actions violate the law (Reiman, 2007). For example, even after it was revealed that Bayer AG—a German pharmaceutical company—had failed to disclose the results of a study that indicated that a widely used heart surgery medicine increases the risk of death and stroke, the Food and Drug Administration (FDA) did not take the drug off the market (G. Harris, 2006). In 2004, the pharmaceutical company GlaxoSmithKline agreed to settle a $2.5 million lawsuit brought by New York State alleging that the company had hidden the results of drug trials showing that its antidepressant Paxil might have deadly side effects, such as increasing suicidal thoughts in children.

At congressional hearings, lawmakers berated executives from GlaxoSmithKline and other drug companies for hiding study results that challenged the effectiveness of their drugs. The companies promised to do better. But according to studies financed by the National Institutes of Health, crucial facts about many clinical trials continue to be withheld from the FDA (cited in Berenson, 2005).

To ease the inconvenience of prosecution for corporate wrongdoers, the U.S. Department of Justice has instituted a form of corporate probation. Several major companies that have been charged with billions of dollars' worth of accounting fraud, bid rigging, and other illegal financial schemes—including American International Group, PNC Financial Services Group, Merrill Lynch, AOL–Time Warner, and American Express—have agreed to *deferred prosecutions*, in which they accept responsibility for wrongdoing, agree not to fight the charges, agree to cooperate with investigations, pay a fine, and implement changes in their corporate structure to prevent future criminal wrongdoing. If a company abides by the agreement for a specified time—usually

12 months—prosecutors will drop all charges (Mokhiber & Weissman, 2004). Between 2005 and 2008, the Department of Justice made deferred prosecution agreements with more than 50 companies accused of criminal activity (Lichtblau, 2008). In 2009, UBS AG, Switzerland's largest bank, entered a deferred prosecution agreement on charges that it had helped U.S. taxpayers hide accounts from the IRS. In exchange for a dismissal of the charges, the bank agreed to pay $780 million in fines, penalties, interest, and restitution; acknowledge responsibility for its actions and omissions; and continue cooperating with Justice Department officials (U.S. Department of Justice, 2009).

Such arrangements are meant to avoid more drastic punishment, which could destroy these companies and cost thousands of innocent employees their jobs. For instance, when the government aggressively prosecuted the Arthur Andersen accounting firm in 2002 for its criminal role in the famous Enron scandal, 28,000 employees lost their jobs (Lichtblau, 2008). But the penalties companies do receive are usually relatively minor and don't do much to deter their future law violations. Fines of hundreds of millions of dollars may sound like a hefty sum to you and me, but for companies that earn hundreds of *billions* of dollars annually, they barely make a dent. For instance, in the five years leading up to the 2010 Gulf of Mexico drilling rig explosion that killed 11 people and dumped nearly 5 million barrels of oil into the water, British Petroleum had received more than $550 million in fines for violations of safety codes, environmental laws, and antitrust statutes. Those fines added up to one tenth of a percent of its revenue over that period. In 2010, the Securities and Exchange Commission imposed a $550 million fine on Goldman Sachs for securities fraud. It was the largest penalty ever paid by a Wall Street firm. However, the company earned $51.7 billion that year, so the fine worked out to about four *days* of earnings ("Do Fines Ever," 2010). It's no wonder that many large corporations consider the punishments they receive for wrongdoing simply a cost of doing business.

The imbalance in the legal response to these crimes versus street crimes is glaring. If you were an individual thief who had robbed a bank at gunpoint, a shop owner who had defrauded your customers of millions of dollars, or a small businessperson who had knowingly manufactured a potentially lethal product, it's highly unlikely that you would be allowed to avoid any criminal prosecution simply by "cooperating with the investigation." Our massive law enforcement and criminal justice machinery would no doubt mobilize its vast resources to see that you were prosecuted to the fullest extent of the law. Yet large corporations engage in such activities every day, largely without much public outcry or moral panic. In fact, most aren't even prosecuted under criminal statutes. Between 1982 and 2002, about 170,000 American workers died on the job. During that same period, federal and state workplace safety agencies investigated 1,798 fatality cases in which companies had *willfully* violated workplace safety laws—for instance, by removing safety devices to speed up production, denying workers proper safety gear, or simply ignoring explicit safety warnings. But only 104 of these cases were ever prosecuted. And of those, only 16 resulted in criminal convictions (Barstow, 2003).

Why aren't these dangerous and costly corporate acts considered deviant the way face-to-face street crimes are? According to sociologist Jeffrey Reiman (2007), the answer resides in the perceived circumstances surrounding these acts. People typically see the injuries caused by corporate crime as unintentional, indirect, and a consequence of an endeavor defined in this culture as legitimate or socially productive: making a profit. In most people's minds, someone who tries to harm someone else is usually considered more evil than someone who harms without intending to.

Moreover, harming someone directly seems more deviant than harming someone indirectly. Finally, harm that results from illegitimate activities is usually considered more serious than harm that is a by-product of standard business activities.

The Menace of "Illegal" Drugs

Different cultures show varying levels of tolerance when it comes to drug use. For instance, throughout the South Pacific, people commonly chew betel nuts for their stimulant effects. In the Bolivian and Peruvian Andes, people chew coca leaves during their ordinary workday. The Huichol of central Mexico ingest peyote—a small cactus that produces hallucinations—as part of their religious rituals.

In the United States, we wink at the use of many substances that alter people's state of mind, such as coffee, chocolate, and alcohol. In 2011, companies began marketing baked goods with names like "Lazy Cakes," "Kush Cakes," and "Lulla Pies" that contain the sleep-inducing substance melatonin. The pastries bear labels warning against operating heavy machinery or driving after eating them. One consumer said, "It knocks you out—in a good way, not a bad way. For me, it's not to chill. For me, it's to get a good night's sleep" (quoted in Saint Louis, 2011, p. 4). Nevertheless, because they look and taste like sweet desserts, these products are considered food, not drugs.

But when it comes to illegal drugs, U.S. attitudes change dramatically. Like the term *terrorist*, the term *drugs* is an easy and popular scapegoat on which to heap our collective hatred. The United States has been characterized as a *temperance culture* (Levine, 1992)—one in which self-control and industriousness are perceived as desirable traits of productive citizens. In such an environment, drug-induced states of altered consciousness are likely to be perceived as a loss of control and thus feared as a threat to the economic and physical well-being of the population.

The United States has been in an ill-defined, undeclared, but highly publicized "war" against illegal drugs for more than 40 years at a cost of about $1 trillion and hundreds of thousands of lives (Mendoza, 2010). The Drug Enforcement Administration, the FBI, and the U.S. Customs Service seized more than 4.8 million pounds of illegal drugs in 2009, more than three times as much as was seized in 2000 (U.S. Bureau of the Census, 2011b). More people are behind bars in the United States for drug offenses than there are people in prison for all crimes in England, France, Germany, and Japan combined (Egan, 1999). Federal spending on antidrug campaigns increased from $420 million in 1973 to $12.7 billion in 2006 (Katel, 2006).

With so much attention and resources now focused on homeland security, it would seem that the fight against drug dealers and users could no longer be a national priority. Indeed, cuts in the federal budget have reduced the availability of resources devoted to drug enforcement, and some antidrug programs and agencies have been folded into antiterrorism efforts. Nevertheless, there remains a widespread belief that although terrorists pose an external danger, drug users and drug dealers are slowly destroying the country from within and therefore need to be stopped.

Many conflict sociologists, however, argue that antidrug campaigns and legislative activities are driven chiefly by political interests (see, e.g., Erich Goode, 1989). The war on drugs in the United States has permitted greater social control over groups perceived to be threatening, such as young minority men, and has mobilized voter support for candidates who profess to be "tough" on drugs. Capitalizing on the "drug menace" as a personal and societal threat is a common and effective political tactic (Ben-Yehuda, 1990).

As with deviance in general, the very definition of which substances are "illegal" is influenced by powerful interests. Behind the phrase "war on drugs" is the assumption that illegal drugs (marijuana, ecstasy, cocaine, methamphetamines, heroin, etc.) are the most dangerous substances and the ones that must be eradicated. However, the difference between legal and illegal drugs is not necessarily a function of their relative danger.

For instance, each year about 1,700 U.S. college students die from alcohol-related injuries, nearly 100,000 are victims of alcohol-related sexual assault and rape, 700,000 are assaulted by another student who has been drinking, and close to 3 million are cited for drunken driving (National Institute on Alcohol Abuse and Alcoholism, 2007). But alcohol is big business: Sales of alcoholic beverages topped $167 billion in 2009 (U.S. Bureau of the Census, 2011b). Hence, efforts to completely criminalize it are few and far between. While most colleges now offer "alcohol-free" housing, encourage students to "drink responsibly," or sponsor alcohol-free social events, few have become "dry" campuses, banning alcohol outright.

And even though it is technically a drug, alcohol rarely enters into conversations on "drug abuse." Indeed, the U.S. Drug Enforcement Administration's Web site contains detailed information on marijuana, heroin, cocaine, methamphetamine, ecstasy, oxycodone (OxyContin), hydrocodone, steroids, LSD, and inhalants but makes no mention of alcohol.

Tobacco is an even clearer health risk than alcohol—or marijuana and heroin for that matter (Reiman, 2007). But aside from some age restrictions, it is legally available to anyone. According to the Centers for Disease Control and Prevention (2011c), cigarette smoking is responsible for one in five deaths annually (or about 443,000 deaths a year). If those figures are accurate, more people die from smoking-related causes than from AIDS, illegal drug use, alcohol use, motor vehicle injuries, suicides, and murders combined. The costs of smoking are financial as well as physical. It's estimated that smoking costs the U.S. economy nearly $193 billion annually in both health care costs and lost productivity due to illness (American Lung Association, 2008).

And tobacco doesn't just affect those who choose to consume it directly. More than 126 million nonsmoking U.S. residents are exposed to secondhand smoke at home, in vehicles, at work, and in public places each year. Such exposure, even for brief periods, can cause health problems. Nonsmokers who inhale secondhand smoke at work or at home increase their risk of heart disease by 30% and risk of cancer by 25% (Centers for Disease Control and Prevention, 2006). Almost 50,000 of the above-cited 443,000 cigarette-related deaths are the result of exposure to secondhand smoke (Centers for Disease Control and Prevention, 2011c). Health experts are now paying attention to the harmful effects of "thirdhand" smoke, the residue of tobacco smoke left on walls, furniture, clothes, and house dust.

In 2003, the U.S. Department of Justice took the unprecedented step of demanding that the nation's biggest cigarette makers forfeit $289 billion in profits derived from more than 50 years of dangerous and "fraudulent" marketing practices, such as manipulating nicotine levels, lying to customers about the health effects of smoking, and directing advertising campaigns at children (Lichtblau, 2003). Yet knowing the hazards of selling and smoking cigarettes has not prompted our society to outlaw them entirely, as we have marijuana smoking and cocaine use. It's true that some states have enacted smoking bans in bars, restaurants, and other enclosed public places and some cities have banned outdoor smoking as well (Springen, 2006). And in 2009, President Obama signed into law the Family Smoking Prevention and Tobacco Control Act, which gives the FDA more power to impose stricter controls on the production and sale of cigarettes (D. Wilson, 2009b). But this bill stopped short of completely criminalizing tobacco, which would have had a disastrous impact on many large corporations and on several states whose economies depend on this crop.

The tobacco industry has one of the most powerful lobbies in Washington. In fact, in 2005, the Justice Department decided to reduce the amount it sought in its case from $289 billion to a mere $10 billion, out of concern over the financial impact that the original amount would have on the tobacco companies (Leonnig, 2005). But as efforts to limit or prohibit smoking in this country become more successful (the proportion of 18- to 25-year-olds who currently smoke dropped from 40% in 2003 to 35.7% in 2008 [U.S. Bureau of the Census, 2011b]), tobacco companies are stepping up efforts to combat regulations in other parts of the world. They are fighting advertising limits in Great Britain, larger health warnings in South America, and higher taxes in the Philippines and Mexico. In addition, tobacco companies are spending billions of dollars each year on promotional advertising in Africa (D. Wilson, 2010).

The response to illegal drug users also shows how conceptions of deviance are socially constructed. Take, for instance, discrepancies in prison sentences for the possession and use of cocaine. Although the two types of cocaine—powdered and crack— cause similar physical reactions, the sentences for those convicted of selling them are vastly different. The average length of a sentence for selling less than 25 grams of crack cocaine is 65 months; for powdered cocaine, it is 14 months (Coyle, 2003). According to federal law, it would take 500 grams of powdered cocaine (or 5,000 doses) to draw the same mandatory minimum sentence of five years in prison that a person convicted of possessing 5 grams (or 10 doses) of crack cocaine would get (L. Greenhouse, 2007a).

Many law enforcement officials argue that the different levels of punishment are justified because crack cocaine is more closely associated with violence than powdered cocaine, it is more dangerous to the user, and it is more likely to cause birth defects in babies whose mothers use it while pregnant. However, a study of the physiological and psychoactive effects of different forms of cocaine found that they are so similar as to make the existing discrepancy in punishment "excessive." In addition, other research has found that the effects of crack use by pregnant women on fetuses are no different from those of tobacco or alcohol use (cited in Coyle, 2003).

Some sociologists argue that the problems associated with crack use have as much to do with class and race as with the drug itself. Harsh sentences for crack offenses have had a disproportionate effect on black and Latino men in poor urban areas, where crack is much more common than the powdered cocaine favored by white users. In 2009, nearly 90% of those convicted of crack possession were black and Latino/a; only 10% were white. In contrast, 28% of those convicted of powdered cocaine possession were black, 17% were white, and 53% were Latino/a (cited in Kurtzleben, 2010). In 2009, the Judiciary Committee of the U.S. House of Representatives began hearings on the mandatory sentence disparity between crack and powdered cocaine, and in 2010, President Obama signed into law the Fair Sentencing Act, which aims to reduce these sentencing disparities. In 2011, the U.S. Sentencing Commission voted unanimously to reduce the unfairly long sentences for crack offenders already in prison so that they are more in line with shorter terms given powder cocaine offenders. Some 12,000 prisoners may find their sentences reduced by as much as three years (Serrano, 2011).

Meanwhile, little has been accomplished in the way of stopping the illegal activities of the rich and powerful interests that participate in the drug industry. Established financial institutions often launder drug money, despite laws against it (Parenti, 1995).

Massive international crime organizations that ensure the flow of illicit drugs into the country have grown bigger and richer, despite a decades-long attempt to stop them (Bullington, 1993). Unlike low-status users and small-time dealers of illegal drugs, these organizations wield tremendous economic power and political influence (Godson & Olson, 1995).

The Medicalization of Deviance

One of the most powerful forces in defining deviance in the United States today is the medical profession. Throughout the 20th century, the medical profession gained in prestige, influence, and authority. This professional dominance gave medicine jurisdiction over anything that could be designated "healthy" or "sick" (Conrad & Leiter, 2004). This trend, what sociologists call *medicalization*, is the process through which deviant behavior is defined as a medical problem or illness and the medical profession is mandated or licensed to provide some type of treatment for it (Conrad, 2005). Each time we automatically refer to troublesome behavior or people as "sick," we help to perpetuate the perception that deviance is like an illness. Many physicians, psychologists, psychiatrists, therapists, and insurance agents, not to mention the entire pharmaceutical industry, benefit from a medicalized view of certain deviant acts.

According to some, we're currently in the midst of an "epidemic of diagnoses" (Welch, Schwartz, & Woloshin, 2007), meaning that more and more actions that were once categorized simply as misbehaviors are being redefined as psychiatric diseases, disorders, or syndromes. Between 1952 and 2000, the number of mental disorders officially recognized by the American Psychiatric Association increased from 110 to close to 400 (P. J. Caplan, 1995; Horwitz, 2002). Many of these designations seem to have nothing to do with illness. Take, for instance a malady called "conduct disorder," a diagnosis restricted to children and adolescents. According to the American Psychiatric Association (2000), the "symptoms" of this disorder include bullying or threatening behavior toward others, physical cruelty, destruction of property, theft, and violations of other rules like staying out late despite parental prohibition. In another era, this sort of misbehavior was called juvenile delinquency. Some psychiatrists have begun discussing a new ailment called "scrupulosity disorder," which they define as excessive doubt about moral behavior, often resulting in compulsive religious observance (C. H. Miller & Hedges, 2008). Conceivably, sufferers of this "disorder" could include people who pray a lot after engaging in behavior that makes them feel extremely guilty.

To accommodate the growing number of "illnesses," the number of psychiatric professionals has almost tripled over the past two decades, as has the number of people seeking psychiatric help. The combined indirect and direct costs of serious mental "illness" in this society, including lost productivity, lost earnings due to illness, disability benefits, and health care expenditures, are estimated to exceed $317 billion annually (National Institute of Mental Health, 2010). According to the National Institute of Mental Health (2009), 26.2% of U.S. adults had suffered from a diagnosable mental disorder during the previous 12-month period and 46.4% had at some point in their lives. Along with alcoholism, drug addiction, and serious mental illness, these disorders now include overeating, undereating, shyness, school stress, distress over a failed romance, poor performance in school, hoarding, addiction to using the Internet, and excessive gambling, shopping, and sex.

For their part, drug companies sometimes create medicalized conceptions of deviance by marketing diseases and selling drugs to treat those diseases. In 1997, Congress passed the Food and Drug Administration Modernization Act, allowing drug companies to advertise directly to the public and create heightened demand for their products. Between 1996 and 2000, drug company spending on television advertising increased by 600%, to $2.5 billion, and it's been rising ever since. They now spend as much money on this direct-to-consumer advertising as they spend on advertising to physicians in medical journals (Conrad, 2005).

In the early 2000s, GlaxoSmithKline sought FDA approval to promote the antidepressant drug Paxil as a treatment for the relatively obscure conditions social anxiety disorder (or social phobias) and generalized anxiety disorder. In general, the principal symptoms of these "disorders" are worry and anxiety in social and performance situations where embarrassment may occur. After receiving approval, the company spent millions to raise public visibility of these conditions. Before this campaign, diagnoses of these disorders had been relatively rare. Today, some mental health organizations maintain that perhaps as many as 30 million people suffer from one of these problems and are in need of diagnosis and pharmaceutical treatment (Mental Health Channel, 2007).

Why has the medical view of deviance become so dominant? One reason is that medical explanations of troublesome social problems and deviant behaviors are appealing to a society that wants simple explanations for complex social problems. If violent behavior is the result of a dysfunction in a person's brain, it then becomes a problem of defective, violent individuals, not of the larger societal context within which violent acts occur. Likewise, when our doctor or therapist tells us our anxiety, depression, crabbiness, and insecurity will vanish if we simply take a drug, we are spared the difficult task of looking at the social complexities of our lives or the structure of our society.

The medicalization of deviance also appeals to our humanitarian values. The designation of a problem as an illness replaces legal punishment and moral scrutiny with therapeutic treatment (Zola, 1986). The alcoholic is no longer a sinner or a criminal but a victim, someone whose behavior is an "illness" beyond her or his control. Children who have trouble learning in school aren't disobedient and disruptive, they are "sick." If people are violating norms because of a disease that has invaded their bodies, they should not be held morally responsible. Medicalization creates less social stigma and condemnation of people labeled deviant.

Despite its enormous public appeal, the tendency to medicalize deviance has serious social consequences (Conrad & Schneider, 1992). These include the individualization of complex social issues and the depoliticization of deviance.

Individualizing Complex Social Issues

U.S. culture often emphasizes the individual over the social structure. Instead of seeing certain deviant behaviors as symptoms of a faulty social system—blocked economic opportunities, neighborhood decay, or unattainable cultural standards—people in the United States tend to see such behaviors as expressions of individual traits or shortcomings. Hence, they can be remedied only through actions aimed at the individual (Kovel, 1980).

Individualistic medical explanations of deviance are not necessarily wrong. Some violent people do have neurological diseases, and some people diagnosed with clinical depression do have imbalances of chemicals in their brains. But when we pursue these explanations for everyone whose behavior diverges from social expectations, the solutions we seek focus on the perpetrator to the exclusion of everything else.

Consider the problem of attention-deficit/hyperactivity disorder (ADHD), one of the most commonly diagnosed maladies among U.S. children today. A child diagnosed with ADHD is difficult to deal with at home and in the classroom. He or she fidgets and squirms, has difficulty remaining seated, can't sustain attention in tasks or play activities, can't follow rules, talks excessively, and is easily distracted (American Psychiatric Association, 2000).

Fifty years ago, such children were considered bad or troublesome and would have been subjected to punishment or even expulsion from school. Today, however, most hyperactive behavior is diagnosed as a symptom of a mental disorder, and drugs are prescribed to treat it. About 9% of all children in the U.S. (and about 13% of boys) will be diagnosed with ADHD at some point in their youth (National Institute of Mental Health, 2010). More than 4 million children in the United States are taking drugs to curb their overactivity or inattentiveness (President's Council on Bioethics, 2003). Between 2000 and 2003, spending for drugs used to treat ADHD increased 183% for all children and 369% for children under the age of five (AIS Health, 2004). The number of prescriptions for these drugs written for U.S. children is growing at a faster rate than for any other drug; more prescriptions are written for them than for antibiotics or asthma medication (Conrad, 2005).

This growth is part of an alarming trend toward the increased use of drugs for children in general (Safer, Zito, & dosReis, 2003). For instance, prescriptions for sleeping pills among children increased 85% between 2000 and 2004 (G. Harris, 2005b). Between one quarter and one half of all kids who attend summer camps take daily prescription medications (J. Gross, 2006). Critics worry not only about the safety of these drugs but also about the mixed messages children receive when they are handed a daily pill to medicate away their troublesome behavior while at the same time they are told to say no to drugs (Koch, 1999).

Despite occasional adverse side effects, the drugs used to treat ADHD are generally successful in quieting unruly and annoying behavior (Whalen & Henker, 1977). And certainly a medical response to ADHD is preferable to harsh punishment. But are we ignoring the possibility that hyperactive behavior may be a child's adaptation to his or her social environment? Some pediatricians, for instance, argue that the symptoms of ADHD may just be children's natural reaction to living in a fast-paced, stressful world (Diller, 1998). According to one neuroscientist, the inability to sustain attention, regulate rage, or tolerate normal types of sensory input may be as much a function of living in a "culture of excess and self-indulgence" as faulty brain wiring (cited in Warner, 2010). Others have argued that ADHD may, in part, be a response to an educational system that discourages individual expression (Conrad, 1975) or that expects more self-control from young children than they're capable of exercising (Duncan, 2007). Narrowly defined norms of acceptable behavior make it difficult if not impossible for children to pursue their own desires and needs.

I'm not suggesting that all children who are diagnosed with ADHD are disruptive simply because they live in a multitasking society, are bored in school, or have had their individual creativity and vitality squashed by unsympathetic teachers. Some children do have neurological disorders that create debilitating behavioral problems in need of treatment. The point is that from an institutional perspective, the tendency to label disruptiveness simply as an individual disorder protects the school system's legitimacy and authority. The institution simply cannot function if disruptiveness is tolerated (Tobin, Wu, & Davidson, 1989). But imagine if our educational system promoted and encouraged free individual expression rather than obedience and discipline. In such an environment, overactivity wouldn't be considered disruptive and wouldn't be a problem in need of a medical solution.

When inconvenient behavior is translated into an individual sickness, medical remedies (usually drugs) become a convenient tool for enforcing conformity and upholding the values of society. When parents say they want "better children," they typically mean they want children who are in line with our culture's values: "well adjusted, well-behaved, sociable, attentive, high-performing, and academically adept" (President's Council on Bioethics, 2003, p. 73). Parents who *don't* want their children to have these characteristics become objects of suspicion.

So it's not surprising that we have come to rely on drugs to help us through many of our common problems in living. Antidepressant drugs, in particular, have become so popular that they are now a prominent feature of the culture.

MICRO-MACRO CONNECTION

The Pharmaceutical Personality

Prozac arrived on the scene in 1987 as a new treatment for depression, and almost as soon as it hit the market, it was being hailed as a miracle drug. Not only was it effective and easy to prescribe, it was relatively free from the weight gain, low blood pressure, irregular heart rhythms, and other side effects common with earlier antidepressant drugs. By 1990, Prozac had become the top-selling antidepressant in the world, a position it held until 2000. At its peak, Prozac brought in $3 billion in annual revenues (Zuckoff, 2000). Sales have dipped recently as cheaper, generic versions have entered the market. Nevertheless, Prozac and chemically similar antidepressant drugs such as Zoloft, Paxil, Celexa, and Wellbutrin earn $10 billion a year in U.S. sales alone (IMS Health, 2010). GlaxoSmithKline spent more money— $91 million—advertising Paxil in 2001 than Nike spent advertising its top shoes (C. Elliott, 2003). At one point, 8.5% of the entire U.S. civilian, noninstitutionalized population had a prescription for an antidepressant (Stagnitti, 2005).

Antidepressants quickly grew to be more than just treatments for depression, however. They are now regularly prescribed for people with eating disorders, obsessive-compulsive disorders, anxiety disorders, social phobias, obesity, gambling addiction, and family problems. A version of Prozac called Sarafem is prescribed for women complaining of premenstrual difficulties. Some people use antidepressants to enhance job performance, improve their alertness and concentration, overcome boredom, think more clearly, become more assertive, or get along better with their mates.

Clearly, the therapeutic realm of antidepressants has expanded beyond clinical depression to include more of what were once thought of as ordinary life stresses. In his book *Listening to Prozac* (1997), psychiatrist Peter Kramer—an avid proponent and energetic prescriber of the drug—argues that Prozac can (and perhaps should) also be used to remove aspects of our personality we find objectionable. He likens the use of Prozac to overcome undesirable psychological traits to the use of cosmetic surgery to overcome undesirable physical ones.

Many people who have benefited from antidepressants describe them in adoring, almost worshipful terms. They weren't healed; they were transformed. Shy introverts report turning into social butterflies, mediocre workers turn into on-the-job dynamos, the bored become interested and alert—even the unattractive begin to feel more beautiful. Some people see drugs like Prozac as nothing short of a divine creation:

> As my husband and I watched the results of Prozac, we knew that the medication was God's gift to us. Breakthroughs . . . like Prozac are evidence of His grace. I now *feel* God's love for me as I never have before. . . . I believe that it is helping me be more true to the person God created me to be. (quoted in Tapia, 1995, p. 17)

According to Kramer (1997), his patients feel "better than well" shortly after they begin taking the drug. They report improvement in their popularity, business sense, self-image, energy, and sexual appeal. One patient was having trouble at work and had recently broken up with her boyfriend. Kramer prescribed Prozac. Within weeks, she was dating several men and handling her job demands smoothly. She even received a substantial pay raise. Convinced that the drug had created these improvements in her life, she happily referred to herself as "Ms. Prozac."

Antidepressants are appealing for economic reasons, too. Because traditional psychotherapy (patients talking to therapists about their problems) is time-consuming and expensive, efforts to cut health care costs work against its use. A psychiatrist can earn $150 for three 15-minute medication visits compared with $90 for a 45-minute talk therapy session (G. Harris, 2011b). Furthermore, many health care plans limit or exclude extensive talk therapy in their coverage, thereby indirectly encouraging greater use of antidepressant drugs. According to one government survey, only about 11% of psychiatrists provide talk therapy to all their patients, even though recent evidence suggests that such an approach may be as good or better than drugs in the treatment of depression (G. Harris, 2011b).

In light of these facts, we should perhaps not be surprised that Prozac is a cultural icon (C. Elliott & Chambers, 2004). The drug pops up in magazine cartoons and the jokes of late-night talk show hosts. As one writer noted, "Prozac has attained the familiarity of Kleenex" (Cowley, 1994, p. 41). Even the word *Prozac* is now an entry in *Webster's New World Dictionary,* defined as a quick-relief cure-all.

Despite claims by some that antidepressants increase suicidal tendencies, they've certainly helped tens of millions of people in serious need. But their popularity raises fundamental sociological questions about the role drugs ought to play in everyday life. Critics fear that antidepressants—as well as other drugs that can modify character—are aimed not just at "sick patients" but at people who already function at a high level and want enriched memory, enhanced intelligence, heightened concentration, and a transformation of bad moods into good ones. In a fast-paced, achievement-oriented society such as the United States, the motivations for gaining a competitive edge—whether in school, on the job, or in interpersonal relations—are obvious. Those who earn higher grades, sell more cars, or come across as more charming and attractive can reap enormous financial and social benefits. Perhaps as many as 16% of college students say they've used stimulants or other prescription drugs to improve their academic performance (cited in Carey, 2008).

But once people begin to use a drug to chemically enhance performance, those who do not use the drug—whether for reasons of principle or because they can't afford it—risk losing out and becoming the less rewarded and less valuable members of the community (President's Council on Bioethics, 2003). Would we, as a society, have to resort to legal regulation—much like the ban on athletic performance enhancers such as anabolic steroids—to prevent a desperate race to keep up?

On a more profound level, if we can use existing pharmaceutical technology to chemically eradicate sadness and despair, why would anyone ever put up with emotional discomfort? In the past, people simply assumed that misery and suffering were part of the human condition. Just as physical pain prevents us from burning ourselves if we get too close to a fire, perhaps mental pain, too, serves a purpose, such as motivating us to change life situations that are getting us into trouble. There's the spiritual element as well: "One reconceives sadness as sickness only by emptying it of psychic or spiritual significance and turning it into a mere thing of the body" (President's Council on Bioethics, 2003, p. 261).

But people today are more inclined to believe they have a right not to be unhappy. Sadness is inconvenient and prevents us from reaching our potential. And if there's a drug to get rid of it quickly and cheaply, then why not use it? And it's not just in the form of pills. Researchers in Japan recently found that prefectures with higher naturally occurring levels of lithium in their water—a mineral that helps balance mood swings—have lower suicide rates than other areas (Ohgami, Terao, Shiotsuki, Ishii, & Iwata, 2009). This finding has led some to speculate that perhaps adding lithium to water supplies can build up a community's resistance to mood swings, not unlike adding fluoride to water supplies has reduced levels of tooth decay.

Mood-altering drugs have not yet completely redefined society. Quite possibly depression, unlike polio or smallpox, will never be essentially wiped out. But the technological possibilities not only of antidepressants but of brain scanning techniques, genetic modification, and drugs as yet unknown raise important issues about the role of medicine in defining deviance, controlling behavior, constructing personality, and ultimately determining social life and the culture that guides it.

Depoliticizing Deviance

The process of individualizing social problems robs deviant behavior of its power to send a message about malfunctioning elements in society. Disruptive behaviors or statements automatically lose their power to prompt social change when they are seen simply as symptoms of individual defects or illnesses. We need not pay attention to the critical remarks of an opponent if that opponent is labeled as mentally ill. Totalitarian regimes often declare political dissidents insane and confine them to hospitals in an attempt to quiet dangerous political criticism. In 2007, a Russian activist was held in a psychiatric clinic for months after publishing an article detailing the harsh treatment of patients in the same hospital. In China, people who file complaints against local government officials often find themselves involuntarily committed to mental institutions. Although there are no reliable statistics on how often these confinements occur, human rights activists say they're increasing because local authorities are under intense pressure to quell social unrest these days. One woman, who was confined for seven months after complaining that she had been unfairly denied a government job, said, "What they are trying to do is completely destroy your mind and weaken your body to the point where you go crazy. That's when you will stop petitioning, they hope" (quoted in LaFraniere & Levin, 2010, p. A14). Such practices are not found only in foreign countries. In the early 1990s, a *Dallas Morning News* investigation discovered that high-ranking U.S. military commanders were trying to discredit and intimidate subordinates who reported security and safety violations or military overpricing by ordering them to undergo psychiatric evaluations or sending them to a mental ward (Timms & McGonigle, 1992). When a low-ranking naval officer reported that fellow sailors had raped three women while stationed in Bermuda, he was committed to a psychiatric hospital for a week (Zwerdling, 2004). A chief petty officer in the Air Force contended that his forced hospitalization was part of retaliation for reporting payroll abuses at the Dallas Naval Air Station. He insightfully describes the power of medical labels to discredit his political criticism:

> What happened was nobody would speak to me. Let's face it. After someone has gone to a mental ward, you kind of question what's going on. It was a nice ploy, and it worked. What they did was totally neutralize me. (quoted in Timms & McGonigle, 1992, p. F1)

Creating the image of deviants as sick people who must be dealt with through medical therapies is a powerful way for dominant groups in society to maintain conformity and protect themselves from those whom they fear or who challenge the way "normal" social life is organized (Pfohl, 1994). The seemingly merciful medical labels not only reduce individual responsibility but also reduce the likelihood that such potentially contagious political criticism will be taken seriously (Hills, 1980).

Conclusion

When we talk about deviance, we usually speak of extreme forms: crime, mental illness, substance abuse, and so on. These activities are indeed troublesome, but for most people they remain comfortably distant phenomena. I think most of us would like to cling to the belief that deviants are "them" and normal people are "us."

The lesson I hope you take away from this chapter, however, is that the issue of deviance is, essentially, an issue of social definition. As a group, community, or society, we decide which differences are benign and which are dangerous. Standards and expectations change. Norms come and go. The consequence is that each of us could be considered deviant to some degree by some audience. We have all broken unspoken interactional norms; many of us have even broken the law. To a lesser degree, we are all potentially like Kelly Michaels, subject to being erroneously labeled deviant and unfairly treated as a result. Given the right—or wrong—circumstances, all of us risk being negatively labeled or acquiring a bad reputation.

This chapter has examined deviance as both a microlevel and a macrolevel sociological phenomenon, as something that plays a profound role in individual lives and in society as a whole. Although sociologists are interested in the broad social and political processes that create cultural definitions of deviance, they are also interested in the ways these definitions are applied in everyday life. Societal definitions have their most potent effect when expressed face to face. We can talk about powerful institutions such as medicine creating definitions of deviance that are consistent with broader political or economic interests, but if these definitions aren't accepted as appropriate to some degree by the majority, they will be ineffectual. Again, we see the value of developing the sociological imagination, which helps us understand the complex interplay between individuals and the culture and community within which they live.

YOUR TURN

People's perceptions of deviant acts and individuals are a crucial element of our understanding of deviance. From a conflict perspective, these perceptions are usually consistent with the goals and interests of those in power. But what exactly are people's perceptions of deviance?

Make copies of the following list, and find 20 to 30 people who would be willing to read it and answer a few questions. Try to get an equal proportion of males and females and younger and older people. Have each person rank the following "deviant" acts in order from 1 to 16, with 16 being the most serious and 1 the least serious. Do not define for them what is meant by "serious."

- Catching your spouse with a lover and killing them both
- Embezzling your employer's funds
- Robbing a supermarket with a gun
- Forcibly raping a stranger in a park

- Selling liquor to minors
- Killing a suspected burglar in your home
- Practicing medicine without a license
- Soliciting for prostitution
- Blowing up a building with people in it
- Hitting your child
- Selling cocaine
- Manufacturing and selling cars known to have dangerous defects
- Forcibly raping a former romantic partner or spouse
- Being drunk in public
- Killing a person for a fee
- Conspiring to fix the prices of machines sold to businesses
  (Most of the 16 items in this exercise are adapted from P. Rossi, Waite, Bose, & Berk, 1974.)

After the volunteers are finished, ask them how they decided on their rankings. What criteria did they use for judging the seriousness of each act? Where did their perceptions come from? Why do they think the "less serious" acts on the list are against the law?

After collecting all your data, compute the average ranking for each of the 16 items (for each item, add all the ranking scores and divide by the number of responses). The larger the average score, the greater the perceived seriousness of that act. Which acts were considered the most serious and which the least serious? Was there a fair amount of agreement among the people in your sample? Were there any differences between the ratings of men and women? Between older and younger people? Between people of different racial or ethnic groups? Use the conflict perspective to discuss the role these perceptions play in the nature and control of deviance.

CHAPTER HIGHLIGHTS

- According to an absolutist definition of deviance, there are two fundamental types of behavior: that which is inherently acceptable and that which is inherently unacceptable. In contrast, a relativist definition of deviance suggests that it is not a property inherent in any particular act, belief, or condition. Instead, deviance is a definition of behavior that is socially created by collective human judgments. Hence, like beauty, deviance is in the eye of the beholder.

- The labeling theory of deviance argues that deviance is a consequence of the application of rules and sanctions to an offender. Deviant labels can impede individuals' everyday social life by forming expectations of them in the minds of others.

- According to conflict theory, the definition of deviance is a form of social control exerted by more powerful people and groups over less powerful ones.

- The criminal justice system and the medical profession have had a great deal of influence in defining, explaining, and controlling deviant behavior. Criminalization is the process by which certain behaviors come to be defined as crimes. Medicalization is the depiction of deviance as a medical problem or illness.

KEY TERMS

absolutism: Approach to defining deviance that rests on the assumption that all human behavior can be considered either inherently good or inherently bad

criminalization: Official definition of an act of deviance as a crime

deterrence theory: Theory of deviance positing that people will be prevented from engaging in deviant acts if they judge the costs of such an act to outweigh its benefits

deviance: Behavior, ideas, or attributes of an individual or group that some people in society find offensive

labeling theory: Theory stating that deviance is the consequence of the application of rules and sanctions to an offender; a deviant is an individual to whom the identity "deviant" has been successfully applied

medicalization: Definition of behavior as a medical problem, mandating the medical profession to provide some kind of treatment for it

relativism: Approach to defining deviance that rests on the assumption that deviance is socially created by collective human judgments and ideas

STUDENT STUDY SITE

Visit the Student Study Site at **www.sagepub.com/newman9e** for these additional learning tools:

- Flashcards
- Web quizzes
- Sociologists at Work features
- Micro-Macro Connection features
- Video links
- Audio links
- Web resources
- SAGE journal articles

PART III

Social Structure, Institutions, and Everyday Life

Up to this point, I have been discussing how our everyday lives are constructed and ordered. But that is only part of the picture. What does social life look like from the top down? Once the architecture is constructed and in place, what influence does it exert on our everyday lives? To answer these questions, the remaining chapters investigate the organizational and institutional pressures on everyday life and the various sources of structural inequality in society: social class and wealth, race and ethnicity, and gender. Global institutions and population trends are other structural influences on everyday life. These facets of society may seem ominous and impenetrable. However, you will see that our lives don't completely fall under the control of the social structure. As the concept of the sociological imagination suggests, the collective actions of individuals often bring about fundamental changes in society.

The Structure of Society

Organizations, Social Institutions, and Globalization

Social Structure and Everyday Life

Social Dilemmas: Individual Interests and Structural Needs

The Structure of Formal Organizations

Organizations and Institutions

Globalization and Social Institutions

History will no doubt mark the 2000 presidential election as one of the most bizarre political events of all time. The chaos began on election night. Early in the evening, Al Gore, the Democratic candidate, was projected as the winner of Florida's 25 electoral votes, giving him the inside track to the presidency; a few hours later, that projection was rescinded, and Florida was labeled "too close to call." In the early morning hours of the following day, George W. Bush, the Republican candidate, was projected as the winner of Florida and therefore of the election, only to have that projection withdrawn when Florida, again, was declared "too close to call." The ensuing month brought a daily dose of street protests, charges of voter fraud, recounts, debates over absentee votes, lawsuits, countersuits, and legal rulings. On November 26, the Florida State canvassing board certified that George Bush was the winner. The Florida Supreme Court overruled and ordered another recount. But on December 13, the U.S. Supreme Court issued its definitive ruling, on a 5–4 vote, that the Florida recount was unconstitutional. George W. Bush was thus declared the next president of the United States, even though he had received over half a million fewer votes nationwide than Gore.

To listen to the domestic and foreign news media describe it at the time, the most powerful country in the world was in a state of utter political confusion. The situation was described in either mocking or apocalyptic terms. U.S. citizens were losing their moral authority to lecture other countries about the virtues of democracy. We were about to face a "constitutional crisis" that could paralyze the government. We were going to be a country without a leader. We were on the brink of anarchy.

Of course, none of that happened. As one journalist put it, "The apparatus of government is still in place, skilled politicians and career civil servants still keep things running, and ultimately nothing apocalyptic is likely to happen. . . . The system will work and life will go on" (Belluck, 2001, p. A9). Indeed, for the average U.S. citizen, nothing really changed during the electoral confusion. Buses, trains, and planes still ran on time. Food was still delivered to grocery store shelves. Municipal services were still provided. Even the stock market remained solid. We all simply went about our business, pausing now and then to witness the political spectacle or to debate with friends, family, and coworkers.

Why didn't the country collapse during this electoral epic? To answer that question, we must turn to one of the key concepts of this book: social structure. Despite strong emotions, dire predictions, and confrontational behavior, the political system remained intact. Whether we agreed with the ultimate outcome of that election or not, our legal and political institutions worked as they were designed to. From local precincts and campaign organizations to state legislatures to the highest court in the land, the system continued to function. To be sure, the motives of some of the individual players were highly partisan. But the structure itself rose above the actions of these individuals and prevented the sort of large-scale catastrophe media pundits predicted. One of the great sociological paradoxes of human existence is that we are capable of producing a social structure that we then experience as something other than a human product. It is ironic that we spend most of our lives either within or responding to the influence of larger structural entities—particularly in a society such as the United States, which so fiercely extols the virtues of rugged individualism and personal accomplishment.

This chapter focuses on our relationship with the social structure we construct and maintain, both locally and globally. This focus requires us to examine the structure not only from the individual's perspective but also from the macrosociological perspective of the organizations and institutions themselves. Many important social issues look quite different depending on the perspective we use to understand them.

Social Structure and Everyday Life

As you recall from Chapter 2, *social structure* is the framework of society that exists above the level of individuals and provides the social setting in which individuals interact with one another to form relationships. It includes the organizations, groups, statuses and roles, cultural beliefs, and institutions that add order and predictability to our lives. The concept of social structure is important because it implies a patterned regularity in the way we live and in the way societies work. We could not draw any meaningful conclusions about human behavior if we started with the notion that society is haphazard and that things occur by chance alone.

If you know what to look for, you can see social structure everywhere. Consider, for instance, the components of social structure that affect the experience of going to high school. Within this broad U.S. educational institution, there are examples of every component of social structure:

- *Organizations:* National Education Association, state teachers' associations, accrediting agencies, local school boards, school districts, and so on
- *Groups:* faculty, administrators, classes, clubs, teams, cafeteria staff, and so on
- *Statuses:* teacher, student, principal, counselor, nurse, secretary, custodian, coach, librarian, and so on
- *Role expectations:* teaching, learning, disciplining, making and taking tests, advising, coaching, feeding, and so on

- *Cultural beliefs:* for example, the belief that education is the principal means of achieving financial success, that it makes possible a complex division of labor, and that it makes a technologically advanced society possible
- *Institutionalized norms:* for example, the expectation that everyone attend school until at least the age of 16, school rules that determine acceptable behavior (not running in the halls, not screaming in class, staying on the school grounds until classes are over; Saunders, 1991)

The massive structure of the educational system is a reality that determines life chances and choices. You can choose which science class to take in high school, whether to go on to college, and what to major in once you get there, but the admissions policies of potential colleges and the availability of jobs to people with and without a college degree are factors beyond your control. You're reading this book right now not because of your fondness for fine literature but because of the structural requirements of being a college student. You know you must graduate to increase your chances of getting a good job, and to graduate you must get good grades in your classes. To get good grades in your classes, you must keep up with the material so you're prepared for exams. You probably would rather be doing a number of other things right now—reading a better book, making love, watching TV, texting, tweeting, blogging, sleeping, staring into space—but personal preferences must take a backseat for the time being to the more immediate structural demands of college life.

The structural requirements of the educational system have a broader impact as well. Course grades, standardized test scores, and class rankings are emphasized so much and create such personal anxiety for students that they may actually overshadow learning and intellectual growth:

> Throughout our school years, we are taught to believe from society that grades display intelligence. Because of this, our motivation, learning, and personal growth are placed second to attaining the ultimate goal—the grade. . . . We are programmed to imitate what the teacher wants. If we don't, we get a bad grade. . . . Imitation, competition, and fear of grades hinders our discovery. (I. Bell & McGrane, 1999, p. 2)

This competitive educational atmosphere can sometimes create incompatibility between the needs of the individual student and the needs of the system. Suppose your sociology instructor told you that she was going to give everyone in the class an A as long as they showed up each day. Your immediate reaction might be joy, because such a grade would no doubt improve your grade point average (GPA). But what if all instructors in all courses at your school decided to do the same thing? Every student who simply showed up for all her or his classes would graduate with a perfect GPA. How would you feel then? Your joy might be tempered by the knowledge that the reputation of your school would suffer. As long as our educational system is structured on the principle of "survival of the fittest"— the assumption that only the smartest or hardest-working students earn the top grades— outsiders would perceive such changes as a sign that your school is academically inferior. Hence, your long-term personal interests may actually be best served by a highly competitive system that ensures that some of your fellow students will get lower grades than you.

Beyond your personal outcomes, the competitive educational structure also influences how schools and teachers are assessed. Consider, for instance, the role of standardized testing. According to the 2001 No Child Left Behind Act, public schools must bring all students up to grade level proficiency in reading and math by 2014. If they fail, administrators can lose their jobs and the schools can be taken over. Low-income schools that receive federal funding risk losing their aid if their students consistently perform poorly on state-administered standardized achievement tests. In addition, about a dozen states take student progress on standardized tests into consideration in teachers' performance reviews. Given such pressures, it's not surprising that more and more educators are tampering with the tests in order to improve students' scores:

- At a charter school in Massachusetts, the principal instructed teachers to look over students' shoulders and point out wrong answers as they took the state test. The state revoked the school's charter.
- In a district outside of Houston, teachers distributed a detailed study guide to students after stealing a look at the state science test (Gabriel, 2010b).
- In Atlanta, an investigation revealed that for about a decade 178 principals and teachers in about 80% of the city's public schools had tampered with standardized tests by erasing students' wrong answers and penciling in the correct ones (Severson, 2011).
- A state examination of standardized test results in Pennsylvania public schools revealed that 89 schools—28 in Philadelphia alone—had been flagged for an improbably high number of erasures as well as questionable gains on reading and math tests (Winerip, 2011).

MICRO-MACRO CONNECTION

Social Structure and Catastrophe

People's dependence on social structure is illustrated most clearly when they face calamitous, life-threatening situations. Remember the 33 Chilean miners who were trapped 2,300 feet underground for 70 days back in 2010? They all survived and most were surprisingly unscathed. Sure, their physical survival required impressive levels of individual stamina, the diligent efforts of rescuers, a constant flow of food and supplies, effective medical advice from doctors at the surface, and some really good luck. But without the well-organized subterranean social structure they created, they never would have made it. Early on in the crisis, the trapped miners determined that every decision they made, no matter how large or small, would be put to a majority vote. They developed a clear authority structure, with every individual assigned to a particular role, such as food organizer, medic, pastor, environmental assistant, communications specialist, and media director. They designated places for eating, exercise, and waste disposal. They split into three groups of 11, each with it's own leadership and assigned tasks. They abided by a regular daily schedule that included meals, showers, exercise, "house" cleaning, and chores done in three shifts around the clock (J. Franklin, 2010). To many observers, the remarkably good shape the miners were in when they emerged could be attributed to all this organization. Social structure literally helped save their lives.

Let's turn the clock ahead to the spring of 2011 and the massive Japanese earthquake and tsunami that devastated the country's northern coast and killed tens of thousands of people. Many villages were wiped off the map. One such place was the tiny fishing hamlet of Hadenya in the town of Minamisanriku. After the tsunami hit, homes were wiped away and loved ones disappeared. Bridges were washed out, vehicles crushed, boats stranded. Electricity and cell phone services were nonexistent. Two hundred and seventy survivors huddled in the frigid cold at a hilltop community center. They had very little food, no fuel, and no news from the outside world. It took nearly two weeks for the military to finally reach them. But they were all alive. Like the Chilean miners, the people of Hadenya realized that the only way they could survive was to create their own social structure, quickly reorganizing themselves along the lines of the original community:

Almost as soon as the waters receded . . . they began dividing tasks along gender lines, with women boiling water and preparing food, while men went scavenging for fire-wood and gasoline. Within days . . . they had re-established a complex community, with a hierarchy and division of labor, in which members were assigned daily tasks.

They had even created a committee that served as an impromptu government body for this and five other nearby refugee centers. . . . Representatives from the centers met daily to swap supplies and assigned tasks. (Fackler, 2011, p. A11)

It soon became apparent that Hadenya wasn't unique. Refugees in scores of other small hamlets all along the coast created similar makeshift organizations to aid their survival. The groups were so successful that when the local government began to plan for the eventual relocation of all the survivors into temporary housing miles away, officials realized that the spontaneous group organizations might have some lasting use:

[The mayor] said the town had originally planned to put people into housing as quickly as possible. Now he thought it best to keep these organizations intact, to help people adapt to new and different living environments.

"They are like extended families," [the mayor] said. "They provide support and com-fort." (Fackler, 2011, p. A11)

But social structure is not always a savior during catastrophes. It can sometimes overwhelm individuals' best efforts to exercise their will. Take, for example, an even bigger tsunami disaster that hit seven years earlier, killing more than 200,000 people in South Asia and Eastern Africa and leaving millions homeless. Millions of ordinary people around the world pledged to help the victims, alongside promises of billions of dollars in aid and military assistance made by 19 nations. Close to 30% of U.S. citizens donated money to the cause, and another 37% indicated that they intended to do so (Lester, 2005). Two weeks after the disaster, the charitable organization Save the Children had received more than $10 million in donations over the Internet alone. In a typical month, the organization receives between $30,000 and $50,000 (Strom, 2005).

But such dramatic individual benevolence was hobbled and almost crushed at the organiza-tional level. When two dozen government and aid organizations arrived in the hardest-hit regions of Indonesia a week or two after the tsunami hit, they found that looters and black market traders had already descended on the wreckage. Some devastated areas had yet to see any relief workers, while others were swarming with doctors and nurses. Moreover, the presence of foreign military and relief workers soon created resentment in the Indonesian government. In response, it imposed travel restrictions on foreign aid workers, citing security concerns, and demanded that all foreign military personnel leave the country within three months. In one of the hardest-hit areas, Banda Aceh, relief organizations found themselves in the middle of a civil war, operating alongside paramilitary rebels (officially regarded as terrorists by the U.S. govern-ment) and an Indonesian military known for its corruption and rights abuses (Wehrfritz & Cochrane, 2005). Despite the presence of thousands of caring and generous individuals who came to help, these structural factors conspired to slow down the relief process.

Even when it's operating as it's designed to, social structure can cause problems. Mistakes are sometimes the end result of a chain of events set in motion by a system that either induces errors or makes them difficult to detect and correct. For instance, an annual study of patient safety in U.S. hospitals estimates that between 2005 and 2007, there were more than 900,000 safety incidents and close to 100,000 preventable deaths attributable to medical errors such as anesthesia complications, drug mix-ups, infections due to medical care, accidental lacerations, and various other postoperative complications. These incidents resulted in nearly $7 billion in excess medical costs (Health Grades, 2009). Another study found that one in five Medicare patients ends up back in the hospital within a month of being discharged and more than half return within a year. The annual cost of these unplanned readmissions is more than $17 billion (S. F. Jencks, Williams, & Coleman, 2009). The tendency to sue individual doctors or nurses for malpractice in such cases demonstrates an overwhelming cultural perception that these errors are caused by personal incompetence.

But what appear to be obvious errors in human judgment or ineptitude are often, on closer inspection, linked to broader structural failures. Up to a quarter of unanticipated injuries and deaths among hospital patients occur because of a systemwide shortage of nurses (Health Resources and Services Administration, 2005). In 2005, 10% of nursing positions were unfilled. That figure is expected to grow to 27% by 2015 and to 36% by 2020 (Health Resources and Services Administration, 2004). The problem is not solely one of too few staff. An analysis of 334 drug errors in hospitals found that structural failure was responsible for most of them—for example, poor dissemination of drug knowledge to doctors, inadequate availability of patient information, faulty systems for checking correct dosage, and inefficient hospital procedure (Leape & Bates, 1995).

More than a decade ago, a report by the Institute of Medicine (1999) recognized that the problem of unnecessary hospital injuries and deaths lies beyond the actions of individual health care workers. It recommended that the health care system build safety concerns into its operations at all levels. It suggested creating a national center for patient safety, establishing a mandatory nationwide reporting system, placing greater emphasis on safety and training in licensing and accreditation evaluations, and developing a "culture of safety" that would help make the reduction of medical errors a top professional priority.

To date, however, the United States, unlike some European countries, has no federal agency charged specifically with hospital oversight. Instead, responsibility for protecting the health and safety of hospital patients lies with a patchwork of state health departments and a nonprofit group called the Joint Commission, which sets quality standards. As a result, bad hospitals are rarely closed and are seldom hit with significant financial penalties for patient suffering (Berenson, 2008).

Some structural improvement is taking place, though. For instance, every year 30,000 patients die from infections associated with their central venous catheters, which are the main devices used to deliver medications to sick patients. For decades, these infections were viewed as inevitable rather than preventable. But hospitals that have implemented a system in which nurses and doctors must fill out a simple checklist of precautions when dealing with central lines—such as washing hands and removing catheters when they're no longer needed—have seen their infection rates plummet. In some medical schools, students must now take workshops on risk reduction in addition to the usual coursework. And at the federal level, hospitals will soon face financial punishments if they don't reduce the number of medical mistakes (Kalb, 2010b).

Social Dilemmas: Individual Interests and Structural Needs

Although social structure can clearly affect the lives of individuals, individual actions can also have an enormous effect on social structure and stability. Sometimes those actions are coordinated to benefit a collection of individuals, and sometimes they're undertaken independently and for personal gain. Let's say a group of residents want to make sure that their neighborhood is free of crime. Each individual could go on a personal crusade to stop crime, but it seems more logical and efficient for everyone to volunteer at some point to "patrol" at night or to chip in money to improve street lighting.

In actuality, though, people seldom voluntarily act to achieve a common objective unless forced to do so. Instead, they usually act to ensure their own personal interests (J. Cross & Guyer, 1980; Dawes & Messick, 2000; Olsen, 1965). Say that your neighbors decide to fight crime by improving street lighting. They ask people in the community for voluntary donations. Some residents may decide that the rational thing to do is not to donate money for a new streetlight because they figure others will do so. That way, they could enjoy the benefits of safer, well-lit streets without spending their own money. But if every person individually decides not to donate, they may save some cash in the short run, but the new streetlights will never be purchased, and everyone will suffer in the long run. The experience of each person in a group pursuing his or her self-interest regardless of the potential ruin for everyone is known as a ***social dilemma*** (Messick & Brewer, 1983).

Major social problems, such as environmental pollution, can be understood as stemming, at least in part, from social dilemmas. If I fling one bag of trash out of my car window and onto the highway, it won't seem significant or destructive. Large numbers of people doing the same thing, though, would be very destructive.

But social dilemmas aren't just the result of selfish or inconsiderate motives. Legitimate economic worries can also create them. For instance, during the current economic recession, more and more individuals have chosen not to seek medical care or have postponed elective surgeries because they can't afford them. According to the American Hospital Association (2008), 31% of hospitals report moderate to significant decreases in elective procedures and 38% report moderate to significant decreases in admissions. At the individual level, delaying such procedures can have serious medical consequences, as when a benign cyst turns into a tumor because a patient didn't have a routine diagnostic procedure. Many young people who lack health insurance and can't afford medical care borrow leftover prescriptions from friends, self-diagnose online, or even set their own broken bones (Buckley, 2009). Indeed, hospitals have reported that emergency rooms are already seeing patients whose dangerous conditions could have been avoided had they not deferred earlier procedures.

Although health insurance companies benefit financially when patients postpone or forgo care (Abelson, 2011), these individual choices can also trigger a chain of events that can have dangerous structural consequences. Elective procedures represent perhaps as much as 25% of a hospital's income (Sack, 2009a). Coupled with other economic woes, the loss of revenue that occurs when large numbers of people decide to cancel or postpone nonurgent surgeries can force some hospitals to trim costs by laying off workers, reducing services, delaying expansions, and canceling equipment updates. As a result, the quality of hospital care may begin to deteriorate, creating potentially hazardous short- and long-term effects for all patients.

If we think of nations as individual actors and the planet as the community to which they belong, many problems that have global significance—including energy shortages, massive climate change, and species extinction—can be understood from this perspective. Two important types of social dilemmas, at both the local level and broader levels, are the tragedy of the commons and the free-rider problem.

The Tragedy of the Commons

The term *commons* was originally used to describe the public pasture ground, often located in the center of medieval towns, where all the local herders could bring their animals to graze. When villagers used the commons in moderation, the grass could regenerate, resulting in a perpetual supply of food for the herds (Hardin & Baden, 1977). However, each herder soon realized that she or he could benefit individually by letting the animals eat as much as they wanted, thereby increasing their size and the price they could fetch at market. Unfortunately, when many of the herders came to this same conclusion and allowed their herds to eat without limit, the grass in the commons could not regenerate fast enough to feed them all. The tragic result was that the commons collapsed and the herds that grazed on it died or were sold off. The short-term needs of the individual overshadowed the long-term collective needs of the group.

In this illustration, the common resource was grazing land, and the group was relatively small. However, the ***tragedy of the commons*** model can be applied to any situation in which indispensable but finite resources are available to everyone. Fisheries in international waters offer a nice contemporary example. If not overfished, they can last forever because there will always be fish around to reproduce. However, without imposed limits, a fisher can take a large amount of fish for himself or herself. The individual obviously benefits, but in doing so he or she does irreparable damage to the stocks and destroys their long-term viability. If nobody else is overfishing, people will be inclined to fish in moderation. However, once others start to overfish, the urge to keep up is powerful. Consequently, the stocks will be damaged and the fish will cease to regenerate. In short, every single person did what was in her or his own best interests, which produced an outcome that was worse for everyone: no more fish.

Or consider the difficulties communities have in conserving energy. People tend to use as much electricity as they are willing to pay for without giving much thought to how their usage affects overall energy supplies. During periods of extremely hot temperatures, they increase their use of fans and air conditioners. Such heightened energy demand can sometimes overwhelm power companies, resulting in isolated or total electrical outages, which hurt everyone.

The impulse to seek individual gain over the collective good becomes particularly tempting when personal well-being is at stake. In the flood-prone summer of 1993, a river overflowed its banks in Des Moines, Iowa, wiping out a filtration system and making the municipal water supply unsafe. To restore full water service, the system had to be refilled with clean water. The situation was urgent. Without full water pressure in the city's water pipes, not only were the residents without regular water service but fire engines also couldn't use the hydrants. Local officials asked everyone to voluntarily refrain from using tap water in their homes and businesses for a few days. If all the city's residents had complied, everyone in the community would have had water within a couple of days. For some individuals, however, the temptation to use water secretly in the privacy of their own homes was too hard to resist. So many residents violated the city's request that the resumption of full water service had to be delayed for many more days (Bradsher, 1993). The entire community suffered as a result of individuals seeking their own short-term benefits.

Why do such dilemmas occur? Part of the problem is lack of communication and lack of trust among individual members of a community. I may want to be a good citizen and conserve water by using it sparingly, but if I think my neighbors are hoarding it, I too will hoard it to make sure I don't go without. Hence, I may follow a line of action that results in a positive outcome for me in the short run but that may eventually have a negative outcome for the community in the long run.

The problem is made worse when individuals think that meeting their individual needs won't have a noticeable effect on the community. "Is my using an extra gallon of water during a drought *really* going to harm the community?" The tragedy of the commons arises when everyone, or at least a substantial number of people, conclude that it will not. As we collectively ignore or downplay the consequences of our actions, we collectively overuse the resource and pave the way for disasters that none of us has caused individually (Edney, 1979).

The Free-Rider Problem

Social dilemmas can also occur when people refrain from contributing something to a common resource because the resource will be available regardless of their contribution. Why pay for something that's available for free? For example, it is irrational, from an individual's point of view, to donate money to public television. I can enjoy *Sesame Street*, *Nova*, and *Frontline* without paying a penny. My small personal donation wouldn't be more than a tiny drop in public television's budgetary bucket anyway. I have no incentive to incur any costs when I don't have to. If everyone acted this way, however, we would all eventually lose the resource. If public television depended solely on voluntary donations made during those annoying fund drives, it would have disappeared a long time ago. Member station fees, grants from universities and the federally funded Corporation for Public Broadcasting, and corporate sponsorships actually keep it going.

Sociologists sometimes refer to this situation as the ***free-rider problem*** (Olsen, 1965). As the term implies, a free rider is an individual who acquires goods or services without risking any personal costs or contributing anything in return. Free-rider behavior can be seen in a variety of everyday activities, from reading a magazine at a newsstand without buying it to downloading music files for free from other people's online collections. We all enjoy the benefits our tax dollars provide—police, firefighters, smooth roads, and many other municipal services. But if taxes were voluntary, would anyone willingly pay for these services?

We can see evidence of the free-rider problem at the institutional level. People often talk about children as a vital resource on whom the future of the country and the planet depend. The care and education of all children can be seen as a public resource. The whole society benefits when our children are well educated and in good physical and psychological health. Yet taxpayers—especially those without children—often protest against tax increases to improve schools, raise teachers' salaries, or hire more youth social workers because they fail to see how such increases will benefit them personally in the long run.

Solutions to Social Dilemmas

Social dilemmas can be solved or at least reduced in several ways. Some sociologists and economists argue that privatization is the best solution. When people own a particular resource, the argument goes, they'll be motivated to preserve it. But privatization creates other problems. For one thing, it's difficult to divide up and sell off resources like air and water. In addition, parties that own a large chunk of a resource may have little interest in seeing that it is shared equitably. For example, several years ago, city leaders in Cochabamba, Bolivia, decided that the best way to save a decrepit municipal water supply system was to sell it to a private corporation that would be motivated to keep it in good repair. But the sale led to exorbitant water bills for city residents and eventually to riots by poor people, who could no longer afford drinkable water (Gardner, 2005).

Establishing communication among individuals is another way in which the negative effects of social dilemmas can be reduced. When everybody knows what everybody else is up to, they may be less likely to hoard a resource and more likely to pay their fair share. In addition, when individual actions are identifiable, feelings of personal responsibility are likely to increase (Edney & Harper, 1978). However, this solution is not very practical when the group or community is quite large, such as an entire country.

The city government of Des Moines set up an emergency hotline that people could call to anonymously turn in violators of the water rules I described earlier. If a city crew found the water meter running, the valve at the curb would be turned off for a week. No appeals were allowed, and water users were never told who turned them in. In addition, the offenders' names and addresses were immediately made known to reporters under Iowa's open records rules and spread across the state by newspapers, radio, and television (Bradsher, 1993). It was a drastic step, but the long-term welfare of the entire community was at stake.

Another solution is centralized control of resources, usually by the government. For instance, in 2010, the U.S. government closed commercial and recreational fishing in the waters off of North Carolina, South Carolina, eastern Florida, and Georgia for six months and imposed strict catch limits thereafter. This action was taken in response to reports that several popular fish species—grouper, black sea bass, red porgy, and red snapper—were seriously depleted and in danger of disappearing entirely. As a consequence, local fishermen, chefs, and restaurateurs have begun catching and preparing previously overlooked but more plentiful species and begun paying more attention to long-term sustainability (Muhlke, 2010).

Often, centralized control of a resource involves coercion—through restrictive rules or laws—to prevent people from seeking their self-interested goals. Requiring people to pay taxes is one example. Another is setting up union "closed shops," meaning that to work in a company an employee must join the union and pay union dues. Without this requirement, individual employees would be able to enjoy the benefits provided by the union—higher wages, shorter hours, and better working conditions—without having to pay anything for them.

The Structure of Formal Organizations

Social life has far more complex functions than simply trying to balance individual and collective interests. Those of us who live in a complex society are all, to varying degrees, organizational creatures. We are born in formal organizations, are educated in them, spend most of our adult lives working for them, and will most likely die in them (E. Gross & Etzioni, 1985). Organizations help meet our most basic needs.

Think about the food on your dinner plate. The farm where the food is produced is probably a huge organization, as are the unions that protect the workers who produce the food and the trucking companies that bring it to your local stores. And all this is controlled by a vast network of financial organizations that set prices and by governmental agencies that ensure the food's safety.

To prepare the food that is produced, delivered, and sold, you have to use products made by other organizations—a sink, a refrigerator, a microwave, a stove. To use those appliances, you have to make arrangements with organizations such as the water and power departments, the gas company, and the electric company. And to pay those bills, you must use still other organizations—the postal service, your Internet provider, your bank, credit companies, and so on.

Most likely, the money to pay the bills comes from a job someone in your household has. If you are employed, you probably work for yet another organization. And when you receive a paycheck, the Internal Revenue Service steps in to take its share.

What about the car you use to get to that job? No doubt a huge, multinational corporation manufactured it. Such corporations also produced and delivered the fuel on which the car runs. The roads you travel on to get to your destinations are built and maintained by massive organizations within the state and federal governments. You aren't even allowed to drive unless you are covered by insurance, which is available only through an authorized organization.

And what if things aren't going well? If you become sick, have an accident, or have a dispute with someone, you have to use organizations such as hospitals, police departments, and courts to rectify the situation.

You get the picture? Life in a complex society is a life touched by public and private organizations at every turn. In such a society, things must be done in a formal, planned, and unified way. For instance, the people responsible for producing our food can't informally and spontaneously make decisions about what to grow and when to grow it, and the people responsible for selling it to us can't make its availability random and unpredictable. Imagine what a mess your life would be if you didn't know when your local supermarket would be open or what sorts of food would be available for purchase. What if one day it sold nothing but elbow macaroni, the next day only mangoes, and the day after that just salad dressing?

In a small-scale community where people grow their own food and the local mom-and-pop store provides everything else, the lack of structure might not be a problem. But this type of informal arrangement can't work in a massive society. There must be a relatively efficient and predictable system of providing goods and services to large numbers of people. The tasks that need to be carried out just to keep that system going are too complex for a single person to manage. This complexity makes bureaucracy necessary.

Bureaucracies: Playing by the Rules

The famous 19th-century sociologist Max Weber (VAY-ber) was vitally interested in understanding the complexities of modern society. He noted that human beings could not accomplish feats such as building cities, running huge enterprises, and governing large and diverse populations without bureaucracies. Bureaucracies were certainly an efficient and rational means of managing large groups of people, although Weber acknowledged that these qualities could easily dehumanize those who work in and are served by those organizations.

Today we tend to see bureaucracies primarily as impersonal, rigid machines that trespass into our personal lives. Bureaucracies conjure up images of rows of desks occupied by faceless workers, endless lines and forms to fill out, and frustration over "red tape" and senseless policies. Indeed, the word *bureaucrat* has taken on such a negative connotation that to be called one is an insult. Keep in mind, however, that in a sociological sense, **bureaucracy** is simply a large hierarchical organization that is governed by formal rules and regulations and that has a clear specification of work tasks.

The bureaucratic organization has three important characteristics:

- *Division of labor:* The bureaucracy has a clear-cut **division of labor**, which is carefully specified by written job descriptions for each position. Theoretically, a clear division of labor is efficient because it employs only specialized experts, every one of whom is responsible only for the effective performance of his or her narrowly defined duties (Blau & Meyer, 1987). Division of labor enables large organizations to accomplish more ambitious goals than would be possible if everyone acted independently. Tasks become highly specific, sometimes to the point that it is illegal to perform someone else's task. In hospitals, for instance, orderlies don't prescribe drugs, nurses don't perform surgery, and doctors don't help patients fill out their insurance forms.
- *Hierarchy of authority:* Not only are tasks divided in a bureaucracy, but they are also ranked in a **hierarchy of authority** (Weber, 1946). Most U.S. bureaucracies are organized in a pyramid shape with a small number of people at the top who have a lot of power and many at the bottom who have virtually none. In such a chain of command, people at one level are responsible to those above them and can exert authority over those below. Authority tends to be attached to the position and not to the person occupying the position, so that the bureaucracy will not stop functioning in the event of a retirement or a death. The hierarchy of authority in bureaucracies not only allows some people to control others, but also justifies paying some people higher salaries than others. When applied to political organizations, the hierarchy of authority can create an **oligarchy**, a system in which many people are ruled by a privileged few (Michels, 1911/1949). In such a setting, leaders can often distance themselves from the public, becoming less accountable for their actions in the process.
- *Impersonality:* Bureaucracies are governed by an elaborate system of rules and regulations that ensure a particular task will be done the same way by each person occupying a position. Rules help ensure that bureaucrats perform their tasks impartially and impersonally. Ironically, the very factors that make the typical bureaucrat unpopular with the public—an aloof attitude, lack of genuine concern—actually allow the organization to run more efficiently. We may want the person administering our driver's license examination to be friendly and to care about us, but think of how you'd feel if the examiner had decided to stop for a bite to eat with the person who was taking the driver's test before you.

Your university is a clear example of a bureaucratic organization. It has a definite division of labor that involves janitors, secretaries, librarians, coaches, professors, administrators, trustees, and students. The tasks that people are responsible for are highly specialized. Professors in the Spanish department don't teach courses in biology. In large universities, the specialization of tasks is even more narrowly defined. Sociology professors who teach criminology probably don't teach courses on family.

Although the power afforded different positions varies from school to school, all universities have some sort of hierarchy of authority. Usually, this hierarchy consists of janitors, groundskeepers, and food service workers at the bottom, followed by students, staff employees, teaching assistants, part-time instructors, professors, and department chairs. At the administrative level are associate deans, deans, vice presidents, and ultimately the president of the university and the board of trustees.

In addition, universities are governed by strict and sometimes exasperating sets of bureaucratic rules. There are rules regarding when students can register for classes and when grades must be turned in by professors, graduation requirements, and behavioral policies. Strict adherence by university employees to these rules and policies is likely to give universities their final characteristic: impersonality.

As people are fitted into roles within bureaucracies that completely determine their duties, responsibilities, and rights, they often become rigid and inflexible and are less concerned about the quality of their work than about whether they and others are playing by the rules. Hence, people become oriented more toward conformity than toward problem solving and critical thinking. They are the source of frustrating procedures and practices that often seem designed not to permit but to prevent things from happening (G. Morgan, 1986). Relief efforts after Hurricane Katrina decimated the Gulf Coast in 2005 were blocked by many bureaucratic obstacles (Goodman, 2005):

- Out-of-state doctors were told they needed a Louisiana license to practice before they could help Katrina victims in New Orleans.
- In cities as far away as Dallas and Houston, attempts to provide shelter were thwarted by building codes and zoning restrictions.
- Both before and after the storm, car owners who offered to haul people out of New Orleans for $5 or $10 were told they were breaking local laws.
- When it came to housing, medical care, and transportation, poor people—as is always the case—did not have the resources to purchase these services on their own and so had to rely on large bureaucratic organizations to provide them, which meant long delays.

Although Weber (1947) stressed the functional necessity of bureaucracies in complex Western societies, he warned that they could take on a life of their own, becoming impersonal "iron cages" for those within them. He feared that bureaucracies might one day dominate every part of society, locking people into a system that allows movement only from one dehumanizing bureaucracy to another. Weber's fears have been largely realized. The bureaucratic model pervades every corner of modern society. The most successful bureaucracies not only dominate the business landscape but have come to influence our entire way of life.

GEORGE RITZER

The McDonaldization of Society

Sociologist George Ritzer (2000) uses the McDonald's restaurant chain as a metaphor for bureaucratization. In 2010, revenues from McDonald's restaurants exceeded $24 billion (McDonald's Corporation, 2011). The 32,000 McDonald's restaurants worldwide can be found in nearly every significant town and city across the United States and on the main thoroughfares in most major foreign locales. Fifty-eight million people eat at a McDonald's restaurant somewhere in the world each day.

For Ritzer (2000), **McDonaldization** is "the process by which the principles of the fast food restaurant are coming to dominate more and more sectors of American society as well as of the rest of the world" (p. 1). Indeed, the phenomenal success of McDonald's has spawned countless other fast food chains that emulate its model. Its formula has also influenced many other types of businesses, among them Toys"R"Us, Starbucks, Pearle Vision, Jiffy Lube, Barnes & Noble bookstores, and the Gap. The model is so powerful that nicknames reflecting McDonald's influence have become ubiquitous: Newly constructed houses in expensive subdivisions are called "McMansions," drive-in medical facilities are called "McHospitals," huge houses of worship with enormous congregations are called "McChurches," and the newspaper *USA Today* is called "McPaper" (Ritzer, 2000, p. 10).

The success of McDonald's is more than just McDonaldization. McDonald's has become a sacred institution, occupying a central place in popular culture. The "golden arches" of McDonald's are among the most identifiable symbols in society today.

McDonald's appeals to us in a variety of ways:

The restaurants themselves are depicted as spick-and-span, the food is said to be fresh and nutritious, the employees are shown to be young and eager, the managers appear gentle and caring, and the dining experience itself seems to be fun-filled. We are even led to believe that we contribute, at least indirectly, to charities by supporting the company that supports Ronald McDonald Houses for sick children. (Ritzer, 2000, pp. 7–8)

According to Ritzer (2000), McDonald's (and every company that imitates it) has been so successful primarily because it fits Weber's model of the classic bureaucracy. It has a clear division of labor and a uniform system of rules that make it highly efficient and predictable. No matter where you are, you know what to expect when you go into a McDonald's. Even without looking at the overhead menu, you know what your choices will be; and once you've ordered your hamburger, you know that the ketchup will be in the same place on the sandwich as it always has been. The appeal of such predictability is unmistakable. As one observer put it, McDonald's customers "are not in search of 'the best burger I've ever had' but rather 'the same burger I've always had'" (Drucker, 1996, p. 47).

In addition, if you've ever watched the workers behind the counter, you know that each has specialized tasks that are narrowly defined:

By combining twentieth-century computer technology with nineteenth-century time-and-motion studies, the McDonald's corporation has broken the jobs of griddleman, waitress, cashier and even manager down into small, simple steps. . . . The corporation has systematically extracted the decision-making elements from filling French fry boxes or scheduling staff. . . . They relentlessly weed out all variables that might make it necessary to make a decision at the store level, whether on pickles or on cleaning procedures. (Garson, 1988, p. 37)

McDonaldization is likely to continue, and even spread, for several reasons:

- It is impelled by economic interests: Profit-making enterprises will go on emulating the McDonald's bureaucratic model because the increased use of nonhuman technology and the uniformity of its product reap greater efficiency and therefore higher profits.
- It has become a culturally desirable process: Our need for efficiency, speed, predictability, and control often blinds us to the fact that fast foods (as well as their household equivalent, microwavable prepared foods) actually cost us more financially and nutritionally than meals we prepare ourselves from scratch. Moreover, most of us have soothing emotional memories of McDonald's: It's where we went after Little League games, hung out as teenagers, stopped on the way to the hospital for the birth of a first child, and so on.
- It parallels other changes occurring in society: With the increasing number of dual-earner couples, families are less likely to have someone with the time or the desire to prepare a meal and clean up afterward. Furthermore, a society that emphasizes mobility is one in which the fast food mentality will thrive.

But McDonaldization does have a downside. Although the efficiency, speed, and predictability of this model may be appealing and comforting to some, the system as a whole has made social life more homogeneous, more rigid, and less personal. The smile on the face of the employee taking your order is a requirement of the position, not a sign of sincere delight in serving you. The fast food model has robbed us of our spontaneity, creativity, and desire for uniqueness, trapping us in Weber's "iron cage"—a bureaucratic culture that requires little thought about anything and leaves virtually nothing to chance.

The Hierarchical Makeup of Organizations

Given the previous descriptions, you might think that everyone within a bureaucracy feels alienated, depersonalized, or perhaps even exploited. But a person's experience in a large bureaucracy depends in part on where she or he fits into the overall hierarchy of the organization. As the conflict perspective points out, although some people are dehumanized by their place in the hierarchy, others may actually benefit from theirs.

The Upper Echelons

People at the top of large organizations have come the furthest within the bureaucracy, are the fewest in number, and get the most out of their position. One interesting and disturbing characteristic of bureaucracies is that, despite the recent influx of women and people of color into executive positions around the world, executives still tend to be homogeneous: predominantly male, members of the dominant ethnic group, and middle or upper class (DiMaggio & Powell, 1983; Kanter, 1977; W. H. Whyte, 1956; Zweigenhaft, 1987). According to the U.S. Bureau of the Census (2011b), over 88% of chief executives in the United States are non-Hispanic Whites and 75% are men. All but 28 of the chief executive officers in the 1,000 largest American companies are men (Catalyst, 2009). In addition, executives' educational, social, and familial experiences are remarkably similar (Kanter, 1977; C. W. Mills, 1956). This homogeneity is caused not only by historical prejudices in hiring and promotion practices but also by the nature of top-level jobs.

Upper-level executives don't have clearly bounded jobs with neatly defined responsibilities. The executive must be prepared to use his or her discretion and be flexible enough to deal with a variety of different problems at all times. However, the bulk of the executive's time is spent not in creating, planning, and making important decisions but in attending meetings, writing memos, responding to phone messages and e-mails, delegating responsibilities to underlings, and participating in company-related social gatherings.

Because the role of the executive is, by nature, vague, no clear-cut criteria exist by which to evaluate whether a person is performing the job effectively. Things such as sales and production figures or profit margins can provide only indirect indicators of an executive's competence. When asked what makes an executive effective, top-level employees indicated as most important imprecise factors such as the ability to communicate and to win acceptance (Kanter, 1977). In such an environment, a common language and a common understanding among executives are important. So, from the perspective of the organization, the best way to ensure efficiency is to limit top-level jobs to people who have had similar experiences and who come from similar backgrounds. The result is a closed circle of executives who resemble one another culturally but who are insulated from the rest of the organization.

The Middle Ground

The middle is in some ways the most depressing segment of a bureaucracy (Kanter & Stein, 1979). Often, the morale of people in the middle is sustained by their belief that they have a shot at the top. If I believe I have a chance to be promoted at some point in the future, my boring and unfulfilling job as a middle-level manager may hold different meaning for me than if I expect to remain in the same position forever (McHugh, 1968). Unpleasant tasks may be minor inconveniences, but they are the price I have to pay. This hope of future promotion may drive people in the middle to concentrate on accumulating bits of status and privilege so they can make enough of an impact to gain recognition from those above.

For most middle-level employees, however, the hope of upward mobility is just that—hope. Because of the pyramid-shaped structure of most bureaucracies, the vast majority of middle-level employees will never move up. Many simply fail in the increasingly competitive push for advancement into the upper echelons of the organization. Others are stuck in jobs that provide little or no opportunity for advancement. Some people are able to develop a comfortable niche in the middle (Kanter & Stein, 1979), but others may grow bitter, angry, and alienated; these feelings can sometimes manifest themselves in attempts to retaliate and punish the company.

The structure of most large organizations often forces middle-level managers to become cautious in their approach to their jobs. Unwilling to jeopardize the limited privileges they have attained, middle-level managers may become controlling, coercive, and demanding in their relationships with the people they supervise (Kanter & Stein, 1979).

For some people in the middle, membership in the organization becomes the focus of their life, often to the detriment of other roles and relationships. More than 50 years ago, sociologist William H. Whyte (1956) described how the personal lives of rising young executives were often overshadowed by their desire to succeed in the corporate world. Large organizations instilled in their employees a corporate social ethic—a belief that "belongingness" to the group was of the utmost importance to their success in the job. Such beliefs encouraged total commitment to the organization and made a person's private life irrelevant.

Whyte's (1956) depiction of the private costs of organizational life rings true today. Organizations still value team players, middle-level employees who place organizational interests above their own (Jackall, 1988). To be a good team player, one must avoid expressing strong political or moral opinions, sacrifice one's home life by putting in long hours, and be obedient to one's superiors. Being seen as a loyal and effective group member and sticking to one's assigned position are also important. Distinctive characteristics such as being abrasive or pushy are dangerous in the bureaucratic world. According to one study, one of the most damaging things that can be said about a middle-level manager is that she or he is brilliant. This judgment usually signals that the individual has publicly asserted her or his intelligence and is perceived as a threat to others (Jackall, 1988).

Interestingly, individuals today seem to be less willing to sacrifice their personal lives and beliefs for the organization than they once were. Two sociologists, Paul Leinberger and Bruce Tucker (1991), interviewed the sons and daughters of the original "organization men" whom Whyte had interviewed back in the 1950s. Leinberger and Tucker found that these individuals were very different from their parents in values and attitudes. They tended to be individualists, more inclined to pursue self-fulfillment than a feeling of belongingness to the organization. Given recent social trends, this finding is not surprising. In an era when corporate mergers, relocations, and downsizing are commonplace, organizational loyalty makes less sense for the individual.

Although few people want to go back to a past when middle-level employees sacrificed everything for their career aspirations, Leinberger and Tucker (1991) point out that today's cultural emphasis on individualism has also created other problems, such as feelings of isolation, an inability to commit to others, and the absence of a sense of community.

The Lower Echelons

Those who stand lowest in the organization's hierarchy are paid the least, valued the least, and considered the most expendable (Kanter & Stein, 1979). The real sign that one is at the bottom is the degree to which he or she is controlled by others. People at the bottom typically don't have the right to define their occupational tasks themselves. They have little discretion, autonomy, freedom, or influence. In the university bureaucracy, for example, students usually don't have much say over the content of their courses, the curriculum of their major, the price of tuition, or the requirements necessary for graduation.

Most corporations are still organized in terms of ideas developed in the early 1900s. The fundamental principle is that a highly specific division of labor increases productivity and lowers costs. Hence, managers usually subdivide the low-level work tasks in a bureaucratic organization into small parts that unskilled workers can perform repetitively. This structure provides management with the maximum control over workers' jobs.

Technological advancements often coincide with the subdivision of low-level jobs and a decline in the level of skills required to do them (Hartmann, Kraut, & Tilly, 1989). For example, in the insurance industry, the skilled work of assigning risks and assessing people's claims has been increasingly incorporated into computer software programs. What once required a great deal of human judgment and discretion is now almost completely routinized. Less skilled, less experienced, and lower-paid clerks can now perform the work once performed by skilled workers and professionals (Hartmann et al., 1989).

This process, called *de-skilling*, creates jobs that require obedience and passivity rather than talent and experience. De-skilling provides organizations and even entire industries with clear financial benefits, but it also creates low levels of job satisfaction among employees. Dull and repetitive tasks that offer little challenge, such as assembly line work, account for a substantial amount of the discontent experienced by workers at the bottom of large bureaucracies.

Not surprisingly, lower-level workers are often subjected to a different set of rules and expectations than their managerial counterparts. Some observers characterize the situation as a two-tier system of morality (Ehrenreich, 2002). Low-paid employees are required to work hard, abide by the law, and respect the company's rules. Their personalities are psychologically scrutinized during the application process, and they may be subjected to random drug tests once they're hired. Sometimes they're even expected to donate their time to the organization free of charge, even though federal and state laws require that hourly employees be paid for every minute they work. In 2004, the U.S. Department of Labor brought enforcement actions against scores of companies, including T-Mobile, Wal-Mart, Starbucks, and RadioShack, that routinely required their employees to work off-the-clock (S. Greenhouse, 2004). Ironically, these cases emerged at the same time that wealthy executives at several large corporations were being accused of concealing debts, lying about profits, and engaging in insider trading.

When workers can take an active role in their jobs—such as making decisions and providing input to superiors on a regular basis—they feel much less alienated and find their jobs more rewarding and satisfying than do workers who lack such autonomy (Hodson, 1996). For instance, over the past 15 years or so, some U.S. hospitals have experimented with redesigning their low-wage, low-skill occupations, such as food service workers, housekeepers, and nursing assistants. These hospitals seek to stabilize the workforce and improve patients' experiences by increasing skill training, diversifying the sorts of tasks workers are responsible for, and creating more autonomy and flexibility. These measures have been shown to reduce turnover and increase job satisfaction (Appelbaum, Berg, Frost, & Preuss, 2003).

Without such workplace innovations, the task facing many workers at the bottom is to make their occupational lives tolerable and more dignified by exerting some kind of control over their work (Hodson, 2001). Lower-level employees are rarely completely powerless and can at times be autonomous, even creative, in their positions. The sheer size of large corporations makes it next to impossible for managers to supervise lower-level workers directly and continuously. Thus, substantial opportunities exist, even in the most highly structured and repetitive jobs, for workers either to redefine the nature of their tasks or to willingly and secretly violate the expectations and orders of superiors. For instance, one study found that clerical, service, and manual workers often figure out ways to do required chores in less than the time allotted by management. They can then spend the rest of their time doing what they want (Hodson, 1991). In workplaces with a union presence and a history of conflict between workers and supervisors, collective worker resistance (such as organized strikes) and individual resistance (such as absenteeism and work avoidance) can give lower-level workers a sense of control (Roscigno & Hodson, 2004).

In sum, lower-level workers are not necessarily powerless automatons whose lives are totally structured from above. In fact, the authority of middle-level managers thoroughly depends on their subordinates' willingness to cooperate and abide by the management's directives. Any sort of worker resistance can be disastrous for the manager and for the organization as a whole (Armstrong, Goodman, & Hyman, 1981). When they are organized, lower-level workers can even exert tremendous influence over the policies of a company through strikes, slowdowns, and collective bargaining arrangements.

The Construction of Organizational Reality

According to the symbolic interactionist perspective, organizations are created, maintained, and changed through the everyday actions of their members (G. Morgan, 1986). The language of an organization is one of the ways it creates its own reality.

At one level, new members must learn the jargon of the organization to survive within it. To function within the military system, for example, a recruit must learn the meaning of a dizzying array of words, phrases, slang, sounds, and symbols that are unintelligible to outsiders (Evered, 1983). Newly arrived professors at my university are frequently befuddled by the plethora of acronyms used to refer to faculty committees, subcommittees, and task forces: COF, COA, FDC, SLAAC, CAPP, MAO, POC, ATAC, RAS, FYS, IEC, DEC, GLCA. More important, language helps generate and maintain the organization by marking boundaries between insiders and outsiders.

For an organization to work well, everyone must also internalize the same rules, values, and beliefs. But people still have their own ideas and may develop their own informal structure within the larger formal structure of the organization (Meyer & Rowan, 1977). For example, many college instructors tell their students that class discussion is important and that it may be used as a criterion for assigning a final grade. Yet rarely does every student in a class, or even a majority of students, participate. Most college students know that a few classmates can usually be counted on to respond to questions asked by the professor or to comment on any issue raised in class. These students relieve the remainder of the class from the burden of having to talk at all (Karp & Yoels, 1976). But although these talkative students are carrying the discussion for the entire class, they tend to be disliked by others. A strong norm among many students is that people shouldn't talk too much in class (Karp & Yoels, 1976). Students who speak up all the time upset the normative arrangement of the classroom and, in the students' eyes, may increase the instructor's expectations, hurting everyone in the long run. Other students indicate their annoyance by audibly sighing, rolling their eyes, or openly snickering when a classmate talks too much.

One of the ironies of large complex organizations is that if everyone followed every rule exactly and literally, the organization would eventually self-destruct. For example, the goal of the highly bureaucratized criminal court system is to ensure justice by punishing those who have violated society's laws. The U.S. Constitution guarantees each person accused of committing a serious crime a timely trial by a jury of peers. However, public defenders, district attorneys, private attorneys, and judges actually work closely together to bypass the courtroom and move offenders through the system in an orderly fashion (Sudnow, 1965). In a typical year, less than 5% of federal convictions result from court trials (U.S. Sentencing Commission, 2008).

If judges and attorneys followed the procedural rules to the letter and provided all their clients with the jury trial that is their constitutional right, the system would break down. The courts, already overtaxed, would be incapable of handling the volume of cases. Thus, the informal system of plea bargaining has taken root, allowing the courts to continue functioning. Those who play exclusively by the rules, such as a young, idealistic public defender who wants to take all her or his cases to trial, are subjected to informal sanctions by judges and superiors, such as inconvenient trial dates or heavier caseloads.

In sum, organizational life is a combination of formal structural rules and informal patterns of behavior. Codified rules are sometimes violated and new, unspoken ones created instead. Stated organizational goals often conflict with the real ones. Despite what may appear to be a clear chain of command, the informal structure often has more of an impact on how things are done.

Organizations and Institutions

Understanding the influence of organizations on our everyday lives tells only part of the story. Organizations themselves exist within a larger structural context, acting as a sort of liaison between people and major social institutions such as the economic system, government, religion, health care, and education. As we saw in Chapter 2, institutions are stable sets of statuses, roles, groups, and organizations that provide the foundation for behavior in certain major areas of social life. They are patterned ways of solving the problems and meeting the needs of a particular society.

Organizational Networks Within Institutions

Like individual people, organizations are born, grow, become overweight, slim down, migrate, form relationships with others, break up, and die. They interact with one another, too, cooperating on some occasions and competing on others, depending on the prevailing economic and political winds. They even lie, cheat, and steal from time to time. As with people, some organizations are extremely powerful and can dictate the manner in which other organizations go about their business.

The state of Texas accounts for about 15% of the entire national textbook market (Stille, 2002). A provision in the Texas Education Code states that textbooks should promote decency, democracy, patriotism, and the free enterprise system. A coalition of various watchdog organizations in Texas scours textbooks each year in search of material they consider inappropriate or offensive. For instance, in 2004, the Texas Board of Education approved new high school health textbooks that emphasized abstinence and contained no mention of condoms. It approved these books only after the publishers agreed to replace the term "married partners" with "husband and wife," and the term "when two people marry" with "when a man and a woman marry" (Gott, 2004). Over the past few years, the Texas Board of Education has also asked publishers to delete favorable references to Islam, discussions of global warming and evolution, and illustrations of breast and testicular self-examinations (Simon, 2009; E. Smith, 2010). In 2010, the Board approved a social studies curriculum that requires history and economics textbooks to stress the superiority of American capitalism, questions the Founding Fathers' commitment to a purely secular government, and presents conservative political philosophy in a more positive light (McKinley, 2010; Shorto, 2010). The economic importance of Texas forces many publishers to write their books with that state's rules in mind.

Similarly, when giant corporations, such as General Electric, Apple, and Coca-Cola, decide to downsize or expand their operations, the effects are felt throughout the entire financial community. But even powerful organizations like these cannot stand alone. Massive networks of organizations are linked by common goals and needs. The networks are often so complex that organizations from very different fields find themselves dependent on one another for survival.

MICRO-MACRO CONNECTION

The U.S. Health Care System

Consider the U.S. health care system, one of our most important social institutions. Think about the vast network of organizations that are necessary for a single patient in a single hospital to receive treatment. First of all, the hospital is tightly linked to all the other hospitals in the area. A change in one hospital, such as a reduction in the number of patients treated in the emergency room or the opening of a new state-of-the-art trauma center, would quickly have consequences for all the others. The linkage among hospitals enables the transfer of equipment, staff, and patients from one to another when necessary.

To be accredited and staffed, the hospital must also connect to formal training organizations, such as medical schools, nursing schools, and teaching hospitals. These organizations usually affiliate with larger universities, thus expanding the links in the network. And, of course, the American Medical Association and various licensing agencies oversee the establishment of training policies and credentials.

To survive financially, the hospital must also make connections to funding organizations. Hospitals have traditionally been owned and operated by a variety of governmental, religious, nonprofit, and for-profit organizations. They must operate under a set of strict regulations, which means they must also link to the city, state, and federal governmental agencies responsible for certification, such as the Joint Commission. Add to these relationships their links to the medical equipment industry, the pharmaceutical industry, food service providers, the legal profession, charities, political action committees working on health care legislation, patients' rights groups, and most notably health insurance companies, and the system becomes even more complex. Indeed, the recent highly contentious debate over and subsequent passage of health care reform legislation was essentially a fight to protect competing economic, political, and personal interests.

The vast network of organizations within the health care system must also work together in response to broader societal demands and crises. For instance, in the wake of the 1995 Oklahoma City bombing, the attacks of September 11, 2001, and the anthrax attacks in the fall of 2001, the Institute of Medicine (2003) published a report warning that the nation's mental health, public health, medical, and emergency systems were not equipped to respond to terrorism. At the organizational level, gaps exist in the coordination of agencies and services, the training and supervision of professionals, and the dissemination of information to the general public. The report concluded that only a multilayered approach—involving the federal Departments of Health and Human Services and Homeland Security, state and local disaster planners, and relevant professionals in all areas of health care—could stave off potential catastrophe.

But despite the health care system's complexity, size, and importance, when patients go to a hospital they don't see it as a node in a vast network. Patients are obviously much less interested in the hospital's organizational links than they are in whether their nurse is friendly, the food is good, or their doctor treats them honestly and compassionately. Yet in a 2003 study, one out of three doctors reported purposely withholding information from patients about potentially helpful treatments because those treatments weren't covered by the patient's health insurance (Wynia, VanGeest, Cummins, & Wilson, 2003). The needs of the larger system can sometimes clash with an individual's health care needs, making even face-to-face interactions problematic and, possibly, even detrimental to the patient's health.

Institutional Pressures Toward Similarity

If you think about how many varieties of organizations exist in the world, you might be tempted to focus on their obvious differences. Some are large, others small. Some are formal and complex, others informal and simple. Some have a pyramid-shaped chain of command; others are more egalitarian (Gross & Etzioni, 1985). Sociologists have long been interested in the unique ways in which different organizations adapt to changing political, economic, cultural, or environmental circumstances. However, organizations seem to be more similar than different and even tend to imitate one another's actions as they become established in a particular institution (DiMaggio & Powell, 1983).

Organizational similarity is not really that surprising. Because of the nature of the problems that organizations in the same industry have to address, they come to adopt similar methods of dealing with them. When Apple sought to corner the electronic gadget market with the popular iPad, it was inevitable that other companies would follow suit with their own tablet devices. The same thing could be said for hybrid cars, Greek yogurt, minimalist running shoes, and 3D televisions.

Often the similarities become overwhelming. There's an old adage among Hollywood filmmakers that goes, "There's no success like a previous box office hit" (Dargis, 2011). Likewise, the major U.S. commercial television networks—NBC, ABC, CBS, and Fox—see the profits one network makes with a particular type of program and try to attract viewers in much the same way. As you well know, the perceived popularity of a certain type of television show creates an irritating avalanche of similar shows on other networks—like shows where people compete with one another to see who will perform the grossest or the most fearsome feats (*Survivor* and *Fear Factor*), home improvement shows (*While You Were Out*, *Flip This House*, and *Trading Spaces*), glorified talent contests (*American Idol*, *America's Got Talent*, *Dancing With the Stars*, and *The X Factor*), model/fashion shows (*Project Runway* and *America's Next Top*

Model), shows about people who save all their junk (*Hoarders* and *Hoarding: Buried Alive*), and weight loss shows (*Biggest Loser* and *Extreme Makeover: Weight Loss Edition*). In short, instead of adjusting directly to changes in the social environment, such as the shifting tastes of the television-viewing public, organizations end up adjusting to what other organizations are doing (DiMaggio & Powell, 1983).

The surprising fact is that the imitated practices are not necessarily more effective or successful. After once-novel strategies have spread throughout an industry, they may no longer improve the organization's performance. Viewers eventually get sick of seeing the same types of shows. The net effect of the imitations is to reduce innovation within the industry.

Indeed, like fads in popular culture, some organizational innovations become popular for a brief period, then fade from view, often after millions of dollars have been invested and lost in a company's attempt to jump on the bandwagon. For instance, in the 1980s, U.S. business analysts openly worried that the Japanese economy was growing faster than that of the United States. Some suggested that American companies should begin adopting Japanese-style business practices, such as "quality circles"—groups that meet regularly and allow workers and managers to discuss how to improve quality and productivity. Hundreds of U.S. corporations underwent expensive reorganizations to establish quality circles. But within a few years—as more and more companies showed little if any improvement in the quality of their products—this fad fell completely out of favor and disappeared from the corporate landscape (Best, 2006).

The tendency for organizations to emulate one another is especially strong in times of institutional uncertainty (DiMaggio & Powell, 1983). When new technologies are poorly understood, when the physical environment is undergoing dramatic changes, or when local, state, and federal governments are creating new regulations or setting new agendas, organizations are likely to be somewhat confused about how things ought to be done. Just as individuals look to one another to help define ambiguous situations and determine an appropriate course of action, so do organizations.

Take changes in the field of higher education. Many colleges and universities across the country face the problem of how to attract more students. Such was the case several years ago at the university where I teach. An outside consultant was called in to design a new marketing program for the school. He had some clear strategies for "packaging" the school's image to make it more attractive to prospective students: redesigned brochures, a new recruitment video, a flashy Web site and Facebook page, and so on. But he was also consulting for several other schools competing for the same shrinking pool of students and admitted that many of the "novel" strategies he advised us to use were things other universities were already using. We were addressing a new and uncertain dilemma by replicating the practices of other organizations in the network.

Organizations also resemble one another because those who run them, particularly professionals, tend to come from similar training backgrounds. In many institutions, the professional career track is so closely guarded that the individuals who make it to the top are practically indistinguishable from one another (DiMaggio & Powell, 1983). For example, medical schools are important centers for the development of organizational norms among doctors. The fact that most doctors belong to the American Medical Association creates a pool of individuals with similar attitudes and approaches across a range of organizations. When these doctors become administrators, they will likely bring this common approach to running a hospital.

Certain organizational forms dominate not necessarily because they are the most effective means of achieving goals but because social forces such as institutional uncertainty and the power of professions to provide individuals with a single normative standard create pressures toward similarity. Such similarity makes it easier for organizations to interact with one another and to be acknowledged as legitimate and reputable within the field (DiMaggio & Powell, 1983). But this homogeneity is not without its costs. When organizations replicate one another, institutional change becomes difficult and the iron cage of bureaucracy becomes harder to escape.

Globalization and Social Institutions

You've seen in this book so far the enormous effect that globalization is having on everyday life. Many of our important social institutions have become international in scope—notably economics, education, and religion. How do such global institutions meet the needs of human beings around the world?

Economics

Looking around my office at this moment, I notice that my cell phone was made in Japan, my desk and chair in the United States, my watch in Switzerland, my stapler in Great Britain, my calculator in Taiwan, my shoes in Korea, my pants in Hong Kong, my bottle of water in Croatia, my briefcase in Indonesia, the frame holding my kids' picture in Thailand, and my paper clips, scissors, computer, and iPod in China. Because of the rapid increase in economic links among producing nations in recent years, your life is probably similarly filled with products made in other countries. Japan is experiencing a troubling shortage of bluefin tuna—the most desirable fish used in sushi—because of growing demand in the United States, Europe, and other countries in Asia (Issenberg, 2007).

Economic globalization is more than just a matter of more goods being shipped from one place to another. For instance, there's a pretty good chance that if you contact someone online or by phone to prepare your taxes, provide legal advice, track your lost luggage, solve your software problem, or review your long-distance phone bill, you'll be dealing with someone working at a call center in India (Friedman, 2005). The large pool of English-speaking, technologically savvy Indian workers willing to work for low wages has attracted the phone service operations of companies such as American Express, Sprint, Citibank, General Electric, Ford, Hewlett-Packard, and IBM (Lakshmi, 2005).

If a product wasn't entirely manufactured in another country, it's a good bet that some of its components were. Even domestic products can have a complex international pedigree. Take, for instance, a loaf of good old American white bread. Its ingredients include honey (Vietnam, Brazil, Uruguay, Canada, Mexico, and Argentina), calcium propionate (Netherlands), guar gum (India), flour enrichments (China), beta-carotene (Switzerland), vitamin D3 (China), and wheat gluten (France, Poland, Russia, and Australia; Barrionuevo, 2007).

The economic processes involved in globalization have made national boundaries less relevant. ***Multinational corporations***, businesses that have extended their markets and production facilities globally, have become increasingly powerful over the past several decades. U.S.-based multinational corporations alone employ more than 33.7 million workers worldwide (U.S. Bureau of the Census, 2011b). These companies control a significant portion of the world's wealth, heavily influence the tastes of people everywhere, and don't owe their allegiance to any one country's political authority or culture. At the same time, international financial organizations, such as the World Bank, the World Trade Organization, and the International Monetary Fund, loan money to countries all over the world to finance development and reconstruction projects. (For more on the global economic impact of international financial organizations and multinational corporations, see Chapter 10.) With the costs of communication and computing falling rapidly, barriers of time and space that traditionally separated national markets have also been falling. Even the most remote rural villagers are linked to the global economy as they carry out transactions over the Internet and send and receive goods around the world.

A global economy has its everyday advantages. Goods manufactured and services provided in a country where wages are lower are less expensive for consumers in other countries. Universally accepted credit cards make international travel more convenient. Snack bars in overseas airports accept American money, as do foreign establishments around the world that are near U.S. borders or military bases. Global economic influence has also enabled a significant portion of the world's population to be healthier, eat better, and live longer than the royalty of past civilizations (Kurtz, 1995).

We may barely be aware of how the taken-for-granted elements of our daily lives connect to the economic well-being of people in faraway places. For instance, most of today's popular electronic gadgets could not work without a little-known gritty, super-heavy mud called coltan. Once it is refined in U.S., Japanese, and European factories, coltan becomes tantalum, a remarkably heat-resistant conductor of electricity. Capacitors made of tantalum can be found inside practically every laptop, tablet, video game system, MP3 player, and cell phone in the world. But there isn't nearly enough coltan in the United States, Europe, or Japan to meet these needs. Its largest quantities lie in the rain forests of eastern Congo, where it is mined in much the same way gold was mined in California in the 1800s. Miners spend days in the muck, digging up mud and sloshing it around in plastic tubs until the coltan settles to the bottom. On a good day, a miner can produce about a kilogram of the stuff. Miners earn up to $50 a week, quite a high figure considering that most people in this region live on the equivalent of $10 a month ("What Is Coltan?" 2002).

But global trade has also created some interesting everyday dilemmas. For instance, for centuries, workers in Spain and other Latin American countries have enjoyed the workday *siesta*, a long afternoon nap or an extended lunch, sometimes lasting until 5 P.M. But the owners of some Spanish factories and retail stores have realized that shutting down operations every afternoon so workers can take their siestas is incompatible with Spain's growing integration into the global economy. As the president of a Spanish research group that advocates doing away with the siesta put it, "In a globalized world, we have to have schedules that are more similar to those in the rest of the world so we can be better connected" (quoted in R. McLean, 2005, p. 4). Spain officially cut lunch breaks from three hours to one hour for government workers in 2006 (R. McLean, 2006).

Global financial institutions must also keep close track of holidays around the world to avoid trying to do business on nonbusiness days. In some countries, holidays are determined by the lunar calendar, which not only varies from year to year but may vary from area to area within a country based on local customs. In other countries, such as France, the dates of some bank holidays are a matter of negotiation between the banks and the unions that represent their employees. Even weekends are defined differently in different countries. In Taiwan, the weekend consists of every Sunday and the second and fourth Saturdays of each month. In Malaysia, it is every Sunday and only the first Saturday of every month. And in Lithuania, one-day weekends are occasionally followed by four-day weekends (Henriques, 1999).

Economic globalization has fostered more serious social problems as well, including higher levels of unemployment in countries that maintain labor and environmental protections and exploitation of workers in poor, developing countries. The result is a worldwide system of inequality, whose problems are often invisible to consumers (see Chapter 10). For instance, many of the best and most beautiful roses Americans buy for their loved ones each year come from the rich volcanic soil of Ecuador. These flowers help generate about $240 million a year and tens of thousands of jobs for this once impoverished region. But the Ecuadorian workers who harvest roses are exposed each day to a toxic mix of pesticides and fungicides (G. Thompson, 2003). They work with severe headaches and rashes for the benefit of wealthier customers around the world, who are largely unaware of the conditions under which these fragrant symbols of romance are produced. We may wish to do our part to make life better for the rose harvesters of Ecuador as well as other poor workers around the world, but it's hard to take any effective action. For instance, boycotts of exploitative manufacturers are a double-edged sword. The origin of products is seldom clear-cut, and local workers are typically glad to have jobs they wouldn't have had otherwise. Pressure to compete in the global marketplace also erodes the ability of governments to set their own economic policies, protect national interests, or adequately protect workers and the environment.

(Text continues on page 310)

The Trail of the Tomato

Deborah Barndt

The life cycle of a tomato reveals how globalization touches us daily. In a collaborative cross-border research project, we followed the trail of a tomato from a Mexican field to a Canadian fast food restaurant. The key characteristic of this process is the many steps between production and consumption. Most of us are unaware of who has planted, picked, sorted, packed, processed, transported, prepared, and sold the food we eat. The trail of the tomato also reflects power relationships between the North and the South (in this case, between Mexico in the South and the United States and Canada in the North), as well as inequalities based on gender, race, and class.

As a northern "gringa" researcher documenting Mexican women, I too reflected and reinforced power differences. When I photographed women picking and packing tomatoes, my camera was a symbol of my privilege. Although it was an awkward reminder of the differences in our social power, some women workers befriended me and invited me to visit them later in their rural community.

Returning to Mexico four months later (the picking season abruptly ended by a premature freeze), I found these women in their homes, no longer salaried workers in a multinational operation. With camera and tape recorder, I followed Teresa through her day as she prepared food for her family. Teresa is a salaried worker for an agro-export company based on monocultural (one-crop) production, which has an impact on the health of both the land and the people who work it. Her story reflects the shifting role of women in the new global economy. It also illustrates how subsistence and market economies coexist and how family economies remain the economic and social base for Mexican peasants.

When I first met Teresa in December, she was picking tomatoes and supervising workers in an agribusiness tomato plantation outside of Sayula in the state of Jalisco, Mexico.

With 40 pails to fill for the 28-peso ($5–$6) daily wage, she couldn't talk much then, so she invited me to visit her sometime in her village, half an hour away.

When I returned to Mexico four months later, the tomato harvest had prematurely ended due to a freeze. I found Teresa, her family, and many coworkers at home in Gomez Farias.

Teresa: I was born in 1930 in a family of five kids. My papa died when I was 2, so my mama had to raise us on her own. I never went to school. They brought books into the rancho, and my brothers taught themselves to read. But not me, I didn't learn; I'm like a burrito (little donkey).

Teresa: We got married when I was 17, and I kept doing the same work. Now I'm 67, and Pedro's 72, five years older than me.

We had 16 children—imagine! The oldest is 47 and the youngest is 21. Nine of them are still alive; seven died of illness, of bronchitis (from the cold).

Our two oldest daughters are married and live in Tlapapa; three married sons and two daughters live here. They visit often and help; we share what we have. While we are alive, as long as God offers us the gift of life, we help each other.

We get eggs from our chickens. From time to time, we eat beef, chicken, squash, carrots, lettuce.

When the day dawns, with God's blessing, we find things to eat, even if it's just beans.

Teresa: Our grandchildren are studying, but when they're not in school, they come to work in the fields on the weekends and during vacations; they get the same pay as others.

Teresa: Everyone has their job. My husband and I are the *cabos* (foremen) for our *tabla* (field). Some are *piscadores* (pickers), others are *vaciadoras* (who empty the pails), others are *aquadores* (they bring us water) and *apuntadoras* (who record the number of pails).

Pedro: Before, we worked harder, we worked with animals. We cultivated three crops together—corn, squash, and beans—in the same field. We rotated from one lot to another.

Before, the tomatoes and corn grew well without chemicals. We used the waste of animals as fertilizer; we put it on the plants; it was very good and would last for two to three years.

The fertilizer we use now only lasts for one season. It's expensive and very strong. It kills the squash, and the *milpa* (field) becomes very sad. The corn grows well, it grows tall, but the fertilizer damages the squash and the beans.

Teresa: The chemicals bother us, if they get into our lungs. Those who don't cover themselves suffer more. We put one handkerchief in the back, one in the front, just leaving a slot open for the eyes. This protects us from the pesticides, the insects, the sun.

Teresa: We all feel the economic crisis. The work in Sayula stopped in February because of the freeze. There is no *chamba* (work) now. We can't keep working, so we don't earn any money. It's very depressing; we're sad when we're not working.

When we find work, we're happy.

In a broader sense, this visual essay exposes only one piece of a globalized food system: Teresa doesn't know where the tomatoes she picks end up, and she can contribute only a small part of the story about where they come from. This has been one of the most powerful and recurring themes in our efforts to trace the trail of the tomato: No one has the whole picture, and most actors in the system understand only their small piece of the long and complex process. Nonetheless, Teresa's story begins to fill a void in our distanced, Northern understanding of where our food comes from and what impact its production has on other people and lands.

Teresa: I've seen big trailer trucks on the highway; I've wondered where they're going. They come from far away and they go far away; we don't know where.

The tomatoes don't stay here.

When I showed these photos to Teresa, she wasn't aware of the work of 500 women in the packing plant just five minutes from where she picks tomatoes.

At the other end of the food chain, Teresa's photo story became a catalyst for conversations with Susan, one of hundreds of supermarket cashiers in Canada who eventually sell these tomatoes to consumers. Susan's responses reflect her curiosity about and empathy with the women working at the other end of the food chain:

> We live in different cultures, with different climates and different life experiences, and yet we're going through the same things. [For example,] Teresa used to make her own tortillas but now she has to go and work. And she's feeling that pull just like the North American women are: Should I stay at home with the kids? Should I go to work? She's feeling the economic thing, obviously because everybody has to survive, everybody

has to eat. She's taking care of the family, that's a priority in her life; I'd like to think that in my life that's a priority.

Teresa had mentioned the freeze that cut short their harvest season and left them unemployed; Susan remembers the impact the freeze in the South had on prices in her store. Signs were posted in the produce department explaining why the vegetables were suddenly so expensive.

The Mexican pickers, when hearing about the Canadians who receive and sell the fruits of their labor, raised this question: "I often wonder what happens to our tomatoes. I wonder if they realize the work we have done so they can eat tomatoes." This, at least, is a connection between women workers nurtured by a red fruit that makes a long journey, passing from one hand to another.

Education

The prospect of international competition in a global economy can foster changes in a country's educational system. For instance, U.S. primary school students attend school an average of 180 days a year, compared with 193 days in Germany, 204 days in Korea, and 210 days in Japan (Bush, 2009). Moreover, during the four years of high school, the average American student devotes approximately 1,462 hours to math, science, language, and social studies. The average Japanese student will spend 3,190 hours studying these subjects. In Germany, the figure is 3,628 hours (cited in Bainbridge, 2005). Not surprisingly, students in these and other industrialized countries consistently outperform U.S. students in fields such as math and science (see Exhibit 9.1). Only about one third of American fourth graders and one fifth of high school seniors score at or above science proficiency levels on the National Assessment of Educational Progress test, and less than 2% can be considered advanced (cited in Dillon, 2011a). Indeed, according to some education experts, American 15-year-olds are about one full school year behind 15-year-olds in other industrialized countries (cited in Dillon, 2010).

Concern over our ability to compete in the global marketplace has led to nationwide calls for educational reforms such as heavier emphasis on math and science; more

Exhibit 9.1 | Student Performance in Math and Science in Selected Countries

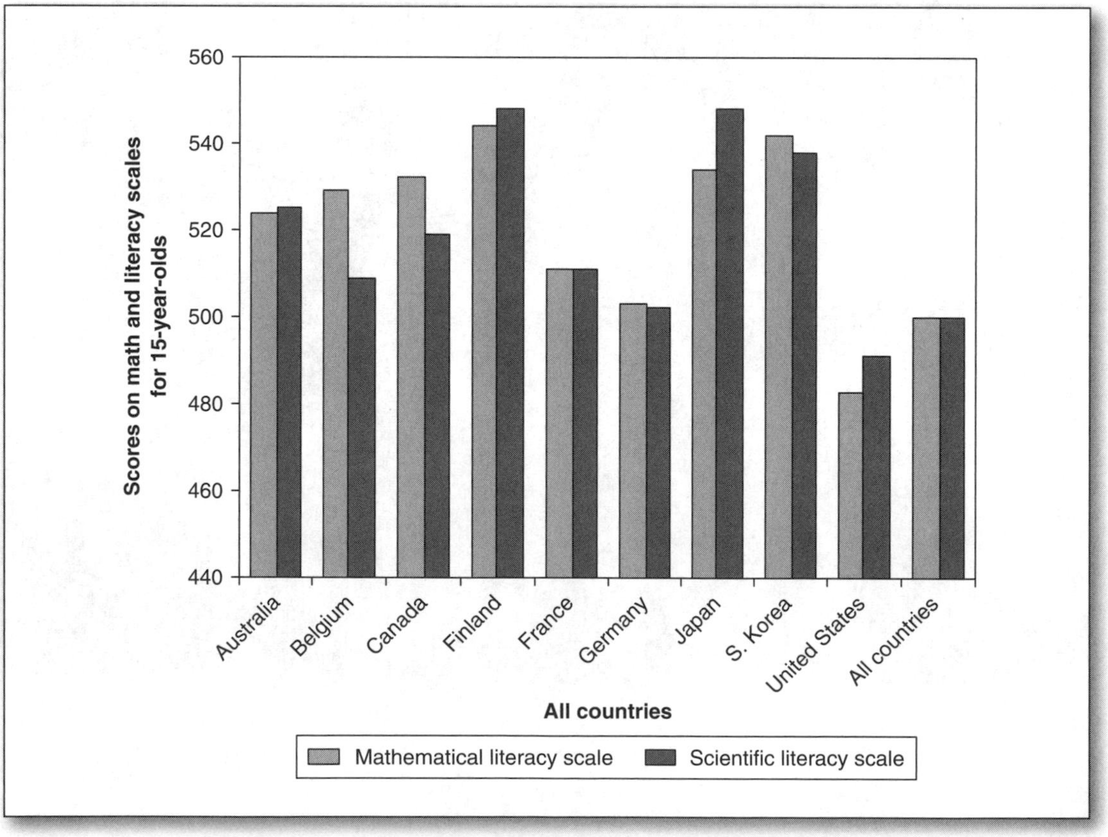

SOURCE: U.S. Bureau of the Census, 2011b, Table 1371

time spent on foundational skills, such as reading and writing; increased computer literacy; and training in political geography and international relations. A few school districts around the country have a year-round schedule to improve student performance (Lehigh, 2005). But competitive pressures have become so great in some schools that administrators have been forced to make students slow down. For instance, school districts across the nation are addressing concerns about stressed-out children by limiting the amount of homework students do on weeknights and banning it altogether on weekends and holidays (Hu, 2011). At a high school in Briarcliff Manor, New York, many students are so caught up in the achievement frenzy that they take classes during lunch period. Some take five or six Advanced Placement classes at a time. To reduce stress levels, school officials decided to rearrange the schedule to cut the number of minutes each class meets over the year and to *require* every student to take a 20-minute lunch break (Hu, 2008).

Pressures to achieve academically are present from the beginning. Even though research shows that play is essential for healthy development, children as early as kindergarten spend significantly more time on lessons and testing than on play, exercise, and imagination. According to a study of New York and Los Angeles kindergartens (E. Miller & Almon, 2009), children spend four to six times as long being instructed and tested in math skills and literacy (two to three hours a day) than in free play (20 to 30 minutes a day). Standardized testing and preparation for testing are now a daily activity in most kindergartens. Play materials like blocks, sand, water tables, and props for dramatic play have largely disappeared from the classroom. Some school districts in Atlanta, New York, Chicago, New Jersey, and Connecticut have opted to eliminate recess, even to the point of building new schools in their districts without playgrounds (Sindelar, 2004).

Education reformers have consistently called for longer school days and shorter vacations so U.S. students can catch up to their peers elsewhere in the world. Some point out that the school calendar—with its six-and-a-half-hour day and 180-day year—was created for the farm-based economy of the past, not today's high-tech one (Ubiñas & Gabrieli, 2011). At his confirmation hearing in 2009, Secretary of Education Arne Duncan stated, "Our school day is too short, our school week is too short, our school year is too short" (quoted in Dillon, 2011b, p. A14). But even at a time when concern over global competitiveness is more acute than ever, economic hard times are forcing schools to cut back rather than expand their educational services. School districts in major cities across the country have laid off thousands of teachers, school psychologists, and custodians. Some districts have trimmed bus service, discontinued field trips, shortened the school day, eliminated summer school, and reduced the school week to four days (Dillon, 2008, 2011b; Ubiñas & Gabrieli, 2011).

Moreover, some critics still feel that we already place far too much emphasis on performance and achievement in this society and that children end up suffering as a result (Mannon, 1997). They often point to Japan, not as a model but as a cautionary tale. Many Japanese children attend classes all day, then go to one of the many private "cram" schools, where they study for college entrance exams until 10 or 11 P.M. Even three-year-olds may spend hours a day memorizing stories, learning vocabulary, and taking achievement tests (WuDunn, 1996a). But Japanese educational accomplishments often come at a steep price. Some Japanese sociologists blame the intense competitive pressures children face for the dramatic rise in youth crime over the past few years. Historically, passing grueling exams and getting into the top high schools and elite colleges was a virtual guarantee of a prestigious job. But Japan's economic stagnation and record unemployment in the 2000s shattered the implicit social contract that once justified all the hard work and sacrifice (French, 1999b). About one in three Japanese elementary school teachers has experienced at least one disruptive classroom incident, such as students mocking their authority, walking out of class, or even physically attacking them (cited in French, 2002).

Few people in the United States would argue that we should emulate the pressurized Japanese educational model. At the same time, though, the demands of the global economy and concerns over Americans' ability to compete internationally will continue to exert influence on legislators and education reformers.

Religion

Another institution influenced by globalization is religion. Despite the enormous variety of cultures and ethnicities that exist today, nearly two thirds of the world's population belongs to just three major religions—Christianity, Hinduism, and Islam—which have successfully crossed national boundaries for centuries. Exhibit 9.2 shows how dominant these world religions are.

Exhibit 9.2   Dominance of World Religions

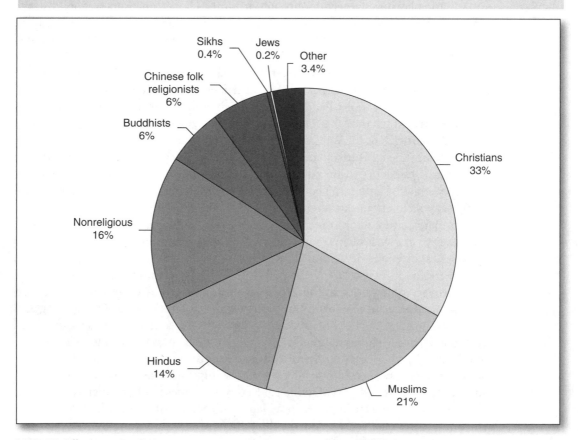

SOURCE: Adherents.com, 2005

Some denominations are globalizing to deal with shrinking memberships in the countries where they originated. For example, outside the United States and Canada, the Mormon Church has grown by over 500% since 1980 (cited in Kress, 2005). The Methodist Church lost 1 million U.S. members between 1980 and 1995 but gained about 500,000 elsewhere, mostly in Africa (Niebuhr, 1998). Indeed, during the 20th century, the population of Christians in Africa grew from 10 million to 360 million. The Anglican Church, in particular, is growing faster in Africa than in its traditional bases, Great Britain and North America; Nigeria alone has 25% of the world's Anglicans (Rice, 2009).

Ironically, this globalization of religion is creating crises for religious communities. Exposure to competing worldviews challenges traditional beliefs. In some cases, religions have reacted with a forceful revitalization of ancient, fundamentalist traditions (Kurtz, 1995). Witness the growing trend toward governments defining themselves in narrowly religious terms. The ascension of fundamentalist Islamic government in Iran, the growing influence of Orthodox Jews in Israeli politics, and the continuing conflict between Hindus and Muslims in Kashmir and between Sunni and Shiite Muslims in Iraq attest to the fact that many people today believe religion cannot be separated from a nation's social and political destiny.

The rise of religious nationalism around the world has created an obvious threat to global security. The attacks of September 11, 2001, are the most glaring illustration. Radical elements sometimes use religious texts—in this case the Qur'an—as justification for violence against societies that they blame for moral decline and economic exploitation. Elsewhere, the possibility of violence by supporters of religious nationalist movements has brought down political regimes, changed the outcomes of elections, strained international relations, and made some parts of the world dangerous places for travelers (Juergensmeyer, 1996).

But religion has also played a positive role in world affairs and has created dramatic social changes. According to Max Weber (1904/1977), the spread of Protestant beliefs throughout Europe made the growth of modern capitalism possible. Protestantism maintained that worldly achievements, such as the accumulation of wealth through hard work, are a sign of God's favor. But the early Protestants also believed that God frowns on vulgar displays of wealth, such as big houses, fancy clothes, and so forth.

So people were motivated to save and reinvest their wealth rather than spend it frivolously. You can see how such beliefs made large-scale and long-term economic growth possible (Weber, 1904/1977). A study of 59 Christian, Buddhist, Muslim, and Hindu countries found that strong religious beliefs tend to stimulate economic growth because of their association with individual traits like honesty, work ethic, thrift, and openness to strangers (Barro & McCleary, 2003).

The influence of religious movements on social life continues. In the 1960s, television pictures of Buddhist monks setting themselves on fire in Vietnam to protest the war fed the growing antiwar movement in the United States. In the 1970s and 1980s, images of Catholic priests and nuns challenging government policies in Central and South America provoked a heightened awareness worldwide of the plight of indigenous people there. In the early 2000s, followers of the Dalai Lama raised global awareness of the plight of Tibetans who seek independence from China, leading to the establishment of the worldwide International Campaign for Tibet. In 2007, tens of thousands of Buddhist monks in Myanmar marched in the streets to protest against that country's oppressive military regime. Their actions sparked organized protests in more than two dozen Asian, European, and North American cities.

Conclusion

More than three centuries ago, John Donne wrote, "No man is an island, entire of itself; every man is a piece of the continent, a part of the main." The same can be said of contemporary social life. We are not isolated individuals whose lives are simply functions of personal characteristics and predispositions. We are social beings. We are part of aggregations of other social beings. We have a powerful need to belong to something larger than ourselves. As a result, we constantly affect and are affected by our associations with others, whether face to face or in well-structured groups, massive bureaucratic organizations, or all-encompassing social institutions.

Throughout Part II of this book, I discussed how society and culture affect everyday experiences and how those experiences help to construct and maintain social order. The development of self and self-controlled behavior, the influence of cultural norms, responses to deviance, and so on are all topics that provide insight into how we are able to live together in a relatively orderly and predictable way. In this chapter, however, you can see that the social structure, though created and maintained by the actions of individuals, is more than just the sum of those actions. Organizations interact at a level well above the individual; institutions are organized in a massive, global system.

Social structure is bigger than any of us, exerts enormous control over our lives, and is an objectified reality that appears to exist independently of us. But it cannot exist without us. I'm reminded of a skit from the old British comedy show *Monty Python's Flying Circus,* in which a high-rise apartment building stood erect only because its inhabitants believed in it. When they doubted its existence, it began to crumble. Like that building, social structure requires constant human support. Once we as a society are no longer able to sustain our organizations or believe in our institutions, they fall apart.

YOUR TURN

One of the major criticisms of complex contemporary society is its sometimes dehumanizing way of life. To see this consequence of bureaucratization firsthand, visit several fast food restaurants close to your home (McDonald's, Taco Bell, Kentucky Fried Chicken, Long John Silver's, etc.). Observe the overall structure of the establishment. How is the work area situated in relation to the customer area? Are the cooking facilities hidden from public view? Note the number of employees and the gender and age configuration of the staff. Observe the way customers are processed. Can you detect a "script" that the employees follow? How do they address customers? How are orders filled? Is there any room for "ad-libbing"? Does each worker seem responsible for a single task (grilling burgers, bagging fries, operating the cash register, cleaning tables, etc.)? Do male employees seem to work in areas different from female employees? Is there an apparent hierarchy among the workers? What is the manager's role? Are you able to detect the ways in which ordinary workers might "resist" on a daily basis (breaking the group's norms, sabotage, labor-management conflicts, etc.)?

Compare your findings across the different restaurants you observed. How much similarity in routine is there? Is some common procedure characteristic of all fast food restaurants, or does each restaurant have a unique way of running? How do diversity and creativity fit into the procedure?

Once you've observed several fast food restaurants, go to other retail businesses in your area. See if you can find any similarities between the way these stores operate and the way the fast food restaurants function.

Drawing from this chapter's discussion of the features of bureaucracies and the notion of McDonaldization, discuss how the systems employed in these businesses maximize efficiency at the cost of dehumanizing the people involved, both workers and customers.

CHAPTER HIGHLIGHTS

- Social structure is both a source of predictability and a source of problems in our everyday life. Sometimes individual interests coincide with structural needs; other times they conflict.

- By virtue of living in society, we are all organizational creatures. We are born in organizations, are educated in them, spend most of our adult lives working in them, and will probably die in them.

- A common form of organization in a complex society is the bureaucracy. A bureaucracy is a large hierarchical organization that is governed by a system of rules and regulations, has a clear specification of work tasks, and has a well-defined division of labor.

- The everyday experience of bureaucratic organizations is determined by where one fits into the hierarchical structure. Bureaucracies look very different depending on whether one is situated at the top, middle, or bottom.

- Organizations are more than structures, rules, policies, goals, job descriptions, and standard operating procedures. Each organization, and each division within an organization, develops its own norms, values, and language.

- Organizations exist within highly interconnected networks. In times of institutional or environmental uncertainty, organizations tend to imitate one another, adopting similar activities, policies, and goals.

- As national borders become increasingly permeable, cultures and social institutions become more global in nature.

KEY TERMS

bureaucracy: Large hierarchical organization governed by formal rules and regulations and having clearly specified work tasks

de-skilling: Subdivision of low-level jobs into small, highly specific tasks requiring less skilled employees

division of labor: Specialization of different people or groups in different tasks, characteristic of most bureaucracies

free-rider problem: Tendency for people to refrain from contributing to the common good when a resource is available without any personal cost or contribution

hierarchy of authority: Ranking of people or tasks in a bureaucracy from those at the top, where there is a great deal of power and authority, to those at the bottom, where there is very little power and authority

McDonaldization: Process by which the characteristics and principles of the fast food restaurant come to dominate other areas of social life

multinational corporation: Company that has manufacturing, production, and marketing divisions in multiple countries

oligarchy: System of authority in which many people are ruled by a privileged few

social dilemma: Potential for a society's long-term ruin because of individuals' tendency to pursue their own short-term interests

social structure: Framework of society social institutions, organizations, groups, statuses and roles, cultural beliefs, and institutionalized norms—that adds order and predictability to our private lives

tragedy of the commons: Situation in which people acting individually and in their own self-interest use up commonly available (but limited) resources, creating disaster for the entire community

STUDENT STUDY SITE

Visit the Student Study Site at **www.sagepub.com/newman9e** for these additional learning tools:

- Flashcards
- Web quizzes
- Sociologists at Work features
- Micro-Macro Connection features
- Video links
- Audio links
- Web resources
- SAGE journal articles

The Architecture of Stratification

Social Class and Inequality

10

Stratification Systems

Sociological Perspectives on Stratification

Class Inequality in the United States

Global Development and Inequality

If you've seen the 1997 Hollywood film *Titanic*, you know that the famous ship had every amenity and comfort: Turkish baths, the finest orchestras, intricately tiled walls, the best cuisine. What it didn't have when it hit an iceberg and began to sink were enough lifeboats. There was room for only 1,178 of the 2,207 passengers and crew members on board. Over the span of two hours on that cold April night in 1912, as the "unsinkable" ocean liner was engulfed by the frigid waters of the North Atlantic, more than 1,500 people lost their lives.

This part of the story is well known. What is less known is that some of the passengers actually had a much better chance of survival than others. More than 60% of the people from the wealthy first-class deck survived, compared with 36% of the people from the second-class deck and 24% of the people from the lowest, or "steerage," class. The figures were even more striking for women and children, who, by virtue of mannerly tradition, were entitled to be spared first. In first class, 97% of the women and children survived; in second class, 89% survived. However, only 42% of the women and children in steerage were saved (W. Hall, 1986).

One reason why so many wealthier passengers survived was that the lifeboats were accessed from the higher first- and second-class decks. The locked doors and other barriers erected to keep third-class passengers from venturing to the upper decks during the cruise remained in place when disaster struck. In addition, little effort was made to save the people in steerage. Some were forcibly kept down by crew members standing guard.

For passengers on the *Titanic*, social inequality meant more than just differences in the comfort of accommodations or the quality of the food. It literally meant life or death. This situation serves as a metaphor for what many people face in today's society. Those at the top have easy access to various "lifeboats" in times of social or economic disaster; others face locked gates, segregated decks, and policies that make even survival exceedingly difficult (Sidel, 1986).

Let's turn the clock ahead to the summer of 2005, when Hurricane Katrina killed more than 1,000 people in the Gulf Coast region of the U.S. South. Most of these people died not because of the hurricane's torrential rains and high winds but because of the flooding that occurred when the levees that ordinarily protect the low-lying areas of New

Orleans (which were in need of repair to begin with) were breached. In addition to the fatalities, hundreds of thousands of people lost everything they owned and were forced to relocate.

The storm and its aftermath did not affect all residents equally. The neighborhoods with significant flooding had a lower median income, a higher poverty rate, and a higher percentage of households without a vehicle than the areas that experienced little or no flooding (J. Schwartz, Revkin, & Wald, 2005). Those of us watching the tragedy unfold on television could not help but notice that the vast majority of the evacuees who suffered for days in the sweltering darkness of the Louisiana Superdome and convention center in New Orleans were poor people of color who came from the most vulnerable parts of the city. These were individuals who either didn't have the necessary transportation to evacuate prior to the hurricane or who stayed behind to tend to sick and elderly relatives who couldn't be moved. Even today, poor, displaced children who were forced to live in ramshackle government trailer parks after the hurricane continue to suffer from various ailments, including anemia, respiratory infections, and depression (Carmichael, 2008). Again we see how lack of economic resources can have direct, physical consequences in people's lives.

In this chapter, I look at class inequality and stratification. In subsequent chapters, I explore two other facets of inequality: race and/or ethnicity and gender. It's important to note, however, that although class, race and ethnicity, and gender are covered in separate chapters, these components of our identities are not experienced separately. They are all interrelated, and they combine to determine individuals' positions in society. For instance, a person doesn't live his life just as a working-class person, just as a man, or just as an Asian American. He is all these things—and more—simultaneously (D. Newman, 2012).

Stratification Systems

Inequality is woven into the fabric of all societies through a structured system of *stratification*, the ranking of entire groups of people that perpetuates unequal rewards and life chances in a society. Just as geologists talk about strata of rock, which are layered one on top of another, the "social strata" of people are arranged from low to high. All societies, past and present, have had some form of stratification, although they vary in the degree of inequality between strata. The four main forms of stratification that sociologists have identified—all of which continue to exist in contemporary societies—are slavery, caste systems, estate systems, and social class systems.

Slavery

One of the most persistent forms of stratification in the world is slavery. *Slavery* is an economic form of inequality in which some people are the property of others. Their lives are owned, controlled, coerced, and restricted. One can become a slave in a variety of ways: through birth, military defeat, debt, or, as in the United States until the mid 19th century, capture and commercial trade (Kerbo, 1991). Because slaves are considered possessions, they are denied the rights and life chances other people take for granted. Slavery has occurred in various forms almost everywhere in the world at some time. Mexico, Great Britain, France, Russia, and Holland all abolished slavery before the United States; Spain, Korea, Cuba, and Brazil did so afterward (D. B. Davis, 2006). Several Middle Eastern countries—Saudi Arabia, Yemen, Oman, United Arab

Emirates—didn't abolish slavery until the latter part of the 20th century. Though theoretically against the law, tens of thousands of people in the West African nations of Niger, Burkina Faso, Mali, and Mauritania are born into slavery today ("A Continuing Abomination," 2008). In South Asia, there are millions of "bonded laborers" whose employers force them to work to pay off a debt (Appiah, 2007).

MICRO-MACRO CONNECTION

Buying and Selling Humans

The United Nations estimates that there are 12.3 million adults and children bought, sold, transported, or kept against their will in the world today (U.S. Department of State, 2010). Other estimates are as high as 27 million. Eighty percent of the victims are women and girls.

Some are forced to labor in sweatshops or become domestic servants. Others are sold into prostitution, sex tourism, or even forced marriage. In Myanmar, children whose parents have no money may be forced into military service. Children in Togo and Benin (in West Africa) are sometimes seized from their villages and sold into servitude in Nigeria, Gabon, and elsewhere. In India, children are sometimes seized, mutilated, and transported to Saudi Arabia to plead for money outside mosques (Crossette, 1997b). In Bangladesh, boys as young as four are sold and put to work as camel jockeys in the Persian Gulf; girls are sent to India and forced to work as prostitutes and maids (Sengupta, 2002). In 2007, a scandal erupted in China when it was discovered that children as young as eight had been kidnapped and forced to work in dangerous brick kilns for no pay and little food (French, 2007b).

Human trafficking is not simply a foreign problem. According to the U.S. Department of State (cited in Ribando, 2007), as many as 17,500 people are trafficked to this country each year. They are forced to work as prostitutes, laborers, or servants. In 2002, police in Plainfield, New Jersey, raided a house expecting to find a brothel. Instead, they found a group of teenage girls from Mexico who were being held captive as sex slaves in squalid conditions (Landesman, 2004). In 2007, a couple who ran a multimillion-dollar perfume business in a wealthy New York suburb were charged with violating a federal antislavery law after it was discovered that they had kept two Indonesian women as sex slaves for years, paying them virtually nothing and forcing them to sleep on mats and to hide when visitors came ("Slaves of New York," 2007).

Traffickers find victims in several ways. Frequently, they take out ads in local newspapers offering good jobs at high pay in exciting cities. In politically unstable countries with high rates of poverty and unemployment, destitute women see these offers as opportunities to help their families financially. Traffickers often use fraudulent modeling, matchmaking, or travel agencies to lure unsuspecting victims. They may even visit families in local villages, assuring them that their daughters will be taught a useful trade or skill or even promising parents that they themselves will marry the daughters. Traffickers deftly target the weakest and most vulnerable populations to victimize. Seventy percent of the world's poor are girls and women (M. A. Clark, 2003). Their low cultural status in many countries makes their victimization that much easier.

What makes human trafficking especially insidious is that victims are at risk in precisely those environments they consider to be safest: their villages and their homes. Impoverished parents, guardians, and husbands—who have nothing else of exchange value—sometimes help to abduct and sell family members, seeing it not as an act of betrayal but as a way of earning money or paying off a debt. A study of Yemeni children trafficked in Saudi Arabia found that the vast majority of cases involved some level of parental agreement and support (cited in Al-Attab, 2005). In China, where males significantly outnumber females, young women and girls may be sold by their impoverished families to potential bridegrooms. Between 1991 and 1996, Chinese police freed about 88,000 women and girls who were being held for this purpose (Goodwin, 2003). Such familial cooperation makes the detection and prosecution of human trafficking even more difficult than it already is.

Caste Systems

Some societies today retain a second form of stratification: a *caste system*. Traditionally, one's caste, which determines lifestyle, prestige, and occupational choices, was fixed at birth and couldn't be changed. Ancient Hindu scriptures, for instance, identified the strict hierarchy of elite, warrior, merchant, servant, and untouchable castes. The rights and duties associated with membership in each caste were clear. In India, "untouchables"—members of the lowest caste—were once required by law to hide from or, if that wasn't possible, to bow in the presence of anyone from a higher caste. They were routinely denied the right to enter Hindu temples or to draw water from wells reserved for members of the higher castes, who feared they would be contaminated if they touched or otherwise came in contact with an untouchable.

According to Human Rights Watch (2009b), more than 260 million people—mostly in India, Nepal, Bangladesh, Pakistan, and Sri Lanka but also in Japan, Yemen, and several African countries—continue to suffer severe caste discrimination. They are victims of exploitation and violence and face massive obstacles to their full attainment of civil, political, economic, and cultural rights.

Things are beginning to change, however. In India, for instance, laws have been passed that prohibit caste-based discrimination. More untouchables (or Dalits, as they prefer to be called) now vote than members of the upper caste (Dugger, 1999). In fact, the benefits Dalits now receive—such as reserved spaces in universities and governmental jobs—have prompted members of the next highest caste of farmers and shepherds to lobby the government to have its caste status downgraded so as to be eligible for these benefits (Gentleman, 2007).

But the caste system still serves as a powerful source of stratification and oppression in India, especially in rural areas. Cultural norms still encourage people to take the occupation of their parents and marry within their caste (Weber, 1970). Even Indians living in the United States find that caste sometimes colors their experiences with friends and business associates (J. Berger, 2004).

Estate Systems

A third form of stratification is the *estate system*, or *feudal system*, which develops when high-status groups own land and have power based on their noble birth (Kerbo, 1991). Estate systems were most commonly found in preindustrial societies. In medieval Europe, the highest "estate" in society was occupied by the aristocracy, who derived their wealth and power from extensive landholdings. The clergy formed the next estate. Although they had lower status than the aristocracy, they still claimed considerable status because the Catholic Church itself owned a great deal of land and exerted influence over people's lives. The last, or "third," estate was reserved for commoners: serfs, peasants, artisans, and merchants. Movement between estates was possible, though infrequent. Occasionally, a commoner might be knighted, or a wealthy merchant might become an aristocrat.

Some reminders of the estate system can still be seen today. In Great Britain, for instance, Parliament's House of Lords is still occupied primarily by people of "noble birth," and a small group of aristocratic families still sit at the top of the social ladder, where they enjoy tremendous inherited wealth and exercise significant political power. For a moment, this system seemed to be changing. In 2007, the British House of Commons (the so-called lower house) voted overwhelmingly to introduce elections to the House of Lords. It also voted to remove the last remaining "hereditary peers," whose presence in the House of Lords is based solely on their noble lineage (Cowell, 2007). A week later, the House of Lords soundly rejected the measure.

Social Class Systems

Stratification systems in contemporary industrialized societies are most likely to be based on social class. A ***social class*** is a group of people who share a similar economic position in society based on their wealth and income. Class is essentially, therefore, an economic stratification system. It is a means of ranking people or groups that determines access to important resources and life chances. Less obviously perhaps, social class standing provides people with a particular understanding of the world and where they fit into it compared with others.

Class systems differ from other systems of stratification in that they raise no legal barriers to ***social mobility***—the movement of people or groups from one level to another. Theoretically, all members of a class system, no matter how destitute they are, can rise to the top. In practice, however, mobility between classes may be difficult for some people. Recent economic studies have found that it takes five or six generations to erase the advantages or disadvantages of a person's economic origins (Krueger, 2002). Within the span of a single generation, there isn't much social mobility—wealthy parents tend to have wealthy children; poor parents tend to have poor children. Likewise, race and gender have historically determined a person's access to educational, social, and employment opportunities. Women of color are especially likely to face barriers to upward mobility, in terms of both economic disadvantage and lack of emotional support from their families (Higginbotham & Weber, 1992).

Sociological Perspectives on Stratification

Sociologists have long been interested in explaining why societies are stratified. Two perspectives—the structural-functionalist perspective and the conflict perspective—offer insights into the sources and purposes of social inequality. They are often presumed to be competing views, but we can actually use them together to deepen our understanding of why social inequality exists, how it develops, and why it is so persistent.

The Structural-Functionalist View of Stratification

From a structural-functionalist perspective, the cause of stratification lies in a society's inevitable need for order. Because social inequality is found in some form in all societies and thus is apparently unavoidable, inequality must somehow be necessary for societies to run smoothly.

As with bureaucracies, the efficient functioning of society requires that various tasks be allocated through a strictly defined division of labor. If the tasks associated with all social positions in a society were equally pleasant and equally important and required the same talents, it wouldn't make a difference who occupied which position. But structural functionalists argue that it does make a difference. Some occupations, such as teaching and medicine, are more important for the well-being of society than others and require greater talent and training. Society's dilemma is to make sure that the most talented people perform the most important tasks. One way to ensure this distribution of tasks is to assign higher rewards—better pay, greater prestige, more social privileges—to some positions in society so that they will be attractive to people with the necessary talents and abilities (Davis & Moore, 1945). Presumably, if these talented people were not offered sufficiently high rewards, they would have no reason to take on the difficult and demanding tasks associated with important positions. Why would someone go through the agony and costs of many years of medical school, for instance, without some promise of compensation and high prestige?

Just because a position is important, however, does not mean it is generously rewarded (Davis & Moore, 1945). Imagine what our society would be like without people who remove our trash. Not only would our streets be unsightly, but our collective health would suffer. Therefore, garbage collectors serve a vital social function. But they don't get paid very much—on average, about $481 a week, according to the U.S. Bureau of Labor Statistics (2010b)—and trash removal is certainly not a highly respected occupation. Why aren't garbage collectors higher up in the hierarchy of occupations? According to the structural-functionalist perspective, it is because we have no shortage of people with the skills needed to collect garbage. Physicians also serve the collective health needs of a society. But because of the skills and training needed to be a doctor, society must offer rewards high enough to ensure that qualified people will want to enter the medical profession. Doctors—even those just starting out—can expect to make, on average, four to five times more than garbage collectors (U.S. Bureau of Labor Statistics, 2010c).

This explanation may make some sense. But when we examine the pay scales of actual occupations, it comes up short. One look at the salary structure in today's society reveals obvious instances of highly paid positions that are not as functionally important as positions that receive smaller rewards. For instance, Oprah Winfrey makes about $315 million a year. Filmmakers Steven Spielberg and Jerry Bruckheimer each earn $100 million a year and comedian Jerry Seinfeld, $75 million. Lady Gaga pulls in $62 million. You might say that talk show hosts, filmmakers, comedians, and singers serve important social functions by providing the rest of us with a recreational release from the demands of ordinary life; and the best entertainers and athletes do have rare skills, indeed. However, society probably can do without another TV show, megahit movie, or concert more easily than it can do without competent physicians, scientists, computer programmers, teachers, or even trash collectors, who earn substantially less in a year than what many celebrities earn in a day.

Furthermore, the structural-functionalist argument that only a limited number of talented people are around to occupy important social positions is probably overstated. Many people have the talent to become doctors. What they lack is access to training. And why are some people—women and members of racial and ethnic minorities—paid less for or excluded entirely from certain jobs? The debates over equal employment opportunity and equal pay for equal work are essentially debates over how the functional importance of certain positions is determined.

Finally, when functionalists claim that stratification serves the needs of society, we must ask, whose needs? A system of slavery obviously meets the economic needs of one group at the expense of another, but that doesn't make it acceptable. In a class-stratified society, individuals who receive the greatest rewards have the resources to make sure they continue receiving such rewards. Over time, the competition for the most desirable positions will become less open and less competitive. The offspring of "talented"—that is, high-status—parents will inevitably have an advantage over equally talented people who are born into less successful families. Hence, social background and not personal aptitude may become the primary criterion for filling important social positions (Tumin, 1953).

The structural-functionalist perspective gives us important insight into how societies ensure that all positions in the division of labor are filled. Every society, no matter how simple or complex, differentiates people in terms of prestige and esteem and possesses a certain amount of institutional inequality. But this perspective doesn't address the fact that stratification can be unjust and divisive, a source of social *disorder* (Tumin, 1953).

The Conflict View of Stratification

Conflict theorists are among those who argue that social inequality is neither a societal necessity nor a source of social order. They see it as a primary source of conflict, coercion, and unhappiness. Stratification ultimately rests on the unequal distribution of resources—some people have them, others don't. Important resources include money, land, information, education, health care, safety, and adequate housing. Those high in the stratification system can control these resources because they are the ones who set the rules. The conflict perspective takes it as a fundamental truth that stratification systems serve the interests of those at the top and not the survival needs of the entire society.

Resources are an especially important source of inequality when they are scarce. Sometimes, their scarcity is natural. For instance, there's only a finite amount of land on earth that can be used, inhabited, and owned. At other times, however, the scarcity of a resource is artificially created. For instance, in 1890, the founder of De Beers, the South African company that currently controls two thirds of the international diamond market, realized that the sheer abundance of diamonds in southern Africa would make them virtually worthless on the international market. So he decided to carefully limit the number of diamonds released for sale each year. This artificially created rarity, coupled with a carefully cultivated image of romance, is what made diamonds so expensive and what continues to make companies such as De Beers so powerful today (Harden, 2000).

Rich and politically powerful individuals frequently work together to create or maintain privilege, often at the expense of the middle and lower classes (Phillips, 2002). The U.S. Congress is dominated by both Republicans and Democrats who are far richer than the citizens they represent. The average wealth of a U.S. senator is well over $10 million; House representatives average over $5 million. Sixty percent of the U.S. senators and 40% of the representatives who were newly elected in 2010 are millionaires—compared with 1% of the general population (Center for Responsive Politics, 2011). Thus, from the conflict perspective, it's not at all surprising that politicians would make decisions that benefit the wealthy over others. For instance, after voting to extend Bush-era tax cuts for the wealthiest Americans in 2011, Congress quickly began to look for ways to cut spending on programs that benefit low-income Americans, such as Medicaid (the health insurance system that covers poor adults and their dependents), low-income housing programs, legal services for the poor, and supplemental nutrition for poor families (Greywolfe359, 2011). To provide financial aid to the victims of Hurricane Katrina, many members of Congress favored cutting the budgets of existing social programs that helped other needy citizens rather than repealing tax cuts for upper-class Americans.

What the conflict perspective gives us that the structural-functionalist perspective doesn't is an acknowledgment of the interconnected roles that economic and political institutions play in creating and maintaining a stratified society.

The Marxian Class Model

Karl Marx and Friedrich Engels (1848/1982) were the original proponents of the view that societies are divided into conflicting classes. They felt that in modern societies, two major classes emerge: *capitalists* (or the bourgeoisie), who own the **means of production**—land, commercial enterprises, factories, and wealth—and are able to purchase the labor of others, and *workers* (or the proletariat), who neither own the means of production nor have the ability to purchase the labor of others. Workers, instead, must sell their own labor to others in order to survive. Some workers, including store managers and factory supervisors, may control other workers, but their power is minimal compared with the power exerted over them by those in the capitalist class. Marx and Engels supplemented this two-tiered conception of class by adding a third tier, the petite bourgeoisie, which is a transitional class of people who own the means of production but don't purchase the labor power of others. This class consists of self-employed skilled laborers and businesspeople who are economically self-sufficient but don't have a staff of subordinate workers (R. V. Robinson & Kelley, 1979). Exhibit 10.1 diagrams the positions of the three classes.

Capitalists have considerable sway over what and how much will be produced, who will get it, how much money people will be paid to produce it, and so forth. Such influence allows them to control other people's livelihoods, the communities in which people live, and the economic decisions that affect the entire society. In such a structure, the rich inevitably tend to get richer, to use their wealth to create more wealth for themselves, and to act in ways that will protect their interests and positions in society.

Ultimately, the wealthy segments of society gain the ability to influence important social institutions such as the government, the media, the schools, and the courts. They have access to the means necessary to create and promote a reality that justifies their exploitative actions. Their version of reality is so influential that even those who are

Exhibit 10.1   Marx's Model of Class

	Control labor of others	Do not control labor of others
Own means of production (land, factories, etc.)	Capitalists	Petite bourgeoisie
Do not own means of production	Workers	Workers

harmed by it come to accept it. Marx and Engels called this phenomenon *false consciousness*. False consciousness is crucial because it is the primary means by which the powerful classes in society prevent protest and revolution. As long as large numbers of poor people continue to believe that wealth and success are solely the products of individual hard work and effort rather than structured inequalities in society—that is, they believe what in the United States has been called the American Dream—resentment and animosity toward the rich will be minimized and people will perceive the inequalities as fair and deserved (R. V. Robinson & Bell, 1978).

Neo-Marxist Models of Stratification

In Marx's time—the heyday of industrial development in the mid 19th century—ownership of property and control of labor were synonymous. Most jobs were either on farms or in factories. Lumping all those who owned productive resources into one class and all those who didn't into another made sense. However, the nature of capitalism has changed a lot since then. Today, a person with a novel idea for a product or service, a computer with high-speed Internet access, and a smartphone can go into business and make a lot of money. Corporations have become much larger and more bureaucratic, with a long, multilevel chain of command. Ownership of corporations lies in the hands of stockholders (foreign as well as domestic), who often have no connection at all to the everyday workings of the business. Thus, ownership and management are separated. The powerful people who run large businesses and control workers on a day-to-day basis are frequently not the same people who own the businesses.

In light of changing realities, more contemporary conflict sociologists, such as Ralf Dahrendorf (1959), have offered models that focus primarily on differing levels of authority among the members of society. What's important is not just who owns the means of production but who can exercise influence over others. *Authority* is the possession of some status or quality that compels others to obey (Starr, 1982). A person with authority has the power to order or forbid behavior in others (Wrong, 1988). Such commands don't require the use of force or persuasion, nor do they need to be explained or justified. Rulers simply have authority over the ruled, as do teachers over students, employers over employees, and parents over children. These authority relationships are not fixed, of course: Children fight with their parents, students challenge their teachers, and workers protest against their bosses. But although the legitimacy of the authority may sometimes be called into question, the ongoing dependence of the subordinates maintains it. The worker may disagree with the boss, and the student may disagree with the teacher; but the boss still signs the paycheck, and the teacher still assigns final grades.

Like Marx and Engels, Dahrendorf believed that relations between classes inherently involve conflicts of interest. Rulers often maintain their position in society by ordering or forcing people with less authority to do things that benefit the rulers. But by emphasizing authority, Dahrendorf argued that stratification is not exclusively an economic phenomenon. Instead, it comes from the social relations between people who possess different degrees of power.

Dahrendorf's ideas about the motivating force behind social stratification have since been expanded. Sociologist Erik Olin Wright and his colleagues (Wright, 1976; Wright, Costello, Hachen, & Sprague, 1982; Wright & Perrone, 1977) have developed a model that incorporates both the ownership of means of production and the exercise of authority over others. The capitalist and petite bourgeoisie classes in this scheme are

Exhibit 10.2   Wright's Model of Class

	Exercise authority	Do not exercise authority
Own means of production	Capitalists	Petite bourgeoisie
Do not own means of production	Managers	Workers

identical to those of Marx and Engels. What is different is that the classes of people who do not own society's productive resources (Marx and Engels's worker class) are divided into two classes: managers and workers (see Exhibit 10.2).

Wright's approach gives us a sense that social class is not simply a reflection of income or the extent to which one group exercises authority over another. Lawyers, plumbers, and cooks, for instance, could each conceivably fall into any of the four class categories. They may own their own businesses and hire assistants (placing them in the capitalist class), work for a large company and have subordinates (placing them in the manager class), work for a large company without any subordinates (placing them in the worker class), or be self-employed (placing them in the petite bourgeoisie; R. V. Robinson & Kelley, 1979).

Wright's approach also emphasizes that class conflict is more than just a clash between the rich and the poor. Societies have, in fact, multiple lines of conflict— economic, political, administrative, and social. Some positions, or what Wright calls *contradictory class locations*, fall between two major classes. Individuals in these positions have trouble identifying with one side or the other. Middle managers and supervisors, for instance, can align with workers because both are subordinates of capitalist owners. Yet because middle managers and supervisors can exercise authority over some people, they may also share the interests and concerns of owners.

Weber's Model of Stratification

Other conflict sociologists have likewise questioned Marx's heavy emphasis on wealth and income as the sole factors that stratify society. Max Weber (1921/1978) agreed with Marx that social class is an important determinant of stratification. However, he observed that the way people are ranked is not just a matter of economic inequality. Weber added two other dimensions—status (or what he called prestige) and power—to his model of stratification, preferring the term ***socioeconomic status***— the prestige, honor, respect, and power associated with different class positions in society—rather than class to describe social inequality (Weber, 1970).

The existence of these other dimensions makes the conflict model of class stratification more complex than simply a battle between the rich and the poor. **Prestige** is the reverence and admiration given to some people in society. It is obviously influenced by wealth and income, but it can also be derived from *achieved* characteristics, such as educational attainment and occupational status, and from *ascribed* characteristics, such as race, ethnicity, gender, and family pedigree. While wealth and prestige often go hand in hand, they don't necessarily have to. Drug dealers, for example, may be multimillionaires, but they aren't well respected and therefore aren't ranked high in the stratification system. On the flip side, professors may earn a modest salary, but they can command a fair amount of respect. **Power**, for Weber, is a person's ability to affect decisions in ways that benefit him or her. Again, power is usually related to wealth and prestige, but it need not be. Sometimes low-income individuals can band together and influence decisions at the societal level, as when workers strike for better working conditions.

Class Inequality in the United States

One of the ideological cornerstones of U.S. society is the belief that all people are created equal and that only individual shortcomings can impede a person's progress up the social ladder. After all, the United States is billed as the "land of opportunity." Our folklore is filled with stories of disadvantaged individuals who use their courage and resolve to overcome all adversity. We don't like to acknowledge that class inequality exists or that some people face immovable obstacles on the path to success that others will never have to face. But sociologists tell us that our place in the stratification system determines the course of our lives, in obvious and subtle ways.

Class and Everyday Life

Class standing in the United States has always determined a whole host of life chances, including access to higher education; better-paying jobs; and healthier, safer, and more comfortable lives:

- In fire-prone regions of the West, insurance companies offer "premium" protection plans to wealthy policyholders. At the first sign of a wildfire in the vicinity, someone will come and spray special fire retardant on the policy owner's house to prevent it from burning (W. Yardley, 2007).
- A study of street repair work in Indianapolis found that the average time it took between the filing of a complaint and the fixing of a pothole was 11 days in neighborhoods with an average annual income of more than $55,000; in neighborhoods with an average income of less than $25,000, it took an average of nearly 25 days (T. Evans & Nichols, 2009).
- For an annual fee, which could be as much as $20,000, wealthy individuals can buy "boutique" or "concierge" medical care, which includes special access to their physician via 24/7 cell phone and e-mail; same-day appointments with a guaranteed waiting time of no more than 15 minutes; nutrition and exercise physiology exams at the patients' homes; nurses to accompany them when they go to see specialists; and routine physicals that are so thorough they can last up to three days (Belluck, 2002; Garfinkel, 2003; Zuger, 2005). The current economic recession has not dampened the desire for this type of personalized health care among the very wealthy (Sack, 2009b).

Perhaps you've experienced the humiliation of being squished into the coach section of an airplane while more affluent passengers luxuriate in the spacious first-class section. First-class cabins usually contain more flight attendants per person than coach, and first-class attendants respond more quickly to call buttons. In addition, most airlines now have special express security lines for first-class passengers so as to avoid unnecessary delays (Squadron, 2005). And it's not just about shorter waits, better service, and roomier seats. Virgin Atlantic Airlines offers its first-class passengers leather armchairs with matching ottomans that turn into double beds. Emirates Airlines offers first-class passengers their own enclosed suites, complete with minibar, 19-inch television, bed, and "dine on demand" room service (Rosato, 2004). Emirates first-class passengers can also take advantage of the two shower spas available on board.

Such exclusive personal attention reinforces feelings of power and privilege. On the other side of the coin, people in the lower classes routinely face frustrating barriers in their daily lives. They must often make use of public facilities (health clinics, Laundromats, public transportation, and so on) to carry out the day-to-day tasks that wealthier people can carry out privately.

Class can also determine access to other resources and thereby contribute to long-term advantages. Consider, for instance, admission to college. We would like to think that admissions decisions are based solely on a student's merit: high academic achievement (reflected in high school grades) and strong intellectual potential (reflected in scores on standardized aptitude tests like the SAT). What could be fairer than the use of these sorts of objective measures as the primary criteria for determining who gets an elite education that will open doors for a lifetime?

Would it disturb you to know that your SAT score may depend as much on your parents' financial status as on your own intellect? Obviously, simply coming from a well-to-do family doesn't guarantee a high score on the SAT, but it can help. If you were fortunate enough to attend high school in an affluent, upper-class neighborhood, chances are your school offered SAT preparation courses. In some of these schools, students take practice SAT exams every year until they take the real one in their senior year. Even if a school doesn't provide such opportunities, private lessons from test preparation coaches are available to those who can afford them. Wealthy high schools are also significantly more likely than midlevel or poor high schools to offer Advanced Placement courses, another important tool that college admissions officers use to measure applicants (Berthelsen, 1999).

Access to these opportunities pays off. In 2010, the average combined SAT score for students whose families earned less than $10,000 a year was 1329. The average score for students whose families earned more than $100,000 a year was 1602 (National Center for Fair and Open Testing, 2011).

Class Distinctions

Class distinctions go beyond differences in access to educational or economic opportunities, however. People create and maintain class boundaries through their perceptions of moral, cultural, and lifestyle distinctions (Lamont, 1992). For example, some communities forbid residents to dry their clothes outdoors on clotheslines because it gives the neighborhood a shabby appearance. A few years ago, the town of Wilson, North Carolina, voted to prohibit people from keeping old sofas on their front porches (Bragg, 1998). For generations, poor people in the area—unable to purchase expensive outdoor furniture—had kept their worn-out sofas and chairs on the porch, where they could still be used. But more affluent residents saw the practice as "low class" and approved the ban to make neighborhoods more presentable.

In the end, class is a statement about self-worth and the quality of one's life:

> It's composed of ideas, behavior, attitudes, values, and language; class is how you think, feel, act, look, dress, talk, move, walk; class is what stores you shop at, restaurants you eat in; class is the schools you attend, the education you attain; class is the very jobs you will work at throughout your adult life. Class even determines when we marry and become mothers. . . . We experience class at every level of our lives; class is who our friends are, where we live . . . even what kind of car we drive, if we own one. . . . In other words, class is socially constructed and all-encompassing. (Langston, 1992, p. 112)

Although the boundaries between classes tend to be fuzzy and subjective, distinct class designations remain a part of everyday thinking, political initiatives, and social research. The *upper class* (which some sociologists define as the highest-earning 5% of the U.S. population) is usually believed to include owners of vast amounts of property and other forms of wealth, major shareholders and owners of large corporations, top financiers, rich celebrities and politicians, and members of prestigious families. The *middle class* (roughly 45% of the population) is likely to include college-educated managers, supervisors, executives, owners of small businesses, and professionals. The *working class* (about 35% of the population) typically includes industrial and factory workers, office workers, clerks, and farm and manual laborers. Most working-class people don't own their own homes and don't attend college. Finally, about 15% of the population consists of people who work for minimum wage or who are chronically unemployed. They are the *poor* (sometimes referred to as the underclass or the lower class; Walton, 1990; E. O. Wright et al., 1982).

The Upper Class

The upper class in the United States is a small, exclusive group that occupies the highest levels of status and prestige. For some, membership in the upper class is relatively recent, acquired through personal financial achievement. These families are usually headed by high-level executives in large corporations and highly compensated lawyers, doctors, scientists, entertainers, and professional athletes. Such individuals may have been born into poor, working-class, or middle-class families, but they have been able to climb the social ladder and create a comfortable life. They are sometimes called "the new rich."

Others, however, are born into wealth gained by earlier generations in their families (Langman, 1988). The formidable pedigree of "old wealth," not to mention the wealth itself, provides them with insulation from the rest of society. Their position in society is perpetuated through a set of exclusive clubs, resorts, charitable and cultural organizations, and social activities that provides members with a distinctive lifestyle and a perspective on the world that distinguishes them from the rest of society.

Sociologists G. William Domhoff (1983, 1998) and C. Wright Mills (1956) have made the case that members of the upper class can structure other social institutions to ensure that their personal interests are met and that the class itself endures. They control the government, large corporations, the majority of privately held corporate stock, the media, universities, councils for national and international affairs, and so on (Domhoff, 1998). Hence, members of this class enjoy political and economic power to a degree not available to members of other classes.

For example, the educational system plays not only a key socializing role (see Chapter 5) but also an important role in perpetuating or reproducing the U.S. class structure. Children of the upper class often attend private schools, boarding schools, and well-endowed private universities (Domhoff, 1998). In addition to the standard curriculum, these schools teach vocabulary, inflection, styles of dress, aesthetic tastes, values, and manners (R. Collins, 1971). Required attendance at school functions; participation in esoteric sports such as lacrosse, squash, and crew; the wearing of school blazers or ties; and other "character-building" activities are designed to teach young people the unique lifestyle of the ruling class. In many ways, boarding schools function like "total institutions" such as prisons and convents (E. Goffman, 1961), isolating members from the outside world and providing them with routines and traditions that are highly effective agents of socialization.

In a study of more than 60 elite boarding schools in the United States and Great Britain, Peter Cookson and Caroline Persell (1985) showed how the philosophies and programs of boarding schools help transmit power and privilege. This school experience forms an everlasting social, political, and economic bond among all graduates, and the schools act as gatekeepers into prestigious universities. After graduates leave these universities, they connect with one another at the highest levels in the world of business, finance, and government. The director of development at Choate, an elite prep school in Connecticut, said this:

> There is no door in this entire country that cannot be opened by a Choate graduate. I can go anywhere in this country and anywhere there's a man I want to see . . . I can find a Choate man to open that door for me. (quoted in Cookson & Persell, 1985, p. 200)

The privileged social status that is produced and maintained through the elite educational system practically guarantees that the people who occupy key political and economic positions will form a like-minded, cohesive group with little resemblance to the majority whose lives depend on their decisions.

The Middle Class

In discussing the U.S. class system, it is tempting to focus on the very top or the very bottom, overlooking the chunk of the population that falls somewhere in the ill-defined center: the middle class. Ironically, the middle class has always been important in defining U.S. culture. Every other class is measured and judged against the values and norms of the middle class. It is a universal class, a class that supposedly represents everyone (Ehrenreich, 1990). Not surprisingly, the middle class is a coveted political constituency. Liberal and conservative politicians alike court it. Policies are proclaimed on its behalf.

But the lofty cultural status of the middle class in U.S. society belies the difficulties it experiences. Economists, pundits, and sociologists have long been fond of talking about the middle class being "under assault," "endangered," or "fragile" (T. A. Sullivan, Warren, & Westbrook, 2000). While corporate profits rose sharply during the early 2000s, the take-home pay of middle-income U.S. workers has failed to keep up (S. Greenhouse & Leonhardt, 2006). Median household incomes rose steadily throughout the 1980s and

1990s but have leveled off and even fallen a bit ever since. In 1980, the median household income (in current dollars) across all ethnoracial groups in the United States was $44,059. By 2010, it had only increased to $49,445 (DeNavas-Walt, Proctor, & Smith, 2011). Between 1980 and 1990, median household income grew by about 8%. But between 2000 and 2007, median income actually shrank by about 1%; between 2009 and 2010, it shrank by an additional 2.3% (DeNavas-Walt, Proctor, & Smith, 2011).

The current economic recession has taken its toll on every sector of the population, including the middle class. Hourly earnings, weekly earnings, and employer-provided benefits like pensions and retirement accounts have all fallen since 2007 (Mishel, Bernstein, & Shierholz, 2009). The number of workers who earn at least $20 an hour (a wage that once symbolized "middle class") has dropped nearly 60% over the past three decades (cited in Uchitelle, 2008). Indeed, after adjusting for inflation, the median hourly wage today is only $16.27 (U.S. Bureau of Labor Statistics, 2010b). In addition to lower wages, many workers across the country are seeing their hours cut—for instance, by being moved from full time to part time or by losing opportunities for overtime. According to data from the U.S. Bureau of Labor Statistics (2011b), in 2011, 8.5 million workers had to cut their hours to fewer than 35 a week due to slack work conditions.

Even before the current recession, only about a third of U.S. adults said they earned enough money to lead the kind of life they wanted, and about two thirds worried that good jobs would move overseas and that workers here would be left with jobs that don't pay enough (Kohut, 1999). Today, even families with good incomes live close to the financial edge, one layoff or medical emergency away from financial crisis. The proportion of middle-class families that could weather an economic emergency equal to three months of lost income decreased from 39% in 2000 to 29% in 2007 (Weller & Logan, 2008). Many urban areas around the country are seeing a new form of homelessness: formerly middle-class families who've lost their homes and now must live week to week in cramped motel rooms (Eckholm, 2009).

To make matters worse, the rising cost of health care coupled with higher insurance premiums, higher out-of-pocket payments, and less extensive coverage is making it increasingly difficult even for middle-class families to afford adequate medical coverage (Abelson & Freudenheim, 2008). Thirty-seven percent of uninsured Americans live in households with incomes of more than $50,000 a year (DeNavas-Walt et al., 2011). According to the Kaiser Family Foundation (2009), because of cost-trimming actions over the past few years, an estimated 11.1 million Americans have lost the health insurance they received through their employer.

Not only do middle-class jobs pay less than they used to, but there are fewer of them to go around. Many people who have followed the institutionalized path to success— getting college degrees, developing marketable skills, building impressive résumés—are finding themselves out of work as companies cut costs to stay afloat. Hundreds of thousands of once solid jobs in high tech, communication, and finance have disappeared. And with a national unemployment rate that hovers around 9%, many people who were once middle class are either marginally attached to the labor force or completely discouraged over their job prospects (U.S. Bureau of Labor Statistics, 2009).

To add insult to injury, economists predict that even as the economy recovers, the job market will be weak. Many companies that are currently laying people off don't plan to rehire at prerecession levels once things get better (Lowenstein, 2009). In 2011, the economy was actually producing as much as it was prior to the recession, but with

7 million fewer workers than there were prior to the recession. In other words, companies learned to produce more cost efficiently with a smaller workforce. Furthermore, since 2010, equipment and software prices have dropped 2.4% while labor costs have risen 6.7%. So when companies grow, they quickly realize that it's much cheaper to buy new machines than to hire more people. Said one executive, "I want to have as few people touching our products as possible. Everything should be as automated as it can be" (quoted in Rampell, 2011a, p. A1).

Moreover, the types of jobs that will be available in the future may not be the sort that will strengthen people's middle-class status. For instance, employers are increasingly turning to temporary workers rather than full-time, permanent workers (who would be eligible for benefits). In 2010, one quarter of the 1.17 million private sector jobs that were added were temporary jobs (cited in Rich, 2010).

And even the permanent jobs that are created may not pay enough to ensure people's middle-class standing. According to the U.S. Bureau of Labor Statistics, 7 out of 10 occupations that are forecasted to show the greatest growth between now and 2018 are in low-wage service fields that require little, if any, education or training: retail sales, customer service, fast food service, office administration, and nursing assistance (U.S. Bureau of Labor Statistics, 2010d). By most accounts, middle-class jobs will continue to be in short supply, meaning that many college-educated people will be thwarted in their attempts to earn a comfortable living. It's no wonder that many middle-class adults feel like they're on a treadmill that constantly threatens to throw them into a less desirable social class.

The Working Class

Members of the working class—people who work in factory, clerical, or low-paying sales jobs—are even more susceptible than those in the middle class to economic fluctuations. Most working-class people have only a high school education and earn an hourly wage rather than a weekly or monthly salary. Although they may earn enough money to survive, they typically don't earn enough to accumulate significant savings or other assets. Under the best circumstances, they usually have difficulty buying a home or paying for a child's education. When times are bad, they live their lives under the constant threat of layoffs, factory closings, and unemployment.

The middle class may be under siege, but the working class always suffers disproportionately from downturns in the U.S. economy. Consequently, they are far more pessimistic about their futures than wealthier Americans. For instance, a recent survey found that people who make less than $30,000 a year are more likely to expect to be laid off or take a pay cut and to say they have had trouble paying for medical care or paying the rent (Pew Research Center, 2011).

Their fears are real. To save money, many large companies first reduce their low-wage workforce. In 2009, during the height of the recession, American employers initiated close to 12,000 "mass layoff events" (when at least 50 employees from a single employer file for unemployment insurance benefits), resulting in the loss of 2.1 million jobs, mostly in manufacturing and retail (U.S. Bureau of Labor Statistics, 2011b). Boeing laid off 10,000 employees that year; Caterpillar cut 22,000 jobs; Chrysler and General Motors fired more than 50,000 employees.

Many working-class people who remain employed haven't had raises in years but have seen the cost of living (in particular, food, energy, and health care) rise steadily. Twenty-two percent of people living in households with an income between $25,000 and $49,000 had no health insurance during 2009 (DeNavas-Walt et al., 2011). And about 80% of low-wage earners get no paid sick days off from work (Herbert, 2007).

To survive psychologically in an economically unstable world, many working-class people begin to define their jobs as irrelevant to their core identity. Instead of focusing on the dreariness or the insignificance of their work, they may come to view it as a noble act of sacrifice. A bricklayer put it simply: "My job is to work for my family" (Sennett & Cobb, 1972, p. 135). Framing their work as sacrifice allows them to escape the disappointment of an unfulfilling job and orient their lives toward their children's and grandchildren's future, something that gives them a sense of control they can't get through their jobs.

But it is especially difficult for working-class parents to sacrifice "successfully." Upper-class and middle-class parents make sacrifices so their children will have a life *like* theirs. Working-class parents sacrifice so their children will *not* have a life like theirs. Their lives are not a "model" but a "warning." The danger of this type of sacrifice is that if the children do fulfill the parents' wishes and rise above their quality of life, the parents may eventually become a burden or an embarrassment to them. Thus, people who struggle to make ends meet are sometimes caught in a vicious trap. In addition, they must deal with public perceptions of them and their work that are decidedly negative.

MIKE ROSE

The Mind at Work

Author Mike Rose (2004) grew up in a modest home, the son of working-class immigrants. Most of the adults in his family and in his neighborhood never graduated from high school, and all of them worked in blue collar or service jobs their whole lives. He was fully aware, early on, that these manual laborers did not occupy a particularly valued place in American society. Low-paying jobs are often labeled "unskilled." Such workers are consistently marginalized, either by more affluent people who treat them as if they are invisible, or by widely held cultural stereotypes that they are unintelligent and unrefined. Because their work doesn't usually require advanced educational credentials, there's a belief that those who do it aren't that bright.

Rose set out to examine these stereotypes. He observed working-class people on the job—waitresses, hair stylists, plumbers, welders, and so on—and took detailed notes of their activities. Once he became aware of the rhythms of their work, he began asking them questions, casual ones to start with and more specific ones as he got to know them better.

What he found was that apparently "mindless" working-class occupations require high levels of skill, judgment, and intelligence. Hair stylists, for example, must show an astonishing amount of aesthetic and mental agility when they turn vague requests ("I want something light and summery") into an actual hairstyle pleasing to the client. They must also have command of a remarkable range of knowledge—nutrition, hair growth patterns, the biology of skin, hair treatment chemicals, and popular images of beauty—in order to provide their clients not only with a look they want but with advice on how to maintain a stylish appearance. As one stylist described it,

> You've got to add up all these pieces of the puzzle, and then at the end you've got to come up with a thought, OK, it's gotta be this length, it's gotta be layered here, it's gotta be textured there . . . It's not like we just start cutting. By the time I take my client to the shampoo bowl, after the consultation, I already have a little road map as to how I'm going to cut this haircut. (quoted in Rose, 2004, p. 33)

Similarly, working-class women who wait on tables in inexpensive diners and coffee shops must have advanced information processing skills, including a sharp memory and the ability to make lightning-fast mathematical calculations. On the surface, restaurant work seems highly structured and determined—from the physical layout that guides people's movements to the norms of dining that are well known to customers and waitstaff. Once seated, customers expect a series of events to unfold along a familiar time line. Indeed, their satisfaction (and the size of the tip they leave) is based on the manner in which the service meets these expectations.

On closer inspection, however, the restaurant environment is exceedingly complex and unpredictable. For instance, customers enter at different times and make requests at different stages of their meals, so each table proceeds at a different pace. This staggering of schedules maximizes the restaurant's flow of trade, but it increases the physical and cognitive demands on waitresses, especially during peak hours or when customers are particularly demanding. The meals themselves develop under their own different timetables. Some items cook quickly; others take a long time. Some meals have only a limited amount of time in which they can be served. So servers must also be aware of the temporal rhythm of the kitchen. And since the restaurant's profit depends on the constant turnover of customers, all this occurs under the pressure to move people along quickly.

Our collective failure to acknowledge the qualities and skills that even lower-status jobs require has helped to undermine a large chunk of the American working-class population. Rose's research is less of an objective assessment of these occupations than it is a plea to broaden our definitions of intelligence and to see dignity in the jobs that keep American society running.

The Poor

In an affluent society like the United States, the people at the very bottom of the social class structure face constant humiliation in their everyday lives. You've heard the old saying "Money can't buy happiness." The implication is that true satisfaction in life is more than just a matter of being wealthy. Indeed, research shows that compared with others, people with high incomes aren't happier, don't spend more time in enjoyable activities, and tend to be more tense (Kahneman, Krueger, Schkade, Schwarz, & Stone, 2006). Yet such information provides little comfort to people who can't pay their bills, don't know where their next meal is coming from or whether their job will exist tomorrow, suffer from ill health, or have no home. The legendary vaudeville singer Sophie Tucker once said, "I've been rich and I've been poor—and believe me, rich is better."

What Poverty Means in the United States

We hear the word *poverty* all the time. In common usage, poverty is usually conceived in economic terms, as the lack of sufficient money to ensure an adequate lifestyle. Sociologists, though, often distinguish between absolute and relative poverty. The term **absolute poverty** refers to the minimal requirements a human being needs to survive. The term **relative poverty** refers to one's economic position compared with the living standards of the majority in a given society. Absolute poverty means not having enough money for minimal food, clothing, and shelter. But relative poverty is more difficult to gauge. It reflects culturally defined aspirations and expectations. Poor people "generally feel better if they know that their position in life does not compare too badly with others in society" (quoted in D. Altman, 2003, p. 21). An annual family income of $5,000, which would constitute abject poverty in the United States, is perhaps five times higher than the *average* income in many developing countries. As Kentucky senator Rand Paul once said, "The poor in our country are enormously better off than the rest of the world" (Paul, 2010, p. 16). Although such a statement reflects a common perception that life in a U.S. slum is luxurious compared with life in destitute regions in other parts of the world, it overlooks the real suffering associated with living in American poverty.

The Poverty Line

The U.S. government uses an absolute definition of poverty to identify people who can't afford what they need to survive. The U.S. ***poverty line*** identifies the amount of yearly income a family requires to meet its basic needs. Those who fall below the line are officially poor. The poverty line is based on pretax money income only, which doesn't include food stamps, Medicaid, public housing, and other noncash benefits. The figure does vary according to family size, and it is adjusted each year to account for inflation. But it doesn't take into account regional differences in cost of living. In 2011, the official poverty line for a family of four—two parents and two children—was an annual income of $22,113.

That dollar amount is established by the U.S. Department of Agriculture and for decades has been computed from something called the Thrifty Food Plan. This plan, developed in the early 1960s, is used to calculate the cost of a subsistence diet, which is the bare minimum a family needs to survive. This cost is then multiplied by three because research at the time showed that the average family spent one third of its income on food each year. The resulting amount was adopted in 1969 as the government's official poverty line. Even though the plan is modified periodically to account for changes in dietary recommendations, the formula itself and the basic definition of poverty have remained the same for about four decades.

Many policymakers, economists, sociologists, and concerned citizens question whether the current poverty line provides an accurate picture of basic needs in the United States. Several things have changed since the early 1960s. For instance, today food costs account for less than 13% of the average family's budget because the price of other things, such as housing and medical care, has inflated at much higher rates (U.S. Bureau of Labor Statistics, 2007). In addition, there were fewer dual-earner and single-parent families in the past, meaning that fewer families had to pay for childcare. In short, today's family has many more expenses and therefore probably spends a greater proportion of its total income on nonfood items. The consequence is that the official poverty line is probably set too low and therefore underestimates the hardships that struggling Americans experience (Swarns, 2008a).

Deciding who is and isn't officially poor is not just a matter of words and labels. When the poverty line is too low, we fail to recognize the problems of the many families who have difficulty making ends meet but who are not officially defined as poor. A needy family earning an amount slightly above the poverty line may not qualify for a variety of public assistance programs, such as housing benefits, Head Start, Medicaid, or Temporary Assistance for Needy Families. As a result, its standard of living may not be as good as that of a family that earns slightly less but qualifies for these programs.

Some economists suggest that the exclusive focus on income in setting the poverty line underestimates the harmful long-term effects of poverty. Obviously, when families don't have enough income, they can't buy adequate food, clothing, and shelter. But when families don't have any assets, such as savings and home equity, they lose economic security and their ability to plan, dream, and pass on opportunities to their children (Boshara, 2002).

The Near-Poor

Interestingly, the government seems to agree implicitly that the poverty line is set too low. The U.S. Bureau of the Census defines individuals or families who earn up to 25% more than the official poverty line amount as the **near-poor** or **working poor**. Their existence is fraught with irony. Because they fall above the poverty line, they escape academic attention and tend not to be the recipients of large-scale governmental assistance programs. At the same time, they are everywhere, doing the tasks with which others come into contact and on which they depend on a daily basis:

> They serve you Big Macs and help you find merchandise at Wal-Mart. They harvest your food, clean your offices, and sew your clothes. In a California factory, they package lights for your kids' bikes. In a New Hampshire plant, they assemble books of wallpaper samples to help you redecorate. (Shipler, 2004, p. 3)

When nothing out of the ordinary happens, the near-poor can manage. But an unexpected event—a sickness, an injury, the breakdown of a major appliance or automobile—can destroy a family financially and sink it into poverty. As one near-poor mother of two put it, "We're O.K. unless something—anything at all—goes wrong" (quoted in Davey, 2011, p. A22).

It has been estimated that about one quarter of U.S. residents hovering just above the poverty line will fall below it at some point in their lives, and then they have some difficult decisions to make. One study of 34,000 people nationwide found that during the cold winter months, families spend less on food and reduce their caloric intake by an average of 10% in order to pay their fuel bills (Bhattacharya, DeLeire, Haider, & Currie, 2003). Imagine being a poor single mother with a sick child. One trip to the doctor might cost an entire week's food budget or a month of rent. Dental work or an eye examination is easily sacrificed when other pressing bills need to be paid. If she depends on a car to get to work and it breaks down, a few hundred dollars to fix it might mean not paying the electric bill that month. When gasoline prices approach $5 a gallon—as they did for a while in 2011—many near-poor families find that they have to cut down on food purchases so they can afford to drive to work. These are choices that wealthier families never face.

The Poverty Rate

The **poverty rate**—the percentage of residents whose income falls below the official poverty line—is the measure that the U.S. government uses to track the success of its efforts to reduce poverty. Exhibit 10.3 shows how the poverty rate has fluctuated over the past few decades. In 2010 (the most recent year for which data are available), 15.1% of the population—or more than 46 million Americans—fell below the poverty line, up from 11.3% in 2000. If we add the near-poor, the number increases to 60.4 million (DeNavas-Walt et al., 2011). Economists project a spike of as many as 10.3 million additional poor people in the next few years, the result of persistently high unemployment and the economic recession (Parrott, 2008).

When used to describe national trends in poverty, the overall poverty rate can obscure important differences among subgroups of the population. For example, in 2010, 9.9% of people who identify themselves as non-Hispanic Whites and 12.1% of Asian Americans fell below the poverty line. That same year, 27.4% of Blacks and 26.6%

Exhibit 10.3   Historical Trends in the U.S. Poverty Rate

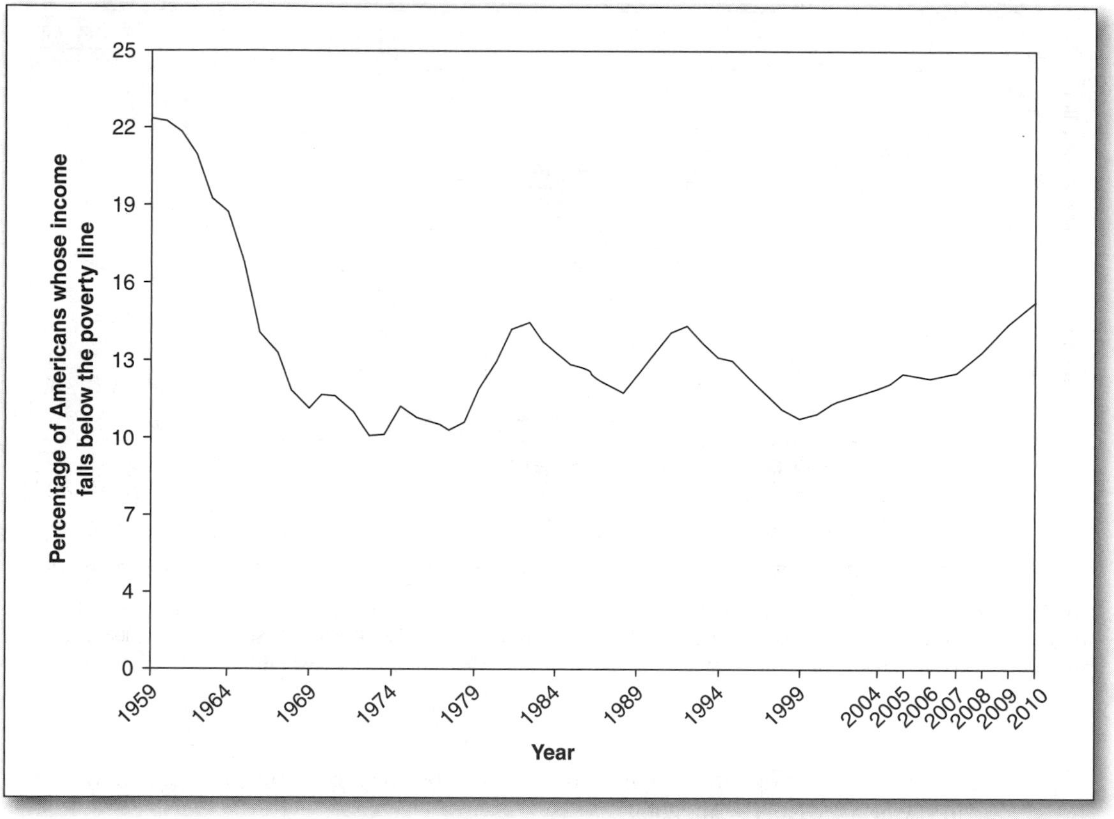

SOURCES: DeNavas-Walt, Proctor, & Smith, 2010, Table 4; DeNavas-Walt, Proctor, & Smith, 2011

of Latino/as (who could be of any race) were considered poor. The poverty rate in the South (16.9%) and West (15.3%) is higher than the rate in the Midwest (13.9%) and Northeast (12.8%). Finally, poverty is higher in rural areas (16.5%) than in metropolitan areas (14.9%), although it's highest in inner cities (19.7%; DeNavas-Walt et al., 2011).

Although racial and ethnic minorities have consistently been rated among the poorest Americans, other groups have seen their status change over time. Before Social Security was instituted in 1935, many of the most destitute were those over age 65. As recently as 1970, 25% of U.S. residents over age 65 fell below the poverty line. Today, only 9% of the people in this age group are poor (DeNavas-Walt et al., 2011). Exhibit 10.4 shows how the poverty rate of older Americans has declined.

Taking their place among the poor, however, are children. Although the rate of child poverty has declined a bit since the mid 1990s, 22% of U.S. residents under the age of 18 (about 16.4 million kids) are poor (DeNavas-Walt et al., 2011). Children make up about 24.4% of the total population yet account for 35.5% of all poor people in this country (DeNavas-Walt et al., 2011). As you would suspect, poverty figures for children vary dramatically along ethnoracial lines. About 34% of African American and 30% of Latino/a children under 18 live in poverty—compared with 15.3% of non-Hispanic white children and 14.2% of Asian children (U.S. Bureau of the Census, 2011b). The 22% poverty rate among U.S. children is the highest of any industrialized country.

Exhibit 10.4   Historical Trends in Poverty by Age

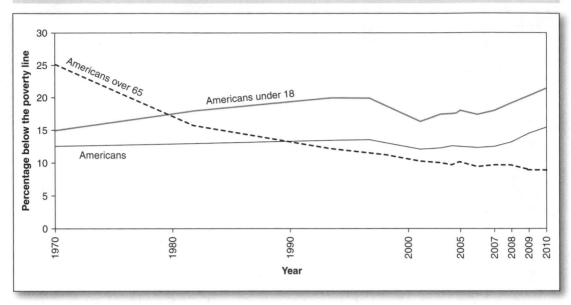

SOURCES: 1970–1999 data from U.S. Bureau of the Census, 2000; 2001 data from Proctor & Dalaker, 2002; 2003 data from DeNavas-Walt, Proctor, & Lee, 2006; 2006–2007 data from DeNavas-Walt, Proctor, & Smith, 2008; 2008–2009 data from DeNavas-Walt, Proctor, & Smith, 2010; 2010 data from DeNavas-Walt, Proctor, & Smith, 2011

In Sweden, Norway, and Finland, for example, between 3% and 4% of all children live in poverty (Mishel et al., 2009).

Several factors explain why the poverty rate among U.S. children is high compared with that of older U.S. residents. For one thing, family structure is closely related to child poverty. The poverty rate for families headed by single mothers is 31.6%, compared with 15.8% for families headed by single fathers and 6.2% for married-couple families (DeNavas-Walt et al., 2011). Half of all poor families are headed by single women. Over half of all children under the age of six who live in a female-headed household are poor—about five times the rate of children in married-couple families (Federal Interagency Forum on Child and Family Statistics, 2007). The current recession affects poverty rates in general but has hit children particularly hard. Between 2007 and 2009, the number of children who live in homes affected by foreclosure and who have at least one unemployed parent more than doubled (cited in Davey, 2011).

In addition, government spending on programs for the elderly (Medicare, Social Security) has increased over the past four decades, while spending on families and children (cash assistance, health care, food and nutritional aid, etc.) has dropped and will continue to drop into the foreseeable future (Davey, 2011; Steuerle, 2007). Worldwide, there is a strong correlation between the amount of money a country spends on social programs and rates of child poverty (see Exhibit 10.5).

The Consequences of Poverty

Poverty isn't just about rates, trends, and official definitions. It is a never-ending burden borne on the shoulders of those who are least equipped to endure it. Being poor clearly influences people's physical and intellectual well-being.

Exhibit 10.5   Government Spending and Child Poverty, 2000

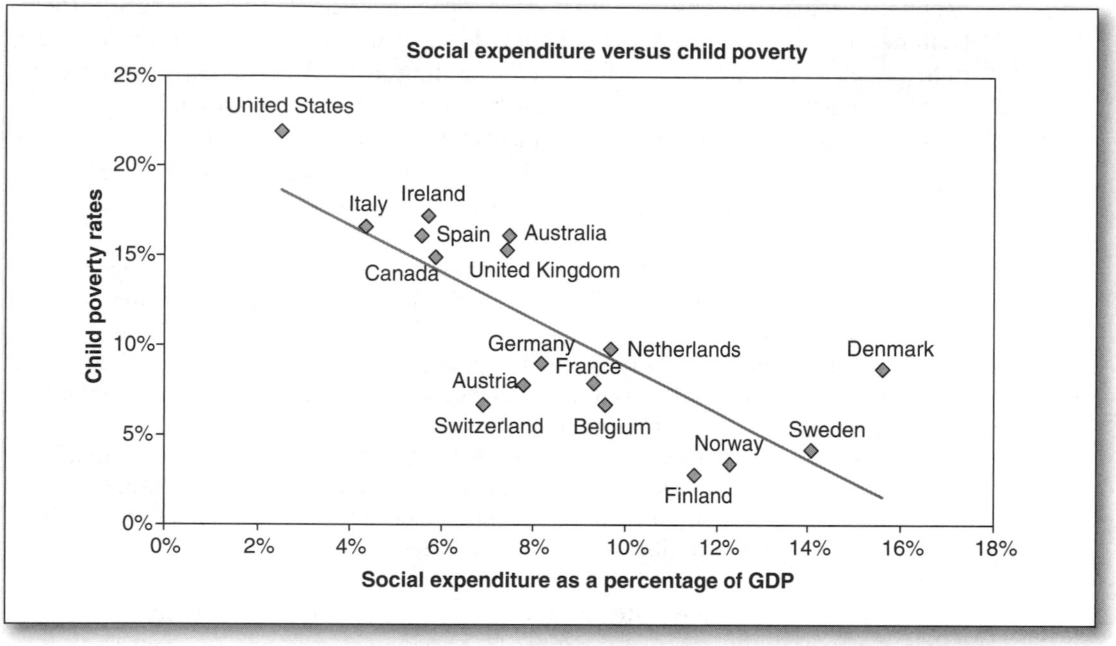

Social expenditure versus child poverty

Child poverty rates vs *Social expenditure as a percentage of GDP*

Data points: United States (~2.5%, ~22%), Italy (~4.5%, ~16.5%), Ireland (~5.5%, ~17%), Spain (~6%, ~15.5%), Canada (~6%, ~15%), Australia (~7.5%, ~15.5%), United Kingdom, Germany (~8%, ~9%), France (~9%, ~8%), Austria (~7.5%, ~7.5%), Netherlands (~9.5%, ~9.7%), Denmark (~15.5%, ~8.5%), Switzerland (~7.5%, ~6.5%), Belgium (~9%, ~6.5%), Norway (~12%, ~3%), Sweden (~14%, ~4%), Finland (~11.5%, ~2.5%)

SOURCE: Reprinted from Lawrence Mishel, Jared Bernstein, and Sylvia Allegretto, *The State of Working America, 2006/2007*

Poverty and Health

With each step down the income ladder comes increased risk of headaches, varicose veins, respiratory infection, hypertension, stress-related illness, low-birth-weight babies, stroke, diabetes, and heart disease (Krugman, 2008; Perez-Peña, 2003; Shweder, 1997). Among children, decades of research show that rates of chronic illness, injury, ear disease, asthma, and physical inactivity all increase as socioeconomic status decreases (E. Chen, Matthews, & Boyce, 2002). And poor children covered by Medicaid/CHIP (Children's Health Insurance Program) are more likely than children with private health insurance to be denied appointments with medical specialists. In addition, they wait an average of 22 days longer for an appointment, even for serious medical problems (Bisgaier & Rhodes, 2011). Lawmakers often seem unsympathetic to the plight of poor people who are sick. In 2010, Arizona legislators voted to cut Medicaid funding for some types of organ transplants, amounting to a death sentence for low-income patients who have little chance of surviving without transplants but who can't afford the hundreds of thousands of dollars needed to pay for them (Lacey, 2010).

Even after controlling for age, sex, race, family size, and education, the risk of death steadily increases as income goes down (Marmot, 2004). And the gap is growing. According to data from the U.S. Department of Health and Human Services, in 1980, the most affluent U.S. citizens could expect to live 2.8 years longer than the poorest citizens; by 1998, the difference had increased to 4.5 years, and it continues to widen today (cited in Pear, 2008a). The health status of poor people in the United States is so bad that volunteer medical groups that were created to provide free medical services in destitute third-world countries like Ghana, Tanzania, and Haiti now set up mobile medical facilities in poor rural areas of the United States (Towell, 2007).

One of the obvious reasons for these health gaps is lack of access to adequate health care. Over the last 20 years, for instance, one quarter of urban and suburban hospitals, particularly those serving poor residents, have closed their emergency rooms (Rabin, 2011). Furthermore, even if they do have access to medical facilities, many poor people aren't able to pay for care. According to the U.S. Bureau of the Census (2011b), 30.4% of poor people have no health insurance, even though they may be eligible for government health insurance (Medicaid). In fact, only 44.5% of poor people receive Medicaid benefits (U.S. Bureau of the Census, 2011b). The dangers of having no health insurance are undeniable:

- Uninsured people are less likely than people who have health insurance to see a doctor when needed and are more likely to report being in poor health (Robert Wood Johnson Foundation, 2005).
- Uninsured people (and those covered by Medicaid) are more likely than those with private health insurance to receive diagnoses of cancer in its late stages, diminishing their chances of survival (Virning, 2008).
- A study of trauma units and emergency departments around the country found that even after controlling for age, gender, and type and severity of injury, uninsured patients were 50% more likely than insured patients to die from their injuries; the gap was worst for ethnoracial minorities (cited in Noonan, 2008).

In addition to inadequate or nonexistent health care, approximately 14% of American households are "food insecure"—meaning that some members don't have enough to eat or the family uses strategies like eating less varied diets, participating in food assistance programs, or getting emergency food from community food pantries (U.S. Bureau of the Census, 2011b). That means that about 49 million poor Americans—including more than 16 million children—now live in households that experience hunger or the risk of hunger, an increase of 13 million since 2007.

As you will recall from Chapter 6, lower-income families actually pay higher-than-average prices for food (Brookings Institution, 2006). Large supermarket chains, for example, hesitate to open stores in very poor neighborhoods because of security fears. Hence, residents who are without transportation must rely on small neighborhood grocery stores, which usually charge more for food than large supermarkets do.

Poverty and Education

The educational deck is likewise stacked against poor people. A report by the Education Trust (2002) showed that in most states, school districts with the neediest students receive far less state and local tax money—on average, just under $1,000 less per student—than districts with the fewest poor students. Teachers in poor districts tend to be less experienced and are paid less than teachers in more affluent districts (LaCoste-Caputo, 2007). Without adequate resources, teachers become frustrated and do not teach; children become cynical and do not learn. Consequently, the lowest-performing school districts typically have the largest percentages of students from poor families (cited in "Student Performance," 2007).

Even if they graduate from high school, most poor children can't afford to attend college. Those who do are more likely to attend community colleges or state universities, which are less expensive but lack the prestige, and often the quality, of their more expensive counterparts.

Despite nationwide efforts to increase access to higher education, a greater proportion of college students today come from wealthy families than was the case two decades ago. Of course, students without family wealth do sometimes attend top universities with the help of need-based scholarships. But these schools, by and large, have no systematic plans for identifying, recruiting, or admitting low-income students. Only 3% of students in elite U.S. universities come from the poorest quarter of the population, and only 10% come from the poorest half (Carnevale & Rose, 2003).

Furthermore, once they get into college, poor students don't fare as well as their more affluent counterparts. According to the Department of Education, a little over 25% of college students from families with annual incomes of under $25,000 earn a bachelor's degree within six years. For students from families with incomes more than $70,000, the figure is 56% (Hebel, 2007). Such a gap is especially significant because a bachelor's degree is essential in today's global economy. According to the U.S. Bureau of the Census (2011b), people with some college experience but no degree earn, on average, about $32,500 a year. College graduates on average earn more than $58,000 a year. Such numbers demonstrate that the educational system often seals the fate of poor people instead of helping them succeed within the U.S. class structure.

Out on the Streets

The most publicly visible consequence of poverty is homelessness. No one knows for sure exactly how many homeless people live in the United States. The National Alliance to End Homelessness (2011) estimates that there are more than 656,000 homeless people, 38% of whom are completely unsheltered. But because people move in and out of homelessness or are homeless for a short period of time, it's estimated that somewhere between 2.3 and 3.5 million people experience some type of homelessness over the course of a year. According to a 2010 survey of 27 major American cities, on an average night, 68% of homeless people are single adults, 31% are persons in families, and 1% are children on their own. Of the homeless, 19% are employed, and 14% are military veterans (U.S. Conference of Mayors, 2010).

The causes of homelessness in the United States are typically institutional ones: stagnating wages, changes in welfare programs, and, perhaps most important, lack of affordable housing. Nearly three quarters of homeless families cite lack of affordable housing as the principal cause of their homelessness (U.S. Conference of Mayors, 2010). When rising wealth at the top of society drives up housing prices, the poor are left unable to afford decent housing and without federal and state programs to help (Shipler, 2004).

According to the federal government, housing is considered "affordable" if it costs 30% of a family's income. The poorest fifth of the population spend about 78% of their wages on housing. By comparison, the wealthiest fifth of the population spend only 19% of their income on housing (cited in Swartz, 2007). In 2011, the nationwide median housing wage—the minimum amount of money a person would have to make to afford two-bedroom rental housing—was $18.46 an hour (or an annual income of $38,400, assuming full-time, year-round employment). That's more than double the federal minimum wage. Nowhere in the United States does a full-time, minimum-wage job provide enough income to afford adequate housing, and in some states— New York, Connecticut, Maryland, and Massachusetts to name a few—a household would need the income of at least three minimum-wage jobs. In Hawaii, *four* minimum-wage jobs wouldn't be enough (National Low Income Housing Coalition, 2011).

With foreclosure rates rising steadily (National Alliance to End Homelessness, 2011), the housing future for the neediest Americans looks even bleaker.

Why Poverty Persists

Even in the best of times, a prosperous country such as the United States has a sizable population of poor people. Why, in such an affluent society, is poverty a permanent fixture? To explain the persistence of poverty, we must look at enduring imbalances in income and wealth, the structural role poverty plays in larger social institutions, and the dominant cultural beliefs and attitudes that help support it.

Enduring Disparities in Income and Wealth

One reason why poverty is so persistent in the United States is the way income and wealth are distributed. According to the U.S. Bureau of the Census (2011b), the average annual income of the top 5% of U.S. households is $180,000 while the average annual income of the bottom 20% of households is under $21,000.

This wide income gap between the richest and poorest segments of the population has been growing steadily over the past few decades (see Exhibit 10.6), although the current recession may have slowed this trend by taking a bite out of sources of income

Exhibit 10.6   The Increasing Gap in Household Incomes

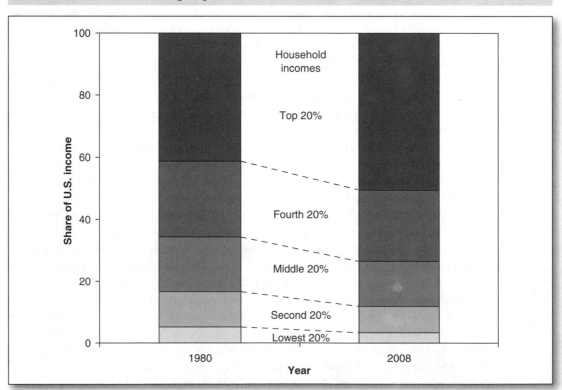

SOURCES: U.S. Bureau of the Census, 2007; 2011b, Table 693

common among the wealthy, such as stock dividends and real estate (Leonhardt & Fabrikant, 2009). Between 1979 and 2009, the incomes of the richest fifth of U.S. families grew by 49%. During that same period, the incomes of the poorest fifth *fell* by 7.4%. Let's look at this another way. In 1973, the bottom 99.5% of the population (in other words, all but the richest 0.5%) earned 93.7% of all the national income. By 2008, that share had fallen to 83.1% (Economic Policy Institute, 2011).

Meanwhile, compensation for those at the very top continues to soar. The average American chief executive makes more than $11 million a year. In 2010, the average annual compensation for the 10 highest-paid U.S. executives was more than $62.4 million (AFL-CIO, 2011). In 1965, chief executives earned $24 for every $1 earned by the average production worker; by 2009, that figure had increased to $185 (Economic Policy Institute, 2011). We may want to believe that personal effort and hard work solely determine our success, but it's hard to imagine that a CEO of, say, an electronics company works 185 times harder than a person who actually assembles the TVs and cell phones.

Over the past few years, the public has become increasingly angry over the escalation of executive pay. Congress has held hearings on the matter. President Obama called Wall Street bankers who gave themselves nearly $20 billion in bonuses as the economy was deteriorating "shameful." In 2009, the Obama administration proposed new rules that would give shareholders greater voice in determining executives' salaries and bonuses. But to date, nothing has been done, and executive compensation remains disproportionately high.

Tax laws also work to the advantage of those at the top. The rich do pay a lot of taxes as a total percentage of all taxes collected; however, they don't pay a lot of taxes as a percentage of what they earn and can afford. In the 1940s, the tax rate for the wealthiest tax bracket was about 90%; today it's 35%. Incidentally, the threshold for that top bracket is $379,150 (Sorkin, 2011). Any income above that is taxed at the same rate. In other words, someone earning $40 million a year pays the same tax percentage as someone earning $380,000 a year.

Although most U.S. residents paid more taxes as a percentage of income during the late 1990s and early 2000s than they had in previous decades, many of the wealthiest citizens paid less. Families earning more than $1 million a year have seen their federal tax rates drop more sharply than those of any other group in the country (Andrews, 2007). In fact, in 2008, the Bush tax cuts had virtually no effect on low-income families. However, families in the top 1% of income earners saw tax savings of more than $50,000 (Mishel et al., 2009).

The United States has the greatest income inequality between poor and wealthy citizens of any industrialized nation. The wealthiest fifth of U.S. families earn almost nine times more than the poorest fifth (U.S. Bureau of the Census, 2011b). In France, the richest fifth earn seven times more than the poorest fifth, and in Japan they earn four times more (Phillips, 2002). But to be fair, the income gap between rich and poor is worse in developing countries. For example, the richest 20% of Brazilians earn 64% of the country's income, whereas the poorest 20% earn 2.5% (Romero, 1999). Similar disparities exist in other Latin American countries and in most of sub-Saharan Africa.

Inequalities in income lead to even more striking inequalities in wealth. A lifetime of high earnings and inheritance from privileged parents creates a lasting advantage in ownership of property; of durable consumer goods such as cars, houses, and furniture; and of financial assets such as stocks, bonds, savings, and life insurance. The wealthiest

1% of U.S. households have an average net worth of $14 million. The bottom 20% of U.S. households have an average net worth of –$27,000—meaning they owe tens of thousands of dollars more than they have (Economic Policy Institute, 2011). There are four times as many households with a net worth of over $10 million today than there were in 1989 (Uchitelle, 2006). We will never live in a society with a perfectly equal distribution of income and wealth. Some people will always earn more, have more, and maybe even deserve more than others. But the magnitude of the gap between rich and poor in the United States challenges the notion that we live in a society where everyone is valued equally. As disparities in income and wealth grow, so does the gap in quality of life and access to opportunity between those at the top of society and those at the bottom.

The Social "Benefits" of Poverty

Recall the structural-functionalist assertion that stratification is necessary because it ensures that the most qualified and valuable people in society will occupy the most important positions. Social conditions exist and persist only if they are functional to society in some way. But functional for whom? If you were to survey people on the street and ask them if poverty is a good or bad thing, most, I'm sure, would say, "Bad." Yet according to sociologist Herbert Gans (1971, 1996), within a free-market economy and competitive society such as the United States, poverty plays a necessary institutional role. Although structural functionalism has often been criticized for its propensity to justify the status quo, Gans combines it with conflict thinking to identify several economic and social "functions" served by poverty that benefit all other classes in society:

- Poverty provides a ready pool of low-wage laborers who are available to do society's "dirty work." Poor people work at low wages primarily because they have little choice. When large numbers of poor people compete for scarce jobs, business owners can pay lower wages.
- Poverty ensures that there will be enough individuals, especially during times of high unemployment, to populate an all-volunteer military. To people with limited educational and occupational opportunities, military service holds the promise of an escape from poverty through stable employment, comprehensive insurance coverage, a living wage, free schooling, and the development of marketable skills. In Iraq and Afghanistan, U.S. military personnel have been disproportionately ethnoracial minorities from poor and working-class families (Halbfinger & Holmes, 2003). As you might guess, American casualties have also been overwhelmingly from families of modest means who live in sparsely populated rural counties (Cushing & Bishop, 2005; Golway, 2004). By 2006, 34% of U.S. military personnel killed in Iraq came from the poorest quarter of families, while only 17% came from the richest quarter (cited in "Price Paid," 2006).
- Poverty supports occupations that either serve the poor or protect the rest of society from them: police officers, penologists, welfare workers, social workers, lawyers, pawnshop owners, and so on. Even drug dealers and loan sharks depend on the presence of a large population of poor people willing to pay for their illegal services.
- Poverty is the reason why some people purchase goods and services that would otherwise go unused: secondhand appliances; day-old bread, fruits, and vegetables; deteriorated housing; dilapidated cars; care from incompetent physicians; and so forth. In 2002, dozens of Coca-Cola employees in Texas revealed that, for years, they had been required to sell expired Coke to stores in poor neighborhoods. They were instructed to strip cans from their boxes, stuff them into fresh boxes with new dates stamped on the side, and stock them on store shelves in poor neighborhoods as if they were new

(Winter, 2002). Clearly, this merchandise had little or no monetary value outside the poverty market; it was believed that the beverages couldn't be sold to wealthier Coke drinkers because they'd have noticed the difference.

- Poverty is a visible reminder to the rest of society of the "legitimacy" of the conventional values of hard work, thrift, and honesty. By violating, or seeming to violate, these mainstream values, the poor reaffirm these virtues. If poor people are thought to be lazy, their presence reinforces the ethic of hard work; if the poor single mother is condemned, the two-parent family is idealized.

- Poverty provides scapegoats for society's institutional problems. The alleged laziness of the jobless poor and the anger aimed at street people and beggars distract us from the failure of the economic system to adequately deal with the needs of all citizens. Likewise, the alleged personal shortcomings of slum dwellers and the homeless deflect attention from shoddy practices within the housing industry.

This explanation of poverty's persistence can easily be dismissed as cold and heartless. We certainly don't want to admit that poor people allow the rest of us to avoid unpleasant or even dangerous tasks and enjoy comfortable and pleasant lifestyles. Yet this explanation is quite compelling. Just as society needs talented people to fill its important occupational positions, it also needs a stable population of poor people to fill its "less important" positions. If society fostered full equality, who would do the dirty work?

If we are truly serious about reducing poverty, we must find alternative ways of performing the societal functions it currently fulfills. But such a change will assuredly come at a cost to those who can now take advantage of poverty's presence. In short, poverty will be eliminated only when it becomes dysfunctional for people who *aren't* poor.

The Ideology of Competitive Individualism

Poverty also persists because of cultural beliefs and values that support the economic status quo. An important component of this value system in U.S. society is the belief in **competitive individualism** (Feagin, 1975; M. Lewis, 1978; Neubeck, 1986). As children, most of us are taught that nobody deserves a free ride. The way to be successful is to work hard, strive toward goals, and compete well against others. We are taught that we are fully responsible for our own economic fates. Rags-to-riches stories of people who rose above terrible conditions to make it to the top reinforce the notion that anybody can be successful if she or he simply has the desire and puts in the necessary effort.

The dark side of the U.S. belief in competitive individualism is that it all too easily justifies the unequal distribution of rewards and the existence of poverty. If people who are financially successful are thought to deserve their advantages, allegedly because of individual hard work and desire, then the people who are struggling financially must likewise deserve their plight—because of their *lack* of hard work and desire. People in the United States have an intense need to believe that good things happen to good people and bad things happen to bad people (Huber & Form, 1973; Lerner, 1970). In short, most of us want to believe that if a poor person is suffering, he or she "must have" done something to deserve it. The people who succeed, in contrast, "must have" been born smarter, stayed in school longer, or worked harder. The belief in competitive individualism gives people the sense that they can control their own fate.

But the depth of such beliefs depends on where people are in the stratification system. When asked why people succeed, lower-income people are more likely than wealthy people to downplay competitive individualism and cite things like "coming from a wealthy family" or "knowing the right people." Upper-class individuals, on the other hand, are more likely than their lower-income counterparts to contend that opportunities for success and advancement are available to everyone, meaning that success is a result of individual merit. They are likely to cite "natural ability," "a good education," and "hard work" as factors that are essential to getting ahead in life. Hence, they can justify inequality by emphasizing equal chances (cited in J. Scott & Leonhardt, 2005). Notice, in the following passage, how this economist blames poverty on the willful actions of poor people who decide not to take advantage of available economic opportunities:

> Some poor people may choose not to work as hard as investment bankers working 70 hours a week....One of the most amazing phenomena of recent years is why so many people . . . have not responded to the opportunities out there. (quoted in Stille, 2001, p. 19)

The belief system that such a comment reflects doesn't take into consideration the possibility that the competition itself may not be fair. Competitive individualism assumes that opportunities to learn a high-level trade or skill or enter a profession are available to everyone. Every person is supposed to have the chance to "be all that she or he can be." But the system may be rigged to favor those who already have power and privilege.

The Culture of Poverty

A variation of the belief in competitive individualism is the argument that poor people as a group possess beliefs, norms, values, and goals that are significantly different from those of the rest of society and that perpetuate a particular lifestyle that keeps them poor. Oscar Lewis (1968), one of the earliest proponents of this *culture-of-poverty thesis*, maintained that poor people, resigned to their position in society, develop a unique value structure to deal with the unlikelihood that they will ever become successful by the standards of the larger society. This culture is at odds with the dominant culture—in the United States, the middle-class belief in self-discipline and hard work.

According to Lewis, although the culture of poverty may keep people trapped in what appears (to the outside observer) to be an intolerable life, it nevertheless provides its own pleasures. Street life in the inner city is exhilarating compared with a world where jobs are dull, arduous, and difficult to obtain and hold (P. Peterson, 1991). It's more fun to hang out, tell exaggerated stories, and exhibit one's latest purchases and conquests than to work and struggle in the "conventional" world. This extreme "present-orientedness"—the inability to live for the future (Banfield, 1970)—and not the lack of income or wealth is the principal cause of poverty, according to this view.

Once the culture of poverty comes into existence, Lewis argued, it is remarkably persistent: You can take the child out of the inner city, but you can't take the inner city out of the child. Furthermore, it is passed down from generation to generation. By age six or seven, he said, most children have absorbed the basic values and attitudes of their subculture, rendering them unable to take advantage of any opportunities that may present themselves later in life. Others have argued that a poor family with a history of welfare dependence tends to raise children who lack ambition, a solid work ethic, and self-reliance (Auletta, 1982).

But the contention that there is a stable, enduring culture of poverty may be overstated. For instance, not all poor people receive public assistance. Only about 28% of poor people receive food stamps, 46% participate in Medicaid, 23% participate in school lunch programs, and 19% receive some kind of housing assistance (U.S. Bureau of the Census, 2007). People receiving government assistance tend to move in and out of the system, making it difficult to sustain a tradition of dependence across generations.

Critics of the culture-of-poverty approach also contend that behavior that seems to be characteristic of poor people is likely to be caused by institutional impediments, such as a tradition of racial or ethnic prejudice and discrimination, residential segregation, limited economic opportunities, and occupational obstacles against advancement (W. J. Wilson, 1980). Poor African Americans, for example, still struggle to overcome the disadvantages of slavery and the Jim Crow laws that subjugated their ancestors. Other root causes of poverty include skyrocketing health care costs, the growing lack of affordable housing, and a changing economy that has all but eliminated entire classes of well-paying, low-skilled jobs.

Despite the lack of supportive evidence, the culture-of-poverty explanation remains popular. Many people strongly believe that poor people live by a different set of moral standards and therefore will remain in poverty unless forced to change their values. If poverty is a "way of life," then giving poor people enough money to raise them out of poverty is not the answer; changing their troublesome culture is. In fact, the contemporary U.S. welfare system reflects the belief that the best way to reduce poverty is to change poor people's lifestyles. In 1994, more than 5 million U.S. families were on government assistance. By 2008, that figure had dropped to 1.6 million (U.S. Bureau of the Census, 2011b). You might think that a booming economy is what helped to reduce U.S. citizens' dependence on government aid, but much of the reduction was actually due to the eligibility limitations of a new welfare system that began in 1996. This system includes a mandatory work requirement (or enrollment in vocational training or community service) after two years of receiving assistance and a five-year lifetime limit to benefits for any family. Despite soaring unemployment rates and the worst economic recession in decades, 18 states cut back their cash-assistance welfare programs in 2009 (DeParle, 2009).

Contrary to popular belief, the financial help that people receive on public assistance is rarely enough to sustain a life that is remotely comfortable. For example, in Indiana—where benefits are among the lowest and eligibility rules among the tightest in the nation—the cash assistance limit for a family of three is a mere $288 per month. To qualify for this assistance, such a family cannot earn more than $378 a month (Groppe, 2010). That works out to an annual "income" below $8,000.

Some of the people who left welfare have, in fact, found sustained employment (Duncan & Chase-Lansdale, 2001). However, more than half of the decrease in welfare rolls in the first decade after welfare reform went into effect reflects a decline in government assistance to families that are poor enough to qualify for aid rather than an increase in the number of families who no longer need the assistance. Indeed, even in the rather affluent 1990s, the poverty rate decreased by only 14% (U.S. Bureau of the Census, 2009), and it has increased significantly ever since. Moreover, the 20.4 million Americans who earn less than half the poverty line represent the highest rate of "deep" poverty in 15 years (DeNavas-Walt et al., 2011; National Center for Law and Economic Justice, 2010).

You'd think that with all the political rhetoric over "ending welfare as we know it," the welfare system would be the largest drain on the federal budget. However, programs to assist the poor constitute only about 21% of the federal budget (cited in Chalt, 2011). In 2008, the federal government paid individuals approximately $55 billion in poverty assistance under the Temporary Assistance for Needy Families and food assistance programs. That same year, it spent more than $1 trillion on Social Security, unemployment insurance, and Medicare—the government-subsidized health care program for the elderly (U.S. Bureau of the Census, 2011b).

Nonetheless, the assumptions behind welfare reform are clear: Making work mandatory will teach welfare recipients important work values and habits, make poor single mothers models of these values for their children, and cut the nation's welfare rolls. The underlying idea is that hard work will lead to the moral and financial rewards of family self-reliance. It will cure poverty and welfare dependence and ensure that new generations of children from single-parent families will be able to enter the American mainstream. Like competitive individualism, however, this ideology protects the non-poor, the larger social structure, and the economic system while blaming poor people for their own plight.

Global Development and Inequality

As you've seen elsewhere in this book, it is becoming increasingly difficult to understand life in any one society without understanding that society's place in the larger global context. The trend toward globalization (see Chapter 9) may have brought the world's inhabitants closer together, but they are not all benefiting equally. Nations have differing amounts of power to ensure that their interests are met. The more developed and less developed countries of the world experience serious inequalities in wealth that have immediate consequences for their citizens.

The Global Economic Gap Just as an economic gap exists between rich and poor citizens within a single country, economic gaps exist between rich and poor countries. Consider these facts:

- The average per capita yearly income in Western Europe, the United States, Canada, and Japan is $32,470; in the less developed countries of the world, it's $5,440 (Population Reference Bureau, 2011a).
- About 0.13% of the world's population controls 25% of the world's financial assets. On the other end of the economic spectrum, more than 2.6 billion people in less developed countries live on the equivalent of less than $2 a day (Shah, 2009), and close to half of all people living in sub-Saharan Africa survive on $1 a day (World Bank, 2006).
- The wealthiest 20% of the world accounts for about 77% of all private consumption (Shah, 2009). Twelve percent of the world's population (who happen to reside in developed countries) uses 85% of its water. The United States alone consumes one quarter of the world's oil ("Burning Through Oil," 2008).

MICRO-MACRO CONNECTION

The Global Health Divide

People around the world are living longer and healthier lives than ever before because of changes in public health policies over the past century—disease control, safe drinking water, effective medical treatment, and the like. Child mortality rates worldwide are at an all-time low (UNICEF, 2007). But these improvements have not been shared equally by all the planet's inhabitants. For the more than 1 billion people worldwide who live on less than one U.S. dollar per day, basic health services and medicines remain virtually nonexistent (Carr, 2004). People living in extreme poverty lack safe drinking water, decent housing, adequate sanitation, effective birth control, sufficient food, health education, professional health care, transportation, and secure employment. Nearly half of all smokers in the world live in the developing countries of China, India, and Indonesia (Marsh, 2008).

Not surprisingly, poor countries lag behind wealthier countries on some of the most important measures of health: infant and child mortality, stunted growth, malnutrition, childhood vaccinations, prenatal and postnatal care, and life expectancy (Population Reference Bureau, 2010c; UNICEF, 2009). Millions of people die prematurely each year from diseases that, in more prosperous countries, are preventable, curable, or nonexistent. In the United States and the developed countries of Western Europe, about 5% of child deaths are attributable to infectious diseases. In Southeast Asia, infectious diseases account for 57% of child deaths, and in Africa the figure increases to 77% (Kent & Yin, 2006). The risk of a woman dying from childbirth complications in a less developed country is 300 times greater than for a woman in a developed country (UNICEF, 2009). Over half of all women who die during pregnancy and childbirth are African; and for every African woman who dies, another 20 suffer from debilitating complications (cited in Grady, 2009).

People in wealthy countries experience less pain as well. Six countries—the United States, Canada, France, Germany, Britain, and Australia—consume 79% of the world's medical narcotics, principally morphine. In contrast, poor and middle-income countries, which are home to 80% of the world's population, consume only 6% (cited in McNeil, 2007).

HIV/AIDS presents the most troubling global imbalance. Although significant progress has been made in the past few years, the vast majority of HIV-infected people around the world are poor and lack access to the effective but extremely expensive drug treatments that are readily available in the West. Consequently, though the number of AIDS cases and AIDS deaths is dropping in Western industrialized countries, rates have stabilized at persistently high levels in less developed countries. Poor countries in sub-Saharan Africa account for 68% of all people living with HIV (Fustos, 2011). Six percent of the adult and child population in these countries are infected with the disease (Ashford, 2006). In 2008, 2.0 million people worldwide died of AIDS, and 1.4 million of them were in sub-Saharan Africa (U.S. Bureau of the Census, 2011b).

The effect HIV/AIDS has had on overall life expectancy is staggering. In the developed regions of North America and Europe, people born today can expect to live until they are close to 80. In the poorest, least developed countries in the world, life expectancy is well below 50. In African countries with high rates of HIV infection (Mozambique, Zimbabwe, Lesotho, and Zambia), life expectancy is now just above 40 (Population Reference Bureau, 2010c). Such startling figures will have severe long-term consequences as millions of the world's poorest children become orphaned and face a lifetime of despair.

Even susceptibility to natural disasters is stratified. Globally, the poorest regions are at the greatest risk for life-threatening drought, tropical storms, earthquakes, tsunamis, and floods (Marsh, 2005). Four out of five poor people in Latin America and over half of the poor people in Asia and Africa live on land that is highly vulnerable to natural degradation and disaster. These people often have no choice but to occupy the least valuable and most disaster-prone areas, such as riverbanks, unstable hills, and deforested lands. Developing countries contain 90% of the victims of natural disasters and bear 75% of the economic damage they cause (DeSouza, 2004).

Politics may sometimes get in the way of improving the health of people in developing countries. Wealthy countries could easily afford to provide regular vaccines, mosquito nets, soil nutrients, sufficient food, and clean water supplies to poor countries to address treatable problems like malaria and malnutrition. In fact, in 2005, the United Nations declared that ending world hunger and disease was "utterly affordable" and would only require that wealthy countries commit one half of 1% of their total incomes to aid poor countries. However, many of these nations have been reluctant to provide such assistance. The United States, for example, provides less than two tenths of 1% of its total income, the smallest percentage among major donor countries (Shah, 2009). As long as expenditures for health care in poor countries remain a politically unpopular budget item in wealthy countries, the global health divide will persist.

Explanations for Global Stratification

How has global stratification come about? The conflict perspective explains not only stratification within a society but also stratification between societies. One way a country can use its power to control another is through *colonization*—invading and establishing control over a weaker country and its people in order to expand the colonizer's markets. Typically, the native people of the colony are forced to give up their culture. The colony serves as a source of labor and raw materials for the colonizer's industries and a market for their high-priced goods. Much of North and South America, Africa, and Asia were at one time or another under the colonial control of wealthier nations:

> Arid Spain and Portugal siphoned off South America's gold; tiny Holland dominated vast Indonesia. Britain, barren except for coal, built an imperial swap shop of grain, lumber, cotton, tea, tobacco, opium, gems, silver and slaves. Japan, less than a century out of its bamboo-armor era, conquered much of China for its iron and coal. (McNeil, 2010, p. 5)

Although the direct conquest of weak countries is rare today, wealthy countries are still able to exploit them for commercial gain. Powerful countries can use weaker countries as a source of cheap raw materials and cheap labor. They can also exert financial pressure on poorer nations by setting world prices on certain goods (Chase-Dunn & Rubinson, 1977). Because their economic base is weak, poor countries often have to borrow money or buy manufactured goods on credit from wealthy countries. The huge debt they build up locks them into a downward spiral of exploitation and poverty. They cannot develop an independent economy of their own and thus remain dependent on wealthy countries for their very survival (Frank, 1969).

But we must note that wealthy countries aren't always exploitative. In 2005, a consortium of the wealthiest nations—the so-called Group of Eight—agreed to cancel more than $40 billion in debts owed by some of the poorest countries in the world in the hope of giving these countries a chance to escape the trap of poverty (Blustein, 2005).

Global Financial Organizations

It's not just powerful nations that have the ability to hold poor nations in their grip. International financial organizations play a significant role in determining the economic and social policies of developing countries. For instance, the World Bank funds reconstruction and development in poor countries through investments and loans. It spends about $55 billion annually to better the lives of destitute people worldwide

(Dugger, 2004b). Similarly, the International Monetary Fund (IMF) tries to foster economic growth and international monetary cooperation through financial and technical assistance. The World Trade Organization (WTO) oversees the rules of trade between nations.

Although these organizations spend a lot of money to improve the standard of living in many poor countries by funding projects such as new roads or water treatment plants, they may, from time to time, do more harm than good. The WTO, for example, can impose fines and sanctions on debtor countries that don't act as it dictates. It has, in the past, forced Japan to accept greater levels of pesticide residue on imported food, prevented Guatemala from outlawing deceptive advertising on baby food, and eliminated asbestos bans and car emission standards in various countries (Parenti, 2006).

In fact, countries that receive the aid of these organizations sometimes end up even more impoverished than before. When the World Bank and the IMF provide development credit, they do so with certain conditions attached. The conditions, referred to as "structural adjustments," typically reflect a Western-style, free-market approach: reducing government spending, lifting import and export restrictions, privatizing public services, removing price controls, and devaluing the country's currency. For instance, countries might be required to lift trade restrictions, enhance the rights of foreign investors, cut social spending, or balance their budgets in exchange for aid.

Conditions like these have at times threatened the welfare of citizens in recipient nations (Brutus, 1999; U.S. Network for Global Economic Justice, 2000):

- In Haiti, the IMF and World Bank blocked the government from raising the minimum wage and insisted that government services, such as sanitation and education, be cut in half. The desperate Haitian government complied, despite the fact that life expectancy is only 61 years for Haitian men and 64 years for women and that infant mortality is about 6% (Population Reference Bureau, 2011a).
- In Mexico, the World Bank advised the government to abolish constitutionally guaranteed free education at the national university, making it virtually impossible for poor Mexicans to go to college.
- In Zimbabwe, the World Bank persuaded the government to shift production supports from food crops such as corn to export crops such as tobacco. As a result, malnutrition increased and infant mortality doubled.

You can see that global financial relationships between international lending institutions and poor countries are a double-edged sword. The countries certainly receive much-needed financial assistance. But in the process, they sometimes become even more dependent and less able to improve conditions for their citizens.

Multinational Corporations

Global stratification has been made even more complex by the growth of massive multinational corporations, which can go outside their country's borders to pursue their financial interests if domestic opportunities aren't promising. They can invest their money in more lucrative foreign corporations or establish their businesses or factories abroad. U.S.-based multinational corporations employ more than 33 million people worldwide and have total assets of $19.9 trillion (U.S. Bureau of the Census, 2011b).

Often such success comes at a price. The largest U.S.-based multinational corporations continue to achieve record earnings while hiring fewer American workers than ever. Between 1980 and 1999, the 500 largest corporations tripled their assets. At the same time, though, they eliminated almost 5 million U.S. jobs (Phillips, 2002). In 2005,

Exhibit 10.7   The Economic Power of Multinational Corporations

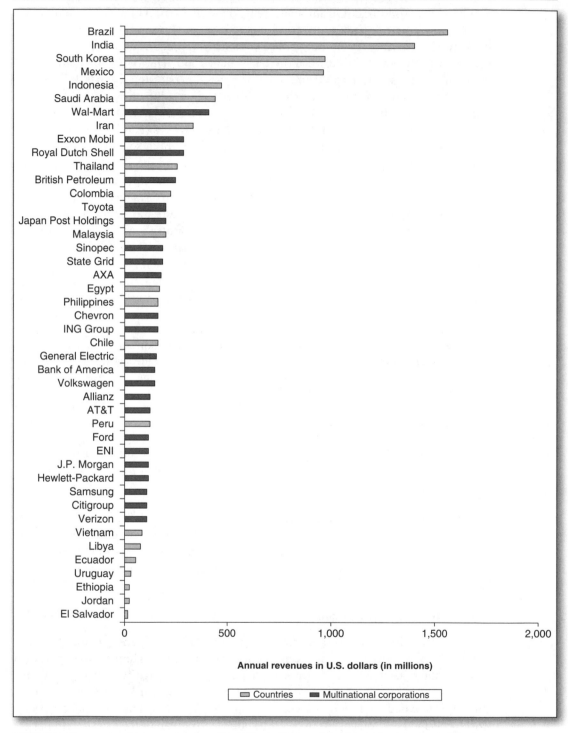

SOURCES: Gross national income data from World Bank, 2011; multinational sales data from CNN Money, 2010

IBM laid off 13,000 American and European workers at the same time that it was adding 14,000 workers in India to its payroll (Lohr, 2005).

With their ability to quickly shift operations to friendly countries, multinational corporations find it easy to evade the governance of any one country. Their decisions reflect corporate goals and not necessarily the well-being or interests of any particular country. In fact, the largest multinational corporations have accumulated more wealth than most countries in the world, as Exhibit 10.7 shows.

From a structural-functionalist perspective, a U.S. company locating a production facility in a poor country would seem to benefit everyone involved. The host country benefits from the creation of new jobs and a higher standard of living. The corporation, of course, benefits from increased profits. And consumers in the country in which the corporation is based benefit from paying lower prices for products that would cost more if manufactured at home. Furthermore, the entire planet benefits because these firms form alliances with many different countries and therefore might help pressure them into settling their political disputes peacefully.

Multinational corporations are indeed a valuable part of the international economy, as we saw in Chapter 9. However, the conflict perspective argues that in the long run multinationals can actually perpetuate or even worsen global stratification. One common criticism of multinationals is that they exploit local workers and communities. Employees in foreign plants or factories often work under conditions that wouldn't be tolerated in wealthier countries. The most obvious inequity is the wage people earn. For example, according to the National Labor Committee for Worker and Human Rights (2001), senior seamstresses with six years' experience at a Bangladesh factory that makes Disney clothing earn 17 cents an hour. Most work more than 15 hours a day, seven days a week.

In addition, environmental regulations and occupational safety requirements that tend to drive up the cost of finished products, such as protection against dangerous conditions or substances, sometimes don't exist in other countries. Hence, local workers may become sicker and the environment more polluted when foreign manufacturers set up facilities. For instance, U.S., Canadian, Australian, and European mining companies are digging mines of unprecedented size and destructiveness around the world. Many of these projects have caused not only significant deforestation but also the release of cyanide, arsenic, lead, and copper into nearby water supplies ("Tarnished Gold," 1999). Conditions in foreign factories were so bad and criticism from human rights organizations so strong that a 1997 presidential task force created a code of conduct on wages, working conditions, and child labor for apparel factories that U.S. companies own and operate around the world.

The host countries themselves are equally likely to be exploited. The money multinational corporations earn is rarely reinvested in the host country. In fact, 85% of the profit from exported products ends up in the hands of the multinational corporations, bankers, traders, and distributors (Braun, 1997). For example, in Brazil, one of the world's largest agricultural exporters, shipments abroad of fruits, vegetables, and soybeans have grown considerably over the past several decades. During the same period, however, the number of Brazilians who were undernourished grew from one third to two thirds of the population (Braun, 1997).

Local economies can suffer as well. For instance, supermarket chains owned by large multinational corporations have revolutionized food distribution worldwide. They are popular with consumers all over the world because of their lower prices and greater variety and convenience (Dugger, 2004a). But these stores tend to get their produce from large conglomerates that have more money and marketing know-how than small, local suppliers and can therefore provide cheaper fruits and vegetables. Hence, the livelihoods of millions of struggling small farmers have been destroyed, widening the gap between the haves and the have-nots in developing countries.

Multinational corporations can also perpetuate global inequality by their decisions on when to develop certain products and where to market them. A case in point is the global pharmaceutical industry. North America, Japan, and Western Europe account for 80% of world drug sales, whereas Africa accounts for about 1% (cited in McNeil, 2000). A significant proportion of medical research today is devoted to drugs that are likely to sell in the lucrative markets of developed countries. These drugs are usually either "blockbuster" drugs (those that can earn upward of $1.5 billion a year) or "lifestyle" drugs (those that enhance the lives of generally healthy people). The astounding popularity—and profit-making capacity—of anti-impotence drugs like Viagra and Cialis and baldness drugs like Propecia and Rogaine are recent examples. Impotence and baldness can be characterized as lifestyle troubles or embarrassing inconveniences but certainly not life-threatening illnesses.

This trend has global significance. Of the drugs introduced between 1975 and 1999 by the world's largest pharmaceutical companies, only 1% were created to combat diseases such as tuberculosis, malaria, sleeping sickness, and acute lower respiratory tract infections, which kill or cripple millions each year in Africa, Asia, and South America (Silverstein, 1999). Cancer kills 76 million people a year. Between 1975 and 1999, 111 new cancer drugs became available. In contrast, tropical diseases kill 128 million people a year. However, only 13 new drugs to fight these diseases were developed between 1975 and 1999 (Cowley, 2005). The last truly new drug to treat tuberculosis—a disease that kills 2 million people a year, mostly in poor, developing countries—was invented more than 40 years ago (McNeil, 2000).

Not all multinationals are hardhearted organizations that ignore the well-being of their workers abroad, the well-being of the workforce at home whose jobs are being exported to other countries, or the health and welfare of poor people in developing nations. For many multinationals, relocating manufacturing facilities to another country where labor is less expensive is a necessary response to global economic pressures as well as the demands of domestic consumers for inexpensive products. But the processes that drive corporate decisions do sometimes drive individuals out of work, contribute to environmental and health problems, and reinforce global inequality.

Conclusion

In Chapter 1, I pondered the question of how free we really are to act as we wish. I described some of the personal, interpersonal, and structural considerations that limit or constrain our choices. In this chapter, you have seen how this fundamental issue is affected by social stratification and inequality. Certain groups of people have a greater capacity to control their own lives than others. Your position in the stratification system can determine not only your ability to influence people and exert authority but a whole host of life chances as well, from financial stability to housing, education, and health care. The unequal distribution of economic resources, whether between wealthy and poor individuals in the same society or between wealthy and poor countries worldwide, has created a seemingly indestructible system of haves and have-nots.

The profound imbalances in wealth, power, and prestige that exist in the United States are especially ironic given how loudly and frequently U.S. citizens boast of their cultural commitment to the values of equality and justice. Nevertheless, the U.S. system is set up, like most others in the world, to promote, enhance, and protect the interests of those who reside at or near the top of the stratification system. Authority, wealth, and influence grant rights that are unknown to the vast majority of people.

It's rather shocking that in a country as wealthy as the United States, a comfortable, healthy, and stable life is well beyond the reach of tens of millions of people. Constant media images of wealth remind poor and working-class people that they are outsiders who can only watch and long to be part of that affluent world. And when disaster strikes, like Hurricane Katrina, poor people receive the message once again that their marginal status in society can have deadly consequences.

We speak of the poor as if they were an unchanging and faceless group to be pitied, despised, or feared. To talk of the "poverty problem" is to talk about some depersonalized, permanent fixture on the U.S. landscape. But poverty is people. It's people standing in soup kitchen lines and welfare lines. It's people living in rat-infested projects. It's people sleeping on sidewalks. It's people struggling to acquire things the rest of society takes for granted. It's people coming up short in their quest for the American Dream.

When we look at the institutional causes of poverty, we see that the personality or "cultural" traits often associated with poverty—low ambition, rejection of the work ethic, inability to plan for the future—might be better understood as the consequences of poverty rather than its causes. As long as the structural obstacles to stable employment, adequate wages, and a decent education continue to exist, so will the characteristic hopelessness associated with poverty.

YOUR TURN

Even people whose income is above the poverty line can sometimes find it difficult to make ends meet. Imagine a family of four living in your hometown. Suppose that both parents work, that one child is seven years old and in elementary school, and that the other is three and must be cared for during the day.

Make a list of all the goods and services this family needs to function at a minimum subsistence level—that is, at the poverty line. Be as complete as possible. Consider food, clothing, housing, transportation, medical care, childcare, entertainment, and so on. Estimate the minimum monthly cost of each item. If you currently live on your own and must pay these expenses yourself, use those figures as a starting point (but remember that you must estimate for a family of four). If you live in a dorm or at home, ask one of your parents (or anyone else who pays the bills) what the expenses are for such goods and services. Call a local day care center to see what it charges for childcare. Go to the local supermarket and compute the family food budget. For expenses that aren't divided on a monthly basis (e.g., clothing and household appliances), estimate the yearly cost and divide by 12.

Once you have estimated total monthly expenses, multiply by 12 to get the annual subsistence budget for the family of four. If your estimate is higher than the government's official poverty line (around $22,113), what sorts of items could you cut out of the budget for the family to be defined as officially poor and therefore eligible for certain government programs? By looking for ways to cut expenses from your minimal subsistence budget, you will get a good sense of what everyday life in poverty is like.

Describe the quality of life of this hypothetical family that makes too much to be officially poor and too little to sustain a comfortable life. What sorts of things are they forced to do without that a more affluent family might simply take for granted (e.g., annual vacations, pocket money, a savings account, a second car, eating out once a week)? What would be the impact of poverty on the lives of the children? How will the family's difficulty in meeting its basic subsistence needs translate into access to opportunities (education, jobs, health care) for the children later in life?

SOURCE: Adapted from M. V. Miller, 1985

CHAPTER HIGHLIGHTS

- Stratification is a ranking of entire groups of people, based on race, gender, or social class, which perpetuates unequal rewards and life chances in society.

- Social class is the primary means of stratification in many societies, including the United States. Contemporary sociologists are likely to define one's class standing as a combination of income, wealth, occupational prestige, and educational attainment. Social class is more than an economic position; it is a way of life that affects how we experience every facet of our lives.

- The structural-functionalist explanation of stratification is that higher rewards, such as prestige and large salaries, are afforded to the most important positions in society, thereby ensuring that the most qualified individuals will occupy the highest positions. Conflict theory argues that stratification reflects an unequal distribution of power in society and is a primary source of conflict and tension.

- The official U.S. poverty line, the dollar cutoff point that defines the amount of income necessary for subsistence living, may actually be set too low, thereby underestimating the proportion of the population that is suffering financially.

- Poverty persists because it serves economic and social functions. The ideology of competitive individualism—that to succeed in life all one has to do is work hard and win in competition with others—creates a belief that poor people are to blame for their own suffering. In addition, poverty receives institutional "support" from a distribution of wealth and income that is growing increasingly unequal.

- Stratification exists not only among different groups within the same society but also among different societies within a global community. Wealthy nations are better able to control the world's financial resources than poor nations are.

KEY TERMS

absolute poverty: Inability to afford the minimal requirements for sustaining a reasonably healthy existence

authority: Possession of some status or quality that compels others to obey one's directives or commands

caste system: Stratification system based on heredity, with little movement allowed across strata

colonization: Process of expanding economic markets by invading and establishing control over a weaker country and its people

competitive individualism: Cultural belief that those who succeed in society are those who work hardest and have the best abilities and that those who suffer don't work hard enough or lack the necessary traits or abilities

culture-of-poverty thesis: Belief that poor people, resigned to their position in society, develop a unique value structure to deal with their lack of success

estate system (feudal system): Stratification system in which high-status groups own land and have power based on noble birth

false consciousness: Situation in which people in the lower classes come to accept a belief system that harms them; the primary means by which powerful classes in society prevent protest and revolution

means of production: Land, commercial enterprises, factories, and wealth that form the economic basis of class societies

middle class: In a society stratified by social class, a group of people who have an intermediate level of wealth, income, and prestige, such as managers, supervisors, executives, small business owners, and professionals

near-poor: Individuals or families whose earnings are between 100% and 125% of the poverty line (see also **working poor**)

poor: In a society stratified by social class, a group of people who work for minimum wage or are chronically unemployed

poverty line: Amount of yearly income a family requires to meet its basic needs, according to the federal government

poverty rate: Percentage of people whose income falls below the poverty line

power: Ability to affect decisions in ways that benefit a person or protect his or her interests

prestige: Respect and honor given to some people in society

relative poverty: Individuals' economic position compared with the living standards of the majority in the society

slavery: Economic form of inequality in which some people are legally the property of others

social class: Group of people who share a similar economic position in a society, based on their wealth and income

social mobility: Movement of people or groups from one class to another

socioeconomic status: Prestige, honor, respect, and lifestyle associated with different positions or groups in society

stratification: Ranking system for groups of people that perpetuates unequal rewards and life chances in society

upper class: In a society stratified by social class, a group of people who have high income and prestige and who own vast amounts of property and other forms of wealth, such as owners of large corporations, top financiers, rich celebrities and politicians, and members of prestigious families

working class: In a society stratified by social class, a group of people who have a low level of wealth, income, and prestige, such as industrial and factory workers, office workers, clerks, and farm and manual laborers

working poor: Employed people who consistently earn wages but do not make enough to survive (see also **near-poor**)

STUDENT STUDY SITE

Visit the Student Study Site at **www.sagepub.com/newman9e** for these additional learning tools:

- Flashcards
- Web quizzes
- Sociologists at Work features
- Micro-Macro Connection features
- Video links
- Audio links
- Web resources
- SAGE journal articles

The Architecture of Inequality

Race and Ethnicity

11

Race and Ethnicity: More Than Just Biology

Histories of Oppression and Inequality

Racial and Ethnic Relations

Global Perspectives on Racism

Just like millions of other Americans, I sat transfixed in front of my television on the night of November 4, 2008, watching the presidential election results trickle in. At about 11:00 P.M. Eastern time, the networks made the astounding projection: Barack Obama—a man with a black Kenyan father and a white American mother—would be the 44th president of the United States. I sat in semi-disbelief. Had this country, one with such a difficult, painful, and deadly racial history, really just elected a black man to the highest office in the land? A development that would have been unthinkable 50, 25, or even 10 years ago had just happened. People of all colors and classes here and abroad danced in the streets. Jesse Jackson, Oprah Winfrey, Colin Powell, and countless other less famous people wept with joy. Parents named their newborns "Barack." One African American columnist wrote a letter to her four-month-old son that night:

> What does Barack Obama's election mean to you? When you are older we will talk about how African American children, like their parents and grandparents, have struggled to overcome the feeling that no matter how hard they study and work and try, there are barriers—some visible, others hidden but still there—that block their way. The feeling that we can rise, but only so far. I did not want you to grow up believing that bitter remnants of the past could hold power over your future. I wanted to be able to tell you that it wasn't true—that you could be anything you wanted to be. But I couldn't quite believe it myself. Now I do. (Kelley, 2008, p. 29)

Sociologists, columnists, and political analysts struggled to find the most memorable and most articulate way to capture the historical significance of the moment. Some speculated that it might mark the end of racial inequality and exclusion in this country; others wondered if we'd become a "postracial" society, where traditional racial categories no longer matter. In a national poll the day before Obama's inauguration, more than two thirds of African Americans said they believed that Martin Luther King's famous 1963 dream (of a country where race and ethnicity are losing their status as major criteria for judging the content of a person's character) had been fulfilled (CNN.com, 2009). And surveys since the election consistently show that college-age Blacks are now more optimistic and upbeat about their economic futures than Whites (Cose, 2011). As I tried to absorb the magnitude of what took place that night,

I began to think about the other important but less dramatic educational, economic, political, and cultural gains that people of color have made over the past few years:

- The percentage of African American and Latino/a college graduates has risen steadily over the past 10 years, as has the proportion of ethnoracial minority families that could be considered middle or upper class.
- The number of black and Latino/a families headed by married couples is increasing.
- More Latino/as, Asian Americans, and Native Americans are in elected offices at the national, state, and local levels than ever before. In 2009, Sonia Sotomayor became the first Latina to be appointed to the U.S. Supreme Court.
- African American artists like Jay-Z, Flo Rida, Kanye West, Beyoncé, and 50 Cent have achieved remarkable crossover success, and Oprah Winfrey is one of the highest-paid entertainers in the country. In recent years, some of the most successful athletes in what were once exclusively white sports—tennis and golf—are black: Serena and Venus Williams and Tiger Woods. Three out of every 10 major league baseball players today is Latino (Lapchick, 2011).

Yet as I think of the significant strides ethnoracial minorities have made, I can't get past a very different reality. Despite the progress they've attained, African Americans, Latino/as, and Native Americans still remain, on average, the poorest and most disadvantaged of all groups in the United States. Their average annual income is still substantially lower than that of Whites and Asian Americans (U.S. Bureau of the Census, 2011b). Half of black men in their 20s who didn't attend college are unemployed (compared with 21% of Whites; Eckholm, 2006b). The rate of home ownership among minority groups passed 50% for the first time in 2004, but rates of foreclosures have more than doubled since then (Bajaj & Nixon, 2006). Of all ethnoracial groups in this society, African Americans have the lowest life expectancy; highest rate of infant mortality; highest rates of most cancers, diabetes, heart disease, high blood pressure, and HIV/AIDS; and highest rates of death from treatable illnesses, gunshot wounds, and drug- or alcohol-induced causes (American Sociological Association, 2005; Centers for Disease Control and Prevention, 2011a; U.S. Bureau of the Census, 2011b).

I also think of specific violent events in the recent past that further belie the image of racial progress and harmony. On the same day in 2009 that the *New York Times* reported that people's views on race relations might be more positive and optimistic than ever before (Stolberg & Connelly, 2009), it ran a story about two white teenagers facing trial for killing a 25-year-old Mexican man after calling him a "spic" and telling him, "This is Shenandoah [Pennsylvania]. You don't belong here" (quoted in Hamill, 2009, p. A3). In one New York suburb, attacks on Latinos are such an established pastime among white youths that attackers have a common derogatory term for it: "Beaner hopping" (Barnard, 2009). According to the Federal Bureau of Investigation (2010), in 2009, there were about 6,700 reported hate-related offenses motivated by race, religion, or ethnicity. Between 2008 and 2009, the number of white supremacist militia groups more than doubled (Hosenball & Isikoff, 2010). In response, the Department of Homeland Security stated that the election of the country's first African American president coupled with the current economic downturn "present unique drivers for right-wing radicalization and recruitment" (quoted in Conant, 2009, p. 32).

So how far have we really come? Which is the real United States? Is it the one that overcame centuries of racial conflict and elected a black president? Or is it the one perpetually plagued by economic inequality, prejudice, and hatred?

In the previous chapter, I examined the class stratification system. But social class doesn't create unequal life chances on its own. This chapter focuses on another important determinant of social inequality: race and ethnicity.

Race and Ethnicity: More Than Just Biology

To most people, *race* is a category of individuals labeled and treated as similar because of common inborn biological traits, such as skin color, color and texture of hair, and shape of eyes, nose, or head. It is widely assumed that people who are placed in the same racial category share behavioral, psychological, and personality traits that are linked to their physical similarities. But sociologists typically use the term *ethnicity* to refer to the nonbiological traits—such as shared culture, history, language, patterns of behavior, and beliefs—that provide members of a group with a sense of common identity. Whereas ethnicity is thought to be something that we learn from other people, race is commonly portrayed as an inherited and permanent biological characteristic that can easily be used to divide people into mutually exclusive groups.

But the concept of race isn't nearly so straightforward. For instance, people who consider themselves "white" may actually have darker skin and curlier hair than some people who consider themselves "black." In addition, some groups have features that do not neatly place them in one race or another. Australian Aborigines have black skin and "Negroid" facial features but also have blond, wavy hair. The black-skinned !Kung who live in the Kalahari Desert of southern Africa have epicanthic eye folds, a characteristic typical of East Asian peoples.

Not surprisingly, there are no universal racial categories. Brazilians have three primary races—*branco* (white), *prêto* (black), and *pardo* (mulatto)—but use dozens of more precise terms to categorize people based on minute differences in skin color, hair texture and length, and facial features. South Africa has four legally defined races—black, white, colored, and Indian—but in England and Ireland the term *black* is used to refer to all people who are not white. In one small Irish town that experienced an unprecedented influx of refugees in the late 1990s, anyone who wasn't Irish was considered black. As one resident put it, "Either Romanians or Nigerians, we don't know the difference. They're all the same. They're all black" (quoted in Lyall, 2000, p. A6). Conversely, some African Americans visiting Ghana are shocked when people there refer to them as *obruni,* or "white foreigner" (Polgreen, 2005).

In some places, racial identification can shift throughout the course of a person's life, reflecting changes in economic standing, not skin color. For instance, Brazilians who climb the class ladder through educational and economic achievement may find themselves in a different racial category, as illustrated by popular Brazilian expressions such as "Money whitens" or "A rich Negro is a white man, and a poor white man is a Negro" (Marger, 1994, p. 441). Educated nonwhite parents in Brazil are significantly more likely to classify their children as white than are less-educated nonwhite parents (Schwartzman, 2007). In Puerto Rico, a U.S. territory, conceptions of race are markedly more fluid than they are in the United States. Race is seen as a continuum of categories with different shades of color as the norm and classifications that can change as one's socioeconomic circumstances change (C. E. Rodriguez & Cordero-Guzman, 2004). But even in this country, racial definitions can fluctuate. A recent nationwide survey showed that over a third of African Americans believe that because of a widening gap between middle-class and poor Blacks, "black" can no longer be thought of as a single race (cited in Gates, 2007).

The complex issue of defining race points to a complicated biological reality. Since the earliest humans appeared, they have consistently tended to migrate and interbreed. Some surveys estimate that at least 75% of U.S. Blacks have some white ancestry (cited in Mathews, 1996). Indeed, there is no gene that is 100% of one form in one race and 100% of a different form in another race (P. Brown, 1998).

That is not to say that race has absolutely *no* connection to biology. Geneticists have known for quite a while that some diseases are not evenly distributed across racial groups. The overwhelming majority of cases of sickle cell anemia, for instance, are among people of African descent; it is rare among non-Hispanic Whites (Blackhealthcare.com, 2003). In 2005, the Food and Drug Administration approved the cardiac drug BiDil, which is intended to be used exclusively by African Americans, who have been shown to be genetically predisposed to heart disease. Hemochromatosis, a digestive disorder that causes the body to absorb too much iron, affects Whites of Northern European descent much more frequently than people of color. Among African Americans, Asian Americans, Latino/as, and American Indians, the disease is virtually nonexistent. Among Whites, about five people out of 1,000—0.5%—carry two copies of the hemochromatosis gene and are susceptible to developing the disease. One out of every 8 to 12 Whites is a carrier of one abnormal gene (National Digestive Diseases Information Clearinghouse, 2011). However, no disease is found *exclusively* in one racial group. Furthermore, it's unclear whether these differences are solely due to some inherited biological trait or to the life experiences and historical, geographical, and/or environmental location of certain groups.

For most sociologists, then, race is more meaningful as a social category than as a biological one (Gans, 2005). That is, the characteristics a society selects to distinguish one ethnoracial group from another shape social rankings and determine access to important resources. But they have less to do with innate physical differences or genetic predispositions than with what the prevailing culture defines as socially significant (American Sociological Association, 2002). For instance, Jews, the Irish, Italians, and even some Germans were once defined as members of inferior races. They came to be seen as "white" only when they entered the mainstream culture and gained economic and political power (Bronner, 1998a). Sociologists have noted that more and more U.S. adults feel comfortable simply shedding the ethnic identities they were born into and taking on new ones (Hitt, 2005).

Historical changes in the categories used by the U.S. government in its decennial population censuses further illustrate shifting conceptions of race (S. M. Lee, 1993):

- In 1790, the first U.S. census used the following classifications: Free White Males, Free White Females, All Other Free Persons, and Slaves.
- In 1870, there were five races: White, Colored (Black), Mulatto (people with some black blood), Chinese, and Indian.
- Race categories in the 1890 census reflected white people's concern about race mixing and racial purity. Eight races were listed, half of them applying to black or partly black populations: White, Colored (Black), Mulatto (people with three-eighths to five-eighths black blood), Quadroon (people with one-fourth black blood), Octoroon (people with one-eighth black blood), Chinese, Japanese, and Indian.
- In 1900, Mulatto, Quadroon, and Octoroon were dropped, so that any amount of "black blood" meant a person had to be classified as "Black."
- In 1910 and 1920, Mulatto returned to the census form, only to disappear for good in 1930.

- Between 1930 and 2000, some racial classifications (such as Hindu, Eskimo, part-Hawaiian, and Mexican) appeared and disappeared. Others (Filipino, Korean, Hawaiian) made an appearance and have remained since.
- Individuals filling out the 2010 census form had a wide array of racial categories from which to choose: White, Black, American Indian or Alaska Native, Asian Indian, Chinese, Filipino, Japanese, Korean, Vietnamese, Native Hawaiian, Guamanian or Chamorro, or Samoan.

You may have noticed that Latino/a or Hispanic is not included in the list of races on the latest census form. With the exception of the inclusion of "Mexican" in 1930, Spanish-speaking people have routinely been classified as "white." But because Latino/as can be members of any race, "Hispanic origin" appears on the census form, not as a race but as an ethnicity. In fact, the 2010 form explicitly states that "Hispanic origins are not races."

This way of thinking has not been received well by all Latino/as. Recent census data show that 87% of Americans born in Cuba and 53% born in Mexico identify themselves as white; but a majority of those born in the Dominican Republic and El Salvador refused to identify themselves by any of the racial categories on the census form (cited in Roberts, 2010). Indeed, in the 2000 census, so many Latino/as refused to racially identify themselves that "some other race" became the fastest-growing racial category in the United States (Swarns, 2004). In the 2010 census, many Latino/as chose to use "American Indian" to identify their race. Consequently, the number of American Indians who also identified themselves as Hispanic tripled between 2000 and 2010 (cited in Decker, 2011).

In short, racial categories are not natural, biological groupings. They are created, inhabited, transformed, applied, and destroyed by people (Omi & Winant, 1992). What ties individuals together in a particular racial group is not a set of shared physical characteristics—because there aren't any physical characteristics shared by all members of a particular racial group—but the shared experience of identifying, and being identified by others, as members of that group (Piper, 1992). The power of this experience is reflected by the fact that people who identify as one race but are perceived by others as a member of another race suffer higher levels of depression and psychological distress than people who are "correctly" classified (M. E. Campbell & Troyer, 2007).

MICRO-MACRO CONNECTION

Why Isn't Barack Obama White?

Definitions of race and the way those definitions are incorporated into people's individual identities are particularly difficult for people whose biological parents are of different races. President Obama, as you well know, is biracial. Although he sometimes jokingly refers to himself as a "mutt," he, like so many biracial individuals before him, is identified as black. He is known as the first black or African American president, usually not the first biracial president and never the first half-white president. Why?

Since the era of slavery, the United States has adhered to the "one-drop rule" regarding racial identity (F. J. Davis, 1991). The term dates back to a common law in the South that a "single drop of black blood" makes a person black. Sociologists call this a *hypodescent* rule, meaning that racially mixed people are always assigned the status of the subordinate group (F. J. Davis, 1991). Conversely, mixed-race people in other groups must meet a hereditary threshold in order to claim a particular ethnoracial identity. For instance, some Native Americans carry a card, known as the CDIB (Certificate of Degree of Indian Blood), that indicates whether they have enough Indian blood to be considered Indian (Hitt, 2005).

People in the United States still tend to see race in mutually exclusive categories: black, white, red, yellow, brown. Even when faced with ambiguities, U.S. residents often try to put people into single-color racial groups. But the dramatic growth in multiracial children has upset traditional views of racial identity. Between 1970 and 2000, the number of children whose parents are of different races grew from 900,000 to more than 3 million (S. M. Lee & Edmonston, 2005). More and more people of mixed racial heritage are fighting against the traditional "one drop" thinking and refusing to identify themselves as one race or another.

In the mid to late 1990s, these individuals lobbied Congress and the Bureau of the Census to add a multiracial category to the 2000 census. They argued that such a change would add visibility and legitimacy to a racial identity that had heretofore been ignored. Even before this debate emerged, some scholars had been arguing that a multiracial category might soften the racial lines that divide the country (Stephan & Stephan, 1989). When people blend two or more races and ethnicities within their own bodies, race becomes a less potent social divider, thereby presenting a biological solution to the problem of racial injustice (J. E. White, 1997). Such a sentiment is echoed by this columnist (a black woman married to a white man):

> [My son] is the exact shade you'd get if you mixed his father and me up in a paint can—a color I call golden. . . . Perhaps as the number of multiracial Americans continues to grow, there will be a plurality of golden people who are impossible to positively identify as one race or the other. And the rest of us who can be easily categorized will be forced to accept that color does not contribute to the content of one's character because we won't know which set of stereotypes to apply to whom. (Kelley, 2009, p. 41)

Not everyone thought such a change to the census form would be a good idea. Many civil rights organizations objected to the inclusion of a multiracial category (R. Farley, 2002). They worried that it would reduce the number of U.S. citizens claiming to belong to long-recognized ethnoracial minority groups, dilute the culture and political power of those groups, and make it more difficult to enforce civil rights laws (Mathews, 1996). Job discrimination lawsuits, affirmative action policies, and federal programs that assist minority businesses or that protect minority communities from environmental hazards all depend on official racial population data from the census.

In the end, the civil rights organizations won. For the 2000 census, the government decided not to add a multiracial category to official forms. Instead, it adopted a policy allowing people, for the first time, to identify themselves on the census form as members of more than one race. These guidelines specify that those who check "white" and another category will be counted as a member of the minority (Holmes, 2000). According to the 2010 census, 9 million people—or about 3% of the population—identify themselves as belonging to more than one race (Humes, Jones, & Ramirez, 2011).

Some sociologists caution, however, that the Census Bureau's method of measuring multiracial identity—checking two or more race categories—does not adequately reflect the way people personally experience race. A recent newspaper article told the story of a female university student whose ethnoracial heritage is Irish, Peruvian, Chinese, Shawnee, and Cherokee. On her 2010 census form, she checked white, Hispanic, Asian, and Native American. However, her father considers her Latina and her best friend thinks she's "mixed race." Her mother describes her as "other," which is how she identifies herself on various surveys (Saulny, 2011b).

Sociologists David Harris and Jeremiah Sim (2002) examined data from the National Longitudinal Study of Adolescent Health, a survey containing information on the racial identity of a nationwide sample of more than 11,000 adolescents. They found that the way people racially classify themselves can change from context to context. For instance, almost twice as many adolescents identify themselves as multiracial when they're interviewed at school as when they're interviewed at home. Furthermore, only 87.6% expressed the same racial identities across different settings. This research is important because it shows that census data on multiracial identity don't necessarily account for people who self-identify as multiracial in everyday situations. Sizable numbers of multiracial adolescents change their racial identity—to that of a single race—as they enter adulthood (J. M. Doyle & Kao, 2007).

Indeed, immediate practical needs can sometimes influence how people racially identify themselves. For instance, high school seniors with a mixed racial heritage find that their chances of being admitted to college or receiving scholarships may depend on which box—or how many boxes—they check on the application form. As one student, who has an Asian mother and a black father, posted on College Confidential (an online bulletin board for conversations about college admissions), "It pains me to say this, but putting down black might help my admissions chances and putting down Asian might hurt it [sic]" (quoted in Saulny & Steinberg, 2011, p. A1). Some commenters to her post agreed and advised her to identify as black. Others suggested selecting both. No one advised marking Asian alone. At Rice University, the admission rate for multiracial students is actually higher than the rate for the applicant pool as a whole. Not surprisingly, the number of applicants checking more than one race has increased from 8 in 2006 to 564 in 2011. So when it comes to determining racial identity, political, social, economic, and personal considerations—not biological ones—are the determining factors.

In this sense, whether Barack Obama is white, black, or a mutt ultimately depends on how *he* defines himself. When he filled out his 2010 census form, Obama chose to identify himself only as "black." But others may define him differently. In a 2010 poll, 55% of black respondents said President Obama is black and only 34% said he was mixed. Among white respondents, 53% said he was mixed, while 24% identified him as black (cited in J. Washington, 2010).

Histories of Oppression and Inequality

A quick glance at the history of the United States reveals a record of not just freedom, justice, and equality but also of conquest, discrimination, and exclusion. Racial and ethnic inequalities have manifested themselves in phenomena such as slavery and fraud; widespread economic, educational, and political deprivation; the violent and nonviolent protests of the civil rights movement; and racially motivated hate crimes. Along the way, such injustices have constricted people's access to basic necessities, including housing, health care, a stable family life, and a means of making a decent living.

Every ethnoracial minority has its own story of persecution. European immigrants—Germans, Irish people, Italians, Poles, Jews, Greeks—were objects of hatred, suspicion, and discrimination when they first arrived in significant numbers in the United States. For instance, Benjamin Franklin once expressed fear that white Pennsylvanians would be "overwhelmed by swarms of swarthy Germans, who 'will soon so out number us, that all the advantages we have will not . . . be able to preserve our language, and even our government will become precarious'" (quoted in Roberts, 2008, p. 6). Nineteenth-century newspaper job ads routinely noted, "No Irish need apply." Jews were refused admission to many U.S. universities until the mid 20th century. The National Origins Act of 1924 restricted immigration from southern Europe (mainly Greece and Italy) until the 1960s. Because these groups had the same skin color as the dominant white Protestants, however, they eventually overcame most of these obstacles and gained entry into mainstream society. Most recently, immigrants from Asia, Latin America, and the Middle East have become popular targets of hostility. For people of color in this country, racial equality has always been elusive.

Native Americans

The story of Native Americans includes racially inspired massacres, takeover of ancestral lands, confinement on reservations, and unending governmental exploitation. Successive waves of white settlers seeking westward expansion in the 18th and 19th centuries pushed Native Americans off any land the settlers considered desirable (U.S. Commission on Human Rights, 1992). A common European belief that Native Americans were "savages" who should be displaced to make way for civilized Whites provided the ideological justification for conquering them.

According to the Fourteenth Amendment to the U.S. Constitution, "All persons born or naturalized in the United States, and subject to the jurisdiction thereof, are citizens of the United States and of the state wherein they reside." But despite the broad wording of this amendment, Native Americans were excluded from citizenship. In 1884, the U.S. Supreme Court ruled that Native Americans owed their primary allegiance to their tribe and so did not automatically acquire citizenship at birth. Not until 1940 were all Native Americans born in the United States considered U.S. citizens (Haney López, 1996).

Despite their history of severe oppression and continuing disadvantaged economic status compared with other groups, some Native Americans have shown a remarkable ability to endure and in a few cases to shrewdly promote their own financial interests. In the Pacific Northwest, for instance, some Indian tribes have successfully protected their rights to lucrative fishing waters (F. G. Cohen, 1986). Casinos and resorts have made some tribes wealthy. The Connecticut Sun, a professional women's basketball franchise, plays its home games on the grounds of a casino owned by the Mohegan tribe. Elsewhere, organizations have been formed to advance the financial concerns of Native Americans in industries such as gas, oil, and coal, where substantial reserves exist on Indian land (Snipp, 1986). However, intense struggles between large multinational corporations and Native American tribes continue today over control of these reserves.

(Text continues on page 372)

"Civilizing" the Indians

Eric Margolis

In 1879, an ex–Indian fighter named Captain Richard Pratt established the Carlisle Indian Industrial School in Carlisle, Pennsylvania. Like other white Americans at the time, Pratt viewed Native Americans as "dirty," "ignorant," and "lazy." He devised a program of boarding schools that he believed would, in one or two generations, eliminate tribal culture by resocializing Indian children. He argued, "The Indian must die as an Indian and live as a man."

The Pratt plan took young children away from their families and tribes in the West and brought them to Pennsylvania and other locations. They had their hair cut and were given military uniforms. Their days were marked by rigid schedules enforced with bells and whistles to teach a sense of time. Half of the day they attended classes and half the time they worked on school farms and in factories intended to socialize young Indians to the dominant white culture. Pratt's Indian schools functioned as "total institutions," in Erving Goffman's terms.

To demonstrate the "success" of his socialization program for Indian children, Pratt made "before" pictures of them when they arrived at the school and "after" pictures when they had been in cloudy Pennsylvania long enough to lose their tans.

The goal was to visibly portray a "whitening" (that is, "civilizing") process. Note that, in the "after" shot, the students were dressed in school uniforms resembling the uniforms of the cavalry that defeated them in the Indian wars.

At the Indian schools, most of the children were trained to do menial work as domestic servants, farmers, and factory workers. Thus, the schools reinforced social class differences in addition to altering the racial identities of Native American children.

Training as domestics, Seneca Training School, 1905

Making tin utensils, Carlisle Indian School, circa 1900 to 1903

The schools reinforced gender distinctions, too. Boys and girls were commonly separated for classes in shop and home economics. Although Native American cultures had diverse family structures, the Indian schools sought to replace that diversity with the 19th-century white American version: the male-dominated nuclear family. Thus girls were prepared for domesticity and boys as breadwinners.

Most important, however, was the curriculum of resocialization. Students were punished if they spoke in their native language or practiced their tribal religion; they were taught to obey Western clock time, work for wages, and cultivate a desire for money and consumer goods. The end product would be an assimilated Indian, one whose traditional way of thinking and tribal lifestyle had been completely obliterated in favor of the individualism and the Protestant work ethic of American life.

Curiously, however, photographs of the school and classroom activities show that what was being taught was not a sense of individualism but regimentation and discipline, illustrated by military uniforms that suppressed individual personality.

Albuquerque Indian School, which was established in 1881 and continued operating until 1982, when its program was transferred to the Santa Fe Indian School.

Indian children did not always take this enforced ethnoracial resocialization quietly. There were many instances of resistance, ranging from stubborn refusal to participate to running away to vandalism and arson. Indian schools became notorious for constant surveillance and for discipline and punishment of resisting students.

Indian schools were the only federally financed education system—except for the military—that the United States ever developed. In 1900, nearly 18,000 Indian children were enrolled not just in Carlisle, Pennsylvania, but in places like Albuquerque, New Mexico; Flandreau, South Dakota; Chemawa, Oregon; Lawrence, Kansas; Mt. Pleasant, Michigan; Riverside, California; and Phoenix, Arizona. Government funding was used to build these imposing institutions and to make a detailed photographic record of the schools.

Most of the schools had jails, like this one at the Sacaton, Arizona, Indian school, where the most intransigent students were imprisoned.

Mt. Pleasant Indian Industrial School, circa 1910

Perhaps we should not be surprised that the Indian schools failed to smoothly assimilate Native Americans into white American culture. Segregated boarding schools were clearly more effective at promoting social exclusion than guiding students into the mainstream of American life. After the schools were through with them, the children were doubly stigmatized: marked by their color in a racist society and miseducated for their tribal culture, whose traditions they had lost and whose language they could no longer speak. Hence, Native Americans remained second-class citizens well into the second half of the 20th century.

Today, remedies are being sought for injustices against Native Americans. In 2003, a class-action lawsuit was filed on behalf of some 100,000 Native Americans who, from 1890 to 1978, were forced to attend boarding schools run by the U.S. government. Alleging sexual, physical, and emotional abuse, the suit seeks damages in the amount of $25 billion.

Indian tribes have also opened a number of their own schools. These schools teach reverence for Indian ways along with the typical school curriculum of English and mathematics. Today's Indian students are thus better prepared to live in either their own culture or the dominant American culture while preserving their own ethnic heritage.

In 1966, the Rough Rock Demonstration School opened in Chinle, Arizona, on the Navajo Reservation. It became a model for many other tribally run schools.

Latino/as

The history of Latino/as in this country has been diverse. Some groups have had a relatively positive experience. For instance, Cuban immigrants who streamed into this country in the late 1950s, fleeing Fidel Castro's communist political regime, received an enthusiastic welcome (Suarez, 1998). Many early Cuban immigrants were wealthy business owners who set up lucrative companies, particularly in South Florida. Today, Cuban American families are the most economically and educationally successful of any Latino/a group.

But other groups have experienced extreme resentment and oppression. For instance, when the United States expanded into the Southwest, white Americans moved into areas already inhabited by Mexicans. After a war that lasted from 1846 to 1848, Mexico relinquished half its national territory to the United States, including what are now the states of Arizona, California, Colorado, New Mexico, Texas, Nevada, and Utah, as well as parts of Kansas, Oklahoma, and Wyoming.

In theory, Mexicans living on the U.S. side of the new border were to be given all the rights of U.S. citizens. In practice, however, their property rights were frequently violated, and they lost control of their mining, ranching, and farming industries. The exploitation of Mexican workers coincided with a developing economic system built around mining and large-scale agriculture, activities that demanded a large pool of cheap labor (J. Farley, 1982). Workers often had to house their families in primitive shacks with no electricity or plumbing for months on end while they performed seasonal labor.

Today, the status of Latino/as is mixed. They account for more than 40% of the 81 million people added to the U.S. population over the last 30 years and now represent a bigger proportion of the U.S. population than Blacks (see Exhibit 11.1). By 2050, three out of every 10 persons in the United States will be Latino/a (Saenz, 2010). Larger numbers mean not only greater influence on the culture but more political clout. An estimated 11.8 million Latino/as voted in the 2008 presidential election (Gimpel, 2009), and they voted for Barack Obama over his Republican opponent John McCain by a margin of more than two to one. In swing states with heavy Latino/a populations, like Florida and California, their vote was key to Obama's victory (Lopez, 2008).

Economically and educationally, however, the situation is less rosy. The average annual income for Latino/a individuals and families is still substantially lower than that of other groups (U.S. Bureau of the Census, 2011b), and they have been hit hardest by the recession. Between 2005 and 2009, median net worth among Latino/as decreased by 66%, compared with 53% for Blacks, 54% for Asians, and 16% for Whites (Kochhar, Fry, & Taylor, 2011). In addition, Latino/as are significantly more likely to drop out of school and less likely to go to college than are white, Asian American, or African American children. Their low levels of education, coupled with geographic concentration in economically distressed areas of the country, has made Latino/as, particularly men, especially vulnerable to downsizing and unemployment (Mather & Jacobsen, 2010).

African Americans

The experience of African Americans has been unique among ethnoracial groups in this country because of the direct and indirect influences of slavery. From 1619, when the first black slaves were sold in Jamestown, Virginia, to 1865, when the Thirteenth Amendment was passed, outlawing slavery, several million Blacks in this country endured the brutal reality of forced servitude. Slave owners controlled every

Exhibit 11.1   Changes in Ethnoracial Composition of the U.S. Population

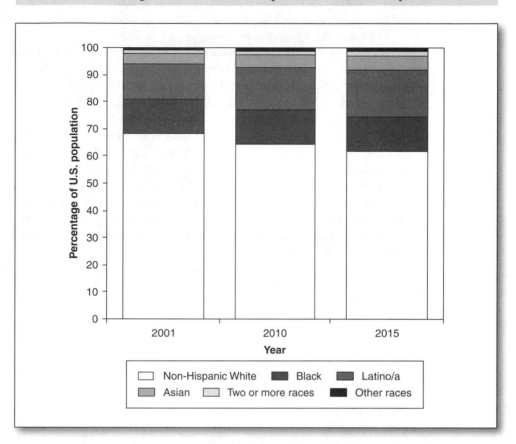

SOURCES: U.S. Bureau of the Census, 2002, Table 14; 2011b, Table 11

aspect of a slave's life. They determined which slaves could marry and which marriages could be dissolved. Wedding vows among slave couples often substituted the phrase "until distance do us part" for "until death"—or "the white man"—"do us part" (Hunter, 2011). The economic value of children (i.e., future slaves) meant that slave owners had an interest in keeping slave marriages intact. But even the possibility of stable family life was an illusion. When economic troubles forced the sale of slaves to raise money, slave owners didn't hesitate to separate the very slave families they had once advocated. The threat of separation hung over every slave family.

Even after slavery was abolished, the conditions of life for U.S. Blacks showed little improvement. Following emancipation, freed Blacks in the South found themselves arrested on trumped up charges like selling produce after dark or talking loudly to white women in public. Vagrancy was criminalized so that Blacks who couldn't show proof of employment were fined and thrown in jail. When they couldn't pay their fines, thousands were "leased" to county officials or private companies and forced to work—sometimes in shackles—under conditions that were actually worse than what they had experienced during slavery (Blackmon, 2009).

Later on, "Jim Crow" laws established rigid lines between the races. In 1896, the U.S. Supreme Court ruled that racial segregation in public facilities was constitutional.

Unequal access to public transportation, schools, hotels, theaters, restaurants, campgrounds, drinking fountains, the military, and practically every other aspect of social life continued until the middle of the 20th century. Conditions were so bad that Blacks often had to take extra precautions simply to engage in everyday activities. For instance, from the 1930s to the 1960s, many Blacks wouldn't embark on a long-distance automobile trip without a guidebook called *The Negro Motorist Green Book.* This book provided Blacks with city-by-city information about where they could drive, sleep, eat, buy gas, or shop without being harassed, humiliated, or attacked (McGee, 2010).

Despite advances, the quality of life for most African Americans remains below that of Whites. The median annual income for black households is $34,218, compared with $52,312 for white households (U.S. Bureau of the Census, 2011b). Black unemployment is twice as high as that of Whites. Fewer than half of African American families own their own homes (47%), compared with 72% of white families (U.S. Bureau of the Census, 2011b). As one author put it, "The era that ushered in the first black president has also introduced the highest levels of unemployment and poverty for African Americans in 20 years" (Samuels, 2011, p. 46). Nevertheless, blatant discrimination has declined in the past four decades, and some economic, educational, and political advances have been made. For instance, black-owned businesses generate more than $89 billion in annual revenues (U.S. Bureau of the Census, 2011b). The average annual household income of $34,218 represents a significant increase over the average income of black households in 1980 ($25,076). And the median income of black women is just a little less than that of white women (U.S. Bureau of the Census, 2009).

Asian Americans

When large numbers of Chinese men came to this country in the second half of the 19th century to work in the mines and on the expanding railroad system, they were treated with hostility. The image of the "yellow peril" was fostered by rampant fears that hordes of Chinese workers would take away scarce jobs and eventually overrun native-born Whites. In the late 19th and early 20th centuries, several laws, such as the Chinese Exclusion Act, the Scott Act, and the Geary Act, barred Chinese immigrants from entering the country and stripped those already here of many of their legal rights. For instance, Chinese laborers were legally prevented from becoming permanent citizens, from bringing their wives with them, and from marrying Whites when they got here.

Early Japanese Americans faced similar circumstances. Like the Chinese, Japanese families created tight-knit, insulated communities where they were able to pool money and resources and achieve relative success. But their perceived success motivated lawmakers to enact legislation that barred all further Japanese immigration. Hostility toward the Japanese reached a peak in 1941, following Japan's attack on Pearl Harbor. President Franklin Roosevelt signed an executive order authorizing the relocation and internment of Japanese immigrants and U.S. citizens of Japanese descent in camps surrounded by barbed wire, watchtowers, and armed guards.

The irony of race for Chinese, Japanese, Koreans, Vietnamese, Cambodians, Laotians, Indians, and other Asian groups is that they are often perceived as "model minorities" or "America's greatest success story." For instance, the average total SAT scores for Asian high school seniors is 1623, compared with 1580 for Whites and 1509 for the general population (National Center for Fair and Open Testing, 2011). Almost twice the percentage of Asian Americans as Whites complete college, and their average household income is actually higher than that of the population as a whole (U.S. Bureau of the Census, 2011b). Over half of the semifinalists in the 2011 Scripps National Spelling Bee were of Asian descent.

But the expectations and resentment associated with being the "model minority" can be as confining and oppressive as those created by more negative labels. Here's how one Asian American author describes it:

> I am Asian American, but I am not good with computers. I cannot balance my checkbook, much less perform calculus in my head. I would like to fail in school, for no reason other than to cast off my freakish alter ego of geek and nerd. . . . I yearn to be an artist, an athlete, a rebel, and, above all, an ordinary person. (Wu, 2002, pp. 39–40)

By overemphasizing Asian American success, the label downplays the problems Asian Americans continue to face from racial discrimination in all areas of public and private life. Furthermore, it portrays Asian American success as proof that the United States provides equal opportunities for those who conform and work hard, even though many ethnoracial groups continue to suffer.

The "model minority" image can also turn ugly when equated with perceptions that Asians are overstudious loners who can't be trusted. These stereotypes bubbled to the surface in the immediate aftermath of the 2007 massacre at Virginia Tech University, in which a Korean American student went on a rampage and killed 32 people. Although it turned out that the gunman suffered from serious mental problems and the feared anti-Korean backlash never materialized, media portrayals continued to highlight both his ethnicity and his lack of social skills, perpetuating the idea that shy, bookish Asian American college students might be ticking time bombs.

Muslim Americans

Although their numbers are small compared with those of other ethnoracial minority groups and their arrival has been more recent, few groups have evoked stronger negative feelings or are as misunderstood as Muslim Americans. While the tendency is to see them as a monolithic, homogeneous group, they are actually quite culturally and racially diverse. Sixty-five percent of Muslim Americans are first-generation immigrants. About a third come from the Arabic-speaking countries of the Middle East and North Africa and another 27% from South Asia. Despite the heavy presence of immigrants, more than three quarters of Muslims in this country are U.S. citizens (Pew Research Center, 2007a).

In terms of educational attainment and income level, Muslim Americans mirror the rest of U.S. society. The proportion of Muslims who have earned college degrees is the same as it is for the general population. In addition, 41% of Muslim American adults report annual household incomes of more than $50,000, compared with 44% of all U.S. adults. In fact, Muslims in the United States are in far better shape economically than those in France, Spain, Germany, or Great Britain (Pew Research Center, 2007a).

Overall, Muslim Americans are quite assimilated into mainstream U.S. society. The vast majority believe that their communities are good places to live in and that hard work will pay off. Most are happy to be in the United States and condemn Islamic extremism. A recent poll found that most Muslim Americans say they are loyal to the United States and optimistic about the future, despite reporting high levels of discrimination (Younis, 2011).

Nevertheless, the equation of Muslims with violent terrorism has been a common prejudice for decades, dating back to the murder of 11 Israeli athletes during the 1972 Summer Olympics in Munich. The September 11, 2001, attacks bolstered anti-Muslim prejudice and continue to make their lives significantly more difficult. Most Muslims believe that the government singles them out for increased surveillance and monitoring (Pew Research Center, 2007a).

Despite knowing more about Muslims than ever before, almost half of U.S. adults have an unfavorable view of them, believing that Islam encourages violence more than other religions (Jost, 2006b). One study found that a high level of anti-Islamic imagery in the media supports the negative portrayal of Muslims and furthers the stereotype that all Muslims are terrorists (Khalema & Wannas-Jones, 2003). In 2010, an NPR news analyst, Juan Williams, stated in an interview, "When I get on a plane, I got to tell you, if I see people who are in Muslim garb and I think, you know, they are identifying themselves first and foremost as Muslims, I get worried. I get nervous" (quoted in Mirkinson, 2010, p. 1). Although he was fired for expressing this view, many people in the country thought he was simply articulating what most people felt.

That same year, proposals to build mosques in places like Murfreesboro, Tennessee, Sheboygan, Wisconsin, and most notably near the site of the World Trade Center in New York were met by angry protests. A national poll found that although 70% of Americans supported the rights of Muslims to build the mosque at the World Trade Center site, 63% believed it would be inappropriate to actually build it (cited in L. Miller, 2010). One Islamic studies professor, describing the bitter tone of the opposition, stated,

> It's one thing to oppose a mosque because traffic might increase, but it's different when you say these mosques are going to be nurturing terrorist bombers, that Islam is invading, that civilization is being undermined by Muslims. (quoted in Goodstein, 2010a, pp. 1, 17)

Indeed, the mere suggestion that someone *is* a Muslim can sometimes be enough to disparage that person. False rumors that Barack Obama is a Muslim dogged him throughout the 2008 election and continue today. The fact that he and his representatives felt this allegation had to be denied reinforced its negative status in the culture.

The expression of anti-Muslim sentiment is more open than such sentiments applied to other ethnoracial groups. According to the Council on American-Islamic Relations, incidents of harassment of and violence against Muslims increased 70% between 2002 and 2003 ("Anti-Muslim Incidents Increase," 2004). Some have even attempted to codify anti-Muslim sentiment into the law. In 2010, voters in Oklahoma approved a ballot measure that would prohibit the use of Sharia law—the body of law based on the Qur'an—in state courts. Although the measure was blocked by a federal judge, several other states are weighing similar legislation. A candidate for the 2012 Republican presidential nomination said publicly that if he was elected president he would not appoint a Muslim to a Cabinet position or judgeship because "there is this creeping attempt to gradually ease Sharia law and the Muslim faith into our government" (quoted in A. Sullivan, 2011, p. 11A). Given such fear and distrust, it's not surprising that Muslim Americans have become one of the most openly despised groups in the country today.

Racial and Ethnic Relations

U.S. society's long history of racial tension is unlikely to fade away anytime soon. Increasing numbers of ethnoracial minorities and an influx of non-English-speaking immigrants are heightening competition and conflict over society's resources, including various forms of wealth, prestige, and power. The unequal distribution of resources is often motivated by *racism*, the belief that humans are subdivided into distinct groups so different in their social behavior and mental and physical capacities that they can be ranked as superior or inferior (Marger, 1994). Racism can be expressed at the personal level through individual attitudes and behavior, at the cultural level in language and collective ideologies, and at the macrostructural level in the everyday workings of social institutions.

Personal Racism

Personal racism is the expression of racist attitudes or behaviors by individual people. This type of racism takes many obvious forms, such as individuals who use derogatory names when they refer to other ethnoracial groups or those who show clear disdain for and hostility toward members of other groups during face-to-face contact. However, subtle forms of personal racism, such as the high school guidance counselor who steers minority students away from "hard" subjects and toward those that do not prepare them for higher-paying jobs, are much more common. Whether blatant or subtle, personal racism rests on two important psychological constructs—stereotypes and prejudice.

Stereotypes

The word *stereotype* was first used by the political commentator Walter Lippmann in 1922. He defined it as an oversimplified picture of the world, one that satisfies our need to see our social environment as a more understandable and manageable place than it really is (Lippmann, 1922). When applied to race, it is the overgeneralized belief that a certain trait, behavior, or attitude characterizes all members of some identifiable group.

Casual observations easily refute the accuracy of common racial or ethnic stereotypes. Most African Americans aren't on welfare, most Jews aren't greedy, few Italians belong to the Mafia, not all Asian Americans excel in math, and so on. Overgeneralizations are never true for every member of a group. Yet despite their obvious inaccuracy, stereotypes remain a common part of our everyday thinking. We all know what the stereotypes are, even if most of us choose not to express them or act on them.

The contemporary view is that stereotyping is a universal aspect of human thought (D. L. Hamilton, 1981). Our brains tend to divide the world into distinct categories: good and bad, strong and weak, them and us (Rothenberg, 1992). By allowing us to group information into easily identifiable categories, stereotypes make the processing of information and the formation of impressions more efficient. As you saw in Chapter 6, our lives would be utterly chaotic if we weren't able to quickly categorize and form expectations about people in terms of gender, race, age, ethnicity, and so on. What's important to remember, though, is that the actual content of stereotypes is by no means natural; it must be learned.

The media provide large audiences with both real and fantasized images of racial, religious, and ethnic groups: the savage American Indian; the sassy, confrontational, overweight black woman; the spoiled, pampered, shopping-obsessed Jewish woman; the fanatical Arab terrorist; and so on. Asians are frequently depicted as camera-wielding tourists, scholastic overachievers, or sinister warlords. Latino/as have historically been cast as "Latin lovers," "banditos," "greasers," or "lazy good-for-nothings" (Reyes & Rubie, 1994).

An analysis of a random sample of television news shows aired in Los Angeles and Orange counties in California revealed that Whites were more likely than African Americans and Latino/as to be portrayed on television news as victims of crime. Conversely, African Americans and Latino/as were more likely to be portrayed on news shows as lawbreakers than as crime victims (Dixon & Linz, 2000). Another study found that although people of color appear regularly in prime-time TV commercials, they usually appear as secondary characters. Furthermore, Whites are more likely to appear in ads for upscale products, beauty products, and home products. People of color, in contrast, are more likely to appear in ads for low-cost, low-nutrition products (like fast foods and soft drinks) and in athletic or sports equipment ads (Henderson & Baldasty, 2003).

Prejudice and Discrimination

When stereotypes form the basis of a set of rigidly held, unfavorable attitudes, beliefs, and feelings about members of a racial or ethnic group, they constitute **prejudice** (Allport, 1954). A good example of how prejudice affects social interaction is a study in which a group of Whites was shown a photograph of a white person holding a razor blade while arguing with a black person on a New York subway. Subjects were shown the picture for a split second and then asked to write down what they saw. More than half said they saw the black man holding the razor against the white man's throat (cited in Helmreich, 1992). The belief that all Blacks are violent was so powerful that it distorted people's perceptions.

These sorts of perceptions can be life threatening. In New York City, for example, undercover black police officers have, on occasion, been shot and wounded or killed by white officers who mistook them for dangerous criminals. As one black officer put it, "If you speak with nine out of 10 [undercover] officers of color they would tell you that when they hear sirens, in their head they are thinking: 'I hope these cops know that I'm one of the good guys'" (quoted in M. Powell, 2009a, p. 18). Over the years, there have been calls for the department to appoint panels to examine the underlying racial assumptions of white officers and to provide cadets with extra training.

Prejudices can change as social conditions change. When people feel their cultural integrity or their economic livelihood is being threatened—by either the real or the perceived infiltration of other ethnoracial groups—prejudicial attitudes can become more open and hostile. For instance, widespread anti-Catholic sentiment became especially virulent in the late 19th and early 20th centuries as waves of Catholic immigrants entered the country looking for a better life (Gusfield, 1963).

Prejudiced beliefs would be of little significance if they didn't lead sometimes to discrimination. **Discrimination** is the unfair treatment of people based on some social characteristic. The 1964 Civil Rights Act prohibits discrimination or segregation on the grounds of race, color, religion, or national origin. This act has produced tremendous progress in U.S. race relations. Nevertheless, discrimination still exists.

When we think of discrimination, we usually think of its most blatant forms—racial epithets, racially inspired hate crimes, barriers to employment, and so on. In 2004, two economists at the University of Chicago sent fictitious résumés in response to help wanted ads in Chicago and Boston newspapers. To some résumés they assigned a very African American–sounding name (like Lakisha or Jamal); to others, they put a very white-sounding name (like Emily or Greg). Résumés with white names received 50% more callbacks than those with African American names (Bertrand & Mullainathan, 2004).

Most of the time, though, discrimination is much more subtle, expressed as suspicion or avoidance; in fact, the person engaging in it may not even realize she or he is doing so. Psychologists Carl O. Word, Mark P. Zanna, and Joel Cooper (1974) created an experimental situation in which white subjects were led to believe they were interviewing applicants for a team position in a group decision making experiment. The applicants, who were really confederates of the researchers, were both black and white. The results showed that the "interviewers" treated black applicants very differently from white ones. For instance, they placed their chairs at a significantly greater distance from the black interviewees. They leaned forward less and made less eye contact with the black applicants. In addition, they ended the interview sooner and tended to trip over their words.

In a second experiment, Word, Zanna, and Cooper sought to determine the effect such behavior would have on the applicants. In this experiment, the interviewers were the confederates of the experimenters. These new interviewers were trained to mimic the behavior found among interviewers in the first experiment. This time, applicants who encountered the "less friendly" behavior—that is, reduced eye contact, greater physical distance, and so on—performed less adequately and showed less composure during the interview than the others.

These experiments illustrate the subtle process by which discrimination sometimes operates, even in people who are not self-consciously prejudiced. We are generally so unaware of our own nonverbal behavior that if we unwittingly give off signs of our dislike, we don't interpret others' subsequent behavior as a reaction to our nonverbal cues. Rather, we attribute it to some inherent trait in them. We may unknowingly prompt the very actions that we then use as evidence of some flaw or deficiency in that group.

These subtle forms of discrimination are often harder to fight than overt bigotry. If you are excluded from a job because you're Asian or denied membership in a club because you're Jewish, you can fight to open those doors. Today, quite a few people have made it in (Blauner, 1992). But once inside, they still have many interpersonal barriers to overcome.

When such subtle behavior becomes common among large numbers of people, prejudice and discrimination become mutually reinforcing. Defining one group as inferior and thus denying its members access to a decent education and jobs becomes a self-fulfilling prophecy, producing the very inferiority that the group was believed to possess in the first place.

Prejudice and discrimination based on skin color may also occur *within* a particular ethnoracial group. Some see this phenomenon, known as ***colorism***, as just as bad a problem as racial hatred expressed toward the group by outsiders. For instance, skin tone has been associated with social advantage among Blacks since the days of slavery, when light-skinned slaves were often allowed to work in the main house but dark-skinned slaves were relegated to the fields (Graham, 1999). During the early to mid 20th century, many African American churches, social clubs, fraternities, and other organizations still used skin color to determine the suitability of candidates for membership. The so-called brown bag test restricted membership to those whose skin was lighter than the color of a brown paper bag (Graham, 1999). Contemporary studies have found that lighter-skinned Blacks have higher educational attainment, more prestigious occupations, and higher annual incomes than darker-skinned Blacks, regardless of their sex, region of residence, age, marital status, or parents' socioeconomic status (M. E. Hill, 2000; Keith & Herring, 1991). As a result, darker-skinned Blacks sometimes resent light-skinned Blacks, accusing them of "selling out" in an attempt to conform to white standards of beauty as well as behavior (F. J. Davis, 1991).

Colorism is not limited to African Americans. Among Latino/as, the degree of "Indianness," or the darkness of one's skin, has long determined a person's status. After controlling for all other relevant factors, researchers have found that dark-skinned Mexican Americans who have a Native American physical appearance have fewer years of education than light-skinned Mexican Americans who appear more European (Murguia & Telles, 1996); they are more likely to live in segregated, low-income neighborhoods (Relethford, Stern, Caskill, & Hazuda, 1983); and they consistently earn lower wages (Telles & Murguia, 1990).

The Privilege of Having No Color

People who are members of a racial majority sometimes have trouble appreciating the humiliating effects of everyday encounters with prejudice and discrimination. They don't have to experience the petty indignities of racism, such as repeatedly being watched with suspicion in stores and on streets. Consequently, many Whites in the United States pay little attention to their own race, think people of color are obsessed with race and ethnicity, and find it difficult to understand the emotional and intellectual energy people of color devote to the subject (Haney López, 1996).

In a society in which they dominate statistically and culturally, U.S. Whites rarely define their identity in terms of race. Whiteness is so obvious and normative that white people's racial identity is, for all intents and purposes, invisible. Whites enjoy the luxury of *racial transparency*, or "having no color" (Haney López, 1996). People in the United States are far more likely to hear "black" or "Asian" or "Latino" used as an adjective (e.g., the black lawyer, the Latino teacher) than "white" (the white lawyer, the white teacher). Whites have the luxury of choosing whether or not to include their specific ancestry in descriptions of their identity (Waters, 2008). In this sense, ethnicity is optional, voluntary, and perhaps even recreational—as when white people celebrate their Irishness on St. Patrick's Day. In short, Whites for the most part enjoy the privilege of not having to constantly think about race or identify their ethnicity:

> Each thing with which "they" have to contend as they navigate the waters of American life is one less thing Whites have to sweat: and that makes everything easier, from finding jobs, to getting loans, to attending college. . . . The virtual invisibility that whiteness affords those of us who have it is like psychological money in the bank, the proceeds of which we cash in every day while others are in a perpetual state of overdraft. (Wise, 2002, pp. 107–108)

Such a luxury provides benefits to Whites whether or not they approve of the way social advantage has been conferred on them. One white author (McIntosh, 2001) catalogued all the everyday privileges she enjoyed (and often didn't notice) simply because she was white. These included the ability to shop alone in a department store without being followed by suspicious salespeople, to buy greeting cards or children's picture books featuring people of her race, and to find bandages that match her skin color. In other words, Whites need not be bigots or feel racially superior or more deserving than others to enjoy the privileges that their skin color brings.

Class, Race, and Discrimination

Some sociologists have argued that discriminatory treatment, as well as the unequal social and political status of some racial groups, is more a function of social class than of race. If this belief were completely accurate, the lives of middle- and upper-class people of color would be relatively free of discrimination. The election of Barack Obama clearly shows that well-educated, highly qualified members of ethnoracial minorities are no longer barred from the highest positions in society. However, some civil rights advocates believe Obama's victory was an isolated one and fear many people will mistakenly conclude that racial discrimination is over (Swarns, 2008b). After all, African Americans still remain twice as likely as Whites to be unemployed, three times as likely to live in poverty, and six times as likely to be incarcerated (National Urban League, 2009). As the former chair of the U.S. Commission on Civil Rights put it, "It's like saying that because some poor white person made it, there's no poverty" (quoted in Cose, 2009, p. 43).

Indeed, even for many financially successful people of color, lack of respect, faint praise, low expectations, and outright harassment and exclusion continue to be common features of their lives (Feagin & McKinney, 2003). Minority professionals often bemoan the tendency of others to assume they bring to every interaction the perspective of their entire group. A successful law professor, who happens to be Chinese American, once said, "I suspect . . . that at every appearance . . . my audience continues to see and hear me as a spokesperson on behalf of Asian Americans" (Wu, 2002, p. 37).

Sociologists Joe Feagin and Karyn McKinney (2003) analyzed data from focus group and individual interviews with several hundred middle-class U.S. Blacks to determine the consequences of the discrimination they experienced at work. These individuals, all of whom were college educated and held professional or managerial jobs, agreed that the work-related stresses they felt did not come from the demands of the jobs themselves but from racially hostile workplace environments that often included the mistrust of colleagues, unfair promotion practices, or outright mistreatment through the use of racial epithets and derogatory names.

Everyday life can be trying as well. Wealthy black residents of affluent neighborhoods all over the country sometimes complain that they are watched closely when shopping in upscale stores or that the police view them with suspicion simply because their skin color doesn't match the neighborhood. Situations like these are disturbing and frustrating not only because of the racist attitudes that lie behind them but also because the people who experience them had come to believe that their upward social mobility protected them from such treatment. A respondent in Feagin and McKinney's (2003) study put it this way:

> I'm always in the process of trying to develop a better and healthier way of working through the inevitable anger about this situation. There's a price you pay in being sensitive and conscious. . . . Have you ever seen a dog really being angry about his condition? If you really were a beast, it wouldn't bother you. The problem is that . . . this treatment bothers you most, because you definitely and clearly aren't what the world thinks you are. (p. 45)

In sum, racial discrimination is still very prevalent in the lives of members of ethnoracial minorities, including those who are affluent. In fact, such discrimination is more apparent than that experienced by low-income people because the affluent individuals have entered previously inaccessible social spaces (Bonilla-Silva, 2008). One study even found that Blacks with college degrees experience more discrimination than those without degrees (Forman, Williams, & Jackson, 1997).

The days of NO NEGROES and NO INDIANS signs on public facilities may be gone, but less blatant contemporary expressions of personal racism serve as a constant reminder that in the 21st century, members of ethnoracial minorities—no matter what their class standing—are still stereotyped, prejudged, and discriminated against every day.

Quiet Racism

Clearly, the nature of public attitudes in the United States toward racial and ethnic groups has changed over the past few decades, prompting many sociologists to rethink their ideas of what constitutes personal racism. One nationwide poll found that the proportion of U.S. residents who feel that race relations are improving and that progress has been made in reducing racial discrimination is the highest it's been since the early 1990s (cited in J. Cohen & Agiesta, 2008). However, other surveys indicate that different groups have very different perceptions of the state of race relations (cited in Blow, 2008, 2009):

- Twice as many Blacks as Whites think racism is a big problem; twice as many Whites as Blacks think that Blacks have achieved racial equality.
- Seventy-two percent of Whites believe that Blacks overestimate the amount of discrimination against them; conversely, 82% of Blacks believe that Whites underestimate the amount of discrimination Blacks suffer.
- Almost half of white respondents oppose programs that make special efforts to help minorities get ahead; 27% feel that too much has been made of the problems facing black people.

These paradoxes have led some to argue that a subtle form of racism has emerged (Ansell, 2000; Bonilla-Silva, 2008; Sniderman & Tetlock, 1986). **Quiet racism** is linked to the traditional forms of personal racism by negative feelings toward certain groups. However, the feelings common to quiet racism are not necessarily hate or hostility but discomfort, uneasiness, and sometimes fear, which tend to motivate avoidance rather than outright confrontation. Quiet racists are people who maintain that discrimination against a person because of his or her race or ethnicity is unfair but who nonetheless cannot entirely escape the cultural forces that give rise to racist beliefs in the first place. What complicates the situation is that this type of racism is often expressed by people who consider themselves unbiased and nonprejudiced.

The changing face of racism has serious institutional consequences as well. When racism remains quiet, people are tempted to assume that it has disappeared and thus to forget about helping groups that have traditionally been the objects of discrimination (Bonilla-Silva, 2003). Recent efforts to eliminate programs designed to help ethnoracial minorities exemplify this trend. Many Whites now believe that the only reason so many Blacks are unsuccessful is that they lack motivation and aren't committed to the "white" values of hard work, individualism, delayed gratification, and so on (Schuman & Krysan, 1999). Although these beliefs are more subtle than overt acts of bigotry, they have the same effect: On the basis of stereotypes, they promote prejudice toward individuals.

JOE FEAGIN AND EILEEN O'BRIEN

Wealthy White Men on Race

The racial views and perspectives of wealthy white men have received virtually no academic attention even though their attitudes have the potential to influence many people's lives. To overcome this deficit, sociologists Joe Feagin and Eileen O'Brien (2003) interviewed about 100 wealthy white male executives, managers, administrators, and professionals about a range of racial issues. Understanding the perceptions of these men is important because many of them have the power to shape policies, laws, and actions involving ethnoracial minorities and majorities.

Because of their socioeconomic status, these men have lived most of their lives in segregated, well-to-do neighborhoods. As children and teenagers, they tended to go to schools that had few, if any, people of color. Only a handful of the interviewees reported long-term friendships with people of other races.

So their first and sometimes most significant encounters with ethnoracial minorities were often with domestic and other service workers, usually female maids or male servants:

> Although I don't remember my first experience of meeting a black person, I would assume it was . . . my grandfather's chauffeur when I was five years old. So to me, Blacks at that point were people that waited on you.

> My very first contact with a black person was with a black maid who essentially raised my sister and [me].

> Honestly, the first black person I ever met was probably a household employee at my parents' house a long time ago. (all quoted in Feagin & O'Brien, 2003, pp. 34–35)

Memories of these initial contacts are usually quite fond. Many men spoke lovingly of household servants because they were people who played an important role in raising them (some respondents even referred to their black maids and nannies as "second mothers").

However, they also were taught, early on, that the social distance between their families and "the help" had to be maintained. Furthermore, it's clear that the men didn't see these individuals as real people with real lives. Most of them were unaware that their maids and chauffeurs had spouses and children of their own or that their jobs made it difficult to sustain those relationships.

Feagin and O'Brien also found that in many ways wealthy white executives are not that different from "ordinary" white Americans when it comes to their stereotypes and prejudices. Some harbor deeply negative attitudes toward Americans of color that seem reminiscent of a bygone age:

> Well, let's look at the statistics. The Negro is about ten percent of the population and eighty percent of the crimes are committed by Negroes, so what does that tell you? . . . What does that tell us? Absolutely, of course, much more crime is committed by them. And anywhere they are, they're criminals. They're criminals here, they're criminals in Africa. (quoted in Feagin & O'Brien, 2003, p. 100)

Furthermore, they often see the advancement of people of color as a threat to the racial privileges they've come to take for granted and to their control over major social institutions. But since they are generally highly educated, most of them are well aware that they should not be too obviously negative in expressing their racial attitudes. Hence, some couch their prejudices in sympathetic-sounding language:

> There are many, many fine black families around. . . . Unfortunately, a large part of the black population has this family problem. . . . It's very, very difficult to generalize why some blacks work out fine while others don't, and the fact that some could work out exactly the same as anyone else leads me to believe that it's not because of the color; it's because of the environment they're brought up in. (quoted in Feagin & O'Brien, 2003, p. 104)

This is a classic example of quiet racism. Notice how this individual distances himself from the prejudices of the past while at the same time embracing the reality of racial inequality.

Not all the men interviewed by Feagin and O'Brien expressed prejudice. A minority of them held very positive attitudes about race relations. These individuals often voiced dismay over racial and class inequality and spoke of the need for a significant shift in the balance of economic and political power in the United States. The factor that seemed to separate these men from the others who held more traditional (and negative) attitudes toward race was the nature of the relationships they'd had with people of color. Those who had long-term friendships or extended contact with members of other races showed a willingness to consider dismantling the structures that perpetuate prejudice and racial inequality. Such a finding supports the idea that regular interpersonal interactions that cross ethnoracial boundaries can diminish stereotypes and prejudice.

The Cultural Ideology of Racism

If I stopped here in my discussion of racism, you might be inclined to consider it an individual-level phenomenon that could best be stopped by changing the way people think or by personal acts of kindness and respect. But the sociologically important thing about racism is that it exists not just in the minds and actions of individuals but in a cultural belief system that both justifies the domination of some groups over others and provides a set of social norms that encourages differential treatment for these groups (O'Sullivan-See & Wilson, 1988). From a conflict perspective, the ideology of racism that exists in our language and in our prevailing cultural beliefs contributes to racial and ethnic inequality.

Racism in Language

Certainly, racial slurs and derogatory words reflect underlying racism. But racism in language is often less obvious. Consider the use of **panethnic labels**—general terms applied to diverse subgroups that are assumed to have something in common (D. Newman, 2012). Today, we use the general terms *Native American* or *American Indian* to refer to all 560 or so native nations living in the United States, despite their different languages and cultures. *Asian American* refers to a variety of peoples from dozens of countries whose ethnic heritages and lifestyles are quite different from one another. Similarly, *Hispanic* or *Latino* refers to people whose backgrounds include culturally diverse areas such as Mexico, the Caribbean, Central America, and South America. To some, even the term *African American*, which is widely considered to be a positive racial label, glosses over the thousands of ethnic groups, class interests, and indigenous religions that exist on the continent of Africa. Reliance on panethnic labels allows users to overlook and ignore variations within a particular labeled group, thereby reinforcing stereotypes.

Racial identifiers often become equated with negative meanings. Consider, for instance, connotations of the words *black* and *white*. Among the definitions of *black* in *Webster's New Universal Unabridged Dictionary* are "soiled and dirty," "thoroughly evil," "wicked," "gloomy," "marked by disaster," "hostile," and "disgraceful." The definition of *white,* in contrast, includes "fairness of complexion," "innocent," "favorable," "fortunate," "pure," and "spotless." The pervasive "goodness" of white and "badness" of black affects children at a very young age and provides white children with a false sense of superiority (R. B. Moore, 1992). Young children know the difference between a black lie, which is harmful and inexcusable, and a white lie, which is small, insignificant, and harmless.

Also important are the political implications of racially tinged terminology. Terms such as *economically disadvantaged, underclass, inner city,* and *underdeveloped* sound unprejudiced, but they are often used as code for racial terms. For instance, a study of the 1995 Louisiana gubernatorial election revealed that the white candidate's stated opposition to affirmative action and his discussion of the crime problems in "inner city" neighborhoods (which everyone knew were black and Latino/a neighborhoods) subtly symbolized his racial attitudes, appealed to many white voters, and thereby contributed to his victory over a black candidate (Knuckey & Orey, 2000).

Language is just a small part of the overall problem of racist ideology in U.S. society. It seemingly pales in comparison with more visible issues such as racial violence and economic discrimination. We must remember, however, that language filters our perceptions. It affects the way people think from the time they first learn to speak. Fortunately, efforts are being made today to address the issue of language and its crucial role in maintaining racism and oppression. People are becoming more aware of the capacity of words to both glorify and degrade (R. B. Moore, 1992).

The Myth of Innate Racial Inferiority

Scientific-sounding theories of the innate inferiority of certain ethnoracial groups have long been used to explain why some groups lag behind others in areas such as educational achievement and financial success. These theories combine with the belief in competitive individualism (see Chapter 10) to justify all forms of prejudice and discrimination.

Appeals to biology and nature have been used throughout history to define the existing stratification system as proper and inevitable (Gould, 1981). What would you think of a person who harbored the following beliefs about Blacks?

> [Blacks] have less hair on the face and body. They secrete less by the kidneys [sic], and more by the glands of the skin, which gives them a very strong and disagreeable odour [sic]. . . . They are at least as brave, and more adventuresome. But this may perhaps proceed from a want of forethought, which prevents their seeing a danger till it be present. . . . In imagination, they are dull, tasteless, and anomalous. . . . The improvement of the blacks in body and mind, in the first instance of their mixture with the whites, has been observed by everyone, and proves that their inferiority is not the effect merely of their condition of life. . . . I advance it therefore . . . that the blacks . . . are inferior to the whites in the endowments both of body and mind.

A white supremacist? A raving bigot? An ignorant fanatic? How would your assessment of this person change if you found out that this passage was written by none other than Thomas Jefferson (1781/1955, pp. 138–143)? In the 18th and 19th centuries, no white person—not even one apparently committed to protecting people's right to "life, liberty and the pursuit of happiness"—doubted the validity of natural racial rankings: Indians below Whites, and Blacks below everyone else. Other idols of Western culture—George Washington, Abraham Lincoln, Charles Darwin—held similar beliefs about the "natural inferiority" of some races, beliefs that were commonly accepted knowledge at the time but would at the very least be considered racially insensitive today.

The approval given by white scientists to conventional racial rankings arose not from objective data and careful research but from a cultural belief in the "goodness" and inevitability of racial stratification. Such beliefs were then twisted into independent, "scientific" support. Scientists, like everybody else, have attitudes and values that shape what they see. Such thinking is not the result of outright dishonesty or hypocrisy; rather, it is the combination of the way human minds work and the generally accepted knowledge of the day.

The belief in innate racial inferiority is not just a historical curiosity. Several years ago, the idea reemerged in a book called *The Bell Curve: Intelligence and Class Structure in American Life* (Herrnstein & Murray, 1994). The authors argued that racial and ethnic differences in intelligence—as measured by IQ scores—must be due, at least in part, to heredity. The book set off a firestorm of debate that continues to this day.

From a conflict perspective, beliefs about racial inferiority provide advantages for the dominant group. These beliefs discourage subordinate groups from questioning their disadvantaged status. In addition, they provide moral justification for maintaining a society in which some groups are routinely deprived of their rights and privileges. Nineteenth-century Whites could justify the enslavement of Blacks, and 20th-century Nazis could justify the extermination of Jews and other "undesirables," by promoting the belief that those groups are biologically subhuman.

Despite energetic searches over the centuries, a link between "inferior" race-based genes and certain traits and abilities has not been found (Hacker, 1992). For one thing, comparing racial groups on, say, intelligence overlooks the range of differences within and between groups. Many African Americans are more intelligent than the average white person; many Whites are less intelligent than the average Native American.

Variations such as these are difficult to explain in terms of the genetic superiority of one race. Moreover, treating the more than 200 million "white" people in the United States as a single (and intellectually superior) group is problematic at best and misleading at worst. It can't account for the wide variation in academic achievement among Whites of different national backgrounds. For instance, at the time *The Bell Curve* was written, 21% of white Americans of Irish descent completed college, whereas 22% of Italian Americans, 33% of Scottish Americans, and 51% of Russian Americans did so (Hacker, 1994).

Moreover, genetic predispositions cannot account for variations in IQ in a particular ethnoracial group over a generation or two. Psychologist James Flynn (1999) examined IQ scores in various populations over 60 years. He found that scores had increased in all countries for which data existed—a phenomenon known as the "Flynn effect" (see Exhibit 11.2). In some countries, average scores had improved by 25 points or more. Increases of such magnitude simply cannot be explained by genetics. Instead, they reflect better education and improvement in things like abstract problem solving across generations.

Finally, such comparisons also ignore a problem I described earlier in this chapter: that race itself is a meaningless biological category. How can we attribute racial differences in intelligence to genes when race itself is not traceable to a single gene?

Nevertheless, the idea that racial inferiority is innate remains appealing. If observable, physical differences among races are inherited, the argument goes, then why not differences in social behavior, intelligence, and leadership ability? Like the belief in competitive individualism we examined in the previous chapter, the belief in innate racial inferiority places the blame for suffering and economic failure on the individual rather than on the society in which that individual exists.

Exhibit 11.2   Improved IQ Scores Over Time

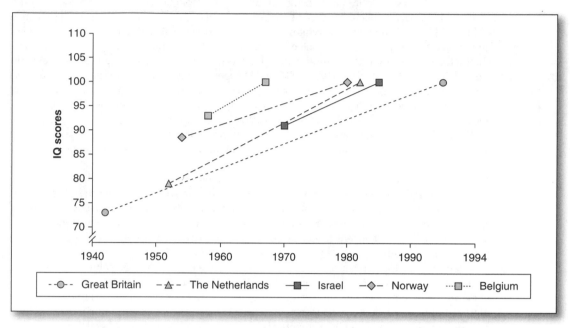

SOURCE: Flynn, 1999, Figure 1

MICRO-MACRO CONNECTION

Racial Superiority and the Dominant Black Athlete

The flip side of the belief in innate racial inferiority is the notion that some racial groups have a biologically rooted superiority in some areas of life. Take, for instance, the widely held belief that some racial groups are biologically predisposed to be more athletically successful than others. Today, black athletes dominate the highest levels of sports such as football, basketball, and track. In the United States, African Americans make up about 13% of the population but constitute 67% of players in the NFL (National Football League), 77% of players in the NBA (National Basketball Association), and 67% of players in the WNBA (Women's National Basketball Association; Lapchick, 2011). Not surprisingly, many people see numbers like these and assume that Blacks must be "naturally" stronger, swifter, and more coordinated than athletes from other races.

In the late 19th century, African Americans were allowed to play professional baseball alongside Whites; boxing, too, was racially integrated. But by the turn of the century, white athletes threatened to quit rather than share the field or the ring with black athletes. Early white heavyweight boxing champions such as John L. Sullivan and Jack Dempsey refused to fight black opponents. In 1888, baseball team owners tacitly agreed not to sign any more African American players. Their formal exclusion lasted until 1947, when Jackie Robinson became the first African American in the 20th century to play baseball in the major leagues (Sage, 2001).

The rationale behind excluding African Americans was not based on their inability to compete. On the contrary, it was based on the common belief that Blacks were athletically superior to Whites. Many 18th- and 19th-century scholars believed black slaves were bred by their owners to be physically strong. In recent decades, such ideas have taken on a scientific cast (Entine, 2000). For instance, some biologists argue that black athletes' muscles are better adapted to hot climates and, therefore, are better at providing energy quickly. Others have cited better power-to-weight ratios and longer Achilles tendons.

Black athletic superiority has become an almost taken-for-granted truth in the sports world. Many athletes have publicly expressed their belief that black success in sports is a consequence of Blacks' physical superiority to Whites. Hall of Fame basketball star Larry Bird (who is white) once voiced his support for the contention that white players don't stack up to black players: "[Basketball] is a black man's game and it will be forever. I mean, the greatest athletes in the world are African-American" ("Bird: NBA," 2004, p. 1). Roger Bannister, a British distance runner who was the first to break the 4:00 mile, once said, "I am prepared to risk political correctness by drawing attention to the seemingly obvious but under-stressed fact that black sprinters and black athletes in general seem to have certain natural anatomical advantages" ("Sports Quiz," 2007, p. 6).

The problem with the belief in black athletic superiority is that physical strength (a seemingly positive characteristic) is all too often associated with alleged social, moral, or intellectual deficiency. A nationally known sportscaster once commonly referred to powerful black athletes (but never white athletes) as "thoroughbreds," a term that simultaneously acknowledged their physical prowess and likened them to horses. As I was writing this chapter, I heard an ESPN commentator say that Vince Young, a black quarterback for the Philadelphia Eagles, was not smart enough to be a starter in the NFL. He said that Young was a gifted and truly phenomenal athlete, but teams need an intelligent leader to be their quarterback. Such comments strengthen the notion that black athletes are athletically superior but deficient in most other ways.

Extending this logic, physically outclassed white athletes must rely on self-discipline, mental acuity, "a tireless work ethic," "fiery determination," and an unwavering attention to discipline and "fundamentals" in order to compete. In this way, successful white athletes become especially praiseworthy because they're able to overcome their "natural" limitations. Such an attitude is reflected in these assessments, the first from a white college basketball player, the second from the former coach of a white player who was being inducted into the Hall of Fame:

> I know I'm not going to beat them with my quickness so I need to see exactly how they're playing me. . . . You have to study the game and watch every little thing to look for some kind of advantage. (quoted in Hutchens, 2002, p. D8)

> He was one of the most creative players that I've ever seen. He wasn't the most athletic, but he made up for it by being creative with his footwork and always finding a way to get his shot off. (quoted in Wells, 2011, p. C8)

Notice how lack of quickness and athleticism becomes a virtue as it opens the way to a superior intellect and work ethic.

Conversely, Blacks' athletic success is often considered a natural by-product of their physical advantages, not the result of hard work or intellect. The famous tennis player Serena Williams once expressed dismay over press coverage of her victories, which commonly emphasized her strength in overpowering her opponents rather than the mental preparation and strategizing required to be the best in the world.

Because of these pervasive stereotypes, the white public often tempers its admiration of black athletic superiority with contempt for what some consider an arrogant, undisciplined style. A few years ago, the NFL decided to penalize players who wore uniforms that didn't conform to tight league regulations, who "trash talked" (taunted opponents), and who choreographed post-touchdown celebrations. These players were almost exclusively black.

Still, the undeniable fact is that Blacks do dominate certain professional sports in the United States. One sociological explanation is that such domination results not from innate physical superiority alone but from a complex set of social conditions that channels a disproportionate number of physically talented Blacks into athletic careers (H. Edwards, 1971). Sport has long been perceived as one of the few avenues of social mobility open to members of certain ethnoracial minorities: baseball for Latinos, football and basketball for African Americans. A national survey found that by a margin of three to one over Whites, Blacks cited financial gain as one of the most important reasons to play sports: "If I am successful at sports, I can make a lot of money" (cited in Price, 1997). Where children from other racial groups are being taught that a good education will pay off, many black children are being taught that a good education may not be enough to overcome the prejudice and discrimination that exist in society. Hence, they are more likely to be encouraged to hone their physical skills and to spend more time perfecting this resource. A high school basketball coach put it this way: "Suburban [white] kids tend to play for the fun of it. Inner-city [black] kids look at basketball as a matter of life or death" (quoted in Price, 1997, p. 35).

Sport has always served as a source of tremendous pride in black and Latino/a communities. Victory is especially sweet because it represents something larger than the athlete herself or himself; it symbolizes the values and aspirations of an entire people (Rhoden, 2006). But highlighting the rags-to-riches stories of a tiny number of successful athletes is a double-edged sword. These high-profile athletes disguise the reality of how little social mobility actually results from sports participation. Only about 3% of all graduating seniors who played basketball in high school will play in college; and only half of them will receive some kind of athletic scholarship (Rhoden, 2006). For African Americans, the odds against becoming a professional athlete (let alone an elite star) are about 5,000 to 1. As one sociologist once remarked, "You have a better chance of getting hit with a meteorite in the next 10 years than getting work as a professional athlete" (quoted in Sage, 2001, p. 283).

An overemphasis on athletic accomplishments can also discourage academic and occupational achievement in favor of physical self-expression, thereby harming ethnoracial minority communities in the long run. The vast majority of African Americans who participate in Division I football, basketball, and track and field never graduate from college. It might be more useful in the long run to focus on the fact that there are 12 times more black lawyers and 15 times more black physicians than there are black professional athletes (Sage, 2001).

Whether or not the emphasis on sports is a good thing and whether or not black athletes do have some anatomical advantage, we must always remember that so-called black athletic superiority is as much a social product as a biological one. Innate talent is never sufficient in itself to explain athletic excellence (D. F. Chambliss, 1989). If we rely simply on innate superiority to explain black success in sports, we overlook the broader social structural context in which everyday life is embedded.

Institutional Racism: Injustice Built Into the System

Anyone can be personally racist, whether overtly or quietly. And members of any ethnoracial group can develop a set of beliefs or a vocabulary that denigrates outsiders. But one form of racism, less obvious and perhaps more dangerous, can work only to the advantage of those who wield power in society: institutional racism. ***Institutional racism*** consists of established laws, customs, and practices that systematically reflect and produce racial inequalities in society, whether or not the individuals maintaining these practices have racist intentions (J. M. Jones, 1986). Thus, a society can be racist even if only a small proportion of its members harbor personally racist beliefs. Because African Americans, Latino/as, Asian Americans, Native Americans, and other groups have historically been excluded from key positions of authority in social institutions, they often find themselves victimized by the routine workings of such structures.

Sometimes institutional discrimination is obvious and codified into the law. Until the early 1990s, for example, South Africa operated under an official system of *apartheid*: Nonwhite groups were legally segregated and subjected to sanctioned forms of political and economic discrimination. In the United States, the forceful relocation of Native Americans in the 19th century, the repressive Jim Crow laws in the 20th-century South, and the internment of Japanese Americans during World War II are all examples of legislated policies that purposely worked to the disadvantage of already disadvantaged groups.

Understanding less obvious forms of institutional racism is a great test of the sociological imagination. Because it is a built-in feature of social arrangements, institutional racism is often much more difficult to detect than acts of personal racism. Consider one well-established practice for granting home mortgage or home improvement loans. Many banks use zip codes to mark off the neighborhoods they consider high risk—that is, where property values are low and liable to drop even further. These practices make it virtually impossible for individuals in such areas to borrow money to buy or improve a home. Unfortunately, these are precisely the areas where minorities, with lower than average incomes, are most likely to find an affordable home to purchase. Thus, although individual bank officers are not denying loans to people because of their race—they are merely following their employers' policy—the resulting discrimination is the same.

Sometimes institutional racism is camouflaged behind claims that seem quite reasonable. For instance, taxi companies protect the safety of their drivers by refusing service to what they consider dangerous neighborhoods. Similarly, home delivery businesses, such as pizza parlors, sometimes refuse to deliver to certain neighborhoods. Several years ago, Domino's Pizza was criticized in the media when it was revealed that the company was distributing software to its outlets to let them mark addresses on computers as green (deliver), yellow (curbside only), or red (no delivery). Businesses defend such policies as a rational response to the threat of sending easy-to-spot, cash-carrying delivery personnel into unsafe areas ("Pizza Must Go," 1996). Although such practices may be considered "good" business policy and are not intentionally racist, their consequences are discriminatory because high-risk neighborhoods tend to be inhabited predominantly by people of color. Institutional racism is difficult to address in these cases because no individual "bad guy," no identifiable bigot, is the source of the discrimination.

MICRO-MACRO CONNECTION

A House Divided—Residential Discrimination

Forty years ago, the Fair Housing Act was enacted, prohibiting housing discrimination based on race, color, religion, or national origin. Yet residential segregation based on class and race is so prevalent in U.S. society that one sociologist once referred to the situation as "American apartheid" (Massey & Denton, 1993). White attitudes toward neighborhood integration have improved over the years (R. Farley & Frey, 1994); however, overall levels of segregation—especially of Blacks and Whites—remain high (Roscigno, Karafin, & Tester, 2009). For instance, 10 years ago, 69% of individuals in large metropolitan areas lived in areas of high segregation between Blacks and Whites; today, that figure has "dropped" to 65% (National Fair Housing Alliance, 2011). And because of the high rate of immigration, Latino/as and Asians are becoming increasingly segregated from Whites (C. Z. Charles, 2003). Residential segregation is not just about people living near others of the same race. Research indicates that it is associated with a variety of negative effects, such as a reduced likelihood of people running successful businesses (Fischer & Massey, 2000) and an increased likelihood of contracting certain deadly diseases (C. Collins & Williams, 1999).

The National Fair Housing Alliance (2011) conservatively estimates that there are approximately 4 million fair-housing violations each year. Apart from incidents of landlords discriminating against families with small children or against people with disabilities, most of these cases involve ethnoracial minorities. Indeed, there were more official reports of such housing discrimination made to private, state, and federal agencies in 2008 than in any previous year. For instance, of the 2,176 cases of racial discrimination in housing filed with the Ohio Civil Rights Commission between 1988 and 2003, 80% involved victims of color (Roscigno et al., 2009). On occasion, such housing discrimination is personal, the result of individuals' blatant "we don't want you people here" attitudes. More commonly, though, it's institutional, politely and subtly driven by company policies (D. Pearce, 1979). Discriminatory policies include making fewer houses or rental units available to minorities, limiting their access to financial assistance, and steering them toward particular neighborhoods.

One study found that African Americans were twice as likely as Whites, and Latino/as one and a half times as likely as Whites, to be denied a conventional 30-year home loan (cited in Kilborn, 1999). When they do receive home loans, African Americans and Latino/as are twice as likely as Whites to have to pay substantially higher "subprime" interest rates (cited in Bajaj & Fessenden, 2007). Some argue that the discrepancy in rates is justified because borrowers who have poor credit histories are higher risks or because Blacks and Latino/as have fewer assets and therefore have less money for down payments than white borrowers (Blanton, 2007). But the discrepancy is even found between minority and white borrowers with similar credit scores (Bocian, Ernst, & Li, 2006). In 2009, the city of Baltimore sued Wells Fargo Bank for systematically steering Blacks into subprime mortgages, which sent hundreds of homeowners into foreclosure and cost the city tens of millions of dollars (M. Powell, 2009b).

Racial Inequality in the Economic System

Institutional racism is readily apparent throughout the U.S. economy. Consider participation in the labor force. With the exception of Asian Americans, workers of color have always been concentrated in lower-paying jobs (see Exhibit 11.3). African Americans make up 10.7% of the entire civilian U.S. workforce but only 4.7% of lawyers, 5.7% of physicians, and 5.5% of architects and engineers. Similarly, Latino/as make up 14% of the labor force but are underrepresented in the fields of law (2.8%), medicine (6.3%), and architecture/engineering (7.2%; U.S. Bureau of the Census, 2011b). This underrepresentation becomes more acute in the higher echelons of certain professions. For instance, while 17% of attorneys in U.S. law firms are members of ethnoracial minorities, only 5% ever become partners in those firms (cited in Glater, 2006).

Because ethnoracial minorities are occupationally concentrated in low-paying jobs, they are particularly vulnerable to economic downturns. The recent economic recession, for instance, has not hit all races equally. The rate of unemployment for Blacks and

Exhibit 11.3   Occupational Concentration by Race and Ethnicity

Occupations with highest proportion of:		
Blacks	**Latino/as**	**Asians**
Home Health Aide	Cook	Computer Software Engineer
Security Guard	Dishwasher	Computer Hardware Engineer
Barber	Maid	Medical Scientist
Baggage Porter/Bellhop	Grounds Maintenance Worker	Physician
Postal Worker	Construction Worker	Tailor/Dressmaker
Bus Driver	Laundry Worker	
Chauffeur	Hand Packer	

SOURCE: U.S. Bureau of the Census, 2011b, Table 615

NOTE: The U.S. Bureau of the Census does not provide data on the proportion of Whites in specific occupations.

Latino/as is consistently higher than that of other groups (U.S. Bureau of the Census, 2011b). In the summer of 2011, the unemployment rate for Blacks was 16.2%, compared with 11.9% for Latino/as, 8.0% for Whites, and 7.0% for Asians (U.S. Bureau of Labor Statistics, 2011a). Members of ethnoracial minorities can sometimes find their employment opportunities limited or blocked by the institutional practices and beliefs found in certain industries. Take, for instance, the restaurant business. Researchers in one study (Restaurant Opportunities Center of New York, 2009) hired white, black, Asian, and Latino/a people to act as job applicants for advertised server positions in 181 upscale New York City restaurants. The applicants were paired up—one white and one nonwhite—and matched for age, appearance, gender, and work experience. They were also trained to have similar mannerisms and answer questions in similar ways. So theoretically, the only thing distinctive about the two people in a pair was their race. Their arrival at restaurants was staggered so that they showed up about 30 minutes apart. This way the restaurant managers had no way of knowing the "applicants" were part of a study. Overall, white applicants were significantly more likely than applicants of color to have their work experience accepted without probing, to be granted an interview, and to be offered a position. The researchers concluded that this differential treatment was not a result of "a few bad apples" with racist intent. Instead, they identified industry-wide trends and practices as the culprit. For instance, a pervasive "culture of informality" exists in the restaurant business. Although such informality creates a casual, "familylike" work environment, it also creates subjective recruitment and hiring practices that rely on word-of-mouth and friendship networks rather than the formal procedures and explicit hiring criteria that could protect against conscious and unconscious biases and stereotypes.

People of color also remain marginal participants in the economy as owners of their own small businesses. Loan companies usually demand a credit history, some form of collateral, and evidence of potential success before they will lend money to prospective businesses. These are standard practices—and not in and of themselves racist—but they perpetuate racial inequalities because members of groups that have been exploited in the past tend to be poorer and thus have poor credit ratings and no collateral. Admittedly, poor people are greater credit risks than those with economic resources, and businesses in poorer communities must pay more for insurance because of the greater likelihood of theft or property damage. But the higher costs of doing business in a poor community usually make small business loans to minority members even more necessary.

Financial concerns, not deep-seated racial hatred, can also work to the disadvantage of retail customers who happen to be members of particular ethnoracial groups. For instance, in 2004, the Cracker Barrel restaurant chain agreed to overhaul its training and management practices after the U.S. Department of Justice accused it of widespread discrimination against African American diners in 50 locations. As a matter of policy, black customers were routinely given tables apart from Whites, seated after white customers who had arrived later, and given inferior service (Lichtblau, 2004). In this case and others like it (e.g., H. Kohn, 1994), senior executives were convinced that customers of color were costing their companies money. Hence, they argued, the policies were not a matter of personal racism but a function of the competitive, profit-driven nature of the marketplace.

As long as companies are motivated to maximize their own interests (and profits), they are likely to adapt to market tastes. To the extent that those tastes reflect underlying prejudice, discrimination will continue. This structural-functionalist explanation of institutional racism is important because it enables us to see why discrimination is so difficult to end. The problem is not individual bigotry; it is the mistreatment that has been built into the system so effectively that it is sometimes difficult to see, let alone remove.

Racial Inequality in the Health Care System

As I pointed out at the beginning of this chapter, the economic and educational advances of ethnoracial minority groups over the past decade or so have been tempered by continuing disadvantages in health and health care. For example, members of ethnoracial minorities are routinely underrepresented as subjects in research on medical and psychiatric drug treatments (Vedantam, 2005). Members of ethnoracial minorities are also less likely than Whites to have access to health insurance. About 31% of Latino/as (especially those from Mexico and Central America) and 21% of African Americans lack any kind of health insurance, compared with 12% of non-Hispanic Whites (DeNavas-Walt, Proctor, & Smith, 2011). As the president of the American Medical Association put it, "When people don't have health insurance, they live sicker and they die younger" (quoted in D. Wilson, 2009a, p. 16).

Ethnoracial health imbalances are most glaring when it comes to the most serious diseases. For instance, a study of heart failure among 5,000 black and white men and women over a 20-year period found that Blacks had a rate 20 times higher than Whites (Bibbins-Domingo, 2009). African Americans account for 43% of all people living with HIV/AIDS in the United States (U.S. Bureau of the Census, 2011b). Death rates from HIV/AIDS also vary widely between different ethnoracial groups (see Exhibit 11.4). It is

Exhibit 11.4   Ethnoracial Differences in Death Rates From HIV/AIDS

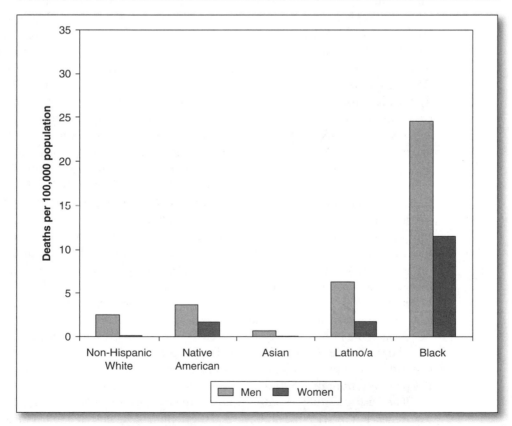

SOURCE: U.S. Bureau of the Census, 2011b, Table 126

now the leading cause of death among African Americans between the ages of 25 and 44—ahead of heart disease, cancer, accidents, and homicides (Andriote, 2005). Furthermore, although rates of new HIV/AIDS cases have remained stubbornly steady among all groups over the past decade, they have increased rapidly among one segment of the population: young gay black men (cited in McNeil, 2011).

Sometimes personal stereotyping and bias are to blame for these outcomes. For instance, in one study, doctors described African American patients—no matter what their education and income levels—as less intelligent, less likely to follow medical advice, less likely to participate in rehabilitation, and more likely to abuse alcohol and drugs than white patients (Van Ryn & Burke, 2000). Another study found that doctors often stereotype Asian patients as compliant and "problem free" (cited in American Sociological Association, 2005). When time and medical resources are limited, such beliefs can drive the treatment decisions doctors make.

But we can't simply blame ruthless and bigoted individuals for all racial imbalances in the health care system. Instead, the financial considerations that drive the health care system create a context ripe for institutional racism. Consider racial differences in organ transplants. According to the Organ Procurement and Transplant Network (2011), the 2011 national kidney transplant waiting list consisted of 38.6% Whites and 34% African Americans. (This figure in and of itself is telling: African Americans make up only about 13% of the population yet account for over one third of people in need of kidney transplants.) However, that same year, Whites received 52.5% of all kidney transplants, while African Americans received only 26%. Such a discrepancy is likely linked to hospitals determining a candidate's ability to pay before approving a procedure. These policies are sometimes referred to as "green screens" or "wallet biopsies." A liver transplant, for example, can cost anywhere from $100,000 to $400,000, so it's not surprising that most hospitals would screen potential recipients for some kind of evidence up front that their insurance will cover the procedure. Because ethnoracial minorities are less likely than Whites to have medical insurance, they are less likely to receive a referral for transplant surgery (Stolberg, 1998). Financial concerns, not outright racial prejudice, lie at the heart of these policies.

Racist ideologies in the field of medicine understandably lead to mistrust of the system among some groups. For instance, African Americans were once routinely used as subjects, frequently without their consent, for new medical treatments, experimental procedures, and medical demonstrations (H. A. Washington, 2006). The most infamous case was the Tuskegee syphilis study. In 1932, the U.S. Public Health Service initiated a study in Tuskegee, Alabama, to determine the natural course of untreated syphilis in black men. In exchange for their participation, the 400 men—all poor and most illiterate—received free meals, free medical exams, and burial insurance. The men were never told they had syphilis. Instead, they were told that they had "bad blood" and would receive treatment. In reality, they received no treatment. When penicillin became available in the early 1950s—the most effective treatment for syphilis—the men were not treated.

In fact, the Public Health Service actively sought to prevent treatment. Even as the men began to die or to go blind or insane, penicillin was withheld. As soon as the experiment was publicized in 1972, it was stopped. Since then, the federal government has paid out more than $9 million in damages to victims and their families and heirs.

The Tuskegee study was driven not by the outright prejudice of individual medical researchers but by scientific rationale and the dominant, taken-for-granted medical "facts" of the time. Prevailing medical opinion in the 1930s was that Blacks were born with strong sexual appetites and a lack of morality, which made them particularly susceptible to sexually transmitted diseases. This belief, coupled with the equally dominant belief that Blacks wouldn't seek treatment even if it were available, led the researchers to conclude that this segment of the population would provide the best subjects for their study.

Such cases of medical maltreatment in the name of research are not merely vestiges of the past. For instance, between 1988 and 2001, researchers at Columbia University Medical Center in New York tested potentially dangerous AIDS drugs on HIV-positive African American foster children living in an orphanage affiliated with the university. Because these children had no parents or had parents who were deemed unfit by the courts, these experiments took place without the consent of their biological parents or legal guardians (H. A. Washington, 2006).

Incidents like these create a pervasive distrust of the health care system among many people of color today, which puts them at even greater disadvantage. Today, many African Americans—as well as Latino/as and Native Americans—avoid participating in medical research (cited in Alvidrez & Areán, 2002). Furthermore, members of ethnoracial minorities are often skeptical that their participation in clinical studies would be a benefit either to them personally or to their communities. Overall mistrust of the medical field has been cited as one of the reasons why African Americans have been slow to come for HIV testing and medical care (Dervarics, 2004), are less likely than Whites to donate organs (Srikameswaran, 2002), and are less likely than Whites to agree to surgery for early stages of lung cancer (Bach, Cramer, Warren, & Begg, 1999).

Sometimes the institutional racism underlying threats to people's health is less obvious than shoddy medical care or unethical research. For instance, people in neighborhoods where hazardous waste treatment plants or other sources of industrial pollution exist are disproportionately exposed to the unhealthful effects of air pollution, water pollution, and pesticides. The decisions on where to place such facilities are usually based not on the ethnoracial makeup of an area but on factors such as the cost of land, population density, and geological conditions. However, because the less desirable residential areas (and hence more desirable industrial areas) are disproportionately inhabited by poor people of color, these decisions have the effect of discriminating against them. For instance, Native American reservations, which have less stringent environmental regulations than other areas, have been targeted by the U.S. military for stockpiles of nuclear, chemical, and biological weapons and by private companies for solid waste landfills, hazardous waste incinerators, and nuclear waste storage facilities (Hooks & Smith, 2004). When it comes to the federal government cleaning up polluted areas, predominantly white communities see faster action, better results, and stiffer penalties for polluters than do communities where ethnoracial minorities predominate (Bullard, 2001).

People of color make up the majority of residents who live in neighborhoods within two miles of the nation's hazardous waste treatment facilities (Dosomething.org, 2007). Poor African American communities often have the worst conditions. Seven oil refineries and several hundred heavy industrial plants are situated along a stretch of the Mississippi River between Baton Rouge and New Orleans known as "cancer alley" (Koeppel, 1999). At one time, a study of toxic emissions in this area by the Environmental Protection Agency showed that 9 of the 10 major sources of industrial pollution were in predominantly black neighborhoods (Cushman, 1993). Overall, the greater the proportion of black residents in a community, the more likely it is that there will be industrial sources of air pollution within a two-mile radius of people's homes (Perlin, Sexton, & Wong,

1999). Indeed, Blacks are 79% more likely than Whites to live in areas where air pollution levels constitute serious health risks (cited in Little, 2007).

Racial Inequality in the Educational System

In 1954, the U.S. Supreme Court ruled in *Brown v. Board of Education of Topeka* that racially segregated schools were unconstitutional because they were inherently unequal. School districts around the country were placed under court order to desegregate. But within the past 10 years, courts have lifted desegregation orders in at least three dozen school districts around the country. In 2007, the Supreme Court reversed itself and ruled that public school systems could not try to achieve or maintain integration through actions that take explicit account of students' race. At the time of the ruling, such programs were in place in hundreds of school districts around the country (L. Greenhouse, 2007b). Some districts have resorted to using integration plans based on children's socio-economic disadvantage, rather than race, to skirt these restrictions (Bazelon, 2008).

You might assume that the court took this action because desegregation plans based on students' race were no longer needed. However, African American and Latino/a students are actually more isolated from white students today than they were 30 years ago (Orfield & Lee, 2007). The average black and Latino/a student attends a school in which at least 70% of the students are not white. In Southern California, two fifths of Latino/a students and one third of black students attend schools where 90% to 100% of the students are not white (Orfield, Siegel-Hawley, & Kucsera, 2011). In contrast, the average white student attends a school in which almost 80% of the students are white (Orfield & Lee, 2007).

And it's not just students who are segregated. In general, white teachers have very little experience with racial diversity. They are currently teaching in schools where almost 90% of their faculty colleagues are white and over 70% of the students are white (Frankenberg, 2006).

Schools where the majority of students are not white are likely to be schools where poverty is concentrated. Almost 86% of schools in which black and Latino/a students represent more than 90% of the enrollment are also schools in which more than half the students came from poor families. This is not the case with majority-white schools, which almost always enroll high proportions of middle-class students. Just 12% of schools with less than 10% black and Latino/a students are schools where a majority of students are poor (Frankenberg, 2006).

The racial mix of the classroom has important implications for the quality of the education students receive. Concentrated poverty tends to be linked to lower educational achievement. Schools in poor communities lack the financial and therefore educational resources that schools in more affluent communities have (see Chapter 10). For instance, poor school districts are less likely than wealthier districts to offer Advanced Placement (AP) programs. And because poor schools tend to be in minority communities, fewer students of color have access to AP courses. So while African Americans make up 14% of high school graduates, they constitute only 8% of those taking AP exams and 4% of those with passing scores (cited in Lewin, 2009a). Furthermore, poor schools hire fewer teachers with credentials in the subjects they're teaching and have more unstable enrollments, higher dropout rates, and more students with untreated health problems. Despite attempts to rectify the problem, black and Latino/a students still lag behind white and Asian students at all levels of the educational system (see Exhibit 11.5).

Exhibit 11.5a   Race, Ethnicity, and Educational Achievement

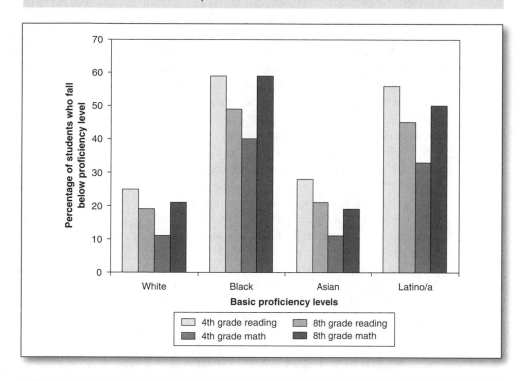

Exhibit 11.5b   High School and College Graduation Rates

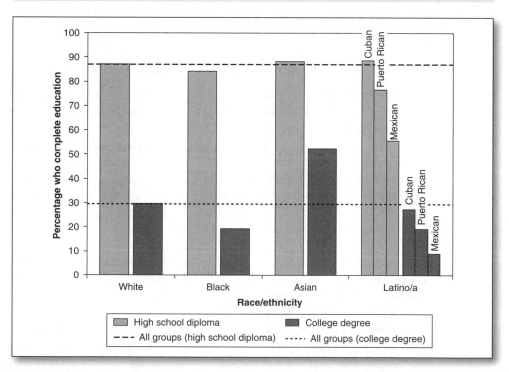

SOURCES: National Center for Education Statistics, 2006; U.S. Bureau of the Census, 2011b, Table 225

Lack of money isn't the only problem, however. Common institutional practices within the educational system can also lead to unequal outcomes. Consider the widespread use of standardized tests, which are often used as the basis for "tracking" students—that is, as Chapter 5 explains, assigning them to different educational programs based on their intellectual abilities. Standardized tests supposedly measure innate intelligence. Many educational experts agree, however, that these tests are culture bound, tapping an individual's familiarity with a specific range of white, middle-class experiences rather than indicating innate intelligence (Hout & Lucas, 2001). Hence, members of ethnoracial minorities consistently score lower on these tests than Whites (C. Jencks & Phillips, 1998).

Despite the potential for bias, more and more states across the country are requiring high school students to pass a standardized test to graduate. And, as you recall from Chapter 9, the government uses standardized test scores to determine school funding under No Child Left Behind laws. At the same time, though, many universities and other educational organizations have begun seeking alternative ways to determine eligibility for admission. For instance, some universities now use a "strivers" approach, whereby college applicants whose SAT scores fall in the borderline range for many selective colleges but who manage to exceed the historical average for students from similar backgrounds by at least 200 points are deemed "strivers" and given special consideration (Cooper, 1999). The Texas legislature went a step further, ordering the University of Texas system to accept all students who graduate in the top 10% of their class, regardless of their SAT scores. In 1999, a U.S. district court judge ruled that the NCAA (National Collegiate Athletic Association) could no longer use SAT scores to determine athletic eligibility. The court concluded that the test is culturally biased and therefore discriminates against underprivileged students.

These changes indicate a significant effort to undermine institutional racism in the educational system, which is, according to some sociologists, the largest barrier to racial equality that exists in this country today (Jencks & Phillips, 1998).

Remedies for Institutional Racism: Affirmative Action

If tomorrow all people in the United States were to wake up harboring absolutely no hatred, prejudice, or animosity toward other groups, institutional racism would still exist. It is part of the structure of society. Thus, it requires a structural solution.

You have already seen how the educational system and the legal system are undertaking limited measures to overcome certain types of institutional racism. However, the most far-reaching structural solution to the problem of institutional racism has been ***affirmative action***. Affirmative action is a governmental policy, developed in the early 1960s, that requires organizations to draft a written plan on how they will seek out members of minority groups and women for educational or occupational positions from which they had previously been excluded. One assumption is that past discrimination has left certain people ill equipped to compete with others as equals today. Another assumption is that organizations will not change discriminatory policies unless they are forced to do so.

Contrary to popular belief, employers and university admissions officers are not compelled to institute hiring or admissions quotas or to compromise standards to meet affirmative action goals. They are simply required to gather all relevant information on all applicants, to interview qualified minority candidates, and to make sure underrepresented groups have access to needed information. For instance, companies doing business with the government can set numerical hiring goals based on the availability of qualified candidates in the particular field. However, affirmative action guidelines specify that such goals cannot be quotas:

> Numerical goals do not create set-asides for specific groups, nor are they designed to achieve proportional representation or equal results. Rather, the goal-setting process in affirmative action planning is used to target and measure the effectiveness of affirmative action efforts to eradicate and prevent discrimination. . . . The regulations . . . specifically prohibit quota and preferential hiring and promotions under the guise of affirmative action numerical goals. In other words, discrimination in the selection decision is prohibited. (United States Department of Labor, 2011, p. 1)

For close to half a century, affirmative action policies have been successful in helping members of ethnoracial minorities get ahead (Katel, 2008). Businesses, unions, universities, and local governments accused of discrimination in hiring or admissions have been sued under the 1964 Civil Rights Act. In part because of such actions, more than 40% of U.S. colleges and universities reported enrollment gains among African Americans and Latino/as during the mid 1990s (cited in Worsnop, 1996). People of color now hold a greater percentage of management, white collar, and upper-level blue collar jobs than ever before. Even young black men—historically the most economically disadvantaged and alienated group in the United States—have made some employment gains (Nasar & Mitchell, 1999). Wages and salaries, relative to those of Whites, have also improved somewhat (although, as we've seen, they still lag behind).

Despite its successes, affirmative action remains highly controversial. In one national survey, for example, 93% of respondents agreed that society has an obligation to help hardworking people overcome disadvantages so they can succeed in life. However, when asked whether a fictitious low-income college applicant who happens to be black should be given preference over a high-income student who happens to be white, only 36% agreed (Carnevale & Rose, 2003).

Opposition to affirmative action comes from all directions. Some politically liberal critics, for example, argue that the lives of people for whom affirmative action policies were originally designed—the poorest and most disadvantaged—remain largely unchanged. Although the percentages of Blacks and Whites earning midrange incomes are roughly the same now, there continues to be a large discrepancy at the top and bottom income levels (U.S. Bureau of the Census, 2011b). Top U.S. colleges are accepting more students of color today than ever before. But these students tend to come from middle- or upper-class backgrounds. For example, of the 8% of Harvard's undergraduates who are black, only a handful are from poor families in which all four grandparents were born in this country and are descendents of slaves (Rimer & Arenson, 2004). In addition, many schools don't provide enough support to ensure that students from historically disadvantaged groups actually graduate. The six-year graduation rate for Native American, Latino/a, and African American students is well below 50%, compared with 60% for white students and 67% for Asian students (National Center for Education Statistics, 2011). Because a college degree is associated with success later in life (bachelor's degree holders earn about twice as much a year as those with high school diplomas), such educational disappointment can have far-reaching social and personal effects.

Conservative critics argue that preferential treatment of any group, even one whose rights have been historically unrecognized, is demeaning to the people it's supposed to help and unfair to everyone else, amounting to a form of "reverse" discrimination. After the Supreme Court's 2007 ruling that barred the use of race in school desegregation plans, the Chief Justice said, "The way to stop discrimination on the basis of race is to stop discriminating on the basis of race" (quoted in L. Greenhouse, 2007b, p. 1). Some go further, arguing that affirmative action isn't needed because discrimination is already illegal and nothing more is required. And others maintain that it's not working because the problems that disadvantaged people face have more to do with economics or with inherent character flaws than with race (Fish, 2000). After four decades of such criticisms, many people have come to believe that affirmative action in all its forms should be abolished.

Ironically, however, other modes of preferential treatment continue to operate with virtually no criticism. For instance, applicants who are most likely to receive favored treatment when it comes to college admissions are white, affluent "legacies," or children of alumni. Playing favorites with alumni children is a common practice at almost every private college and many public institutions as well. At some highly selective universities, legacies are twice as likely to be accepted as unconnected applicants with similar or better credentials (Larew, 2003). Some schools reserve a certain number of spaces for legacies. In one recent year at Harvard, marginally qualified white legacies outnumbered all African American, Mexican American, Puerto Rican, and Native American students combined.

Yet all around the country, voters have been approving bans on race-based affirmative action. Five states—California, Florida, Michigan, Nebraska, and Washington—forbid racial preferences for historically underrepresented groups in college admissions as well as employment. The California case has served as a model for other states considering bans on racial preferences. In 1996, voters there approved Proposition 209, a landmark referendum that bans the consideration of race, ethnicity, and sex in the public sector, including college admissions. Prior to the ban, African Americans, Latino/as, and Native Americans made up 23.1% of first-year students in the University of California system. The first year after the ban went into effect, that figure fell to 10.4% (Bronner, 1998b). In California, Blacks and Latino/as make up 42% of the state's population. However, they accounted for only about 15% of first-year admissions in the University of California system in 2006. At the same time, Asians, who make up about 12% of the state's population, accounted for about half of first-year admissions (Egan, 2007). That year, UCLA had its lowest first-year black enrollment in 30 years (Lewin, 2007).

Clearly, affirmative action remains a divisive issue. In a society with a tradition of racial stratification, what is the best way to overcome institutional inequality? Does it take discriminating in the opposite direction to "make things equal," or is it enough simply to treat people equally from this point on?

Here's one way to think about these questions: Imagine a fictitious championship game of a basketball tournament between University A and University B. The rules of the game clearly favor University A. Its team is allowed five players on the court, but Team B is allowed only four. Team A gets 4 points for every basket made; Team B gets 2. Team A is given 2 points for each free throw made; Team B gets 1. Team A is allowed to physically impede the progress of the opposing players without being called for a foul, and so on. At halftime, Team A leads Team B by a score of 70 to 15. During halftime, tournament officials decide that the current rules have made the game completely unfair and have harmed the interests of Team B. They declare that from now on, each team will have the same number of players on the court and receive the same number of points per basket. But there's a slight problem—when the game resumes after halftime, the score is still 70 to 15!

In other words, just because opportunities have been equalized in the present doesn't mean that the accumulated disadvantages of the past have been entirely overcome (Shapiro, 2008). Such is the problem we face today. We can legislate hiring and admission policies that do away with unfair advantages to any group, but is that action enough to address a long history of exclusion? For a long time to come, members of certain groups will continue to be underrepresented in traditionally white positions. Can U.S. citizens achieve complete equality without forcing those who have benefited historically to give up some of their advantages? The answer to this question is complex, controversial, and emotionally charged and will have a great impact on the nature of ethnoracial relations in the United States in the foreseeable future.

Global Perspectives on Racism

Given the focus of this chapter so far, you might be tempted to conclude that racism and racial inequality are purely U.S. phenomena. Certainly, these problems are very obvious in a society such as the United States, which is so ethnically and racially diverse and which has had such a long history of bitter conflict. But ethnoracial tension is the worldwide rule, not the exception.

Like disadvantaged ethnoracial groups in the United States, minority groups in other countries suffer discrimination that ruins their opportunities for success:

- Between 2004 and 2008, negative attitudes toward Jews and Muslims increased significantly in Spain, Poland, Russia, Germany, and France (Pew Global Attitudes Project, 2008).
- During soccer matches all across Europe, black players are routinely subjected to racist taunts, derisive chanting, monkey noises, and hurled bananas from white fans (Longman, 2006).
- Police in Paris, France, stop young Arab and black men for identity checks in train stations about seven times more often than young Whites (Erlanger, 2009).
- In 2011, France became the first country in Europe to ban Muslim women from wearing facial veils in public (De La Baume, 2011).
- In Eastern European countries such as Slovakia, Romania, Hungary, and the Czech Republic, discrimination against the Roma—or Gypsies—is the norm. They have been despised for centuries as thieving subhumans with no respect for the law and are stereotyped as loud, dirty, indecent, and sloppy (Erlanger, 2000). As a result of such attitudes, Gypsies suffer disproportionately from poverty, interethnic violence, discrimination, illiteracy, and disease (Wood, 2005). In Ostrovany, Slovakia, a 500-foot-long, 7-foot-high concrete wall separates a Roma ghetto from a handsome *gadzo*, or white neighborhood, on the other side even though two thirds of the city's population are Romas (Bilefsky, 2010). Such treatment is not confined to countries where Romas have long resided. In 2010, France embarked on a major push to reduce crime and illegal immigration by forcibly expelling some Romas, even though such mass expulsion based on ethnicity violates European Union law (Erlanger, 2010).
- In Mexico, all citizens are considered legally equal under the country's constitution. Yet it is a society deeply divided along racial lines, particularly between dark-skinned people of Indian descent and light-skinned people of Spanish descent. Ironically, most Mexicans are of mixed lineage, so that nearly all of them could be considered at least part Indian. But Mexicans who are considered Indians are the object of severe discrimination. More than 80% of Mexico's Indian communities suffer high levels of poverty. Nearly half of all Indians are illiterate, and only 14% complete sixth grade (DePalma, 1996).

Sociologists once believed that the global forces of industrialization and modernization would create ethnoracially diverse societies where people's loyalty would be directed to the national society rather than their racial or ethnic community (Deutsch, 1966). But the opposite has happened. At a time when people from every corner of the globe are linked technologically, economically, and ecologically and when mass migrations mix people from different races, religions, and cultures in unprecedented numbers, racial and ethnic hostilities are at an all-time high (Barber, 1992).

It's tempting to view ethnic conflict as the pent-up expression of age-old ethnic loyalties and cultural differences. However, in many areas of the world, the origins of conflict can be traced to the lingering effects of colonialism and the manipulation of political leaders. Consider, for instance, the ethnic violence that occurred between Hutus and Tutsis in Rwanda in the mid 1990s. The way the conflict was presented in the media led many outside observers to assume that these two groups had some deep-seated, centuries-old ethnic hatred of one another that had reached its boiling point. It turns out, though, that prior to German colonization in the 19th century and Belgian colonization in the early 20th century, Rwandans didn't consider themselves Hutu or Tutsi. They saw themselves as one group. People drew their identity from where they were born or by how much wealth they had (Bowen, 1996). It was the colonizers who decreed that each person had to have an "ethnic identity" that determined their place in society. By pitting one group against another, colonial rulers, whose numbers were always quite small, could seek out allies among certain ethnic groups. Belgian rulers formed such an alliance with the Tutsis. Their suppression of the Hutus created a sense of collective Hutu identity and outrage. In the 1950s, Hutus successfully rebelled against Tutsis. Eventually, Tutsi resentment led to the creation of their own rebel army. The conflict reached its bloody conclusion in the civil war of 1994, in which hundreds of thousands of Tutsis and moderate Hutus were killed.

Regardless of its source, so much ethnic conflict is going on in the world today that we might conclude that hostility between groups is among the most universal of human feelings (Schlesinger, 1992). Look at any online news service and you will see stories of ethnic, religious, or racial conflict: Jews and Palestinians in Israel and Gaza, Chechens and Russians in the former Soviet Union, Janjaweed and Darfurians or Sudanese and Nubans in Sudan, Hindus and Muslims or Bengalis and Gurkhas in India, the Han and Uighurs in western China, Lendus and Hemas in the Democratic Republic of the Congo, Georgians and Ossetians in Georgia, Sunis and Shiites in Iraq, Tajiks and Pashtuns in Afghanistan, the Kyrgyz and Uzbeks in Kyrgyzstan, and the Ijaw and Itsekiri in Nigeria. In Great Britain, France, and Germany, loud and sometimes violent resentment occurs between the native born and immigrants from Africa, Eastern Europe, and the Middle East. In the United States, such animosity is likely to be directed toward immigrants from Latin America and Asia (see Chapter 13 for more details). When people feel that their survival is threatened, they often blame others for their problems, particularly newly arrived others who look and act differently. Racial and ethnic hatred costs the lives of millions of people each year.

But global forces don't just increase ethnoracial tension and inequality; sometimes they help to resolve it. In South Africa, for example, the end of apartheid in the early 1990s was the result of an international boycott. In the 1980s, the global media brought the world pictures and stories of the brutal treatment of South African Blacks. When consumers in the United States and other industrial nations stopped buying products from companies that held investments in South Africa, the companies began to withdraw their money. The minority white government felt the sting as domestic economic problems mounted. As a result of these pressures, the white population of South Africa voted to abolish apartheid. Shortly thereafter, the first black president, Nelson Mandela, was elected. In 1996, a new constitution was adopted that officially and peacefully completed South Africa's transition from white supremacy to nonracial democracy. The document renounces the racism of the past and guarantees all South Africans broad freedoms of speech, movement, and political activity (Daley, 1996). Although serious inequalities and animosities remain, the country is well on its way toward unity and stability.

More recently, we've seen how political developments in one country can reverberate around the globe. Shortly after the 2008 U.S. presidential election, social observers in Europe began to speculate on how Barack Obama's ascendency to the highest office in the land would influence race relations in their own countries. As an editor of a French blog put it, "They always said, 'You think race relations are bad here in France, check out the U.S.' But that argument can no longer stand" (quoted in Erlanger, 2008, p. 1). France's defense minister pondered how Obama's victory might serve as a lesson to the French on dealing with issues of immigration and integration. However, others in Italy, Great Britain, and Germany were more skeptical about the ultimate impact it would have on race relations there. I guess we'll just have to wait and see.

Conclusion

On April 16, 1963, the Reverend Martin Luther King, Jr., was arrested and jailed for leading a civil rights demonstration in Birmingham, Alabama. At that time, not only were Blacks being subjected to daily doses of fear, violence, and humiliation, but they also had to constantly fight what Dr. King called "a degenerating sense of nobodiness." Torn between the brutal reality of a racist society and a fierce optimism for the future, he wrote from his jail cell,

> Let us all hope that the dark clouds of racial prejudice will soon pass away and the deep fog of misunderstanding will be lifted from our fear-drenched communities and in some not too distant tomorrow the radiant stars of love and brotherhood will shine over our great nation with all of their scintillating beauty. (King, 1991, p. 158)

A half century later, our society—like most societies around the globe—still struggles with the debilitating effects of personal and institutional discrimination based on race, religion, and ethnicity. In the United States, lynchings and state-supported segregation have given way to a form of racism that resides not in bloodshed and flagrant exclusion but in the day-to-day workings of our major social institutions. Despite recent gains, people of color still suffer noticeable disadvantages in economics, education, politics, employment, health care, vulnerability to crime, and many other areas. When opportunities to learn, legislate, and make a living are unequally distributed according to race, all facets of life remain unequal.

Fifty years after racial segregation was ruled unconstitutional in the United States, the complete integration of fundamental social institutions such as public schools, government, and business has only partially been achieved. And some are questioning the very value of integration. One reason why race relations are so problematic today is that public debate over the issue confuses personal racism and institutional racism. Different types of racism require different solutions. We cannot put an end to economic deprivation or massive residential segregation by trying to convince people not to stereotype other groups.

I realize that this chapter has been rather depressing. After reading it, you may have a hard time imagining a society without racial or ethnic stratification, one where skin color is about as relevant in determining people's life chances as eye color.

We must remember, however, that differences do not have to imply inequality. The transformation from difference to disadvantage is a social construction. The people of every society decide which differences should be irrelevant and which should be the primary criteria for making social and legal distinctions between groups of people. The good news is that because we construct these differences, we can tear them down.

YOUR TURN

A curious and disturbing feature of prejudice is that many of our beliefs and attitudes about other racial or ethnic groups are formed without any direct contact with members of those groups. The media—most notably television—play a significant role in providing the public with oversimplified and often inaccurate ethnoracial information, which indirectly shapes public attitudes.

For one week, observe several prime-time television shows that feature prominent African American, Latino/a, Asian, or Middle Eastern characters. The shows can be either comedies or dramas. Note the number of characters on each show who are people of color. Pay particular attention to the way the characters are portrayed. For instance, are they college educated? Gainfully employed? Happily married? What is their apparent social class standing? How do their mannerisms, appearances, and speech patterns conform to common stereotypes associated with members of these groups? How frequently do their words or actions refer to their own race or ethnicity? Do the plots of the shows revolve around what you might consider "racial" themes? That is, how often does the issue of race or ethnicity come up during the course of the show?

If you have time, you can expand your analysis to examine the role of race and ethnicity in stand-up comedy. What proportion of comedians of color use race as part of their act compared with white comedians? What are the consequences of comedians such as Chris Rock, Margaret Cho, George Lopez, and Carlos Mencia playing on racial stereotypes in their acts?

Interpret your observations sociologically. What are the implicit messages communicated by the portrayal of ethnoracial minorities in American media? What role does humor play in reinforcing or fighting prejudice? Are characters who do not act in stereotypical ways conforming instead to a white, middle-class standard? If so, how will this portrayal ultimately affect public perceptions of race?

CHAPTER HIGHLIGHTS

- The history of race and ethnicity in U.S. society is an ambivalent one. Famous sayings about equality conflict with the experiences of most ethnoracial minorities—experiences of oppression, violence, and exploitation. Opportunities for life, liberty, and the pursuit of happiness have always been distributed along racial and ethnic lines.

- Personal racism is manifested in the form of bigotry, prejudice, and individual acts of discrimination. Quiet racism is expressed not directly but rather indirectly through anxiety about or avoidance of minorities.

- Racism can also be found in language and norms prescribing differential treatment of certain groups.

- Institutional racism exists in established institutional practices and customs that reflect, produce, and maintain ethnoracial inequality. Institutional racism is more difficult to detect than personal racism and hence is more difficult to stop. Because such racism exists at a level above personal attitudes, it will not disappear simply by reducing people's prejudices.

- Ethnoracial conflict is not just an American phenomenon. It is a global reality.

KEY TERMS

affirmative action: Program designed to seek out members of minority groups for positions from which they had previously been excluded, thereby seeking to overcome institutional racism

colorism: Skin color prejudice within an ethnoracial group, most notably between light-skinned and dark-skinned Blacks

discrimination: Unfair treatment of people based on some social characteristic, such as race, ethnicity, or sex

ethnicity: Sense of community derived from the cultural heritage shared by a category of people with common ancestry

institutional racism: Laws, customs, and practices that systematically reflect and produce racial and ethnic inequalities in a society, whether or not the individuals maintaining these laws, customs, and practices have racist intentions

panethnic labels: General terms applied to diverse subgroups that are assumed to have something in common

personal racism: Individual expression of racist attitudes or behaviors

prejudice: Rigidly held, unfavorable attitudes, beliefs, and feelings about members of a different group based on a social characteristic such as race, ethnicity, or gender

quiet racism: Form of racism expressed subtly and indirectly through feelings of discomfort, uneasiness, and fear, which motivate avoidance rather than blatant discrimination

race: Category of people labeled and treated as similar because of allegedly common biological traits, such as skin color, texture of hair, and shape of eyes

racial transparency: Tendency for the race of a society's majority to be so obvious, normative, and unremarkable that it becomes, for all intents and purposes, invisible

racism: Belief that humans are subdivided into distinct groups that are different in their social behavior and innate capacities and that can be ranked as superior or inferior

stereotype: Overgeneralized belief that a certain trait, behavior, or attitude characterizes all members of some identifiable group

STUDENT STUDY SITE

Visit the Student Study Site at **www.sagepub.com/newman9e** for these additional learning tools:

- Flashcards
- Web quizzes
- Sociologists at Work features
- Micro-Macro Connection features
- Video links
- Audio links
- Web resources
- SAGE journal articles

The Architecture of Inequality

Sex and Gender

12

Sexism at the Personal Level

The Ideology of Sexism: Biology as Destiny

Institutions and Gender Inequality

The Global Devaluation of Women

At a women's rights convention held in Seneca Falls, New York, participants created a modified version of the Declaration of Independence. They called it the Declaration of Sentiments and Resolutions. Here are some excerpts from that document:

> We hold these truths to be self-evident: that all men and women are created equal. . . . The history of mankind is a history of repeated injuries . . . on the part of man toward woman, having in direct object the establishment of an absolute tyranny over her:
>
> > He has compelled her to submit to laws, in the formation of which she had no voice.
> >
> > He has monopolized nearly all profitable [occupations], and from those she is permitted to follow, she receives but a scanty remuneration. He closes against her all the avenues to wealth and distinction which he considers most honorable to himself.
> >
> > He has endeavored, in every way that he could, to destroy her confidence in her own powers, to lessen her self-respect, and to make her willing to lead a dependent and abject life.
>
> In view of their social degradation and in view of the unjust laws above mentioned, and because women do feel themselves aggrieved, oppressed, and fraudulently deprived of the most sacred rights, we insist that they have immediate admission to all the rights and privileges which belong to them as citizens of the United States.

The women who wrote this declaration were not the women's liberationists of the 1960s and 1970s or the radical feminists of the 1990s and 2000s. They were participants in the first convention in support of women's rights ever held in the United States—in 1848 ("Declaration of Sentiments and Resolutions," 2001, pp. 449–450). We tend to think that women of the past were either content with their second-class status or unaware that it could be otherwise. As you can see from the preceding declaration, though, 164 years ago U.S. women were anything but passive, ignorant victims of discrimination.

Many people are also inclined to believe that the battle against gender inequality has been won. Beginning with the civil rights movement of the 1960s and the so-called sexual revolution of the 1970s, a process of liberation has given contemporary U.S. women opportunities that equal men's. After all, as many U.S. women as men work in the paid labor force, the majority of college students these days are women, and women play a prominent role in business, politics, and entertainment. In 2011, six states had female governors, and there were seven women in the president's Cabinet. Perhaps you will be surprised to learn in this chapter, then, that women's struggle to overcome economic, legal, and social inequality is no less relevant in the 21st century than it was in 1848.

In Chapter 5, I discussed the difference between sex and gender and how we learn to become boys and girls and men and women within the appropriate social and cultural contexts. Being placed in a gender category affects everything we do in life. But gender is more than just a source of personal identity that sets societal expectations; it is a location in the stratification system and a major criterion for the distribution of important resources in most societies.

In this chapter, I will address several important questions: What are sexism and gender discrimination? How are they expressed and felt at the personal level? How is inequality based on sex and gender supported by cultural beliefs and symbols? At the institutional level, how is inequality related to family and work roles? What are its legal and economic consequences? And finally, how pervasive is gender inequality around the world?

Sexism at the Personal Level

What do you think of when you hear the word *sexism*? The husband who won't let his wife work outside the home? The construction worker who whistles and shouts vulgar comments at female passersby? Perhaps you think of the woman who mocks men's interpersonal skills or their clumsy attempts at romance? Sexism is all those things, to be sure. But sociologically speaking, *sexism* refers to a system of beliefs that assert the inferiority of one sex and that justify discrimination based on gender—that is, on feminine or masculine roles and behaviors. At the personal level, sexism refers to attitudes and behaviors communicated in everyday interaction.

In male-dominated societies, or *patriarchies*, which exist in every quadrant of the globe, cultural beliefs and values typically give higher prestige and importance to men than to women. Throughout such societies, inequality affects girls and women in everything from the perceptions, ambitions, and social interactions of individuals to the organization of social institutions. Above all, gender inequality in a patriarchy provides men with privileged access to socially valued resources and furnishes them with the ability to influence the political, economic, and personal decisions of others. *Matriarchies*, which are societies that give preference to women, are rare in the contemporary world.

Even the most democratic societies tend to be patriarchal to some degree. Research on U.S. gender stereotypes, for instance, has shown that they have changed little over the years (D. L. Berger & Williams, 1991). Some researchers have shown that women are consistently perceived as more passive, emotional, easily influenced, and dependent than men (Broverman, Vogel, Broverman, Clarkson, & Rosenkrantz, 1972; Deaux & Kite, 1987; Tavris & Offir, 1984). Others have noted the myriad ways personal sexism is expressed in U.S. society, both overtly and subtly, through physical domination, condescending comments, sabotage, and exploitation (Benokraitis & Feagin, 1993). One study found that although some forms of personal sexism are motivated by hostility, others are motivated by benevolence, as when men assume women are helpless and thus feel compelled to offer assistance (Glick & Fiske, 1996). Such attitudes and behaviors not only place women in a lower-status position compared with men but also channel them into less advantageous social opportunities.

Men, of course, aren't the only ones who can be personally sexist. Certainly, some women dislike men, judge them on the basis of stereotypes, hold prejudiced attitudes toward them, objectify them sexually, consider them inferior, and even discriminate against them socially or professionally. We must keep in mind, though, that male sexism occupies a very different place in society from female sexism. The historical balance of power in patriarchal societies has allowed men as a group to subordinate women socially and sometimes legally to protect male interests and privileges. Because men dominate society, their sexism has more cultural legitimacy, is more likely to be reflected in social institutions, and has more serious consequences than women's sexism.

Sexism and Social Interaction

Everyday social life is fraught with reminders of gender imbalances. Men and women interact with each other a lot, but rarely do these interactions occur between two people who are of equal status (Ridgeway & Smith-Lovin, 1999). The average woman is reminded frequently of her subordinate position, through subtle—and sometimes not so subtle—ways. Men often have a hard time understanding women's reactions to personal encounters between the sexes. Just as white people enjoy racial transparency (see Chapter 11), members of the dominant sex take for granted the social arrangements that serve their interests.

For example, consider the following tongue-in-cheek quote from a female newspaper columnist:

> By whistling and yelling at attractive but insecure young men, we women may actually help them feel better about themselves, and give them new appreciation of their bodies. Some might say women were descending to the level of male street-corner oafs, but I'm willing to take that risk. If, with so little effort, I can bring joy to my fellow man, then I am willing to whistle at cute guys going down the street. (Viets, 1992, p. 5)

If you're a man, you may wonder why the columnist is bothering to make fun of "wolf whistles." The answer simply is that this behavior means different things when directed at men versus women. Unsolicited sexual attention may be an enjoyable, esteem-enhancing experience for men, but it doesn't have the weight of a long tradition of subordination attached to it, nor is it linked in any way to the threat of violence. Men aren't subjected to **objectification**—that is, to being treated like objects rather than people—in the same way that women are. Sure, women gawk at and swoon over good-looking men from time to time (just watch reruns of *Sex and the City* sometime). But men's entire worth is not being condensed into a quick and crude assessment of their physical appearance. For women, who must often fight to be taken seriously in their social, private, and professional lives, whistles and lewd comments serve as a reminder that their social value continues to be based primarily on their looks.

Communication patterns also show the effects of unconscious personal sexism. Research in the symbolic interactionist tradition suggests that women and men converse in different ways (Parlee, 1989; Tannen, 1990). For instance, women are more likely than men to use a tag question at the end of a statement: "She's a good professor, *don't you think?*" They are also more likely to use modifiers and hedges such as *sort of* and *kind of* and to be more polite and deferential in their speech (Lakoff, 1975). But such techniques may make the speaker sound less powerful and therefore call into question her credibility and qualifications. Imagine if your math professor always said things like, "The answer to the problem is $3x + y$, isn't it?" Or if your boss said, "We're going to pursue the Johnson account; is that OK?"

The implicit, nonverbal messages of social interaction—body movements, facial expressions, posture—also have more serious implications and consequences for women than for men. For example, femininity is typically gauged by how little space women take up; masculinity is judged by men's expansiveness and the strength of their gestures. Women's bodily demeanor tends to be restrained and restricted (Henley, 1977). What is typically considered "ladylike"—crossed legs, folded arms—is also an expression of submission. Men's freedom of movement—feet on the desk, legs spread, straddling a chair—conveys power and dominance. Such interactional norms place women who are in authoritative positions in a no-win situation. If, on the one hand, they meet cultural definitions of femininity by being passive, polite, submissive, and vulnerable, they fail to meet the requirements of authority. If, on the other hand, they exercise their authority by being assertive, confident, dominant, and tough, their femininity may be called into question (J. L. Mills, 1985).

Nonverbal cues can also play an important role in providing people with information about their social worth. Thus, they sometimes serve to keep women "in their place." It is the rare female subway traveler in New York who hasn't been groped on a crowded train. Preparing for these unwanted encounters is as taken for granted as making sure you have the proper fare:

> Women know the drill.... Pull in your backside.... Wedge a large bag for protection between yourself and the nearest anonymous male rider.... Put on your fiercest face, and brace yourself for contact. (Hartocollis, 2006, p. B11)

In Japan, unwanted fondling has gotten so bad on crowded trains that rail companies have introduced "women only" cars to protect women. Similarly, Mexico City began running single-sex buses in 2008. The fact that men can more freely touch women than vice versa serves as a reminder that women's bodies are not considered entirely their own.

U.S. women are also routinely exposed to unwelcome leers, comments, requests for sexual favors, and unwanted physical contact in a variety of institutional settings, from schools to workplaces. According to the American Association of University Women (2001), about 83% of girls have been subjected to sexual harassment in elementary, middle, and high school, ranging from the spread of sexual rumors about them to coerced sexual activity. A third of teenage girls are bullied at school and another 5% report being cyber-bullied (U.S. Bureau of the Census, 2011b). And nearly two thirds of female college students experience sexual harassment at some point during their college careers, though fewer than 10% tell a university official and an even smaller number file an official complaint (C. Hill & Silva, 2006).

The Equal Employment Opportunity Commission (2011) resolved close to 12,000 cases of workplace sexual harassment in 2010, but these figures obviously don't include incidents that are never reported. According to one national poll, close to one third of female workers reported being sexually harassed on the job (cited in Sexual Harassment Support, 2009). In 2010, the Congressional Office of Compliance reported that U.S. taxpayers fund about $1 million per year in settlements to congressional employees who have been harassed by their bosses (Lovley, 2010).

Some occupations are particularly vulnerable to sexual harassment and assault. For instance, sexual affronts from male guests are an everyday safety hazard for female hotel workers (S. Greenhouse, 2011). It is so common, in fact, that hotel managers routinely provide their housekeeping staff with a list of safety precautions, for example, to always carry a panic button (or mace) in your pocket, always clean rooms in tandem with another housekeeper, and always prop the door open when cleaning a room (J. Bernstein & Ellison, 2011).

From a conflict perspective, cases of sexual harassment are expressions of and attempts to reinforce positions of dominance and power (Uggen & Blackstone, 2004). Indeed, the vast majority of harassment cases involve male assertions of power over women. But women aren't the only victims. Sometimes an overbearing, sexually aggressive female boss may harass a male subordinate; but more commonly, it's men who create a hostile environment for other men through bullying, hazing, goosing, various sexual insults, and other boorish behaviors. According to the Equal Employment Opportunity Commission (2011), sexual harassment charges filed by men increased from 11.6% of all cases in 1997 to 16.4% of all cases in 2010. Sometimes men are victimized in settings where you'd least expect it. In 2010, more than 110 male soldiers filed confidential reports of sexual assault by other men, nearly three times as many as in 2007 (cited in Ellison, 2011). As troubling as this trend is, however, women face a far less welcoming and more dangerous environment in the military.

LAURA MILLER

Gender, Power, and Harassment in the Military

When a woman fought a legal battle in the mid 1990s to be admitted into the Citadel—at that point, an all-male military academy of more than 1,900 students—she became a target of harassment and ridicule. Alumni sold T-shirts that read "1,952 Bulldogs and One Bitch" (Vojdik, 2002, p. 68).

Misconduct against women is pervasive in the entire military system. A survey conducted by the General Accounting Office found that 59% of female students at the Air Force Academy, 50% at the Naval Academy, and 76% at West Point reported experiencing one or more forms of sexual harassment (cited in N. Katz, 2003). The Pentagon reported that in the fiscal year that ended in September 2008, there were 2,908 reports of sexual abuse involving military personnel as assailants or victims (Myers, 2009). Nine out of 10 victims were women (U.S. Department of Defense, 2008). That year there were 251 reported sexual assaults of female American soldiers by fellow male military personnel in Iraq, Afghanistan, and other combat regions, a 44% increase over 2007 (cited in Myers, 2009). Female soldiers are statistically more likely to be assaulted by a fellow soldier than killed in combat (Ellison, 2011). And such figures don't even include the countless number of female soldiers who regularly face degradation, hostility, and loneliness instead of the camaraderie every soldier depends on for comfort and survival. Many female military personnel end up waging what amounts to two wars—one against the enemy and one against their fellow soldiers (Benedict, 2009). It's not surprising that one in seven female veterans who visit a Veterans Affairs Center for medical care report being a victim of sexual assault or harassment during their active duty (cited in M. Elias, 2008).

The problem goes beyond individually violent soldiers. As far back as 2004, the Pentagon concluded that the root cause of the problem was a decade's worth of failure on the part of commanding officers to acknowledge its severity (cited in Shanker, 2004). Things got so bad that in 2005, the Department of Defense rewrote its rules so that female soldiers could report sexual assaults confidentially and gain access to counseling and medical services without setting off an official investigation. It now pursues complaints more aggressively and sponsors a "Sexual Assault Prevention and Response" Web site to provide "guidance and other information for victims of sexual assault, unit commanders, first responders, and others who deal with this sensitive issue."As a result, the number of reported incidents jumped 40% compared with the previous year (Corbett, 2007). However, few cases end in a prosecution. Of the more than 2,000 suspects of investigations in 2008, only 317 faced a court-martial and 515 faced administrative punishment or discharge; half the investigations were deemed "unsubstantiated or unfounded" (Myers, 2009). Frustration over this lack of action led 15 female soldiers—and two male soldiers—to file a federal lawsuit in 2011 accusing the Department of Defense of permitting a military culture that failed to prevent sexual harassment and abuse and of mishandling cases that came to its attention (A. Parker, 2011).

The U.S. military has been almost exclusively male for most of its history, except for female medical, clerical, and logistics personnel. Men still make up the vast majority of the armed forces and hold all the highest positions of authority. Even today, depending on the branch of service, women make up a small, albeit growing, percentage of our active military force. At the time of this writing, there were more than 213,000 women in active duty in the Army, Marine Corps, Navy, and Air Force and another 190,000 in the Reserves and National Guard. That represents a higher number of women in the armed services than at any other time in history (during the Vietnam War, for instance, women made up 2% of active duty servicepeople) but still accounts for less than 16% of all U.S. military personnel (Alvarez, 2009; The Women's Memorial, 2011).

Some women have been able to climb the military ladder and achieve the rank of lieutenant, captain, major, or general. In 2011, a female general became the first woman in history to take charge of the famed Marine Corps training depot at South Carolina's Parris Island. Women in leadership positions create a special dilemma for male soldiers because female officers simultaneously occupy a subordinate position (because they are women) and a superior position (because they are commanding officers in a highly stratified military hierarchy). So how do lower-level male soldiers—whose gender grants them power but whose military rank makes them inferior—respond?

Sociologist Laura Miller (1997) set out to answer this question by conducting field research at eight U.S. Army posts and two national training centers. She also lived with U.S. Army personnel overseas, in Somalia and Haiti. In addition, she collected survey data from more than 4,000 American soldiers, both enlisted personnel and officers. On the basis of her research, Miller draws a distinction between sexual harassment (unwanted sexual comments or advances) and the more common gender harassment (harassment used to enforce traditional gender roles or in response to the violation of those roles). She considered statements such as "Women can't drive trucks" or "Women can't fire heavy artillery" to be gender harassment. Gender harassment is also often used against men, as when they fail to live up to the masculine ideal and are called "ladies" or "girls" by their comrades or commanding officers.

Many of the men Miller studied strongly believed that they were the disadvantaged sex in the military. They were convinced that women's physical training requirements are easier than men's, that women can "get away with more," and that women receive special breaks, such as avoiding demanding physical duty because of menstrual cramps.

As one enlisted man stated, "They want equal rights, but don't want to do what it takes to become equal" (quoted in Miller, 1997, p. 48). In short, many male soldiers had come to believe that any woman's power in the military is gained illegitimately.

Often men resorted to subtle forms of gender harassment to express their disapproval of women's power positions in the military. Because of their abiding loyalty to the military "chain of command," these men were not about to overtly disobey orders from a superior officer. Nor were they likely to use traditional forms of harassment, such as blatant sexual comments or sexual advances. Instead, they often used what sociologists refer to as "weapons of the weak"—strategies that subordinates employ to resist oppression from above. Such techniques include foot dragging, feigned ignorance, gossip and rumors, and sabotage. According to one male officer interviewed by Miller, most soldiers at one time or another try to undermine the authority of their female superiors.

Gender harassment is more subtle, and therefore more difficult to trace, than sexual harassment. Furthermore, Miller's study shows us that positions of power are not sufficient to guarantee respect and authority. Rather, it shows that harassment lies at the crossroads of power and gender.

Sexual Orientation

Prejudices expressed at the personal level often combine gender and sexual orientation. For many decades, gays and lesbians have been rejected, ridiculed, and condemned on moral, religious, criminal, or even psychiatric grounds. Today, homosexuals and bisexuals—as well as people assumed to be or accused of being gay or bisexual—routinely experience discrimination, interpersonal rejection, or even violence (Herek, 2000a). Such sexual prejudice varies along gender lines. According to one study (Herek, 2000b), women tend to express fewer antigay attitudes, beliefs, and behaviors than men. But the object of attitudes is also gender specific. Heterosexual men tend to have more negative attitudes toward and feel more discomfort around gay men than they feel toward lesbians. Heterosexual women, in contrast, hold similar attitudes toward gay men and lesbians. Demonstrating one's heterosexuality and one's conformity to traditional gender roles seems to be of greater concern to men than women, which may explain the heightened male hostility toward gay men.

Often the attitudes are unabashedly virulent. According to the Federal Bureau of Investigation (2010), there were close to 1,500 documented cases of anti-homosexual hate crimes in 2009. Several years ago, a gay college student in Wyoming, Matthew Shepard, was pistol-whipped, tied to a fence, and left to die. At his funeral, protestors from a church in Topeka, Kansas, held up signs reading "God Hates Fags!" The church's Web site had a picture of Matthew depicted burning in hell. The same Web site had a similar photo of a lesbian who was mauled to death by two dogs a few years earlier. Above her picture, it read, "God used literal dogs to kill a figurative dog." More recently, nine attackers lured a 30-year-old gay man into a house, where they stripped him, tied him to a chair, burned his nipples and penis with a cigarette, whipped him with a chain, and sodomized him with a baseball bat while shouting anti-gay slurs at him (M. Wilson & Baker, 2010). According to one researcher, gay, lesbian, and bisexual youth are about five times as likely as heterosexuals to attempt suicide (Hatzenbuehler, 2011). In 2010, a rash of suicides among harassed and bullied gay teenagers in New Jersey, California, Texas, and Indiana focused national attention on the problem.

Harassment can also occur in settings purported to be more tolerant, such as universities. In a nationwide study of gay, lesbian, and bisexual college students, 89% had been the recipient of derogatory remarks, 49% had received verbal threats, and 2% had been physically assaulted. Close to 20% feared for their physical safety because of their sexual orientation (Rankin, 2003). These students are not only more likely than heterosexuals to be harassed by fellow students, but also at greater risk of being harassed by teachers and school employees (C. Hill & Silva, 2006).

Violence Against Women

The epitome of sexual domination expressed at the personal level is sexual violence. Forcible rape and other forms of sexual assault exist throughout the world, in the most democratic societies as well as in the most repressive.

In the United States, rape is the most frequently committed but least reported violent crime. Only 55% of these crimes ever come to the attention of the police—compared with 68% of robberies and 58% of aggravated assaults (Truman & Rand, 2010). According to the National Crime Victimization Survey—an annual assessment of crime victimization carried out by the U.S. Bureau of Justice Statistics (Truman & Rand,

2010)—more than 203,000 women over the age of 12 said they'd been raped or sexually assaulted in 2008, more than double the roughly 90,000 incidents of forcible rape and attempted rape officially reported to the police in a given year (U.S. Bureau of the Census, 2011b).

Rape is the most personal of violent crimes. In 79% of rapes and sexual assaults, the victim knows the attacker (Truman & Rand, 2010). On college campuses, where about 3% of college women experience a completed or attempted rape during a typical college year, 90% of the victims know their attackers (U.S. Bureau of Justice Statistics, 2001).

Rape as a Means of Social Control

According to the conflict perspective, stratification along sex and gender lines has long distorted our understanding of rape. Throughout history, women have been viewed socially and legally as the property of men, as either daughters or wives. Thus, in the past, rape was defined as a crime against men or, more accurately, against men's property (Siegel, 2004). Any interest a husband took in another man sexually assaulting his wife probably reflected a concern with his own status, the loss of his male honor, and the devaluation of his sexual possession. Even when women are not seen as men's property, their lives are controlled by rape and sexual assault. Lesbians in South Africa are sometimes raped by men who believe it will "cure" them of their sexual orientation. These violent acts are known as "corrective rapes." As one woman put it,

> We get insults every day, beatings if we walk alone, you are constantly reminded that . . . you deserve to be raped, they yell, "if I rape you then you will go straight . . . you will buy skirts and start to cook because you will have learned how to be a real woman." (quoted in ActionAid, 2009, p. 15)

Globally, rape is a time-tested wartime tactic of terror, revenge, and intimidation, not only against female victims but also against husbands, sons, and fathers whose idea of honor is connected to their ability to protect "their" women (Amnesty International, 2004b; Enloe, 1993; Sengupta, 2004). In the Democratic Republic of the Congo, for example, bands of soldiers have been "waging a war of rape and destruction against women" since the 1980s (Herbert, 2009, p. A17). Congolese girls and women of all ages have been publicly gang-raped, had their reproductive organs deliberately destroyed, and been violated with loaded guns. In one four-day stretch during 2010, gangs of marauding Congolese soldiers raped at least 200 women in one village, despite the fact that United Nations peacekeepers were based just up the road (Gettleman, 2010). The devastation of these atrocities extends beyond the psychological humiliation, physical wounds, and deaths of individual victims. Entire families and neighborhoods are traumatized when husbands are forced to watch their wives being raped, parents their daughters, or children their mothers.

According to some feminist sociologists, men have used rape and the threat of rape throughout history to exert control over women (Brownmiller, 1975). The mere existence of rape limits women's freedom of social interaction, denies them the right of self-determination, and makes them dependent on and ultimately subordinate to men (Griffin, 1986). All forms of oppression—whether against ethnic Darfurians in Sudan, peasants in Bolivia, or women in the United States—employ the threat of violence to ensure compliance. The subordination of women depends on the power of men to intimidate and punish them sexually.

The fear of rape goes beyond simply making life terrifying and uncomfortable for women. It also can restrict their economic opportunities. Women may avoid some neighborhoods with affordable housing because of potential danger. If a woman has a job that requires night work, she may be forced to buy a car to avoid walking at night or using public transportation. The threat of sexual assault restricts where and when she is able to work, thereby limiting her money-earning choices and perhaps keeping her financially dependent on others.

Women are also harmed by the larger cultural ideology surrounding rape and rapists. I think most of us are inclined to believe that men who rape must be insane or abnormally violent. All one has to do to avoid being raped, then, is to avoid strange guys. However, rapists as a group have not been shown to be any more disturbed than nonrapists (Griffin, 1986; Warshaw, 1988). In fact, most rapists are quite "normal" by usual societal standards. As I mentioned earlier, almost 80% of rapes involve people the victim knows—friends, acquaintances, classmates, coworkers, or relatives. But when rape is generally perceived to be perpetrated by psychologically defective strangers, it doesn't implicate the dominant culture or established social arrangements. In other words, rape isn't considered the fault of society; it's the fault of flawed men who can't abide by society's rules. This assumption may explain why date or acquaintance rape, marital rape, and other forms of sexual violence that don't fit the typical image have, until quite recently, been ignored or trivialized.

We must therefore examine the crime of rape within a broader cultural context that encourages certain types of behavior between men and women (S. Jackson, 1995). When we do so, rape becomes less an act of deviance and more an act of overconformity to cultural expectations; less an act of abnormal individuals and more an act of "normal" men taking cultural messages about power and assertiveness to their violent extreme. As one author wrote, rape is the "all-American crime," involving precisely those characteristics traditionally regarded as desirable in American men: strength, power, domination, and control (Griffin, 1989).

Victim Blaming

Globally, cultural beliefs about gender, sexuality, and intimacy influence societal and legal responses to rape and rape victims (Morgan, 1996):

- In Colombia, a man who rapes a woman—whether he knows her or not—can be absolved of all charges if he offers to marry her.
- In Senegal, single women who are rape victims may be killed by their families because as nonvirgins they can no longer command a high dowry; a married woman who's been raped may be killed by her "dishonored" husband.
- In Iran, because Islamic tradition forbids the execution of virgins, any woman condemned to die must first lose her virginity through rape.
- In Afghanistan, women are forbidden by law to refuse to have sex with their husbands.

Arguably, the United States has a more sympathetic reaction to rape victims. But the legal response here still tends to be consistent with men's interests, focusing on women's complicity or blameworthiness. In rape cases, unlike any other crime, victims typically must prove their innocence rather than the state having to prove the guilt of the defendant. Many women who have been victimized come to the conclusion that reporting their experiences would, at best, be embarrassing and useless (Sanday, 1996).

And, to some extent, they may be right. Consider, for example, the way a victim is treated in the immediate aftermath of a rape. When she reports being victimized, she is physically examined, photographed, probed, and swabbed for the assailant's DNA. This process—which can last several hours in a hospital—produces what's known as a "rape kit." The kit is then sent to a crime lab, where, after thorough DNA analysis, it becomes the key piece of physical evidence in criminal proceedings. National studies have found that rape cases in which there is a rape kit containing DNA evidence are significantly more likely to lead to a conviction than cases where there is no kit. You would think that the process that produces such an important component of a legal case would be quick and efficient. However, according to a recent study of rape cases in Los Angeles County, there are more than 12,000 *untested* rape kits sitting in police storage facilities; 450 of them have been there for more than 10 years (Human Rights Watch, 2009a). Such delays can be tragic. California has a 10-year statute of limitations for rape (the maximum period after a crime when a defendant can be prosecuted) that can be lifted only if a rape kit is tested within two years of the date of the crime. It's no wonder that so many women are reluctant to report being sexually victimized.

The conflict perspective provides one explanation for the widespread tendency to hold women responsible for their own victimization: The common definition of rape is based on a traditional model of sexual intercourse—penile-vaginal penetration—rather than on the violent context within which the act takes place. The primary focus on the sexual component of the crime requires that information about the intimate circumstances of the act and about the relationship between the people involved be taken into consideration—all of which tends to put female rape victims at a disadvantage during criminal proceedings. Research consistently shows that observers attribute more blame to the victims and minimize the seriousness of the assault when the perpetrator is an acquaintance, date, or steady partner (S. T. Bell, Kuriloff, & Lottes, 1994). One study of convicted rapists found that those who assaulted strangers received longer prison sentences than those who were acquaintances or partners of their victims, regardless of the amount of force used or physical injury to the victim (McCormick, Maric, Seto, & Barbaree, 1998).

Moreover, public attitudes toward rape and rapists continue to be influenced by the relationship between the people involved. One study of college students found that some people (mostly men) still believe it is acceptable for a man to force his wife to have sex with him and that when compared with other types of violent offenses, marital rape is considered less serious than rape committed by a previously unknown assailant (Kirkwood & Cecil, 2001). In fact, until 1976, state rape laws defined rape as nonconsensual sexual intercourse between a man and a woman, *not his spouse*. Although every state at least partially abolished this marital exemption by the early 1990s, only 24 states treat marital rape cases just as they do any other rape cases (McMahon, 2007). For instance, some states exempt husbands from rape prosecutions when the degree of violence is minimal or when the couple is not living apart or separated at the time of the incident. Four states—Connecticut, Iowa, Minnesota, and West Virginia—extend these privileges to unmarried cohabiters (Bergen, 1999). With rare exception, courts have validated state laws that treat marital rape cases differently from other rapes (Hasday, 2000).

Even when rape victims are not married to or living with their attackers, they are often expected to provide clear evidence that they were "unwilling" and tried to resist. Anything short of vigorous and repeated resistance can still call the victim's motives into question. Indeed, research suggests that police, prosecutors, and juries are less likely to believe allegations of rape if there is no evidence of violence (McEwan, 2005).

No other serious crime requires that the victim prove lack of consent. People aren't asked if they wanted their house broken into or if they enticed someone to beat them up and steal their wallet. Yet if women cannot prove that they resisted or cannot find someone to corroborate their story, consent (or even latent desire) may be presumed (Siegel, 2004). A few years ago, while in a hospital waiting room after being brutally raped, a woman from Madison, Wisconsin, was required to submit a "statement of nonconsent" swearing that she hadn't given her knife-wielding assailant permission to rape, cut, and rob her (Lueders, 2006).

Certain states have reconsidered the issue of what constitutes consent. In Connecticut and Kansas, for example, a woman may withdraw her consent to have sex at any time, and if the man continues, he is committing rape. However, in North Carolina, once a woman gives consent, she cannot rescind it. Such an understanding of consent rests on the belief that at a certain point during arousal, a man loses the ability to stop (Lee-St. John, 2007).

Public perceptions are slow to change. Many people regard female rape victims as at least partly to blame if they put themselves in risky situations, for instance, by behaving seductively, wearing "provocative" clothing, drinking too much, or telling dirty jokes. In one study, male and female high school students were given a list of statements and asked to indicate the extent to which they agreed with them (Kershner, 1996). Of the male and female subjects, 52% agreed that most women fantasize about being raped by a man, 46% felt that women encourage rape by the way they dress, and 53% said they felt that some women provoke men into raping them. Moreover, 31% agreed that many women falsely report rapes, and 35% felt that the victim should be required to prove her innocence during a rape trial. Research has linked such attitudes to an increased likelihood of holding rape victims responsible (Frese, Moya, & Megías, 2004) as well as a heightened risk of rape and sexual assault occurring (Ching & Burke, 1999).

The important sociological point of these findings is that many men and even some women don't always define violent sexual assault as a form of victimization. They think it is either something women bring on themselves or something men understandably do under certain circumstances. These views have become so entrenched that many women have internalized the message, blaming themselves to some degree when they are assaulted. Apart from fear, self-blame is the most common reaction to rape and is more frequent than anger (Janoff-Bulman, 1979). When rape victims say things such as, "I shouldn't have walked alone," "I should have known better than to go out with him," or "I shouldn't have worn that dress to the party," they are at least partly taking the blame for a crime they didn't commit. Such guilt and self-blame make recovery all the more difficult and tend to increase rates of depression, posttraumatic stress, shame, anxiety, and even suicidal thoughts (Kubany et al., 1995).

As a consequence of victim blaming, women are forced to bear much of the responsibility for preventing rape. I frequently pose this question to students in my introductory sociology class: What can people do to stop rape from occurring? Their responses always echo the standard advice: Don't walk alone at night. Don't get drunk at parties where men are present, and if you do drink, know where your drink is at all times. Don't flirt or engage in foreplay if you have no intention of "going all the way." Don't miscommunicate your intentions. Don't wear revealing clothes. Certainly all these safety measures are smart, sensible things to do. But note how all of these suggestions focus exclusively on things that *women* should avoid in order to prevent rape and say nothing about the things *men* can do to stop it. Confining discussions of rape prevention to women's behavior and vulnerability suggests that if a woman doesn't take these precautions, she is "inviting trouble." And "inviting trouble" implies that violent male behavior either is a natural response to provocation or is likely to happen if precautions aren't taken to discourage it.

Some progress is being made regarding cultural perceptions of rape. Myths are being debunked, the violent sexual exploitation of women in the media is being protested, and the rules governing admissible evidence in rape trials are being changed. The recent increase in attention paid to rape, particularly to rape between acquaintances and intimate partners, has increased public awareness of the problem. Rates of officially reported rapes and attempted rapes have dropped steadily since the 1990s (see Exhibit 12.1). However, as long as we live in a culture that objectifies women and glorifies male assertiveness, we will continue to have sexual violence.

Exhibit 12.1   Trends in Forcible Rape

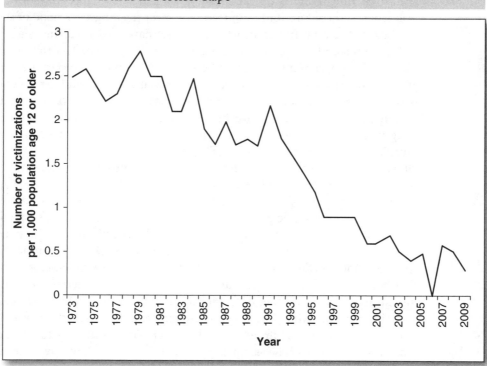

SOURCE: U.S. Bureau of Justice Statistics, 2010

The Ideology of Sexism: Biology as Destiny

The domination of one group over another is always endorsed by a set of beliefs that explains and justifies that domination. You saw in the previous chapter that racism is often justified by the belief in innate racial inferiority. With sexism, it is the belief that men and women are biologically and naturally different.

For 19th- and early-20th-century physicians, few facts were more incontestable than the fact that women were the products and prisoners of their anatomy. One French scientist noted a century ago that women have smaller brains than men, which explained their "fickleness, inconstancy, absence of thought and logic, and incapacity to reason" (quoted in Angier & Chang, 2005, p. A1). Even today, there's no shortage of books purporting to show that female tendencies in self-control, risk taking, intuition, empathy, anxiety, aggression, emotions, and even decision making can all be traced to the structure and function of their brains (Baron-Cohen, 2003; Brizendine, 2006; Mansfield, 2006).

Likewise, women's reproductive systems have been the object of scientific attention and concern for centuries (Scull & Favreau, 1986). Everything supposedly known about women that made them different from men—their subordinate place in society, their capacity for affection, their love of children and aptitude for child rearing, their "preference" for domestic work, and so on—could be explained by the their uterus and ovaries (Ehrenreich & English, 1979; Scull & Favreau, 1986). Scholars in the past warned that young women who studied too much were struggling against nature, would badly damage their reproductive organs, and would perhaps even go insane in the process (Fausto-Sterling, 1985). So the exclusion of women from higher education was not only justifiable but necessary for health reasons and for the long-term good of society.

Some structural-functionalist sociologists have also used the bodily differences between men and women to explain gender inequality. The fact that men tend to be physically stronger and that women bear and nurse children has created many culturally recognized sex-segregated social roles, especially at work and in the family (Parsons & Bales, 1955). This specialization of roles is the most effective way to maintain societal stability, structural functionalists believe. By giving birth to new members, by socializing very young children, and by providing affection and nurturing, women make invaluable contributions to society. The common occupations women have traditionally had outside the home—teacher, nurse, day care provider, maid, social worker, and so on—tend simply to be extensions of their "natural" tendencies.

Similarly, men's physical characteristics have been presumed to better suit them for the roles of economic provider and protector of the family. If it's true that men are "naturally endowed" with traits such as strength, assertiveness, competitiveness, and rationality, then they are best qualified to enter the serious and competitive world of work and politics (Kokopeli & Lakey, 1992). Sociologist Steven Goldberg (1999) argues that because male rule and male dominance seem to characterize the vast majority of human societies, this gender difference must be rooted in evolutionary biology.

The problem with depicting masculinity and femininity as natural, biological phenomena is that it confuses sex with gender. The underlying assumption of sexist ideology—that gender is as unchangeable as sex—overlooks extensive similarities between the sexes and extensive variations within each sex. The distributions of men and women on most personality and behavioral characteristics generally overlap. For instance, men as a group do tend to be more aggressive than women as a group. Yet some women are much more aggressive than the average man, and some men are much less aggressive than the average woman. Indeed, social circumstances may have a greater impact on aggressive behavior than any innate, biological traits. Some studies show that when women are rewarded for behaving aggressively, they can be just as violent as men (Hyde, 1984).

Furthermore, the reliance on biology ignores the wide cultural and historical variation in conceptions of masculinity and femininity. For instance, although every known society has a division of labor based on sex, what's considered "men's work" and "women's work" differs. In most societies, men fish, hunt, clear land, and build boats and houses, but in some societies, women regularly perform these tasks. In most societies, women do the cooking; but in some societies, cooking is typically a male responsibility (Eitzen & Baca Zinn, 1991).

Although women have become prominent in the U.S. workforce, many people still believe that they are less capable than men of performing certain tasks outside the home (Wagner, Ford, & Ford, 1986). Some in the United States still may find female doctors or lawyers unusual. Legislators and military officials continue to debate the role of female soldiers in direct ground combat. The controversy in several churches over whether or not women should be ordained as ministers and priests illustrates the depth and intensity of people's feelings about gender-appropriate career pursuits.

Moreover, the qualities we consider naturally feminine are usually seen as less socially valuable than those considered masculine. Girls do suffer sometimes when their behavior is considered "boylike." But accusing a boy of acting like a girl is the ultimate schoolyard insult. Even when they get older, many men can be easily whipped into aggressive responses by accusations of femininity, such as when coaches call their male players "girls" or "ladies."

The biological rationale for gender inequality is difficult to justify these days. Technological advances—including bottled baby formula, contraceptives that give women more choices over childbearing, and innovations that lessen the need for sheer physical strength—have made it possible for women and men to fulfill many of the same responsibilities. Nevertheless, as long as people believe that gender-linked roles and societal contributions are determined by nature, they will continue to accept inequality in women's and men's opportunities, expectations, and outcomes. If people consider it "natural" for women to play nurturing, weak, and dependent roles, then limiting women to such positions seems neither unfair nor oppressive.

Institutions and Gender Inequality

The subordination of women that is part of the everyday workings of social institutions (or *institutional sexism*) has far greater consequences for women as a group than personal expressions of sexism. When sexism in social institutions becomes part of the ongoing operation of large-scale organizations, it perpetuates and magnifies women's disadvantages, making social equality all the more difficult to attain. But not only can social institutions be sexist, they can also be gendered. In other words, institutions and organizations segregate, exploit, and exclude women solely on the basis of their physical characteristics and then compound the impact of their sexism by incorporating values and practices based on traditional expectations for women and men (Kimmel, 2004).

Masculinized Institutions

More often than not, institutions incorporate masculine values—which is not surprising because, historically, men have developed, dominated, and interpreted most institutions. Take competitive sports, for example. Most of us would agree that to be successful, an athlete must be aggressive, strong, and powerful—attributes typically associated with masculinity. By celebrating these traits, a sport such as football symbolically declares itself an arena that women cannot or should not enter (except, of course, as spectators or cheerleaders). But even sports such as gymnastics and figure skating, which have traditionally valued more "feminine" traits like grace, beauty, and balance, have now made their judging criteria more masculine. For a woman to be a world-class gymnast or skater these days, she must also be physically strong and exhibit explosive acrobatic power. Indeed, the popularity of women's team sports in this country coincides with the increasing presence of traditionally male traits such as physical strength and competitive vigor in female athletes.

In most high schools, student culture revolves around sports, especially football. In such an environment, privilege and power are conferred on successful male athletes. Some sociologists and educators fear that high schools are now being pressured to apply an equally aggressive, competitive, "masculinized" approach to the curriculum as well, through emphases on academic rigor, high-stakes test taking, zero-tolerance discipline policies, and increased efforts in math, science, and technology (Lesko, 2008).

The masculine traits necessary for successful athletic and educational competition can be seen in other institutions. For instance, we don't often associate the practice of religion with masculine traits like aggression, strength, and power. However, some evangelical pastors have become disdainful of mainstream American Protestantism for what they perceive as its softening or "feminizing" of Christ. They believe that too much attention is paid to sensitivity and tolerance and not enough to damnation and salvation:

> What really grates is the portrayal of Jesus as a wimp, or worse. Paintings depict a gentle man embracing children and cuddling lambs. Hymns celebrate his patience and tenderness. . . . The mainstream church . . . has transformed Jesus into a "Richard Simmons, hippie, queer Christ," a "neutered and limp-wristed popular Sky Fairy of pop culture that . . . would never talk about sin or send anyone to hell." (quoted in Worthen, 2009, p. 22)

To counteract this trend, some evangelical churches have begun to incorporate a hypermasculine, hard-edged, smackdown approach to the Gospel into their religious services.

Similarly, most bureaucracies in institutional areas such as business, politics, and the military operate according to taken-for-granted masculine principles. Successful leaders and organizations are usually portrayed as aggressive, goal oriented, competitive, and efficient—all characteristics associated with masculinity in this society. Rarely are strong governments, prosperous businesses, or efficient military units described as supportive, nurturing, cooperative, kind, and caring (Acker, 1992). When institutions are gendered in these ways, everyday inequalities become apparent.

Gender Inequality in Health and Health Care

Gender inequality has created some curious discrepancies in the way the medical establishment treats men and women. For instance, prior to the health care reform bill signed into law in 2010, it was legal in most states for insurance companies selling individual policies—those for people who don't have group insurance coverage through their employers—to charge women more than men for the same medical coverage. The difference in price ranged from 4% to 48%. The obvious justification was that because of all the medical procedures associated with childbirth, women used the health care system more than men. But discrepancies exist even for policies that don't cover maternity costs (Pear, 2008b). Moreover, nonsmoking women have sometimes been charged higher health insurance premiums than men who smoke (Grady, 2010). At the time of this writing, health care reform had not yet been fully implemented, so it remains to be seen if the changes will lower the health-care-related cost of being a woman.

Ironically, men tend to have more health problems and a shorter life expectancy than women (Legato, 2006). They occupy more physically demanding jobs and engage in more dangerous physical activity. Hence, they've historically been at greater risk for various bodily injuries and stress-related ailments. According to figures from the U.S. Bureau of the Census (2011b), men also have higher rates of cancer (excluding breast, cervical, and ovarian types) than women.

Yet women have historically been the focus of intrusive medical attention more than men (B. K. Rothman, 1984). Women are far more likely than men to undergo surgical and diagnostic procedures. Indeed, the three most common short-stay surgical procedures for women—repair of lacerations during childbirth, cesarean sections, and hysterectomy—all deal with female anatomy and physiology. The three most common short-stay procedures for men—cardiac catheterization, reduction of fractures, and coronary artery bypass grafting—are not sex specific (U.S. Bureau of the Census, 2011b). Similarly, physicians often specialize in *women's* health care, but rarely do they specialize in *men's*. Obstetricians and gynecologists deal exclusively with the reproductive and sexual matters of female patients. There are no comparable specialties of medicine devoted solely to men's reproductive health (urologists address men's reproductive issues, but they also see female patients).

Normal biological events in women's lives—menstruation, pregnancy, childbirth, and menopause—have long been considered problematic conditions in need of medical intervention. For instance, the board of trustees of the American Psychiatric Association continues to debate the inclusion of a psychiatric diagnosis called "premenstrual dysphoric disorder" in its official manual of mental disorders. Indisputably, many women around the world experience irritability, moodiness, and other symptoms related to hormonal cycles. The issue, however, is whether these symptoms ought to be labeled as a medical and/or mental problem (Lander, 1988). To do so not only promotes the selling of drugs to healthy women (C. A. Bailey, 1993; Figert, 1996) but fosters the belief that women, biologically frail and emotionally erratic because of their hormones, cannot be allowed to work too hard or be trusted in positions of authority (Fausto-Sterling, 1985).

From a sociological perspective, it seems highly likely that women's experiences with the "symptoms" surrounding menstruation are related to the place that menstruation occupies in the larger society. We live in a culture that, by and large, has tried either to ignore menstruation or to present it as shameful. Only relatively recently—as evidenced by the glut of commercials and advertisements for "feminine hygiene" products—has it come out of the closet. But, of course, the attention we as a culture devote to menstruation continues to be almost exclusively negative, focusing on overcoming bothersome premenstrual symptoms or camouflaging the unsightly or otherwise unappealing by-products of menstruation itself. A Web site called Beinggirl.com (2010) regularly posts advice for adolescent girls on the use of tampons. One recent blog, titled "Keeping it quick and quiet," reinforces the idea that menstruation is shameful by providing advice such as, "Be discreet when you're bringing a tampon into the girls' room. . . . Anyone can bring a purse to the restroom (a classic hiding spot) but try tucking it in your waistband, bra, sock, or cell phone case. No one needs to suspect a thing" and "For better hiding potential, try compact tampons."

Given the special attention women's health problems receive, it's ironic that, outside obstetrics and gynecology, research on women's general health needs has been rather limited. More than 20 years ago, the U.S. Public Health Service reported that a lack of medical research on women limited our understanding of their health concerns (B. K. Rothman & Caschetta, 1999). The reason often given for their exclusion from medical studies was that their menstrual cycles complicated the interpretation of research findings. In addition, medical researchers have historically been reluctant to perform research on women of childbearing age for fear that exposing them to experimental manipulations might harm their reproductive capabilities. In fact, in the 1970s and 1980s, federal policies and guidelines actually called for the blanket exclusion of women of childbearing potential from certain types of drug research. That meant that any woman who was physically capable of becoming pregnant, regardless of her own desire to do so, could be excluded. Concerns were less about threats to women's health than they were about the possibility of liability if reproductive damage due to exposure to the experimental drug occurred (J. A. Hamilton, 1996).

The exclusion of women from medical research became so problematic that Congress passed a law in 1993 stipulating that women must be included in clinical trials in numbers sufficient to provide evidence of the different ways men and women respond to drugs, surgical treatments, and changes in diet or behavior. Nevertheless, a study in 2000 found that many researchers were not complying with the law (cited in Pear, 2000). In 2003, the Agency for Healthcare Research and Quality reported that research on coronary heart disease (CHD) still either excludes women entirely or includes them only in limited numbers. Consequently, the therapies used to treat women with CHD—a disease that kills 250,000 women a year—are still based on studies conducted primarily on middle-aged men (cited in "Research Findings Affirm," 2003).

Gender Inequality in the Media

You saw in Chapter 5 that the media's portrayal of men and women contributes to gender socialization. But the media as an institution can also contribute to the cultural devaluation of women and perpetuate gender inequality.

Worldwide, men tend to control the creation and production of media images. Women hold only about 3% of key decision making positions in mainstream media (The Women's Media Center, 2011). In key behind-the-scenes roles like creators, producers, directors, writers, editors, and directors of photography, men outnumber women four to one (Media Report to Women, 2009). It wasn't until 2009 that a woman received an Academy Award for Best Director (Kathryn Bigelow for the film *The Hurt Locker*). Such an imbalance in productive and creative control means that what we see in theaters and on television is likely to reflect men's perspectives.

Hence, apart from the occasional powerful female character—like Alicia Florrick in *The Good Wife*, Brenda Johnson in *The Closer*, or Jane Timoney in *Prime Suspect*—the portrayal of women in film and on prime-time television remains rather traditional and stereotypical. Although fewer women are portrayed as housewives than in the past, men are still more likely than women to be shown working outside the home (D. Smith, 1997). Women express emotions much more easily and are significantly more likely to use sex and charm to get what they want than are men. An analysis of 18 prime-time-television situation comedies found that female characters are significantly more likely than male characters to receive derogatory comments about their appearance from other characters. These comments are typically reinforced by audience laughter (Fouts & Burggraf, 2000). Similarly, an analysis of more than 1,600 television commercials showed that female characters were less prevalent, more likely to be shown in families, and less likely to be employed outside the home than male characters (Coltrane & Adams, 1997).

A glimpse at the portrayal of modern women in U.S. advertising, fashion, television, music videos, and films further reveals a double-edged stereotype. On the one hand, we see the successful woman of the 21st century: the perfect wife/mother/career woman, the triumphant professional who leaps gracefully about the pages of fashion magazines. She is the high-powered lawyer or surgeon that we commonly see on prime-time television: outgoing, bright, and assertive. No occupation is beyond her reach.

Coexisting with this image, though, is the stereotypical image of the "exhibited" woman: the seductive sex object displayed in beer commercials, magazine advertisements, soap operas, and the swimsuit issue of *Sports Illustrated*. More generally, television continues to present stereotypes that show women as shallow, vain, and materialistic characters whose looks overshadow all else. Popular dating-themed reality shows like *The Bachelor* reinforce the belief that sexual charm and physical attractiveness are lures that women can use to attract men.

But because the blatant sexual exploitation of female television characters is frowned upon these days, networks are setting their shows in earlier periods when attitudes were quite different. For instance, one of the most popular and critically acclaimed television shows in recent years, *Mad Men*, chronicles the sexual escapades of men working in an early 1960s ad agency. Because the show takes place half a century ago, its male characters can unabashedly express attitudes that would not be tolerated in a more contemporary setting: "We see sexist jokes, chronic philandering, and office parties in which executives tackle secretaries in order to see what color their panties are" (S. Doyle, 2010, p. 1). Sensing a lucrative market for such shows, in 2011 NBC began airing *The Playboy Club*, a drama set in 1960s Chicago that depicts the lives of voluptuous Playboy Bunnies with names like "Bunny Janie" and "Bunny Alice." That same year, ABC trotted out *Pan Am*, another 1960s-era show that was advertised as "a drama full of sexy entanglements" between male pilots and their female "stewardesses." An ad for this show said, "They do it all—and they do it at 30,000 feet." As one columnist put it, "Jiggle TV is back" (Dowd, 2011, p. 8).

In sum, young women today are not only expected to achieve educationally and economically at unprecedented levels; they also must look sexy doing it. These images, created mainly by and for men, produce the illusion that success or failure is purely a personal, private achievement and ignore the complex social, economic, and political forces that continue to prevent real-life women from achieving success.

MICRO-MACRO CONNECTION

Can Media Images Be Hazardous to Your Health?

What is especially troublesome about media images of female beauty is that they are artificial and largely unattainable. The average American woman is 5'4" tall and weighs 140 pounds. The average American fashion model is 5'11" tall and weighs 117 pounds and thus is thinner than 98% of adult American women (National Eating Disorders Association, 2011). Researchers at Johns Hopkins University compiled data on the heights and weights of Miss America pageant winners between 1922 and 1999. They found that the weights of these women steadily decreased, reaffirming the cultural value of thinness (Rubinstein & Caballero, 2000). Recent winners have had a height-weight ratio that places them in the range of what the World Health Organization defines as "undernourished."

Nonetheless, television, magazine, and Internet images of sticklike models and celebrities continue to appeal to young women who equate thinness with popularity and success. It's not surprising, therefore, that girls and young women who regularly view these images spend a great deal of time and energy trying to emulate them through extreme dieting and other disordered eating patterns (J. L. Wilson, Peebles, Hardy, & Litt, 2006). The following statistics were compiled by the National Eating Disorders Association (2011):

- Forty-two percent of first- to third-grade girls want to be thinner, 51% of 9- to 10-year-old girls feel better about themselves when they're on a diet, and 81% of 10-year-olds are afraid of being fat.

- Ninety-one percent of college women attempt to control their weight through dieting.
- On any given day, about half of American women are on a diet, even though 95% of them will likely regain the weight they've lost within one to five years.
- About 91% of the 11 million Americans diagnosed with eating disorders (anorexia, bulimia, binge eating) are girls or women.

Although many people view such figures with alarm, others see them as benign or even positive. An Internet movement, called "pro-ana" (for pro-anorexia) or "pro-mia" (for pro-bulimia), encourages young women to view eating disorders not as dangerous medical conditions but as positive lifestyle choices. Hundreds of pro-ana Web sites and blogs provide young women with dieting challenges, discussion groups, and inspirational messages or "pep talks" about the desirability of limiting food intake and the appeal of extreme thinness. Some contain declarations such as "Food is Poison." Pro-anas also post their messages and pictures celebrating extreme thinness on social network sites like Facebook, Myspace, Tumblr, and Xanga (Peng, 2008; A. Williams, 2006). Other sites provide "thinspiration" (or "thinspo") videos, visual celebrations of skeletal women, including some celebrities and models. Soundtracks to these videos include songs with messages like "Skeleton, you are my friend" and "Bones are beautiful" (Heffernan, 2008).

Supporters of this media movement argue that they are simply providing young anorexic and bulimic women a place to go where they can get support and not be judged. However, critics worry that the movement glorifies dangerous and potentially life-threatening conditions. Research seems to support this position. A study of 10- to 22-year-olds with diagnosed eating disorders found that those who frequented pro-ana Web sites remained sicker for longer periods than those who visited prorecovery sites. About 96% said they'd learned new tips for purging and weight loss from the pro-ana sites, and two thirds used these methods (J. L. Wilson et al., 2006). The potential for harm is so great that the Academy for Eating Disorders (2006) called on government officials and Internet service providers to require warning screens for pro-ana Web sites much like the warning labels found on cigarette packs.

Gender Inequality in Families

Much of the inequality women face revolves around the traditional view of their family role: keepers of the household and producers, nurturers, and socializers of children. Although in other times and places, women have had different levels of responsibility for homemaking, they have always been responsible for reproduction.

One of the major consequences of the industrial revolution of the 18th and 19th centuries was the separation of the workplace and the home. Prior to industrialization, most countries were primarily agricultural. People's lives centered on the farm, where husbands and wives were partners not only in making a home but also in making a living (Vanek, 1980). The farm couple were interdependent; each needed the other for survival. It was taken for granted that women provided for the family along with men (J. Bernard, 1981). Although the relationship between husbands and wives on the farm was never entirely equal—wives still did most if not all of the housekeeping and family care—complete male dominance was offset by women's indispensable contributions to the household economy (Vanek, 1980).

With the advent of industrialization, things began to change. New forms of technology and the promise of new financial opportunities and a good living drew people (mostly men) away from the farms and into cities and factories. For the first time in history, the family economy in some societies was based outside the household. Women no longer found themselves involved in the day-to-day supervision of the family's business as they had once been. Instead, they were consigned to the only domestic responsibilities that remained necessary in an industrial economy: the care and nurturing of children and the maintenance of the household. Because this work was unpaid and because visible goods were no longer being produced at home, women quickly found their labor devalued in the larger society (Hareven, 1992).

However, as we saw in Chapter 7, men weren't the only ones who left home each day to work in factories. At the turn of the century, hundreds of thousands of children worked in mines, mills, and factories (Coontz, 1992). And contrary to popular belief, one fifth of U.S. women worked outside the home in 1900, especially women of color (Staggenborg, 1998).

Today, the devaluation of "women's work" is the result of a separation of the public and private spheres (Sidel, 1990). As long as men dominate the public sphere—the marketplace and the government—they will wield greater economic and political power within society and also be able to translate that power into authority at home. "Women's work" within the relatively powerless private sphere of the home will continue to be hidden and undervalued.

According to the conflict perspective, the problem is not that housewives don't work; it's that they work for free outside the mainstream economy, in which work is strictly defined as something one is paid to do (Ciancanelli & Berch, 1987; Voyandoff, 1990). Ironically, however, domestic work is actually invaluable to the entire economic system.

If a woman were to be paid the minimum going rate for all her labor as mother and housekeeper, including childcare, transportation, housecleaning, laundry, cooking, bill paying, and grocery shopping, her yearly salary would be comparable to that of women who are employed full time, year round. One recent study found that if we apply average hourly wage rates to the typical daily amounts of childcare mothers of children under 12 provide, a low-end estimate of the monetary value of this work is about $33,000 a year (Folbre & Yoon, 2006). But because societal and family power is a function of who brings home the cash, such unpaid work does not afford women the prestige it might if it were paid labor.

Despite significant shifts in U.S. attitudes toward gender roles and the accelerated entry of women into the paid labor force in the past few decades, housework continues to be predominantly female (see Exhibit 12.2). Husbands do play a more prominent role in the raising of children than they did two decades ago, and they've increased their contribution to housework somewhat (Bianchi, Robinson, & Milkie, 2006), especially when compared with men in other industrialized countries (Fuwa, 2004). But the household work that husbands do is typically quite different from the work that wives do. Women's tasks tend to be essential to the daily functioning of the household (Fuwa, 2004); men's chores are typically infrequent, irregular, or optional:

> They take out the garbage, they mow the lawns, they play with children, they occasionally go to the supermarket or shop for household durables, they paint the attic or fix the faucet; but by and large, they do not launder, clean, or cook, nor do they feed, clothe, bathe, or transport children. These . . . most time-consuming activities . . . are exclusively the domain of women. (Cowan, 1991, p. 207)

Exhibit 12.2 Engagement in Household Activities

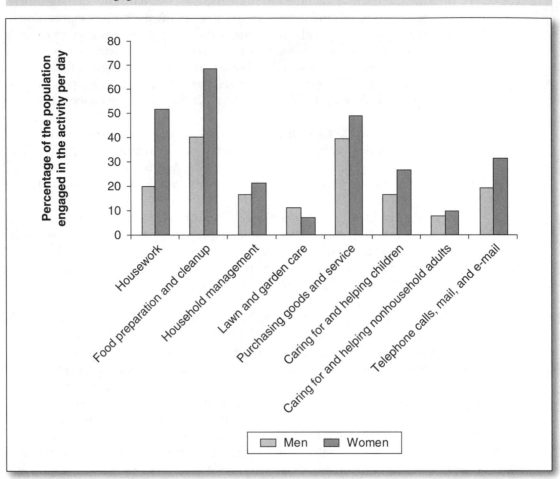

SOURCE: U.S. Bureau of Labor Statistics, 2010a, Table 1

From a structural-functionalist perspective, one could argue that traditional gendered household responsibilities actually reflect an equitable, functional, interdependent division of labor. That is, the husband works in the paid labor force and supports the family financially; the wife takes care of the household work and childcare. Each person provides essential services in exchange for those provided by the other. But research in this area indicates that the gender discrepancy in housework responsibilities does not diminish when women work full time outside the home. On average, working women spend about 19 hours per week on housework, while men spend only about 10 hours (Bianchi et al., 2006). The hours that women spend on housework are down from 35 hours in the mid 1960s, and men have increased their contribution from 4 hours per week, but still men contribute only half as much time as women do to the maintenance of the household. According to a survey conducted by the U.S. Bureau of Labor Statistics (2010a), employed women spend more than an hour a day more than employed men caring for children under the age of six. When they have older children, these women spend more than 6 hours a day on so-called "secondary care," like shopping with children in tow, while men spend only 4 hours a day on such activities.

Because working women continue to be primarily responsible for housework, they often end up working what amounts to two full-time jobs. Even when a husband is unemployed, he does less housework than a wife who puts in a 40-hour week. Indeed, recently laid-off men tend to take on fewer household tasks—rather than more—when they lose their jobs. In contrast, laid-off women double the time they spend on child-care and household chores (Dokoupil, 2009).

The dynamics of retirement, too, are a factor. Because wives, in general, are younger than their husbands, millions of women continue to work for pay after their husbands retire. These women sometimes come to resent retired husbands, who have lots of free time on their hands but who don't contribute much more around the house than they did while they were employed. One study of retirement-age men and women found that working women whose husbands are retired were the least happy with their marriages of all types of couples; working men whose wives stayed home were the happiest (cited in Leland, 2004).

Interestingly, couples who profess egalitarian, nonsexist values also experience discrepancies in the division of household labor (P. Blumstein & Schwartz, 1983). Husbands who say that all the housework should be shared still spend significantly less time doing it than their wives (Institute for Policy Research, 2002). The fact that house-work is still predominantly women's work gives us some sense of how pervasive and powerful our sexist ideology continues to be.

Gender Inequality in Education

Another institutional setting in which gender inequality persists is education. In elementary school and beyond, teachers are likely to treat their male and female students differently (Sadker, Sadker, Fox, & Salata, 2004):

- Girls receive less teacher attention and less useful feedback than boys.
- Girls talk significantly less in class than boys, and when they do speak up, they are more likely than boys to be reminded to raise their hands.
- Students rarely see mention of the contributions of women in their textbooks, which continue to emphasize male accomplishments.
- Girls are more likely than boys to be the focus of unwanted sexual attention in school.

Over the course of their school careers, such differential treatment takes its toll on girls. Since it is sometimes quite subtle, most people are unaware of the hidden sexist lessons and quiet losses it creates (Sadker & Sadker, 1999).

In elementary school and middle school, girls outperform boys on almost every standard measure of academic achievement (Tyre, 2006). Boys are more likely than girls to repeat a grade, drop out, be put in special education, or be diagnosed as hav-ing an emotional problem, a learning disability, or attention-deficit disorder (Lewin, 1998). Yet boys have higher expectations for themselves and higher self-esteem than girls, a gap that widens with each passing year in the school system. According to one study, around the ages of eight and nine, about two thirds of both boys and girls report feeling confident and positive about themselves. By high school, however, the percentage drops to 29% for young women (Freiberg, 1991). As girls make the tran-sition from childhood to adolescence, they are faced with a conflict between the way they see themselves and the way others, particularly teachers, see them (Gilligan, 1990).

These gender-typed patterns pervade high school. Teenage boys' sense of their own masculinity tends to be derived primarily from their achievements, such as participation in organized sports (Messner, 2002). Boys are also likely to be encouraged by counselors and teachers to formulate ambitious career goals. In contrast, prestige and popularity for teenage girls are still likely to come largely from their physical appearance and from having a boyfriend (Lott, 1987). Not surprisingly, by the end of high school, boys perform better than girls. For instance, although 54% of all SAT takers are girls, boys' average total score is higher (1523 for boys vs. 1498 for girls; National Center for Fair and Open Testing, 2011).

Gender differences in academic performance are usually a cultural by-product as opposed to some innate intellectual difference. Take, for instance, the common belief that boys are naturally better at science and mathematics than girls. Cross-cultural evidence shows that many Asian and Eastern European countries consistently produce girls with strong mathematical abilities, while other countries (chiefly the United States) do not (Andreescu, Gallian, Kane, & Mertz, 2008). In fact, girls in developing countries are far more likely than girls in industrialized countries to indicate that they like math and science and would like to work in those fields (M. Charles, 2011). In the United States, girls who excel in national and international mathematical competitions are likely to be the daughters of immigrants. Researchers locate the reason for this discrepancy in a culture that doesn't value, actively discourages, or even socially penalizes mathematical excellence in girls.

Gender inequality is evident in postsecondary education, too. Since 1980, more U.S. women than men have enrolled in college (U.S. Bureau of the Census, 2011b). And women earn 59% of all associate's, bachelor's, and advanced college degrees. Moreover, college women study more and have higher grade point averages than men. They're also more likely to complete their bachelor's degrees in four or five years (cited in Lewin, 2006). However, men are more likely to take rigorous courses geared for math and science majors and achieve higher grades in those courses than women (The College Board, 1998). Many of the majors that lead to high-paying or high-prestige careers remain dominated by men (engineering, economics, mathematics, earth sciences, etc.), whereas women are concentrated in fields such as nursing, education, and social services (Dey & Hill, 2007). Here too, however, we see cross-cultural differences. In countries that we typically view as repressive when it comes to women's rights—such as Iran, Saudi Arabia, and Malaysia—women earn the majority of science degrees (M. Charles, 2011).

To overcome the cumulative impact of this differential treatment in this country, some educational reformers have advocated sex-segregated private schools as well as single-sex classrooms in coeducational public schools. They argue that girls who go to single-sex schools are more assertive, more confident, and more likely to take classes in math, computer science, and physics than girls in coeducational schools. They also have higher career aspirations than girls who attend coeducational schools (C. M. Watson, Quatman, & Edler, 2002). Boys in single-sex environments are less likely to get into trouble and more likely to pursue interests in art, music, and drama than their counterparts in coeducational schools (National Association for Single Sex Public Education, 2011).

Across the country, the number of single-sex public schools increased from three in 1995 to more than 240 in 2006 (Schemo, 2006a), and more than 500 public coeducational schools offer single-sex classes in subjects like math and science (National Association for Single-Sex Public Education, 2011). Some private schools now offer a combination of mixed-sex and single-sex education, with boys and girls learning together in elementary school and high school but being taught separately during the turbulent middle school years. As one prominent educator put it, "Girls who are 'confident at 11 and confused at 16' will more likely be creative thinkers and risk-takers as adults if educated apart from boys in middle school" (quoted in J. Gross, 2004b, p. A16).

Trends in college enrollments and innovation in educational policy give us reason to believe that in the future, sex and gender might become less significant factors in determining people's educational tracks.

Gender Inequality in the Economy

Because of their difficulty converting educational achievements into high pay, women have historically been prevented from taking advantage of the occupational opportunities and rewards to which most men have had relatively free access. Today, women continue to have much less earning power in the labor market than men (P. N. Cohen & Huffman, 2003).

The unequal economic status of women not only results from the personal sexism of potential employers but is tied to larger economic structures and institutional forces. The standard assumptions that drive the typical workplace often work against women, both at work and at home. For instance, during the current economic recession, many mortgage lenders have become skittish about approving home loans for expectant parents. They fear that these couples will inevitably experience a temporary drop in income if the mother goes on temporary maternity leave—or perhaps a permanent loss of income if she decides to leave the workforce entirely—and therefore will be unable to make their mortgage payments (T. S. Bernard, 2010).

More generally, think of the things one generally has to do to be considered a good worker by a boss: work extra hours, travel to faraway business meetings, go to professional conferences, attend training programs, be willing to work unpopular shifts, or entertain out-of-town clients. These activities assume that employees have the time and the freedom from familial obligations to do them. Because women, especially mothers, still tend to have the lion's share of responsibility at home, they are less able than their male colleagues to "prove" to management that they are good, committed employees. Even if women are able to commit extra time to work, employers frequently assume that, because they are women, they won't.

Such assumptions are even present in professional, academic environments. In its assessment of the underrepresentation of women in science and engineering positions, the National Academy of Sciences (2007) concluded that the traditional scientific or engineering career rests on the assumption that the faculty member will be thoroughly committed to his or her occupation throughout his or her working life. It found that attention to other obligations, such as family, is often interpreted as a lack of dedication to one's career. Because the burden of family and household care still generally falls more heavily on women than on men—and because women seldom have substantial spousal support—women scientists and engineers experience greater conflict between their family and professional roles than male scientists and engineers do.

It's not surprising, therefore, that women in these fields experience widespread bias. It's not just that there are relatively few of them, both in academic positions and in leadership positions in professional organizations. They also typically receive fewer resources and less institutional support than their male colleagues (National Academy of Sciences, 2007).

Segregation in the Workplace

U.S. women have made remarkable progress in overcoming traditional obstacles to employment. In 1950, a little over 30% of adult women were employed in the paid labor force; today, that figure is almost 60%, and it increases to 69.8% for married mothers, 72% for single mothers, and 79.2% for widowed, separated, and divorced mothers (U.S. Bureau of the Census, 2011b). Over half of all U.S. workers today are female.

The increase in female labor force participation has been particularly dramatic in some traditionally male-dominated fields such as medicine and law. For instance, in 1983, 15% of lawyers and 16% of physicians in the United States were women; by 2009, those figures had doubled (U.S. Bureau of the Census, 2004, 2011b).

Although such a trend is encouraging, sex segregation in the workplace is still the rule. Women constitute 96.8% of all secretaries, 92% of all registered nurses, 95% of all childcare workers, 96.6% of all dental hygienists, and 97.8% of all preschool and kindergarten teachers (U.S. Bureau of the Census, 2011b). Despite their increased presence in traditionally male occupations, women still tend to be underrepresented among dentists (30.2%), physicians (32.2%), engineers and architects (13.8%), lawyers (32.4%), police officers (15.5%), and firefighters (3.4%).

Most of the changes that have taken place in the sex distribution of different occupations have been the result of women entering male lines of work, not vice versa. Although women have entered traditionally male occupations at a steady clip since the 1980s, men have not noticeably increased their representation in female-dominated occupations. The number of male nurses, kindergarten teachers, and secretaries has increased only minimally, if at all (see Exhibit 12.3). One study found that some men would rather suffer unemployment than accept "women's jobs," even high-paying ones, because of the potential damage to their sense of masculinity (Epstein, 1989).

This kind of "one-way" occupational shift may cause problems in the long run. Historically, when large numbers of women enter a particular occupation previously closed to them, the number of men in that occupation decreases. Given that greater value is usually awarded to male pursuits, such occupations become less prestigious as men leave them. In fact, the higher the proportion of female workers in an occupation, the less both male and female workers earn in that occupation (Padavic & Reskin, 2002).

Greater female entry into traditionally male lines of work doesn't necessarily mean sexual equality either. For instance, women now make up over half of students in divinity schools but account for only 3% of pastors who lead large congregations—defined as more than 350 attendees at Sunday services—in mainline Protestant churches (N. Banerjee, 2006). Often, sex segregation occurs in jobs *within* a profession. In the field of medicine, for example, female physicians are substantially overrepresented in specialties such as family practice, pediatrics, and obstetrics and gynecology and underrepresented in more prestigious and lucrative areas such as surgery. Seventy-three percent of pediatric residents and 77% of obstetrics/gynecology residents today are women; but only 30% of surgical residents are women (Women Physicians

Exhibit 12.3   Employment Trends in "Male" and "Female" Occupations,1983–2009

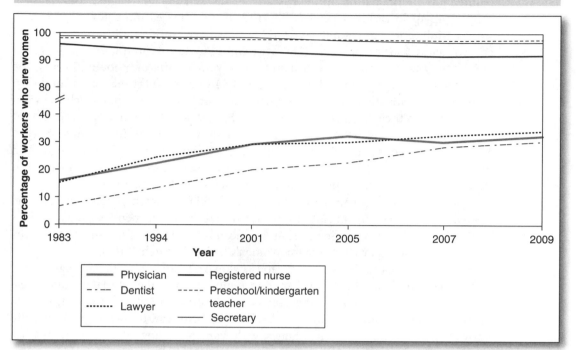

SOURCES: U.S. Bureau of Labor Statistics, 2008, Table 11; U.S. Bureau of the Census, 1995, Table 649; 2002, Table 588; 2011b, Table 615

Congress, 2008). Among lawyers, women are promoted at a lower rate than their male counterparts, and they remain underrepresented in private practice, in law firm partnerships, and in high positions such as judges on the federal courts, district courts, and circuit courts of appeals (Hull & Nelson, 2000).

In sum, although more women than ever work in the paid labor force, we continue to have some jobs that employ almost exclusively women and others that employ almost exclusively men. When people are allocated jobs on the basis of sex rather than ability to perform the work, chances for self-fulfillment are limited (Reskin & Hartmann, 1986). Society also loses, because neither men nor women are free to do the jobs for which they might best be suited. However, segregation is most harmful to individual women, because the occupations they predominantly hold tend to be less prestigious and to pay lower wages than those held predominantly by men.

The Wage Gap

> The Lord spoke to Moses and said, "When a man makes a special vow to the Lord which requires your valuation of living persons, a male between twenty and sixty years old shall be valued at fifty silver shekels. If it is a female, she shall be valued at thirty shekels." (Leviticus 27:1–4)

You don't have to go back to biblical times to find evidence of the practice of setting women's pay at less than men's. Even though the 1963 Equal Pay Act guaranteed equal pay for equal work in the United States, and Title VII of the 1964 Civil Rights Act banned job discrimination on the basis of sex (as well as race, religion, and national origin), a gap in earnings persists. In 2010, the average earnings for all U.S. men working full time, year round was $47,715. All women working full time, year round earned about $36,931 per year (DeNavas-Walt, Proctor, & Smith, 2011). To put it another way, for every dollar a U.S. man earns, a woman earns only about 77 cents. The gap widens with age. Women between 25 and 34 working full time, year round earn about 87% of what their male counterparts do. But by the time they reach the years leading up to retirement (between the ages of 55 and 64), they earn only 73% of what men earn. That means that over a 40-year career, the average working woman will earn $431,000 less than the average working man (Boushey, Arons, & Smith, 2010). And because women earn less when they're employed, their retirement pensions are also significantly smaller than men's (National Women's Law Center, 2006).

Moreover, the wage gap is especially pronounced for women of color. In 2010, the annual earnings for African American women were 69.6% of men's earnings. Latinas earned 59.8% of men's earnings. Asian American women were more successful, earning 90.9% of men's pay (Institute for Women's Policy Research, 2011).

I should point out that the wage gap is a global phenomenon. To varying degrees, in every country around the world, men earn more than women. In Japan and Korea, women earn 30% to 40% less than men earn. In other countries, however, such as Belgium, Greece, Hungary, Italy, New Zealand, and Norway, the wage gap is actually narrower than it is in the United States, with women earning 90% or more of what men earn (Organization for Economic Cooperation and Development, 2011).

Why is the wage gap so persistent? One reason, of course, is occupational segregation and the types of jobs women are most likely to have. For five of the "most female" jobs in the United States (i.e., those that are around 95% female)—namely, preschool teacher, teacher's assistant, secretary, childcare worker, and dental assistant—the overall average weekly salary is $549. For five of the "most male" jobs (those around 95% male)—namely, airplane pilot, firefighter, aircraft engine mechanic, plumber, and steel worker—the overall average weekly salary is $990 (U.S. Bureau of Labor Statistics, 2010c). However, even in the same occupations, men's and women's earnings diverge (see Exhibit 12.4).

Some economists and policymakers argue that the wage gap is essentially an institutional by-product that exists because men on the whole work more hours per year, are more likely to work a full-time schedule than women, and have more work experience and training (Dey & Hill, 2007). Now, you will recall from Chapter 10 that due to the current economic recession, large numbers of both men and women have been forced to work part time because their employers have cut back. But women are particularly susceptible to this trend. According to the U.S. Bureau of Labor Statistics (2010e), 14% of employed men work part time, compared with 27.8% of employed women. Not only do part-time workers earn less, but during hard times, they are usually the first ones pushed out of employment—not because they're women but because their jobs are the most expendable.

However, even after controlling for differences in experience, age, and education—factors that might justify discrepancies in salary—the wage gap between men and women remains (Weinberg, 2007). For instance, the average income of female workers in the United States is significantly lower than that of men with the same level of

Exhibit 12.4   Male and Female Earnings in "Male" and "Female" Occupations

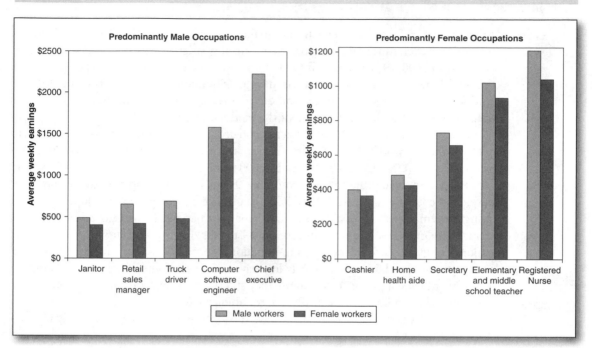

SOURCE: Institute for Women's Policy Research, 2011, Table 1. Figure reproduced with permission from the Institute for Women's Policy Research, originally published in "The Gender Wage Gap by Occupation (April 2011)" by Ariane Hegewisch, Claudia Williams, and Amber Henderson.

educational attainment. Men with bachelor's degrees earn, on average, 65% more than women with bachelor's degrees. In fact, women with bachelor's degrees can expect to earn only around $4,400 a year more than men who attended college but never earned a degree (mean annual earnings of $44,078 compared with $39,635). Similarly, women with doctoral degrees (with mean annual earnings of $70,898) earn *less* than men with bachelor's degrees (with mean annual earnings of $72,868; U.S. Bureau of the Census, 2011b).

One possible remedy for the wage gap is to increase women's access to occupations that have traditionally been closed to them. As I noted earlier, this is already happening, to a certain degree, although sex segregation is still the rule.

Another solution is ***pay equity***. The principle behind this remedy is that the pay for particular jobs shouldn't be low simply because those jobs happen to be filled predominantly by women. Different jobs that are of equal value to society and require equal levels of training ought to have equal pay. In 2007, a bill was introduced in the U.S. Senate called "The Fair Pay Act." It sought to end wage discrimination against those who work in female-dominated jobs by establishing equal pay guidelines for equivalent work. For example, within an individual company, employers could not pay less for jobs held predominately by women than for jobs held predominately by men if those jobs were similarly important to the employer (National Committee on Pay Equity, 2007). However, the bill was defeated. In 2009, President Obama signed into law a stripped-down version of the bill, which makes it easier for women to file equal-pay lawsuits.

The Global Devaluation of Women

At first glance, women seem to be making tremendous advances worldwide—becoming better educated and more economically independent than ever before. For instance, in 1990, 79 girls were enrolled in secondary schools for every 100 boys around the world; by 2010, that figure had risen to 97 (Population Reference Bureau, 2011b). And over the past several decades, women in most regions of the world have increased their representation in most sectors of the paid labor force.

Nevertheless, women remain physically and economically disadvantaged in most societies around the world. In sub-Saharan Africa, women make up close to 60% of all HIV-infected adults (UNAIDS, 2008). About 536,000 women around the world die each year in pregnancy and childbirth, but an astounding 99.5% of these deaths occur in poor, less developed countries (UNICEF, 2009). The chances of a woman in a developed country dying from maternal causes are one in 3,600; for a woman in a less developed country, the chances are one in 90 (Population Reference Bureau, 2011b). Women make up the vast majority of global factory workers in multinational corporations, often working in unsafe and unhealthy conditions at extremely low pay. And while women have made significant strides worldwide in access to education, they still lag far behind men in top political and decision making roles (Hausmann, Tyson, & Zahidi, 2008).

In many countries, women do not have the same legal, familial, and bodily protections that men enjoy:

- The Iranian constitution states that the value of a woman's life is half that of a man's. An Iranian woman cannot travel anywhere without her husband's permission (I. Watson, 2005).
- In Kenya, when a woman's husband dies, she loses her land, her livestock, and all her household property. In addition, a widow is transferred to a male relative of her deceased husband, who takes control of the property (Lacey, 2003).
- In Kyrgyzstan, it's estimated that more than half of all married women were abducted by their soon-to-be husbands in a centuries-old legal custom known as *ala kachuu* (which literally means "grab and run"). If the woman is kept in the man's home overnight, her virginity becomes suspect, her name disgraced, and her future marriage chances destroyed. So most women (about 80%, according to estimates) eventually relent and marry their abductor, often at the urging of their own families (C. S. Smith, 2005).
- In Sri Lanka, an estimated 600,000 women have been forced by economic need to leave their own families and migrate to affluent Persian Gulf countries, where they work as maids for wealthy families. Saudi Arabians refer to Sri Lanka as "the country of housemaids" (Waldman, 2005). These women are considered heroines at home because of their economic contributions to their families, but they are often subjected to severe beatings and mistreatment at the hands of their foreign employers.
- In Syria, girls who bring dishonor to their families by having premarital sex are sometimes killed by relatives. Under Syrian law, these killings, called *ghasalat al arr* ("washing away the shame"), are not considered murder. If the killer is convicted of the lesser charge of "crime of honor" and sentenced to prison, he is typically released within months (Zoepf, 2007).
- In 2009, almost 90,000 Indian women were tortured by their husbands or relatives, and 8,383—an average of 23 a day—were killed by their husbands for not providing adequate dowries (National Crime Records Bureau, 2009). Even though India officially banned dowry (gifts that a woman receives from her parents on marriage) in 1961, it is still an essential part of premarital negotiations and now encompasses the wealth that the bride's family pays the groom. Young brides, who by custom live with their new husbands' parents, are commonly subjected to severe abuse if the promised money is not paid. Sometimes dowry harassment ends in suicide or murder.

The globalization of the world economy also helps create a market for the international exploitation of women. In many poor countries, one of the fastest-growing criminal enterprises is forcing naive and desperately poor women to work as prostitutes in other countries. In some of these countries, prostitution is legal; in others it may be illegal, but enforcement is inconsistent and punishment light. Without any other means of support and often without knowledge of the native language, these women become completely dependent on men who are perfectly willing to exploit them.

However, the public devaluation of women can sometimes hide a very different private reality. For instance, Japanese women have historically occupied a visibly subservient position in society and in families. Wives are still legally prohibited from using different surnames from their husbands. Women in the workforce suffer discrimination in hiring, salary, and promotion despite the presence of equal-opportunity laws there. Only 40% of women currently work outside the home, even though many economists argue that their inclusion could help boost an economy that has been slumping for decades (French, 2003). They are expected to clean, cook, and tend to the needs of their husbands within the home.

Yet many Japanese wives dominate their husbands. Typically, they control the household finances, giving their husbands monthly allowances as they see fit. If a man wants to withdraw money from the family account, the savings bank will usually phone the wife to get her approval. Japanese men are even starting to take on some of the housework responsibilities, which would have been unthinkable a couple of decades ago.

Women are making significant strides in other parts of the world where they have traditionally suffered. In places like Uganda, Burundi, and Tunisia, women now account for around 30% of elected officials. For women in Rwanda, the figure is 56%—the highest in the world—up from just 17% in 2000 (Population Reference Bureau, 2011b). Women in Iran, Afghanistan, Somalia, and Liberia are at the forefront of local and national reform movements (Foroohar, 2010). In Algeria, women now make up 60% of university students, 70% of lawyers, and 60% of judges. They also contribute more to household income than men (Slackman, 2007).

To some extent, the improvement of women's lives in some parts of the world can be attributed to global forces for change, which sometimes spread democratic values and humanitarian principles (Giddens, 2005). In 1979, the United Nations General Assembly adopted a treaty known as the Convention on the Elimination of All Forms of Discrimination Against Women (Division for the Advancement of Women, 2009). By accepting the treaty, countries agreed to take measures to end discrimination against women in all forms by

- incorporating the principle of equality of men and women into their legal systems, abolishing all discriminatory laws, and adopting appropriate ones prohibiting discrimination against women;
- establishing tribunals and other public institutions to ensure the effective protection of women against discrimination; and
- ensuring elimination of all acts of discrimination against women by persons, organizations, or enterprises.

All but eight of the 192 member countries of the United Nations have ratified this agreement, which legally binds them to put its provisions into practice (Crary, 2009). The only holdouts are Sudan, Somalia, Qatar, Iran, Nauru, Palau, Tonga . . . and the United States.

Conclusion

Inequality based on sex and gender goes beyond the degrading media and cultural images of women, the face-to-face interactions that reinforce the devaluation of women, and the stereotypical beliefs of individual people. It is woven into the institutional and cultural fabric of societies around the world. In the United States, it is as much a part of the social landscape as baseball, apple pie, and Fourth of July fireworks. Every woman has felt sexism at some level, whether as personal violence, annoying harassment, sexually suggestive leers and comments, fear of going out at night, job discrimination, legal obstacles, or subtle encouragement toward "appropriate" pursuits—whether they be sports, hobbies, or careers.

Men tend to benefit from living in a society where language, identity, intimacy, history, culture, and social institutions are built on gender distinctions, even if the men themselves do not support such inequality. Like most people whose interests are being served by the system, men are largely unaware of the small and large advantages the social structure provides them (W. J. Goode, 1981). Thus, most men don't see sex and gender inequality as their problem—it's a "women's issue"—and they are less likely than women to see a need for large-scale social change.

So the first step toward gender equality is that men will have to come to understand their role in the process, even in the absence of blatant, personal sexism. All men are tacitly involved in the oppression of women each time they automatically giggle at sexist jokes, mistake female doctors for nurses, see women in purely physical terms, expect less from women on the job or in school, or expect more of them at home.

The next step will require a fundamental transformation of institutional patterns and cultural values. Such a solution sounds too massive to be possible. But today, we are seeing early steps in that direction: changing conceptions of family roles, women's increasing (though not yet equal) participation in the labor force, their growing (but not yet equal) political power, and greater awareness of sexual exploitation and violence worldwide. How far these changes will take us in the future remains to be seen.

YOUR TURN

To understand how beliefs are translated into action, examine how sexism influences people's activities. One fruitful area of examination is the home. Locate a few of each of the following types of couples in which both partners work full time outside the home:

- Newly married without children (married less than one year)
- Married without children (married 10 years or more)
- Married (older or younger) with at least one child living at home
- Nonmarital cohabiting (heterosexual or homosexual)
- Remarried

Ask each person in the couple to make a list of all the household chores that need to be done during the course of a week. Ask each to be as specific and exhaustive as possible (e.g., "cleaning windows" rather than "cleaning the house"). After the lists are completed, ask each person to indicate which of these tasks she or he is primarily responsible for, which her or his partner is responsible for, and which are shared. Ask the participants also to estimate the total amount of time spent each week on all these tasks combined. Finally, ask them to estimate how many hours they work at their jobs during a typical week. (*Note:* To ensure that you're gauging each individual's perceptions, interview each partner separately.) Compare people's responses to see if you can find any differences—in terms of time spent doing housework and the number of tasks for which each one is responsible—between

- partners in the same couple,
- men and women,
- younger and older couples,
- married and cohabiting couples,
- couples with and without children at home,
- married and remarried couples, and
- heterosexual and homosexual couples.

Do women who work outside the home still bear the primary responsibility for housework? Is the traditional gender division of labor absent in certain types of couples? How does the presence of children affect the household division of labor? If partners have different ideas about housework responsibilities, to what do you attribute this lack of agreement? Describe the tensions that men and women experience when trying to balance work and home responsibilities.

CHAPTER HIGHLIGHTS

- Personal sexism is most apparent during the course of everyday interaction in the form of communication patterns and gestures. It can be particularly dangerous when expressed in the form of sexual harassment and sexual violence.

- Gender stratification is perpetuated by a dominant cultural ideology that devalues women on the basis of alleged biological differences between men and women. This ideology overlooks the equally important role of social forces in determining male and female behavior.

- Institutional sexism exists in the media, in the law, in the family, in the educational system, and in the economy. Women have entered the paid labor force in unprecedented numbers, but they still tend to occupy jobs that are typically considered "female" and still earn significantly less than men.

- Not only are social institutions sexist in that women are systematically segregated, exploited, and excluded; they are also "gendered." Institutions themselves are structured along gender lines so that traits associated with success are usually stereotypically male characteristics: tough-mindedness, rationality, assertiveness, competitiveness, and so forth.

- Despite recent advances worldwide, women still tend to suffer physically, psychologically, economically, and politically in most societies.

KEY TERMS

institutional sexism: Subordination of women that is part of the everyday workings of economics, law, politics, and other social institutions

matriarchy: Female-dominated society that gives higher prestige and value to women than to men

objectification: Practice of treating people as objects

patriarchy: Male-dominated society in which cultural beliefs and values give higher prestige and value to men than to women

pay equity: Principle that women and men who perform jobs that are of equal value to society and that require equal training ought to be paid equally

sexism: System of beliefs that asserts the inferiority of one sex and justifies gender-based inequality

STUDENT STUDY SITE

Visit the Student Study Site at **www.sagepub.com/newman9e** for these additional learning tools:

- Flashcards
- Web quizzes
- Sociologists at Work features
- Micro-Macro Connection features
- Video links
- Audio links
- Web resources
- SAGE journal articles

Demographic Dynamics

13

Population Trends

The Influence of Birth Cohorts

Demographic Dynamics

Population Trends in the United States

I admit it. I said those seven words I once vowed I'd never say. The ones that permanently tag you as an over-the-hill relic: "I just don't understand you kids today!"

It all started several years ago when I was arguing with my two sons—one 16 at the time, the other 13—over what to watch on television. They wanted to watch the X Games on ESPN; I wanted to watch a rerun of the sixth game of the 1975 World Series on ESPN Classic. I told them that my choice was a priceless piece of U.S. sports history; the best World Series game ever played. Besides, I still don't understand the allure of the X Games. I know it's an annual alternative sports festival based on recreational activities such as skateboarding, Moto X, freestyle BMX, snowboarding, freestyle snowmobiling, and so on. But I don't care to know the difference between an "acid drop" and a "backside disaster." To me, "grinding" is what you do with coffee beans in the morning and "getting clean air" means moving out of Los Angeles.

They told me that I was a dinosaur and that I had better wake up and smell the 21st century. The X Games, they claimed, was the future. And you know what? They turned out to be right. "Extreme" sports, as they have come to be called, have become part of a broader youth subculture with its own hard-edged language, fashion, and music. In fact, the word *extreme* has become a modifying adjective for any activity that pushes beyond what's commonly accepted: extreme camping, extreme bartending, extreme paintball, extreme pumpkin carving, extreme chess, extreme tanning, and even extreme childbirth.

It would seem that the trend in society today is to eliminate risk for young people. For instance, some cities are installing "managed playgrounds"—public areas where adult "play workers" supervise children's play and guide all their activities (Carey, 2007). An elementary school in Newark, New Jersey, employs a $14-an-hour "recess coach" to ensure that children aren't left to their own devices (Hu, 2010). Other communities have removed swings and monkey bars from parks to avoid liability in the event of an injury. Extreme sports are self-consciously designed to be the opposite: thrilling, dangerous, subversive, and rebellious. Their appeal lies not so much in grace, strategy, or face-to-face competition as in the chance of disaster striking. "The fact that they're called 'extreme' sports means, if you make a mistake, you die," said one admirer (quoted in Clemmitt, 2009, p. 301).

For the most part, extreme athletes bear little resemblance to athletes in more traditional sports. They tend to despise rules, regulations, and standard conceptions of the competitive spirit. Indeed, many extreme sports don't have objective measures of success—like finishing first in a race or scoring more points than an opponent—but are instead judged on their degree of risk and danger.

The allure has been powerful. One survey found that more teens and preteens prefer watching extreme sports on television than watching college basketball, college football, auto racing, hockey, tennis, or golf (G. Bennett, Henson, & Zhang, 2003). Indeed, the number of Americans who ride skateboards tripled between 1995 and 2005; during that same period, the number of baseball players dropped by 7%. There are now more skateboarders in this country than football players. Worldwide, there are more than 18.5 million snowboarders, ranging in age from 5 to 75 (Clemmitt, 2009). Tens of millions of people now regularly participate in other extreme sports such as wall climbing, mountain biking, and wakeboarding ("Extreme Facts," 2005).

Ironically, although extreme sports appear to be solidly antiestablishment, they have clearly become a marketing gold mine, generating tens of billions of dollars a year (Longman & Higgins, 2005). Corporate America has been scrambling to co-opt the language, image, and culture of extreme athletes in order to tap into a booming market. Extreme sports have also achieved a significant degree of societal acceptance. Events like freestyle skiing, snowboarding, and BMX racing are now in the Olympics. Nevertheless, many older people still fail to understand the appeal of these sports.

What my sons didn't realize was that they had identified one of the most crucial dividing lines in society today. They and I may be members of the same family. We may share the same genes, ethnicity, social class, and political views. But we're also members of two extremely different, sometimes antagonistic, social groups that are distinguished by one simple and unchangeable fact: our ages.

In the past several chapters, I examined various interconnected sources of social stratification: class, race and ethnicity, and sex and gender. You have seen that the distance between the haves and the have-nots—both locally and globally—continues to grow wider as a result of their different levels of access to important cultural, economic, and political resources. But within the United States, as well as most other societies, imbalances between various age groups will also be a defining feature of social life in the decades to come. This chapter examines the relationship between broad population trends—which include not only a changing age structure but also population growth and immigration—and everyday life. How are these changes affecting the ability to provide people with the resources they need for a comfortable life? How are important social institutions functioning as a result of these population shifts?

The Influence of Birth Cohorts

If you're like most college students, you've no doubt asked yourself questions like these: Will I get a job after I graduate? Where will I live? Will I be able to afford a house? Will I have a spouse or lifetime partner? Will I ever be a parent? How will I save for my retirement? The answers to these questions are obviously influenced by your personal desires, traits, values, ambitions, and abilities. And as you've already read in this book so far, your social class, gender, race, religion, and ethnicity will shape the answers too.

But they will also be influenced by your place in the population at a given point in time. **Birth cohorts** are sets of people who were born during the same time period and who face similar societal circumstances brought about by their position in the age

structure of the population. Birth cohorts affect people's everyday lives in two fundamental ways (Riley, 1971):

- People born within a few years of one another tend to experience life course events or social rites of passage—such as puberty, marriage, childbearing, graduation, entrance into the workforce, and death—at roughly the same time. Sociologists call these experiences *cohort effects*. The size of your birth cohort, relative to other cohorts, can have a significant impact on your life experiences: It can determine things like the availability of affordable housing, high-paying jobs, and attractive potential mates and can also affect how satisfied you feel with your own life. One study found that large cohorts in developed countries tend to have higher rates of suicide than small cohorts because people face more economic disadvantage and have more difficulty integrating into their communities when there are large numbers of people in the same age range competing for limited resources (Stockard & O'Brien, 2002).
- Members of the same birth cohort also share a common history. A cohort's place in time tells us a lot about the opportunities and constraints placed on its members. Unexpected historical events (wars, epidemics, natural disasters, economic depressions, etc.), changing political conditions, and major cultural trends, called *period effects*, contribute to the unique shape and outlook of each birth cohort. Many historians, for instance, believe that a period of drought and famine caused the people of the Mayan civilization to abandon their great cities nearly a thousand years ago. Those who were young when this period began enjoyed comfortable lives, reveled in the high culture of the Mayans, and had tremendous prospects for the future. But for their children, born just a generation later, starvation, death, and social dislocation were the basic facts of life (Clausen, 1986).

Cohort and period effects combine to give each birth cohort its distinctive properties, such as ethnic composition, average life expectancies, and age-specific birthrates. For instance, women who experienced the Great Depression during their peak childbearing years—their 20s and early 30s—had the lowest birthrate of women in any cohort during the 20th century. Therefore, women born between 1900 and 1910 tended as a group to have smaller families to rely on in their old age, which for them occurred roughly between 1970 and 1980. These experiences contrast sharply with those of women born a mere 10 years later, who were too young to have children during the Great Depression but entered adulthood during the prosperous years after World War II. They tended to have large families and therefore more sources of support in their old age (Soldo & Agree, 1988).

Cohort and period effects also influence your worldview and self-concept. Think how different your goals and ambitions would be had you experienced childhood during a time of economic uncertainty as opposed to a period of relative affluence, such as the late 1990s. Rights and privileges considered unattainable dreams by one cohort are likely to be taken for granted by a different one.

As we grow older, we develop and change in a society that itself is developing and changing. We start our lives in one historical period with a distinct set of social norms, and we end our lives in another. Early in the 20th century, for example, most people went to school for only six or seven years, which yielded an adequate education for the types of jobs their parents and older siblings held. Today, 85% of U.S. residents go to school for at least 12 years (U.S. Bureau of the Census, 2011b). As a result, older cohorts on the whole tend to score substantially lower on standardized intelligence tests than younger cohorts. Because of such test results, social scientists long assumed that intelligence declines markedly with age. But we now know that these differences are the result not of aging but of changing societal values regarding education (Clausen, 1986).

Even the way people personally experience the aging process is affected by the social, cultural, and environmental changes to which their cohort is exposed in moving through the life course. Because of advances in nutrition, education, sanitation, medical treatment, working conditions, transportation safety, and environmental quality, younger cohorts can expect to live longer and healthier than older cohorts.

As you can see, birth cohorts are more than just a collection of individuals born around the same time; they are distinctive generations tied together by historical circumstances, population trends, and societal changes. However, we must also realize that when many individuals in the same cohort are affected by social events in similar ways, the changes in their collective lives can produce changes in society. Each succeeding cohort leaves its mark on the prevailing culture. In other words, cohorts are not only affected by social changes but contribute to them as well (Riley, Foner, & Waring, 1988).

Baby Boomers

The birth cohort that has received the most national attention is, without a doubt, the Baby Boom generation, the 79 million or so people born between 1946 and 1964. They make up close to 26% of the entire U.S. population (U.S. Bureau of the Census, 2011b).

The passing of this massive cohort through the life course has been described metaphorically as "a pig in a python." If you've ever seen one of those nature shows on TV where snakes devour and digest small rodents, you know how apt the metaphor is. In 1980, the largest age group in the United States consisted of people between 15 and 24 years of age. In 1990, the largest group was 25- to 34-year-olds. In 2010, it was people between 45 and 54 (U.S. Bureau of the Census, 2011b). As this cohort bulge works its way through the life course, it stretches the parameters of the relevant social institutions at each stage. Baby Boomers packed hospital nurseries as infants, school classrooms as children, and college campuses, employment lines, and the housing market as young adults (Light, 1988). In middle age, they are prime movers in the burgeoning markets for adventure travel, diet, nutrition, and wellness products as well as relaxed-fit fashion, high-tech gadgets, and financial services. Advertisers for companies like Kellogg's cereal, Skechers shoes, and 5-Hour Energy drinks have already begun to shift their marketing focus from young people to those over 55 (B. Carter & Vega, 2011).

The trend will continue into the future. By the year 2030, there will be more than 72 million Baby Boomers of retirement age, about twice the number of retirees today (U.S. Bureau of the Census, 2011b). As they reach their golden years, programs concerned with later life—pension plans, Social Security, medical and personal care—will be seriously stretched. For instance, the number of older Americans covered by Medicare will increase by 30 million over the next two decades (Greenblatt, 2011). And sometime in the middle of the 21st century, there will likely be a surge in business for the funeral industry as this generation reaches the end of its collective life cycle (Schodolski, 1993).

Baby Boomers have so dominated the cultural landscape that they have evoked a fair amount of resentment from younger generations. As one syndicated columnist put it,

> We grew up in the shadow of the baby boomers, who still manage, in their [old age], to commandeer disproportionate attention. Every time they hit a life cycle milestone it's worth 10 magazine covers. When they retire, the Social Security system will go under! When they die, narcissism will be so much lonelier. (A. O. Scott, 2010, p. 4)

Baby Boomers have left an especially influential mark on the institution of family. Their generation was the first to redefine families to include a variety of living arrangements, such as cohabitation, domestic partnerships, and never-married women with dependent children (Wattenberg, 1986). They were also the first to acknowledge the expectation of paid work as a central feature of women's lives. And they were the first to grow up with effective birth control, enabling delayed childbearing, voluntary childlessness, and low birthrates.

Consequently, as the Baby Boomers reach old age, they will have fewer children to turn to for the kind of help they gave their own grandparents and parents (Butler, 1989). Hence, they will be more likely than previous generations to turn to social service and health care organizations to care for them. Not surprisingly, most Baby Boomers are quite pessimistic about their ability to sustain their quality of life (Pew Research Center, 2010b).

Generation X

Although Baby Boomers have dominated the cultural spotlight for decades, U.S. society has also taken notice of the generation to follow them, known in the media as "Generation X." Today, there are more than 61 million U.S. residents who were born between 1965 and 1979 (U.S. Bureau of the Census, 2011b). The birthrate during the 1970s, when most of these individuals were born, was about half what it was during the post–World War II years of the Baby Boom.

More Generation Xers—roughly 40% of them—experienced the divorce of their parents than any previous generation. As a result, they are emotionally conflicted about marriage. They are less likely to get married than older generations and more likely to delay marriage and childbearing if they do (Carlson, 2009). In addition, they're more likely to be single—with or without children—than previous generations (Sayer, Casper, & Cohen, 2004).

Even more Generation Xers grew up as so-called latchkey children, the first generation of children to experience the effects of having two working parents. For many of these children, childhood was marked by dependence on secondary relationships—teachers, friends, babysitters, and day care workers.

The Millennium Generation

The 85 million or so individuals born between 1980 and the late 1990s make up the next noticeable cohort, known as the Millennium Generation. This cohort is comparable to the Baby Boom in size but differs in almost every other way. For one thing, unlike the Baby Boomers, Millennials are not evenly distributed across the nation. States that have large minority and immigrant populations (e.g., California, Florida, and Texas) account for a relatively high proportion of the Millennium Generation (Faust, Gann, & McKibben, 1999). Consequently, its members are more ethnically diverse than previous cohorts; one in three is not white (Mather, 2007). They are also more likely than preceding cohorts to grow up in a nontraditional family. One in four lives in a single-parent household; three in four have working mothers. In addition, compared with older cohorts, they are less religious, less likely to serve in the military, and on track to become the most educated cohort in American history. Although entry into their careers has been set back by the recession, they are

Exhibit 13.1   Use of Technology Across Generations

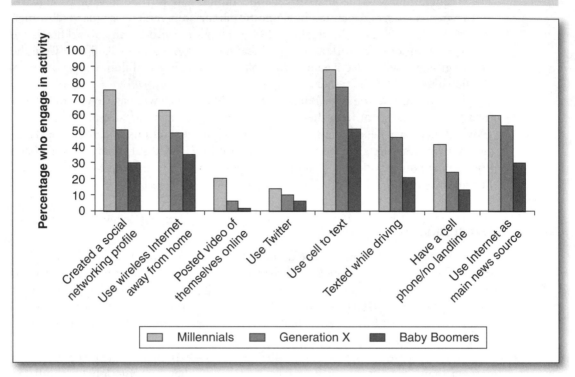

SOURCE: Pew Research Center, 2010b, pp. 25, 35

significantly more upbeat about their futures than their elders (Pew Research Center, 2010b).

The Millennium Generation is the most media connected of any cohort. According to a Kaiser Family Foundation report (Rideout, Roberts, & Foehr, 2005), children between the ages of 8 and 18 spend more than eight hours a day with some kind of communication or entertainment medium: watching TV, listening to CDs or MP3 players, playing video games, sending e-mails, and talking or texting on cell phones. In addition, they are the first generation to see computer technology as a birthright (see Exhibit 13.1).

Although this preoccupation with computers and other forms of technology may create a generation less interpersonally adept than generations of the past, the exposure to other cultures that the Internet provides will make these individuals significantly more worldly than any generation in history. And as the Millennium Generation enters and exits college, it will come to the workforce with unprecedented technological savvy, forcing companies to think more creatively about how to meet its needs (Trunk, 2007). Indeed, some have argued that this cohort's seemingly constant participation in social network sites, online games, and video sharing sites and its constant use of gadgets such as iPods and smartphones actually give its members the technological skills they'll need to succeed in the contemporary world. They have also become adept at maintaining and navigating intimate connections in an "always on," full-time technological community via texting, instant messaging, tweeting, mobile phones, and the Internet (Ito et al., 2008).

On some issues, members of the Millennium Generation seem to be more socially conservative than prior generations. For instance, close to 70% of young people in a nationwide survey support so-called zero-tolerance policies against drug use in high school (Howe & Strauss, 2000). The proportion of high school students who have had sexual intercourse within the preceding three months decreased from 37.5% in 1991 to 34.2% in 2009 (Centers for Disease Control and Prevention, 2011d). Indeed, rates of pregnancy, abortion, and births for girls between 15 and 19 have all declined since 1990 (U.S. Bureau of the Census, 2011b).

At the same time, though, members of the Millennium Generation are more likely than older cohorts to self-identify as liberals (Pew Research Center, 2010b). They also seem even less eager to get married in their early 20s than either the Generation Xers or the Baby Boomers. The median age at first marriage in the early 1970s—when Baby Boomers were young—was 21 for women and 23 for men; by 2009, it had increased to 26 for women and 28 for men (cited in Henig, 2010). In addition, compared with older cohorts, they are more inclined to be tolerant of single women having children, people living together without being married, mothers of young children working outside the home, people of different races marrying one another, and gay couples legally marrying and raising children. However, tolerance is not the same as outright approval; only about a third of Millennials see any of these trends as good for society (Pew Research Center, 2010b).

As this cohort ages and begins to control important social institutions, these attitudes and behaviors will shape reality for other cohorts in U.S. society.

Demographic Dynamics

Many aspects of our personal lives are influenced by our birth cohort, but our lives are also affected by society-wide and worldwide population trends. Sociologists who study fluctuations in population characteristics are called *demographers*. Demographers examine several important and interrelated population processes to explain current social problems or to predict future ones: birth or fertility rates, death or mortality rates, and patterns of migration. These three processes influence a population's growth, overall age structure, and geographic distribution.

Population Growth

The most fundamental population characteristic is, of course, size. Changes in population size are mostly a function of birth and death rates. As long as people are dying and being born at similar rates, the size of the population remains stable (barring large changes caused by migration). But when birthrates increase and death rates decrease, the population grows.

It took hundreds of thousands of years, from the beginning of humanity to the early 19th century, for Earth's human population to reach 1 billion. However, it took only an additional hundred years for it to reach 2 billion. Then, 3 billion was reached 30 years later; 4 billion, 16 years later; and 5 billion, a little over 10 years after that. Today's population is 7 billion and will likely exceed 10 billion by 2100 (Haub & Gribble, 2011; United Nations, 2011).

People disagree about the consequences of such growth. In the past, large numbers of people were seen as a precious resource. The Bible urged humanity to be fruitful and multiply. One 18th-century British scholar, referring to the strategic importance of a large population, called a high birthrate "the never-failing nursery of Fleets and Armies" (quoted in Mann, 1993, p. 49).

Although few individuals today sing the praises of massive population growth, some argue that it isn't particularly troublesome. A larger population creates greater division of labor and a larger market to support highly specialized services. More people are available to contribute to the production of needed goods and services.

Others, however, aren't so optimistic. When a particular population is excessively large, people are forced to compete for limited food, living space, and jobs. According to some contemporary demographers, population growth can compound, magnify, or even create a wide variety of social problems, such as pollution, environmental degradation, housing shortages, high inflation, energy shortages, illiteracy, and the loss of individual freedom (J. Weeks, 1995).

Global Imbalances in Population Growth

On a global scale, population growth could widen the gap between rich and poor nations, perpetuate social and economic inequality within nations, give rise to racial and ethnic separatism, and increase the already high levels of world hunger and unemployment (Ehrlich & Ehrlich, 1993). Environmental threats are growing too. Humanity's use of once plentiful natural resources—fossil fuel, rich soil, and certain plant and animal species—is now 50% higher than Earth's biologically productive capacity. Overall, we need one and a half earths to support the consumption of all humans (World Wildlife Fund, 2010).

The problem, however, is not just that the overall population is growing rapidly but also that different countries are experiencing vastly different rates of growth. Populations in poor, developing countries tend to expand rapidly, whereas those in wealthy, developed countries have either stabilized or are declining. The annual growth rate of the world's population is approximately 1.2% (Population Reference Bureau, 2011a). But that figure masks the dramatic regional differences that will exist for several decades to come (see Exhibit 13.2). Consider these facts:

- In Africa, the rate of natural population increase (i.e., without taking migration into consideration) is about 2.4% each year; Europe, in contrast, experiences a growth rate of 0%. If current trends continue, by the middle of the 21st century, the population of Poland will be 11% smaller, Germany's 15% smaller, and Bulgaria's 24% smaller than it is today. In contrast, Liberia's population will be 163% bigger, Zambia's, 233%, and Niger's 244% bigger (Population Reference Bureau, 2011a).
- In 1950, half of the 10 most populous nations were in the industrialized world. In 2011, two industrialized countries were in the top 10: Japan and the United States. By 2050, demographers predict that the United States will be the only developed country among the world's 10 most populous nations. The rest will be developing countries in Asia, Africa, and South America (Crossette, 2001; Population Reference Bureau, 2011a).
- In 1950, over 28% of the world's population lived in North America and Europe. Today, it's 15.5%, and by 2050, about 12.5% will live in these regions. The rest of the world's population will reside in the developing countries of Africa, Asia, and Latin America (Population Reference Bureau, 2011a; United Nations Population Division, 2005).

Exhibit 13.2 World Population Growth by Region

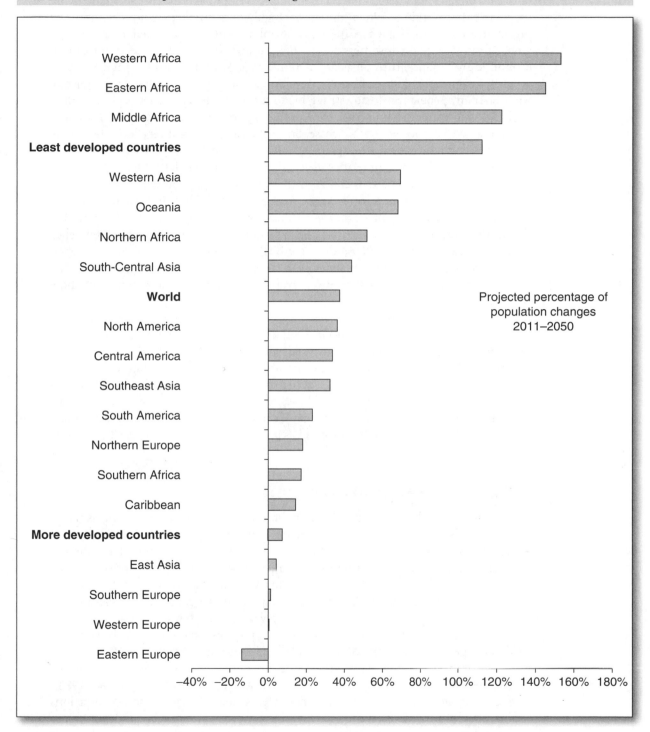

Projected percentage of population changes 2011–2050

SOURCE: Population Reference Bureau, 2011a

These imbalances will influence how people view one another, affect global and domestic policies, and determine the availability of food, energy, and adequate living space (Kennedy, 1993). When the most highly industrialized and economically productive countries begin to experience shrinking populations, their role as major global producers and consumers of goods is thrown into doubt. The result can be economic and political turmoil as other countries jockey for global advantage.

Why would populations in poor, developing countries grow at such a high rate when so many people are already struggling to survive? When societies begin to industrialize, living conditions improve. New technology often means better food supplies and increased knowledge about disease. Societies learn how to keep their water supplies clean and how to dispose of garbage and sewage. So death rates begin to fall.

But for a considerable time after the death rate begins to fall, the birthrate remains high, resulting in a dramatic increase in the size of the population. In sub-Saharan Africa, for instance, women will bear an average of 5.2 children in their lifetimes. By comparison, U.S. women have, on average, 2.0 children. In Canada, the figure is 1.7, and in the countries of Southern Europe, it's a minuscule 1.4 (Population Reference Bureau, 2011a). In the mid 2000s, some low-birthrate countries in the more developed world were beginning to show an increase in the number of babies being born. But the current global recession has slowed or reversed this trend in the majority of these countries (Haub, 2010).

One of the reasons why birthrates are so high in less developed countries is the lack of access to effective contraception. Only 44% of women in these regions use some form of modern contraception, compared with 62% in the more developed world (Population Reference Bureau, 2011a). In sub-Saharan Africa, the figure is 19%. In contrast, 73% of U.S. women and 78% of Northern European women use modern contraception. In addition, established laws, customs, and religious norms often continue to exert strong influences on people's reproductive behavior. In developing nations, children are likely to be perceived as productive assets and "social security" for old age (Mann, 1993).

Politics, Culture, and Population Growth

You may have the impression that population growth is a "natural" process working relentlessly and inevitably on unsuspecting populations. Yet human intervention—government intervention, more specifically—has at times purposefully altered the size or even the configuration of a population for political or economic reasons.

Take China, for example. Because of its massive population of more than 1.3 billion and its limited resources, Chinese leaders have been struggling for decades to limit family size. One of every five humans alive today is Chinese, but China has only 7% of Earth's farmland, much of it of poor quality. In response, the government enacted a strict birth policy in the early 1970s. Couples had to wait until their mid 20s to marry. Provinces and cities were assigned yearly birth quotas. Neighborhood committees determined which married couples could have a baby and when (Ignatius, 1988). Women who lacked approval to be pregnant were often subjected to forced abortions (Kahn, 2007). In the 1990s, more than 80% of all Chinese couples of childbearing age were sterilized (Crossette, 1997a). Couples who had only one child were rewarded with salary bonuses, better educational opportunities, and housing priorities. Couples who had more than one child faced fines of more than a year's salary, lost access to apartments and schools, or were fired from their jobs (Ignatius, 1988). A 2010 report by the Chinese Human Rights Defenders found that the government still uses a variety of coercive family planning tactics, such as financial penalties for households that violate the restrictions, financial rewards for citizens who divulge the reproductive secrets of their neighbors, and forced sterilizations of women who have already had one child (cited in Jacobs, 2010).

The effectiveness of China's birth policy has amazed population experts. The average number of births per woman has decreased from more than 7 in the 1960s to 1.5 today (Population Reference Bureau, 2011a). In contrast, the average number of births per woman in India, a country with similar population problems, is 2.6. Without the policy, there would likely be hundreds of millions more Chinese citizens than there are now (Kahn, 2004).

But the success of China's birth policy has created some serious social problems. So few babies are being born now—and so many more elderly people are living longer—that the overall age of the population is growing steadily. Chinese officials fear that the country will likely encounter what is sometimes called the "four-two-one problem"—a generation of only children who will have to find the resources to care for two aging parents and four elderly grandparents ("One Child Left Behind," 2009). Today, there are six Chinese working adults for every one retired person; by 2040, there will be just two (French, 2007a). It's estimated that by that same year, China will have an older population than the United States but with only about one fourth the average per capita income (Kahn, 2004). Retirement funds and pension plans are scarce. Only 40% of elderly men and 13% of elderly women receive any kind of support from a pension. And the social networks that once supported aging Chinese are no longer there. Migration to urban areas and the work pressures of an increasingly industrialized economy have fractured family ties (Population Reference Bureau, 2010a). The problem has become so bad that the Chinese government is considering a law that would require children to take care of their elderly parents ("China Law to Make Children Visit Parents," 2011).

Like those in China, officials in many other countries are now starting to worry that their populations aren't growing enough. In contemporary Russia, for instance, many couples postpone childbearing or decide not to have children altogether because of severe economic instability and uncertainty about the future. Russia now has one of the world's lowest birthrates. At the same time, because of skyrocketing rates of poverty, stress, and alcoholism, Russians are dying much earlier than the rest of the world. As a result, over the past decade and a half, the Russian population has shrunk by about 700,000 people a year ("Vladimir Putin on Raising Russia's Birth Rate," 2006). Population experts project that it will decrease by an additional 11.7% between now and 2050 (Population Reference Bureau, 2011a). Fearing that such a dramatic population decline will lead to economic catastrophe, Russian politicians have promoted a variety of policies to reverse the trend, such as a nationwide ban on abortions, financial incentives for couples to have children, increased funds for prenatal care and maternity leave, and a tax on childlessness ("Fearing Demographic Abyss," 2006; Karush, 2001). In one central Russian region, the governor has decreed September 12 to be a "Day of Conception," in which couples are given the day off from work to . . . well . . . procreate. Those who have a baby nine months later receive money, cars, and other prizes ("Baby, and a Car," 2011). Other countries have tried a variety of tactics to encourage people to have more babies:

- A few years ago, the French government approved a package of parenting incentives that included generous allowances; tax incentives; housing payments; and "large-family" discounts on public transportation, household goods, and leisure activities for families with three or more children (Schofield, 2005).
- In Iran, each child born in 2010 received a deposit of US$950 in a government bank account and will receive an additional US$95 every year until he or she reaches 18 ("Iran's Leader Introduces," 2010).
- For a few years, the Spanish government paid US$3,300 for every child, but they suspended the program in 2011 as part of general budget cuts (Haub, 2011).
- In 2010, the Taiwanese government announced a nationwide contest for the most creative slogan that would motivate couples to procreate, with a prize of about US$32,000. But 2010 was the Year of the Tiger, an inauspicious year for childbearing according to the Chinese zodiac, so the plan backfired (Haub, 2010).

Cultural tradition also continues to play a powerful role in people's decisions about having children. Some patriarchal cultures express a deep preference for male children because only they can perpetuate the family line. As one Chinese mother put it, "If you have only girls, you don't feel right inside. You feel your status is lower than everyone else" (quoted in Jacobs, 2009, p. 8).

Parents in such cultures may take extreme measures to have sons rather than daughters. In rural China—where the one-child policy coupled with a tradition of favoring boys over girls has led many parents to fear they will be left to take care of themselves in old age—the abduction and sale of baby boys has become a thriving business (Jacobs, 2009). Elsewhere, female babies are aborted, killed at birth, abandoned, neglected, or given up for foreign adoption (Kristof, 1993). Although it is illegal, couples often seek to determine the sex of their fetus through sonograms, and if it's a girl, they have an abortion. In South Korea, for instance, one out of 12 female fetuses—or 30,000 girls a year—is aborted, even though disclosure of the sex of a fetus and abortion are against the law (WuDunn, 1997). In India, as many as 10 million female fetuses have been aborted over the past 20 years as families have tried to secure male heirs (Gentleman, 2006).

Such practices have led to a conspicuous shortage of females in many developing countries. Under normal circumstances in every society, there are between 103 and 107 boys born for every 100 girls; but higher male infant mortality works to even the distribution of boys to girls. In India, however, there are 109 males for every 100 females (Gentleman, 2006). In some areas of China, the ratio is 120 males for every 100 females. There are 32 million more Chinese males under 20 than females; in 2005 alone, there were 1.1 million more boys born than girls (Zhu, Lu, & Hesketh, 2009). Demographers have identified similar shortages of females in South Korea, Pakistan, Bangladesh, Nepal, and Papua New Guinea, and some estimate that about 163 million females are "missing" from Asia's population (Hvistendahl, 2011).

Incidentally, such gender biases are not confined to foreign countries. In this country, a similar bias is found among U.S.-born children of Chinese, Korean, and Indian immigrants. Census data indicate that couples from these ethnic groups will keep trying to have a son—and perhaps make use of sex-selection procedures—if their first and second children are daughters. Among firstborn children, the ratio of male children to female children is relatively equal. But when the firstborn child is a girl, male second children outnumber female second children 117 to 100. And when the first two children are girls, the sex ratio for third children soars to 151 boys for every 100 girls. No such sex imbalance exists in other racial or ethnic groups (Almond & Edlund, 2008).

Age Structure

In addition to population growth, demographers also study the ***age structure*** of societies—the balance of old and young people. Age structure, like the size of a population, is determined principally by birthrates and life expectancy.

The proportion of old people in the world has been growing steadily for decades. Currently, 8% of the global population is over 65 (Population Reference Bureau, 2011a). By 2045, that figure is projected to be 15.2% (Sanderson & Scherbov, 2008). During the same period, the proportion of the "oldest old" (those over 80) will increase more than fivefold (United Nations Population Division, 2003).

But as with population growth in general, the global growth of the elderly population is not spread evenly across countries. In developing countries where recent population growth is exceedingly rapid and where life expectancy remains low—as in most countries of Southeast Asia, Latin America, the Indian subcontinent, the Middle East, and especially Africa—the age structure tends to be dominated by young people. Forty-three percent of the population in sub-Saharan Africa is under the age of 15 (Population Reference Bureau, 2011a). The median age of the population in the world's three youngest countries—Uganda, Mali, and Niger—is about 16 (United Nations, 2011). In contrast, developed countries that are experiencing low birthrates coupled with increasing life expectancy have a very different age structure, as Exhibit 13.3 shows. More old people are living, and fewer people are being born. Only 16% of Europe's population is under 15 (Population Reference Bureau, 2011a). The median age of the population in the world's three oldest countries (Italy, Japan, and Germany) is about 44 (United Nations, 2011). Demographers project that by 2050 the median age in Europe will be an unprecedented 52.3 years (cited in R. Bernstein, 2003).

The global implications of these different age structures cannot be understated. In Germany, Austria, France, and other European countries, a decreasing number of young people are paying into a pension system that must support a growing number of older people (R. Bernstein, 2003). Governments have reacted to the aging of their populations by reducing social services, including the pensions that millions of retirees have been counting on.

In contrast, when young people outnumber the elderly in a particular country, they are likely to overwhelm labor markets and educational systems (K. Davis, 1976). The result is a steady decline in living standards. When combined with a skewed sex ratio—due to a shortage of young females and an overabundance of young males—the likelihood of instability and sometimes violent political unrest increases (Hvistendahl, 2011). In the spring of 2011, we witnessed massive angry demonstrations in many parts of the Middle East. Not surprisingly, over 60% of the populations of Syria, Saudi Arabia, Iraq, Yemen, Jordan, Oman, Egypt, and Libya are now under 30 years of age (U.S. Bureau of the Census, 2011a). Increasing rates of unemployment leave more and more young people angry and dissatisfied. Some authors even go so far as to predict that if these young men cannot find spouses or jobs, they will pose such a threat to the internal stability of these countries that their governments may decide they have to go to war with other countries simply to occupy the surplus male population (Hudson & den Boer, 2004).

The obvious consequence of today's trends is that developing nations will have the burden of trying to accommodate populations dominated by young people, whereas developed nations will have the burden of trying to support millions of people over the age of 65.

Exhibit 13.3   Changing Age Distributions in Less Developed and More Developed Regions

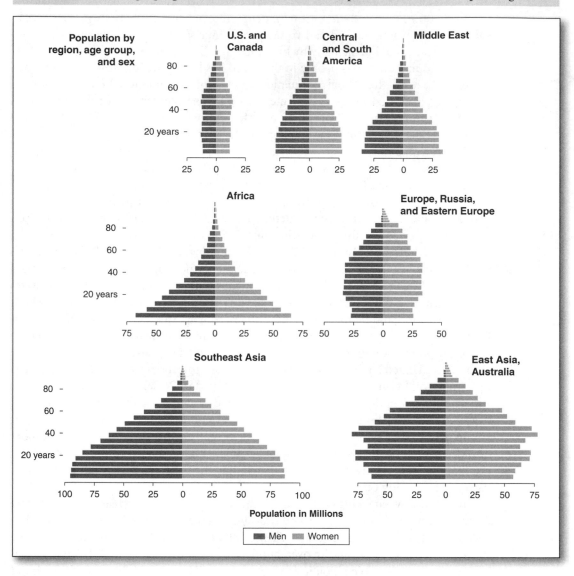

SOURCE: Copyright © 2008 The New York Times Company. Reprinted with permission.

Geographic Distribution

Many people seek to escape these kinds of problems through *migration*, or moving to another place where prospects for a comfortable life are brighter. Through the centuries, migration has played a crucial role in history as people have contended for territory and the resources that go with it ("Workers of the World," 1998). Today, global media expose people more quickly and more consistently than ever to appealing lifestyles elsewhere. Large-scale migration includes both within-country movement and cross-border movement.

Migration Within a Country

Migration trends within a country can have a considerable effect on social life. In the United States, such internal migration usually consists of people moving from colder to warmer climates or from large cities to outer suburbs (Lalasz, 2006). But in less developed countries these days, in-country migration is more likely to reflect ***urbanization***, the process by which people leave rural areas and begin to concentrate in large cities. For instance, in 1950, less than 30% of the world's population lived in cities. In 2010, that figure topped 50% (Population Reference Bureau, 2010c), and it's estimated that by 2050, almost 70% of the world's population will be urban dwellers (United Nations Population Division, 2008). In Asia and Africa, four times more people live in cities today than in 1950 (Population Reference Bureau, 2008). It's estimated that in India alone, 700 million people will move from villages to cities by 2050 (cited in Giridharadas, 2007).

This transformation has changed assumptions about what urban living means worldwide. In the past, cities were meccas of commerce and culture and tended to have higher standards of living and better health conditions than rural areas. But when cities grow rapidly, as many are in the developing world, their economies and infrastructures can't keep up. In sub-Saharan Africa, only about 43% of city dwellers have access to adequate sanitation facilities, compared with 99% in more developed countries (Population Reference Bureau, 2010c). Moreover, cities typically have much higher rates of poverty, crime, violence, and sexually transmitted diseases than rural areas.

Migration From One Country to Another

Population movement from one country to another is equally significant. It's estimated that about 200 million people worldwide live outside their countries of birth (cited in DeParle, 2007). Most have left their homelands in search of a better life somewhere else. In the process, they bring together an extraordinary diversity of ethnicities and cultures:

> A woman gynecologist from Romania sells bananas in a downtown supermarket [in the United States]. Polish engineers pick grapes in Swiss alpine vineyards. . . . Thai bar girls in Tokyo ride the Japanese economic boom together with 700,000 workers from Korea. . . . Among the 2.8 million foreign workers . . . in the Middle East last year were 17,000 Vietnamese. Hundreds of thousands of Indonesians harvest rubber and copra in Malaysia for the same pocketbook reasons that Mexicans pump gasoline in Los Angeles. In Germany, there are more than 1,000 mosques for resident Turkish workers. (McMichael, 1996, p. 187)

International migration is encouraged by disparities in opportunities. Poverty, political instability, war, famine, environmental deterioration, high unemployment, and the lure of high wages in richer countries continue to drive the world's poorest people to give up their life savings and risk death to find a better life in more prosperous nations. According to the United Nations, each year hundreds of thousands of illegal immigrants from poor countries in Africa, Central Asia, and the Middle East try to enter the wealthy nations of Western Europe (cited in Cowell, 2002).

You might think that when people migrate from underdeveloped, overcrowded countries to more developed, technologically advanced countries, everyone would benefit. After all, migration lowers population pressures and unemployment at home while offsetting the problems of negative population growth and an aging workforce in developed destination countries. Indeed, the only way Japan and Western Europe will be able to sustain a stable population in the future is through immigration.

From a sociological point of view, however, international migration often creates conflict. The immigrants themselves often experience tension between the values of their new home and the values of their country of origin. Take, for instance, cultural mores regarding virginity and premarital sex. As the Middle Eastern immigrant population in Europe grows, young Muslim women are caught between the relative sexual freedoms of European society and the deep, and often very restrictive, traditions of their parents and grandparents. Although there are no reliable statistics, French cosmetic surgeons report increasing numbers of young Muslim women seeking a surgical procedure called hymenoplasty—the restoration of the hymen, the vaginal membrane that breaks during the first act of intercourse—to give the appearance of virginity (Sciolino & Mekhennet, 2008).

People seeking opportunities can no longer move to uncharted areas but rather must push into territories where other people already live. Instead of seeing immigrants for their contribution to the overall economy, the people already in residence see immigrants as an immediate and personal threat. The immigrants require jobs, housing, education, and medical attention, all of which are in limited supply. They also bring with them foreign habits, traditions, and norms.

Immigration creates a variety of cultural fears: fear that a nation can't control its own borders, fear that an ethnically homogeneous population will be altered through intermarriage, fear of the influx of a "strange" way of life, and fear that newcomers will encroach on property, clog the educational system, and suck up social benefits owned and largely paid for by "natives" (Kennedy, 1993). Many people also express concern that immigrants are responsible for outbreaks of diseases such as AIDS, tuberculosis, measles, and cholera, which strain health care systems and thus create even more resentment. Above all, they fear that immigrants and their offspring may one day become a statistical majority, rendering the "natives" powerless in their own country.

Even though laws in most countries ban discrimination against immigrants, antiforeigner resentment and prejudice are global phenomena. For instance, legislators in Denmark, France, and Italy are currently seeking ways to tighten their borders so they can limit the free flow of immigrants, chiefly from North Africa. In Great Britain, the antipathy is usually directed toward immigrants from India and Pakistan. In Australia, politicians talk of being swamped by South and East Asians. And in the United States, immigrants from Latin America bear the brunt of the public's anti-immigrant animosity. In Japan, the resentment is directed toward almost anyone who isn't Japanese. Despite a severe labor shortage that could cripple its economy, Japan has done little to loosen its tight restrictions on immigration. In fact, the government actively encourages foreign workers and foreign graduates of its universities to return home as quickly as possible (Tabuchi, 2011).

Antiforeigner sentiment tends to be more pronounced in places with a large proportion of foreign populations, where economies are less prosperous, and where there is greater support for extreme right-wing political parties (Semyonov & Raijman, 2006). It's important to note, though, that such hostility is not inevitable. Peaceable contact with immigrants at work, at school, or in the community can reduce feelings of threat and the willingness to expel legal immigrants from the country

(McLaren, 2003). In any case, the trend toward greater immigration is unlikely to slow down as long as communication and transportation technologies continue to shrink the globe and economic disparities between countries continue to exist.

Population Trends in the United States

In the United States, two important demographic trends will exert a profound effect on the population in the future: the growing proportion of nonwhite, non-English-speaking immigrants and their children and the shifting age structure of the population, marked by a growing proportion of elderly and a shrinking proportion of young people. These two trends together will strain the social fabric in years to come, raising questions about the fair distribution of social resources.

Immigration and the Changing Face of the United States

Because the U.S. population is currently growing at a manageable rate, residents may have trouble understanding the impact of population explosions in other countries on their everyday lives here. But as populations burst the seams of national boundaries elsewhere, many of those seeking better opportunities end up in the United States. Newly arrived immigrants believe that chances to get ahead, protection of women's rights, treatment of the poor, and availability of schools are all better here than in their countries of origin (Rieff, 2005). Some arrive legally by plane, boat, or train. Others arrive illegally by foot or are smuggled in the backs of trucks or the holds of cargo ships.

The Immigrant Surge

In the mid 1980s, the U.S. Bureau of the Census predicted that by the year 2050 the United States would have a population of 300 million (Pear, 1992). But that number has already been surpassed. Subsequently, the Census Bureau has revised its estimate to 439 million by 2050 (U.S. Bureau of the Census, 2011b).

Part of the reason this projection had to be adjusted was that immigration increased more than had been anticipated. About 3,100 legal and 2,000 undocumented immigrants arrive in the United States each day (P. Martin & Midgley, 2010). The share of the U.S. population that is foreign born rose from 5% in 1967 to 12% in 2009 (U.S. Bureau of the Census, 2011b). Between 1990 and 2010, the number of foreign-born U.S. residents almost doubled from 20 million to 40 million. Hence, immigration directly contributed one third of overall growth in the U.S. population. And if you count the U.S. born children and grandchildren of immigrants, immigration accounted for half of U.S. population growth (P. Martin & Midgley, 2010). This isn't the first time a surge of immigration has radically increased the U.S. population. In the first decade of the 20th century, nearly 9 million immigrants entered the country. By 1915, foreign-born residents constituted 15% of the population (U.S. Bureau of the Census, 2006). What makes contemporary immigration different, though, is that fewer of today's newcomers are of European descent (see Exhibit 13.4).

Exhibit 13.4 Shifting Sources of Legal Immigrants to the United States

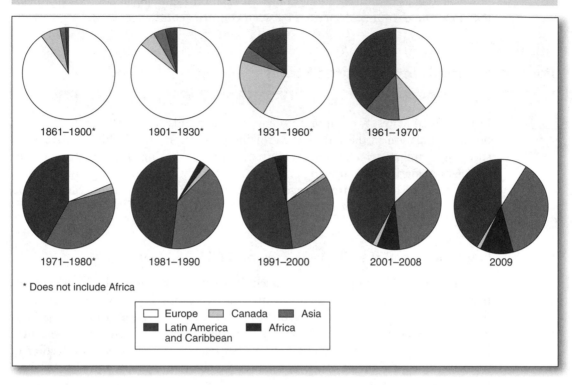

1861–1900* 1901–1930* 1931–1960* 1961–1970*

1971–1980* 1981–1990 1991–2000 2001–2008 2009

* Does not include Africa

Europe   Canada   Asia
Latin America   Africa
and Caribbean

SOURCES: Daniels, 1990; U.S. Bureau of the Census, 2000; 2011b, Table 50

Not surprisingly, then, the racial and ethnic composition of the United States has changed dramatically over the past century. In 1900, one out of every eight U.S. residents was of a race other than white; in 2010, the ratio was one in three; and by 2050, it is projected to be one in two (P. Martin & Midgley, 2010). Over the past decade or so, the fastest-growing surnames in the United States were Garcia, Rodriguez, Martinez, Hernandez, Lopez, and Gonzalez (Roberts, 2007). Latino/as currently constitute a little over 16% of the population, but they accounted for over half of the population increase between 2000 and 2010 (Mather, Pollard, & Jacobsen, 2011). Experts estimate that by the year 2050, one out of four U.S. residents will be Latino/a, and by 2100, one out of three will be Latino/a (Saenz, 2004).

Until quite recently, the non-European immigrant population was not spread evenly across the country. Immigrants tended to settle in large urban areas that serve as ports of entry, such as New York, Los Angeles, Houston, and Miami. In the mid 1980s, for example, two thirds of Mexican immigrants lived in California and 20% more lived in Texas and Illinois (G. Thompson, 2009). Of the 20 metropolitan areas with the largest proportion of Asian immigrants in the early 2000s, eight were in California and six were cities in the eastern corridor that runs from Boston to Washington, D.C. (Zhao, 2002).

However, new immigrants can now be found all across the United States. Just like everyone else, they're motivated to go where jobs exist. In the past decade, the growth of the immigrant population has been largest in counties where immigrants composed less than 5% of the population in 2000. In fact, more immigrants now settle in suburbs and small towns than in large urban centers (cited in Tavernise & Gebeloff, 2010). Consequently, the need for people to teach English as a second language has grown most rapidly in school districts in these regions. Between 1993 and 2002, the number of students in Idaho, Nebraska, Tennessee, and Georgia who speak little if any English tripled. In North Carolina, the number of such students increased sixfold (Zhao, 2002). Students who do not know English represent the fastest-growing group of students in the nation (G. Thompson, 2009). Questions of how best to integrate immigrants and their children are now being debated in every corner of the country.

Social Responses to Immigrants

U.S. residents have always had a love-hate relationship with immigrants. In good times, immigrants have been welcome contributors to the economy. Early in the 20th century, their labor helped build roads and the U.S. rail system. Immigrants have filled unwanted jobs, opened businesses, and improved the lives of many U.S. residents by working cheaply as housekeepers, dishwashers, and gardeners.

When times are bad, however, or when the political winds shift, many U.S. residents are inclined to shut the door and blame immigrants for many of the country's economic and social woes. During these periods, people often describe the influx of immigrants as a "flood," subtly equating their arrival with disaster. As in Europe, immigrants to the United States often find they are targets of a variety of social anxieties, from economic tension to outright hostility (Sontag, 1992).

MICRO-MACRO CONNECTION

The Peculiar Politics of Immigration

Immigration is one of the hot-button political issues of our time. But it's not one of those issues where liberals and conservatives line up neatly on opposing sides.

As you might expect, some conservative politicians consider the millions of illegal immigrants in this country to be invaders who threaten national security, take away jobs from U.S. citizens, and change the culture by refusing to assimilate (Katel, 2005). They typically support legislation that would provide funds to toughen border security. The number of border patrol agents assigned to the U.S.-Mexico border has increased steadily since the early 1990s. In 1992, there were 3,555 agents assigned to this region; by 2000, that number had increased to 8,580. Since 2000, the number of agents has more than doubled to 20,119 agents (Haddal, 2010). Some also advocate laws that would deny all benefits to children of illegal immigrants, block states from issuing drivers' licenses to illegal immigrants, or make it a crime to employ or rent to illegal immigrants (Robertson, 2011).

In 2006, Congress passed the Secure Fence Act, allocating $2.7 billion for the construction of a 700-mile reinforced wall along the Mexican border. In 2010, Arizona attracted national attention when it enacted a law that makes the failure to carry immigration documents a crime and gives police broad powers to detain anyone who "appears" to be in the country illegally. Polls taken at the time indicated that a majority of Americans support such a measure, even though they feel it may lead to racial profiling (Archibold & Thee-Brenan, 2010). Georgia and

Alabama passed similar laws in 2011. In Utah, a group called Concerned Citizens of the United States sent a letter to law enforcement organizations and media outlets containing the names of 1,300 alleged undocumented immigrants. For each name, an address, telephone number, date of birth, and, in the case of pregnant women, delivery due date were provided. The letter urged immediate deportation of the people listed, promised more lists in the future, and ominously concluded with, "We will be listening and watching" (K. Johnson, 2010). Indeed, some members of Congress have recently begun questioning the validity of the Fourteenth Amendment to the Constitution, which stipulates that any baby born in the United States, regardless of the citizenship status of his or her parents, is automatically a U.S. citizen.

But addressing the problem of illegal immigration is not as simple as locking down borders, detaining people who "look" illegal, and kicking individuals out of the country. In fact, such a position may actually conflict with other conservative ideals, such as the importance of intact families. About 350,000 children are born to at least one unauthorized immigrant each year (Passel & Cohn, 2011). Because people born in the United States automatically become American citizens, the political desire for deportations can create serious problems for these families. It's estimated that of the 2.2 million illegal immigrants deported between 1997 and 2007, more than 100,000 were the parents of children born in the United States. So what should happen to these children? If a child is deported along with her or his parents, then technically the government is deporting an American citizen. On the other hand, if the parents are allowed to remain in the country, they are being given a special—and in some people's minds, unwarranted—benefit (Falcone, 2009).

Some liberal politicians have also called on the government to seal the U.S. borders. Their primary concern is that foreign immigrants, both legal and illegal, hurt poor U.S. residents by directly competing with them for low-level jobs (Danziger & Gottschalk, 2004). And because they're usually willing to work for less money, some economists point out, undocumented workers depress wages among the less skilled native-born workers (Broder, 2006; Lowenstein, 2006). In 2011, the Obama administration began cracking down on employers who hire illegal immigrants while at the same time it moved away from arresting the workers themselves (Preston, 2011). In addition, some members of liberal environmentalist groups, like the Sierra Club, oppose unlimited immigration. They believe that it taxes the already strained natural resources and renders an already overcrowded country unable to protect its environment (Barringer, 2004).

But pro-immigrant sentiment can be found on both ends of the political spectrum as well. To some fiscal conservatives, immigrants make important contributions to the economy (Swarns, 2006). Fifteen percent of U.S. workers are born outside the United States (P. Martin & Midgley, 2010). One study found that a 1% increase in employment in a state due to immigration produces an income increase of 0.5% in that state (Peri, 2009). About a third of foreign-born workers are here illegally (cited in Broder, 2006). Most of them work in jobs that citizens don't want. For instance, nationwide, one out of every four low-wage workers in fishing, construction, housekeeping, and forestry is an illegal immigrant (Broder, 2006; "Laboring in the U.S.," 2006). About 75% of workers on U.S. crop farms were born abroad and over two thirds of them are here illegally (P. Martin, 2010). As one journalist put it, without illegal workers,

> fruit and vegetables would rot in fields. Toddlers in Manhattan would be without nannies. Towels at hotels in states like Florida, Texas, and California would go unlaundered. Commuters at airports from Miami to Newark would be stranded as taxi cabs sat driverless. Home improvement projects across the Sun Belt would grind to a halt. And bedpans and lunch trays at nursing homes in Chicago, New York, Houston, and Los Angeles would go uncollected. (D. E. Murphy, 2004, p. 1)

In addition, some conservative economists argue that Social Security would go broke without the $7 billion or so in annual payments from undocumented workers, many of whom—contrary to popular perceptions—pay their share of income taxes (D. E. Murphy, 2004; Porter, 2005).

For many liberal-leaning civil rights organizations and advocates for ethnic minorities, immigration is a human rights issue, and hostility toward immigrants is seen as fundamentally racist (Holmes, 1995). They point to the fact that immigrants, in general, tend to have lower educational achievement, higher rates of poverty, more families without health insurance, and more families on public assistance than native-born U.S. residents (Camarota, 2004).

The public, too, tends to have mixed feelings about immigration. We are, as two researchers for the Population Reference Bureau put it, "a nation of immigrants unsure about immigration" (P. Martin & Midgley, 2010, p. 6). About as many people believe that immigrants strengthen U.S. society as say they threaten traditional American values. As you might expect, proximity to immigrants affects those attitudes. People who live in areas with high concentrations of immigrants are less likely to see them as a burden or a threat to society. However, they're more likely to see immigration as an important social problem in their local communities (Pew Research Center, 2006a). One nationwide poll found that while 30% of people believed illegal immigrants take jobs away from citizens, almost 60% believed they mostly take jobs native-born workers don't want. And almost two thirds felt that illegal immigrants should be allowed to apply for legal status after living in the country for two years (cited in Preston & Connelly, 2007).

As with a whole host of other controversial issues, the current economic recession will no doubt affect the way citizens and politicians perceive and treat immigrants. Because of their willingness to work for lower wages, immigrant workers have always had lower rates of unemployment than native-born Americans. However, that has changed recently. Between 2007 and 2009, the number of employed immigrants dropped by 9%. In contrast, the number of native-born workers dropped by 3.7%. In 2011, the unemployment rate for all immigrants was 10%; it was 12% for Latino/a immigrants. If we add to these figures those who want to work but have not looked recently, and those forced to work part time, the rates increase to 20% for all immigrants and 25% for Latino/a immigrants (Camarota, 2011).

Just how this trend will affect public attitudes and political action is unclear. Heightened competition over a shrinking supply of jobs could lead to increased hostility against immigrants and louder calls for more restrictive laws or tougher enforcement of existing laws. Government limitations on the number of immigrants entering the country could improve the employment prospects of poor, less educated, native-born workers, who are likely to be hardest hit by the recession.

But such political action may be unnecessary. The flow of illegal immigrants from Latin America into the United States has slowed in recent years. After peaking at 12 million in 2007, the number of undocumented immigrants dropped to 11.1 million in 2009, the first decline in two decades (Passel & Cohn, 2011). The drop has been particularly steep among undocumented Mexican immigrants. Between 2000 and 2004, there were more than 500,000 illegal border crossings per year; in 2010, the figure dropped to 100,000 (cited in Cave, 2011). Experts attribute the decrease not only to economic slowdowns and immigration crackdowns in the United States but to expanding economic and educational opportunities and declining birthrates in Mexico.

The immigration issue illustrates a clash of political and economic forces. To politicians of all stripes, immigration is a crucial and sometimes volatile issue. But as long as powerful business interests see the need for a pool of cheap, mobile labor that is willing to work outside union and regulatory constraints, attempts to crack down on illegal immigration will remain ineffective. As long as jobs are available, poor foreigners will continue to come here seeking a better life.

(Text continues on page 468)

Immigrant Nation

Liz Grauerholz and Rebecca Smith

All around the world, immigration is a function of economic imbalances and political conflict. Gaps between rich people and poor people are increasing in most countries, and the gap between rich and poor countries is growing as well. Wars and oppression are never ending. These forces keep people moving across national borders in search of a better life.

Immigration has shaped U.S. society since its beginning. The United States is a land of immigrants. In the early 20th century, a large influx of immigrants, mostly from Europe, enriched U.S. culture and provided the labor to fuel the nation's rise as an industrial powerhouse. At the time, the need to incorporate so many new Americans was considered a societal problem, but today we take for granted the Italian, Polish, Irish, Jewish, and other once-foreign names and faces in our midst.

In the early 20th century, most immigrants arrived by boat, ferried across the Atlantic Ocean to Ellis Island in New York. There they were processed in massive numbers, sometimes for days or weeks, before establishing their new homes in the United States.

More recent immigrants are like earlier arrivals in their keen desire for a better life. But they are also different in some important ways. For one thing, they are likely to be from Latin America or Asia rather than Europe. For another, they typically make the trip in a fraction of the time that it took early-20th-century arrivals. Many simply book a flight to the United States. An airport processing area is their first stop, but as soon as their papers are determined to be in order, they're on their way.

Poor immigrants who have difficulty obtaining the proper documentation often take a more harrowing route, however. Cubans and Haitians may cross the ocean in small boats and attempt to sneak ashore in Florida. Many Mexicans and other Latin Americans try to cross the southwestern U.S. border on foot. So common are accidents involving these pedestrians that signs like this one have been posted on many highways near the border.

Undocumented immigrants face many difficulties. Not the least is the U.S. law enforcement system and the antagonism of many U.S. citizens. Illegal immigration is considered by many to be a threat to national security, especially since the attacks of September 11, 2001. Beefed-up security at airports is a hurdle for many would-be immigrants.

But the porous southern border seems to be a greater concern. So many illegal immigrants come from Mexico that government officials use an acronym, OTMs, to describe illegal immigrants "other than Mexicans." The men at this holding center in Brownsville, Texas, are all OTMs who have crossed the U.S.-Mexico border illegally. Mexican detainees are far more numerous.

The legitimate path, of course, is to seek naturalization after a period in which immigrants contribute to the social fabric and learn how to be Americans. More than 700,000 took their oaths as naturalized U.S. citizens in 2009 (U.S. Bureau of the Census, 2011b).

Among the roughly 2,000 people naturalized in this 2002 ceremony are immigrants who joined the armed forces and pledged to sacrifice their lives for their adopted country before they were even citizens.

In the past, intermittent amnesty programs have allowed longtime undocumented residents to become citizens, but given current security concerns, this policy has become controversial. Meanwhile, babies born in the United States to illegal immigrants are considered U.S. citizens from birth and therefore enjoy all the privileges associated with citizenship. Some Mexican women deliberately seek to give birth in the United States, despite the hardships they face themselves as illegal immigrants.

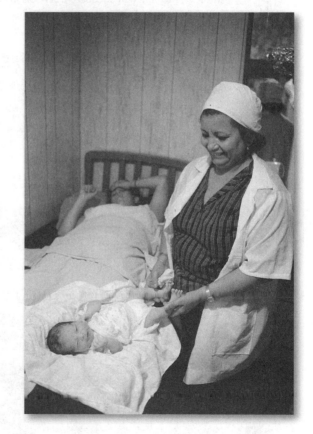

The sheer number of new immigrants—both legal and illegal—strains the capacity of many social institutions to function adequately. Schools in some communities are struggling to educate students who need to learn not only reading, writing, arithmetic, science, and social studies but also English.

Businesses and governments have to provide information in a variety of languages, as in this Chicago street sign.

Poverty is another possible consequence of large-scale immigration, as the economy struggles to accommodate the influx of new workers. Unemployed immigrants strain the government's already dwindling ability to house, feed, and clothe those who are at a disadvantage in the competitive, individualistic American system.

Anti-immigrant sentiment tends to be fueled by this sort of competition over scarce resources, as well as fear of outsiders and perhaps even outright racism. Many people regard immigrants, legal and illegal alike, with suspicion or outright hostility. During harsh economic times, social conflict over immigration issues may intensify.

Still, not all sentiment is anti-immigrant. Immigrants serve important economic functions in the labor market. First, they become servants, gardeners, cooks, and nannies, providing the middle class with the accoutrements of the rich. Second, they compete with the most disadvantaged groups for the least desirable jobs, thereby keeping wages (and prices) low and lessening the pressure to address other economic problems. In the process, consumers have the benefit of products made with cheap labor.

Despite concerns, immigration is likely to continue as long as the United States remains a vibrant and open society. In fact, cultural diversity keeps things lively. Fifty or so years ago, who knew that American culture would embrace these once-foreign artifacts and many others?

New ideas: Buddhism and other Eastern religions

New dining options

New holidays: Cinco de Mayo

We also have something to look forward to: the contributions of today's immigrant children. They will become tomorrow's dedicated workers and citizens—perhaps even the trendsetters and innovators of the new generation. Fifty years from now, we are likely to take their once-foreign names and faces for granted.

The "Graying" of the United States

At the same time that the United States grapples with the changing ethnic and racial configuration of its population, it also must address its shifting age structure. Perhaps the most important and most problematic demographic trend in the United States today involves the increasing average age of the population. In 1910, 38% of the U.S. population was under 18; today, that figure is 24% (Mather, Pollard, & Jacobsen, 2011). Two hundred years ago, the median age for U.S. residents was 16; in 1980, it was 30; today, it is 36.2. And it's expected to be close to 40 by the middle of this century, as the massive Baby Boom cohort reaches old age (U.S. Bureau of the Census, 2011b).

Two developments in the past few decades have conspired to alter the U.S. age structure. The first has been a decrease in the number of children being born. In 1960, there were approximately 24 births per 1,000 people in the population. By 2007, the rate had dropped to 14.3 per 1,000 (U.S. Bureau of the Census, 2011b). More U.S. women than ever are choosing not to have children at all (Dye, 2008). Like many countries in the developed world, the U.S. fertility rate is barely at the level necessary to replace the current population in the next generation. Most of the conditions that have helped lower fertility—improved educational and employment opportunities for women and more effective contraception, for example—are not likely to reverse in the future.

The other development has been a rapid increase in the number of people surviving to old age. The number of Americans over the age of 65 has nearly doubled in the last four decades (Greenblatt, 2011). Technological advances in medicine and nutrition have extended the lives of countless U.S. residents, whose historical counterparts would not have lived nearly as long. Life expectancy has risen from 67.1 for males and 74.7 for females born in 1970 to 75.7 for males and 80.8 for females born in 2010 (U.S. Bureau of the Census, 2011b). By 2050, the United States will have more old people than children (see Exhibit 13.5). The number of people over 85, an age group for which health care costs are exceptionally high, will grow fastest of all, increasing from 5.7 million today to more than 8 million by 2030 and soaring to more than 19 million by 2050 (U.S. Bureau of the Census, 2011b). Some demographers project that by 2050 there will be 10 times the number of centenarians (people living to 100) that we have today (cited in Dominus, 2004).

Why should we be concerned about the "graying" of the U.S. population? The answer is that a society with an aging population will inevitably experience increased demands for pensions, health care, and other social services for the elderly. Although older people in the United States tend to be healthier than their counterparts in the past, a significant proportion suffer from health problems and chronic disease and will eventually need some kind of long-term care (National Institute on Aging, 2006). The ability and willingness of society, and in particular the working population, to bear the additional burden of caring for the growing number of elderly people is an open question.

Political debate rages today over how—or even whether—the Social Security system should be transformed to accommodate the growing number of people who will turn 65 in the coming years. One survey found that 18% of Americans feel that the Social Security system is in crisis, 53% believe it has major problems, and 24% feel it has minor problems. About 60% of people fear that by the time they retire, there will not be enough money in the system to pay the benefits they're entitled to (Pew Research Center, 2005). Unless elderly Americans are better able to support themselves

Exhibit 13.5   Changing Age Makeup of the U.S. Population

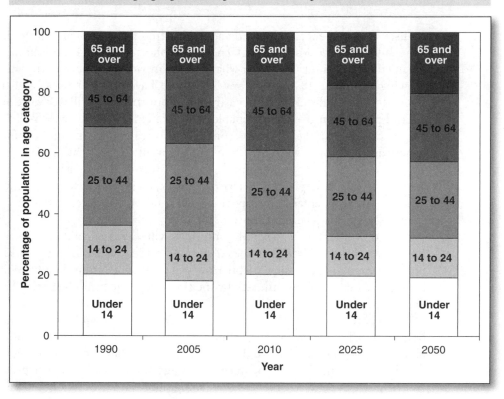

SOURCES: U.S. Bureau of the Census, 2004, 2009

financially in the future than they are today, the government will have to play an even larger role in providing health care and other services. To do that, it will have to devote more tax dollars to the needs of older citizens, a prospect that seems unlikely given the current congressional atmosphere that advocates reduced rather than increased government spending.

The graying of the United States is also challenging employers to restructure the workplace. Already, fewer young workers are available to replace retiring workers. Some employers will be forced to pay higher wages or provide additional benefits to attract new workers or will be forced to focus more attention on employee productivity, perhaps turning to machines to replace workers.

On the positive side, however, employers will have to find innovative ways to keep older workers interested in the job. Business owners are beginning to realize that older workers are more stable employees than younger workers. Indeed, the turnover rate for workers under 30 is 6 times higher than the rate for workers over 50 (The Silver Lining at Borders, 2011). So employers are developing new strategies to recruit older employees. Home Depot, for example, offers its older workers "snowbird specials"—winter jobs in warm-climate regions like Florida and summer jobs in cooler states like Maine. Employers may also have to keep older workers interested in continuing to work by offering substantial bonuses or by creating prestigious and well-paid part-time positions.

Conclusion

In discussing current and future demographic trends, I can't help but think about my own children. Their Millennium Generation cohort is the first to reach the teen years during the 21st century. I wonder what kind of impact being born in the late 1980s and growing up in the 1990s and early 2000s will have on their lives. Will the world's population reach the predicted catastrophic proportions, or will we figure out a way to control population growth and enable all people to live quality lives? Will the growing ethnic diversity of U.S. society continue to create tension and conflict, or will Americans eventually learn how to be a truly multicultural nation? What will be the single, most definitive "punctuating" event for my sons' cohort: a war, an assassination, a severe economic depression, a terrorist attack, a natural disaster, a political scandal, or some environmental catastrophe? Or will it be world peace, an end to hunger and homelessness, and a cure for cancer?

I also wonder how well social institutions will serve my children's generation. Will jobs be waiting for them when they're ready to settle down and go to work? What will be their share of the national debt? How will they perceive family life? Will marriage be an outdated mode of intimacy by the time they reach middle age? What will be a desirable family size?

As a parent, of course, I'm more than a little curious about how these questions will be answered. But as a sociologist, I realize that they will emerge only from the experiences and interactions of my kids, and others their age, as they progress through their lives. Herein lies the unique and fundamental message of the sociological perspective.

As powerful and relentless as the demographic and generational forces described in this chapter are in determining my children's life chances, the responsibility for shaping and changing this society in the 21st century ultimately rests in the hands of their generation. This topic—the ability of individuals to change and reconstruct their society—is the theme of the next and final chapter.

YOUR TURN

Demographers often use population pyramids (refer back to Exhibit 13.3) to graphically display the age and sex distributions of a population. These pictures are often used to draw conclusions about a population's most pressing economic, educational, and social needs. To see what these pyramids look like for different countries, visit the U.S. Bureau of the Census Web site (www.census.gov/ipc/www/idb/informationGateway.php). Once there, you can select a particular country and then click on the "Population Pyramids" tab to display its age and sex distribution.

Using information from the most recent U.S. census (available in the government documents section of your school's library or at www.census.gov), construct population pyramids for several different types of U.S. cities:

- A college town (e.g., Ann Arbor, Michigan; Princeton, New Jersey)
- A military town (e.g., Norfolk, Virginia; Annapolis, Maryland)
- A large city (e.g., New York City, Chicago, Los Angeles)
- A small rural town
- An affluent suburb
- A city with a large elderly retirement community (e.g., St. Petersburg, Florida; Sun City, Arizona)

Exhibit 13.6 Population Pyramid Form

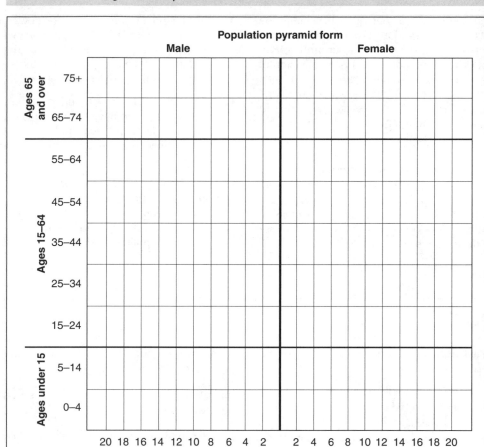

Exhibit 13.6 is a form you can copy and then use to construct your population pyramids.

After constructing your population pyramids, describe how the age and sex profiles of these cities differ. What other characteristics of these cities would be different as a result of the shape of their populations? Consider the following:

- The nature of the educational system
- The types of businesses that would succeed or fail
- The sorts of recreational opportunities available
- Political issues considered important and the degree of citizen involvement in political activity
- Important health care issues
- Crime rates
- Divorce rates
- Suicide rates

From these differences, draw some general conclusions about how people's lives are influenced by the age and sex distribution of the population in which they live.

CHAPTER HIGHLIGHTS

- Often overlooked in our quest to identify the structural factors that shape our everyday experiences are the effects of our birth cohort. Birth cohorts are more than just a collection of individuals born within a few years of each other; they are distinctive generations tied together by historical events, national and global population trends, and large-scale societal changes.

- Earth's population is growing at an unprecedented rate. But different countries experience different rates of growth. Poor, developing countries are expanding rapidly, whereas the populations in wealthy, developed countries have either stabilized or, in some cases, declined.

- When the population of a country grows rapidly, the age structure is increasingly dominated by young people. In slow-growth countries with low birthrates and high life expectancy, the population is much older, on average.

- As conditions in developing countries grow worse, pressures to migrate increase, creating a variety of cultural, political, and economic fears in countries experiencing high levels of immigration.

- The changing age structure of the U.S. population—more older people and fewer younger people—suggests that a number of adjustments will have to be made in both employment policies and social programs.

KEY TERMS

age structure: Population's balance of old and young people

birth cohort: Set of people who were born during the same era and who face similar societal circumstances brought about by their shared position in the overall age structure of the population

cohort effect: Phenomenon in which members of a birth cohort tend to experience a particular life course event or rite of passage—puberty, marriage, childbearing, graduation, entry into the workforce, death—at roughly the same time

demographer: Sociologist who studies trends in population characteristics

migration: Movement of populations from one geographic area to another

period effect: Phenomenon in which a historical event or major social trend contributes to the unique shape and outlook of a birth cohort

urbanization: Process by which people leave rural areas and begin to concentrate in large cities

STUDENT STUDY SITE

Visit the Student Study Site at **www.sagepub.com/newman9e** for these additional learning tools:

- Flashcards
- Web quizzes
- Sociologists at Work features
- Micro-Macro Connection features
- Video links
- Audio links
- Web resources
- SAGE journal articles

Architects of Change

Reconstructing Society

14

Social Change

Social Movements

The Sociological Imagination Revisited

Jonathan Simms, a 17-year-old student from a working-class family in Belfast, Northern Ireland, was a gifted soccer player who some felt had a chance of playing professionally. In September 2001, however, things began to change. He seemed to lose interest in soccer, and his playing suffered. Around the house, he became clumsy and began falling down, dropping things, and so on. He slurred his words. His parents suspected that he was drinking or taking drugs.

Within weeks, Jonathan became so weak that he had to be rushed to the hospital. He was diagnosed with a condition called variant Creutzfeldt-Jakob disease, popularly known as mad cow disease. This malady is a debilitating condition that results from eating infected beef. It can incubate in the body for years, even decades, before manifesting itself by attacking the brain (Belkin, 2003). By the middle of 2002, Jonathan could no longer walk or talk. His parents had to bathe him. Soon he became totally unresponsive, lying in bed in a vegetative state.

Doctors told Jonathan's parents that there was no hope and that he wouldn't live more than a year. But his father, Don, refused to accept the prognosis. And so he set out on a single-minded mission: to save his son's life. Don quit his job and spent days on the Internet trying to find doctors, researchers, anybody who could commute his son's death sentence.

Don Simms eventually found a researcher, Steven Dealler, who had been experimenting with a powerful and sometimes lethal new drug called pentosan polysulfate (PPS). PPS had shown some effectiveness in treating animals suffering from a similar disease called scrapie but had never been tested on humans. The problem with PPS is that it must be injected directly into the brain to achieve its intended effect. Most doctors were convinced that injecting this drug directly into a human's brain would be fatal.

So Don embarked on another quest: to find someone who would be willing to use this technique on his son. He found Dr. Nikolai Rainov, a neurosurgeon who was an expert on injecting cancer drugs directly into the brain. Dr. Rainov agreed to treat Jonathan, but the board of neurosurgery at Rainov's hospital refused to approve the treatment plan, stating that it was simply too dangerous (Belkin, 2003). Britain's Committee on Safety of Medicines entered the fray, saying that there was no rational basis for prescribing the drug ("Family of VCJD Victim Claim Untried Treatment Is a Success," 2003).

Don didn't give up. He found a hospital in Germany that would allow the PPS treatment. He chartered a medical transport plane—at his own expense—and prepared his

473

son for the trip. But days before the family was set to leave, the German Department of Health blocked them. Germany had no cases of mad cow disease and wanted to keep it that way.

Again, Don refused to give up. He hired a lawyer and took the case to court in Great Britain. Numerous legal battles ensued. But in December 2002, 15 months after the initial diagnosis, a High Court judge ruled that the family could proceed with the treatment.

Jonathan began PPS treatments in February 2003. After several months, his doctors noticed that his heart rhythms were improving, that he had regained his ability to swallow, and that he was more responsive to light and pain. There were none of the adverse side effects that critics had predicted. By all accounts, the disease had been brought under control. In 2008, his condition was upgraded from "critical" to "non–life threatening." However, in 2011, Jonathan Simms finally died. Nevertheless, he lived for a decade with the disease—about a decade longer than anyone except his father thought possible at the time of his diagnosis. He is the world's longest known survivor of mad cow disease.

The message of the Jonathan Simms case is sociologically compelling: An individual was able to overcome the institutional obstacles of a massive international medical establishment to find an answer to a seemingly insoluble problem. As we have seen throughout this book, institutions must operate in a highly structured, standardized, and impersonal way, at a level above the interests and personalities of the individual people they are created to serve. Imagine the chaos that would ensue if the system were set up so that any parent with a terminally ill child could compel researchers, physicians, and hospitals to concoct unique and risky treatments. The entire health care system would quickly collapse. That hasn't stopped some patient advocacy groups from lobbying for laws that would allow the "compassionate use" of not yet approved experimental drugs for seriously ill patients who have run out of other options (Harmon, 2009).

But from an institutional perspective, new drugs must be tested meticulously—and sometimes slowly—to determine their effectiveness and to identify all potentially dangerous side effects before they are made available to the public. A sharp line must be drawn between the need to satisfy the principles of sound scientific method and the desire to help people who are suffering (D. J. Rothman & Edgar, 1992). Insurance companies usually won't pay for drugs that have not completed rigorous scientific testing (Harmon, 2009). Indeed, in 2005, the Food and Drug Administration slowed down its drug approval process in response to several reports of unsafe drugs on the market (G. Harris, 2005a). But Jonathan's story shows that individuals can overcome bureaucratic slowness and actually change a part of the social structure. As a result of Don Simms's actions, the standard medical approach to treating people infected with mad cow disease changed.

In the past, only the most dedicated individuals, such as Don Simms, were able to become highly involved in medical decisions. Today, however, when a doctor mentions a diagnosis or prescribes a drug, patients can immediately go online and consult one of the thousands of medical Web sites or blogs that offer information (some of it more trustworthy than others) on everything from common colds to exotic diseases. And when they visit their doctors, more and more patients arrive with information they've downloaded from the Internet (Kolata, 2000).

By working together, individuals with the same illnesses or medical concerns have also been able to act as their own best advocates. For instance, in the early 1990s, AIDS deaths were mounting while the slow progress of the government drug approval process kept drugs out of the hands of the people who needed them. But AIDS activists demanded that the Food and Drug Administration loosen rules for clinical trials and speed up the approval process (L. K. Altman, 2011). They were successful and thus changed the way AIDS drugs are developed and regulated. Effective treatments—called antiretroviral therapies—are now being produced more quickly and are making an impact. Mother-to-child transmission of HIV/AIDS in the United States, for example, has been all but eliminated (Santora, 2005), and for many people who are HIV positive, AIDS has become merely a chronic illness, not the inevitable death sentence it once was. Some studies have even found that antiretrovirals are effective in *preventing* infection (D. Brown, 2011).

AIDS activists have also successfully pressured pharmaceutical companies to allow developing countries in sub-Saharan Africa to import cheaper, generic antiretrovirals (Swarns, 2001). In 2006, for instance, Bristol-Myers agreed to license its newest and most powerful AIDS drugs to pharmaceutical companies in India and South Africa so they could be made more cheaply (McNeil, 2006). These activists have worked together to magnify the influence none of them could have had acting individually. The reach of their achievements goes beyond sick individuals to global institutions and concerns.

This theme—the power of individuals acting collectively to change the structural elements of their society—guides this final chapter of the book. I have spent the previous 13 chapters discussing how our society and everything in it is socially constructed and how these social constructions, in turn, shape the lives of individuals. You may feel a little helpless when considering how much control culture, bureaucracies, institutions, and systems of social stratification have over our lives. It's only fitting, then, to end this book on a more encouraging note, with a discussion of social change and the ways individuals can reconstruct their society.

Social Change

Change is the preeminent characteristic of modern human societies, whether it occurs in personal relationships, cultural norms and values, systems of stratification, or institutions. Everywhere you look—your school, your job, your home, your government, and every aspect of your very way of life—institutional and cultural change is the rule, not the exception.

As a result of substantive changes affecting many social institutions simultaneously, the United States and other technologically advanced societies have become what sociologists call **postindustrial societies**. Economies that once centered on farms and agriculture or factories and the production of material goods now revolve around information and service industries, including communication, mass media, research and development, tourism, insurance, banking and finance, and technology. The everyday lives of ordinary people in these societies are qualitatively different from the lives of those in agricultural or industrial societies.

Change is clear when we look at specific institutions. Consider how the nature of education has changed in the past half century. If you had taken this sociology course 50 years ago, your instructor would have needed only a few tools: a good collection of books on the subject, a manual typewriter, some pencils, a ditto machine, a stack of carbon paper, and a love of the discipline. Good instructors today still need a love of the discipline (I hope!), but it's becoming difficult to teach interestingly, effectively, and efficiently without taking advantage of state-of-the-art technology: a high-speed computer; in-class access to the Internet; e-mail; databases, blogs, and course materials available online; computerized test banks; and a DVD library. My university goes so far as to offer financial incentives to professors who want to revise their courses to incorporate the latest technology. Indeed, technological advances have made similar inroads into almost every occupation—as well as almost every social institution.

Family life in the United States has also changed considerably over the past 50 years. Divorce rates were low in the 1950s, skyrocketed in the 1960s and 1970s, stabilized in the 1980s and 1990s, and have dropped a bit in the 2000s. Women have entered the workforce in unprecedented numbers. People are waiting longer to marry, and once they do, they are having fewer children. Cultural concerns about gender equality have altered the way men and women relate to one another inside and outside the home. Social and sexual rules that once seemed permanent and natural have disintegrated: Unmarried couples can live openly together, unmarried women can have and keep their babies without community condemnation, and remaining single and remaining childless have become acceptable lifestyle options (Skolnick & Skolnick, 1992). In short, today's family bears little resemblance to the cultural ideal of the 1950s.

These changes in family life have, in turn, affected other institutions. Because so many families are headed by dual-earner couples these days, children spend less time with their parents than they did in the past, forcing families to depend on others to look after their children: paid caregivers, friends, neighbors, and/or teachers. More parents than ever rely on professional day care centers to watch over their preschool-age children. Many of these centers require that children be toilet trained before they enroll, compelling parents to exert premature pressure on their children to comply. As a result, many pediatricians report an increase in children with toilet training problems, such as lack of daytime and nighttime urine control (Erica Goode, 1999).

Schools are also being called on to address many of the problems families used to deal with at home. They now routinely provide students with training in moral values, technological and financial "literacy," adequate nutrition, and practical instruction to help them avoid drug and alcohol abuse, teen pregnancy, and sexually transmitted diseases.

Not surprisingly, the very nature of childhood is also changing. Contemporary social critics argue that childhood has all but disappeared in the modern world. In the United States, children are exposed to events, devices, images, and ideas that would have been inconceivable to their Baby Boom grandparents or Generation X parents when they were young. Moreover, the increasingly competitive nature of childhood is making some parents feel obligated to give their young children every conceivable edge to help them succeed.

MICRO-MACRO CONNECTION

Parental Pressure in Childhood Sports

In the past, childhood sports were simply for fun and recreation. But sports are now a multibillion-dollar business (Greene, 2004). With the promise of lucrative careers looming large, parents often encourage young children who show some athletic promise to hone their skills early on. For instance, gymnasts and figure skaters must start training for their athletic futures when they're toddlers if they have any desire to succeed later on. Companies with names like athleticBaby and Baby Goes Pro now market sports DVDs to parents who want to get their children started in athletics—sometimes even before they're old enough to walk. The

Little Gym in Scottsdale, Arizona, offers exercise classes for children as young as four months (Hyman, 2010).

In communities all across the country, parents encourage and sometimes force their children to specialize in one sport and play it year round, making sports look, for all intents and purposes, like work. When asked how long the baseball season is for his team of nine-year-olds, one coach replied, "Labor Day to Labor Day" (quoted in Pennington, 2003, p. C16). Ironically, such early specialization is making children less athletically well rounded and more prone to injury.

Furthermore, it has become rather common for children to be turned over to professionals for training for future athletic careers. Affluent towns often have youth soccer clubs run by paid directors and coached by professionals rather than parent volunteers. Some parents go even further. At IMG Academies in Bradenton, Florida, for instance, potential sports prodigies—in team sports like baseball, basketball, and soccer as well as individual sports like tennis and golf—practice their sport over four hours a day for five days a week from September to May. In addition, they participate in hours of intense physical and mental conditioning each week. Tuition plus room and board can cost more than $50,000 a year, and that's not counting extras like private coaching sessions, which can go for an additional $500 an hour. In the end, some parents end up investing hundreds of thousands of dollars in their children's athletic futures (Sokolove, 2004).

Parents who pressure their children to succeed athletically defend their actions by citing studies that show that adolescents involved in sports are less likely to use drugs and are more likely to get good grades in school than children who aren't involved. The ultra-organized model of sports teams, they believe, is a valuable way to teach children qualities they will need down the road, like teamwork, responsibility, and self-reliance.

But not everyone is in favor of specialized, pressurized sports experiences for children. Grassroots organizations with names like "Putting Family First" and "Ready, Set, Relax" have sprung up in recent years to help parents and children return relaxation to lives that are crammed with games, practices, and other activities (Tugend, 2006). Some communities have established "Silent Saturdays," days on which soccer coaches are asked not to coach their players and parents are asked not to cheer or guide their children in any way. There is no shouting, swearing, or yelling at referees by coaches and, according to supporters, no pressure on children. They are free to have fun (R. A. Powell, 2004).

As we saw in Chapter 9, the pressure on children to excel at younger and younger ages reflects a growing concern with young people's ability to compete in an increasingly tight economic marketplace. In the pressure-packed world of contemporary childhood sports, we see the interconnections of large-scale social change and everyday life.

More seriously, children are increasingly having trouble getting along in society. A 2005 nationwide study found that about 7 out of every 1,000 three- and four-year-old preschoolers are expelled each year for misbehavior, a rate more than three times as high as for K–12 students (Gilliam, 2005). We read about 12-year-olds becoming pregnant and seven-year-olds being tried for crimes such as rape and drug smuggling. In Pensacola, Florida, a five-year-old girl faced assault charges for beating a 51-year-old school counselor. In Columbus, Ohio, an eight-year-old girl was charged with attempted murder for allegedly pouring poison into her great-grandmother's drink because the two didn't get along. A six-year-old in Michigan shot and killed a classmate. A seven-year-old boy in Tampa beat his seven-month-old sister to death with a two-by-four (Chachere, 2005).

In 1990, about 66,000 juveniles in the United States were arrested for the sale, manufacture, or possession of illegal drugs; in 2008, that figure increased to more than 134,000 (U.S. Bureau of the Census, 2011b). The National Longitudinal Study of Adolescent Health found that one in four young people between the ages of 12 and

17 has used a gun or a knife or has been in a situation where someone was injured by a weapon in the past year ("Study Finds Increase in Weapons Use," 2000). About 7% of teachers nationwide have been threatened with injury or physically attacked by a student (National Center for Education Statistics, 2010). No wonder that since the late 1980s, 44 states have adopted new laws enabling courts to try more children as adults. Between 1990 and 2008, the number of juveniles sent to adult jails and prisons increased by over 300% (Minton & Sabol, 2009). In fact, nearly three times as many youthful offenders are held in adult facilities as are held in juvenile detention centers (Minton, 2011).

The state of childhood is even more precarious in other parts of the world:

- About 830,000 children around the globe die each year from preventable accidents, such as drowning, burns, car crashes, poisoning, and falls (cited in McNeil, 2008).
- The United Nations estimates that about 1.1 million children worldwide are deprived of their liberty and detained in prisons, military facilities, immigration detention centers, welfare centers, or educational facilities (Hamilton, Anderson, Barnes, & Dorling, 2011).
- More than 158 million children under 14 are engaged in child labor, many in hazardous conditions involving mines, agricultural chemicals and pesticides, and heavy machinery (UNICEF, 2011). Some are as young as five or six. Often they're not even paid for their labor (Wines, 2006).
- More than 250,000 children—sometimes as young as nine—have been exploited as child soldiers and are taking part in armed conflicts in places such as Sudan, Colombia, Myanmar, Iraq, and Afghanistan (United Nations, 2007).

Clearly, social change has made children's lives less carefree than we would wish.

The Speed of Social Change

In the distant past, societies tended to change slowly, almost imperceptibly, during the course of one's lifetime. Family and community traditions typically spanned many generations. Although the traditional societies that exist today still change relatively slowly, change in postindustrial societies is particularly fast paced. Even while writing this book, I've had to revise several examples at the last minute because things have changed so abruptly. The pre-Facebook, pre-Twitter early 2000s already seem like a long-gone era.

Because we live in a world that seems to be in a constant state of flux, we're often tempted to believe that rapid social change is an exclusively contemporary issue. Keep in mind, however, that sociologists and other scholars have long expressed deep concern over the effects that social change has on people. The 19th-century sociologist Émile Durkheim (1897/1951) argued that rapid social change creates a vacuum in norms, which he called *anomie*, where the old cultural rules no longer apply. When things change quickly—through sudden economic shifts, wars, natural disasters, population explosions, or rapid transitions from a traditional to a modern society—people become disoriented and experience anomie as they search for new guidelines to govern their lives.

Widespread anomie affects the larger society as well. When rapid change disrupts social norms, it unleashes our naturally greedy impulses. Without norms to constrain our unlimited aspirations and with too few resources to satisfy our unlimited desires, we are in a sense doomed to a frustrating life of striving for unattainable goals

(Durkheim, 1897/1951). The result, Durkheim felt, is higher rates of suicide and criminal activity as well as weakened ties to family, neighborhood, and friends.

But rapid change isn't always bad. Sometimes speedy change is necessary to effectively address shifting social conditions. For instance, over the span of a few years in the late 1990s, school districts around the country drastically modified their curricula in response to the sudden ascendancy of the Internet in students' everyday lives, forever changing the face of U.S. education. In the wake of the September 11, 2001, attacks and the subsequent military actions in Iraq and Afghanistan, universities around the country scrambled to offer more courses on Islam and the politics of the Middle East.

The velocity of change today has affected the way sociologists go about their work, too. When U.S. society was understood to be relatively stable, sociological study was fairly straightforward. Most social researchers in the 1950s believed that one could start a 5- or 10-year study of some social institution, say the family or higher education, and assume that the institution would still be much the same when the study ended (Wolfe, 1991). Today, such assumptions about the staying power of institutions are dubious at best.

There is no such thing as a permanent social institution. Thus, sociologists, like everyone else in contemporary society, have had to adjust their thinking and their methods to accommodate the rapid pace of social change.

Causes of Social Change

The difficulty of pinning down any aspect of society when change is so rapid has led sociologists to study change itself. Following in the footsteps of Durkheim, they ask, what causes all these technological, cultural, and institutional changes? On occasion, massive change—in the private lives of individuals as well as in entire social institutions—can result from a single dramatic historical event, such as the attacks of September 11, 2001, Hurricane Katrina in 2005, the global economic meltdown of 2008, or the Japanese earthquake and tsunami of 2011. We can be thankful that such colossal events are relatively rare. Sociologists who focus on change tell us that institutional transformations are more likely to be caused over time by a variety of social forces, including environmental and population pressures, cultural innovation, and technological and cultural diffusion.

Environmental and Population Pressures

As you saw in Chapter 13, the shifting size and shape of the population—globally and locally—is enough by itself to create change in societies. As populations grow, more and more people move either into urban areas, where jobs are easier to find, or into previously uninhabited areas, where natural resources are plentiful.

Environmental sociologists note the complex interplay among humans, social structure, and natural resources as previously undeveloped territories are settled. For instance, one social scientist has argued that many civilizations throughout history—such as the Easter Islanders, the Mayans, and the Norse colony in Greenland—collapsed because deforestation led to soil erosion, which led to food shortages and ultimately political and social collapse (Diamond, 2005).

Even when new areas are developed for food production, environmental damage often occurs. Of course, improved food supplies have had obvious benefits for societies around the world. Fewer and fewer people today die from famine and malnutrition than ever before. But the positive effects of a growing global food supply have been tempered by the serious environmental harm that new production techniques have caused. For instance, pesticide use has increased 17-fold over the past several decades, threatening the safety of water supplies. Some insects have developed resistance, which leads to increased pesticide use. New crop varieties often require more irrigation than old varieties, which has been accompanied by increased erosion and water runoff. As demand for meat products increases, cattle ranches expand, destroying natural habitats, displacing native animal species, and polluting water sources. Modern factory farming practices helped spread mad cow disease throughout Great Britain (Cowley, 2003), affecting people like Jonathan Simms.

More broadly, the clearing of forests and the burning of fossil fuels, such as coal, oil, and natural gas, have been implicated as the chief cause of ***global climate change***—a steady rise in Earth's average temperature as a result of increasing amounts of carbon dioxide in the atmosphere. We are already seeing the consequences of climate change: Polar ice caps and glaciers are melting; sea levels are rising; plants and animals are being forced out of their habitats; certain diseases, like malaria, are spreading to higher altitudes; and the number of severe storms, heat waves, and droughts is increasing. Many scientists believe that the long-term effects of global climate change may lead to unprecedented worldwide catastrophe.

Cultural and Technological Innovation

But population and environmental pressures have the potential to create more positive social change in the form of cultural and technological innovation. For example, natural disasters, such as earthquakes, hurricanes, and tornadoes, often inspire improvements in emergency response technology, home safety products, and architectural design that improve everyone's lives. Likewise, concerns about pollution and global climate change have fostered innovative changes in people's behavior (e.g., recycling and conserving energy), the creation of environmentally safe, "green" products and services (low-watt light bulbs, low-flow showerheads, and biodegradable detergent), and the development of energy-efficient hybrid vehicles and non-polluting energy sources, such as solar power and wind power. The result is felt not only on an individual level but also on a societal level, as eco-efficient and environmentally sustainable businesses grow around these innovations and attract investors. The Apollo Alliance (2011), a coalition of business, labor, environmental, and community groups, estimates that a $500 billion investment over 10 years could produce 5 million jobs in renewable energy, hybrid cars, and infrastructure replacement. Many universities, companies, and even city governments now employ full-time "sustainability directors" to look for cost-saving ways to minimize the wasting of electricity and natural gas, improve energy efficiency, and reduce harmful greenhouse gasses (Greenblatt, 2009).

Sometimes, these scientific discoveries and technological inventions spur further innovations within a society. Improvements in motor vehicle safety, such as air bags, safety belts, child safety seats, and motorcycle helmets, have contributed to large reductions in motor vehicle deaths and fundamentally changed the way we drive. Water fluoridation is credited for a 40% to 60% reduction in tooth loss in adults. Safer and healthier foods have all but eliminated nutritional deficiency diseases such as rickets, goiter, and pellagra in the United States (Centers for Disease Control and Prevention, 1999).

Often, revolutionary innovations seem insignificant at first. Imagine what life would be like without the invention of corrective eyeglasses, which dramatically extended the activities of near- and farsighted people and fostered the belief that physical limitations could be overcome with a little ingenuity. The invention of indoor plumbing, the internal combustion engine, television, the microchip, nuclear fusion, and effective birth control have been instrumental in determining the course of human history. Sometimes the smallest innovation has the largest impact: According to one author, without the machine-made precision screw—the most durable way of attaching one object to another—entire fields of science would have languished, routine maritime commerce would have been impossible, and there would have been no machine tools and hence no industrial products and no industrial revolution (Rybczynski, 1999).

But social institutions can sometimes be slow to adjust to scientific and technological innovations. Consider, for instance, the medical treatment of infertility. Artificial insemination, in vitro fertilization, surrogate motherhood, and other medical advances have increased the number of previously infertile people who can now bear and raise children. And more and more same-sex couples are utilizing infertility treatments to have children. According to one of the nation's largest sperm banks, about one third of its clients are lesbian couples (Holson, 2011b). Yet these technological developments were changing the face of parenthood well before society began to recognize and address the ethical, moral, and legal issues they raised. For instance, close to half a million embryos created through in vitro fertilization are kept frozen at fertility clinics around the country. Many of them belong to couples that no longer need them because they are finished having children. But it's unclear exactly what should be done with the embryos. Some couples are opposed to destroying them for moral or religious reasons. Most couples don't want to donate them to other couples because of genetic links to their own children. (In fact, state and federal regulations make donation to other couples difficult because they require donors to come back to the clinics to be tested for infectious diseases.) Still others would like to donate them for research, but that option is not always available (Grady, 2008).

The very definition of family and parenthood can also become complicated when technology plays a role in childbearing. Surrogacy—an arrangement in which a woman agrees to become pregnant and give birth to a child others will raise—divides motherhood into three distinct roles, which may be occupied by three separate people: the *genetic* mother (the one who supplies the egg from which the fetus develops), the *gestational* mother (the one who becomes pregnant and gives birth), and the *social* mother (the one who raises the child). Add to the mix the *genetic* father and the *social* father, and you can see how difficult it can sometimes be to establish legal parenthood. There is little uniformity between states about whether to recognize and enforce surrogacy agreements. Some states grant preference to surrogacy contracts; others assume the woman giving birth to the child is the mother and will reverse that determination only when the commissioning couple files a prebirth order to legally adopt the child after he or she is born (Shapo, 2006).

Moreover, the technological innovations that are meant to improve our lives can also change people's behavior in unanticipated, and sometimes dangerous, ways. Consider these examples:

- Antibiotics were a revolutionary advance in the treatment of infectious diseases. But doctors soon began prescribing them for minor illnesses just to be safe. As a result of the overuse of antibiotics, some infectious and highly dangerous organisms have become resistant to the drugs. Some public health experts estimate that perhaps as many as 100,000 deaths a year in the United States occur as a result of antibiotic-resistant infections (cited in Interlandi, 2010).
- Low-tar, low-nicotine cigarettes cut down the amount of dangerous substances, but in doing so they encourage people to continue smoking.
- The distractions caused by technological devices used in cars—cell phones, onboard navigation systems, entertainment centers, even fax machines—may be responsible for as many as 1.5 million crashes each year. The risk of a truck driver getting into an accident or near accident is 23 times greater when she or he is texting while driving than when she or he is not doing so (Richtel & Wald, 2009).
- Not only do hybrid cars reduce air pollution and reliance on fossil fuels, but they also reduce noise pollution. However, pedestrians and bicyclists sometimes have difficulty hearing these cars coming their way, thereby increasing the risk of being clipped or run over. At intersections, parking lots, and other places where cars travel slowly, pedestrians and bicyclists get hit by hybrids at up to twice the normal rate. To address the problem, manufacturers are now marketing fake car noise so unwary people can hear them (Mihm, 2009).
- Smartphones have improved our ability to communicate with others and remain technologically connected, but they've also created a workday and a workweek that never end. With these devices, the unspoken expectation is that a person will always be reachable. Hence, we no longer have any excuse to be "away" from work.

MICRO-MACRO CONNECTION

Technology and the Erosion of Privacy

Computer technology has revolutionized our lives by making purchasing, communicating, and information gathering easy and efficient (see Exhibit 14.1). The Internet in particular has all but eliminated the constraints of time and place, whether we're conversing with friends, researching a topic of interest for a school paper, seeking guidance on an important decision, or conducting everyday business.

In some ways, the anonymity of the Internet allows people to do or say things they wouldn't do or say if they were identifiable. For instance, although anonymity allows dissidents and whistle blowers to post critical comments about powerful individuals and organizations that they would be reluctant to post if their identities were known, it also invites the posting of inflammatory and sometimes threatening messages online, known as trolling (Bazelon, 2011). Funeral-related Web sites have become quite popular in the past few years, giving distant mourners opportunities to post remembrances of the dead that range from simple text messages to multimedia presentations (Holson, 2011a). But the anonymity and one-click immediacy of these sites has emboldened some people to say nasty things about the deceased they wouldn't say in a letter or in person. The posting of angry tirades, petty insults, accusations of incest or criminal activity, and revelations of adultery have become so common that some sites have been forced to employ full-time screeners to catch personal attacks and inappropriate comments (Urbina, 2006).

Our reliance on the Internet has also made us much more vulnerable to invasions of privacy. Just ask Anthony Weiner, the former U.S. representative from New York who was forced to resign in 2011 after the sexually suggestive photos of himself that he sent to several women via Twitter went public. A mobile GPS tracking application called FourSquare allows users to locate their friends. It keeps a running tally of how many times people "check in" at

Exhibit 14.1   Technological Changes, 2000–2010

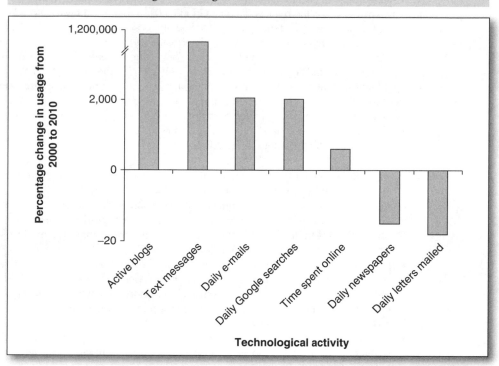

SOURCE: "Exactly How Much," 2010, p. 56

every location, automatically building a diary of their movements and habits (Wolf, 2010). Companies in the multibillion-dollar data mining industry collect and sell personal and behavioral data to anyone willing to buy them. These data include information about religious preference, political affiliation, annual income, educational history, entertainment likes and dislikes, purchasing activities, and so on (J. Stein, 2011).

Furthermore, the Internet never forgets; it retains every bit of information ever posted, sometimes making it impossible to escape one's past. "Like a metastasized cancer . . . incriminating data [embeds] itself into the nether reaches of cyberspace, etched into archives, algorithms, and a web of hyperlinks" (Bilton, 2011, p. 1). Employers routinely scan the Internet for information about job applicants. The chief security officer at an encryption software company once warned, "You should always assume anything you write online is stapled to your résumé" (quoted in Clemmitt, 2006a, p. 629). In the medical field, for instance, the Department of Health and Human Services helps potential employers with a Web site called the National Practitioner Data Bank. Here, state licensing boards, hospitals, and other health care facilities can find out whether a doctor's license has been revoked in another state or if the doctor has ever been disciplined.

In pre-Internet days, people could essentially leave "childish things" and youthful transgressions behind them as they matured into adulthood. No one had to know that as a youth you smoked a lot of pot, engaged in petty shoplifting, said really stupid things, followed Phish around the country for a year and a half, or slept with the wrong people. Today, however, those experiences have an unbounded shelf life.

In 2010, an Albuquerque police officer flippantly listed "human waste disposal" as his occupation on his Facebook profile. Several months later, after he was involved in a fatal on-duty shooting, a local television station—using sleuthing techniques any contemporary eight-year-old with a laptop has mastered—dug up his profile. He issued a public apology calling his cynical job description "extremely inappropriate" (Erica Goode, 2011a, p. A1). But it was too late. He'd already been placed on desk duty. In Indiana, a television station discovered photos of a drunken state trooper on his Facebook page. He had also posted a comment about a homeless man who'd been beaten by officers in California: "These people should have died when they were young anyway, I'm just doing them a favor" (Erica Goode, 2011a, p. A18). He was forced to resign.

With so much private material available online, the posting of false or misleading information can quickly tarnish reputations. So it was only a matter of time before someone came up with a way for people to clean their stained identities. For an annual fee of $1,000, a British Web site, ICorrect, now gives individuals or companies who have been the target of unflattering gossip or misstated facts a chance to wipe away the mud that has been slung in their direction by posting corrections online. Others have turned to practitioners of a new Web specialty known as "online reputation management" to expunge negative posts; bury unfavorable search results on Google, Facebook, or Twitter; and generally monitor a client's digital image (Bilton, 2011).

And it's not just the Internet that invades our privacy:

- Since September 11, 2001, there has been a huge increase in the use of surveillance cameras—some run by law enforcement, others by private businesses—in airports, stores, banks, schools, hospitals, busy urban sidewalks, and quiet suburban neighborhoods (D. E. Murphy, 2002). It's estimated that London residents are photographed more than 300 times a day by the more than 1.5 million surveillance cameras placed around the city (Clemmitt, 2006b).
- In 2004, the Food and Drug Administration approved the manufacture of under-the-skin computer chips that when scanned at the proper frequency can provide access to individuals' medical information. Although supporters believe access to such information will improve medical care and save lives, opponents fear that the chips will further erode our personal privacy (Feder & Zeller, 2004).
- About two thirds of all cars manufactured in 2005 were equipped with "black boxes" that record data, such as speed, steering wheel movement, and how hard the brakes are pressed (Clemmitt, 2006b).
- Over half of American universities now use some type of anti-plagiarism service to monitor students and their work so they can detect cheating. When test proctors at the University of Central Florida see what they suspect is student cheating, they can direct an overhead camera to zoom in and photograph the student; images are then burned onto a CD and retained for evidence (Gabriel, 2010a).

As you can see, technological innovation can be a double-edged sword. It has the potential to make our everyday lives more efficient, convenient, and productive. But it can also chip away at the thing we hold most dear: our personal privacy.

Diffusion of Technologies and Cultural Practices

Another cause of social change is **cultural diffusion**: the process by which beliefs, technology, customs, and other cultural items are spread from one group or society to another. You may not realize it, but most of the taken-for-granted aspects of our daily lives originally came from somewhere else. For instance, pajamas, clocks, toilets, glass, coins, newspapers, and soap were initially imported into Western cultures from elsewhere (Linton, 1937). Even a fair amount of the English language has been imported, as can be seen from the following examples:

algebra (Arabic)	*barbeque* (Taino)
anatomy (Greek)	*boondocks* (Filipino Tagalog)
bagel (Yiddish)	*catamaran* (Tamil)

coyote, poncho (Spanish)

dynamite (Swedish)

medicine (Latin)

safari (Swahili)

sherbet (Turkish)

tycoon (Chinese)

vogue (French)

Diffusion often occurs because one society considers the culture or technology of another society to be useful. However, the diffusion process is not always friendly, as you may recall from the discussion of colonization in Chapter 10. When one society's territory is taken over by another society, the indigenous people may be required to adapt to the customs and beliefs of the invaders. When Europeans conquered the New World, Native American peoples were forced to abandon their traditional ways of life and become more "civilized." Hundreds of thousands of Native Americans died in the process, not only from violent conflict but also from malnutrition and new diseases inadvertently brought by their conquerors. Whether diffusion is invited or imposed, the effect is the same: a chain reaction of social changes that affect both individuals and the larger social structure.

Social Movements

One danger of talking about the sources of social change or its cultural, environmental, and institutional consequences is that we then tend to see change as a purely macrolevel structural phenomenon, something that happens to us rather than something we create. But social change is not some huge, invisible hand that descends from the heavens to arbitrarily alter our routine way of life. It is, in the end, a phenomenon driven by human action.

Collective action by large numbers of people has always been a major agent of social change, whether it takes the form of mothers marching on Washington, D.C., to demand gun control legislation; people holding a pray-in outside the Capitol building to encourage lawmakers to pass a budget "that is more reflective of the moral values of our nation" ("Religious Groups Gather," 2005); or a sit-in by students in the Harvard University president's house to demand higher wages for the school's blue collar workers. When people organize and extend their activities beyond the immediate confines of the group, they may become the core of a ***social movement*** (Zurcher & Snow, 1981)

Underlying all social movements is a concern with social change: the desire to enact it, stop it, or reverse it. That desire may be expressed in a variety of ways, from peaceful activities such as signing petitions, participating in civil demonstrations, donating money, and campaigning during elections to violent activities such as rioting and overthrowing a government.

Types of Social Movements

Depending on the nature of their goals, social movements can be categorized as reform movements, countermovements, or revolutionary movements. A ***reform movement*** attempts to change limited aspects of a society but does not seek to alter or replace major social institutions. Take the U.S. civil rights movement of the 1960s. It did not call for an overhaul of the U.S. economic system (capitalism) or political system (two-party democracy). Instead, it advocated a more limited change: opening up existing institutions to full and equal participation by members of minority groups (DeFronzo, 1991). Similarly, the anti–Vietnam War movement questioned government policy (and in the process brought down two presidents—Lyndon Johnson and Richard Nixon), but it didn't seek to change the form of government itself (Fendrich, 2003). Other recent examples of reform movements include the women's movement, the nuclear freeze movement, the labor union movement, the school prayer movement, and the environmental movement. The recent Tea Party movement is a political movement that espouses the values of individual liberty and limited government. Their message resonated with enough voters in 2010 that several Tea Party candidates won election to Congress. However, although adherents express a desire to dismantle the federal government for what they perceive to be out-of-control spending, debt, and deficits, the politicians they helped elect still must enact any change within the confines of the present system of government.

Because reform movements seek to alter some aspect of existing social arrangements, they are usually opposed by some people and groups. **Countermovements** are designed to prevent or reverse the changes sought or accomplished by an earlier movement. A countermovement is most likely to emerge when the reform movement against which it is reacting becomes large and effective in pursuing its goals and therefore comes to be seen as a threat to personal and social interests (Chafetz & Dworkin, 1987; Mottl, 1980).

For instance, the emergence in the 1980s and 1990s of a conservative social countermovement often called the "religious right" or the "Christian right" was provoked by a growing perception among its members of enormous social upheaval in U.S. society: the breakdown of traditional roles and values and a concerted challenge to existing institutions such as education, religion, and the family. Although members of the religious right blamed these changes on the civil rights, antiwar, student, and women's movements of the 1960s and 1970s (Klatch, 1991), they perceived the women's movement as particularly dangerous. Indeed, the leaders of the religious right were the first, in modern times, to articulate the notion that the push for women's equality is responsible for the unhappiness of many individual women and the weakening of the American family (Faludi, 1991). Access to legal abortion, the high divorce rate, and the increased number of children who grow up with working mothers are often offered as proof that the moral bases of family life are eroding (Klatch, 1991). Even today, the Christian right's fear of shifting definitions of gender due to earlier reform movements motivates them to action:

> In an era when sexual liberation has saturated American culture, when women are climbing the corporate ladder and bearing fewer children, and mainline churches are ordaining women and homosexuals, conservative evangelicals are escalating their counteroffensive. Many call themselves complementarians, signalling their belief that God ordained complementary—not identical or flexible—roles for men and women. (Worthen, 2010, p. 54)

Over the past few decades, the religious right has had some success in shifting the political and social mood of the country. It first gained legitimacy in 1980, when presidential candidate Ronald Reagan and several Senate candidates who were supported by the group won the election. It reasserted its influence in 1994 with the takeover of Congress by conservative Republicans. And it gained even more power and visibility with the election and reelection of George W. Bush, who promoted many religious right themes. Today, it remains a formidable and influential wing of the Republican party.

In the late 2000s, the religious right turned its focus to opposing the increasing visibility of homosexuality in U.S. society. Through organizations such as the Eagle Forum, the Christian Coalition, the Family Research Council, the Traditional Values Coalition, Concerned Women for America, Focus on the Family, the Alliance for Marriage, and many smaller groups around the United States, it has achieved some notable triumphs at the state and local levels. It has succeeded in influencing public school curricula as well as promoting anti-gay-rights legislation and defense of marriage acts at the city and state levels.

Over the years, the religious right has been especially effective in limiting access to abortion. Even though the majority of U.S. citizens still favor the legal right to abortion, virtually every state in the nation has enacted new restrictions on abortion since 1996, such as mandatory waiting periods and parental notification. In recent years, legislatures in states such as Kansas, Oklahoma, and Indiana have been successful in passing restrictive laws that make it even more difficult or uncomfortable for women to get abortions, such as requiring doctors to show the woman a picture of the fetus or regulating the amount and type of equipment, drugs, and resources available in clinics. Few medical schools or residency programs in obstetrics and gynecology provide training in abortion techniques, although pressure from medical student advocacy groups has led a few programs to reinstate abortion instruction into the curriculum (Bazelon, 2010).

Given such an environment, it's not surprising that abortion services have become less and less available. About 87% of all U.S. counties (and 97% of rural counties) have no abortion provider. These counties are home to 35% of all American women. Nationwide, the number of abortion providers decreased by 37% between 1982 and 2001 (Henshaw & Finer, 2003) and another 2% between 2000 and 2008 (Alan Guttmacher Institute, 2011; Kaiser Family Foundation, 2008). In addition, rates of legal abortion have declined steadily over the past two decades. In 1980, there were about 29 abortions per 1,000 women between the ages of 15 and 44; today, that figure is less than 20 per 1,000 (Alan Guttmacher Institute, 2008; U.S. Bureau of the Census, 2011b).

The women's movement, the gay rights movement, and the religious right all remain quite active today, creating numerous colorful conflicts in the national political arena. However, it is important to remember that all these movements are pursuing their interests within the existing social system—as do all reform movements and countermovements. In contrast, ***revolutionary movements*** attempt to overthrow the entire system itself, whether it is the government or the existing social structure, in order to replace it with another (Skocpol, 1979). The American Revolution of 1776, the French Revolution of 1789, the Russian Revolution of 1917, the Iranian Revolution of 1979, and the Afghan Revolution of 1996 are examples of movements that toppled existing governments and created a new social order.

Revolutionary change in basic social institutions can be brought about through nonviolent means, such as peaceful labor strikes, democratic elections, and civil disobedience. However, most successful revolutions have involved some level of violence on the part of both movement participants and groups opposing the revolution (DeFronzo, 1991).

Elements of Social Movements

Whichever type they are, social movements occur when dissatisfied people see their condition as resulting from society's inability to meet their needs. Movements typically develop when certain segments of the population conclude that society's resources—access to political power, higher education, living wages, legal justice, medical care, a clean and healthy environment, and so on—are distributed unequally and unfairly (Roger Brown, 1986). People come to believe that they have a moral right to the satisfaction of their unmet expectations and that this satisfaction cannot or will not occur without some effort on their part. This perception is often based on the experience of past failures in working within the system.

As individuals and groups who share this sense of frustration and unfairness interact, the existing system begins to lose its perceived legitimacy (Piven & Cloward, 1977). Individuals who ordinarily might have considered themselves helpless come to believe that as a social movement they have the capacity to change things and significantly alter their lives and the lives of others:

- In 2006, a Web site called MomsRising.org was launched, bringing mothers together to talk about ways to change public policy. In "house parties" all across the country, small groups of mothers meet regularly to discuss ways to lobby legislators on issues like family leave, health insurance, childcare, and after-school activities. They now have 90,000 members nationwide and have helped change paid family leave policies in several states (St. George, 2007).
- In the early 2000s, tens of thousands of janitors all around the country went on strike to demand health insurance and better wages. Typically, janitors are among the most invisible and least appreciated workers. But in Chicago, they banded together to block downtown traffic. In Los Angeles, they walked off their jobs. In New York, they marched down Park Avenue. In San Diego, some went on a hunger strike. In several cities, the janitors won new contracts.
- In several dozen cities across the country, day laborers—typically immigrants who congregate at well-known locations like street corners or parking lots, waiting for building contractors, landscapers, plumbers, or other potential employers to offer a day's work—have organized to set their own minimum wages (S. Greenhouse, 2006).

Ideology

Any successful social movement must have an ***ideology***, a coherent system of beliefs, values, and ideas that justifies its existence (R. W. Turner & Killian, 1987; Zurcher & Snow, 1981). An ideology fulfills several functions. First, it helps frame the issue in moral terms. Once people perceive the moral goodness of their position, they become willing to risk arrest, personal financial costs, or more for the good of the cause. Second, the ideology defines the group's interests and helps to identify people as either supporters or detractors, creating identifiable "good guys" and "villains." Finally, an ideology provides participants with a collective sense of what the specific goals of the movement are or should be.

Consider the antiabortion (or pro-life) movement. Its ideology rests on several assumptions about the nature of childhood and motherhood (Luker, 1984). For instance, it assumes that each conception is an act of God and so abortion violates God's will. The ideology also states that life begins at conception, the fetus is an individual who has a constitutional right to life, and every human life should be valued

(Michener, DeLamater, & Schwartz, 1986). This ideology reinforces the view among adherents that abortion is immoral, evil, and self-indulgent.

The power of an ideology to mobilize support for a social movement often depends on the broader cultural and historical context in which the movement exists. For instance, it would have seemed in the 2003 buildup to the invasion of Iraq that antiwar activists would be able to make a strong case against going to war by using an ideology based on a portrayal of the United States as a hostile aggressor. After all, the country we were set to invade, Iraq, posed no direct threat to the United States, hadn't undertaken a large-scale military mobilization, wasn't involved in planning or carrying out the 9/11 attacks that precipitated our military action, and wasn't harboring those who were involved. Internationally, the sympathetic response that we received from other countries immediately after 9/11 was short lived, replaced by a growing perception that the United States was a global bully whose policies ignore the interests of people in other countries. The vast majority of nations around the world—foes and allies alike—were strongly opposed to the invasion.

But the post–9/11 cultural atmosphere in this country was a mixture of anger, fear, lingering shock, and heightened patriotism, which made an ideology of military restraint intolerable to many Americans. Enduring memories of earlier antiwar protestors' hostility toward soldiers returning from Vietnam during the late 1960s and early 1970s complicated the task. Reluctant to disrespect the individual soldiers in Iraq who were willing to put their lives at risk, antiwar activists had to walk a thin line between opposing U.S. aggression and expressing support for the young men and women who were being asked to carry out that aggression on the front lines. Against such a backdrop, the ideology of the 2003 antiwar movement—which advocated a diplomatic, reflective, and measured approach—sounded unpatriotic, weak, and inadequate, not to mention disloyal to the thousands who died in the 9/11 attacks. Not surprisingly, the movement failed to prevent the onset of war.

Although an ideology might be what attracts people to a movement, it must be spread through social networks of friends, family, coworkers, and other contacts (Zurcher & Snow, 1981). For some people, in fact, the ideology of the movement is secondary to other social considerations. Potential participants are unlikely to join without being introduced to the movement by someone they know (Gladwell, 2010). The ideological leaders of a social movement might want to believe that participants are there because of "the cause," but chances are the participants have a friend or acquaintance who persuaded them to be there (Gerlach & Hine, 1970; Stark & Bainbridge, 1980).

Sometimes the activities required to promote or sustain a particular movement run counter to the ideological goals of the movement itself. The leaders of successful political revolutions, for example, soon realize that to run the country they now control, they must create highly structured bureaucracies not unlike the ones they have overthrown. At the time of this writing, leaders of the Egyptian pro-democracy movement were struggling to find ways to govern in the aftermath of a revolution that toppled a dictatorial regime that had been in power for 30 years. Furthermore, an ill-defined, unarticulated ideology—or one that is too broadly defined—may in the end muffle any headway the movement is able to make in the first place. In 2011, disorganized protests sprung up all over Europe. The motivation was less about specific discontent than it was about generalized anger and political estrangement. As one journalist put it,

> The unrest . . . appears to be a brushfire revolt, with no common denominators like class or ideology and an agenda that's all over the map. Its members seem united only by their rejection of government plans and by a sense that no one listens to them. . . . Today's protests offer no coherent alternative to the status quo. (Giglio, 2011, p. 5)

Participants in reform movements and countermovements may also have to engage in behaviors that conflict with the ideological beliefs of the movement. The religious right movement's pro-family, pro-motherhood positions are clearly designed to turn back the feminist agenda. However, early in the movement, it became clear that to be successful it would have to enlist high-profile women to campaign against feminist policies. Women on the religious right frequently had to leave their families, travel the country to make speeches, and display independent strength—characteristics that were anything but the models of traditional womanhood they were publicly promoting. Note how the following description of a popular female minister in the Christian right movement could apply to just about any modern-day, female professional:

> Priscilla [Shirer] now accepts about 20 out of some 300 speaking invitations each year, and she publishes a stream of Bible studies, workbooks and corresponding DVDs. . . . Jerry [her husband] does his share of housework and childcare so that Priscilla can study and write. He travels with his wife everywhere. Whenever possible, they take their sons along on her speaking trips, but they often deposit the boys with Jerry's mother. (Worthen, 2010, p. 54)

Ironically, social movements sometimes require the involvement of individuals from outside the group whose interests the movement represents. For example, many of the people who fought successfully for Blacks' right to vote in Alabama and Mississippi during the civil rights movement of the 1950s and 1960s were middle-class white college students from the North. Similarly, it wasn't until mainstream religious organizations, labor groups, and college students got involved that the *living wage movement*—an effort to require cities and counties to pay their low-wage workers an amount above the federal minimum wage—became successful. As of 2006, 140 cities had passed living wage laws (Living Wage Resource Center, 2006). The Chicago City Council, for instance, passed an ordinance requiring large retail stores, such as Wal-Mart and Home Depot, to pay a minimum wage that was almost twice as high as the federal minimum wage (Eckholm, 2006a). In 2007, Maryland became the first state to require a living wage for all state employees.

The ideology of a social movement gains additional credibility when voiced by those whose interests seem contrary to its goals. In the mid 2000s, opposition to the war in Iraq gained some traction not because people took a second look at the original antiwar ideology or because street protests and rallies suddenly gained their attention. Instead, it grew because many U.S. soldiers who fought there and saw the conditions firsthand started speaking out in opposition, often under the threat of disciplinary action (Houppert, 2005). Combatants knew the reality of war in ways that civilian protestors never could (Utne, 2006). Some even spoke out while on the front lines, posting daily blogs that criticized the condition of military equipment and resources, our lack of understanding of Iraqi insurgents, and ultimately our very involvement in the war (Finer, 2005). Membership in organizations with names like Operation Truth, Gold Star Families for Peace, and Iraq and Afghanistan Veterans of America grew during the early years of the war (N. Banerjee, 2005).

(Text continues on page 499)

Portraits of Grief

Samira Alic, Diler Erdengiz, Paul Joseph, Elizabeth Park, Katherine Porter, and Julia Torgovitskaya

War photography has a long, compelling, and conflicted history. The medium has a remarkable capacity to bring the public closer to the battlefield and to the physical and human costs of violence. Many photographers have attempted to deepen antiwar sentiment by focusing deliberately—sometimes graphically—on the devastating consequences of combat. While the impact of "real" pictures of war on antiwar opposition is by no means automatic, generations of photographers and movement activists have fed the public grim and telling visuals.

The influence of war images is also recognized by political and military leaders. Their impulse has been to control public perceptions of the face of battle through total censorship or strict guidelines. In more sophisticated strategies they have encouraged substitute images that highlight the less devastating and occasionally heroic features of human conduct under arduous conditions. Thus, war could liberate people from evil, alleviate suffering, inspire courageous behavior, and establish powerful bonds among those waging it. War has been presented as if it were fought between weapons rather than between humans. Finally, from bombed-out buildings to "shock and awe," photographs can underline the spectacular quality of war. On the other hand, political leaders have argued, pictures that convey pain or grief are in "poor taste."

The tension between the subversive and enabling impact of photography on war has played out in different historical circumstances. The clash has been especially acute during the war in Iraq, where both visual criticism and war management through public relations have reached new levels. With digital technology, well-organized Web sites, search engines, and the Internet, it is not difficult for viewers to find extremely disturbing pictures that on balance undermine the formal justifications for the war. Yet, until recently, newspaper and television editors were reluctant to publish images showing traumatized bodies, particularly of injured or dead Americans. Liberation rather than occupation, military efficiency instead of civil war, and competence over mismanagement were the dominant themes. The Bush administration banned photographs of body containers returning through Dover Airfield. The Pentagon followed a double-sided policy of embedding photojournalists who in theory operate with relative freedom while simultaneously discouraging pictures of downed helicopters, actual combat, and collateral damage. "Discouragement" has included preventing journalists from taking pictures, seizing cameras, and even dire physical threats.

The essay that follows focuses on grief following the loss of life or the severe wounds caused by the war. As with most emotions, the expression of grief differs from one individual to the next and is influenced by a range of social factors such as culture, religion, and family. Many of these differences can be traced in the photographs that follow. Yet the loss of a loved one due to sudden, unexpected, often brutal violence has crucial commonalities as well. Death and injury result not from disease, accident, or natural catastrophe, but from the deliberate actions of other human beings. This makes it particularly difficult to adjust no matter where one lives. Many never do, because the pain created by the sudden rupture can never be understood in a way that brings acceptance and personal peace. For them, the war lasts forever.

In chronicling the devastating reactions, we pay attention to the body, and especially to the face. The photographs are classified into themes common to the war experience: the loss of a comrade, the funeral, the relationship between parent and child now suddenly layered with pain, and the mutual

SOURCE: *Contexts*, Vol. 6, Number 3, pp. 48–55. ISSN 1536-5042, electronic ISSN 1537-6052. © 2007 by the American Sociological Association.

support of women as they share a loss. These expressions of grief transcend the presumed boundary between the dangers of the battlefield and the safety of civilian life.

The photographs are of Americans and Iraqis. Although, with one exception, they do not portray directly the physical consequences of violence, these photographs invite—and even demand—a moral accounting of the war.

This photo essay is derived from a class on the sociology of war and peace at Tufts University. While working together, we discovered our shared tendency either to pass between cultures or to live at their outer extremities. Samira came from Bosnia to Manchester, New Hampshire; Julia from Moscow to Los Angeles; Diler is a Turkish Cypriot. Even the two students born in the United States straddled boundaries: Elizabeth is from upstate New York near the Canadian border and Katie from northern Maine. Paul is the exception: He was born and raised in New York City—the center of the universe. We thank Lynn Wiles, Jim Glaser, and the Tufts University Undergraduate Research Fund for their support.

Comrades

Fallujah: U.S. Marines pray over a comrade killed while fighting insurgent strongholds in April 2004.

This photograph captures the powerful solidarity that often emerges among those sharing grief. Though the body of the Marine is partly visible, the focus is on the entire unit as they form a shield around their fallen brother. The uniforms contribute to their common sorrow while the military equipment in the background stands in stark contrast to the more human huddling, touching, and bowed heads among the men. Only the legs of the dead Marine can be seen—a framing that reflects government, media, and public sensitivities to the casualties of war.

Funerals

U.S. Marine pallbearers wait in formation to escort the remains of fallen Marine Pfc. Bufford "Kenny" VanSlyke, who died in February 2007 after being shot at a checkpoint in Anbar province.

Kim Hitzges, mother of Army Spc. Chad Keith, is comforted by her husband Mark Hitzges as they attend funeral services for Keith in August 2003 at Arlington National Cemetery. Keith was killed when a roadside bomb exploded as he was patrolling Baghdad.

Iraqis pray during a mass funeral in Baghdad for the bodies of 22 Iraqis found blindfolded with their hands tied. The bodies were found in October 2005 near the Iraq and Iran border.

Funerals are settings of collective and ritualistic grieving. The photographs show soldiers carrying the casket of a comrade to his grave (top, previous page), parents grieving over the loss of their son (bottom, previous page), and an Iraqi community performing a funeral prayer for war victims (above). The flags present in each picture symbolize the connection between immediate grief and the larger community but also tell somewhat different stories: of military protocol, as the embodiment of a cradled son, and of the significantly larger scale of casualties in Iraq.

Parents

Father Saleh Ahmed carries the body of his daughter Diar, four, out of a hospital in Kirkuk in northern Iraq, December 2005, after she was shot dead while sitting in her family's house, during an exchange of fire between unidentified gunmen in the town.

Melissa Storey hugs her daughter Adella Claire during a graveside service for her husband, Staff Sgt. Clint Storey, in Enid, Oklahoma, August 2006. Storey died after a roadside bomb blast in Ramadi.

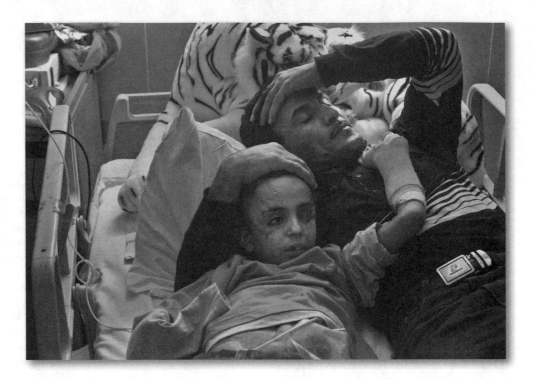

Saleh Khalaf, a nine-year-old Iraqi boy, was severely maimed by an explosion in October 2003. His strong spirit—which earned Saleh the nickname Lion Heart—moved Air Force surgeons in Iraq to launch an international mercy mission to bring him to the United States. Throughout the ordeal Saleh's father, Raheem, stayed at the boy's side. Raheem was still grieving the death of his oldest son, Dia, when Saleh was maimed. Two months after the incident Raheem had not told Saleh his brother was dead.

Parental grief is particularly poignant. In one photograph on the previous page, a mother shares the loss of her husband with her child, who has lost her father. In another photograph on that page, a father's anguish following the death of his child speaks directly to all. In the photograph above, we can see a father struggling to remain strong for his son and for himself, but it is evident that the future will be extremely difficult and that he too is overwhelmed.

Women

Widows Richelle Hecker, right, and Ursula Pirtle hug at a help center for families of fallen soldiers located at Fort Hood, Texas, February 2007. Both women's husbands were killed in Iraq.

Women grieve outside a hospital after a suicide car bomb attack in Baghdad's Shiite enclave of Sadr City, in March 2007, killed at least 20 people.

Seemingly separated by geography and culture, the losses American and Iraqi women share with each other are continuities that form another parallel of war. In the top photograph above, two American women let each other know that they know what the other has been feeling. In the subsequent picture, shadows profile the grieving of two Iraqi women and remind us of the multitudes who have mourned and who have died in the war. Though specific expressions of grief vary across circumstances, individuals, and cultures, women also display a mutualism that is nearly universal.

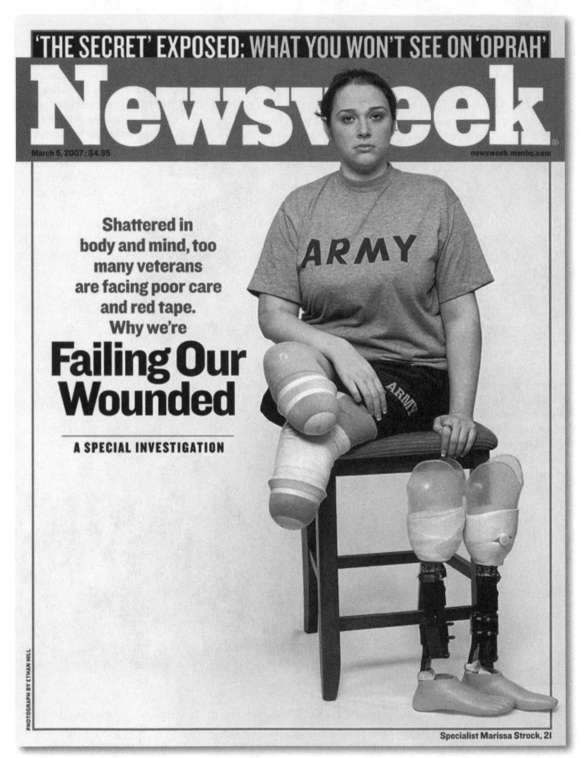

'THE SECRET' EXPOSED: WHAT YOU WON'T SEE ON 'OPRAH'

Newsweek

March 5, 2007; $4.95

newsweek.msnbc.com

Shattered in body and mind, too many veterans are facing poor care and red tape. Why we're

Failing Our Wounded

A SPECIAL INVESTIGATION

PHOTOGRAPH BY ETHAN HILL

Specialist Marissa Strock, 21

Specialist Marissa Strock's maimed legs dominate a 2007 issue of *Newsweek*. The physical trauma stands in contrast to her facial expression and posture, which suggest considerable reserves of strength and pride. But is there a viewer who cannot feel her loss?

The magazine cover also reminds readers of the changing gender composition of the military, and that women as well as men are now in harm's way. How will this fact affect public perceptions of the legitimacy of war?

Furthermore, people who are already disadvantaged by particular social conditions may not be as effective as others in promoting their cause because they lack the money, time, skills, and connections that successful movements require. For instance, the people who would stand to benefit the most from environmental improvement—individuals in poor, polluted communities—have historically been uninvolved in the environmental movement. Residents tend to see environmentalists as middle- and upper-middle-class outsiders whose own neighborhoods are relatively unpolluted and who don't appreciate the community's concerns (Bullard, 1993). Nobody wants garbage dumps, landfills, incinerators, or polluting factories in their backyards. But if these are the only ventures that will provide steady employment for residents, poor communities are left with little choice but to support them. Consequently, they often fear that outside environmentalists will take away their jobs and economic livelihoods. Recently, however, many members of poor communities have joined the environmental movement, motivated not by a "Save the earth" ideology but by a more immediately relevant one that emphasizes the unfairness and discrimination to which they are exposed. As one successful local activist put it, "People here aren't going to install solar panels on their roofs or drive a Prius, but they can demand institutional change and decent business practices" (quoted in Breslau, 2007, p. 69). In some developing nations, poor communities have mobilized resistance to commercial tree plantations, oil drilling, mining, or dam construction when these developments are perceived to constitute a threat to people's livelihoods (Martinez-Alier, 2003).

Rising Expectations

You might think that major social movements, particularly revolutionary ones, would be most likely to occur when many people's lives are at their lowest and most desperate point. Certainly, huge numbers of disadvantaged people who see little chance of things improving, and who perceive the government as unwilling or unable to meet their needs, are necessary for any massive movements for change (Tilly, 1978).

But some sociologists argue that social movements are actually more likely to arise when social conditions begin to improve than when they are at their worst (Brinton, 1965; Davies, 1962). Constant deprivation does not necessarily make people want to revolt. Instead, they are more likely to be preoccupied with daily survival than with demonstrations and street protests. Heightened expectations brought about by small improvements in living conditions, however, show those who are deprived that their society is capable of being different, sparking a desire for large-scale change. As one historian put it, "'Ironically, revolutions happen at times when things are getting better'—when people realize they have more control over their lives" (quoted in Dokoupil, 2011, p. 7). When these new expectations aren't met, deprived people become angry. The gap between what they expect and what they have now feels intolerable. Although they may actually be somewhat better off than in the past, their situation relative to their expectations now appears much worse (Davies, 1962). Such frustration makes participation in protest or revolutionary activity more likely.

Consider the short-lived pro-democracy movement in China in 1989. During the early 1980s, the Chinese government began to introduce economic reforms that opened up markets and created faster growth. It also enacted political reforms that provided citizens with more freedom. The lives of ordinary Chinese were improving, but only slightly and not quickly enough. Because they could now imagine even greater freedom and democracy, young people began to actively protest for more reforms. The result was a wide-scale student movement. The government quickly and violently squashed the movement, although after a while, it did continue to gradually liberalize Chinese society.

Resource Mobilization

At any given point, numerous problems in a society need to be fixed, and people's grievances remain more or less constant from year to year. Yet relatively few major social movements exist at any one time. If widespread dissatisfaction and frustration were all that is needed to sustain a social movement, "the masses would always be in revolt" (Trotsky, 1930/1959). What else is needed for a social movement to get started, gain support, and achieve its goals?

According to *resource mobilization theory*, the key ingredient is effective organization. No social movement can exist unless it has an organized system for acquiring needed resources: money, labor, participants, legal aid, access to the media, and so on (J. D. McCarthy & Zald, 1977). How far a movement goes in attaining its goals depends on its ability to expand its ranks, build large-scale public support, and transform those who join into committed participants (Zurcher & Snow, 1981).

Most large, long-term social movements involve a national, and even international, coalition of groups. Such widespread organization makes the movement more powerful by making recruiting and fundraising more efficient. For example, most of us first heard of the movement against corporate globalization in 1999, when thousands of people in Seattle protested against a meeting of the World Trade Organization (WTO). News reports of the event gave the impression that the protestors were a bunch of renegade anarchists who spontaneously took to the streets to vandalize local outlets of corporate giants such as McDonald's and Starbucks. Although a few of the protesters were, in fact, destructive, the vast majority were longtime nonviolent supporters of the movement. The mobilization that was required to get so many people involved was accomplished by various established organizations, such as the AFL-CIO, the Sierra Club, the Humane Society, Global Exchange, Public Citizen, and Rainforest Action Network. In fact, more than 1,200 labor, environmental, consumer, religious, farm, academic, and human rights groups from more than 90 nations had already been working to halt the expansion of the WTO long before the Seattle protest took place (Nichols, 2000; Rothschild, 2000).

Moreover, movements that historically have lasted the longest—the women's movement, the antiabortion movement, the civil rights movement, the environmental movement—are those supported by large bureaucracies. The National Organization for Women, the Christian Coalition, the National Association for the Advancement of Colored People (NAACP), the Sierra Club, and the like have full-time lobbyists or political action committees in Washington that connect them to the national political system. Few movements can succeed without such connections, because achieving social change often requires changing laws or convincing courts to interpret laws in particular ways.

Another important feature of highly organized social movements is an established network of communication (J. D. McCarthy & Zald, 1977). Movements need an effective system both for getting information to all participants and for recruiting and fundraising (Tarrow, 1994). The ability to quickly mobilize large numbers of people for, say, a flash mob or a march to the nation's capital depends on the ability to tell them what is going to happen and when and where it will happen. Modern social movements must use Web sites, Facebook, Twitter, direct mailing strategies, and networked phone and computer systems to be successful.

In 2009, a crowd of more than 10,000 youth in Moldova gathered to protest the country's communist leadership. Protestors ransacked government buildings and clashed with the police. To older observers and government officials, the sea of young people seemed to materialize out of nowhere. What they didn't realize was that protest organizers had mobilized participants through Twitter (E. Barry, 2009). Similar technological mobilization occurred during the so-called Arab Spring in 2011 when anti-government protestors in Egypt, Tunisia, Yemen, Morocco, Libya, Syria, Bahrain, Saudi Arabia, Jordan, and elsewhere used Twitter, Facebook, and YouTube to mobilize collective actions and export images of their plight around the world. Cell phones replaced traditional reporters as the world's "eyes and ears" on the protests (Preston & Stelter, 2011). Media outlets referred to the movement variously as the Facebook Revolution, the Twitter Revolution, and the Keystroke Revolution.

The mass media play an equally important part in the success of a social movement by helping to validate and enlarge the scope of its cause. In other words, the media play a key role in constructing a particular social reality useful to the movement. The media spotlight sends the message that the movement's concerns are valid and that the movement is an important force in society. A small group of people disrupting a town hall meeting on health care reform is, for all intents and purposes, a nonevent without media coverage. Media recognition is often a necessary condition before those who are the targets of influence respond to the movement's claims and demands (Gamson & Wolfsfeld, 1993).

In sum, movements that succeed in enacting substantial social change are not necessarily those with the most compelling ideological positions or the greatest emotional appeal (Ferree, 1992). Instead, they are the ones with the necessary high-level organization and communication networks to mobilize supporters and the necessary media access and technological savvy to neutralize the opposition and transform the public into sympathizers.

Bureaucratization

It makes sense that the most successful social movements are those that are the best organized. However, high-level organization can backfire if it leads to rigidity and turf wars, common to any bureaucracy. When organizations within a movement differ in their philosophies and tactics, tremendous infighting and bickering may break out among organizations ostensibly working toward the same goal.

For instance, the U.S. civil rights movement during the 1950s and 1960s included many diverse, seemingly incompatible organizations. The NAACP was large, racially integrated, legalistic, and bureaucratic in form; the Student Non-violent Coordinating Committee (SNCC) was younger and more militant in its tactics and after a while excluded Whites from participation; the Southern Christian Leadership Conference (SCLC) was highly structured, had a religious ideology, and was dominated by male clergy; the Black Muslims and the Black Panthers advocated violent methods to achieve civil rights. The ideologies and methods of these diverse civil rights groups often conflicted, which arguably slowed down the extension of civil rights to African Americans.

No matter their shape, size, or motive, social movements require sustained activity over a long period (R. W. Turner & Killian, 1987). Thus, unlike riots, which are of limited duration, social movements may become permanent fixtures in the political and social environment. Ironically, a social movement whose goal is the large-scale alteration of some aspect of society can, in time, become so large and bureaucratic itself that it becomes part of the establishment it seeks to change. For instance, Sinn Féin was a movement founded in 1905 to end British rule in Ireland. Among its off-shoots over the years was the Irish Republican Army, which carried out a bombing and terror campaign in Northern Ireland and England for decades. In recent years, most of the violence has been stopped, and the people of Ireland have won some autonomy. Sinn Féin is now the third-largest political party in Ireland, with its own news organi-zation, a highly structured network of local branches, and representatives in both the Irish Parliament and the European Parliament.

In addition, people who devote their lives to a movement come to depend on it for their own livelihood. Hence, social movements organized for the purpose of enacting social change actually provide structure and order in the lives of their members, acting as sources of opportunities, careers, and rewards (Hewitt, 1988).

Political Opportunity Structure

Social movements also depend on conditions outside their reach. One such con-dition is the structure of existing political institutions. Political systems are more or less vulnerable and more or less receptive to challenge at different times (McAdam, McCarthy, & Zald, 1988). These ebbs and flows of political opportunities produce cycles of protest and movement activity. When political systems are firm, unyielding, and stable, people have to deal individually with their problems or air their griev-ances through existing channels. But when a system opens up and people realize it is vulnerable—that they can actually make a difference—movements are likely to develop.

Sometimes these opportunities are unintentional and exist quite independently of the actions of movement members. For instance, in the 1970s, similar antinuclear movements arose in (what was then West) Germany and France. The movements had similar ideologies and used similar mobilization techniques. However, the German movement flourished and remains highly influential in national politics today. The French movement was weak and quickly died off. Why were the outcomes of these two movements so different? In Germany, the government procedure for reviewing nuclear power facilities provided opportunities for those opposed to nuclear power to legally intervene. The procedure in place in France was closed and unresponsive to public sentiment (Nelkin & Pollak, 1981). Similarly, the emergence in the 1970s of the contemporary environmental movement in the United States was possible because government agencies were already sympathetic to environmental concerns (Gale, 1986).

The idea that unintentional political opportunities can encourage social move-ments for change was dramatically supported during the 1989 pro-democracy move-ment in the former Soviet Union and Eastern Europe. In the mid 1980s, the Soviet government under Mikhail Gorbachev embarked on a massive program of economic and structural reforms (*perestroika*) as well as a relaxation of constraints on freedom of expression (*glasnost*). The ensuing liberties encouraged open criticism of the political order and created new opportunities for political action (Tarrow, 1994). Protest movements took advantage of these opportunities, leading to the sometimes violent struggles for independence on the part of small, ethnically homogeneous republics that we saw during the 1990s and continue to see today in a few remaining areas. In other words, only when the political structure became less repressive could these monumental changes take place.

Political instability can sometimes spawn less dramatic reform movements. The changing fortunes of a government can create uncertainty among supporters and encourage challengers to try to take advantage of the situation. Consider once more the civil rights movement in the United States in the 1950s and 1960s. During the 1950s, as the first calls for racial equality were being heard, many conservative Southern Democrats defected to the Republican Party, where their segregationist leanings met with more sympathy. The ensuing decline of Southern white support for the Democratic Party, coupled with the movement of African Americans to large cities in the North, where they were more likely to vote, forced the Democrats to seek black support in the presidential election of 1960. The black vote is widely credited with John Kennedy's narrow victory that year (McAdam, 1982). Hence, the Kennedy administration (and later the Johnson administration) felt compelled to campaign for civil rights (Tarrow, 1994). Increased political power, in turn, enhanced the bargaining position of civil rights forces, culminating in two landmark pieces of legislation: the Civil Rights Act of 1964 and the Voting Rights Act of 1965.

At other times, existing political regimes intentionally create or actively support structural opportunities for change. For example, from the beginning, the George W. Bush administration accepted political and financial support from Christian fundamentalist groups and organizations. In return, it attempted to support things like school prayer, the teaching of "intelligent design" in science classes, and funding for faith-based organizations, as well as efforts to limit abortion access, prohibit same-sex marriage, and prevent stem cell research. The success of these initiatives further fortified the growth and development of the religious groups and organizations and cemented their political power on the national scene.

Similarly, the U.S. anti-drunk-driving movement is strong and influential today because it enjoys substantial support from federal, state, and local governments; state and federal highway agencies; and state and local police departments (J. D. McCarthy & Wolfson, 1992). When in the 1980s the movement advocated a national drinking age of 21, many state legislatures balked, fearing a backlash from powerful alcohol producers, distributors, and retailers. However, the federal government enacted legislation threatening to withhold significant amounts of federal highway funds from states that didn't establish a drinking age of 21—a strong incentive for states to pass such a law.

Political opportunities provide the institutional framework within which social movements operate. Movements form when ordinary citizens respond to changes in the opportunity structure that lower the costs of involvement and reveal where the authorities are vulnerable. Unlike money and power, these conditions are external to the movement. If political opportunities exist, then even groups with fairly mild grievances or few resources can develop a successful movement (see also J. C. Jenkins & Perrow, 1977). In contrast, groups with deep grievances and ample resources—but few political opportunities—may never get their movements off the ground (Tarrow, 1994).

The Sociological Imagination Revisited

In the summer of 1981 with my brand new bachelor's degree in hand, I had the good fortune to visit Florence, Italy. While there, I made a point of visiting the Galleria dell'Accademia, the museum where one of my favorite works of art, Michelangelo's statue of David, resides. To my eye, it is truly a masterpiece of sculpture, nearly flawless in its detail. I stood there admiring this amazing work of art for close to two hours. As I left, I noticed several sculptures that had escaped my attention when I first entered the museum. I soon discovered that they, too, were created by Michelangelo. What made them particularly interesting was that they were all unfinished. Some were obviously near completion, but others looked to me like shapeless blocks of granite. As I looked closer, I could see the actual chisel marks the great sculptor had made. I imagined the plan Michelangelo had in his head as he worked. I envisioned him toiling to bring form to the heavy stone.

These imperfect slabs of rock showed evidence of human creation in a way that the perfect, finished statue of David never could. At that moment, I saw Michelangelo as a real guy who fashioned beauty from shapelessness. I began to admire the genius of the creator and not just the creation. I went back to look at *David* again with a new-found appreciation.

Society isn't nearly as perfect as Michelangelo's *David*, yet we can still fall into the trap of seeing social structure as a product that exists on its own and not as something that people have collectively chiseled. We sometimes forget that many of the realities of our lives that we take for granted were the result, at some point in history, of the handiwork of individuals. One generation's radical changes become another's common features of everyday life. The fact that you can't be forced to work 70 or 80 hours a week, can't be exposed to dangerous working conditions without your knowledge, and are entitled to a certain number of paid holidays a year are a result of the actions of real people in early labor union movements.

Because we take many of our freedoms, rights, and desires for granted, we may not only overlook the struggles of those who came before us but also downplay the extent to which inequities and injustices existed in the past. For instance, many young women today have never even considered that they are only a generation or two removed from a time when they might have been prohibited from attending the college or pursuing the career of their choice, when they might have been expected to abandon their own dreams and ambitions to provide the support their husbands needed to succeed, or when they might have had to take sole responsibility for household chores and their children's daily care while their husbands focused on work and the outside world. The majority of young women polled in a survey a few years ago indicated that they didn't know that abortion was once illegal (Zernike, 2003). Like most beneficiaries of past movements, young women today simply take their freedoms and opportunities for granted, sometimes even expressing contempt for the feminists responsible for winning the rights they so casually enjoy (Stacey, 1991). The irony of social movements, then, is that the more profound and far reaching their accomplishments, the more likely we are to eventually forget the original inequities that fostered them and the efforts of the individuals who produced them.

Fundamentally, societies remain stable because enough individuals define existing conditions as satisfactory, and societies change because enough individuals define situations that were once tolerable as problems that must be acknowledged and solved. As one author wrote regarding the antiwar movement of the 1960s and 1970s:

> Ten years and 12 days after the first busloads of demonstrators rolled into Washington to protest U.S. involvement in Indochina, the last planeloads of Americans left Saigon. . . . The standard American histories of the Vietnam War, when they are culled from the memoirs of the generals and politicians . . . are unlikely to record this coincidence. But the decisions about the pursuit of those generals' and politicians' objectives in Indochina were not made only in their carpeted offices. They were also made in the barracks, in the schools, in the streets, by the millions of Americans—Blacks and Whites, students, workers, nuns and priests, draftees and draft resisters—who made up the Anti-War Movement. (Cluster, 1979, p. 131)

Some influential acts of individuals may at first blush appear rather insignificant. Early in 1960, four black students at North Carolina Agricultural and Technical State University, in Greensboro, engaged in a series of discussions in their dormitory room about the state of the civil rights movement. They came to the conclusion that things weren't progressing quickly enough in the still segregated South and that it was time for action. So they decided to go to the lunch counter at the local Woolworth's store and order coffee and doughnuts. Now that might not sound like much. But in the early-1960s South, public eating facilities that weren't reserved for Blacks were forbidden by law to serve Blacks. And Greensboro at the time was the sort of place where any act of racial rebelliousness was routinely met with violence (Gladwell, 2010).

After purchasing some school supplies in another part of the store, the four students sat down at the lunch counter and placed their orders. As anticipated, the reply was, "I'm sorry, we don't serve you here" (McCain, 1991, p. 115). They remained seated for 45 minutes, citing the fact that they had been served in another part of the store without any difficulty. They were subjected to the verbal taunts, racial slurs, and even violence of angry Whites in the store.

Their actions attracted the attention of area religious leaders, community activists, and students from other local colleges, both black and white. Despite the abuses they knew awaited them, these four young men returned to Woolworth's a few days later, only this time with more demonstrators. At one point, they and their fellow protestors occupied 63 of the 65 seats available at the lunch counter. This was the first social movement covered by television too, so word of their actions spread quickly. They received endorsements from religious organizations like the North Carolina Council of Churches. Within weeks, young African Americans and sympathetic Whites had engaged in similar acts in nine states and 54 cities in the South as well as several areas in the North, where stores were picketed. After several months of protests, Woolworth's integrated its lunch counter.

Some historians argue that many of the political movements for change that burst onto the scene in the 1960s—including the women's movement, the antiwar movement, and the student free speech movement—could trace their philosophical and tactical roots to this small act by four students (Cluster, 1979). Admittedly, the participants in all these movements might have developed the sit-in as a tactic on their own, even if in 1960 the four students *had* been served coffee and doughnuts at

Woolworth's. The point is, though, that the collective movement that arose from the actions of these seemingly insignificant individuals in 1960 had an enormous impact on the massive changes that occurred in the United States over the next 50 years and probably beyond.

We re-create society not only through acts of defiance and organized social movements but also through our daily interactions. The driving theme throughout this book has been that society and its constituent elements are simultaneously human creations and phenomena that exist independently of us, influencing and controlling our private experiences at every turn.

Organizations and institutions exist and thrive because they implicitly or explicitly discourage individuals from challenging the rules and patterns of behavior that characterize them. Imagine what would happen to the system of higher education if you and others like you challenged the authority of the university. You could establish a new order in which students would dictate the content of courses, take control of the classroom, abolish grading or any other evaluative mechanism used for assessing student performance, do away with tuition, and so on. But because you have an education and a career to gain from the institutional structure as it stands, you're not very likely to do something to jeopardize it.

Are we then to believe that we are all leaves in the wind, buffeted here and there by the powerful and permanent forces of a structure that dwarfs us? To some extent, the answer is yes. I subscribe to the sociological imagination and strongly believe that to fully understand our lives, we must acknowledge that processes larger than ourselves determine some of our private experiences. Along the way, though, we sometimes lose sight of our important role as shapers of society. Although society presents itself as largely unchangeable, U.S. culture is based at least in part on the "can do" attitude. I recall, as a child in 1969, sitting in a darkened living room with my parents on a warm July evening. The only light in the room came from the gray-blue glow of our little black-and-white television. I watched with great amazement the fuzzy, almost imperceptible image of astronaut Neil Armstrong taking the first tentative steps on the moon and stating, "That's one small step for man, one giant leap for mankind." I didn't realize at the time how far beyond the space program the power of that statement stretched. But since then, I have come to realize that people do indeed leave footprints on the world in which they live.

Conclusion and Farewell

Sociology is not one of those disciplines that draws from a long-standing body of scientific facts and laws. We do have some useful explanations for why certain important social phenomena happen, and we can make reasonable projections about future developments. But sociology is not inherently a discipline of answers. It's a discipline of questions, one that provides a unique and useful method for identifying the puzzles of your life and your society.

This discipline scrutinizes, analyzes, and dissects institutional order and its effects on our thinking. It exposes the vulnerable underbelly of both objective and official reality and, by doing so, prods us into taking a closer look at ourselves and our private worlds—not an easy thing to do. Sociology makes life an unsafe place. I don't mean that it makes people violent or dangerous; I mean that it makes perceptions of social stability unstable or at least fair game for analysis. It's not easy to admit that our reality may be a figment of our collective minds and just one of many possible realities. We live under a belief system that tells us that our unchallenged assumptions are simply the way things are.

Sociology is thus a "liberating" perspective (Liazos, 1985). It forces us to look at the social processes that influence our thoughts, perceptions, and actions and helps us see how social change occurs and the impact we can have on others. In doing so, sociology also points out the very limits of liberation. We become aware of the chains that restrict our "movements." But sociology also gives us the tools to break those chains. The sociological imagination gives us a glimpse of the world both as it is and as it could be. To be a sociologically astute observer of the world as it is, you must be able to strip away fallacies and illusions and see the interconnected system underneath. Only then can you take full advantage of your role as a cocreator of society.

I leave you with one final thought: If you now look at your life and the lives of those around you differently, if you now question things heretofore unquestionable, if you now see where you fit in the bigger societal picture, if you now see orderly patterns in areas you previously thought were chaotic, or chaos in areas you previously thought were orderly, then you are well on your way to understanding the meaning—and the promise—of sociology.

YOUR TURN

Reading about people taking an active role in reconstructing a part of their personal lives or of their society is one thing, but it's quite another to see such people in action. Most communities contain people who were at one time active in a major movement for social change: the labor movement, the antiwar movement, the women's movement, the civil rights movement, the antiabortion movement, and so forth. Find a few people who were involved in one such movement. Ask them to describe their experiences. What was their motive for joining the movement? What sorts of activities did they participate in? What were the goals they wanted to accomplish? Looking back, do they feel the movement accomplished those goals? If not, why not? What else needs to be done?

For purposes of historical comparison, see if you can identify a movement that is currently under way in your community. It might be a drive in support of a broad societal concern, such as environmental awareness or health care reform; a group organized to address a political issue of local interest, such as an antismoking ordinance; or an attempt to stop something that some people think might harm the local area, like the construction of a factory or the arrival of a particular type of business.

Try to attend a gathering in which the movement is involved. It might be an organizational meeting, a city council meeting, an open town hall meeting, a protest march, a fundraiser, or a demonstration.

What happened at the gathering? What seemed to be the overall atmosphere? Was it festive, solemn, angry, or businesslike? Was any opposition present?

Interview some of the participants. Ask them the same questions you asked the participants who were in past movements. Do people get involved in social movements for the same reasons they did in the past?

Most social movement organizations now have their own Web sites on the Internet. Visit some of these sites to get a sense of the kinds of information these organizations provide. Do they tend to be primarily informational, focusing on the history and current state of the issue at hand, or are they primarily recruitment tools, designed to attract new participants and financial donors? How are these sites presented? Do they appeal to the emotions, or do they rely on factual argument? Do these Web sites contain links to the sites of other organizations that have similar ideologies?

Relate your observations from the interviews and the Internet to the discussion of social movements in this chapter. What are the most effective tactics and strategies? How are resources mobilized? Why do some movements succeed and others fail?

CHAPTER HIGHLIGHTS

- Whether at the personal, cultural, or institutional level, change is the preeminent feature of modern societies.

- Social change is not some massive, impersonal force that arbitrarily disrupts our routine way of life; it is a human creation.

- Social change has a variety of causes: adaptation to environmental pressures, internal population changes, technological discoveries and innovations, and the importation of cultural practices from other countries.

- Social movements are long-term collective actions that address an issue of concern to large numbers of people.

- Societies remain stable because enough people define existing conditions as satisfactory and they change because enough people define the once accepted conditions as problems that must be solved.

KEY TERMS

anomie: Condition in which rapid change has disrupted society's ability to adequately regulate and control its members and the old rules that governed people's lives no longer seem to apply

countermovement: Collective action designed to prevent or reverse changes sought or accomplished by an earlier social movement

cultural diffusion: Process by which beliefs, technology, customs, and other elements of culture spread from one group or society to another

global climate change: Steady rise in Earth's average temperature as a result of increasing amounts of carbon dioxide in the atmosphere

ideology: Coherent system of beliefs, values, and ideas

postindustrial society: Society in which knowledge, the control of information, and service industries are more important elements of the economy than agriculture or manufacturing and production

reform movement: Collective action that seeks to change limited aspects of a society but does not seek to alter or replace major social institutions

revolutionary movement: Collective action that attempts to overthrow an entire social system and replace it with another

social movement: Continuous, large-scale, organized collective action motivated by the desire to enact, stop, or reverse change in some area of society

STUDENT STUDY SITE

Visit the Student Study Site at **www.sagepub.com/newman9e** for these additional learning tools:

- Flashcards
- Web quizzes
- Sociologists at Work features
- Micro-Macro Connection features
- Video links
- Audio links
- Web resources
- SAGE journal articles

References

Abelson, R. (2011, May 14). Health insurers profit as many postpone care. *The New York Times.*

Abelson, R., & Freudenheim, M. (2008, May 4). Even the insured feel the strain of health costs. *The New York Times.*

Abrams, K. K., Allen, L., & Gray, J. J. (1993). Disordered eating attitudes and behaviors, psychological adjustment and ethnic identity: A comparison of black and white female college students. *Journal of Eating Disorders, 14,* 49–57.

Academy for Eating Disorders. (2006). *Academy for Eating Disorders calls for warning labels on "pro-ana" Web sites.* www.aedweb.org/public/proana.cfm. Accessed July 10, 2007.

Acitelli, L. (1988). When spouses talk to each other about their relationship. *Journal of Social and Personal Relationships, 5,* 185–199.

Acker, J. (1992). From sex roles to gendered institutions. *Contemporary Sociology, 21,* 565–569.

ActionAid. (2009). *Hate crimes: The rise of "corrective" rape in South Africa.* www.actionaid.org/assets/pdf/CorrectiveRapeRep_final.pdf. Accessed June 3, 2009.

Aday, D. P. (1990). *Social control at the margins.* Belmont, CA: Wadsworth.

Adherents.com. (2005). *Major religions of the world ranked by number of adherents.* www.adherents.com/Religions_By_Adherents.html. Accessed June 22, 2007.

Adler, P. (1985). *Wheeling and dealing.* New York, NY: Columbia University Press.

AFL-CIO. (2011). *CEO pay database: 100 highest paid CEOs.* www.aflcio.org/corporatewatch/paywatch/ceou/top100_2011.cfm. Accessed June 14, 2011.

Ahrons, C. R., & Rodgers, R. H. (1987). *Divorced families: A multidisciplinary developmental view.* New York, NY: Norton.

Ainlay, S. C., Becker, G., & Coleman, L. M. (1986). *The dilemma of difference.* New York, NY: Plenum Press.

AIS Health. (2004). *Medco says pediatric drug costs soar, driven by ADHD, depression.* www.aishealth.com/DrugCosts/DCMRMedcoPediatricCosts.html. Accessed June 3, 2005.

Alan Guttmacher Institute. (2008). *Facts on induced abortion in the United States.* www.guttmacher.org/pubs/fb_induced_abortion.html. Accessed June 10, 2009.

Alan Guttmacher Institute. (2011). *Facts on induced abortion in the United States.* www.guttmacher.org/pubs/fb_induced_abortion.html. Accessed June 30, 2011.

Al-Attab, M. (2005, February 5). Parents, children complicit in human trafficking. *Yemen Observer.* www.yobserver.com. Accessed June 7, 2005.

Allport, G. (1954). *The nature of prejudice.* Reading, MA: Addison-Wesley.

Almond, D., & Edlund, L. (2008). Son-biased sex ratios in the 2000 United States Census. *Proceedings of the National Academy of Sciences, 105,* 5681–5682.

Alter, J. (2007, May 7). Trials of the truth seekers. *Newsweek.*

Alter, J. (2010, September 6). The illustrated man. *Newsweek.*

Altman, D. (2003, April 26). Does a dollar a day keep poverty away? *The New York Times.*

Altman, L. K. (2011, May 31). 30 years in, we are still learning from AIDS. *The New York Times.*

Alvarez, L. (2009, August 16). G.I. Jane quietly breaks the combat barrier. *The New York Times.*

Alvidrez, J., & Areán, P. A. (2002). Psychosocial treatment research with ethnic minority populations: Ethical considerations in conducting clinical trials. *Ethics and Behavior, 12,* 103–116.

Amato, P. R. (2000). The consequences of divorce for adults and children. *Journal of Marriage and the Family, 62,* 126–288.

Amato, P. R., & Sobolewski, J. M. (2001). The effects of divorce and marital discord on adult children's psychological well-being. *American Sociological Review, 66,* 900–921.

American Association of University Women. (2001). *Hostile hallways: Teasing and sexual harassment in school.* www.aauw.org/research/girls_education/hostile.cfm. Accessed July 31, 2004.

American Hospital Association. (2008). *Report on the economic crisis: Initial impact on hospitals.* www.aha

.org/aha/content/2008/pdf/081119econcrisisreport .pdf. Accessed May 22, 2009.

American Lung Association. (2008). *State of tobacco control: 2008.* www.stateoftobaccocontrol.org/ 2008/ALA_SOTC_08.pdf. Accessed January 14, 2009.

American Psychiatric Association. (2000). *Diagnostic and statistical manual of mental disorders* (4th ed., text revision). Washington, DC: Author.

American Religion Data Archive. (2002). *Religious groupings: Full U.S. report.* www.thearda.com. Accessed May 27, 2005.

American Society of Plastic Surgeons. (2011). *2010 plastic surgery procedural statistics.* www.plastic surgery.org/News-and-Resources/Statistics .html. Accessed May 31, 2011.

American Sociological Association. (2002). *Statement of the American Sociological Association on the importance of collecting data and doing social scientific research on race.* www.asanet.org/ governance/racestmt.htm. Accessed June 18, 2003.

American Sociological Association. (2005, July). *Race, ethnicity, and the health of Americans* (ASA Series on How Race and Ethnicity Matter). Washington, DC: Author.

Ammerman, N. T. (1987). *Bible believers: Fundamentalists in the modern world.* New Brunswick, NJ: Rutgers University Press.

Amnesty International. (2004a). *Death penalty facts.* www.amnestyusa.org/abolish/racialprejudices .html. Accessed July 25, 2004.

Amnesty International. (2004b). *Rape as a tool of war: A fact sheet.* www.amnestyusa.org/ women/pdf/rapeinwartime.pdf. Accessed September 4, 2009.

Anderson, D. J. (2003). The impact on subsequent violence of returning to an abusive partner. *Journal of Comparative Family Studies, 34,* 93–112.

Anderson, E. (1990). *Streetwise: Race, class and change in an urban community.* Chicago: University of Chicago Press.

Andreescu, T., Gallian, J. A., Kane, J. M., & Mertz, J. E. (2008). Cross-cultural analysis of students with exceptional talent in mathematical problem solving. *Notices of the American Mathematical Society, 55,* 1248–1260.

Andrews, E. L. (2007, January 8). Bush tax cuts offer most for very rich, study finds. *The New York Times.*

Andriote, J. M. (2005, March). *HIV/AIDS and African Americans: A "state of emergency"* (PRB Report). Washington, DC: Population Reference Bureau. www.prb.org. Accessed March 16, 2005.

Ang, A. (2004, December 13). Pageant is paean to plastic surgery. *Indianapolis Star.*

Angier, N. (1997a, May 13). New debate over surgery on genitals. *The New York Times.*

Angier, N. (1997b, March 14). Sexual identity not pliable after all, report says. *The New York Times.*

Angier, N., & Chang, K. (2005, January 24). Gray matter and the sexes: Still a scientific gray area. *The New York Times.*

Ansell, A. E. (2000). The new face of race: The metamorphosis of racism in the post-civil rights era United States. In P. Kivisto & G. Rundblad (Eds.), *Multiculturalism in the United States.* Thousand Oaks, CA: Pine Forge Press.

Antill, J. K., Goodnow, J. J., Russell, G., & Cotton, S. (1996). The influence of parents and family context on children's involvement in household tasks. *Sex Roles, 34,* 215–236.

Anti-Muslim incidents increase. (2004, May 4). *The New York Times.*

Apollo Alliance. (2011). *Mission.* http://apolloalliance .org/about/mission/. Accessed June 29, 2011.

Appelbaum, E., Berg, P., Frost, A., & Preuss, G. (2003). The effects of work restructuring on low-wage, low-skilled workers in U.S. hospitals. In E. Appelbaum, A. Bernhardt, & R. J. Murname (Eds.), *Low-wage America.* New York, NY: Russell Sage.

Appiah, K. A. (2007, March 18). A slow emancipation. *The New York Times Magazine.*

Archer, D. (1985). Social deviance. In G. Lindzey & E. Aronson (Eds.), *Handbook of social psychology* (3rd ed., Vol. 2). New York, NY: Random House.

Archibold, R. C. (2007, September 8). San Diego diocese settles lawsuit for $200 million. *The New York Times.*

Archibold, R. C., & Thee-Brenan, M. (2010, May 4). Poll finds serious concern among Americans about immigration. *The New York Times.*

Arendell, T. (1995). *Fathers and divorce.* Thousand Oaks, CA: Sage.

Ariès, P. (1962). *Centuries of childhood: A social history of family life.* New York, NY: Vintage Books.

Armstrong, P. J., Goodman, J. F. B., & Hyman, J. D. (1981). *Ideology and shop-floor industrial relations.* London, UK: Croom Helm.

Ashford, L. S. (2006). *How HIV and AIDS affect populations* (PRB Report). Washington, DC: Population Reference Bureau. www.prb.org. Accessed May 1, 2007.

Associated Press. (2007). *Deployed troops fight for lost custody of kids.* www.msnbc.msn.com/id/18506417. Accessed June 14, 2007.

Astbury, J. (1996). *Crazy for you: The making of women's madness.* Melbourne, Victoria, Australia: Oxford University Press.

Auletta, K. (1982). *The underclass.* New York, NY: Random House.

Averett, S., & Korenman, S. (1999). Black and white differences in social and economic consequences of obesity. *International Journal of Obesity, 23,* 166–173.

Babbie, E. (1986). *Observing ourselves: Essays in social research.* Belmont, CA: Wadsworth.

Babbie, E. (1992). *The practice of social research.* Belmont, CA: Wadsworth.

Babbie, E. (2007). *The practice of social research* (11th ed.). Belmont, CA: Wadsworth.

Baby, and a car! Russians hold Conception Day. (2011, September 11). MSNBC Online. www.msnbc.msn.com/id/20730526/ns/world_news-europe/t/baby-car-russians-hold-conception-day/#.Tm4l8k_b8xk. Accessed September 12, 2011.

Baca Zinn, M., & Eitzen, D. S. (1996). *Diversity in families* (4th ed.). New York, NY: HarperCollins.

Bach, P. B., Cramer, L. D., Warren, J. L., & Begg, C. B. (1999). Racial differences in the treatment of early-stage lung cancer. *The New England Journal of Medicine, 341,* 119–205.

Bagdikian, B. H. (1991). Missing from the news. In J. H. Skolnick & E. Currie (Eds.), *Crisis in American institutions.* New York, NY: HarperCollins.

Bai, M. (2009, May 24). Queer developments. *The New York Times Magazine.*

Bailey, B. L. (1988). *From front porch to back seat: Courtship in 20th century America.* Baltimore, MD: Johns Hopkins University Press.

Bailey, C. A. (1993). Equality with difference: On androcentrism and menstruation. *Teaching Sociology, 21,* 121–129.

Bailey, J. (2007, March 18). Airlines learn to fly on a wing and an apology. *The New York Times.*

Bailey, W. C. (1990). Murder, capital punishment, and television: Execution publicity and homicide rates. *American Sociological Review, 55,* 628–633.

Bainbridge, W. L. (2005, February 5). Longer school year would benefit students. *Columbus Dispatch.*

Baird, J. (2010, July 12). Too hot to handle. *Newsweek.*

Bajaj, V., & Fessenden, F. (2007, November 4). What's behind the race gap? *The New York Times.*

Bajaj, V., & Nixon, R. (2006, February 22). For minorities, signs of trouble in foreclosures. *The New York Times.*

Baker, P., & Herszenhorn, D. M. (2010, April 23). Obama chastises Wall St. in call to stiffen rules. *The New York Times.*

Baker, P. L. (1997). And I went back: Battered women's negotiation of choice. *Journal of Contemporary Ethnography, 26,* 55–74.

Bald, M. (2000, December). Disputed dams. *World Press Review.*

Baldas, T. (2010). Jurors may be swayed by a pretty face, study finds. www.law.com/jsp/article.jsp?id=1202458388657&Jurors_May_Be_Swayed_by_a_Pretty_Face_Study_Finds&slreturn=1&hbxlogin=1. Accessed May 19, 2010.

Ballard, C. (1987). A humanist sociology approach to teaching social research. *Teaching Sociology, 15,* 7–14.

Bandura, A., & Walters, R. H. (1963). *Social learning and personality development.* New York, NY: Holt, Rinehart & Winston.

Banerjee, A. V., & Duflo, E. (2006). *The economic lives of the poor.* MIT Department of Economics Working Paper Series, #06-29. Cambridge, MA.

Banerjee, N. (2005, January 23). Aided by elders and Web, Iraq veterans turn critics. *The New York Times.*

Banerjee, N. (2006, August 26). Clergywomen find hard path to bigger pulpit. *The New York Times.*

Banfield, E. (1970). *The unheavenly city.* Boston, MA: Little, Brown.

Banks, J., Marmot, M., Oldfield, Z., & Smith, J. P. (2006). Disease and disadvantage in the United States and in England. *Journal of the American Medical Association, 295,* 2037–2045.

Barber, B. (1992, March). Jihad vs. McWorld. *Atlantic Monthly,* pp. 53–65.

The Barna Group. (2007). *Barna's annual tracking study shows Americans stay spiritually active, but biblical views wane.* www.barna.org/barna-update/article/18-congregations/103-barnas-annual-tracking-study-shows-americans-stay-spiritually-active-but-biblical-views-wane. Accessed September 4, 2009.

Barnard, A. (2009, January 9). In attacks on Latinos, seeing a pattern of hate. *The New York Times.*

Baron-Cohen, S. (2003). *The essential difference: Men, women, and the extreme male brain.* London, UK: Allen Lane.

Barringer, F. (2004, March 16). Bitter division for Sierra Club on immigration. *The New York Times.*

Barrionuevo, A. (2007, June 16). Globalization in every loaf. *The New York Times.*

Barro, R. J., & McCleary, R. M. (2003). Religion and economic growth across countries. *American Sociological Review, 68,* 760–781.

Barry, D. (2000, February 27). What to do if you're stopped by the police. *The New York Times.*

Barry, E. (2009, April 8). Protests in Moldova explode, with a call to arms on Twitter. *The New York Times.*

Barstow, D. (2003, December 22). U.S. rarely seeks charges for deaths in workplace. *The New York Times.*

Bazelon, E. (2008, July 20). The next kind of integration. *The New York Times Magazine.*

Bazelon, E. (2010, July 18). The new abortion providers. *The New York Times Magazine.*

Bazelon, E. (2011, April 24). Trolls, the bell tolls for thee. *The New York Times Magazine.*

Beaman, A. L., Klentz, B., Diener, E., & Svanum, S. (1979). Objective self-awareness and transgression in children: A field study. *Journal of Personality and Social Psychology, 37,* 1835–1846.

Bearak, B. (2010, September 6). Dead join the living in a family celebration. *The New York Times.*

Beauboeuf-Lafontant, T. (2009). *Behind the mask of the strong black woman: Voice and the embodiment of a costly performance.* Philadelphia, PA: Temple University Press.

Becker, H. S. (1963). *Outsiders: Studies in the sociology of deviance.* New York, NY: Free Press.

Becker, H. S., & Geer, B. (1958). The fate of idealism in medical school. *American Sociological Review, 23,* 50–56.

Begley, S. (2011, January 31). Why almost everything you hear about medicine is wrong. *Newsweek.*

Beinggirl.com. (2010). *Keeping it quick and quiet.* www.beinggirl.com/en_US/articledetail .jsp?ContentId=ART11906. Accessed June 25, 2010.

Belkin, L. (2003, May 11). Why is Jonathan Simms still alive? *The New York Times Magazine.*

Bell, I., & McGrane, B. (1999). *This book is not required.* Thousand Oaks, CA: Pine Forge Press.

Bell, S. T., Kuriloff, P. J., & Lottes, I. (1994). Understanding attributions of blame in stranger rape and date rape situations: An examination of gender, race, identification, and students' social perceptions of rape victims. *Journal of Applied Social Psychology, 24,* 1719–1734.

Bellah, R., Madsen, R., Sullivan, W. M., Swidler, A., & Tipton, S. M. (1985). *Habits of the heart.* New York, NY: Harper & Row.

Belluck, P. (1998, March 20). Black youths' rate of suicide rising sharply. *The New York Times.*

Belluck, P. (2001, January 20). A nation's voices: Concern and solace, resentment and redemption. *The New York Times.*

Belluck, P. (2002, January 15). Doctors' new practices offer deluxe service for deluxe fee. *The New York Times.*

Belluck, P. (2004, November 14). To avoid divorce, move to Massachusetts. *The New York Times.*

Belson, K. (2004, June 27). I want to be alone. Please call me. *The New York Times.*

Benedict, H. (2009). *The lonely soldier: The private war of women serving in Iraq.* Boston, MA: Beacon Press.

Bennett, G., Henson, R. K., & Zhang, J. (2003). Generation Y's perceptions of the action sports industry segment. *Journal of Sports Management, 17,* 95–115.

Bennett, J. (2008, February 25). Say "cheese" and now say "airbrush." *Newsweek.*

Bennett, J. (2010, July 28). The beauty advantage. *Newsweek.*

Benokraitis, N. V., & Feagin, J. R. (1993). Sex discrimination: Subtle and covert. In J. Henslin (Ed.), *Down-to-earth sociology* (7th ed.). New York, NY: Free Press.

Ben-Yehuda, N. (1990). *The politics and morality of deviance.* Albany: State University of New York Press.

Berenson, A. (2005, May 31). Despite vow, drug makers still withhold data. *The New York Times.*

Berenson, A. (2008, December 8). Weak patchwork of oversight lets bad hospitals stay open. *The New York Times.*

Berg, B. (1992). The guilt that drives working mothers crazy. In J. Henslin (Ed.), *Marriage and family in a changing society.* New York, NY: Free Press.

Bergen, R. K. (1999). Marital rape. *Violence Against Women Online Resources.* www.vaw.umn.edu. Accessed June 13, 2005.

Berger, D. L., & Williams, J. E. (1991). Sex stereotypes in the United States revisited: 1972–1988. *Sex Roles, 24,* 413–423.

Berger, J. (2004, October 24). Pressure to live by an outmoded tradition is still felt among Indian immigrants. *The New York Times.*

Berger, P. L. (1963). *Invitation to sociology.* Garden City, NY: Anchor Books.

Berger, P. L., & Kellner, H. (1964). Marriage and the construction of reality: An exercise in the microsociology of knowledge. *Diogenes, 46,* 1–23.

Berger, P. L., & Luckmann, T. (1966). *The social construction of reality.* Garden City, NY: Anchor Books.

Bernard, J. (1972). *The future of marriage.* New York, NY: Bantam Books.

Bernard, J. (1981). The good provider role: Its rise and fall. *American Psychologist, 36,* 1–12.

Bernard, T. S. (2010, July 19). Need a mortgage? Don't get pregnant. *The New York Times.*

Berndt, T. J., & Heller, K. A. (1986). Gender stereotypes and social inferences. *Journal of Social and Personality Psychology, 50,* 889–898.

Bernstein, J., & Ellison, J. (2011, June 5). Hotel confidential. *Newsweek.*

Bernstein, R. (2003, June 29). Aging Europe finds its pension is running out. *The New York Times.*

Bertenthal, B. I., & Fischer, K. W. (1978). Development of self-recognition in the infant. *Developmental Psychology, 14,* 44–50.

Berthelsen, C. (1999, July 28). Suit says advanced-placement classes show bias. *The New York Times.*

Bertrand, M., & Mullainathan, S. (2004). Are Emily and Greg more employable than Lakisha and Jamal? A field experiment on labor market discrimination. *American Economic Review, 94,* 991–1013.

Best, J. (2006). *Flavor of the month: Why smart people fall for fads.* Berkeley: University of California Press.

Bhatnagar, P. (2005). Were Barbie's holiday dreams dashed? *CNNMoney.com* http://money.cnn.com/2005/12/29/news/fortune500/holiday_barbie/index.htm. Accessed June 3, 2007.

Bhattacharya, J., DeLeire, T., Haider, S., & Currie, J. (2003). Heat or eat? Cold-weather shocks and nutrition in poor American families. *American Journal of Public Health, 93,* 1149–1154.

Bianchi, S. M., Robinson, J. P., & Milkie, M. A. (2006). *Changing rhythms of American family life.* New York, NY: Russell Sage.

Bibbins-Domingo, K. (2009). Racial differences in incident heart failure among young adults. *The New England Journal of Medicine, 360,* 1179–1190.

Bilefsky, D. (2010, April 3). Walls, real and imagined, surround the Roma in Slovakia. *The New York Times.*

Billings, A. C., Angelini, J. R., & Eastman, S. T. (2005). Diverging discourses: Gender differences in televised golf announcing. *Mass Communication and Society, 8,* 155–171.

Bilton, N. (2011, April 3). Erasing the digital past. *The New York Times.*

Bird: NBA "a black man's game." (2004). *ESPN Online.* http://sports.espn.go.com/nba/news/story?id=1818396. Accessed June 10, 2004.

Birenbaum, A., & Sagarin, E. (1976). *Norms and human behavior.* New York, NY: Praeger.

Bisgaier, J., & Rhodes, K. V. (2011). Auditing access to specialty care for children with public insurance. *The New England Journal of Medicine, 364,* 2324–2333.

Blackhealthcare.com. (2003). *Sickle-cell anemia: Description.* www.blackhealthcare.com/BHC/SickleCell/Description.asp. Accessed June 17, 2003.

Blackmon, D. A. (2009). *Slavery by another name: The re-enslavement of black Americans from the Civil War to World War II.* New York, NY: Anchor.

Blakeslee, S. (1998, October 13). Placebos prove so powerful even experts are surprised. *The New York Times.*

Blanton, K. (2007, March 16). A "smoking gun" on race, subprime loans. *The Boston Globe.*

Blass, T. (2004). *The man who shocked the world: The life and legacy of Stanley Milgram.* New York, NY: Basic Books.

Blau, P. M., & Meyer, M. W. (1987). The concept of bureaucracy. In R. T. Schaeffer & R. P. Lamm (Eds.), *Introducing sociology.* New York, NY: McGraw-Hill.

Blauner, R. (1992). The ambiguities of racial change. In M. L. Anderson & P. H. Collins (Eds.), *Race, class and gender: An anthology.* Belmont, CA: Wadsworth.

Blow, C. M. (2008, August 9). Racism and the race. *The New York Times.*

Blow, C. M. (2009, February 21). A nation of cowards? *The New York Times.*

Blow, C. M. (2010, June 12). Friends, neighbors, and Facebook. *The New York Times.*

Blumstein, P., & Schwartz, P. (1983). *American couples.* New York, NY: Morrow.

Blustein, P. (2005, June 12). Debt cut is set for poorest nations. *The Washington Post.*

Bocian, D. G., Ernst, K. S., & Li, W. (2006). *Unfair lending: The effect of race and ethnicity on the price of subprime mortgages.* Durham, NC: Center for Responsible Lending. www.responsiblelending.org. Accessed October 10, 2007.

Bonilla-Silva, E. (2003). *Racism without racists: Color-blind racism and the persistence of racial inequality in the United States.* Lanham, MD: Rowman & Littlefield.

Bonilla-Silva, E. (2008). "New racism," color-blind racism, and the future of whiteness in America. In S. J. Ferguson (Ed.), *Mapping the social landscape.* New York, NY: McGraw-Hill.

Bonner, R., & Fessenden, F. (2000, September 22). States with no death penalty share lower homicide rates. *The New York Times.*

Bonnie, R. J., & Whitebread, C. H. (1974). *The marijuana conviction.* Charlottesville: University of Virginia Press.

Booth, A., Johnson, D. R., Branaman, A., & Sica, A. (1995). Belief and behavior: Does religion matter in today's marriage? *Journal of Marriage and the Family, 57,* 661–671.

Boshara, R. (2002, September 29). Poverty is more than a matter of income. *The New York Times.*

Bosman, J. (2009, February 20). Newly poor swell lines at nation's food banks. *The New York Times.*

Boston Archdiocese closing 65 parishes. (2004, May 25). *The New York Times.*

Boushey, H., Arons, J., & Smith, L. (2010). *Families can't afford gender wage gap.* Center for American Progress. www.americanprogress.org/issues/2010/04/pdf/equal-pay-day.pdf. Accessed June 21, 2011.

Bowen, J. R. (1996). The myth of global ethnic conflict. *Journal of Democracy, 7,* 3–14.

Bowker, L. H. (1993). A battered woman's problems are social, not psychological. In R. J. Gelles & D. R. Loeske (Eds.), *Current controversies on family violence.* Newbury Park, CA: Sage.

Brabant, S., & Mooney, L. A. (1999). The social construction of family life in the Sunday comics: Race as a consideration. *Journal of Comparative Family Studies, 30,* 113–133.

Bradsher, K. (1993, July 22). Mark Twain would understand the water crisis that's corrupting Iowans. *The New York Times.*

Bragg, R. (1998, January 4). Proposal to ban sofas from porches creates culture clash. *The Indianapolis Star.*

Bramlett, M. D., & Mosher, W. D. (2002). *Cohabitation, marriage, divorce, and remarriage in the United States.* Hyattsville, MD: National Center for Health Statistics. www.cdc.gov/nchs/data/series/sr_23/sr23_022.pdf. Accessed August 11, 2006.

Braun, D. (1997). *The rich get richer: The rise of income inequality in the United States and the world.* Chicago, IL: Nelson-Hall.

Breaking the rules of engagement. (2002, July/August). *American Demographics,* p. 35.

Breslau, K. (2007, December 25). Majora Carter. *Newsweek.*

Brewis, A. A., Wutich, A., Falletta-Cowden, A., & Rodriguez-Soto, I. (2011). Body norms and fat stigma in global perspective. *Current Anthropology, 52,* 269–276.

Brint, S. (1998). *Schools and societies.* Thousand Oaks, CA: Pine Forge Press.

Brinton, C. (1965). *The anatomy of revolution.* New York, NY: Vintage Books.

Brizendine, L. (2006). *The female brain.* New York, NY: Broadway.

Broder, J. M. (2006, April 2). Immigrants and the economics of hard work. *The New York Times.*

Brodey, D. (2005, September 20). Blacks join the eating-disorder mainstream. *The New York Times.*

Bronner, E. (1998a, January 10). Inventing the notion of race. *The New York Times.*

Bronner, E. (1998b, April 1). U of California reports big drop in black admission. *The New York Times.*

Bronson, P., & Merryman, A. (2010, July 19). The creativity crisis. *Newsweek.*

Brooke, J. (2004, October 18). Strangers in life join hands in death as the Web becomes a tool for suicide in Japan. *The New York Times.*

Brookings Institution. (2006). *From poverty, opportunity: Putting the market to work for lower income families.* www.brookings.edu/metro/pubs/20060718_PovOp.pdf. Accessed July 18, 2006.

Broverman, I., Vogel, S., Broverman, D., Clarkson, F., & Rosenkrantz, P. (1972). Sex role stereotypes: A current appraisal. *Journal of Social Issues, 28,* 59–78.

Brown, D. (2011, July 13). Two studies show that drugs used to treat AIDS can be used to prevent HIV infection too. *The Washington Post.*

Brown, P. (1998). Biology and the social construction of the "race" concept. In J. Ferrante & P. Brown (Eds.), *The social construction of race and ethnicity in the United States.* New York, NY: Longman.

Brown, P. L. (2011, March 6). Bill to ban Chinese delicacy has some fuming. *The New York Times.*

Brown, Robbie. (2009, January 22). Nashville won't make English official language. *The New York Times.*

Brown, Roger. (1986). *Social psychology.* New York, NY: Free Press.

Brown, T. (2010, September 7). Learning to talk the talk in a hospital. *The New York Times.*

Browne, B. A. (1998). Gender stereotypes in advertising on children's television in the 1990s: A cross-national analysis. *Journal of Advertising, 27,* 83–96.

Brownmiller, S. (1975). *Against our will: Men, women, and rape.* New York, NY: Simon & Schuster.

Brutally Honest. (2004). *Jimmy Swaggart. Just. Shut. Up.* www.brutallyhonest.org/brutally_honest/2004/09/jimmy_swaggart_html. Accessed June 2, 2005.

Brutus, D. (1999). Africa 2000 in the new global context. In T. J. Gallagher (Ed.), *Perspectives: Introductory sociology.* St. Paul, MN: Coursewise.

Buckley, C. (2009, February 18). For uninsured young adults, do-it-yourself medical care. *The New York Times.*

Buckley, C. (2010, December 9). To test housing program, some are denied aid. *The New York Times.*

Bullard, R. D. (1993). Anatomy of environmental racism and the environmental justice movement. In R. D. Bullard (Ed.), *Confronting environmental racism.* Boston, MA: South End Press.

Bullard, R. D. (2001). Decision making. In L. Westra & B. E. Lawson (Eds.), *Faces of environmental racism: Confronting issues of global justice.* Lanham, MD: Rowman & Littlefield.

Bullington, B. (1993). All about Eve: The many faces of United States drug policy In F. Pearce & M. Woodiwiss (Eds.), *Global crime connections.* Toronto, Ontario, Canada: University of Toronto Press.

Bunk busters unravel the art of spin. (2007). *National Public Radio.* www.npr.org/templates/story/story.php?storyId=10416827. Accessed September 5, 2009.

Bureau of Transportation Statistics. (2011). *Number of U.S. aircraft, vehicles, vessels, and other conveyances.* http://www.bts.gov/publications/national_transportation_statistics/html/table_01_11.html. Accessed August 31, 2011.

Burger, J. M. (2009). Replicating Milgram: Would people still obey today? *American Psychologist, 64,* 1–11.

Burke, T. W., & Owen, S. S. (2006, January/February). Same-sex domestic violence: Is anyone listening? *Gay & Lesbian Review, 8*(1), 6–7.

Burning through oil, or conserving it. (2008, April 20). *The New York Times.*

Burros, M., & Warner, M. (2006, May 4). Bottlers agree to a school ban on sweet drinks. *The New York Times.*

Bush, M. (2009). *International benchmarking—time.* Education Commission of the States. www.ecs.org/clearinghouse/80/66/8066.pdf. Accessed June 12, 2011.

Butler, R. (1989). A generation at risk: When the baby boomers reach Golden Pond. In W. Feigelman (Ed.), *Sociology full circle.* New York, NY: Holt, Rinehart & Winston.

Butterfield, F. (1999, January 10). Eliminating parole boards isn't a cure-all, experts say. *The New York Times.*

Butterfield, F. (2000, April 26). Racial disparities seen as pervasive in juvenile justice. *The New York Times.*

Butterfield, F. (2005, February 13). In rural America, guns and a "culture of suicide." *The New York Times.*

Cahill, S. (1999). Emotional capital and professional socialization: The case of mortuary science students (and me). *Social Psychology Quarterly, 62,* 101–116.

Caldwell, C. (2005, January 23). The triumph of gesture politics. *The New York Times.*

Camarota, S. A. (2004). *Economy slowed, but immigration didn't: The foreign-born population, 2000–2004.* Washington, DC: Center for Immigration Studies. www.cis.org. Accessed June 9, 2005.

Camarota, S. A. (2011). *A need for more immigrant workers?* Center for Immigration Studies. http://www.cis.org/articles/2011/need-more-immigrant-workers-q1-2011.pdf. Accessed July 21, 2011.

Cameron, D. (2000). Styling the worker: Gender and the commodification of language in the globalized service economy. *Journal of Sociolinguistics, 4/3,* 323–347.

Cameron, P. (2003). Domestic violence among homosexual partners. *Psychological Reports, 93,* 410–416.

Campbell, A. (1987). Self-definition by rejection: The case of gang girls. *Social Problems, 34,* 451–466.

Campbell, A., Converse, P. E., & Rodgers, W. L. (1976). *The quality of American life*. New York, NY: Russell Sage.

Campbell, M. E., & Troyer, L. (2007). The implications of racial misclassification by observers. *American Sociological Review, 72*, 750–765.

Campo-Flores, A. (2008). A gay marriage surge. *Newsweek Online*. www.newsweek.com/id/172399/output/print. Accessed May 18, 2009.

Canadian Broadcasting Corporation. (2003). *What border? The Americanization of Canada*. www.tv.cbc.ca/national/pgminfo/border/culture.html. Accessed May 27, 2003.

Caplan, B. (2011). *Selfish reasons to have more kids: Why being a great parent is less work and more fun than you think*. New York, NY: Basic Books.

Caplan, P. J. (1995). *They say you're crazy: How the world's most powerful psychiatrists decide who's normal*. Reading, MA: Addison-Wesley.

Carey, B. (2007, January 14). Can Johnny come out and (be taught) to play? *The New York Times*.

Carey, B. (2008, March 9). Brain enhancement is wrong, right? *The New York Times*.

Carey, B. (2009, April 7). When all you have left is your pride. *The New York Times*.

Carlson, E. (2009). 20th-century U.S. generations. *Population Bulletin, 64*, 1–17.

Carmichael, M. (2008, December 1). Katrina kids: Sickest ever. *Newsweek*.

Carnevale, A. P., & Rose, S. J. (2003). *Socioeconomic status, race/ethnicity, and selective college admissions*. Washington, DC: Century Foundation. www.tcf.org/Publications/Education/carnevale_rose.pdf. Accessed September 4, 2009.

Carr, D. (2004). *Improving the health of the world's poorest people* (Health Bulletin No. 1). Washington, DC: Population Reference Bureau.

Carr, D. (2011, April 17). Keep your thumbs still when I'm talking to you. *The New York Times*.

Carr, D., & Friedman, M. A. (2006). Body weight and the quality of interpersonal relationships. *Social Psychology Quarterly, 69*, 127–149.

Carroll, J. (2007). Most Americans approve of interracial marriages. *Gallup News Service*. www.gallup.com/poll/28417/Most-Americans-Approve-Interracial-Marriages.aspx. Accessed May 18, 2009.

Carter, B., & Vega, T. (2011, May 14). In shift, ads try to entice over-55 set. *The New York Times*.

Carter, H., & Glick, P. C. (1976). *Marriage and divorce: A social and economic study*. Cambridge, MA: Harvard University Press.

Cashdan, E. (2008). Waist-to-hip ratio across cultures: Trade-offs between androgen- and estrogen-dependent traits. *Current Anthropology, 49*, 1099–1107.

Cast, A. D. (2004). Role taking and interaction. *Social Psychology Quarterly, 67*, 296–309.

Catalyst. (2009). *Women CEOs of the Fortune 1000*. www.catalyst.org/publication/322/women-ceos-of-the-fortune-1000. Accessed May 23, 2009.

Cave, D. (2011, July 6). Better lives for Mexicans cut allure of going north. *The New York Times*.

Cellular Telecommunications and Internet Association. (2011). *CTIA semi-annual wireless industry survey*. www.ctia.org/advocacy/research/index.cfm/AID/10316. Accessed May 25, 2011.

Center for Public Integrity. (2008). *Iraq: The war card*. www.publicintegrity.org/projects/entry/276. Accessed May 3, 2009.

Center for Responsive Politics. (2011). *Freshmen in 112th Congress exceedingly wealthy despite struggling national economy*. Open Secrets Blog. www.opensecrets.org/news/2011/03/as-a-class-congressional-freshmen-e.html. Accessed June 13, 2011.

Center for Science in the Public Interest. (2011). *Taxing sugared beverages would help trim state budget deficits, consumers' bulging waistlines, and health care costs*. www.cspinet.org/liquid candy/. Accessed May 18, 2011.

Centers for Disease Control and Prevention. (1999). Ten great public health achievements in the United States, 1900–1999. *Mortality and Morbidity Weekly Report, 48*, 241–243.

Centers for Disease Control and Prevention. (2006). *Smoking and tobacco use*. www.cdc.gov/tobacco/data_statistics/Factsheets/index.htm. Accessed June 18, 2007.

Centers for Disease Control and Prevention. (2007). Suicide trends among youths and young adults aged 10–24 years—United States 1990–2004. *Morbidity and Mortality Weekly Report, 56*, 905–908.

Centers for Disease Control and Prevention. (2009). *Intimate partner violence fact sheet*. www.cdc.gov/violenceprevention/pdf/IPV_factsheet-a.pdf. Accessed July 2, 2010.

Centers for Disease Control and Prevention. (2010). *Suicide: Facts at a glance*. www.cdc.gov/ViolencePrevention/suicide/index.html. Accessed May 16, 2011.

Centers for Disease Control and Prevention. (2011a). *Highlights in minority health & health disparities.* www.cdc.gov/omhd/Highlights/Highlight.htm#DISPARITIES0. Accessed June 17, 2011.

Centers for Disease Control and Prevention. (2011b). *Occupational cancer.* www.cdc.gov/niosh/topics/cancer. Accessed June 8, 2011.

Centers for Disease Control and Prevention. (2011c). *Tobacco-related mortality.* www.cdc.gov/tobacco/data_statistics/fact_sheets/health_effects/tobacco_related_mortality/index.htm. Accessed June 8, 2011.

Centers for Disease Control and Prevention. (2011d). *Trends in prevalence of sexual behaviors: National YRBS: 1991–2009.* www.cdc.gov/healthyyouth/yrbs/pdf/us_summary_all_trend_yrbs.pdf. Accessed June 23, 2011.

Chachere, V. (2005, June 3). Young killers a quandary for states. *The Indianapolis Star.*

Chafetz, J. S. (1978). *A primer on the construction and testing of theories in sociology.* Itasca, IL: Peacock.

Chafetz, J. S., & Dworkin, A. G. (1987). In the face of threat: Organized anti-feminism in comparative perspective. *Gender & Society, 1,* 33–60.

Chalt, J. (2011, April 18). War on the weak. *Newsweek.*

Chambliss, D. F. (1989). The mundanity of excellence: An ethnographic report on stratification and Olympic swimmers. *Sociological Theory, 7,* 70–86.

Chambliss, W. (1964). A sociological analysis of the law of vagrancy. *Social Problems, 12,* 66–77.

Chapkis, W. (2010). Patients, "potheads," and dying to get high. In D. M. Newman & J. O'Brien (Eds.), *Sociology: Exploring the architecture of everyday life: Readings.* Thousand Oaks, CA: Pine Forge Press.

Charles, C. Z. (2003). The dynamics of racial residential segregation. *Annual Review of Sociology, 29,* 167–207.

Charles, M. (2011, Spring). What gender is science? *Contexts.* http://contexts.org/articles/spring-2011/what-gender-is-science/. Accessed June 21, 2011.

Charon, J. (1992). *Ten questions: A sociological perspective.* Belmont, CA: Wadsworth.

Charon, J. (1998). *Symbolic interactionism.* Upper Saddle River, NJ: Prentice Hall.

Chase-Dunn, C., & Rubinson, R. (1977). Toward a structural perspective on the world system. *Politics and Society, 7,* 453–476.

Chaudhry, L. (2006, April 7). Acting your race. *In These Times.*

Chen, D. W. (2010, August 2). On television, playing down an image of wealth. *The New York Times.*

Chen, E., Matthews, K. A., & Boyce, W. T. (2002). Socioeconomic differences in children's health: How and why do these relationships change with age? *Psychological Bulletin, 128,* 295–329.

Cherlin, A. J. (1992). *Marriage, divorce, remarriage.* Cambridge, MA: Harvard University Press.

Cherlin, A. J., Furstenberg, F. F., Jr., Chase-Lansdale, P. L., Kiernan, K. E., Robins, P. K., Morrison, D. R., & Teitler, J. O. (1991). Longitudinal studies of effects of divorce on children in Great Britain and the United States. *Science, 252,* 1386–1389.

Cherney, I. D., & London, K. (2006). Gender-linked differences in the toys, television shows, computer games, and outdoor activities of 5- to 13-year-old children. *Sex Roles, 54,* 717–726.

CHILD, Inc. (2011). *Religious exemptions from health care for children.* http://childrenshealthcare.org/?page_id=24. Accessed May 18, 2011.

Child Welfare Information Gateway. (2010). *Child abuse and neglect fatalities: Statistics and interventions.* www.childwelfare.gov/pubs/factsheets/fatalities.pdf. Accessed June 6, 2011.

China changes death penalty law. (2006, October 31). *The New York Times.*

China law to make children visit parents. (2011, January 6). *BBC News–Asia Pacific.* www.bbc.co.uk/news/world-asia-pacific-12130140. Accessed June 23, 2011.

Ching, C. L., & Burke, S. (1999). An assessment of college students' attitudes and empathy toward rape. *College Student Journal, 33,* 573–584.

Chotiner, I. (2010, May 31). Globish for beginners. *The New Yorker.*

Christakis, N. A., & Fowler, J. H. (2007). The spread of obesity in a large social network over 32 years. *The New England Journal of Medicine, 357,* 370–379.

Chua, A. (2011). *Battle hymn of the Tiger Mother.* New York, NY: Penguin.

Ciancanelli, P., & Berch, B. (1987). Gender and the GNP. In B. B. Hess & M. M. Ferree (Eds.), *Analyzing gender: A handbook of social science research.* Newbury Park, CA: Sage.

Clarity, J. F. (1999, March 14). Lost youth in Ireland: Suicide rate is climbing. *The New York Times.*

Clark, B. (1960). The "cooling out" function in higher education. *American Journal of Sociology, 65,* 569–576.

Clark, C. (1997). *Misery and company: Sympathy in everyday life.* Chicago, IL: University of Chicago Press.

Clark, M. A. (2003). Trafficking in persons: An issue of human security. *Journal of Human Development, 4,* 247–263.

Clausen, J. A. (1986). *The life course: A sociological perspective.* Englewood Cliffs, NJ: Prentice Hall.

Clear Channel Communications. (2011). *Corporate fact sheet.* www.clearchannel.com/Corporate/ PressRelease.aspx?PressReleaseID=1564&p=hi dden. Accessed May 24, 2011.

Clemmitt, M. (2006a). Cyber socializing. *CQ Researcher, 16,* 625–648.

Clemmitt, M. (2006b). Privacy in peril. *CQ Researcher, 16,* 961–984.

Clemmitt, M. (2009). Extreme sports. *CQ Researcher, 19,* 297–320.

Clinard, M. B., & Meier, R. F. (1979). *Sociology of deviant behavior.* New York, NY: Holt, Rinehart & Winston.

Cluster, D. (1979). *They should have served that cup of coffee.* Boston, MA: South End Press.

CNN.com. (2009). *Most blacks say MLK's vision fulfilled, poll finds.* http://edition.cnn.com/2009/ POLITICS/01/19/king.poll/. Accessed August 13, 2009.

CNN Money. (2010). *Global 500.* http://money.cnn .com/magazines/fortune/global500/2010/full- list. Accessed June 14, 2011.

Cohen, A. K. (1955). *Delinquent boys: The culture of the gang.* New York, NY: Free Press.

Cohen, A. K. (1966). *Deviance and control.* Englewood Cliffs, NJ: Prentice Hall.

Cohen, F. G. (1986). *Treaties on trial: The continuing controversy over Northwest Indian fishing rights.* Seattle: University of Washington Press.

Cohen, J., & Agiesta, J. (2008, June 22). 3 in 10 Americans admit to race bias. *The Washington Post.*

Cohen, N. (2006, August 6). So English is taking over the globe. So what? *The New York Times.*

Cohen, P. (2003, April 5). Visions and revisions of child-raising experts. *The New York Times.*

The College Board. (1998). *SAT and gender differences* (Research Summary RS-04). http:// professionals.collegeboard.com/profdownload/ pdf/rs04_3960.pdf. Accessed August 13, 2009.

Collegiate Employment Research Institute. (2011). *Recruiting trends: 2010–2011.* www.ceri.msu .edu/recruiting-trends-2010-2011/. Accessed May 16, 2011.

Collins, C., & Williams, D. R. (1999). Segregation and mortality: The deadly effects of racism. *Sociological Forum, 14,* 495–523.

Collins, G. (2011, April 7). Medicine on the move. *The New York Times.*

Collins, R. (1971). Functional and conflict theories of educational stratification. *American Sociological Review, 36,* 1002–1019.

Collins, R. (1981). On the microfoundations of macro-sociology. *American Journal of Sociology, 86,* 984–1014.

Coltrane, S., & Adams, M. (1997). Work-family imagery and gender stereotypes: Television and the reproduction of difference. *Journal of Vocational Behavior, 50,* 32–47.

Comer, J. P., & Poussaint, A. F. (1992). *Raising black children.* New York, NY: Plume.

Conant, E. (2009, May 4). Rebranding hate in the age of Obama. *Newsweek.*

Conant, E. (2010, October 4). Do ask, do tell. *Newsweek.*

Conrad, P. (1975). The discovery of hyperkinesis: Notes on the medicalization of deviant behavior. *Social Problems, 23,* 12–21.

Conrad, P. (2005). The shifting engines of medicalization. *Journal of Health and Social Behavior, 46,* 3–14.

Conrad, P., & Leiter, V. (2004). Medicalization, markets, and consumers. *Journal of Health and Social Behavior, 45,* 158–176.

Conrad, P., & Schneider, J. W. (1992). *Deviance and medicalization: From badness to sickness.* Philadelphia, PA: Temple University Press.

A continuing abomination. (2008, November 1). *The Economist.*

Cookson, P., & Persell, C. (1985). *Preparing for power.* New York, NY: Basic Books.

Cooley, C. H. (1902). *Human nature and social order.* New York, NY: Scribner.

Coolidge, S. (2005, August 20). Parents must pay $7M. *The Cincinnati Enquirer.*

Coontz, S. (1992). *The way we never were.* New York, NY: Basic Books.

Coontz, S. (2005). *Marriage, a history: From obedience to intimacy, or how love conquered marriage.* New York, NY: Viking.

Cooper, K. J. (1999). Admissions models for inclusion. *Black Issues in Higher Education, 16,* 3–5.

Corbett, S. (2007, March 18). The women's war. *The New York Times Magazine.*

Cose, E. (2009, February 2). Revisiting "The rage of the privileged class." *Newsweek.*

Cose, E. (2011, May 23 & 30). Meet the new optimists. *Newsweek.*

Coser, R. L. (1960). Laughter among colleagues: A study of the social functions among staff of a mental hospital. *Psychiatry, 23,* 81–95.

Coulson, M. A., & Riddell, C. (1980). *Approaching sociology.* London, UK: Routledge & Kegan Paul.

Counterterrorism Communications Center. (2008, March 14). *Words that work and words that don't: A guide for counterterrorism communication.* www.investigativeproject.org/documents/misc/id/127. Accessed May 22, 2011.

Cowan, R. (1991). More work for mother: The postwar years. In L. Kramer (Ed.), *The sociology of gender.* New York, NY: St. Martin's Press.

Cowell, A. (2002, April 28). Migrants feel chill in a testy Europe. *The New York Times.*

Cowell, A. (2007, March 8). Commons moves again to erode nobles' power in Britain. *The New York Times.*

Cowley, G. (1994, February 7). The culture of Prozac. *Newsweek.*

Cowley, G. (1997, May 9). Gender limbo. *Newsweek.*

Cowley, G. (2003, May 5). How progress makes us sick. *Newsweek.*

Cowley, G. (2005, Summer). Chasing black fever. *Newsweek* [Special issue].

Coyle, M. (2003). *Race and class penalties in crack cocaine sentencing* (Sentencing Project Report No. 5077). www.sentencingproject.org/doc/publications/5077.pdf. Accessed September 4, 2009.

Crandall, M., Nathens, A. B., Kernic, M. A., Holt, V. L., & Rivara, F. P. (2004). Predicting future injury among women in abusive relationships. *Journal of Trauma: Injury, Infection, and Critical Care, 56,* 906–912.

Cranz, G. (1998). *The chair: Rethinking culture, body, and design.* New York, NY: Norton.

Crary, D. (2003, June 1). Internet can speed up divorces. *The Indianapolis Star.*

Crary, D. (2007, June 3). TB case raises ethical questions. *The Indianapolis Star.*

Crary, D. (2009, March 8). Women's rights pact worries right, left. *The Indianapolis Star.*

Critchell, S. (2005, November 8). All in a haze about parenting's good old days. *The Indianapolis Star.*

Critser, G. (2000, March). Let them eat fat: The heavy truths about American obesity. *Harper's Magazine.*

Cross, G. (1997). *Kids' stuff: Toys and the changing world of American childhood.* Cambridge, MA: Harvard University Press.

Cross, J., & Guyer, M. (1980). *Social traps.* Ann Arbor: University of Michigan Press.

Crossette, B. (1997a, November 2). How to fix a crowded world: Add people. *The New York Times.*

Crossette, B. (1997b, July 27). What modern slavery is, and isn't. *The New York Times.*

Crossette, B. (2001, February 28). Against a trend, U.S. population will bloom, UN says. *The New York Times.*

Croteau, D., & Hoynes, W. (2000). *Media/society: Industries, images, and audiences.* Thousand Oaks, CA: Pine Forge Press.

Crystal, D. (2003). *English as a global language.* Cambridge, UK: Cambridge University Press.

Curra, J. (2000). *The relativity of deviance.* Thousand Oaks, CA: Sage.

Currie, J., DellaVigna, S., Moretti, E., & Pathania, V. (2009). *The effect of fast food restaurants on obesity* (Working Paper No. 14721). Cambridge, MA: National Bureau of Economic Research. www.nber.org/papers/w14721.pdf. Accessed May 15, 2009.

Curtin, J. S. (2004). Suicide also rises in land of rising sun. *Asia Times Online.* www.atimes.com/atimes/Japan/FG28Dh01.html. Accessed November 19, 2004.

Cushing, R., & Bishop, B. (2005, July 20). The rural war. *The New York Times.*

Cushman, J. H. (1993, November 19). U.S. to weigh Blacks' complaints about pollution. *The New York Times.*

Dahrendorf, R. (1959). *Class and class conflict in industrial society.* Stanford, CA: Stanford University Press.

Daley, S. (1996, May 9). A new charter wins adoption in South Africa. *The New York Times.*

Daley, S. (2000, April 9). More and more, Europeans find fault with U.S. *The New York Times.*

Daniels, R. (1990). *Coming to America.* New York, NY: HarperCollins.

Danziger, S., & Gottschalk, P. (2004, December). *Diverging fortunes: Trends in poverty and inequality* (PRB Report). Washington, DC: Population Reference Bureau. www.prb.org. Accessed January 19, 2005.

Dao, J. (2010a, February 12). Single mother is spared court-martial. *The New York Times.*

Dao, J. (2010b, July 8). V.A. is easing rules to cover stress disorder. *The New York Times.*

Dao, J. (2011, May 14). Unfounded suspicions wreak havoc on lives of two Muslim soldiers. *The New York Times.*

Dargis, M. (2011, May 25). 3 men and a monkey-baby. *The New York Times.*

Davey, M. (2010, December 2). In Illinois, lawmakers approve legislation allowing civil unions. *The New York Times.*

Davey, M. (2011, September 7). Families feel sharp edge of state budget cuts. *The New York Times.*

Davies, J. C. (1962). Toward a theory of revolution. *American Sociological Review, 27,* 5–19.

Davis, D. B. (2006). *Inhuman bondage: The rise and fall of slavery in the New World.* New York, NY: Oxford University Press.

Davis, F. J. (1991). *Who is black?* University Park: Pennsylvania State University Press.

Davis, K. (1937). The sociology of prostitution. *American Sociological Review, 2,* 744–755.

Davis, K. (1976). The world's population crisis. In R. K. Merton & R. Nisbett (Eds.), *Contemporary social problems.* New York, NY: Harcourt Brace Jovanovich.

Davis, K., & Moore, W. (1945). Some principles of stratification. *American Sociological Review, 10,* 242–247.

Davis, S. (2003). Sex stereotypes in commercials targeted toward children: A content analysis. *Sociological Spectrum, 23,* 407–424.

Dawes, R. M., & Messick, D. M. (2000). Social dilemmas. *International Journal of Psychology, 35,* 111–116.

Dean, C. (2007, May 19). Evolution opponent is in line for schools post. *The New York Times.*

Deane, D. (2007, July 4). Justice is unequal for parents who host teen drinking parties. *The New York Times.*

Death Penalty Information Center. (2010). *Facts about death penalty.* www.deathpenaltyinfo.org/FactSheet.pdf. Accessed July 2, 2010.

Deaux, K., & Kite, M. E. (1987). Thinking about gender. In B. B. Hess & M. M. Ferree (Eds.), *Analyzing gender: A handbook of social science research.* Newbury Park, CA: Sage.

DeCastro, J. M. (1994). Family and friends produce greater social facilitation of food-intake than other companions. *Physiology and Behavior, 56,* 445–455.

DeCastro, J. M. (2000). Eating behaviors: Lessons from the real world of humans. *Ingestive Behavior and Obesity, 16,* 800–813.

Decker, G. (2011, July 4). More Hispanics are identifying themselves as Indians. *The New York Times.*

Declaration of sentiments and resolutions, Seneca Falls Convention, 1848. (2001). In P. S. Rothenberg (Ed.), *Race, class, and gender in the United States.* New York, NY: Worth.

DeFronzo, J. (1991). *Revolutions and revolutionary movements.* Boulder, CO: Westview Press.

De La Baume, M. (2011, May 12). Enforcing veil ban, the French have stopped 46 violators. *The New York Times.*

DeLeire, T. (2000). The unintended consequences of the Americans with Disabilities Act. *Regulation, 23,* 21–24.

Deming, D., & Dynarski, S. (2008). *The lengthening of childhood* (Working Paper No. 14124). Cambridge, MA: National Bureau of Economic Research. www.nber.org/papers/w14124.pdf?new_window=1. Accessed May 14, 2009.

DeNavas-Walt, C., Proctor, B. D., & Lee, C. H. (2006). *Income, poverty, and health insurance: Coverage in the United States: 2005* (U.S. Census Bureau, Current Population Reports, P60-231). Washington, DC: Government Printing Office.

DeNavas-Walt, C., Proctor, B. D., & Smith, J. C. (2008). *Income, poverty, and health insurance coverage in the United States: 2007* (U.S. Census Bureau, Current Population Reports, P60-235). www.census.gov/prod/2008pubs/p60-235.pdf. Accessed September 4, 2009.

DeNavas-Walt, C., Proctor, B. D., & Smith, J. C. (2010). *Income, poverty, and health insurance coverage in the United States: 2009* (U.S. Census Bureau, Current Population Reports, P60-238). www.census.gov/prod/2010pubs/p60.238.pdf. Accessed September 16, 2010.

DeNavas-Walt, C., Proctor, B. D., & Smith, J. C. (2011). *Income, poverty, and health insurance coverage in the United States: 2010.* (U.S. Census Bureau, Current Population Reports, P60-239). www.census.gov/prod/2011pubs/p60-239.pdf. Accessed September 13, 2011.

Denizet-Lewis, B. (2011, August 7). It's not U, it's me :(. *The New York Times Magazine.*

Denzin, N. (1977). *Childhood socialization: Studies in the development of language, social behavior, and identity.* San Francisco, CA: Jossey-Bass.

Denzin, N. (1989). *The research act: A theoretical introduction to sociological methods.* Englewood Cliffs, NJ: Prentice Hall.

DePalma, A. (1996, January 13). For Mexico's Indians, new voice but few gains. *The New York Times.*

DeParle, J. (2007, April 22). A good provider is one who leaves. *The New York Times Magazine.*

DeParle, J. (2009, February 2). Welfare system failing to grow as economy lags. *The New York Times.*

Derber, C. (1979). *The pursuit of attention.* New York, NY: Oxford University Press.

Dervarics, C. (2004, March). *Conspiracy beliefs may be hindering HIV prevention among African Americans* (PRB Report). Washington, DC: Population Reference Bureau. www.prb.org. Accessed March 16, 2005.

DeSouza, R.-M. (2004, October). *In harm's way: Hurricanes, population trends, and environmental change* (PRB Report). Washington, DC: Population Reference Bureau. www.prb.org. Accessed December 30, 2004.

Deutsch, K. W. (1966). *Nationalism and social communication.* Cambridge, MA: MIT Press.

Deutscher, G. (2010, August 29). You are what you speak. *The New York Times Magazine.*

Dewan, S. (2008, May 7). Releases from Death Row raise doubts about quality of defense. *The New York Times.*

Dey, J. G., & Hill, C. (2007). *Behind the pay gap.* Washington, DC: American Association of University Women Educational Foundation. www.aauw.org. Accessed April 1, 2007.

Diamond, J. (2005). *How societies choose to succeed or fail.* New York, NY: Viking.

Diekman, A. B., & Murnen, S. K. (2004). Learning to be little women and little men: The inequitable gender equality of nonsexist children's literature. *Sex Roles, 50,* 373–385.

Diekmann, A., & Engelhardt, H. (1999). The social inheritance of divorce: Effects of parent's family type in postwar Germany. *American Sociological Review, 64,* 78–93.

Diller, L. H. (1998). *Running on Ritalin.* New York, NY: Bantam Books.

Dillon, S. (2008, September 1). Hard times hitting students and schools in double blow. *The New York Times.*

Dillon, S. (2010, March 10). Many nations passing US in education, experts say. *The New York Times.*

Dillon, S. (2011a, January 26). Few students show proficiency in science, federal tests show. *The New York Times.*

Dillon, S. (2011b, July 6). Saving money means less time for school. *The New York Times.*

DiMaggio, P. J., & Powell, W. W. (1983). The iron cage revisited: Institutional isomorphism and collective rationality in organizational fields. *American Sociological Review, 48,* 147–160.

DiMaggio, P. J., & Powell, W. W. (1991). Introduction. In W. W. Powell & P. J. DiMaggio (Eds.), *The new institutionalism in organizational analysis.* Chicago, IL: University of Chicago Press.

Dion, K., Berscheid, E., & Walster, E. (1972). What is beautiful is good. *Journal of Personality and Social Psychology, 24,* 285–290.

Division for the Advancement of Women. (2009). *Convention on the elimination of all forms of discrimination against women: Overview of the convention.* New York, NY: Author. www.un.org/womenwatch/daw/cedaw/. Accessed June 4, 2009.

Dixon, T. L., & Linz, D. (2000). Race and the misrepresentation of victimization on local television news. *Communication Research, 27,* 547–573.

Dobash, R. E., & Dobash, R. P. (1979). *Violence against wives: A case against the patriarchy.* New York, NY: Free Press.

Do fines ever make corporations change? (2010, September 13). *Newsweek.*

Dokoupil, T. (2009, March 2). Men will be men. *Newsweek.*

Dokoupil, T. (2011, June 6). Mad as hell. *Newsweek.*

Domhoff, G. W. (1983). *Who rules America now? A view from the eighties.* Englewood Cliffs, NJ: Prentice Hall.

Domhoff, G. W. (1998). *Who rules America? Power and politics in the year 2000.* Mountain View, CA: Mayfield.

Domino's. (2011). *About Domino's Pizza.* www.dominosbiz.com/Biz-Public-EN/Site+Content/Secondary/About+Dominos/Fun+Facts/. Accessed May 26, 2011.

Dominus, S. (2004, February 22). Life in the age of old, old age. *The New York Times Magazine.*

Donadio, R. (2010a, April 5). Comments by cardinal on sexuality create a stir. *The New York Times.*

Donadio, R. (2010b, April 30). In abuse crisis, a church is pitted against society and itself. *The New York Times.*

Dosomething.org. (2007). *11 facts about environmental racism.* www.dosomething.org/tipsandtools/11-facts-about-environmental-racism. Accessed June 19, 2011.

Dowd, M. (2011, May 15). Corsets, cleavage, and fishnets. *The New York Times.*

Doyle, J. M., & Kao, G. (2007). Are racial identities of multiracials stable? Changing self-identification among single and multiple race individuals. *Social Psychology Quarterly, 70,* 405–423.

Doyle, S. (2010, August 2). *Mad Men*'s very modern sexism problem. *The Atlantic.* www.theatlantic .com/entertainment/archive/2010/08/mad-mens-very-modern-sexism-problem/60788/. Accessed April 12, 2011.

Drucker, S. (1996, March 10). Who is the best restaurateur in America? *The New York Times Magazine.*

Dugger, C. W. (1996, February 29). Immigrant cultures raising issues of child punishment. *The New York Times.*

Dugger, C. W. (1999, April 25). India's poorest are becoming its loudest. *The New York Times.*

Dugger, C. W. (2004a, December 28). Supermarket giants crush Central American farmers. *The New York Times.*

Dugger, C. W. (2004b, July 28). World Bank challenged: Are the poor really helped? *The New York Times.*

Duncan, G. J. (2007). School readiness and later achievement. *Developmental Psychology, 43,* 1428–1446.

Duncan, G. J., & Chase-Lansdale, P. L. (2001). For better and for worse: Welfare reform and the well-being of children and families. In G. J. Duncan & P. L. Chase-Lansdale (Eds.), *For better and for worse.* New York, NY: Russell Sage.

Durkheim, É. (1947). *The division of labor in society* (G. Simpson, Trans.). Glencoe, IL: Free Press. (Original work published 1893)

Durkheim, É. (1951). *Suicide.* New York, NY: Free Press. (Original work published 1897)

Durkheim, É. (1954). *The elementary forms of religious life* (J. Swain, Trans.). New York, NY: Free Press. (Original work published 1915)

Durkheim, É. (1958). *Rules of sociological method* (G. E. G. Catlin, Ed.; A. Solovay & J. H. Mueller, Trans.). Glencoe, IL: Free Press. (Original work published 1895)

Dye, J. L. (2008). *Fertility of American women: 2006* (U.S. Census Bureau, Current Population Reports, P20-558). www.census.gov/prod/2008pubs/p20-558.pdf. Accessed September 4, 2009.

Ebaugh, H. R. F. (1988). *Becoming an ex.* Chicago, IL: University of Chicago Press.

Eckholm, E. (2006a, July 27). Chicago orders "big box" stores to raise wages. *The New York Times.*

Eckholm, E. (2006b, March 20). Plight deepens for black men, study warns. *The New York Times.*

Eckholm, E. (2009, March 11). As jobs vanish, motel rooms become home. *The New York Times.*

Eckholm, E. (2010, September 29). Saying no to "I do," economy in mind. *The New York Times.*

Eckholm, E. (2011, March 22). With few jobs, a single pastor points to a bias. *The New York Times.*

Economic Policy Institute. (2011). *The state of working America.* www.stateofworkingamerica .org/. Accessed June 13, 2011.

Edidin, P. (2005, March 6). How to shake hands or share a meal with an Iraqi. *The New York Times.*

Edney, J. J. (1979, August). Free riders en route to disaster. *Psychology Today,* pp. 80–102.

Edney, J. J., & Harper, C. S. (1978). The commons dilemma: A review of contributions from psychology. *Environmental Management, 2,* 491–507.

The Education Trust. (2002). *The funding gap: Low-income and minority students receive fewer dollars.* www.edtrust.org. Accessed January 16, 2003.

Edwards, H. (1971, November). The sources of black athletic superiority. *The Black Scholar, 3,* 32–41.

Edwards, T. M. (2000, August 28). Flying solo. *Time.*

Egan, T. (1999, February 28). The war on crack retreats, still taking prisoners. *The New York Times.*

Egan, T. (2007, January 7). Little Asia on the hill. *The New York Times.*

Ehrenreich, B. (1990). Is the middle class doomed? In B. Ehrenreich (Ed.), *The worst years of our lives.* New York, NY: Harper & Row.

Ehrenreich, B. (2002, June 30). Two-tiered morality. *The New York Times.*

Ehrenreich, B., & English, D. (1979). *For her own good: 150 years of the experts' advice to women.* Garden City, NY: Anchor Books.

Ehrlich, P. R., & Ehrlich, A. H. (1993). World population crisis. In K. Finsterbusch & J. S. Schwartz (Eds.), *Sources: Notable selections in sociology.* Guilford, CT: Dushkin.

Einhorn, C. (2007, November). Nun pleads no contest in sex abuse. *The New York Times.*

Eitzen, D. S., & Baca Zinn, M. (1991). *In conflict and order: Understanding society.* Boston, MA: Allyn & Bacon.

Elder, G. H., & Liker, J. K. (1982). Hard times in women's lives: Historical influences across 40 years. *American Journal of Sociology, 88,* 241–269.

Eldridge, R. I., & Sutton, P. D. (2007, May). *Births, marriages, divorces, and deaths: Provisional data for October 2006* (National Vital Statistics Reports, Vol. 55, pp. 1–6). Hyattsville, MD: National Center for Health Statistics.

Elias, M. (2008, October 29). Study: 1 in 7 female vets report sexual trauma. *The Indianapolis Star.*

Elias, P. (2006, February 18). Execution reignites medical debate. *The Indianapolis Star.*

Eliot, L. (2010). *Pink brain, blue brain: How small differences grow into troublesome gaps and what we can do about it.* New York, NY: Mariner Books.

Elliott, C. (2003, June). American bioscience meets the American dream. *The American Prospect.*

Elliott, C., & Chambers, T. (2004). *Prozac as a way of life.* Chapel Hill: University of North Carolina Press.

Elliott, D., & Simmons, T. (2011). *Marital events of Americans: 2009.* (U.S. Bureau of the Census, American Community Survey Report ACS-13). www.census.gov/prod/2011pubs/acs-13 .pdf. Accessed September 4, 2011.

Ellison, J. (2011, April 11). The military's secret shame. *Newsweek.*

England, P., & Thomas, R. J. (2007). The decline of the date and the rise of the college hook-up. In A. S. Skolnick & J. H. Skolnick (Eds.), *Family in transition.* Boston, MA: Allyn & Bacon.

English, C. (1991). Food is my best friend: Self-justifications and weight loss efforts. *Research in the Sociology of Health Care, 9,* 335–345.

Enloe, C. (1993). *The morning after: Sexual politics at the end of the cold war.* Berkeley: University of California Press.

Entine, J. (2000). *Taboo: Why black athletes dominate sports and why we're afraid to talk about it.* New York, NY: PublicAffairs.

Epstein, C. F. (1989). Workplace boundaries: Conceptions and creations. *Social Research, 56,* 571–590.

Equal Employment Opportunity Commission. (2011). *Sexual harassment charges, EEOC & FEPAs combined: FY 1997–FY 2010.* www.eeoc .gov/eeoc/statistics/enforcement/sexual_ harassment.cfm. Accessed June 20, 2011.

Erikson, K. (1966). *Wayward Puritans.* New York, NY: Wiley.

Erlanger, S. (2000, April 2). Across a new Europe, a people deemed unfit for tolerance. *The New York Times.*

Erlanger, S. (2008, November 12). After U.S. breakthrough, Europe looks in mirror. *The New York Times.*

Erlanger, S. (2009, June 30). Study says Blacks and Arabs face bias from Paris police. *The New York Times.*

Erlanger, S. (2010, August 19). France intensifies effort to expel Roma, raising questions. *The New York Times.*

Evans, L., & Davies, K. (2000). No sissy boys here: A content analysis of the representation of masculinity in elementary school reading textbooks. *Sex Roles, 42,* 255–270.

Evans, T., & Nichols, M. (2009, March 22). Waiting for help in Indy. *The Indianapolis Star.*

Evans-Pritchard, E. E. (1937). *Witchcraft, oracles and magic among the Azande.* Oxford, UK: Oxford University Press.

Evered, R. (1983). The language of organizations: The case of the Navy. In L. R. Pondy, P. J. Frost, G. Morgan, & T. C. Dandridge (Eds.), *Organizational symbolism.* Greenwich, CT: JAI Press.

Exactly how much are the times a-changing? (2010, July 26). *Newsweek.*

Extreme facts. (2005, June 4). *The Indianapolis Star.*

Fackler, M. (2011, March 24). Severed from the world, villagers survive on tight bonds and to-do lists. *The New York Times.*

Falcone, M. (2009, February 13). 100,000 parents of citizens were deported over 10 years. *The New York Times.*

Faludi, S. (1991). *Backlash: The undeclared war against women.* New York, NY: Crown.

Family of VCJD victim claim untried treatment is a success. (2003). *Vegsource Newsletter.* www .vegsource.com/talk/madcow/messages/422 .html. Accessed June 30, 2003.

Farb, P. (1983). *Word play: What happens when people talk.* New York, NY: Bantam Books.

Farley, J. (1982). *Majority-minority relations.* Englewood Cliffs, NJ: Prentice Hall.

Farley, R. (2002). *Identifying with multiple races: A social movement that succeeded but failed?* (Population Studies Center Research Report No. 01-491). Ann Arbor: University of Michigan, Institute for Social Research.

Farley, R., & Frey, W. H. (1994). Changes in the segregation of Whites from Blacks during the 1980s: Small steps toward a more integrated society. *American Sociological Review, 59,* 23–45.

Farmer, R. (2002, Spring). Same sex couples face post–September 11 discrimination. *National NOW Times.*

Farrar, L. (2010). Chinese companies "rent" white foreigners. *CNN Online.* www.cnn.com/2010/ BUSINESS/06/29/china.rent.white.people/ index.html. Accessed June 1, 2011.

Faust, K., Gann, M., & McKibben, J. (1999). The boomlet goes to college. *American Demographics, 21,* 4–5.

Fausto-Sterling, A. (1985). *Myths of gender: Biological theories about women and men.* New York, NY: Basic Books.

Fausto-Sterling, A. (2000). *Sexing the body: Gender politics and the construction of sexuality.* New York, NY: Basic Books.

Feagin, J. R. (1975). *Subordinating the poor.* Englewood Cliffs, NJ: Prentice Hall.

Feagin, J. R., & McKinney, K. D. (2003). *The many costs of racism.* New York, NY: Rowman & Littlefield.

Feagin, J. R., & O'Brien, E. (2003). *White men on race: Power, privilege, and the shaping of cultural consciousness.* Boston, MA: Beacon Press.

Fearing demographic abyss, Putin promises mums more money. (2006, May 10). *Agence France Presse—English.*

Fears, D., & Deane, C. (2001, July 5). Biracial couples report tolerance. *The Washington Post.*

Feder, B. J., & Zeller, T. (2004, October 14). Identity badge worn under skin approved for use in health care. *The New York Times.*

Federal Bureau of Investigation. (2010). *Hate crime statistics: 2009.* www2.fbi.gov/ucr/hc2009/victims .html. Accessed June 15, 2011.

Federal Interagency Forum on Child and Family Statistics. (2007). *America's children: Key national indicators of well-being, 2007.* www .childstats.gov/pdf/ac2007/ac_07.pdf. Accessed July 20, 2007.

Feldmann, L., Marlantes, L., & Bowers, F. (2003, March 14). The impact of Bush linking 9/11 and Iraq. *Christian Science Monitor.*

Felmlee, D., Sprecher, S., & Bassin, E. (1990). The dissolution of intimate relationships: A hazard model. *Social Psychology Quarterly, 53,* 13–30.

Fendrich, J. M. (2003). The forgotten movement: The Vietnam antiwar movement. *Sociological Inquiry, 73,* 338–358.

Ferguson, N. (2004, April 4). Eurabia? *The New York Times Magazine.*

Ferree, M. M. (1992). The political context of rationality. In A. D. Morris & C. M. Mueller (Eds.), *Frontiers in social movement theory.* New Haven, CT: Yale University Press.

Festinger, L., Riecken, H., & Schacter, S. (1956). *When prophecy fails.* New York, NY: Harper & Row.

Feuer, A. (2004, May 15). Vatican discourages marriage with Muslims for Catholic women. *The New York Times.*

Fields, J. (2004). *America's families and living arrangements: 2003* (U.S. Census Bureau, Current Population Reports, P20-553). www .census.gov/prod/2004pubs/p20-553.pdf. Accessed September 4, 2009.

Fiese, B. H., & Skillman, G. (2000). Gender differences in family stories: Moderating influence of parent gender role and child gender. *Sex Roles, 43*(5/6), 267–283.

Figert, A. (1996). *Women and the ownership of PMS.* New York, NY: Aldine de Gruyter.

Fincham, F., & Bradbury, T. N. (1987). The impact of attributions in marriage: A longitudinal analysis. *Journal of Personality and Social Psychology, 53,* 510–517.

Finer, J. (2005, August 12). The new Ernie Pyles: Sgtlizzie and 67shdocs. *The Washington Post.*

Fischer, M. J., & Massey, D. S. (2000). Residential segregation and ethnic enterprise in U.S. metropolitan areas. *Social Problems, 47,* 408–424.

Fish, S. (2000). The nifty nine arguments against affirmative action in higher education. *Journal of Blacks in Higher Education, 27,* 79–81.

Fisher, I., & Goodstein, L. (2005, November 23). In strong terms, Rome is to ban gays as priests. *The New York Times.*

Flaccus, G. (2007, July 16). L.A. archdiocese apologizes. *The Indianapolis Star.*

Fleischaker, D. T. (2004). Dead man pausing: The continuing need for a nationwide moratorium on executions. *Human Rights, 31,* 14–18.

Flynn, J. (1999). Searching for justice: The discovery of IQ gains over time. *American Psychologist, 54,* 5–20.

Folbre, N., & Yoon, J. (2006, January 5). *The value of unpaid child care in the U.S. in 2003.* Paper presented at the meeting of the Allied Social Science Association, Boston, MA. (Cited with permission of author)

Forman, T. A., Williams, D., & Jackson, J. (1997). Race, place, and discrimination. *Perspectives on Social Problems, 9,* 231–261.

Foroohar, R. (2010, April 26). The Burqa revolution. *Newsweek.*

Fountain, H. (2005, June). Unloved, but not unbuilt. *The New York Times.*

Fouts, G., & Burggraf, K. (2000). Television situation comedies: Female weight, male negative comments, and audience reactions. *Sex Roles, 42,* 925–932.

Fowler, J. H., & Christakis, N. A. (2008). Dynamic spread of happiness in a large social network: Longitudinal analysis over 20 years in the Framingham Heart Study. *British Medical Journal, 338,* 23–31.

Fox, J. A., & Zawitz, M. W. (2007). *Homicide trends in the United States.* Washington, DC: U.S. Bureau of Justice Statistics. www.ojp.usdoj .gov/bjs/pub/pdf/htius.pdf. Accessed May 18, 2009.

Frank, A. G. (1969). *Capitalism and under-development in Latin America.* New York, NY: Monthly Review Press.

Frankenberg, E. (2006). *The segregation of American teachers.* Cambridge, MA: Civil Rights Project at Harvard University.

Franklin, D. (2006, August 15). Patient power: Making sure your doctor really hears you. *The New York Times.*

Franklin, J. (2010, September 9). Chilean miners: A typical day in the life of a subterranean miner. *The Guardian.*

Free Press. (2010). *Media consolidation.* www .freepress.net/media_issues/consolidation. Accessed May 24, 2011.

Free the Children. (2011). *Progress.* www.freethe children.com/aboutus/progress.php. Accessed May 17, 2011.

Freiberg, P. (1991). Self-esteem gender gap widens in adolescence. *APA Monitor, 22,* 29.

French, H. W. (1999a, November 15). "Japanese only" policy takes body blow in court. *The New York Times.*

French, H. W. (1999b, October 12). Japan's troubling trend: Rising teen-age crime. *The New York Times.*

French, H. W. (2000, May 3). Japan unsettles returnees, who yearn to leave again. *The New York Times*

French, H. W. (2002, September 23). Educators try to tame Japan's blackboard jungles. *The New York Times.*

French, H. W. (2003, July 25). Japan's neglected resource: Female workers. *The New York Times.*

French, H. W. (2007a, March 22). China scrambles for stability as its workers age. *The New York Times.*

French, H. W. (2007b, June 16). Reports of forced labor at brick kilns unsettle China. *The New York Times.*

Frese, B., Moya, M., & Megias, J. L. (2004). Social perception of rape: How rape myth acceptance modulates the influence of situational factors. *Journal of Interpersonal Violence, 19,* 143–161.

Freund, P. E. S., & McGuire, M. B. (1991). *Health, illness, and the social body: A cultural sociology.* Englewood Cliffs, NJ: Prentice Hall.

Friedman, T. L. (2005, April 3). It's a flat world after all. *The New York Times Magazine.*

Frosch, D. (2011, March 30). A trip to these principals may mean a paddling. *The New York Times.*

Fryer, R. G. (2006, Winter). "Acting white": The social price paid by the best and brightest minority students. *Education Next,* pp. 53–59.

Furstenberg, F. F., & Harris, K. M. (1992). The disappearing American father? Divorce and the waning significance of biological parenthood. In S. J. South & S. E. Tolnay (Eds.), *The changing American family: Sociological and demographic perspectives.* Boulder, CO: Westview Press.

Fustos, K. (2010a, June). *Marriage and partnership turnover for American families.* Population Reference Bureau. http://www.prb.org/ Articles/2010/usmarriagepolicyseminar.aspx. Accessed August 28, 2011.

Fustos, K. (2010b). *Marriage benefits men's health.* Population Reference Bureau. www.prb.org/ Articles/2010/usmarriagemenshealth .aspx?p=1. Accessed June 5, 2011.

Fustos, K. (2011). *Gender-based violence increases risk of HIV/AIDS for women in sub-Saharan Africa.* Population Reference Bureau. www.prb .org/Articles/2011/gender-based-violence-hiv .aspx?p=1. Accessed April 26, 2011.

Fuwa, M. (2004). Macro-level gender inequality and the division of household labor in 22 countries. *American Sociological Review, 69,* 751–767.

Gabriel, T. (2010a, July 6). To stop cheats, colleges learn their trickery. *The New York Times.*

Gabriel, T. (2010b, June 10). Under pressure, teachers tamper with tests. *The New York Times.*

Gale, R. P. (1986). Social movements and the state: The environmental movement, countermovement and governmental agencies. *Sociological Perspectives, 29,* 202–240.

Galinsky, E., Bond, J. T., Kim, S. S., Backon, L., Brownfield, E., & Sakai, K. (2006). *Overwork in America: When the way we work becomes too much.* New York, NY: Families and Work Institute. www.familiesandwork.org/summary/ overwork2005.pdf. Accessed July 19, 2006.

Galles, G. M. (1989, June 8). What colleges really teach. *The New York Times.*

Galliher, J. M., & Galliher, J. F. (2002). A "commonsense" theory of deterrence and the "ideology" of science: The New York State death penalty debate. *Journal of Criminal Law and Criminology, 92,* 307–333.

Gamson, W. A., Fireman, B., & Rytina, S. (1982). *Encounters with unjust authority.* Homewood, IL: Dorsey Press.

Gamson, W. A., & Wolfsfeld, G. (1993). Movements and media as interactive systems. *Annals of the American Academy of Political and Social Science, 528,* 114–125.

Gans, H. (1971, July/August). The uses of poverty: The poor pay for all. *Social Policy,* pp. 20–24.

Gans, H. (1996). Positive functions of the undeserving poor: Uses of the underclass in America. In J. Levin & A. Arluke (Eds.), *Snapshots and portraits of society.* Thousand Oaks, CA: Pine Forge Press.

Gans, H. (2005). Race as class. *Contexts, 4,* 17–21.

Garcia-Moreno, C., Jansen, H., Ellsberg, M., Heise, L., & Watts, C. H. (2006). Prevalence of intimate partner violence: Findings from the WHO multi-country study on women's health and domestic violence. *Lancet, 368,* 1260–1269.

Gardner, G. (2005, March/April). Yours, mine, ours—or nobody's? *World Watch.*

Garfinkel, J. (2003, February 24). Boutique medical practices face legal, legislative foes. *Cincinnati Business Courier.* www.bizjournals.com/cincinnati/stories/2003/02/24/focus2.html. Accessed July 12, 2004.

Garner, B. A. (2010, February 28). Webinar: What makes for a successful mash-up neologism. *The New York Times Magazine.*

Garson, B. (1988). *The electronic sweatshop.* New York, NY: Penguin Books.

Gates, H. L. (2007, November 18). Forty acres and a gap in wealth. *The New York Times.*

Gaubatz, K. T. (1995). *Crime in the public mind.* Ann Arbor: University of Michigan Press.

Gelles, R. J., & Straus, M. A. (1988). *Intimate violence.* Newbury Park, CA: Sage.

Gentleman, A. (2006, January 10). Millions of abortions of female fetuses reported in India. *The New York Times.*

Gentleman, A. (2007, June 3). Indian shepherds stoop to conquer caste system. *The New York Times.*

Gergen, K. J. (1991). *The saturated self.* New York, NY: Basic Books.

Gerlach, P., & Hine, V. H. (1970). *People, power, change: Movements of social transformation.* Indianapolis, IN: Bobbs-Merrill.

Getlin, J., & Wilkinson, T. (2003, April 3). "Embedded" reporters are mixed blessing for the military. *The Seattle Times.*

Gettleman, J. (2010, October 4). 4-day frenzy of rape in Congo reveals U.N. troops' weakness. *The New York Times.*

Giddens, A. (1984). *The construction of society: Outline of the theory of structuration.* Berkeley: University of California Press.

Giddens, A. (2005). The global revolution in family and personal life. In A. S. Skolnick & J. H. Skolnick (Eds.), *Family in transition.* Boston, MA: Allyn & Bacon.

Giglio, M. (2011, January 10, 17). Germany is mad as hell. *Newsweek.*

Gillen, B. (1981). Physical attractiveness: A determinant of two types of goodness. *Personality and Social Psychology Bulletin, 7,* 277–281.

Gilliam, W. S. (2005). *Prekindergarteners left behind: Expulsion rates in state prekindergarten systems.* New York, NY: Foundation for Child Development. www.fcd-us.org/PDFs/NationalPreK ExpulsionPaper03.02_new.pdf. Accessed May 17, 2005.

Gilligan, C. (1990). Teaching Shakespeare's sister: Notes from the underground of female adolescence. In C. Gilligan, N. P. Lyons, & T. J. Hanmer (Eds.), *Making connections.* Cambridge, MA: Harvard University Press.

Gilman, S. (2004). *Fat boys.* Lincoln: University of Nebraska Press.

Gimpel, J. G. (2009). *Latino voting in the 2008 election: Part of a broader electoral movement.* Washington, DC: Center for Immigration Studies. www.cis.org/latinovoting. Accessed May 31, 2009.

Ginzel, L. E., Kramer, R. M., & Sutton, R. I. (2004). Organizational impression management as a reciprocal influence process: The neglected role of the organizational audience. In M. J. Hatch & M. Schultz (Eds.), *Organizational identity.* New York, NY: Oxford University Press.

Giridharadas, A. (2007, November 25). Rumbling across India: Stories of urban migration. *The New York Times.*

Giridharadas, A. (2010a, August 8). Getting in (and out of) line. *The New York Times.*

Giridharadas, A. (2010b, April 11). Where a cellphone is still cutting edge. *The New York Times.*

Gitlin, T. (1979). Prime time ideology: The hegemonic process in television entertainment. *Social Problems, 26,* 251–266.

Gladwell, M. (2010, October 4). Small change. *The New Yorker*.

Glater, J. D. (2006, December 3). Straight "A" students? Good luck making partner. *The New York Times*.

Glaze, L. E., & Bonczar, T. P. (2010). *Probation and parole in the United States, 2009* (NCJ 231674). U.S. Bureau of Justice Statistics. http://bjs.ojp .usdoj.gov/content/pub/pdf/ppus09.pdf. Accessed March 31, 2011.

Glick, P., & Fiske, S. T. (1996). The ambivalent sexism inventory: Differentiating hostile and benevolent sexism. *Journal of Personality and Social Psychology, 70,* 491–512.

Godofsky, J., Zukin, C., & Van Horn, C. (2011). *Unfulfilled expectations: Recent college graduates struggle in a troubled economy.* John J. Heldrich Center for Workforce Development. www .heldrich.rutgers.edu. Accessed May 19, 2011.

Godson, R., & Olson, W. J. (1995). International organized crime. *Society, 32,* 18–29.

Goffman, A. (2009). On the run: Wanted men in a Philadelphia ghetto. *American Sociological Review, 74,* 339–357.

Goffman, E. (1952). On cooling the mark out: Some aspects of adaptation to failure. *Psychiatry, 15,* 451–463.

Goffman, E. (1959). *The presentation of self in everyday life.* Garden City, NY: Doubleday.

Goffman, E. (1961). *Asylums.* Garden City, NY: Doubleday.

Goffman, E. (1963). *Stigma: Notes on the management of spoiled identity.* Englewood Cliffs, NJ: Prentice Hall.

Goffman, E. (1967). *Interaction ritual.* Chicago, IL: Aldine-Atherton.

Goldberg, C. (2001, April 22). In some states, sex offenders serve more than their time. *The New York Times*.

Goldberg, S. (1999). The logic of patriarchy. *Gender Issues, 17,* 53–69.

Goleman, D. (1989, October 10). Sensing silent cues emerges as key skill. *The New York Times*.

Goleman, D. (1990, December 25). The group and the self: New focus on a cultural rift. *The New York Times*.

Goleman, D. (1993, May 4). Therapists find some patients are just hateful. *The New York Times*.

Golway, T. (2004, August 2–9). Redrafting America. *America*.

Gomstyn, A. (2009). Good P.R. or guilt? Rich get discreet. *ABC News*. http://abcnews.go.com/ Business/Economy/story?id=6823310&page=1. Accessed April 28, 2009.

Gonnerman, J. (2004). *Life on the outside.* New York, NY: Farrar, Strauss, & Giroux.

Goode, Erica. (1999, January 12). Pediatricians renew battle over toilet training. *The New York Times*.

Goode, Erica. (2011a, April 7). Police lesson: Network tools have 2 edges. *The New York Times*.

Goode, Erica. (2011b, May 21). States seeking new registries for criminals. *The New York Times*.

Goode, Erich. (1989). *Drugs in American society.* New York, NY: McGraw-Hill.

Goode, Erich. (1994). *Deviant behavior.* Englewood Cliffs, NJ: Prentice Hall.

Goode, W. J. (1971). World revolution and family patterns. *Journal of Marriage and the Family, 33,* 624–635.

Goode, W. J. (1981). Why men resist. In B. Thorne & M. Yalom (Eds.), *Rethinking the family: Some feminist questions.* New York, NY: Longman.

Goodman, J. C. (2005). *Aid to Katrina victims: A right/left consensus.* Dallas, TX: National Center for Policy Analysis. www.ncpa.org/pub/ba529. Accessed May 23, 2009.

Goodnough, A. (2005, April 27). Florida expands right to use deadly force in self-defense. *The New York Times*.

Goodstein, L. (2003, September 11). Survey finds slight rise in Jews' intermarrying. *The New York Times*.

Goodstein, L. (2009, April 3). Early alarm for church on abusers in the clergy. *The New York Times*.

Goodstein, L. (2010a, August 8). Around nation, heated debates on new mosques. *The New York Times*.

Goodstein, L. (2010b, December 2). $30 million is award over abuse by priest. *The New York Times*.

Goodstein, L. (2011, May 11). Presbyterians approve ordination of gay people. *The New York Times*.

Goodwin, J. (2003). The ultimate growth industry: Trafficking in women and girls. In E. Disch (Ed.), *Reconstructing gender: A multicultural anthology.* New York, NY: McGraw-Hill.

Gootman, E. (2006, October 19). Those preschoolers are looking older. *The New York Times*.

Gorbis, E., & Kholodenko, Y. (2005, September 1). Plastic surgery addiction in patients with body dysmorphic disorder. *Psychiatric Times*.

Gordon, M. M. (1964). *Assimilation in American life.* New York, NY: Oxford University Press.

Gordon, R. G. (2005). *Ethnologue: Languages of the world* (15th ed.). Dallas, TX: SIL International.

Gott, N. (2004, November 6). Textbooks OK'd after marriage redefined. *The Indianapolis Star.*

Gould, S. J. (1981). *The mismeasure of man.* New York, NY: Norton.

Gould, S. J. (1997, June). Dolly's fashion and Louis's passion. *Natural History.*

Gove, W., Hughes, M., & Geerkin, M. R. (1980). Playing dumb: A form of impression management with undesirable effects. *Social Psychology Quarterly, 43,* 89–102.

Gove, W., Style, C. B., & Hughes, M. (1990). The effect of marriage on the well-being of adults. *Journal of Family Issues, 11,* 34–35.

Governors Highway Safety Association. (2011). *Cell phone and texting laws.* www.ghsa.org/html/ stateinfo/laws/cellphone_laws.html. Accessed May 27, 2011.

Gracey, H. L. (1991). Learning the student role: Kindergarten as academic boot camp. In J. Henslin (Ed.), *Down-to-earth sociology.* New York, NY: Free Press.

Grady, D. (2008, December 4). Parents torn over extra frozen embryos from fertility procedures. *The New York Times.*

Grady, D. (2009, May 24). Where life's start is a deadly risk. *The New York Times.*

Grady, D. (2010, March 30). Overhaul will lower the costs of being a woman. *The New York Times.*

Graham, L. O. (1999). *Our kind of people: Inside America's black upper class.* New York, NY: HarperCollins.

Grall, T. S. (2007). *Custodial mothers and fathers and their child support: 2005* (U.S. Census Bureau, Current Population Reports, P60-234). www .census.gov/prod/2007pubs/p60-234.pdf. Accessed September 4, 2009.

Greenblatt, A. (2009). Confronting warming. *CQ Researcher, 19,* 1–24.

Greenblatt, A. (2011). Aging population. *CQ Researcher, 21,* 577–600.

Greencastle Banner Graphic. 1992, March 7. [Letter to the editor].

Greene, M. F. (2004, November 28). Sandlot summer: Hyperscheduled, overachieving children learn how to play. *The New York Times Magazine.*

Greenhouse, L. (2005, June 7). Justices say U.S. may prohibit the use of medical marijuana. *The New York Times.*

Greenhouse, L. (2007a, June 12). Court to weigh disparities in cocaine laws. *The New York Times.*

Greenhouse, L. (2007b, June 29). Justices, 5–4, limit use of race for school integration plans. *The New York Times.*

Greenhouse, S. (2004, November 19). Forced to work off the clock, some fight back. *The New York Times.*

Greenhouse, S. (2006, July 14). On dusty corner, laborers band together for more pay. *The New York Times.*

Greenhouse, S. (2009, May 16). Bill would guarantee up to 7 paid sick days. *The New York Times.*

Greenhouse, S. (2011, May 21). Sexual affronts a known hotel hazard. *The New York Times.*

Greenhouse, S., & Leonhardt, D. (2006, August 28). Real wages fail to match a rise in productivity. *The New York Times.*

Greywolfe359. (2011, March 9). The must see chart (This is what class war looks like) [Web log post]. www.dailykos.com/story/2011/03/09/ 954301/-The-Must-See-Chart-(This-is-What-Class-War-Looks-Like). Accessed June 14, 2011.

Griffin, S. (1986). *Rape: The power of consciousness.* New York, NY: Harper & Row.

Griffin, S. (1989). Rape: The all-American crime. In L. Richardson & V. Taylor (Eds.), *Feminist frontiers II.* New York, NY: Random House.

Griswold, W. (1994). *Cultures and societies in a changing world.* Thousand Oaks, CA: Pine Forge Press.

Groppe, M. (2010, July 19). More get welfare in hard times, right? Not here. *The Indianapolis Star.*

Gross, E., & Etzioni, A. (1985). *Organizations and society.* Englewood Cliffs, NJ: Prentice Hall.

Gross, E., & Stone, G. P. (1964). Embarrassment and the analysis of role requirements. *American Journal of Sociology, 70,* 1–15.

Gross, J. (2004a, February 24). Older women team up to face future together. *The New York Times.*

Gross, J. (2004b, May 31). Splitting up boys and girls, just for the tough years. *The New York Times.*

Gross, J. (2006, July 16). Checklist for camp: Bug spray. Sunscreen. Pills. *The New York Times.*

Grossbard, L. (2011, June 5). Does Twitter make you stupid? *The New York Times.*

Gunnell, J. J., & Ceci, S. J. (2010). When emotionality trumps reason: A study of individual processing style and juror bias. *Behavioral Sciences and the Law, 28,* 850–877.

Gusfield, J. R. (1963). *Symbolic crusade: Status politics and the American temperance movement.* Urbana: University of Illinois Press.

Hacker, A. (1992). *Two nations: Black and white, separate, hostile, unequal.* New York, NY: Scribner.

Hacker, A. (1994, October 31). White on white. *The New Republic.*

Haddal, C. C. (2010). *Border security: The role of the U.S. Border Patrol.* Congressional Research Service. http://assets.opencrs.com/rpts/RL 32562_20100303.pdf. Accessed June 26, 2011.

Hafferty, F. W. (1991). *Into the valley: Death and socialization of medical students.* New Haven, CT: Yale University Press.

Hagan, J. (1985). *Modern criminology: Crime, criminal behavior and its control.* New York, NY: McGraw-Hill.

Hagan, J. (2000). The poverty of a classless criminology: The American Society of Criminology 1991 presidential address. In R. D. Crutchfield, G. S. Bridges, J. G. Weis, & C. Kubrin (Eds.), *Crime readings.* Thousand Oaks, CA: Pine Forge Press.

Hagerty, B. B. (2011, May 23). Doomsday believers cope with an intact world. *NPR Online.* www .npr.org/2011/05/23/136560695/doomsday-believers-cope-with-an-intact-world. Accessed May 23, 2011.

Halbfinger, D. M., & Holmes, S. A. (2003, March 30). Military mirrors a working-class America. *The New York Times.*

Hall, P. (1990). The presidency and impression management. In J. W. Heeren & M. Mason (Eds.), *Sociology: Windows on society.* Los Angeles, CA: Roxbury.

Hall, W. (1986). Social class and survival on the *S.S. Titanic. Social Science and Medicine, 22,* 687–690.

Hallin, D. C. (1986). We keep America on top of the world. In T. Gitlin (Ed.), *Watching television.* New York, NY: Pantheon Books.

Hamill, S. D. (2009, April 29). 2 white youths on trial for killing of a Mexican. *The New York Times.*

Hamilton, C., Anderson, K., Barnes, R., & Dorling, K. (2011). *Administrative detention of children: A global report.* UNICEF. www.unicef.org/protection/files/Administrative_detention_discussion_paper_April2011.pdf. Accessed June 29, 2011.

Hamilton, D. L. (1981). *Cognitive processes in stereotyping and intergroup behavior.* Hillsdale, NJ: Erlbaum.

Hamilton, J. A. (1996). Women and health policy: On the inclusion of women in clinical trials. In C. F. Sargent & C. B. Brettell (Eds.), *Gender and health: An international perspective.* Upper Saddle River, NJ: Prentice Hall.

Hamilton, V. L., & Sanders, J. (1995). Crimes of obedience and conformity in the workplace: Surveys of Americans, Russians, and Japanese. *Journal of Social Issues, 51,* 67–88.

Hampton, K., Sessions, L., Her, E. J., & Rainie, L. (2009). *Social isolation and new technology.* Pew Internet and American Life Project. www .pewinternet.org/~/media//Files/Reports/2009/PIP_Tech_and_Social_Isolation.pdf. Accessed June 3, 2011.

Haney López, I. E. (1996). *White by law: The legal construction of race.* New York, NY: New York University Press.

Hankiss, E. (2001). *Symbols of destruction: After September 11.* Brooklyn, NY: Social Science Research Council. http://essays.ssrc.org/sept11/essays/hankiss.htm. Accessed September 4, 2009.

Harden, B. (2000, April 6). Africa's gems: Warfare's best friend. *The New York Times.*

Hardin, G., & Baden, J. (1977). *Managing the commons.* New York, NY: Freeman.

Hareven, T. K. (1978). *Transitions: The family and the life course in historical perspective.* New York, NY: Academic Press.

Hareven, T. K. (1992). American families in transition: Historical perspectives on change. In A. S. Skolnick & J. H. Skolnick (Eds.), *Family in transition* (7th ed.). New York, NY: HarperCollins.

Harmon, A. (2009, May 17). Fighting for a last chance at life. *The New York Times.*

Harrington, B., Van Deusen, F., & Ladge, J. (2010). *The new dad: Exploring fatherhood within a career context.* Boston College Center for Work & Family. http://www.bc.edu/content/dam/files/centers/cwf/pdf/BCCWF_Fatherhood_Study_The_New_Dad1.pdf. Accessed August 28, 2011.

Harris, D. R., & Sim, J. J. (2002). Who is multiracial? Assessing the complexity of lived race. *American Sociological Review, 67,* 614–627.

Harris, G. (2003, December 7). If shoe won't fit, fix the foot? Popular surgery raises concern. *The New York Times.*

Harris, G. (2005a, August 6). F.D.A. responds to criticism with new caution. *The New York Times.*

Harris, G. (2005b, October 19). Sleeping pill use by youths soars, study says. *The New York Times.*

Harris, G. (2006, September 30). F.D.A. says Bayer failed to reveal drug risk study. *The New York Times.*

Harris, G. (2009, January 12). F.D.A. is lax on oversight during trials, inquiry finds. *The New York Times.*

Harris, G. (2011a, May 27). Study questions treatment used in heart disease. *The New York Times.*

Harris, G. (2011b, March 6). Talk doesn't pay, so psychiatry turns instead to drug therapy. *The New York Times.*

Harris, M. C. (1996). Doctors implicated in Tutsi genocide. *Lancet, 347,* 684.

Hart, T. C. (2003). *Violent victimization of college students* (Bulletin NCJ 196143). Washington, DC: Bureau of Justice Statistics. www.ojp.usdoj.gov/bjs/pub/pdf/vvcs00.pdf. Accessed June 18, 2007.

Hartmann, H., Kraut, R. E., & Tilly, L. A. (1989). Job content: Job fragmentation and the deskilling debate. In D. S. Eitzen & M. Baca Zinn (Eds.), *The reshaping of America.* Englewood Cliffs, NJ: Prentice Hall.

Hartocollis, A. (2006, June 24). Women have seen it all on subway, unwillingly. *The New York Times.*

Hasday, J. E. (2000). Contest and consent: A legal history of marital rape. *California Law Review, 88,* 1373–1506.

Hass, N. (1995, September 10). Margaret Kelly Michaels wants her innocence back. *The New York Times Magazine.*

Hatzenbuehler, M. L. (2011). The social environment and suicide attempts in lesbian, gay, and bisexual youth. *Pediatrics, 127,* 896–903.

Haub, C. (2010). *Recession putting brakes on increases in birth rates.* Population Reference Bureau. www.prb.org/Articles/2010/lowfertilitytfr.aspx?p=1. Accessed August 26, 2010.

Haub, C. (2011). *Birth rate trends in low-fertility countries.* Population Reference Bureau. www.prb.org/Articles/2011/low-fertility-countries-tfr.aspx?p=1. Accessed March 28, 2011.

Haub, C., & Gribble, J. (2011). The world at 7 billion. *Population Bulletin, 66,* 1–12.

Hausmann, R., Tyson, L. D., & Zahidi, S. (2008). *The global gender gap report: 2008.* Geneva, Switzerland: World Economic Forum. www.weforum.org/pdf/gendergap/report2008.pdf. Accessed June 3, 2009.

Health Grades. (2009). *The sixth annual Health Grades Patient Safety in American Hospitals Study.* www.healthgrades.com/media/DMS/pdf/PatientSafetyinAmericanHospitalsStudy2009.pdf. Accessed May 22, 2009.

Health Resources and Services Administration. (2004). *What is behind HRSA's projected supply, demand, and shortage of registered nurses?* ftp://ftp.hrsa.gov/bhpr/workforce/behindshortage.pdf. Accessed June 21, 2007.

Health Resources and Services Administration. (2005). *Nursing education in five states: 2005.* http://bhpr.hrsa.gov/healthworkforce/reports/nursing/nursinged5/default.htm. Accessed June 21, 2007.

Hebel, S. (2007, March 23). The graduation gap. *Chronicle of Higher Education.* http://chronicle.com/weekly/v53/i29/29a02001.htm. Accessed August 8, 2007.

Heffernan, V. (2008, May 25). Narrow minded. *The New York Times Magazine.*

Helmreich, W. B. (1992). The things they say behind your back: Stereotypes and the myths behind them. In H. E. Lena, W. B. Helmreich, & W. McCord (Eds.), *Contemporary issues in sociology.* New York, NY: McGraw-Hill.

Henderson, J. J., & Baldasty, G. J. (2003). Race, advertising, and prime-time television. *Howard Journal of Communication, 14,* 97–112.

Henig, R. M. (2010, August 18). What is it about 20-somethings? *The New York Times.*

Henley, N. (1977). *Body politics.* Englewood Cliffs, NJ: Prentice Hall.

Henrich, J., Heine, S. J., & Norenzayan, A. (2010). The weirdest people in the world? *Behavioral and Brain Sciences, 33,* 61–135.

Henriques, D. B. (1999, August 24). New take on perpetual calendar. *The New York Times.*

Henriques, D. B. (2009, June 30). Madoff, apologizing, is given 150 years. *The New York Times.*

Henshaw, S. K., & Finer, L. B. (2003). The accessibility of abortion services in the United States, 2001. *Perspectives on Sexual and Reproductive Health, 35,* 16–24.

Henslin, J. (1991). *Down-to-earth sociology.* New York, NY: Free Press.

Herbert, B. (2007, May 15). The right to paid sick days. *The New York Times.*

Herbert, B. (2009, February 21). The invisible war. *The New York Times.*

Herek, G. M. (2000a). The psychology of sexual prejudice. *Current Directions in Psychological Science, 9,* 19–22.

Herek, G. M. (2000b). Sexual prejudice and gender: Do heterosexuals' attitudes toward lesbians and gay men differ? *Journal of Social Issues, 56,* 251–266.

Herman, N. J. (1993). Return to sender: Reintegrative stigma-management strategies of ex-psychiatric patients. *Journal of Contemporary Ethnography, 22,* 295–330.

Herrnstein, R. J., & Murray, C. (1994). *The bell curve: Intelligence and class structure in American life.* New York, NY: Free Press.

Hewitt, J. P. (1988). *Self and society: A symbolic interactionist social psychology.* Boston, MA: Allyn & Bacon.

Hewitt, J. P., & Hewitt, M. L. (1986). *Introducing sociology: A symbolic interactionist perspective.* Englewood Cliffs, NJ: Prentice Hall.

Hewitt, J. P., & Stokes, R. (1975). Disclaimers. *American Sociological Review, 40,* 1–11.

Heymann, J., Earle, A., & Hayes, J. (2007). *The work, family, and equity index: How does the United States measure up?* Boston, MA: Project on Global Working Families, Harvard School of Public Health. http://www.mcgill.ca/files/ihsp/WFEI2007.pdf. Accessed September 4, 2009.

Hibbler, D. K., & Shinew, K. J. (2005). The social life of interracial couples. In R. H. Lauer & J. C. Lauer (Eds.), *Sociology: Windows on society.* Los Angeles, CA: Roxbury.

Higginbotham, E., & Weber, L. (1992). Moving up with kin and community: Upward social mobility for black and white women. *Gender & Society, 6,* 416–440.

Hill, C., & Silva, E. (2006). *Drawing the line: Sexual harassment on campus.* Washington, DC: American Association of University Women. www.aauw.org/research/upload/DTLFinal.pdf. Accessed September 5, 2009.

Hill, M. E. (2000). Color differences in the socioeconomic status of African American men: Results from a longitudinal study. *Social Forces, 78,* 1437–1460.

Hill, N. E. (1997). Does parenting differ based on social class? African American women's perceived socialization for achievement. *American Journal of Community Psychology, 25,* 67–97.

Hills, S. (1980). *Demystifying social deviance.* New York, NY: McGraw-Hill.

Hirschi, T. (1969). *Causes of delinquency.* Berkeley: University of California Press.

Hitt, J. (2005, August 21). The new Indians *The New York Times Magazine.*

Hochschild, A. R. (1983). *The managed heart.* Berkeley: University of California Press.

Hochschild, A. R. (1997). *The time bind: When work becomes home and home becomes work.* New York, NY: Metropolitan Books.

Hodson, R. (1991). The active worker: Compliance and autonomy at the workplace. *Journal of Contemporary Ethnography, 20,* 47–78.

Hodson, R. (1996). Dignity in the workplace under participative management: Alienation and freedom revisited. *American Sociological Review, 61,* 719–738.

Hodson, R. (2001). *Dignity at work.* New York, NY: Cambridge University Press. Hofferth, S. L., & Sandberg, J. F. (2001). How American children spend their time. *Journal of Marriage and the Family, 63,* 295–308.

Hoffman, J. (1997, January 16). Crime and punishment: Shame gains popularity. *The New York Times.*

Hoffman, J. (2005, January 25). Sorting out ambivalence over alcohol and pregnancy. *The New York Times.*

Hollander, J. A., Renfrow, D. G., & Howard, J. A. (2011). *Gendered situations, gendered selves.* Lanham, MD: Rowman & Littlefield.

Holmes, S. A. (1995, December 31). The strange politics of immigration. *The New York Times.*

Holmes, S. A. (2000, March 11). New policy on census says those listed as white and minority will be counted as minority. *The New York Times.*

Holson, L. M. (2011a, January 25). For the funeral too distant, mourners gather on the Web. *The New York Times.*

Holson, L. M. (2011b , July 5). Who's on the family tree? Now it's complicated. *The New York Times.*

Holtzworth-Munroe, A., & Jacobson, N. S. (1985). Causal attributions of married couples: When do they search for causes? What do they conclude when they do? *Journal of Personality and Social Psychology, 48,* 1398–1412.

Hooks, G., & Smith, C. L. (2004). The treadmill of destruction: National sacrifice areas and Native Americans. *American Sociological Review, 69,* 558–575.

Horon, I. L., & Cheng, D. (2001). Enhanced surveillance for pregnancy-associated mortality— Maryland, 1993–1998. *Journal of the American Medical Association, 285,* 1455–1459.

Horwitz, A. V. (2002). *Creating mental illness.* Chicago, IL: University of Chicago Press.

Hosenball, M., & Isikoff, M. (2010, April 12). Extremist reaction. *Newsweek.*

Houppert, K. (2005, March 28). The new face of protest? *The Nation.*

House, J. (1981). Social structure and personality. In M. Rosenberg & R. H. Turner (Eds.), *Social psychology: Sociological perspectives.* New York: Basic Books.

Hout, M., & Lucas, S. R. (2001). Narrowing the income gap between rich and poor. In P. Rothenberg (Ed.), *Race, class, and gender in the United States.* New York, NY: Worth.

Howe, N., & Strauss, W. (2000). *Millennials rising: The next great generation.* New York, NY: Vintage Books.

Hu, W. (2008, May 24). Too busy to eat, students get a new required course: Lunch. *The New York Times.*

Hu, W. (2010, March 15). Forget goofing around: Recess has a new boss. *The New York Times.*

Hu, W. (2011, June 16). Anti-homework rebels gain a new recruit: The principal. *The New York Times.*

Huber, J., & Form, W. H. (1973). *Income and ideology.* New York, NY: Free Press.

Hubert, C. (2005, June 7). Cell phone addictive for users. *The Indianapolis Star.*

Hudson, V. M., & den Boer, A. (2004). *Bare branches: The security implications of Asia's surplus male population.* Cambridge, MA: MIT Press.

Hughes, D., & Chen, L. (1997). When and what parents tell children about race: An examination of race-related socialization among African American families. *Applied Developmental Science, 1,* 200–214.

Hull, K. E., & Nelson, R. L. (2000). Assimilation, choice, or constraint? Testing theories of gender differences in the careers of lawyers. *Social Forces, 79,* 229–264.

Human Rights Campaign. (2009). *Marriage equality and other relationship recognition laws.* www.hrc.org/documents/Relationship_Recognition_Laws_Map.pdf. Accessed May 18, 2009.

Human Rights Campaign. (2011a). *HRC statement on new data on domestic partner benefits.* www.hrc.org/15780.htm. Accessed September 4, 2011.

Human Rights Campaign. (2011b). *LGBT equality at the Fortune 500.* www.hrc.org/issues/fortune500.htm. Accessed June 3, 2011.

Human Rights Watch. (2009a). *Testing justice: The rape kit backlog in Los Angeles City and County.* www.hrw.org/sites/default/files/reports/rapekit0309.pdf. Accessed May 4, 2009.

Human Rights Watch. (2009b). *Time to tear down the wall of caste.* www.hrw.org/en/news/2009/10/09/time-tear-down-wall-caste. Accessed June 15, 2011.

Humes, K. R., Jones, N. A., & Ramirez, R. R. (2010). *Overview of race and Hispanic origin: 2010* (2010 Census Briefs, C2010BR-02). www.census.gov/prod/cen2010/briefs/c2010br-02.pdf. Accessed April 1, 2011.

Humphreys, L. (1970). *The tearoom trade: Impersonal sex in public places.* Chicago, IL: Aldine-Atherton.

Hunsinger, D. (2009, March 15). New college grads scramble for jobs. *The Indianapolis Star.*

Hunt, J. (1985). Police accounts of normal force. *Urban Life, 13,* 315–341.

Hunter, T. W. (2011, August 2). Putting an antebellum myth to rest. *The New York Times.*

Hutchens, T. (2002, December 21). Coverdale gives IU its heart and soul. *The Indianapolis Star.*

Hvistendahl, M. (2011). *Unnatural selection: Choosing boys over girls, and the consequences of a world full of men.* New York, NY: PublicAffairs.

Hyde, J. S. (1984). How large are gender differences in aggression? A developmental meta-analysis. *Developmental Psychology, 20,* 722–736.

Hyman, M. (2010, December 1). For the goal-oriented parent, a jump start in toddler sports. *The New York Times.*

Ignatieff, M. (2005, June 26). Who are Americans to think that freedom is theirs to spread? *The New York Times Magazine.*

Ignatius, A. (1988, July 14). China's birthrate is out of control again as one-child policy fails in rural areas. *The Wall Street Journal.*

IMS Health. (2010). *IMS Health reports U.S. prescription sales grew 5.1 percent in 2009 to $300.3 billion.* www.imshealth.com/portal/site/imshealth. Accessed June 8, 2011.

Inciardi, J. A. (1992). *The war on drugs II.* Mountain View, CA: Mayfield.

Institute for Policy Research. (2002). Housework in double-income marriages still divides unevenly. *Institute for Policy Research News, 24,* 1–2. www.northwestern.edu/ipr/publications/newsletter/iprn0212/housework.html. Accessed September 5, 2009.

Institute for Women's Policy Research. (2011). *The gender wage gap by occupation* (IWPR #C350a). www.iwpr.org/publications/pubs/the-gender-wage-gap-by-occupation-updated-april-2011/at_download/file. Accessed June 21, 2011.

Institute of Medicine. (1999). *To err is human: Building a safer health care system.* Washington, DC: Committee on Quality of Health Care in America, National Academy Press.

Institute of Medicine. (2003). *Preparing for the psychological consequences of terrorism: A public health strategy.* Washington, DC: National Academies Press. www.nap.edu. Accessed June 10, 2003.

InterfaithFamily.com. (2011). *Jewish intermarriage statistics.* www.interfaithfamily.com/news_and_opinion/synagogues_and_the_Jewish_community?Jewish_Intermarriage_Statistics.shtml. Accessed June 3, 2011.

Interlandi, J. (2010, December 13). Are we running out of antibiotics? *Newsweek.*

International Centre for Prison Studies. (2011). *Entire world—prison population rates per 100,000 of the national population.* www.prisonstudies.org/info/worldbrief/wpb_stats.php?area=all&category=wb_poprate. Accessed June 8, 2011.

International Committee of the Red Cross. (2007). *ICRC report on the treatment of fourteen "high value detainees" in CIA custody.* www.nybooks.com/icrc-report.pdf. Accessed September 5, 2009.

Ioannidis, J. P. A. (2005). Contradicted and initially stronger effects in highly cited clinical research. *Journal of the American Medical Association, 294,* 218–228.

Iran's leader introduces plan to encourage population growth by paying families. (2010, July 27). *The New York Times.*

Isidore, C. (2010). 7.9 million jobs lost—many forever. *CNN Money.* http://money.cnn.com/2010/07/02/news/economy/jobs_gone_forever/index.htm. Accessed May 16, 2011.

Issenberg, S. (2007). *The sushi economy.* New York, NY: Gotham Books.

Is there a Santa Claus? (1897, September 21). *The New York Sun.*

Ito, M., Horst, H., Bittanti, M., Boyd, D., Herr-Stephenson, B., Lange, P. G., . . . Robinson, L. (2008). *Living and learning with new media: Summary of findings from the Digital Youth Project* (Reports on Digital Media and Learning). Chicago, IL: MacArthur Foundation. http://digitalyouth.ischool.berkeley.edu/files/report/digitalyouth-WhitePaper.pdf. Accessed June 7, 2009.

Jackall, R. (1988). *Moral mazes: The world of corporate managers.* New York, NY: Oxford University Press.

Jackson, D. (2011, February 15). Obama's citizenship questioned by GOP voters, polling firm says. *USA Today.* http://content.usatoday.com/communities/theoval/post/2011/02/obamas-citizenship-questioned-by-gop-voters-polling-firm-says/1. Accessed May 24, 2011.

Jackson, S. (1995). The social context of rape: Sexual scripts and motivation. In P. Searles & R. J. Berger (Eds.), *Rape and society.* Boulder, CO: Westview Press.

Jacobs, A. (2009, April 5). Rural China's hunger for sons fuels traffic in abducted boys. *The New York Times.*

Jacobs, A. (2010, December 22). Abuses cited in enforcing China policy of one child. *The New York Times.*

Jacobs, A. (2011, April 15). For many bachelors in China, no property means no dates. *The New York Times.*

Jamail, D. (2007). *Another casualty: Coverage of the Iraq war.* New York, NY: Global Policy Forum. http://globalpolicy.org/component/content/article/168-general/36698.html. Accessed September 5, 2009.

Janoff-Bulman, R. (1979). Characterological versus behavioral self-blame: Inquiries into depression and rape. *Journal of Personality and Social Psychology, 37,* 1798–1809.

Japanese railways hope soothing lights will curb suicides. (2009, November 5). *The New York Times.*

Japan suicides rise to 33,000 in 2009. (2010). *China Daily.* www.chinadaily.com.cn/world/2010-05/13/content_9845670.htm. Accessed May 17, 2011.

Jefferson, T. (1955). *Notes on the State of Virginia.* Chapel Hill: University of North Carolina Press. (Original work published 1781)

Jencks, C., & Phillips, M. (1998). *The black-white test score gap.* Washington, DC: Brookings Institute.

Jencks, S. F., Williams, M. V., & Coleman, E. A. (2009). Rehospitalizations among patients in the Medicare fee-for-service program. *The New England Journal of Medicine, 360,* 1418–1428.

Jenkins, H. (1999, July). Professor Jenkins goes to Washington. *Harper's Magazine.*

Jenkins, J. C., & Perrow, C. (1977). Insurgency of the powerless: Farm worker movements (1946–1972). *American Sociological Review, 42,* 249–268.

Jennings, D. (2010, March 16). With cancer, let's face it: Words are inadequate. *The New York Times.*

Johnson, D. (2009, January 21). Trials loom for parents who embraced faith over medicine. *The New York Times.*

Johnson, K. (2010, July 14). "Immigrant" list sets off fears. *The New York Times.*

Johnson, R. (1987). *Hard time: Understanding and reforming the prison.* Pacific Grove, CA: Brooks/Cole.

Johnston, D. (2002, April 7). Affluent avoid scrutiny on taxes even as I.R.S. warns of cheating. *The New York Times.*

Jones, A. (2010). Your guide to dormcest: Avoiding the pitfalls, scoring the perks. *Her campus: A collegiate guide to life.* www.hercampus.com/love/your-guide-dormcest-avoiding-pitfalls-scoring-perks. Accessed June 6, 2011.

Jones, E. E., Farina, A., Hastorf, A. H., Markus, H., Miller, D. T., & Scott, R. A. (1984). *Social stigma: The psychology of marked relationships.* New York, NY: Freeman.

Jones, E. E., & Pittman, T. S. (1982). Toward a general theory of strategic self-presentation. In J. Suls (Ed.), *Psychological perspectives on the self* (Vol. 1). Hillsdale, NJ: Lawrence Erlbaum.

Jones, J. M. (1986). The concept of racism and its changing reality. In B. P. Bowser & R. G. Hunt (Eds.), *Impacts of racism on white Americans.* Beverly Hills, CA: Sage.

Jones, M. (2006, January 15). Shutting themselves in. *The New York Times Magazine.*

Jordan, M. (2009, May 20). Pupils abused for decades in Irish schools; panel finds misconduct by priests, nuns until 1990. *The Washington Post.*

Jost, K. (2002). Sexual abuse and the clergy. *CQ Researcher, 12,* 393–416.

Jost, K. (2006a). Transgender issues. *CQ Researcher, 16,* 385–408.

Jost, K. (2006b). Understanding Islam. *CQ Researcher, 16,* 913–936.

Juergensmeyer, M. (1996, November). Religious nationalism: A global threat? *Current History.*

Justice Policy Institute. (2002). *Cellblocks or classrooms? The funding of higher education and corrections and its impact on African American men.* www.justicepolicy.org/images/upload/02-09_REP_CellblocksClassrooms_BB-AC.pdf. Accessed September 5, 2009.

Kahn, J. (2004, May 30). The most populous nation faces a population crisis. *The New York Times.*

Kahn, J. (2007, May 22). Harsh birth control steps fuel violence in China. *The New York Times.*

Kahneman, D., Krueger, A. B., Schkade, D., Schwarz, N., & Stone, A. A. (2006). Would you be happier if you were richer? A focusing illusion. *Science, 312,* 1908–1910.

Kain, E. (1990). *The myth of family decline.* Lexington, MA: Lexington Books.

Kaiser Family Foundation. (2008). *Abortion in the U.S.: Utilization, financing, and access.* www.kff.org/womenshealth/upload/3269-02.pdf. Accessed September 5, 2009.

Kaiser Family Foundation. (2009). *Rising unemployment, Medicaid, and the uninsured* (Publication No. 7850). www.kff.org/uninsured/7850.cfm. Accessed June 7, 2009.

Kalb, C. (2010a, March 14). Culture of corpulence. *Newsweek.*

Kalb, C. (2010b, October 4). Do no harm. *Newsweek.*

Kalmijn, M. (1994). Assortive mating by cultural and economic occupational status. *American Journal of Sociology, 100,* 422–452.

Kalmijn, M., & Flap, H. (2001). Assortive meeting and mating: Unintended consequences of organized settings for partner choices. *Social Forces, 79,* 1289–1312.

Kanter, R. M. (1977). *Men and women of the corporation.* New York, NY: Basic Books.

Kanter, R. M., & Stein, B. A. (1979). *Life in organizations: Workplaces as people experience them.* New York, NY: Basic Books.

Kantor, J. (2007, January 8). As obesity fight hits cafeteria, many fear a note from school. *The New York Times.*

Kaptchuk, T. J., Friedlander, E., Kelley, J. M., Sanchez, M. N., Kokkotou, E., Singer, J. P., . . . Lembo, A. J. (2010). Placebos without deception: A randomized control trial in irritable bowel syndrome. *PLoS ONE, 5,* 1–14.

Karabel, J. (1972). Community colleges and social stratification. *Harvard Educational Review, 42,* 521–559.

Karp, D. A., & Yoels, W. C. (1976). The college classroom: Some observations on the meanings of student participation. *Sociology and Social Research, 60,* 421–439.

Karraker, K. H., Vogel, D. A., & Lake, M. A. (1995). Parents' gender stereotyped perceptions of newborns: The eye of the beholder revisited. *Sex Roles, 33,* 687–701.

Karush, S. (2001, May 6). Russia's population drain could open a floodgate of consequences. *Los Angeles Times.*

Katbamna, M. (2009, October 27). Half a good man is better than none at all. *The Guardian.*

Katel, P. (2005). Illegal immigration. *CQ Researcher, 15,* 393–420.

Katel, P. (2006). War on drugs. *CQ Researcher, 16,* 649–672.

Katel, P. (2008). Affirmative action. *CQ Researcher, 18,* 841–864.

Katz, J. (1975). Essences as moral identities: Verifiability and responsibility in imputations of deviance and charisma. *American Journal of Sociology, 80,* 1369–1390.

Katz, N. (2003). *Rapes/sexual assault at the Air Force Academy.* http://womensissues.about.com/cs/militarywomen/a/aaairforcerapes.htm. Accessed August 2, 2003.

Kaufman, D. (2011, June 5). Does Twitter make you stupid? [Letter to the editor]. *The New York Times.*

Kearl, M. C. (1980). Time, identity and the spiritual needs of the elderly. *Sociological Analysis, 41,* 172–180.

Kearl, M. C., & Gordon, C. (1992). *Social psychology.* Boston, MA: Allyn & Bacon.

Keith, V. M., & Herring, C. (1991). Skin tone and stratification in the black community. *American Journal of Sociology, 97,* 760–778.

Kelley, R. (2008, November 17). A letter to my son on election night. *Newsweek.*

Kelley, R. (2009, February 2). Beyond just black and white. *Newsweek.*

Kennedy, P. (1993). *Preparing for the 21st century.* New York, NY: Random House.

Kent, M. (2010). *Young U.S. adults vulnerable to injuries and violence.* Washington, DC: Population Reference Bureau. www.prb.org/Articles/2010/usyoungadultinjury.aspx?p=1. Accessed August 8, 2010.

Kent, M., & Lalasz, R. (2006, June). *In the news: Speaking English in the United States.* Washington, DC: Population Reference Bureau. www.prb.org. Accessed July 20, 2006.

Kent, M., & Yin, S. (2006). *Controlling infectious diseases.* Washington, DC: Population Reference Bureau. www.prb.org. Accessed May 1, 2007.

Kerbo, H. R. (1991). *Social stratification and inequality.* New York, NY: McGraw-Hill.

Kershaw, S. (2004, July 21). It's a long, lonely search for men looking for love in Alaska. *The New York Times.*

Kershaw, S. (2005, January 26). Old law shielding a woman's virtue faces an updating. *The New York Times.*

Kershaw, S. (2008, October 30). Move over, my pretty, ugly is here. *The New York Times.*

Kershner, R. (1996). Adolescent attitudes about rape. *Adolescence, 31,* 29–33.

Kessler, S. J., & McKenna, W. (1978). *Gender: An ethnomethodological approach.* Chicago, IL: University of Chicago Press.

Kessler-Harris, A. (1982). *Out to work: A history of wage-earning women in the United States.* New York, NY: Oxford University Press.

Khalema, N. E., & Wannas-Jones, J. (2003). Under the prism of suspicion: Minority voices in Canada post-September 11. *Journal of Muslim Minority Affairs, 23,* 25–39.

Kilborn, P. T. (1999, September 16). Bias worsens for minorities buying homes. *The New York Times.*

Kilgannon, C., & Singer, J. E. (2010, June 22). Shoplifting suspects' choice: Pay or be shamed. *The New York Times.*

Kim, K. H., & Van Tassel–Baska, J. (2010). The relationship between creativity and behavior problems among underachieving elementary and high school students. *Creativity Research Journal, 22,* 185–193.

Kimmel, M. S. (2004). *The gendered society.* New York, NY: Oxford University Press.

King, M. L., Jr. (1991). Letter from Birmingham City jail. In C. Carson, D. J. Garrow, G. Gill, V. Harding, & D. Clark Hine (Eds.), *The eyes on the prize civil rights reader.* New York, NY: Penguin Books.

Kirkwood, M. K., & Cecil, B. K. (2001). Marital rape: A student assessment of rape laws and the marital exemption. *Violence Against Women, 7,* 1234–1253.

Kirn, W. (2009, May 10). More than a numbers game. *The New York Times Magazine.*

Kirp, D. L. (2006, July 23). After *The Bell Curve. The New York Times Magazine.*

Kishor, S., & Johnson, K. (2004). *Profiling domestic violence: A multi-country study.* www.measuredhs.com/pubs/pdf/OD31/DV.pdf. Accessed June 1, 2005.

Klatch, R. (1991). Complexities of conservatism: How conservatives understand the world. In A. Wolfe (Ed.), *America at century's end.* Berkeley: University of California Press.

Kleck, R. (1968). Physical stigma and nonverbal cues emitted in face-to-face interaction. *Human Relations, 21,* 19–28.

Kleck, R., Ono, H., & Hastorf, A. (1966). The effects of physical deviance and face-to-face interaction. *Human Relations, 19,* 425–436.

Klevens, R. M., Edwards, J. R., Richards, C. L., Horan, T. C., Gaynes, R. P., Pollock, D. A., & Cardo, D. M. (2007). Estimating health care-associated infections and deaths in U.S. hospitals, 2002. *Public Health Report, 122,* 160–166. www.cdc.gov/ncidod/dhqp/pdf/hicpac/infections_deaths.pdf. Accessed September 5, 2009.

Knight, D. (2006, May 21). Hiring frenzy. *The Indianapolis Star.*

Knuckey, J., & Orey, B. D. (2000). Symbolic racism in the 1995 Louisiana gubernatorial election. *Social Science Quarterly, 81,* 1027–1035.

Kobrin, F. E. (1976). The fall in household size and the rise of the primary individual in the United States. *Demography, 31,* 127–138.

Koch, K. (1999, October 22). Rethinking Ritalin. *CQ Researcher* [Special issue].

Kochhar, R., Fry, R., & Taylor, P. (2011). *Wealth gaps rise to record highs between Whites, Blacks, and Hispanics.* Pew Research Center Publications. http://pewresearch.org/pubs/2069/housing-bubble-subprime-mortgages-hispanics-blacks-household-wealth-disparity. Accessed September 8, 2011.

Kocieniewski, D. (2006, October 10). A history of sex with students, unchallenged over the years. *The New York Times.*

Koeppel, B. (1999, November 8). Cancer Alley, Louisiana. *The Nation.*

Kohlberg, L. A. (1966). A cognitive-developmental analysis of children's sex-role concepts and attitudes. In E. Maccoby (Ed.), *The development of sex differences.* Stanford, CA: Stanford University Press.

Kohn, H. (1994, November 6). Service with a sneer. *The New York Times Magazine.*

Kohn, M. L. (1979). The effects of social class on parental values and practices. In D. Reiss & H. A. Hoffman (Eds.), *The American family: Dying or developing.* New York, NY: Plenum Press.

Kohut, A. (1999, December 3). Globalization and the wage gap. *The New York Times.*

Kokopeli, B., & Lakey, G. (1992). More power than we want: Masculine sexuality and violence. In M. L. Anderson & P. H. Collins (Eds.), *Race, class and gender: An anthology.* Belmont, CA: Wadsworth.

Kolata, G. (2000, March 6). Web research transforms visit to the doctor. *The New York Times.*

Kolata, G. (2004, July 13). Experts set a lower low for cholesterol levels. *The New York Times.*

Kolata, G. (2011, February 6). Mysterious maladies. *The New York Times.*

Kole, W. J. (2006, August 24). Pluto is no longer a planet, astronomers say. *The Washington Post.*

Korean girls take poison to aid kin. (1989, March 3). *Hartford Courant.*

Kosmin, B. A., & Keysar, A. (2009). *American religious identification survey (ARIS 2008).* Hartford, CT: Trinity College. www.livinginliminality.files.wordpress.com/2009/03/aris_report_2008.pdf. Accessed May 6, 2009.

Kosmin, B. A., & Mayer, E. (2001). *American religious identification survey.* http://www.gc.cuny.edu/faculty/research_studies/aris.pdf. Accessed September 5, 2009.

Kovel, L. (1980). The American mental health industry. In D. Ingleby (Ed.), *Critical psychiatry.* New York, NY: Pantheon Books.

Kramer, P. (1997). *Listening to Prozac.* New York, NY: Penguin Books.

Kreider, R. M. (2005). *Number, timing, and duration of marriages and divorces: 2001* (U.S. Census Bureau, Current Population Reports, P70-97). Washington, DC: Government Printing Office.

Kreider, R. M., & Ellis, R. (2011). *Number, timing, and duration of marriages and divorces: 2009* (U.S. Census Bureau, Current Population Reports, P70-125). www.census.gov/prod/2011pubs/p70-125.pdf. Accessed June 3, 2011.

Kress, M. (2005, April 20). Mormonism is booming in the U.S. and overseas. *The News-Sentinel.*

Kristof, N. D. (1993, July 21). Peasants of China discover new way to weed out girls. *The New York Times.*

Kristof, N. D. (2008, December 18). Miracle tax diet. *The New York Times.*

Kristof, N. D. (2010, May 22). Moonshine or the kids? *The New York Times.*

Krueger, A. B. (2002, November 14). The apple falls close to the tree, even in the land of opportunity. *The New York Times.*

Krugman, P. (2008, February 18). Poverty is poison. *The New York Times.*

Kubany, E. S., Abueg, F. R., Owens, J. A., Brennan, J. M., Kaplan, A. S., & Watson, S. B. (1995). Initial examination of a multidimensional model of trauma-related guilt: Applications to combat veterans and battered women. *Journal of Psychopathology and Behavioral Assessment, 17,* 353–376.

Kulick, D., & Machado-Borges, T. (2005). Leaky. In D. Kulick & A. Meneley (Eds.), *Fat: The anthropology of an obsession.* New York, NY: Tarcher/Penguin.

Kurtz, L. R. (1995). *Gods in the global village.* Thousand Oaks, CA: Pine Forge Press.

Kurtzleben, D. (2010, August 3). Data show racial disparity in crack sentencing. *U.S. News & World Report.*

Kurutz, S. (2008, December 14). Fast food zoning. *The New York Times.*

Laboring in the U.S. (2006, June 19). *The New York Times.*

Lacey, M. (2003, March 5). Rights group calls for end to inheriting African wives. *The New York Times.*

Lacey, M. (2006, December 14). Rwandan priest sentenced to 15 years for allowing deaths of Tutsi in church. *The New York Times.*

Lacey, M. (2010, December 3). Transplant patients put at risk by a state's financial distress. *The New York Times.*

LaCoste-Caputo, J. (2007, June 21). Academic ratings, teacher pay tied. *San Antonio Express-News.*

LaFraniere, S. (2007, July 4). Seeking to end an over-fed ideal. *The New York Times.*

LaFraniere, S. (2009, June 13). All-nighter? For this test Chinese cram all year. *The New York Times.*

LaFraniere, S. (2011, April 24). For many Chinese, new wealth and a fresh face. *The New York Times.*

LaFraniere, S., & Levin, D. (2010, November 12). Assertive Chinese marooned in mental wards. *The New York Times.*

Lakoff, R. (1975). *Language and woman's place.* New York, NY: Harper & Row.

Lakshmi, R. (2005, February 27). India call centers suffer storm of 4-letter words. *The Washington Post.*

Lalasz, R. (2006). *Americans flocking to outer suburbs in record numbers.* Washington, DC: Population Reference Bureau. www.prb.org. Accessed May 9, 2006.

Lamont, M. (1992). *Money, morals and manners: The culture of the French and American upper middle class.* Chicago, IL: University of Chicago Press.

Lander, L. (1988). *Images of bleeding: Menstruation as ideology.* New York, NY: Orlando.

Landesman, P. (2004, January 25). The girls next door. *The New York Times.*

Landler, M. (1996, September 10). Corporate insurer to cover cost of spin doctors. *The New York Times.*

Landler, M. (2002, December 1). For Austrians, HoHoHo is no laughing matter. *The New York Times.*

Lang, S. (1998). *Men as women, women as men: Changing gender in Native American cultures.* Austin: University of Texas Press.

Langan, P. A., & Levin, D. J. (2002). *Recidivism of prisoners released in 1994* (NCJ 193427). Washington, DC: Bureau of Justice Statistics. www.ojp.usdoj.gov/bjs/abstract/rpr94.htm. Accessed January 20, 2003.

Langman, L. (1988). Social stratification. In M. B. Sussman & S. K. Steinmetz (Eds.), *Handbook of marriage and the family.* New York, NY: Plenum Press.

Langston, D. (1992). Tired of playing monopoly? In M. L. Anderson & P. H. Collins (Eds.), *Race, class and gender: An anthology.* Belmont, CA: Wadsworth.

Lanvers, U. (2004). Gender in discourse behaviour in parent-child dyads: A literature review. *Child: Care, Health, and Development, 30,* 481–493.

Lapchick, R. (2011). *The racial and gender report card.* www.bus.ucf.edu/sportbusiness/?page=1445. Accessed June 15, 2011.

Lareau, A. (2003). *Unequal childhoods: Class, race, and family life.* Berkeley: University of California Press.

Larew, J. (2003). Why are droves of unqualified, unprepared kids getting into our top colleges? Because their dads are alumni. In K. E. Rosenblum & T. C. Travis (Eds.), *The meaning of difference: American constructions of race, sex and gender, social class, and sexual orientation.* New York, NY: McGraw-Hill.

Larson, L. E., & Goltz, J. W. (1989). Religious participation and marital commitment. *Review of Religious Research, 30,* 387–400.

Lasch, C. (1977). *Haven in a heartless world.* New York, NY: Basic Books.

Lauer, R., & Handel, W. (1977). *Social psychology: The theory and application of symbolic interactionism.* Boston, MA: Houghton Mifflin.

Lawson, C. (1993, February 11). Stereotypes unravel, but not too quickly, in new toys for 1993. *The New York Times.*

Leape, L. L., & Bates, D. W. (1995). Systems analysis of adverse drug events. *Journal of the American Medical Association, 274,* 35–43.

LeBesco, K. (2004). *Revolting bodies? The struggle to redefine fat identity.* Amherst: University of Massachusetts Press.

Lee, M. (2006). *The neglected link between food marketing and childhood obesity in poor neighborhoods.* Washington, DC: Population Reference Bureau. www.prb.org. Accessed July 12, 2006.

Lee, S. M. (1993). Racial classifications in the U.S. Census: 1890–1990. *Ethnic and Racial Studies, 16,* 75–94.

Lee, S. M., & Edmonston, B. (2005). New marriages, new families: U.S. racial and Hispanic intermarriage. *Population Bulletin, 60,* 1–36.

Lee-St. John, J. (2007, February 12). A time limit on rape. *Time.*

Legato, M. J. (2006, June 17). The weaker sex. *The New York Times.*

Lehigh, S. (2005, January 19). The case for longer school days. *The Boston Globe.*

Leinberger, P., & Tucker, B. (1991). *The new individualists: The generation after the organization man.* New York, NY: HarperCollins.

Leland, J. (2004, March 23). He's retired, she's working, they're not happy. *The New York Times.*

Leland, J. (2005, July 7). Just a minute, Boss. My cellphone is ringing. *The New York Times.*

Lemert, E. (1972). *Human deviance, social problems, and social control.* Englewood Cliffs, NJ: Prentice Hall.

Leonhardt, D. (2011, June 26). Even for cashiers, college pays off. *The New York Times.*

Leonhardt, D., & Fabrikant, G. (2009, August 21). After 30-year run, rise of the super-rich hits a sobering wall. *The New York Times.*

Leonnig, C. D. (2005, June 8). Tobacco escapes huge penalty. *The New York Times.*

Lerner, M. (1970). The desire for justice and reactions to victims. In J. Macauley & L. Berkowitz (Eds.), *Altruism and helping behavior.* New York, NY: Academic Press.

Lesko, N. (2008). Our guys/good guys: Playing with high school privilege and power. In S. J. Ferguson (Ed.), *Mapping the social landscape.* New York, NY: McGraw-Hill.

Lester, W. (2005, January 8). Poll: 29% in U.S. give tsunami aid. *The Indianapolis Star.*

Levine, H. G. (1992). Temperance cultures: Concern about alcohol problems in Nordic and English-speaking cultures. In M. Lader, G. Edwards, & D. C. Drummond (Eds.), *The nature of alcohol and drug-related problems.* New York, NY: Oxford University Press.

Levinson, D. (1989). *Family violence in cross-cultural perspective.* Newbury Park, CA: Sage.

Levitt, S. D., & Dubner, S. J. (2009). *Freakonomics: A rogue economist explores the hidden side of everything.* New York, NY: Harper Perennial.

Levy, A. (2006, May 29). Dirty old women. *The New York Magazine.* http://nymag.com/news/features/17064/index1.html. Accessed September 5, 2009.

Lewin, T. (1998, December 13). How boys lost out to girl power. *The New York Times.*

Lewin, T. (2000, April 11). Disabled student is suing over test-score labeling. *The New York Times.*

Lewin, T. (2001, October 21). Shelters have empty beds: Abused women stay home. *The New York Times.*

Lewin, T. (2006, July 9). At colleges, women are leaving men in the dust. *The New York Times.*

Lewin, T. (2007, January 26). Colleges regroup after voters ban race preferences. *The New York Times.*

Lewin, T. (2009a, February 5). A.P. program is growing, but black students lag. *The New York Times.*

Lewin, T. (2009b, December 10). College dropouts cite low money and high stress. *The New York Times.*

Lewis, M. (1978). *The culture of inequality.* New York, NY: New American Library.

Lewis, M. M. (1948). *Language in society.* New York, NY: Social Science Research Council.

Lewis, O. (1968). The culture of poverty. In D. P. Moynihan (Ed.), *On understanding poverty: Perspectives from the social sciences.* New York, NY: Basic Books.

Lewis, P. H. (1998, August 15). Too late to say "extinct" in Ubykh, Eyak or Ona. *The New York Times.*

Lewis, R., & Yancey, G. (1997). Racial and nonracial factors that influence spouse choice in black/white marriages. *Journal of Black Studies, 28,* 60–78.

Liazos, A. (1985). *Sociology: A liberating perspective.* Boston, MA: Allyn & Bacon.

Liben, L. S., & Bigler, B. R. (2002). The developmental course of gender differentiation: Conceptualizing, measuring, and evaluating constructs and pathways. *Monographs of the Society for Research in Child Development, 67,* 1–112.

Lichtblau, E. (2003, March 18). U.S. lawsuit seeks tobacco profits. *The New York Times.*

Lichtblau, E. (2004, May 4). Cracker Barrel agrees to plan to address reports of bias. *The New York Times.*

Lichtblau, E. (2008, April 9). In justice shift, corporate deals replace trials. *The New York Times.*

Light, P. (1988). *Baby boomers.* New York, NY: Norton.

Lindesmith, A. R., Strauss, A. L., & Denzin, N. K. (1991). *Social psychology.* Englewood Cliffs, NJ: Prentice Hall.

Link, B. G., Mirotznik, J., & Cullen, F. T. (1991). The effectiveness of stigma-coping orientations: Can negative consequences of mental illness labeling be avoided? *Journal of Health and Social Behavior, 32,* 302–320.

Link, B. G., & Phelan, J. C. (2001). Conceptualizing stigma. *Annual Review of Sociology, 27,* 363–385.

Lino, M. (2010). *Expenditures on children by families, 2009.* Center for Nutrition Policy and Promotion, U.S. Department of Agriculture. www.cnpp.usda.gov/publications/crc/crc2009 .pdf. Accessed June 5, 2011.

Linton, R. (1937). One hundred percent American. *American Mercury, 40,* 427–429.

Lippmann, L. W. (1922). *Public opinion.* New York, NY: Harcourt Brace Jovanovich.

Lips, H. M. (1993). *Sex and gender: An introduction.* Mountain View, CA: Mayfield.

Liptak, A. (2003, June 3). For jailed immigrants, a presumption of guilt. *The New York Times.*

Liptak, A. (2004, March 17). Bans on interracial unions offer perspective on gay ones. *The New York Times.*

Liptak, A. (2006, August 7). 15 states expand victims' rights on self-defense. *The New York Times.*

Little, A. G. (2007, September 2). Not in whose backyard? *The New York Times Magazine.*

Living Wage Resource Center. (2006). *Living wage wins.* Brooklyn, NY: Author. www.livingwage campaign.org/index.php?id=1959. Accessed June 10, 2009.

Loe, V. (1997, September 21). New nuptial license gets cool reception. *The Indianapolis Star.*

Lofland, L. H. (1973). *A world of strangers: Order and action in urban public space.* New York, NY: Basic Books.

Lohr, S. (2005, June 24). Cutting here, but hiring over there. *The New York Times.*

Longman, J. (2006, June 4). Surge in racist mood raises concerns on eve of World Cup. *The New York Times.*

Longman, J., & Higgins, M. (2005, August 3). Rad dudes of the world, unite. *The New York Times.*

Lopez, M. H. (2008). *How Hispanics voted in the 2008 election.* Washington, DC: Pew Research Center. http://pewresearch.org/pubs/1024/ exit-poll-analysis-hispanics. Accessed June 2, 2009.

Lorber, J. (1989). Dismantling Noah's Ark. In B. J. Risman & P. Schwartz (Eds.), *Gender in intimate relationships: A microstructural approach.* Belmont, CA: Wadsworth.

Lorber, J. (2000). *Gender and the social construction of illness.* Walnut Creek, CA: AltaMira Press.

Lott, B. (1987). *Women's lives: Themes and variations in gender learning.* Pacific Grove, CA: Brooks/Cole.

Lovley, E. (2010). *Abused staffers net nearly $1M a year.* www.politico.com/news/stories/0710/39637 .html. Accessed July 22, 2010.

Lowenstein, R. (2006, July 9). The immigration equation. *The New York Times.*

Lowenstein, R. (2009, July 26). The new joblessness. *The New York Times Magazine.*

Lueders, B. (2006). *Cry rape: The true story of one woman's harrowing quest for justice.* Madison, WI: Terrace Books.

Luker, K. (1984). *Abortion and the politics of motherhood.* Berkeley: University of California Press.

Luo, F., Florence, C., Quispe-Agnoli, M., Ouyang, L., & Crosby, A. (2011). Impact of business cycles on US suicide rates, 1928–2007. *American Journal of Public Health, 101,* 1139–1146.

Luo, M. (2007, July 22). God '08: Whose, and how much, will voters accept? *The New York Times.*

Luo, M. (2009, May 28). Still working, but making do with less. *The New York Times.*

Luo, M. (2011, July 3). Mixing guns and mental illness. *The New York Times.*

Lyall, S. (2000, July 8). Irish now face the other side of immigration. *The New York Times.*

Lyman, R. (2005, April 4). Gay couples file suit after Michigan denies benefits. *The New York Times.*

Lytton, H., & Romney, D. M. (1991). Parents' differential socialization of boys and girls: A meta-analysis. *Psychology Bulletin, 109,* 267–296.

Lytton, T. D. (2007, February 4). Legal legacy. *The Boston Globe.*

MacAndrew, C., & Edgerton, R. B. (1969). *Drunken comportment: A social explanation.* Chicago, IL: Aldine-Atherton.

MacDonald, K., & Parke, R. D. (1986). Parent-child physical play: The effects of sex and age on children and parents. *Sex Roles, 15,* 367–378.

Macgillivray, I. K. (2000). Educational equity for gay, lesbian, bisexual, transgendered, and queer/ questioning students: The demands of democracy and social justice for America's schools. *Education and Urban Society, 32,* 303–323.

Mann, C. C. (1993, February). How many is too many? *Atlantic Monthly.*

Manning, L. (2007). Nightmare at the day care: The Wee Care case. *Crime Magazine.* www.crime magazine.com/nightmare-day-care-wee-care-case. Accessed June 7, 2011.

Manning, W. D., & Smock, P. J. (1999). New families and nonresident father-child visits. *Social Forces, 78,* 87–117.

Mannon, J. (1997). *Measuring up.* Boulder, CO: Westview Press.

Mansfield, H. (2006). *Manliness.* New Haven, CT: Yale University Press.

Marger, M. N. (1994). *Race and ethnic relations: American and global perspectives.* Belmont, CA: Wadsworth.

Marger, M. N. (2005). The mass media as a power institution. In S. J. Ferguson (Ed.), *Mapping the social landscape.* New York, NY: McGraw-Hill.

Markets and Markets. (2011). *Global weight loss & diet management products & services market (2010–2015)* (Report code PH1300). www.marketsandmarkets.com/Market-Reports/weight-loss-industry-224.html. Accessed June 2, 2011.

Marla Olmstead. (2004). *About Marla.* www.marlaolmstead.com. Accessed November 23, 2004.

Marmot, M. (2004). *The status syndrome: How social standing affects our health and longevity.* New York, NY: Times Books.

Marsh, B. (2005, January 2). The vulnerable become more vulnerable. *The New York Times.*

Marsh, B. (2008, February 24). A growing cloud over the planet. *The New York Times.*

Martin, C. L., & Ruble, D. (2004). Children's search for gender cues. *Current Directions in Psychological Science, 13,* 67–70.

Martin, P. (2010). *Migration's economic tradeoffs: Farm worker wages and food costs.* Population Reference Bureau. www.prb.org/Articles/2010/usfarmworkersfoodprices.aspx?p=1. Accessed July 14, 2010.

Martin, P., & Midgley, E. (2010). *Immigration in America 2010* (Population Bulletin Update). www.prb.org/pdf10/immigration-update2010.pdf. Accessed July 6, 2010.

Martinez-Alier, J. (2003). *The environmentalism of the poor.* Cheltenham, UK: Edward Elgar.

Marx, K. (1963). *The 18th Brumaire of Louis Bonaparte.* New York, NY: International. (Original work published 1869)

Marx, K., & Engels, F. (1982). *The communist manifesto.* New York, NY: International. (Original work published 1848)

Massey, D. S., & Denton, N. A. (1993). *American apartheid: Segregation and the making of the underclass.* Cambridge, MA: Harvard University Press.

Mather, M. (2007). *The new generation gap.* Washington, DC: Population Reference Bureau. www.prb.org/Articles/2007/NewGenerationGap.aspx. Accessed May 19, 2007.

Mather, M., & Adams, D. (2006). *The risk of negative child outcomes in low-income families.* Washington, DC: Population Reference Bureau. www.prb.org/pdf06/RiskNegOut_Families.pdf. Accessed July 27, 2006.

Mather, M., & Jacobsen, L. A. (2010). *Hard times for Latino men in U.S.* Population Reference Bureau. www.prb.org/Articles/2010/latinomen.aspx. Accessed June 16, 2011.

Mather, M., Pollard, K., & Jacobsen, L. A. (2011). *First results from the 2010 Census.* Population Reference Bureau. www.prb.org/pdf11/reports-on-america-2010-census.pdf. Accessed July 20, 2011.

Mathews, L. (1996, July 6). More than identity rides on a new racial category. *The New York Times.*

MBA vs. prison. (1999, May/June). *The American Prospect.*

McAdam, D. (1982). *Political process and the development of black insurgency, 1930–1970.* Chicago, IL: University of Chicago Press.

McAdam, D., McCarthy, J. D., & Zald, M. N. (1988). Social movements. In N. J. Smelser (Ed.), *Handbook of sociology.* Newbury Park, CA: Sage.

McCain, F. (1991). Interview with Franklin McCain. In C. Carson, D. J. Garrow, G. Gill, V. Harding, & D. Clark Hine (Eds.), *The eyes on the prize civil rights reader.* New York, NY: Penguin Books.

McCall, G. J., & Simmons, J. L. (1978). *Identities and interactions.* New York, NY: Free Press.

McCarthy, J. D., & Wolfson, M. (1992). Consensus movements, conflict movements, and the cooptation of civic and state infrastructures. In A. D. Morris & C. M. Mueller (Eds.), *Frontiers in social movement theory.* New Haven, CT: Yale University Press.

McCarthy, J. D., & Zald, M. N. (1977). Resource mobilization and social movements: A partial theory. *American Journal of Sociology, 82,* 1212–1241.

McCarthy, T. (2001, May 14). He makes a village. *Time.*

McCormick, J. S., Maric, A., Seto, M. C., & Barbaree, H. E. (1998). Relationship to victim predicts sentence length in sexual assault cases. *Journal of Interpersonal Violence, 13,* 413–420.

McDonald's Corporation. (2011). *Financial press release.* http://phx.corporate-ir.net/phoenix.zhtml?c=97876&p=irol-newsArticle&ID=1518914&highlight=. Accessed June 10, 2011.

McEwan, J. (2005). Proving consent in sexual cases: Legislative change and cultural evolution. *International Journal of Evidence and Proof, 9,* 1–28.

McGee, C. (2010, August 23). The open road wasn't quite open to all. *The New York Times.*

McHale, S. M., Crouter, A. C., & Whiteman, S. D. (2003). The family contexts of gender development in childhood and adolescence. *Social Development, 12,* 125–148.

McHugh, P. (1968). *Defining the situation.* Indianapolis, IN: Bobbs-Merrill.

McIntosh, P. (2001). White privilege: Unpacking the invisible knapsack. In P. Rothenberg (Ed.), *Race, class, and gender in the United States.* New York, NY: Worth.

McKenry, P. C., & Price, S. J. (1995). Divorce: A comparative perspective. In B. B. Ingoldsby & S. Smith (Eds.), *Families in multicultural perspective.* New York, NY: Guilford Press.

McKinley, J. (2010, March 13). Conservatives on Texas panel carry the day on curricular change. *The New York Times.*

McKinley, J. (2011, February 17). "Non-English" tip policy raises eyebrows, then fades. *The New York Times.*

McLaren, L. M. (2003). Anti-immigrant prejudice in Europe: Contact, threat perception, and preferences for the exclusion of migrants. *Social Forces, 81,* 909–936.

McLean, C., & Singer, P. W. (2010, June 14). Don't ask. Tell. *Newsweek.*

McLean, R. (2005, January 12). Spaniards dare to question the way the day is ordered. *The New York Times.*

McLean, R. (2006, January 21). In the new year, a novel idea for Spanish government workers: A literal lunch hour. *The New York Times.*

McLoyd, V. C., Cauce, A. M., Takeuchi, D., & Wilson, L. (2000). Marital processes and parental socialization in families of color: A decade review of research. *Journal of Marriage and the Family, 62,* 1070–1094.

McMahon, J. (2007, August 11). *Marital rape laws, 1976–2002: From exemptions to prohibitions.* Paper presented at the annual meeting of the American Sociological Association, New York, NY.

McMichael, P. (1996). *Development and social change: A global perspective.* Thousand Oaks, CA: Pine Forge Press.

McNeil, D. G. (2000, May 21). Drug companies and the third world: A case study of neglect. *The New York Times.*

McNeil, D. G. (2006, February 15). Bristol-Myers allows 2 major AIDS drugs to be sold cheaply. *The New York Times.*

McNeil, D. G. (2007, September 10). Drugs banned, world's poor suffer in pain. *The New York Times.*

McNeil, D. G. (2008, December 10). Report sounds alarm on child accidents. *The New York Times.*

McNeil, D. G. (2010, June 20). The curse of plenty. *The New York Times.*

McNeil, D. G. (2011, August 4). New H.I.V. cases remain steady over a decade. *The New York Times.*

McPhee, J. (1971). *Encounters with the archdruid.* New York, NY: Noonday.

McPherson, M., Smith-Lovin, L., & Brashears, M. E. (2006). Social isolation in America: Changes in core discussion networks over two decades. *American Sociological Review, 71,* 353–375.

McVeigh, R., & Diaz, M. D. (2009). Voting to ban same-sex marriage: Interests, values, and communities. *American Sociological Review, 74,* 891–915.

Mead, G. H. (1934). *Mind, self and society.* Chicago, IL: University of Chicago Press.

Media Awareness Network. (2005). *Gender stereotyping.* Ottawa, Ontario, Canada: Author. www.media-awareness.ca/english/parents/video_games/concerns/gender_videogames.cfm. Accessed January 8, 2005.

Media Report to Women. (2009). *Industry statistics.* www.mediareporttowomen.com/statistics.htm. Accessed June 15, 2010.

Mehan, H., & Wood, H. (1975). *The reality of ethnomethodology.* New York, NY: Wiley.

Meier, B. (2004, June 15). Group is said to seek full drug-trial disclosure. *The New York Times.*

Mendoza, M. (2010, May 14). U.S. drug war is "on going tragedy." *The Indianapolis Star.*

Mental Health Channel. (2007). *"General anxiety disorder" and "social phobias."* Northampton, MA: Author. www.mentalhealthchannel.net. Accessed June 18, 2007.

Merton, R. (1948). The self-fulfilling prophecy. *Antioch Review, 8,* 193–210.

Merton, R. (1957). *Social theory and social structure.* New York, NY: Free Press.

Messick, D. M., & Brewer, M. B. (1983). Solving social dilemmas: A review. In L. Wheeler & P. Shaver (Eds.), *Review of personality and social psychology.* Beverly Hills, CA: Sage.

Messner, M. (2002). Boyhood, organized sports, and the construction of masculinities. In D. M. Newman &

J. O'Brien (Eds.), *Sociology: Exploring the architecture of everyday life (Readings)*. Thousand Oaks, CA: Pine Forge Press.

Meyer, J. W., & Rowan, B. (1977). Institutionalized organizations: Formal structure as myth and ceremony. *American Journal of Sociology, 83,* 340–363.

Miall, C. E. (1989). The stigma of involuntary childlessness. In A. S. Skolnick & J. H. Skolnick (Eds.), *Family in transition*. Boston, MA: Little, Brown.

Michaels, K. (1993). Eight years in Kafkaland. *National Review, 45,* 36–38.

Michels, R. (1949). *Political parties*. Glencoe, IL: Free Press. (Original work published 1911)

Michener, H. A., DeLamater, J. D., & Schwartz, S. H. (1986). *Social psychology*. San Diego, CA: Harcourt Brace Jovanovich.

Mihm, S. (2009, December 13). Artificial car noise. *The New York Times Magazine*.

Milbank, D., & Deane, C. (2003, September 6). Hussein link to 9/11 lingers in many minds. *The Washington Post*.

Milgram, S. (1974). *Obedience to authority*. New York, NY: Harper & Row.

Miller, C. H., & Hedges, D. W. (2008). Scrupulosity disorder: An overview and introductory analysis. *Journal of Anxiety Disorders, 22,* 1042–1058.

Miller, C. L. (1987). Qualitative differences among gender-stereotyped toys: Implications for cognitive and social development. *Sex Roles, 16,* 473–488.

Miller, E., & Almon, J. (2009). *Crisis in the kindergarten: Why children need to play in school*. College Park, MD: Alliance for Childhood.

Miller, L. (1997). Not just weapons of the weak: Gender harassment as a form of protest for army men. *Social Psychology Quarterly, 60,* 32–51.

Miller, L. (2008, May 5). An algorithm for Mr. Right. *Newsweek*.

Miller, L. (2010, September 27). Our state of disgrace. *Newsweek*.

Miller, L. (2011, July 25). How to raise a global kid. *Newsweek*.

Miller, M. V. (1985). Poverty and its definition. In R. C. Barnes & E. W. Mills (Eds.), *Techniques for teaching sociological concepts*. Washington, DC: American Sociological Association.

Millman, M. (1980). *Such a pretty face*. New York, NY: Norton.

Mills, C. W. (1940). Situated actions and vocabularies of motive. *American Sociological Review, 5,* 904–913.

Mills, C. W. (1956). *The power elite*. New York, NY: Oxford University Press.

Mills, C. W. (1959). *The sociological imagination*. New York, NY: Oxford University Press.

Mills, J. L. (1985, February). Body language speaks louder than words. *Horizons*.

Minton, T. D. (2011). *Jail inmates at midyear 2010: Statistical tables* (NCJ 233431). U.S. Bureau of Justice Statistics. http://bjs.ojp.usdoj.gov/content/pub/pdf/jim10st.pdf. Accessed June 29, 2011.

Minton, T. D., & Sabol, W. J. (2009). *Jail inmates at midyear 2008: Statistical tables* (NCJ 225709). Washington, DC: Bureau of Justice Statistics. http://www.ojp.usdoj.gov/bjs/pub/pdf/jim08st.pdf. Accessed June 10, 2009.

Mirkinson, J. (2010, October 21). Juan Williams fired: NPR sacks analyst over Fox News Muslim comments. *Huffington Post*. www.huffingtonpost.com/2010/10/21/juan-williams-fired-npr_n_770901.html. Accessed June 16, 2011.

Mishel, L., Bernstein, J., & Allegretto, S. (2007). *The state of working America: 2006/2007*. Washington, DC: Economic Policy Institute.

Mishel, L., Bernstein, J., & Shierholz, H. (2009). *The state of working America 2008/2009*. Washington, DC: Economic Policy Institute.

Mnookin, S. (2011, January 10, 17). Autism and the affluent. *Newsweek*.

Mobius, M. M., & Rosenblat, T. S. (2006). Why beauty matters. *American Economic Review, 96,* 222–235.

Moffatt, M. (1989). *Coming of age in New Jersey*. New Brunswick, NJ: Rutgers University Press.

Mogelson, L. (2011, May 1). A beast in the heart. *The New York Times Magazine*.

Mokhiber, R. (1999, July/August). Crime wave! The top 100 corporate criminals of the 1990s. *Multinational Monitor,* pp. 1–9.

Mokhiber, R. (2000, July/August). White collar crime spree. *Multinational Monitor,* p. 38.

Mokhiber, R., & Weissman, R. (2004, December). The ten worst corporations of 2004. *Multinational Monitor,* pp. 8–21.

Molloy, B. L., & Herzberger, S. D. (1998). Body image and self-esteem: A comparison of African-American and Caucasian women. *Sex Roles, 38,* 631–643.

Molotch, H., & Lester, M. (1974). News as purposive behavior: On the strategic use of routine events, accidents, and scandals. *American Sociological Review, 39,* 101–112.

Molotch, H., & Lester, M. (1975). Accidental news: The great oil spill as local occurrence and national event. *American Journal of Sociology, 81,* 235–260.

Monk-Turner, E., Kouts, T., Parris, K., & Webb, C. (2007). Gender role stereotyping in advertisements for three radio stations: Does musical genre make a difference? *Journal of Gender Studies, 16,* 173–182.

Moore, R. B. (1992). Racist stereotyping in the English language. In M. L. Anderson & P. H. Collins (Eds.), *Race, class and gender: An anthology.* Belmont, CA: Wadsworth.

Moore, S. (2009, March 3). Study shows high cost of criminal corrections. *The New York Times.*

Moore, S. A. D. (2003). Understanding the connection between domestic violence, crime, and poverty: How welfare reform may keep battered women from leaving abusive relationships. *Texas Journal of Women and the Law, 12,* 451–484.

Morgan, G. (1986). *Images of organizations.* Newbury Park, CA: Sage.

Morgan, M. (1982). Television and adolescents' sex role stereotypes: A longitudinal study. *Journal of Personality and Social Psychology, 48,* 1173–1190.

Morgan, M. (1987). Television sex role attitudes and sex role behavior. *Journal of Early Adolescence, 7,* 269–282.

Morgan, R. (1996). *Sisterhood is global.* New York, NY: Feminist Press at the City University of New York.

Morrongiello, B. A., & Hogg, K. (2004). Mothers' reactions to children misbehaving in ways that can lead to injury: Implications for gender differences in children's risk taking and injuries. *Sex Roles, 50,* 103–118.

Morson, B. (2008, December 10). Colorado educators ban selling sodas at schools. *Rocky Mountain News.*

Mottl, T. L. (1980). The analysis of countermovements. *Social Problems, 27,* 620–635.

Muhlke, C. (2010, January 31). Field report: Catch me if you can. *The New York Times Magazine.*

Mulrine, A. (2003, May 5). Echoes of a scandal. *U.S. News & World Report.*

Mummolo, J. (2006, July 3–10). Privacy: Cell-phone sanctuaries. *Newsweek.*

Murdock, G. P. (1949). *Social structure.* New York, NY: Macmillan.

Murdock, G. P. (1957). World ethnography sample. *American Anthropologist, 59,* 664–687.

Murguia, E., & Telles, E. E. (1996). Phenotype and schooling among Mexican Americans. *Sociology of Education, 69,* 276–289.

Murphy, D. E. (2002, September 29). As security cameras sprout, someone's always watching. *The New York Times.*

Murphy, D. E. (2004, January 11). Imagining life without illegal immigrants. *The New York Times.*

Murphy, K. (2008, May 31). Job climate for the class of 2008 is a bit warmer than expected. *The New York Times.*

Mydans, S. (1995, February 12). A shooter as vigilante, and avenging angel. *The New York Times.*

Mydans, S. (2007, April 9). Across cultures, English is the word. *International Herald Tribune.*

Mydans, S. (2009, May 7). Recalculating happiness in a Himalayan kingdom. *The New York Times.*

Myers, S. L. (2009, December 28). Another peril in war zones: Sexual abuse by fellow GI's. *The New York Times.*

Nanda, S. (1994). *Cultural anthropology.* Belmont, CA: Wadsworth.

Nasar, S., & Mitchell, K. B. (1999, May 23). Booming job market draws young black men into the fold. *The New York Times.*

National Academy of Sciences. (2007). *Beyond bias and barriers: Fulfilling the potential of women in academic science and engineering.* Washington, DC: National Academies Press.

National Alliance to End Homelessness. (2011). *State of homelessness in America 2011.* www.endhomelessness.org/content/article/detail/3668. Accessed June 13, 2011.

National Association for Single Sex Public Education. (2011). *Single-sex schools/schools with single-sex classrooms/What's the difference?* www.singlesexschools.org/schools-schools.htm. Accessed June 21, 2011.

National Center for Education Statistics. (2006). *2005 trial urban district results.* Washington, DC: Author. http://nces.ed.gov/nationsreportcard/nrc/tuda_reading_mathematics_2005/. Accessed July 5, 2007.

National Center for Education Statistics. (2010). *Indicators of school crime and safety: 2010,* http://nces.ed.gov/programs/crimeindicators2010/ind_05.asp. Accessed July 1, 2011.

National Center for Education Statistics. (2011). *Fast facts.* http://nces.ed.gov/fastfacts/display.asp?id=40. Accessed July 20, 2011.

National Center for Fair and Open Testing. (2011). *2010 college-bound seniors average SAT scores.*

http://fairtest.org/2010-collegebound-seniors-average-sat-scores. Accessed April 13, 2011.

National Center for Health Statistics. (2005). *Self-inflicted injury/suicide. Tables 46 & 58*. Atlanta, GA: Author. www.cdc.gov/nchs/data/hus/hus04trend.pdf#059. Accessed April 11, 2005.

National Center for Health Statistics. (2010). *Health, United States, 2010*. Atlanta, GA: Author. www.cdc.gov/nchs/data/hus/hus10.pdf. Accessed May 16, 2011.

National Center for Law and Economic Justice. (2010). *Poverty in the United States: A snapshot*. www.nclej.org/poverty-in-the-us.php. Accessed June 14, 2011.

National Committee on Pay Equity. (2007). *Current legislation*. Washington, DC: Author. www.pay-equity.org/info-leg.html. Accessed July 11, 2007.

National Conference of State Legislatures. (2009). *State laws regarding marriage between first cousins*. Washington, DC: Author. www.ncsl.org/programs/cyf/cousins.htm. Accessed April 28, 2009.

National Crime Records Bureau. (2009). *Crime in India: 2009*. http://ncrb.nic.in/CII-2009-NEW/Home.htm. Accessed June 21, 2011.

National Digestive Diseases Information Clearinghouse. (2011). *Hemochromatosis*. http://digestive.niddk.nih.gov/ddiseases/pubs/hemochromatosis. Accessed April 1, 2011.

National Eating Disorders Association. (2011). *Statistics: Eating disorders and their precursors*. www.nationaleatingdisorders.org/information-resources/general-information.php#facts-statistics. Accessed June 20, 2011.

National Fair Housing Alliance. (2011). *The big picture: How fair housing organizations challenge systematic and institutionalized discrimination* (NFHA Trend Report). www.national-fairhousing.org/FairHousingResources/ReportsandResearch/tabid/3917/Default.aspx. Accessed June 19, 2011.

National Institute of Mental Health. (2009). *Statistics*. www.nimh.nih.gov/health/topics/statistics/index.shtml. Accessed September 5, 2009.

National Institute of Mental Health. (2010). *Statistics*. www.nimh.nih.gov/statistics/index.shtml. Accessed June 9, 2011.

National Institute on Aging. (2006). *Dramatic changes in U.S. aging highlighted in new Census* (NIH report). Bethesda, MD: Author. www.nia.nih.gov/NewsAndEvents/PressReleases/PR2006030965PLusReport.htm. Accessed July 31, 2006.

National Institute on Alcohol Abuse and Alcoholism. (2007). *What colleges need to know now: An update on college drinking research* (NIH Publication 07-5010). Bethesda, MD: Author. www.collegedrinkingprevention.gov/1College_Bulletin-508_361C4E.pdf. Accessed September 5, 2009.

National Labor Committee for Worker and Human Rights. (2001). *Shah Haksdum Garments Factory, Dhaka, Bangladesh*. Pittsburgh, PA: Author. www.nlcnet.org/campaigns/shahmakhdum/0502/sm0201.shtml. Accessed June 16, 2003.

National Low Income Housing Coalition. (2011). *Out of reach 2011*. www.nlihc.org/oor/oor2011/oor2011pub.pdf. Accessed June 13, 2011.

The National Marriage Project. (2010). *When marriage disappears: The new middle America*. www.virginia.edu/marriageproject/pdfs/Union_11_12_10.pdf. Accessed September 4, 2011.

National Partnership for Women and Families. (2005). *Expecting better: A state-by-state analysis of parental leave programs*. Washington, DC: Author. www.nationalpartnership.org/site/DocServer/ParentalLeaveReportMay05.pdf?docID=1052. Accessed September 5, 2009.

National Urban League. (2009). *The state of black America 2009: Message to the President. Executive Summary*. www.nul.org/thestateofblackamerica.html. Accessed September 5, 2009.

National Women's Law Center. (2006). *The Paycheck Fairness Act: Helping to close the wage gap for women*. Washington, DC: Author. www.pay-equity.org/PDFs/PaycheckFairnessActApr06.pdf. Accessed September 5, 2009.

Nelkin, D., & Pollak, M. (1981). *The atom besieged*. Cambridge, MA: MIT Press.

Nestle, M. (2002). *Food politics*. Berkeley: University of California Press.

Neubeck, K. (1986). *Social problems: A critical approach*. New York, NY: Random House.

Neuman, W. L. (1994). *Social research methods: Qualitative and quantitative approaches*. Boston, MA: Allyn & Bacon.

Newman, D. (2009). *Families: A sociological perspective*. New York: McGraw-Hill.

Newman, D. (2012). *Identities and inequalities: Exploring the intersections of race, class, gender, and sexuality* (2nd ed.). New York, NY: McGraw-Hill.

Newman, K. (2005). Family values against the odds. In A. S. Skolnick & J. H. Skolnick (Eds.), *Family in transition* (13th ed.). Boston, MA: Allyn & Bacon.

Newport, F. (2011). *For first time, majority of Americans favor legal gay marriage.* Gallup, Inc. www.gallup.com/poll/147662/First-Time-Majority-Americans-Favor-Legal-Gay-Marriage.aspx. Accessed July 5, 2011.

Nichols, J. (2000, January). Now what? WTO protests: Seattle is just a start. *The Progressive.*

Niebuhr, G. (1998, April 12). Makeup of American religion is looking more like a mosaic, data say. *The New York Times.*

The nocebo response. (2005, March). *Harvard Mental Health Letter*, pp. 6–7.

Noonan, D. (2008, November 10). No insurance? That's a killer. *Newsweek.*

Nugman, G. (2002). *World divorce rates.* Washington, DC: Heritage Foundation. www.divorcereform.org/gul.html. Accessed July 6, 2003.

Nunberg, G. (2004, July 11). How much wallop can a simple word pack? *The New York Times.*

O'Connell Davidson, J. (2002). The practice of social research. In D. M. Newman & J. O'Brien (Eds.), *Sociology: Exploring the architecture of everyday life (Readings).* Thousand Oaks, CA: Pine Forge Press.

Office of Presidential Advance. (2002). *Presidential advance manual.* www.aclu.org/pdfs/freespeech/presidential_advance_manual.pdf. Accessed June 1, 2011.

Ohgami, H., Terao, T., Shiotsuki, I., Ishii, N., & Iwata, N. (2009). Lithium levels in drinking water and risk of suicide. *British Journal of Psychiatry, 194,* 464–465.

Oldenburg, R., & Brissett, D. (1982). The third place. *Qualitative Sociology, 5,* 265–284.

Olds, J., & Schwartz, R. S. (2009). *The lonely American: Drifting apart in the twenty-first century.* Boston, MA: Beacon Press.

Olsen, M. (1965). *The logic of collective action.* Cambridge, MA: Harvard University Press.

Omi, M., & Winant, H. (1992). Racial formations. In P. S. Rothenberg (Ed.), *Race, class and gender in the United States.* New York, NY: St. Martin's Press.

One child left behind. (2009, March/April). *UTNE Reader.*

Onishi, N. (2002, October 3). Globalization of beauty makes slimness trendy. *The New York Times.*

Onishi, N. (2004a, March 30). On U.S. fast food, more Okinawans grow super-sized. *The New York Times.*

Onishi, N. (2004b, December 16). Tokyo's flag law: Proud patriotism, or indoctrination? *The New York Times.*

Onishi, N. (2005, April 27). In Japan crash, time obsession may be culprit. *The New York Times.*

Orenstein, P. (2008, February 10). Girls will be girls. *The New York Times Magazine.*

Orfield, G., & Lee, C. (2007). *Historical reversals, accelerating resegregation, and the need for new integration strategies.* The Civil Rights Project. www.civilrightsproject.ucla.edu/research/deseg/reversals_reseg_need.pdf. Accessed September 5, 2009.

Orfield, G., Siegel-Hawley, G., & Kucsera, J. (2011). *Divided we fail: Segregated and unequal schools in the Southland.* The Civil Rights Project. www.civilrightsproject.ucla.edu. Accessed June 17, 2011.

Organization for Economic Cooperation and Development. (2011). *Gender pay gaps for full-time workers and earnings differentials by educational attainment.* www.oecd.org/dataoecd/29/63/38752746.pdf. Accessed June 22, 2011.

Organ Procurement and Transplant Network. (2011). *Transplants in the U.S. by recipient ethnicity.* http://optn.transplant.hrsa.gov/latestData/rptData.asp. Accessed April 26, 2011.

O'Sullivan-See, K., & Wilson, W. J. (1988). Race and ethnicity. In N. Smelser (Ed.), *Handbook of sociology.* Newbury Park, CA: Sage.

Padavic, I., & Reskin, B. (2002). *Women and men at work* (2nd ed.). Thousand Oaks, CA: Sage.

Pagan, J. A., & Davila, A. (1997). Obesity, occupational attainment, and earnings. *Social Science Quarterly, 78,* 756–770.

Parenti, M. (1986). *Inventing reality.* New York, NY: St. Martin's Press.

Parenti, M. (1995). *Democracy for the few.* New York, NY: St. Martin's Press.

Parenti, M. (2006). Mass media: For the many, by the few. In P. S. Rothenberg (Ed.), *Beyond borders: Thinking critically about global issues.* New York, NY: Worth.

Parker, A. (2011, February 16). Lawsuit says the military is rife with sexual abuse. *The New York Times.*

Parker, S., Nichter, M., Nichter, M., Vuckovic, N., Sims, C., & Ritenbaugh, C. (1995). Body image and weight concerns among African American and white adolescent females: Differences that make a difference. *Human Organization, 54,* 103–114.

Parker-Pope, T. (2011, March 31). Fat stigma is fast spreading around the globe. *The New York Times.*

Parlee, M. B. (1989). Conversational politics. In L. Richardson & V. Taylor (Eds.), *Feminist frontiers II.* New York, NY: Random House.

Parrott, S. (2008). *Recession could cause large increases in poverty and push millions into deep poverty.* Washington, DC: Center on Budget and Policy Priorities. www.cbpp.org/cms/index.cfm?fa=view&id=1290. Accessed May 26, 2009.

Parsons, T. (1951). *The social system.* New York, NY: Free Press.

Parsons, T. (1971). Kinship and the associational aspect of social structure. In F. L. K. Hsu (Ed.), *Kinship and culture.* Chicago, IL: Aldine-Atherton.

Parsons, T., & Bales, R. F. (1955). *Family, socialization and interaction process.* Glencoe, IL: Free Press.

Parsons, T., & Smelser, N. (1956). *Economy and society.* New York, NY: Free Press.

Pascoe, C. J. (2010). Dude, you're a fag? In S. Ferguson (Ed.), *Mapping the social landscape.* New York, NY: McGraw-Hill.

Passel, J. S., & Cohn, D. (2011). *Unauthorized immigrant population: National and state trends, 2010.* http://pewhispanic.org/files/reports/133.pdf. Accessed June 24, 2011.

Pattillo-McCoy, M. (1999). *Black picket fences: Privilege and peril among the black middle class.* Chicago, IL: University of Chicago Press.

Paul, R. (2010, July 26). Perspectives. *Newsweek.*

Payer, L. (1988). *Medicine and culture.* New York, NY: Penguin Books.

Pear, R. (1992, December 4). New look at U.S. in 2050: Bigger, older and less white. *The New York Times.*

Pear, R. (2000, April 30). Studies find research on women lacking. *The New York Times.*

Pear, R. (2008a, March 23). Gap in life expectancy widens for the nation. *The New York Times.*

Pear, R. (2008b, October 30). Women buying health policies pay a penalty. *The New York Times.*

Pear, R. (2010, June 22). Gay workers will get time to care for partner's sick child. *The New York Times.*

Pearce, D. (1979). Gatekeepers and homeseekers: Institutional patterns in racial steering. *Social Problems, 26,* 325–342.

Pearce, L. D., & Axinn, W. G. (1998). The impact of family religious life on the quality of mother child relations. *American Sociological Review, 63,* 810–828.

Peng, T. (2008, November 22). Out of the shadows. *Newsweek Online.* www.newsweek.com/2008/11/22/out-of-the-shadows.html. Accessed April 12, 2011.

Pennington, B. (2003, November 12). As team sports conflict, some parents rebel. *The New York Times.*

Perez-Peña, R. (2003, April 19). Study finds asthma in 25% of children in central Harlem. *The New York Times.*

Peri, G. (2009). *The effect of immigration on productivity: Evidence from U.S. states* (National Bureau of Economic Research Working Paper 15507). www.nber.org/papers/w15507.pdf?new_window=1. Accessed July 5, 2010.

Perlez, J. (1991, August 31). Madagascar, where the dead return, bringing joy. *The New York Times.*

Perlin, S. A., Sexton, K., & Wong, D. W. S. (1999). An examination of race and poverty for populations living near industrial sources of air pollution. *Journal of Exposure Analysis and Environmental Epidemiology, 9,* 29–48.

Perlman, D., & Fehr, B. (1987). The development of intimate relationships. In D. Perlman & S. Duck (Eds.), *Intimate relationships: Development, dynamics and deterioration.* Newbury Park, CA: Sage.

Pescosolido, B. A. (1986). Migration, medical care and the lay referral system: A network theory of role assimilation. *American Sociological Review, 51,* 523–540.

Pescosolido, B. A., Grauerholz, E., & Milkie, M. A. (1997). Culture and conflict: The portrayal of Blacks in U.S. children's picture books through the mid- and late-twentieth century. *American Sociological Review, 62,* 443–464.

Peterson, I. (2005, March 14). Casino with weight policy finds boon in controversy. *The New York Times.*

Peterson, P. (1991). The urban underclass and the poverty paradox. In C. Jencks & P. Peterson (Eds.), *The urban underclass.* Washington, DC: Brookings Institution.

Peterson, R. D., & Bailey, W. C. (1991). Felony murder and capital punishment: An examination of the deterrence question. *Criminology, 29,* 367–395.

Peterson, S. B., & Lach, M. A. (1990). Gender stereotypes in children's books: Their prevalence and influence in cognitive and affective development. *Gender and Education, 2,* 185–197.

Pew Forum on Religion and Public Life. (2004). *The American religious landscape and politics, 2004.* Washington, DC: Pew Research Center. www.pewforum.org/publications/surveys/green.pdf. Accessed December 31, 2004.

Pew Forum on Religion and Public Life. (2008). *U.S. religious landscape survey: Religious affiliation, diverse and dynamic.* http://religions.pewforum.org/pdf/report-religious-landscape-study-full.pdf. Accessed May 30, 2011.

Pew Forum on Religion and Public Life. (2010a). *Religion among the millennials.* http://pewforum.org/Age/Religion-Among-the-Millennials.aspx. Accessed May 30, 2011.

Pew Forum on Religion and Public Life. (2010b). *U.S. religious knowledge survey.* http://pewforum.org/Other-Beliefs-and-Practices/U-S-Religious-Knowledge-Survey.aspx. Accessed May 30, 2011.

Pew Forum on Religion and Public Life. (2011). *The future of the global Muslim population.* http://pewforum.org/The-Future-of-the-Global-Muslim-Population.aspx. Accessed June 10, 2011.

Pew Global Attitudes Project. (2008). *Unfavorable views of Jews and Muslims on the increase in Europe.* Washington, DC: Pew Research Center. http://pewglobal.org/reports/display.php?ReportID=262. Accessed June 2, 2009.

Pew Research Center. (2005). *Social security polling: Cross-currents in opinion about private accounts.* Washington, DC: Author. http://people-press.org/commentary/pdf/106.pdf. Accessed September 5, 2009.

Pew Research Center. (2006a). *America's immigration quandary.* Washington, DC: Author. http://people-press.org/reports/display.php3?ReportID=274. Accessed July 16, 2007.

Pew Research Center. (2006b). *Less opposition to gay marriage, adoption, and military service.* Washington, DC: Author. http://people-press.org/report/273/less-opposition-to-gay-marriage-adoption-and-military-service. Accessed May 20, 2009.

Pew Research Center. (2007a). *Muslim Americans: Middle class and mostly mainstream.* Washington, DC: Author. http://pewresearch.org/assets/pdf/muslim-americans.pdf. Accessed September 5, 2009.

Pew Research Center. (2007b). *Trends in political values and core attitudes: 1987–2007.* Washington, DC: Author. http://people-press.org/reports/pdf/312.pdf. Accessed September 5, 2009.

Pew Research Center. (2010a). *The decline of marriage and rise of new families.* http://pewsocialtrends.org/files/2010/11/pew-social-trends-2010-families.pdf. Accessed June 2, 2011.

Pew Research Center. (2010b). *Millennials: A portrait of generation next.* http://pewsocialtrends.org/2010/12/20/files/2010/10/millennials-confident-connected-open-to-change.pdf. Accessed June 23, 2011.

Pew Research Center. (2011). *Pessimism about national economy rises, personal financial views hold steady.* http://people-press.org/2011/06/23/section-2-views-of-personal-finances/. Accessed June 27, 2011.

Pfohl, S. J. (1994). *Images of deviance and social control.* New York, NY: McGraw-Hill.

Phillips, K. (2002). *Wealth and democracy.* New York, NY: Broadway Books.

Piore, A. (2003, March 17). Home alone. *Newsweek.*

Piper, A. (1992). Passing for white, passing for black. *Transition, 58,* 4–32.

Piven, F. F., & Cloward, R. A. (1977). *Poor people's movements: Why they succeed, how they fail.* New York, NY: Vintage Books.

Pizza must go through: It's the law in San Francisco. (1996, July 14). *The New York Times.*

Polgreen, L. (2005, December 27). Ghana's uneasy embrace of slavery's diaspora. *The New York Times.*

Polgreen, L. (2010, March 31). Suicides, some for separatist cause, jolt India. *The New York Times.*

Pollan, M. (2007, January 28). Unhappy meals. *The New York Times Magazine.*

Pope exalts women for roles as wife, mom. (2003, June 7). *The Indianapolis Star.*

Popenoe, D. (1993). American family decline, 1960–1990: A review and appraisal. *Journal of Marriage and the Family, 55,* 527–555.

Popenoe, R. (2005). Ideal. In D. Kulick & A. Meneley (Eds.), *Fat: The anthropology of an obsession.* New York, NY: Tarcher/Penguin.

Population Reference Bureau. (2008). *2008 world population data sheet.* Washington, DC: Author. www.prb.org/pdf08/08WPDS_Eng.pdf. Accessed May 27, 2009.

Population Reference Bureau. (2010a). China's rapidly aging population. *Today's Research on Aging, 20,* 1–5.

Population Reference Bureau. (2010b). *Female genital mutilation/cutting: Data and trends.* www.prb.org/pdf10/fgm-wallchart2010.pdf. Accessed March 9, 2010.

Population Reference Bureau. (2010c). *2010 world population data sheet.* www.prb.org/pdf10/10wpds_eng.pdf. Accessed June 14, 2011.

Population Reference Bureau. (2011a). *2011 world population data sheet.* Washington, DC: Author. www.prb.org/pdf11/2011population-data-sheet_eng.pdf. Accessed September 8, 2011.

Population Reference Bureau. (2011b). *The world's women and girls.* www.prb.org/pdf11/world-women-girls-2011-data-sheet.pdf. Accessed June 21, 2011.

Porter, E. (2005, April 5). Illegal immigrants are bolstering Social Security with billions. *The New York Times.*

Porter, E. (2006, October 17). Law on overseas brides is keeping couples apart. *The New York Times.*

Powell, B., Bolzendahl, C., Geist, C., & Steelman, L. C. (2010). *Counted out: Same-sex relations and Americans' definitions of family.* New York, NY: Russell Sage.

Powell, M. (2009a, May 31). On diverse force, Blacks still face special peril. *The New York Times.*

Powell, M. (2009b, June 7). Suit accuses Wells Fargo of steering Blacks to subprime mortgages in Baltimore. *The New York Times.*

Powell, R. A. (2004, November 5). No yelling, no cheering. Shhhhh! It's silent Saturday. *The New York Times.*

Prah, P. M. (2006). Domestic violence. *CQ Researcher, 16,* 1–24.

President's Council on Bioethics. (2003). *Beyond therapy: Biotechnology and the pursuit of happiness.* Washington, DC: Government Printing Office.

Preston, J. (2011, May 30). A crackdown on employing illegal workers. *The New York Times.*

Preston, J., & Connelly, M. (2007, May 25). Immigration bill provisions gain wide support in poll. *The New York Times.*

Preston, J., & Stelter, B. (2011, February 18). Cellphone cameras become the world's eyes and ears on protests across the Middle East. *The New York Times.*

Price, S. L. (1997, December 8). Whatever happened to the white athlete? *Sports Illustrated.*

Price paid in military lives equal to 9/11 toll. (2006, September 23). *Banner Graphic.*

Proctor, B. D., & Dalaker, J. (2002). *Poverty in the United States: 2001* (U.S. Census Bureau, Current Population Reports, P60–219). Washington, DC: Government Printing Office.

Project for Excellence in Journalism. (2005). *Embedded reporters: What are Americans getting?* Washington, DC: Pew Research Center. www.journalism.org/sites/journalism.org/files/pejembedreport.pdf. Accessed September 5, 2009.

Project for Excellence in Journalism. (2006). *Change in stations owned by top companies: 1999–2005.* Washington, DC: Pew Research Center. www.journalism.org/node/1325. Accessed June 18, 2007.

Protestant church insurers' data give look at sexual abuse. (2007, June 16). *The Indianapolis Star.*

Prothero, S. (2007). *Religious literacy.* San Francisco, CA: Harper.

Provine, R. R. (2000). *Laughter: A scientific investigation.* New York, NY: Penguin Books.

Pugliesi, K. (1987). Deviation in emotion and the labeling of mental illness. *Deviant Behavior, 8,* 79–102.

Puhl, R., & Brownell, K. D. (2001). Bias, discrimination, and obesity. *Obesity Research, 9,* 788–805.

Putnam, R. D. (1995). Bowling alone: America's declining social capital. *Journal of Democracy, 6,* 65–78.

Quart, A. (2008, March 16). When girls will be boys. *The New York Times Magazine.*

Quinney, R. (1970). *The social reality of crime.* Boston, MA: Little, Brown.

Rabin, R. C. (2008, December 16). Living with in-laws linked to heart risks in Japanese women. *The New York Times.*

Rabin, R. C. (2011, May 18). Study finds fewer emergency rooms as need rises. *The New York Times.*

Raftery, I. (2011, May 30). Changes in Oregon law put faith-healing parents on trial. *The New York Times.*

Raley, S., & Bianchi, S. (2006). Sons, daughters, and family processes: Does gender of children matter? *Annual Review of Sociology, 32,* 401–421.

Rampell, C. (2011a, June 10). Companies spend on equipment, not workers. *The New York Times.*

Rampell, C. (2011b, May 19). Many with new college degrees find the job market humbling. *The New York Times.*

Rand, M. R. (2008). *Criminal victimization, 2007* (NCJ 224390). Washington, DC: Bureau of Justice Statistics. www.ojp.usdoj.gov/bjs/pub/pdf/CV07.pdf. Accessed June 3, 2009.

Rankin, S. R. (2003). *Campus climate for gay, lesbian, bisexual, and transgender people: A national perspective.* Washington, DC: National Gay and Lesbian Task Force. www.thetaskforce.org/downloads/reports/reports/CampusClimate.pdf. Accessed September 5, 2009.

Ray, R. T., Gornick, J. C., & Schmitt, J. (2009). *Parental leave policies in 21 countries: Assessing generosity and gender equality.* Center for Economic and Policy Research. www.cepr.net/documents/publications/parental_2008_09.pdf. Accessed June 5, 2011.

Reddy, G. (2005). *With respect to sex: Negotiating hijra identity in South Asia.* Chicago, IL: University of Chicago Press.

Redstone, J. (2003). *The language of war.* Worldwatch. www.omegastar.org/worldwatch/America/Language_of_War.html. Accessed May 23, 2003.

Reiman, J. (2007). *The rich get richer and the poor get prison.* Boston, MA: Allyn & Bacon.

Reinharz, S. (1992). *Feminist methods in social research.* New York, NY: Oxford University Press.

Relethford, J. H., Stern, M. P., Caskill, S. P., & Hazuda, H. P. (1983). Social class, admixture, and skin color variation in Mexican Americans and Anglo Americans living in San Antonio, Texas. *American Journal of Physical Anthropology, 61,* 97–102.

Religious groups gather for "Justice Wednesday" pray in. (2005, April 26). *Worldwide Faith News.* www.wfn.org/2005/04/msg00274.html. Accessed July 24, 2005.

Rennison, C. M., & Welchans, S. (2000). *Intimate partner violence* (Special Report No. NCJ 178247). Washington, DC: United States Bureau of Justice Statistics.

Renzetti, C. M., & Curran, D. J. (2003). *Women, men and society: The sociology of gender.* Boston, MA: Allyn & Bacon.

Research findings affirm health of women hinges on reform of clinical research. (2003, August 14). *Women's Health Weekly.*

Reskin, B., & Hartmann, H. (1986). *Women's work, men's work: Sex segregation on the job.* Washington, DC: National Academy Press.

Restaurant Opportunities Center of New York. (2009). *The great service divide: Occupational segregation & inequality in the New York City restaurant industry.* www.rocunited.org/files/GREATSERVICEDIVIDE.pdf. Accessed June 17, 2011.

Reyes, L., & Rubie, P. (1994). *Hispanics in Hollywood: An encyclopedia of film and television.* New York, NY: Garland Press.

Rhoden, W. C. (2006). *Forty million dollar slaves: The rise, fall, and redemption of the black athlete.* New York, NY: Crown.

Ribando, C. M. (2007). *Trafficking in persons: U.S. policy and issues for Congress.* Congressional Research Service. www.humantrafficking.org/uploads/publications/20070806_120229_RL30545.pdf. Accessed August 6, 2007.

Rice, A. (2009, April 12). Mission from Africa. *The New York Times Magazine.*

Rich, M. (2010, December 20). Weighing costs, companies favor temporary help. *The New York Times.*

Richtel, M. (2007, November 2). Devices enforce cellular silence, sweet but illegal. *The New York Times.*

Richtel, M. (2009, June 15). Providing cellphones for the poor. *The New York Times.*

Richtel, M., & Wald, M. L. (2009, August 5). Federal agency plans forum on driving while distracted. *The New York Times.*

Rideout, V., Roberts, D. E., & Foehr, U. G. (2005). *Generation M: Media in the lives of 8–18 year olds.* www.kff.org/entmedia/upload/Generation-M-Media-in-the-Lives-of-8–18-Year-olds-Report.pdf. Accessed September 5, 2009.

Ridgeway, C. L., & Smith-Lovin, L. (1999). The gender system and interaction. *Annual Review of Sociology, 25,* 191–216.

Rieff, D. (2005, November 6). Migrant worry. *The New York Times Magazine.*

Rieff, D. (2006, July 2). America the untethered. *The New York Times Magazine.*

Riesman, D. (1950). *The lonely crowd.* New Haven, CT: Yale University Press.

Riley, M. W. (1971). Social gerontology and the age stratification of society. *Gerontologist, 11,* 79–87.

Riley, M. W., Foner, A., & Waring, J. (1988). Sociology of age. In N. J. Smelser (Ed.), *Handbook of sociology.* Newbury Park, CA: Sage.

Rimer, S. (2002, June 4). Suspects lacking lawyers are freed in Atlanta. *The New York Times.*

Rimer, S., & Arenson, K. W. (2004, June 24). Top colleges take more Blacks, but which ones? *The New York Times.*

Ritzer, G. (2000). *The McDonaldization of society.* Thousand Oaks, CA: Pine Forge Press.

Robbins, A. (2004). *Pledged: The secret life of sororities.* New York, NY: Hyperion.

Roberts, S. (1995, December 24). Alone in the vast wasteland. *The New York Times.*

Roberts, S. (2006, February 12). So many men, so few women. *The New York Times.*

Roberts, S. (2007, November 17). In the U.S. name count, Garcias are catching up with the Joneses. *The New York Times.*

Roberts, S. (2008, August 17). A nation of none and all of the above. *The New York Times.*

Roberts, S. (2010, January 21). Census figures challenge views of race and ethnicity. *The New York Times.*

Roberts, S. (2011, May 19). A judicial rite: Suspects on parade (bring a raincoat). *The New York Times.*

Robertson, C. (2011, August 14). Alabama law criminalizes Samaritans, bishops say. *The New York Times.*

Robert Wood Johnson Foundation. (2005). *Characteristics of the uninsured: A view from the states.* www.rwjf.org/files/research/Full_SHADAC.pdf. Accessed September 5, 2009.

Robinson, B. A. (1999). *Facts about inter-faith marriages.* www.religioustolerance.org/ifm_fact.htm. Accessed July 6, 2003.

Robinson, R. V., & Bell, W. (1978). Equality, success and social justice in England and the United States. *American Sociological Review, 43,* 125–143.

Robinson, R. V., & Kelley, J. (1979). Class as conceived by Marx and Dahrendorf: Effects on income inequality and politics in the United States and Great Britain. *American Sociological Review, 44,* 38–58.

Rodriguez, C. E., & Cordero-Guzman, H. (2004). Placing race in context. In C. A. Gallagher (Ed.), *Rethinking the color line: Readings in race and ethnicity.* New York, NY: McGraw-Hill.

Rodriguez, M. N., & Emsellem, M. (2011). *65 million "need not apply."* The National Employment Law Project. www.nelp.org/page/-/65_Million_Need_Not_Apply.pdf?nocdn=1. Accessed March 31, 2011.

Roehling, M. V. (1999). Weight-based discrimination in employment: Psychological and legal aspects. *Personnel Psychology, 52,* 969–1017.

Roethlisberger, E. J., & Dickson, W. J. (1939). *Management and the worker.* Cambridge, MA: Harvard University Press.

Rohter, L. (2004, December 29). Learn English, says Chile, thinking upwardly global. *The New York Times.*

Rohter, L. (2005, January 30). Divorce ties Chile in knots. *The New York Times.*

Rohter, L. (2007, January 14). In the land of bold beauty, a trusted mirror cracks. *The New York Times.*

Roland, A. (1988). *In search of self in India and Japan.* Princeton, NJ: Princeton University Press.

Romero, S. (1999, July 24). Cashing in on security woes. *The New York Times.*

Rosato, D. (2004, August). Flights of fancy: Part 2. Airlines' class warfare. *Money.*

Roscigno, V. J., & Hodson, R. (2004). The organizational and social foundations of worker resistance. *American Sociological Review, 69,* 14–39.

Roscigno, V. J., Karafin, D. L., & Tester, G. (2009). The complexities and processes of racial housing discrimination. *Social Problems, 56,* 49–69.

Rose, M. (2004). *The mind at work.* New York, NY: Viking.

Rosenberg, D. (2006, November 27). A renewed war over "Don't ask, don't tell." *Newsweek.*

Rosenblatt, P. C., Karis, T. A., & Powell, R. D. (1995). *Multiracial couples.* Thousand Oaks, CA: Sage.

Rosenfeld, M. J. (2005). A critique of exchange theory in mate selection. *American Journal of Sociology, 110,* 1284–1325.

Rosenthal, E. (2002, November). Study links rural suicides in China to stress and ready poisons. *The New York Times.*

Rosenthal, R., & Jacobson, L. (1968). *Pygmalion in the classroom.* New York, NY: Holt, Rinehart & Winston.

Ross, C. E., Mirowsky, J., & Goldstein, K. (1990). The impact of family on health: The decade in review. *Journal of Marriage and the Family, 52,* 1059–1078.

Rossi, A. (1968). Transition to parenthood. *Journal of Marriage and the Family, 30,* 26–39.

Rossi, P., Waite, E., Bose, C. E., & Berk, R. E. (1974). The seriousness of crimes: Normative structure and individual differences. *American Sociological Review, 39,* 224–237.

Rothenberg, P. S. (Ed.). (1992). *Race, class and gender in the United States.* New York, NY: St. Martin's Press.

Rothman, B. K. (1984). Women, health and medicine. In J. Freeman (Ed.), *Women: A feminist perspective.* Palo Alto, CA: Mayfield.

Rothman, B. K., & Caschetta, M. B. (1999). Treating health: Women and medicine. In S. J. Ferguson (Ed.), *Mapping the social landscape: Readings in sociology.* Mountain View, CA: Mayfield.

Rothman, D. J., & Edgar, H. (1992). Scientific rigor and medical realities: Placebo trials in cancer and AIDS research. In E. Fee & D. M. Fox (Eds.), *AIDS: The making of a chronic disease.* Berkeley: University of California Press.

Rothschild, M. (2000, January). Soothsayers of Seattle. *Progressive.*

Rothstein, R. (2001, December 12). An economic recovery will tell in the classroom. *The New York Times.*

Royte, E. (2008, August 10). A tall, cool drink of . . . sewage? *The New York Times Magazine.*

Rubin, J. Z., Provenzano, F. J., & Luria, Z. (1974). The eye of the beholder: Parents' views on sex of newborns. *American Journal of Orthopsychiatry, 44,* 512–519.

Rubin, L. (1994). *Families on the fault line.* New York, NY: HarperCollins.

Rubinstein, S., & Caballero, B. (2000). Is Miss America an undernourished role model? *Journal of the American Medical Association, 283,* 1569.

Rucker, P. (2009, April 8). Some link economy with spate of killings. *The New York Times.*

Ruethling, G. (2005, June 22). Chicago police put arrest photos of prostitution suspects online. *The New York Times.*

Rusbult, C. E., Zembrodt, I. M., & Iwaniszek, J. (1986). The impact of gender and sex-role orientation on responses to dissatisfaction in close relationships. *Sex Roles, 15,* 1–20.

Rwandan Stories. (2011). *With me, he behaved nicely.* www.rwandanstories.org/genocide/strangness_of_mind.html. Accessed May 19, 2011.

Rybczynski, W. (1999, April 18). One good turn. *The New York Times Magazine.*

Sack, K. (2009a, March 14). Bad economy leads patients to put off surgery, or rush it. *The New York Times.*

Sack, K. (2009b, May 11). Despite recession, personalized health care remains in demand. *The New York Times.*

Sadker, M., & Sadker, D. (1999). Failing at fairness: Hidden lessons. In S. Ferguson (Ed.), *Mapping the social landscape.* Mountain View, CA: Mayfield.

Sadker, M., Sadker, D., Fox, L., & Salata, M. (2004). Gender equity in the classroom: The unfinished agenda. In M. S. Kimmel (Ed.), *The gendered society reader.* New York, NY: Oxford University Press.

Saenz, R. (2004, August). *Latinos and the changing face of America* (PRB Report). Washington, DC: Population Reference Bureau. www.prb.org. Accessed September 3, 2004.

Saenz, R. (2010). *Latinos in the United States: 2010.* Population Reference Bureau. www.prb.org/Publications/PopulationBulletins/2010/latinosupdate1.aspx. Accessed June 16, 2011.

Safer, D. J., Zito, J. M., & dosReis, S. (2003). Concomitant psychotropic medication for youths. *American Journal of Psychiatry, 160,* 438–449.

Safire, W. (2006, January 15). Mideastisms. *The New York Times Magazine.*

Sage, G. H. (2001). Racial equality and sport. In D. S. Eitzen (Ed.), *Sport in contemporary society.* New York, NY: Worth.

Saint Louis, C. (2010, July 4). What big eyes you have, dear, but are those contacts risky? *The New York Times.*

Saint Louis, C. (2011, May 15). Dessert, laid-back and legal. *The New York Times.*

Salganik, M. J., Dodds, P. S., & Watts, D. J. (2006). Experimental study of inequality and unpredictability in an artificial cultural market. *Science, 311,* 854–856.

Samuels, A. (2011, September 5). Reliving MLK's last hours. *Newsweek.*

Sanday, P. R. (1996). *A woman scorned: Acquaintance rape on trial.* New York, NY: Doubleday.

Sanderson, W., & Scherbov, S. (2008). Rethinking age and aging. *Population Bulletin, 63,* 1–16.

Santora, M. (2005, January 30). U.S. is close to eliminating AIDS in infants, officials say. *The New York Times.*

Sapir, E. (1929). The status of linguistics as a science. *Language, 5,* 207–214.

Sapir, E. (1949). *Selected writings* (D. G. Mandelbaum, Ed.). Berkeley: University of California Press.

Saul, L. (1972). Personal and social psychopathology and the primary prevention of violence. *American Journal of Psychiatry, 128,* 1578–1581.

Saulny, S. (2009a, November 8). Overweight Americans push back with vigor in the health care debate. *The New York Times.*

Saulny, S. (2009b, February 25). They stand when called upon, and when not. *The New York Times.*

Saulny, S. (2011a, March 20). Black and white and married in the deep south: A shifting image. *The New York Times.*

Saulny, S. (2011b, February 10). In a multiracial nation, many ways to tally. *The New York Times.*

Saulny, S., & Richtel, M. (2011, January 26). States' lawmakers turn attention to the dangers of distracted pedestrians. *The New York Times.*

Saulny, S., & Steinberg, J. (2011, June 14). On college forms, a question of race, or races, can perplex. *The New York Times.*

Saunders, J. M. (1991). Relating social structural abstractions to sociological research. *Teaching Sociology, 19,* 270–271.

Savage, D. (2008, November 12). Anti-gay, anti-family. *The New York Times.*

Sayer, L., Casper, L., & Cohen, P. (2004, October). *Women, men, and work* (PRB Report). Washington, DC: Population Reference Bureau. www.prb.org. Accessed December 30, 2004.

Schemo, D. J. (2006a, October 25). Federal rules back single-sex public education. *The New York Times.*

Schemo, D. J. (2006b, October 21). Turmoil at college for deaf reflects broader debate. *The New York Times.*

Schlesinger, A. (1992). *The disuniting of America.* New York, NY: Norton.

Schlosser, E. (2001). *Fast food nation.* New York, NY: Houghton Mifflin.

Schmitt, E., & Shanker, T. (2005, July 25). New name for "War on Terror" reflects wider U.S. campaign. *The New York Times.*

Schodolski, V. J. (1993, December 26). Funeral industry, pitching videos, 2-for-1 specials to baby boomers. *The Indianapolis Star.*

Schoenborn, C. A. (2004). Marital status and health: United States, 1999–2002. Centers for Disease Control and Prevention. *Vital and Health Statistics, 351.* http://www.cdc.gov/nchs/data/ad/ad351.pdf. Accessed September 5, 2009.

Schofield, H. (2005, September 22). France announces new measures to encourage large families. *Agence France Presse—English.*

Schooler, C. (1996). Cultural and social structural explanations of cross-national psychological differences. *Annual Review of Sociology, 22,* 323–349.

Schott, B. (2007, February 25). Who do you think we are? *The New York Times.*

Schrobsdorff, S. (2006, October 30). Skinny is the new fat. *Newsweek.*

Schuman, H., & Krysan, M. (1999). A historical note on Whites' beliefs about racial inequality. *American Sociological Review, 64,* 847–855.

Schur, E. M. (1984). *Labeling women deviant: Gender, stigma and social control.* New York, NY: Random House.

Schutt, R. K. (2006). *Investigating the social world.* Thousand Oaks, CA: Pine Forge Press.

Schwartz, C. R., & Mare, R. D. (2005). Trends in educational assertive marriage from 1940 to 2003. *Demography, 42,* 621–646.

Schwartz, J. (2010, December 6). Extreme makeover: Criminal court edition. *The New York Times.*

Schwartz, J., Revkin, A. C., & Wald, M. L. (2005, September 12). In reviving New Orleans, a challenge of many tiers. *The New York Times.*

Schwartzman, L. F. (2007). Does money whiten? Intergenerational changes in racial classification. *American Sociological Review, 72,* 940–963.

Sciolino, E., & Mekhennet, S. (2008, June 11). Muslim world and virginity: 2 worlds collide. *The New York Times.*

Scott, A. O. (2010, May 9). Gen X has a midlife crisis. *The New York Times.*

Scott, J., & Leonhardt, D. (2005, May 15). Class in America: Shadowy lines that still divide us. *The New York Times.*

Scott, L. D. (2003). The relation of racial identity and racial socialization to coping with discrimination among African American adolescents. *Journal of Black Studies, 33,* 520–538.

Scott, M., & Lyman, S. (1968). Accounts. *American Sociological Review, 33,* 46–62.

Scull, A., & Favreau, D. (1986). A chance to cut is a chance to cure: Sexual surgery for psychosis in three nineteenth-century societies. In S. Spitzer & A. T. Scull (Eds.), *Research in law, deviance and social control* (Vol. 8). Greenwich, CT: JAI Press.

Seelye, K. Q. (2009, August 15). Competing ads on health care plan swamp the airwaves. *The New York Times.*

Segal, D. (2009, March 12). Financial fraud rises as target for prosecutors. *The New York Times.*

Semyonov, M., & Raijman, R. (2006). The rise of anti-foreigner sentiment in European societies, 1988–2000. *American Sociological Review, 71,* 426–449.

Sen, S. (2007, July 16). The newest parent trap. *Newsweek.*

Sengupta, S. (2002, April 29). Child traffickers prey on Bangladesh. *The New York Times.*

Sengupta, S. (2004, October 26). Relentless attacks on women in West Sudan draw an outcry. *The New York Times.*

Sennett, R. (1984). *Families against the city: Middle-class homes in industrial Chicago.* Cambridge, MA: Harvard University Press.

Sennett, R., & Cobb, J. (1972). *Hidden injuries of class.* New York, NY: Vintage Books.

Serrano, R. A. (2011, June 30). Federal panel OKs shorter sentences for crack offenders. *The Seattle Times.*

Severson, K. (2011, July 6). Systematic cheating is found in Atlanta's school system. *New York Times.*

Sex offender's case denied in court. (2001, January 16). *Associated Press Online.* www.highbeam.com/doc/1P1-39751038.html. Accessed October 2, 2011.

Sexual Harassment Support. (2009). *Sexual harassment in the workplace.* www.sexualharassmentsupport.org/SHworkplace.html. Accessed July 2, 2010.

Shah, A. (2009). Poverty facts and statistics. *Global Issues.* www.globalissues.org/article/26/poverty-facts-and-stats#src1. Accessed May 28, 2009.

Shakin, M., Shakin, D., & Sternglanz, S. H. (1985). Infant clothing: Sex labeling for strangers. *Sex Roles, 12,* 955–964.

Shanker, T. (2004, December 8). Inquiry faults commanders in assaults on cadets. *The New York Times.*

Shapiro, T. M. (2008). The hidden cost of being African American. In S. J. Ferguson (Ed.), *Mapping the social landscape.* New York, NY: McGraw-Hill.

Shapo, H. S. (2006). Assisted reproduction and the law: Disharmony on a divisive social issue. *Northwestern University Law Review, 100,* 465–479.

Shear, M. D. (2010, April 16). Obama extends hospital visitation rights to same-sex partners of gays. *The Washington Post.*

Shenk, D. (2010, May/June). Are you a genius? *Brown Alumni Magazine.*

Shibutani, T. (1961). *Society and personality: An interactionist approach to social psychology.* Englewood Cliffs, NJ: Prentice Hall.

Shipler, D. K. (2004). *The working poor: Invisible in America.* New York, NY: Knopf.

Shorto, R. (2010, February 14). Founding father? *The New York Times Magazine.*

Shugart, H. A. (2003). She shoots, she scores: Mediated construction of contemporary female athletes in coverage of the 1999 U.S. Women's soccer team. *Western Journal of Communication, 67,* 1–31.

Shweder, R. A. (1997, March 9). It's called poor health for a reason. *The New York Times.*

Sidel, R. (1986). *Women and children last.* New York, NY: Penguin Books.

Sidel, R. (1990). *On her own: Growing up in the shadow of the American dream.* New York, NY: Penguin Books.

Siegel, R. B. (2004). A short history of sexual harassment. In C. A. MacKinnon & R. B. Siegel (Eds.), *Directions in sexual harassment law.* New Haven, CT: Yale University Press.

Signorielli, N. (1990). Children, television, and gender roles. *Journal of Adolescent Health Care, 11,* 50–58.

The silver lining at Borders. (2011, October 2). *HR Management.* www.hrmreport.com/article/The-silver-lining-at-Borders/. Accessed October 2, 2011.

Silverman, D. (1982). *Secondary analysis in social research: A guide to data sources and methods with examples.* Boston, MA: Allen & Unwin.

Silverstein, K. (1999, July 19). Millions for Viagra, pennies for the poor. *The Nation.*

Simmel, G. (1950). *The sociology of Georg Simmel* (K. Wolff, Ed.). New York, NY: Free Press. (Original work published 1902)

Simon, S. (2009, April 13). Education board in Texas faces curbs. *The Wall Street Journal.*

Simons, M. (2001, April 30). An awful task: Assessing 4 roles in death of thousands in Rwanda. *The New York Times.*

Simons, M. (2011, June 25). Official gets life sentence for genocide in Rwanda. *The New York Times.*

Simpson, I. H. (1979). *From student to nurse: A longitudinal study of socialization.* Cambridge, UK: Cambridge University Press.

Sinclair Broadcast Group. (2011). *Company profile.* www.sbgi.net/about/profile.html. Accessed May 24, 2011.

Sindelar, R. (2004). *Recess: Is it needed in the 21st century?* Champaign, IL: Clearinghouse on Early Education and Parenting. http://ceep.crc.uiuc.edu/poptopics/recess.html. Accessed May 23, 2009.

Singer, N. (2009, August 5). Medical papers by ghostwriters pushed therapy. *The New York Times.*

Singer, N. (2010, August 13). Eat an apple (doctor's orders). *The New York Times.*

Skocpol, T. (1979). *States and social revolutions: A comparative analysis of France, Russia and China.* New York, NY: Cambridge University Press.

Skolnick, A. S. (1991). *Embattled paradise.* New York, NY: Basic Books.

Skolnick, A. S., & Skolnick, J. H. (Eds.). (1992). *Family in transition* (7th ed.). New York, NY: HarperCollins.

Slackman, M. (2006, August 6). The fine art of hiding what you mean to say. *The New York Times.*

Slackman, M. (2007, May 26). A quiet revolution in Algeria: Gains by women. *The New York Times.*

Slaves of New York. (2007, May 20). *The New York Times.*

Smith, C. S. (2002, May 5). Risking limbs for height and success in China. *The New York Times.*

Smith, C. S. (2005, April 30). Abduction, often violent, a Kyrgyz wedding rite. *The New York Times.*

Smith, D. (1997, May 1). Study looks at portrayal of women in media. *The New York Times.*

Smith, E. (2010, April 26). The Texas curriculum massacre. *Newsweek.*

Smith, S. L., & Choueiti, M. (2010). *Gender inequality in cinematic content? A look at females onscreen and behind-the-camera in top-grossing 2008 films.* Annenberg School for Communication and Journalism Report. http://annenberg.usc .edu. Accessed May 30, 2011.

Smith, W. (2002, April 5). Eroica trio offers beauty of more than one kind. *The Indianapolis Star.*

Snell, T. L. (2010). *Capital punishment, 2009— statistical tables* (NCJ231676). http://bjs.ojp .usdoj.gov/content/pub/pdf/cp09st.pdf. Accessed June 7, 2011.

Sniderman, P. M., & Tetlock, P. E. (1986). Symbolic racism: Problems of motive attribution in political analysis. *Social Forces, 42,* 129–150.

Snipp, C. M. (1986). American Indians and natural resource development. *American Journal of Economics and Sociology, 45,* 457–474.

Sokolove, M. (2004, November 28). Constructing a teen phenom. *The New York Times Magazine.*

Sokolove, M. (2005, February 13). Clang! *The New York Times Magazine.*

Soldo, B. J., & Agree, E. M. (1988). America's elderly. *Population Bulletin, 43,* 1–45.

Sontag, D. (1992, December 11). Across the U.S., immigrants find the land of resentment. *The New York Times.*

Sontag, S. (2004, May 23). Regarding the torture of others. *The New York Times Magazine.*

Sorkin, A. R. (2011, May 15). Rich and sort of rich. *The New York Times.*

Soukup, E. (2004, August 2). Till blog do us part. *Newsweek.*

South, S. J., & Lloyd, K. M. (1995). Spousal alternatives and marital dissolution. *American Sociological Review, 60,* 21–35.

Sports quiz: White men can't jump and other assumptions about sports and race (Assumption 6). (2007). Arlington, VA: American Anthropological Association. www.understandingrace.org/ lived/sports/index.html. Accessed May 30, 2009.

Springen, K. (2006, February 27). States: Time to stub out smoking. *Newsweek.*

Squadron, D. (2005, June 1). United we stand (in line). *The New York Times.*

Srikameswaran, A. (2002, July 23). Minorities lag in receiving transplants and heart surgeries. *Pittsburgh Post-Gazette.*

Stacey, J. (1991). Backward toward the postmodern family. In A. Wolfe (Ed.), *America at century's end.* Berkeley: University of California Press.

Staggenborg, S. (1998). *Gender, family, and social movements.* Thousand Oaks, CA: Pine Forge Press.

Stagnitti, M. N. (2005). *Antidepressant use in the U.S. civilian noninstitutionalized population, 2002* (Brief No. 77). Rockville, MD: Medical Expenditure Panel Survey. www.meps.ahrq .gov. Accessed June 3, 2005.

Staples, R. (1992). African American families. In J. M. Henslin (Ed.), *Marriage and family in a changing society.* New York, NY: Free Press.

Starbucks. (2011). *Starbucks company profile.* http:// assets.starbucks.com/assets/aboutuscompany profileq12011fina113111.pdf. Accessed May 26, 2011.

Stark, R., & Bainbridge, W. S. (1980). Networks of faith: Interpersonal bonds and recruitment in cults and sects. *American Journal of Sociology, 85,* 1376–1395.

Starr, P. (1982). *The social transformation of American medicine.* New York, NY: Basic Books.

Stein, J. (2011, March 10). Data mining: How companies now know everything about you. *Time.*

Stein, R. (2007, May 27). Critical care without consent. *The Washington Post.*

Steinhauer, J. (2005, May 29). When the Joneses wear jeans. *The New York Times.*

Steinmetz, S. K., Clavan, R., & Stein, K. F. (1990). *Marriage and family realities: Historical and contemporary perspectives.* New York, NY: Harper & Row.

Stephan, C. W., & Stephan, W. G. (1989). After intermarriage: Ethnic identity among mixed heritage Japanese-Americans and Hispanics. *Journal of Marriage and the Family, 51,* 507–519.

Stephens, W. N. (1963). *The family in cross-cultural perspective.* New York, NY: University Press of America.

Steuerle, C. E. (2007). *Crumbs for children?* Washington, DC: Urban Institute. www.urban.org/publications/901068.html. Accessed June 24, 2007.

Stevenson, B., & Wolfers, J. (2007). *Marriage and divorce: Changes and their driving forces* (Working Paper No. 12944). Cambridge, MA: National Bureau of Economic Research. http://bpp.wharton.upenn.edu/jwolfers/Papers/MarriageandDivorce(JEP).pdf. Accessed May 12, 2007.

Stewart, A. J., Copeland, A. P., Chester, A. L., Malley, J. E., & Barenbaum, N. B. (1997). *Separating together: How divorce transforms families.* New York, NY: Guilford Press.

St. George, D. (2007, May 13). Pushing the motherhood cause. *The Washington Post.*

Stille, A. (2001, December 15). Grounded by an income gap. *The New York Times.*

Stille, A. (2002, June 29). Textbook publishers learn to avoid messing with Texas. *The New York Times.*

Stinnett, N., & DeFrain, J. (1985). *Secrets of strong families.* Boston, MA: Little, Brown.

St. John, W. (2006, June 2). Sports, songs, and salvation on Faith Night at the stadium. *The New York Times.*

Stobbe, M. (2010, October 16). Study: Obesity weighs in at nearly 17% of health care costs. *The Indianapolis Star.*

Stockard, J., & O'Brien, R. M. (2002). Cohort effects on suicide rates: International variation. *American Sociological Review, 67,* 854–872.

Stokes, R., & Hewitt, J. P. (1976). Aligning actions. *American Sociological Review, 41,* 837–849.

Stolberg, S. G. (1998, April 5). Live and let die over transplants. *The New York Times.*

Stolberg, S. G. (2004, March 21). When spin spins out of control. *The New York Times.*

Stolberg, S. G. (2010, April 15). Obama widens medical rights for same-sex partners. *The New York Times.*

Stolberg, S. G., & Connelly, M. (2009, April 29). Obama nudging views on race, a survey finds. *The New York Times.*

Stone, G. P. (1981). Appearance and the self: A slightly revised version. In G. P. Stone & H. A. Farberman (Eds.), *Social psychology through symbolic interaction.* New York, NY: Wiley.

Straus, M. A. (1977). A sociological perspective on the prevention and treatment of wife beating. In M. Roy (Ed.), *Battered women.* New York, NY: Van Nostrand Reinhold.

Straus, M. A., & Gelles, R. J. (1990). How violent are American families? Estimates from the National Family Violence Resurvey and other studies. In M. A. Straus & R. J. Gelles (Eds.), *Physical violence in American families.* New Brunswick, NJ: Transaction.

Strom, S. (2005, January 13). U.S. charity overwhelmed by disaster aid. *The New York Times.*

Strom, S., & Gay, M. (2010, May 21). Pay-what-you-want has patrons perplexed. *The New York Times.*

Strube, M. J., & Barbour, L. S. (1983). The decision to leave an abusive relationship: Economic dependence and psychological commitment. *Journal of Marriage and the Family, 45,* 785–793.

Stryker, J. (1980). *Symbolic interactionism.* Menlo Park, CA: Benjamin/Cummings.

Stryker, J. (1997, July 13). The age of innocence isn't what it once was. *The New York Times.*

Student performance, poverty link seen again. (2007, June 7). *Banner Graphic.*

Study finds increase in weapons use. (2000, November 30). *The New York Times.*

Suarez, Z. (1998). The Cuban-American family. In C. H. Mindel, R. W. Habenstein, & R. Wright (Eds.), *Ethnic families in America: Patterns and variations.* Upper Saddle River, NJ: Prentice Hall.

Sudarkasa, N. (2001). Interpreting the African heritage in Afro-American family organization. In S. Ferguson (Ed.), *Shifting the center: Understanding contemporary families.* Mountain View, CA: Mayfield.

Sudnow, D. (1965). Normal crimes: Sociological features of the penal code in a public defender's office. *Social Problems, 12,* 255–264.

Sullivan, A. (2011, June 13). The Sharia myth sweeps America. *USA Today.*

Sullivan, R. (2006, June 25). A slow-road movement. *The New York Times Magazine.*

Sullivan, T. A., Warren, E., & Westbrook, J. L. (2000). *The fragile middle class: Americans in debt.* New Haven, CT: Yale University Press.

Sulzberger, A. G. (2011, February 11). Hospitals shift smoking bans to smoker bans. *The New York Times.*

Sussman, D. (2010, February 28). A question of what to ask. *The New York Times.*

Sutherland, E., & Cressey, D. (1955). *Criminology.* Philadelphia, PA: Lippincott.

Swanson, B. (2006). *Is thin really in? New subzero clothing line fashion faux pas.* East Lansing, MI: Lansing Lowdown. www.lansinglowdown .com/index.php/article/402. Accessed May 16, 2009.

Swanson, G. (1992). Doing things together: On some basic forms of agency and structuring in collective action and on some explanations for them. *Social Psychology Quarterly, 55,* 94–117.

Swarns, R. L. (2001, April 20). Drug makers drop South Africa suit over AIDS medicines. *The New York Times.*

Swarns, R. L. (2004, October 24). Hispanics resist racial grouping by census. *The New York Times.*

Swarns, R. L. (2006, March 29). Republican split on immigration reflects nation's struggle. *The New York Times.*

Swarns, R. L. (2008a, September 2). Bipartisan calls for new federal poverty measure. *The New York Times.*

Swarns, R. L. (2008b, August 25). Blacks debate civil rights risk in Obama's rise. *The New York Times.*

Swarns, R. (2008c, September 16). Capitol strives to define "homeless." *The New York Times.*

Swartz, M. (2007, June 10). Shop stewards on Fantasy Island? *The New York Times Magazine.*

Swinburn, B. A., Sacks, G., Hall, K. D., McPherson, K., Finegood, D. T., Moodie, M. L., & Gortmaker, S. L. (2011). The global obesity pandemic: Shaped by global drivers and local environments. *The Lancet, 378,* 804–814.

Sykes, G., & Matza, D. (1957). Techniques of neutralization: A theory of delinquency. *American Sociological Review, 22,* 664–670.

Tabuchi, H. (2011, January 3). Despite shortage, Japan keeps a high wall for foreign labor. *The New York Times.*

Takayama, H. (2003, January 13). The Okinawa way. *Newsweek.*

Talbot, M. (2000a, February 27). A mighty fortress. *The New York Times Magazine.*

Talbot, M. (2000b, January 9). The placebo prescription. *The New York Times Magazine.*

Talbot, M. (2010, October 25). Pride and prejudice. *The New Yorker.*

Tannen, D. (1990). *You just don't understand: Women and men in conversation.* New York, NY: Ballantine.

Tanner, L. (2007, February 11). Youth suicides rise after years of decline. *The Indianapolis Star.*

Tapia, A. T. (1995, December). Christian faith in the age of Prozac. *Harper's Magazine.*

Tarnished gold. (1999, October). *Harper's.*

Tarrow, S. (1994). *Power in movement.* New York, NY: Cambridge University Press.

Taub, E. A. (2001, November 22). Cell yell: Thanks for (not) sharing. *The New York Times.*

Tauber, M. A. (1979). Parental socialization techniques and sex differences in children's play. *Child Development, 50,* 225–234.

Tavernise, S. (2011a, August 25). New numbers, and geography for gay couples. *The New York Times.*

Tavernise, S. (2011b, April 20). Ohio county losing its young to painkillers' grip. *The New York Times.*

Tavernise, S. (2011c, August 16). Parents skip marriage for cohabitation, report finds. *The New York Times.*

Tavernise, S. (2011d, April 21). Youth, mobility, and poverty help drive cellphone-only status. *The New York Times.*

Tavernise, S., & Gebeloff, R. (2010, December 15). Immigrants make paths to surburbia, not cities. *The New York Times.*

Tavris, C., & Offir, C. (1984). *The longest war: Sex differences in perspective.* New York, NY: Harcourt Brace Jovanovich.

Taylor, S. J., & Bogdan, R. (1980). Defending illusions: The institution's struggle for survival. *Human Organization, 39,* 209–218.

Teachman, J. D. (1991). Contributions to children by divorced fathers. *Social Problems, 38,* 358–371.

Tejada-Vera, B., & Sutton, P. D. (2009). Births, marriages, divorces, and deaths: Provisional data for July 2008. *National Vital Statistics Reports, 57,* 13. www.cdc.gov/nchs/data/nvsr/nvsr57/ nvsr57_13.htm. Accessed May 18, 2009.

Telles, E. E., & Murguia, E. (1990). Phenotypic discrimination and income differences among Mexican Americans. *Social Science Quarterly, 71,* 682–696.

Terry, K. (2004). *The nature and scope of the problems of sexual abuse of minors by priests and deacons.* New York, NY: John Jay College of Criminal Justice. www.bishop-accountability .org/reports/2004_02_27_JohnJay/index .html#credits. Accessed May 21, 2009.

This American Life. (2011a). *The invention of money.* www.thisamericanlife.org/radio-archives/ episode/423/the-invention-of-money. Accessed May 19, 2011.

This American Life. (2011b). *The psychopath test.* www .thisamericanlife.org/radio-archives/episode/436/ the-psychopath-test. Accessed June 8, 2011.

Thoits, P. (1985). Self-labeling process in mental illness: The role of emotional deviance. *American Journal of Sociology, 91,* 221–249.

Thomas, J. (2010, June 14). Mixing makes for matching. *The Indianapolis Star.*

Thompson, G. (2003, February 13). Behind roses' beauty, poor and ill workers. *The New York Times.*

Thompson, G. (2009, March 15). Where education and assimilation collide. *The New York Times.*

Thompson, T. L., & Zerbinos, E. (1995). Gender roles in animated cartoons: Has the picture changed in 20 years? *Sex Roles, 32,* 651–673.

Thomson, D. S. (2000). The Sapir-Whorf hypothesis: Worlds shaped by words. In J. Spradley & D. W. McCurdy (Eds.), *Conformity and conflict.* Boston, MA: Allyn & Bacon.

Thornton, M. (1997). Strategies of racial socialization among black parents: Mainstreaming, minority, and cultural messages. In R. Taylor, J. Jackson, & L. Chatters (Eds.), *Family life in black America.* Thousand Oaks, CA: Sage.

Tietz, J. (2006, April 20). The killing factory. *Rolling Stone.*

Tilly, C. (1978). *From mobilization to revolution.* Reading, MA: Addison-Wesley.

Timms, E., & McGonigle, S. (1992, April 5). Psychological warfare. *The Indianapolis Star.*

Tjaden, P., & Thoennes, N. (2000). *Extent, nature, and consequences of intimate partner violence* (NCJ 181867). Washington, DC: Bureau of Justice Statistics. www.ncjrs.gov/pdffiles1/nij/181867.pdf. Accessed September 5, 2009.

Tobin, J. J., Wu, D. Y. H., & Davidson, D. H. (1989). *Preschool in three cultures: Japan, China and the United States.* New Haven, CT: Yale University Press.

Tönnies, F. (1957). *Community and society* [Gemeinschaft und Gesellschaft] (C. P. Loomis, Ed.). East Lansing: Michigan State University Press. (Original work published 1887)

Towell, L. (2007, November 18). Patients without borders. *The New York Times Magazine.*

Toymakers study troops, and vice versa. (2003, March 30). *The New York Times.*

Triandis, H. C., McCusker, C., & Hui, C. H. (1990). Multimethod probes of individualism and collectivism. *Journal of Personality and Social Psychology, 59,* 1006–1020.

Trotsky, L. (1959). *The history of the Russian Revolution* (F. W. Dupee, Ed.). Garden City, NY: Doubleday. (Original work published 1930)

Trotter, R. T., & Chavira, J. A. (1997). *Curanderismo: Mexican American folk healing.* Athens: University of Georgia Press.

Truman, M., & Rand, J. (2010). *Criminal victimization, 2009* (NCJ 231327). U.S. Bureau of Justice Statistics. http://bjs.ojp.usdoj.gov/content/pub/pdf/cv09.pdf. Accessed June 20, 2011.

Trunk, P. (2007, July 16). What Gen Y really wants. *Time.*

Tsushima, T., & Gecas, V. (2001). Role taking and socialization in single-parent families. *Journal of Family Issues, 22,* 267–288.

Tugend, A. (2006, April 15). Pining for the kickback weekend. *The New York Times.*

Tumin, M. (1953). Some principles of stratification: A critical analysis. *American Sociological Review, 18,* 387–393.

Turkheimer, E., Haley, A., Waldron, M., D'Onofrio, B., & Gottesman, I. I. (2003). Socioeconomic status modifies heritability of IQ in young children. *Psychological Science, 14,* 623–628.

Turkle, S. (2011). *Alone together: Why we expect more from technology and less from each other.* New York, NY: Basic Books.

Turner, E. H., Matthews, A. M., Linardatos, E., Tell, R. A., & Rosenthal, R. (2008). Selective publication of antidepressant trials and its influence on apparent efficacy. *The New England Journal of Medicine, 358,* 252–260.

Turner, J. H. (1972). *Patterns of social organization.* New York, NY: McGraw-Hill.

Turner, R. W., & Killian, L. M. (1987). *Collective behavior.* Englewood Cliffs, NJ: Prentice Hall.

Tyagi, A. W. (2004, March 22). Why women have to work. *Time.*

Tyre, P. (2006, January 30). The trouble with boys. *Newsweek.*

Ubel, P., Zell, M. M., Miller, D. L., Fischer, G. S., Peters-Stefani, D., & Arnold, R. M. (1995). Elevator talk: Observational study of inappropriate comments in a public space. *American Journal of Medicine, 99,* 190–194.

Ubiñas, L. A., & Gabrieli, C. (2011, August 23). Shortchanged by the bell. *The New York Times.*

Uchitelle, L. (2005, January 13). College degree still pays, but it's leveling off. *The New York Times.*

Uchitelle, L. (2006, November 27). Very rich are leaving the merely rich behind. *The New York Times.*

Uchitelle, L. (2008, April 20). The wage that meant middle class. *The New York Times.*

Uchitelle, L. (2010, July 7). A new generation, an elusive American dream. *The New York Times.*

Uggen, C., & Blackstone, A. (2004). Sexual harassment as a gendered expression of power. *American Sociological Review, 69,* 64–92.

UNAIDS. (2008). *2008 report on the global AIDS epidemic.* Geneva, Switzerland: Author. http://data.unaids.org/pub/GlobalReport/2008/JC1511_GR08_ExecutiveSummary_en.pdf. Accessed September 5, 2009.

UNICEF. (2007). *The state of the world's children 2007.* Geneva, Switzerland: Author. www.unicef.org/sowc07/statistics/statistics.php. Accessed September 24, 2007.

UNICEF. (2009). *The state of the world's children 2009.* Geneva, Switzerland: Author. www.unicef.org/sowc09/docs/SOWC09-FullReport-EN.pdf. Accessed September 5, 2009.

UNICEF. (2011). *Child protection from violence, exploitation, and abuse.* www.unicef.org/protection/index_childlabour.html. Accessed July 1, 2011.

United Nations. (2007). *Situations of concern.* Geneva, Switzerland: Office of the Special Representative of the Secretary-General for Children and Armed Conflict. www.un.org/children/conflict/english/conflicts2.html. Accessed September 5, 2009.

United Nations. (2011). *World population prospects.* Department of Economic and Social Affairs. http://esa.un.org/unpd/wpp/index.htm. Accessed June 23, 2011.

United Nations Population Division. (2003). *World population prospects: The 2002 revision.* Geneva, Switzerland: Author. www.un.org/esa/population/publications/wpp2002/wpp2002-highlightsrev1.pdf. Accessed June 26, 2003.

United Nations Population Division. (2005). *World population prospects: The 2004 revision population database.* Geneva, Switzerland: Author. http://esa.un.org/unpp/index.asp?panel=2. Accessed July 15, 2005.

United Nations Population Division. (2008). *World urbanization prospects: The 2007 revision.* Geneva, Switzerland: Author. http://esa.un.org/unup/. Accessed June 15, 2009.

United States Bureau of Justice Statistics. (2001). *The sexual victimization of college women* [Press release]. Washington, DC: Author. www.ojp.usdoj.gov/bjs/pub/press/svcw.pr. Accessed September 5, 2009.

United States Bureau of Justice Statistics. (2009). *Sourcebook of criminal justice statistics online.* www.albany.edu/sourcebook/. Accessed June 30, 2010.

United States Bureau of Justice Statistics. (2010). *National crime victimization survey: Violent crime trends, 1973–2009.* http://bjs.ojp.usdoj.gov/content/glance/tables/viortrdtab.cfm. Accessed June 20, 2011.

United States Bureau of Justice Statistics. (2011). *Homicide trends in the U.S.* http://bjs.ojp.usdoj.gov/content/homicide/relationship/cfm. Accessed May 24, 2011.

United States Bureau of Labor Statistics. (2007). *Consumer expenditures in 2005* (Report No. 998). Washington, DC: Author. www.bls.gov/cex/csxann05.pdf. Accessed September 5, 2009.

United States Bureau of Labor Statistics. (2008). *Women in the labor force: A databook 2008.* Washington, DC: Author. www.bls.gov/cps/wlf-databook2008.htm. Accessed September 5, 2009.

United States Bureau of Labor Statistics. (2009). Ranks of discouraged workers and others marginally attached to the labor force rise during recession. *Issues in Labor Statistics,* Summary 09-04. www.bls.gov/opub/ils/pdf/opbils74.pdf. Washington, DC: Author. Accessed September 5, 2009.

United States Bureau of Labor Statistics. (2010a). *American time use survey—2009 results* (USDL-10-0855). www.bls.gov/news.release/atus.nr0.htm. Accessed June 21, 2011.

United States Bureau of Labor Statistics. (2010b). *May 2010 national occupational employment and wage estimates—United States.* www.bls.gov/oes/current/oes_nat.htm#00-0000. Accessed June 14, 2011.

United States Bureau of Labor Statistics. (2010c). *Median weekly earnings of full-time and salary workers by detailed occupation and sex—Table 39.* ftp://ftp.bls.gov/pub/special.requests/lf/aat39.txt. Accessed June 15, 2011.

United States Bureau of Labor Statistics. (2010d). *Occupations with the largest job growth—Table 14.* www.bls.gov/emp/ep_table_104.htm. Accessed June 13, 2011.

United States Bureau of Labor Statistics. (2010e). *Women in the labor force: A databook.* www.bls.gov/cps/wlf-databook-2010.pdf. Accessed June 22, 2011.

United States Bureau of Labor Statistics. (2010f). *Workplace injuries and illnesses—2009.*

www.bls.gov/news.release/osh.nr0.htm. Accessed June 8, 2011.

United States Bureau of Labor Statistics. (2011a). *The employment situation: May 2011* (USDL-11-10809). www.bls.gov/news.release/pdf/empsit.pdf. Accessed June 16, 2011.

United States Bureau of Labor Statistics. (2011b). *Extended mass layoffs—first quarter 2011* (USDL-11-0678). www.bls.gov/news.release/pdf/mslo.pdf. Accessed June 15, 2011.

United States Bureau of Labor Statistics. (2011c). *Revisions of the 2009 census of fatal occupational injuries (CFOI) counts.* www.bls.gov/iif/oshwc/cfoi/cfoi_revised09.pdf. Accessed June 8, 2011.

United States Bureau of the Census. (1995). *Statistical abstract of the United States.* Washington, DC: Author. www.census.gov/prod/1/gen/95statab/labor.pdf. Accessed September 5, 2007.

United States Bureau of the Census. (2000). *Statistical abstract of the United States.* Washington, DC: Government Printing Office.

United States Bureau of the Census. (2002). *Statistical abstract of the United States.* Washington, DC: Government Printing Office.

United States Bureau of the Census. (2004). *Statistical abstract of the United States.* Washington, DC: Author. www.census.gov/prod/www/statistical-abstract-04.html. Accessed June 15, 2005.

United States Bureau of the Census. (2005). *Current population survey (CPS): Definitions and explanations.* Washington, DC: Author. www.census.gov/population/www/cps/cpsdef.html. Accessed September 21, 2005.

United States Bureau of the Census. (2006). *Special edition: 300 million.* Washington, DC: Author. www.census.gov/Press-Release/www/releases/archives/facts_for_features_special_editions/007276.htm. Accessed July 12, 2007.

United States Bureau of the Census. (2007). *Statistical abstract of the United States.* Washington, DC: Author. www.census.gov/prod/2006pub/07statab/pop.pdf. Accessed March 29, 2007.

United States Bureau of the Census. (2009). *Statistical abstract of the United States.* Washington, DC: Author. www.census.gov/compendia/statab/2009edition.html. Accessed March 27, 2009.

United States Bureau of the Census. (2010). *America's families and living arrangements: 2010. Table C3.* www.census.gov/populaton/www/socdemo/hh-fam/cps2010.html. Accessed May 24, 2011.

United States Bureau of the Census. (2011a). *International data base.* www.census.gov/ipc/www/idb. Accessed June 23, 2011.

United States Bureau of the Census. (2011b). *Statistical abstract of the United States.* Washington, DC: Author. www.census.gov/compendia/statab/2011edition.html. Accessed July 4, 2011.

United States Commission on Human Rights. (1992). Indian tribes: A continuing quest for survival. In P. S. Rothenberg (Ed.), *Race, class and gender in the United States.* New York, NY: St. Martin's Press.

United States Conference of Catholic Bishops. (2011). *The causes and context of sexual abuse of minors by Catholic priests in the United States, 1950–2010.* www.usccb.org/mr/causes-and-context-of-sexual-abuse-of-minors-by-catholic-priests-in-the-united-states-1950-2010.pdf. Accessed June 6, 2011.

United States Conference of Mayors. (2010). *Hunger and homelessness survey: A status report on hunger and homelessness in America's cities.* www.usmayors.org/pressreleases/uploads/2010_Hunger-Homelessness_Report-final_Dec_21_2010.pdf. Accessed April 15, 2011.

United States Department of Agriculture. (2001, June 17). *USDA estimates child rearing costs.* Washington, DC: Author.

United States Department of Defense. (2008). *FY07 report on sexual assault in the military.* Washington, DC: Author. www.sapr.mil/contents/references/2007%20Annual%20Report.pdf. Accessed September 5, 2009.

United States Department of Health and Human Services. (2006). *Sustaining state programs for tobacco control: Data highlights 2006.* www.cdc.gov/tobacco/data_statistics/state_data/data_highlights/2006/pdfs/dataHighlights06rev.pdf. Accessed September 5, 2009.

United States Department of Justice. (2008). *Criminal victimization in the United States, 2006 statistical tables* (Table 27) (NCJ 223436). Washington, DC: Author. www.ojp.usdoj.gov/bjs/pub/pdf/cvus06.pdf. Accessed September 5, 2009.

United States Department of Justice. (2009). *UBS enters into deferred prosecution agreement.* Washington, DC: Author. www.usdoj.gov/opa/pr/2009/February/09-tax-136.html. Accessed May 21, 2009.

United States Department of Labor. (2004). *The Americans with Disabilities Act of 1990.* Washington, DC: Author. www.dol.gov. Accessed December 14, 2004.

United States Department of Labor. (2007). *Family and Medical Leave Act regulations: A report on the Department of Labor's request for information.* Washington, DC: Author. www.dol.gov/ESA/WHD/FMLA2007Report/Chapter11.pdf. Accessed July 9, 2007.

United States Department of Labor. (2011). *Facts on Executive Order 11246—Affirmative action.* Office of Federal Contract Compliance Programs. www.dol.gov/OFCCP/regs/compliance/aa.htm. Accessed June 17, 2011.

United States Department of State. (2010). *Trafficking in persons report 2010.* www.state.gov/g/tip/rls/tiprpt/2010/. Accessed June 13, 2011.

United States Network for Global Economic Justice. (2000). *False profits: Who wins, who loses when the IMF, World Bank, and WTO come to town.* Washington, DC: Author. www.50years.org/april16/booklet.html. Accessed June 22, 2000.

United States Sentencing Commission. (2008). *U.S. Sentencing Commission 2008 Annual Report.* Washington, DC: Author. www.ussc.gov/ANNRPT/2008/Chap5_08.pdf. Accessed May 22, 2009.

United States Sentencing Commission. (2009). *Sourcebook of federal sentencing statistics.* www.ussc.gov/ANNRPT/2009/SBTOC09.htm. Accessed July 2, 2010.

Upton, R. L. (2010). "Fat eggs": Gender and fertility as important factors in HIV/AIDS prevention in Botswana. *Gender & Development, 18,* 515–524.

Upton, R. L. (in press). *The next one changes everything.* Ann Arbor: University of Michigan Press.

Urbina, I. (2006, November 5). Sites invite online mourning, but don't speak ill of the dead. *The New York Times.*

Urbina, I. (2009, February 25). In push to end death penalty, some states cite cost-cutting. *The New York Times.*

U.S. English. (2011). *Fact sheets: States with official English.* www.us-english.org/view/302. Accessed May 26, 2011.

Utne, L. (2006, March/April). Soldiers for peace. *Utne Reader.*

Van Ausdale, D., & Feagin, J. R. (2001). *The first R: How children learn race and racism.* Lanham, MD: Rowman & Littlefield.

van den Haag, E. (1975). *Punishing criminals: Concerning a very old and painful question.* New York, NY: Basic Books.

Vanek, J. (1980). Work, leisure and family roles: Farm households in the United States: 1920–1955. *Journal of Family History, 5,* 422–431.

Van Ryn, M., & Burke, J. (2000). The effect of patient race and socio-economic status on physicians' perceptions of patients. *Social Science and Medicine, 50,* 813–820.

Vaughan, D. (1986). *Uncoupling.* New York, NY: Vintage Books.

Vedantam, S. (2005, June 26). Patients' diversity is often discounted. *The Washington Post.*

Viets, E. (1992, November 29). Give a whistle, he'll love it. *St. Louis Post-Dispatch.*

Virning, B. A. (2008). Associating insurance status with cancer stage at diagnosis. *The Lancet Oncology, 9,* 189–191.

Vladimir Putin on raising Russia's birth rate. (2006). *Population and Development Review, 32,* 385–389.

Vojdik, V. K. (2002). Gender outlaws: Challenging masculinity in traditionally male institutions. *Berkeley Women's Law Journal, 17,* 68–122.

Voyandoff, P. (1990). Economic distress and family relations: A review of the eighties. *Journal of Marriage and Family, 52,* 1099–1115.

Wagner, D. G., Ford, R. S., & Ford, T. W. (1986). Can gender inequalities be reduced? *American Sociological Review, 51,* 47–61.

Wahl, O. (1999). *Telling is risky business.* New Brunswick, NJ: Rutgers University Press.

Waite, L. J., & Gallagher, M. (2000). *The case for marriage: Why married people are happier, healthier, and better off financially.* New York, NY: Doubleday.

Waldman, A. (2003, March 28). Broken taboos doom lovers in an Indian village. *The New York Times.*

Waldman, A. (2005, May 8). Sri Lankan maids' high price for foreign jobs. *The New York Times.*

Walker, R. (2010, July 2). Having a blast. *The New York Times Magazine.*

Wal-Mart. (2011). *About us.* http://walmartstores/AboutUs/. Accessed May 26, 2011.

Walton, J. (1990). *Sociology and critical inquiry.* Belmont, CA: Wadsworth.

Wang, W., & Morin, R. (2009). *Home for the holidays . . . and every other day.* Pew Research Center. http://pewsocialtrends.org/2009/11/24/home-for-the-holidays-and-every-other-day/. Accessed June 6, 2011.

Wansink, B. (2006). *Mindless eating: Why we eat more than we think.* New York, NY: Bantam.

Ward, L. M., & Friedman, K. (2006). Using TV as a guide: Associations between television viewing and adolescents' sexual attitudes and behavior. *Journal of Research on Adolescence, 16,* 133–156.

Warner, J. (2010, June 20). Dysregulation nation. *The New York Times.*

Warren, E., & Tyagi, A. W. (2007). Why middle-class mothers and fathers are going broke. In A. S. Skolnick & J. H. Skolnick (Eds.), *Family in transition.* Boston, MA: Allyn & Bacon.

Warshaw, R. (1988). *I never called it rape.* New York, NY: Harper & Row.

Wartik, N. (2003, September 9). Muting the obsessions over perceived flaws. *The New York Times.*

Washington, H. A. (2006). *Medical apartheid: The dark history of medical experimentation on black Americans from Colonial times to the present.* New York, NY: Doubleday.

Washington, J. (2010). Black or biracial? Census forces a choice for some. *The Grio.* www.thegrio.com/news/black-or-biracial-census-forces-a-choice-for-some.php. Accessed May 27, 2010.

Waters, M. C. (2008). Optional ethnicities: For Whites only? In D. Newman & J. O'Brien (Eds.), *Sociology: Exploring the architecture of everyday life (Readings).* Thousand Oaks, CA: Pine Forge Press.

Watson, C. M., Quatman, T., & Edler, E. (2002). Career aspirations of adolescent girls: Effects of achievement level, grade, and single-sex school environment. *Sex Roles, 46,* 323–335.

Watson, I. (2005, June 13). As elections near, Iranian women stage protest. *National Public Radio.* www.npr.org/templates/story/story.php?storyID=4700486. Accessed June 13, 2005.

Wattenberg, E. (1986). The fate of baby boomers and their children. *Social Work, 31,* 20–28.

Watts, D. J. (2007, April 15). Is Justin Timberlake a product of cumulative advantage? *The New York Times Magazine.*

Watzlawick, P. (1976). *How real is real?* Garden City, NY: Doubleday.

Watzlawick, P. (1984). Self-fulfilling prophecies. In P. Watzlawick (Ed.), *The invented reality: How do we know what we believe we know? Contributions to constructivism.* New York, NY: Norton.

Weber, M. (1946). Bureaucracy. In H. H. Gerth & C. W. Mills (Eds.), *From Max Weber: Essays in sociology.* New York, NY: Oxford University Press.

Weber, M. (1947). *The theory of social and economic organization.* New York, NY: Free Press.

Weber, M. (1970). *From Max Weber: Essays in sociology* (H. H. Gerth & C. W. Mills, Eds.). New York, NY: Oxford University Press.

Weber, M. (1977). *The Protestant ethic and the spirit of capitalism.* New York, NY: Macmillan. (Original work published 1904)

Weber, M. (1978). *Economy and society* (G. Roth & C. Wittich, Trans.). Berkeley: University of California Press. (Original work published 1921)

Weeks, J. (1995). *Population: An introduction to concepts and issues* (Rev. 5th ed.). Belmont, CA: Wadsworth.

Weeks, L. (2011, June 23). The end of gender? *National Public Radio.* www.npr.org/2011/06/24/137342682/the-end-of-gender?sc=17&f=1001. Accessed June 24, 2011.

Wehrfritz, G., & Cochrane, J. (2005, January 17). Charity and chaos. *Newsweek.*

Weil, E. (2006, September 24). What if it's (sort of) a boy and (sort of) a girl? *The New York Times Magazine.*

Weil, E. (2007, June 3). When should a kid start kindergarten? *The New York Times Magazine.*

Weinberg, D. H. (2007, July/August). Earnings by gender: Evidence from Census 2000. *Monthly Labor Review,* pp. 26–34.

Weismantel, M. (2005). White. In D. Kulick & A. Meneley (Eds.), *Fat: The anthropology of an obsession.* New York, NY: Tarcher/Penguin.

Weitzman, L., Eifler, D., Hodada, E., & Ross, C. (1972). Sex-role socialization in picture books for preschool children. *American Journal of Sociology, 77,* 1125–1150.

Welch, H. G., Schwartz, L., & Woloshin, S. (2007, January 2). What's making us sick is an epidemic of diagnoses. *The New York Times.*

Weller, C. E., & Logan, A. (2008). *America's middle class still losing ground.* Washington, DC: Center for American Progress. www.americanprogress.org/issues/2008/07/pdf/middleclasssqueeze.pdf. Accessed September 5, 2009.

Wells, M. (2011, August 11). Mullin left indelible mark on Pacers over 3 seasons. *The Indianapolis Star.*

West, H. C. (2010). *Prison inmates at midyear 2009—statistical tables* (NCJ 230113). U.S. Bureau of Justice Statistics. http://bjs.ojp.usdoj.gov/content/pub/pdf/pim09st.pdf. Accessed June 30, 2010

Whalen, C. K., & Henker, B. (1977). The pitfalls of politicization: A response to Conrad's "The discovery of hyperkinesis: Notes on the medicalization of deviance." *Social Problems, 24,* 590–595.

What is coltan? (2002, January 21). *ABCNews.com.* http://abcnews.go.com/Nightline/story?id=128631&page=1. Accessed September 5, 2009.

White, J. E. (1997, May 5). Multiracialism: The melding of America. *Time.*

White, L., & Brinkerhoff, D. (1981). The sexual division of labor: Evidence from childhood. *Social Forces, 60,* 170–181.

The White House Blog. (2010). *A look behind the scenes of presidential advance.* www.whitehouse.gov/blog/2010/01/21/a-look-behind-scenes-presidential-advance. Accessed June 1, 2011.

Whorf, B. (1956). *Language, thought and reality.* Cambridge, MA: MIT Press.

Whyte, M. K. (1990). *Dating, mating and marriage.* New York, NY: Aldine de Gruyter.

Whyte, W. H. (1956). *The organization man.* Garden City, NY: Doubleday.

Wilcox, W. B. (2000). Conservative Protestant child discipline: The case of parental yelling. *Social Forces, 79,* 856–891.

Wildman, S. M., & Davis, A. D. (2002). Making systems of privilege visible. In P. S. Rothenberg (Ed.), *White privilege: Essential readings on the other side of racism.* New York, NY: Worth.

Wilford, J. N. (2007, September 19). Languages die, but not their last words. *The New York Times.*

Wilgoren, J. (2003, January 12). Governor assails system's errors as he empties Illinois death row. *The New York Times.*

Wilkinson, L. C., & Marrett, C. B. (1985). *Gender influences in classroom interaction.* Orlando, FL: Academic Press.

Williams, A. (2006, April 2). Before spring break, the anorexic challenge. *The New York Times.*

Williams, A. (2009, June 22). At meetings, it's mind your BlackBerry or mind your manners. *The New York Times.*

Williams, C. L. (2006). *Inside toyland: Working, shopping, and social inequality.* Berkeley: University of California Press.

Williams, W. L. (1992). *The spirit and the flesh: Sexual diversity in American Indian culture.* Boston, MA: Beacon Press.

Williamson, R. C. (1984). A partial replication of the Kohn-Gecas-Nye thesis in a German sample. *Journal of Marriage and the Family, 46,* 971–979.

Wilmer, F. (2002). *The social construction of man, the state, and war: Identity, conflict, and violence in former Yugoslavia.* New York, NY: Routledge.

Wilson, D. (2009a, August 30). Race, ethnicity, and care. *The New York Times.*

Wilson, D. (2009b, June 12). Senate approves tight regulation over cigarettes. *The New York Times.*

Wilson, D. (2010, November 14). Cigarette giants in a global fight on tighter rules. *The New York Times.*

Wilson, J. L., Peebles, R., Hardy, K. K., & Litt, I. F. (2006). Surfing for thinness: A pilot study of pro-eating disorder website usage in adolescents with eating disorders. *Pediatrics, 118,* 1635–1643.

Wilson, M., & Baker, A. (2010, October 8). Lured into a trap, then tortured for being gay. *The New York Times.*

Wilson, W. J. (1980). *The declining significance of race.* Chicago, IL: University of Chicago Press.

Winerip, M. (2011, August 1). Pennsylvania joins the list of states facing a school cheating scandal. *The New York Times.*

Wines, M. (2006, August 24). Africa adds to miserable ranks of child workers. *The New York Times.*

Winter, G. (2002, May 19). Workers say Coke sold old soda. *The New York Times.*

Wise, T. (2002). Membership has its privileges: Thoughts on acknowledging and challenging whiteness. In P. S. Rothenberg (Ed.), *White privilege: Essential readings on the other side of racism.* New York, NY: Worth.

Witt, S. (2005). How television shapes children's gender roles. In R. H. Lauer & J. C. Lauer (Eds.), *Sociology: Windows on society.* Los Angeles, CA: Roxbury.

Wolf, G. (2010, May 2). The data-driven life. *The New York Times Magazine.*

Wolfe, A. (1991). *America at century's end.* Berkeley: University of California Press.

Women Physicians Congress. (2008). *Statistics and history.* Chicago, IL: Author. www.ama-assn.org/ama/pub/about-ama/our-people/member-groups-sections/women-physicians-congress/statistics-history.shtml. Accessed June 5, 2009.

The Women's Media Center. (2011). *Statistics summary.* http://womensmediacenter.com/index.php?option=com_contents&view=article&id=157&Itemid=167. Accessed April 12, 2011.

The Women's Memorial. (2011). *Statistics on women in the military.* www.womensmemorial.org/PDFs/StatsonWIM.pdf. Accessed June 20, 2011.

Wood, N. (2005, February 6). Eight nations agree on plan to lift status of Gypsies. *The New York Times.*

Word, C. O., Zanna, M. P., & Cooper, J. (1974). The nonverbal mediation of self-fulfilling prophecies in interracial interaction. *Journal of Experimental Social Psychology, 10,* 109–120.

Workers of the world. (1998, January 30). *Economist.*

World Bank. (2006). *Global monitoring report 2006.* Washington, DC: Author. http://web.world bank.org. Accessed August 9, 2007.

World Bank. (2011). *World development indicators—Table 1.1.* www.data.worldbank.org/ data-catalog/world-development-indicators. Accessed June 14, 2011.

World Wildlife Fund. (2010). *Living planet report.* http://wwf.cn/newsroom/reports/living_planet_ report-2010.cfm. Accessed June 24, 2011.

Worsnop, R. (1996). Getting into college. *CQ Researcher, 6,* 169–192.

Wortham, J. (2010, May 14). Everyone is using cell-phones, but not so many are talking. *The New York Times.*

Worthen, M. (2009, January 11). Who would Jesus smack down? *The New York Times Magazine.*

Worthen, M. (2010, November 14). Housewives of God. *The New York Times Magazine.*

Wright, E. O. (1976). Class boundaries in advanced capitalist societies. *New Left Review, 98,* 3–41.

Wright, E. O., Costello, C., Hachen, D., & Sprague, J. (1982). The American class structure. *American Sociological Review, 47,* 709–726.

Wright, E. O., & Perrone, L. (1977). Marxist class categories and income inequality. *American Sociological Review, 42,* 32–55.

Wright, J. D., & Wright, S. R. (1976). Social class and parental values for children: A partial replication and extension of the Kohn thesis. *American Sociological Review, 41,* 527–537.

Wrong, D. (1988). *Power: Its forms, bases, and uses.* Chicago, IL: University of Chicago Press.

Wu, F. H. (2002). *Yellow. Race in America beyond black and white.* New York, NY: Basic Books.

WuDunn, S. (1996a, January 23). In Japan, even toddlers feel the pressure to excel. *The New York Times.*

WuDunn, S. (1996b, September 11). A taboo creates a land of Romeos and Juliets. *The New York Times.*

WuDunn, S. (1997, January 14). Korean women still feel demands to bear a son. *The New York Times.*

Wuthnow, R. (1994). *Sharing the journey.* New York, NY: Free Press.

Wynia, M. K., VanGeest, J. B., Cummins, D. S., & Wilson, I. B. (2003). Do physicians not offer useful services because of coverage restrictions? *Health Affairs, 22,* 190–198.

Xiao, H. (2000). Class, gender, and parental values in the 1990s. *Gender & Society, 14,* 785–803.

Yardley, J. (2000, March 25). Unmarried and living together, till the sheriff do us part. *The New York Times.*

Yardley, W. (2007, August 28). When wildfires threaten, wealthy get extra shield. *The New York Times.*

Yardley, W. (2011, March 26). Catholic order reaches $166 million settlement with sexual abuse victims. *The New York Times.*

Yi, C.-C., Chang, C.-E., & Chang, Y.-H. (2004). The intergenerational transmission of family values: A comparison between teenagers and parents in Taiwan. *Journal of Comparative Family Studies, 35,* 523–545.

Yong, W. (2010, December 7). Divorce soars in Iran as women say no, and work the system. *The New York Times.*

Yoshino, K. (2006). *Covering: The hidden assault on our civil rights.* New York, NY: Random House.

Young, L. M., & Powell, B. (1985). The effects of obesity on the clinical judgments of mental health professionals. *Journal of Health and Social Behavior, 26,* 233–246.

Younis, M. (2011). *Muslim Americans identify with God and country.* Abu Dhabi Gallup Center. www.gallup.com/poll/148799/Muslim-Americans-Identify-God-Country.aspx. Accessed September 8, 2011.

Yum! Brands. (2011). *Yum! Brands.* www.yum.com/ company/default.asp. Accessed May 26, 2011.

Zernike, K. (2003, January 20). 30 years after *Roe v. Wade,* new trends but the old debate. *The New York Times.*

Zernike, K. (2004, December 19). Does Christmas need to be saved? *The New York Times.*

Zhao, Y. (2002, August 5). Wave of pupils lacking English strains schools. *The New York Times.*

Zhu, W. X., Lu, L., & Hesketh, T. (2009). China's excess males, sex selective abortion, and one child policy: Analysis of data from 2005 national intercensus survey. *British Medical Journal, 338,* 1211–1213.

Zimbardo, P. (2007). *The Lucifer effect: Understanding how good people turn evil.* New York, NY: Random House.

Zoepf, K. (2007, September 23). A dishonorable affair. *The New York Times Magazine.*

Zola, I. (1986). Medicine as an institution of social control. In P. Conrad & R. Kern (Eds.), *The sociology of health and illness.* New York, NY: St. Martin's Press.

Zoll, R. (2005, June 7). Poll reveals U.S. leads in religious devotion. *The Indianapolis Star.*

Zuckoff, M. (2000, June 8). Lawsuit accuses drug maker Eli Lilly of concealing Prozac data from trial. *The Boston Globe.*

Zuger, A. (1999, April 30). Take some strychnine and call me in the morning. *The New York Times.*

Zuger, A. (2005, October 30). For a retainer, lavish care by "boutique doctors." *The New York Times.*

Zurcher, L. A., & Snow, D. A. (1981). Collective behavior: Social movements. In M. Rosenberg & R. H. Turner (Eds.), *Social psychology: Sociological perspectives.* New York, NY: Basic Books.

Zweigenhaft, R. L. (1987). Minorities and women of the corporation. In G. W. Domhoff & T. R. Dye (Eds.), *Power elites and organizations.* Newbury Park, CA: Sage.

Zwerdling, D. (2004). U.S. military whistle blowers face retribution. *National Public Radio.* www.npr.org/templates/story/story.php?storyId=1905858. Accessed June 19, 2007.

Photo Credits

Chapter 2 Visual Essay, "The Old Ball Game"

Photos, pages 38–39: Photos by Douglas Harper

Photos, pages 40–41: © Reuters/CORBIS

Photo, page 42: © Barton Silverman/The New York Times/Redux

Photos, pages 43–45: Photos by Douglas Harper

Chapter 3 Visual Essay, "Personal Billboards"

Photo, page 73, left: © Owen Franken/CORBIS

Photo, page 73, right: © Lynn Goldsmith/CORBIS

Photo, page 74, top: © Mark Petersen/CORBIS SABA

Photo, page 74, bottom: © Phil Schermeister/CORBIS

Photo, page 75, top: © Tom Bean/CORBIS

Photo, page 75, bottom: © Robert Holmes/CORBIS

Photo, page 76, top: © Bob Rowan, Progressive Images/CORBIS

Photo, page 76, bottom: © Tariq Mahmood/AFP/Getty Images

Photo, page 77, top: © Robert Holmes/CORBIS

Photo, page 77, center: © Ed Eckstein/CORBIS

Photo, page 77, bottom: © Gideon Mendel/CORBIS

Photo, page 78, top left: © Penny Tweedle/CORBIS

Photo, page 78, top right: © Owen Franken/CORBIS

Photo, page 78, bottom: © Ferdaus Shamin/Sygma/CORBIS

Photo, page 79, top: © Robert Maass/CORBIS

Photo, page 79, bottom: © Tony Savino/Sygma/CORBIS

Photo, page 80: © Matthew Polak/Sygma/CORBIS

Chapter 4 Visual Essay, "Funeral Rituals in the Netherlands"

Photos, pages 119–128: from Marrie Bot, *A Last Farewell: Funeral and Mourning Rituals in the Multicultural Society of the Netherlands,* Rotterdam: M. Bot, 1998

Chapter 5 Visual Essay, "Becoming a Mariner"

Photo, page 155: © James L. Amos/CORBIS

Photo, page 156, top: © Swim Ink 2, LLC/CORBIS

Photo, page 156, bottom: © Judy Griesedieck/CORBIS

Photos, page 157–page 159, top: © Michael S. Yamashita/CORBIS

Photo, page 159, center: U.S. Merchant Marine Academy

Photos, page 159, bottom–page 160: © Michael S. Yamashita/CORBIS

Chapter 7 Visual Essay, "The Blending of America: Mixed Race"

Photos, page 204; page 205, top left; page 205, top center: © CORBIS

Photos, page 205, top right, center: © Bettmann/CORBIS

Photo, page 205, bottom: © Underwood & Underwood/CORBIS

Photo, page 206, top left: Photo by Jerome Krase

Photo, page 206, top right: © John David Mercer/AP Images

Photo, page 206, center: © Associated Press

Photo, page 206, bottom left: © Laura Rauch/AP Images

Photo, page 206, bottom center: Photo by Jerome Krause

Photo, page 206, bottom right: © Associated Press

Chapter 8 Visual Essay, "A Culture of Tramps"

Photos, pages 243–247: Photos by Douglas Harper

Chapter 9 Visual Essay, "The Trail of the Tomato"

Photos, pages 302–309: Photos by Deborah Barndt

Chapter 11 Visual Essay, "'Civilizing' the Indians"

Photo, page 366: National Archives

Photo, page 367, top: Courtesy of The Denver Public Library, Western History Collection, DPL X-32086

Photo, page 367, bottom: Courtesy of The Denver Public Library, Western History Collection, DPL X-32085

Photo, page 368, top: National Archives and Records Administration

Photo, page 368, bottom: Courtesy of the Library of Congress

Photo, page 369: Photo from National Archives–Rocky Mt. Region, Denver, CO

Photo, page 370, top: Collection of Jeremy Rowe Vintage Photography, vintagephoto.com

Photo, page 370, bottom: Courtesy of the Library of Congress

Photo, page 371: Children at the Round Rock school in Round Rock, Arizona

Chapter 13 Visual Essay, "Immigrant Nation"

Photo, page 460: © Bettmann/CORBIS

Photo, page 461, top: © Hulton-Deutsch Collection/CORBIS

Photo, page 461, bottom: © Chase Swift/Corbis

Photo, page 462, top: © David Turnley/CORBIS

Photo, page 462, bottom: © Danny Lehman/CORBIS

Photo, page 463, top: © Hector Mata/AFP/Getty Images

Photo, page 463, bottom: © Danny Lehman/CORBIS

Photo, page 464, top: © Kim Kulish/CORBIS

Photo, page 464, bottom left: © James Marshall/CORBIS

Photo, page 464, bottom right: © Sandy Felsenthal/CORBIS

Photo, page 465, top: © Scott Nelson/Getty Images

Photo, page 465, bottom: © Najlah Feanny/CORBIS

Photo, page 466, top: © David Turnley/CORBIS

Photo, page 466, center left: © Gerhard Steiner/CORBIS

Photo, page 466, center right: Photo courtesy of Nevdon Jamgochian

Photo, page 466, bottom: © Catherine Karnow/CORBIS

Photo, page 467, top: © Mark Peterson/CORBIS SABA

Photo, page 467, center: © Julie Plasencia/San Francisco

Photo, page 467, bottom: © Ralf-Finn Hestoft/CORBIS

Chapter 14 Visual Essay, "Portraits of Grief"

Photo, page 492: © Murad Sezer/AP Images

Photo, page 493, top: © The Bay City Times, Kevin Hagen

Photo, page 493, bottom: © Ron Edmonds/AP Images

Photo, page 494: © Mohamed Messara/epa/CORBIS

Photo, page 495, top: © Yahya Ahmed/AP Images

Photo, page 495, bottom: © Sue Ogrocki/AP Images

Photo, page 496: © Deanne Fitzmaurice/San Francisco Chronicle/Corbis

Photo, page 497, top: © LM Otero/AP Images

Photo, page 497, bottom: © Samir Mizban/AP Images

Photo, page 498: *Newsweek* magazine cover

Glossary/Index

Unobtrusive research: Research technique in which the researcher, without direct contact with the subjects, examines the evidence of social behavior that people create or leave behind, 88–89

Upper class: In a society stratified by social class, a group of people who have high income and prestige and who own vast amounts of property and other forms of wealth, such as owners of large corporations, top financiers, rich celebrities and politicians, and members of prestigious families, 329–330

Urbanization: The process by which people leave rural areas and begin to concentrate in large cities, 453

SAGE Research Methods Online
The essential tool for researchers